THE LAW OF
TRUSTS

THE LAW OF
TRUSTS

By

GEORGE W. KEETON

M.A., LL.D.(Cantab.), Hon.LL.D.
(Sheffield and Hong Kong), F.B.A.

Of Gray's Inn, Barrister-at-Law
Associate Professor of
Brunel University
Emeritus Professor of the
University of London

and

L. A. SHERIDAN

LL.D.(London), Ph.D.(Belfast),
Hon.LL.D.(Singapore)

Of Lincoln's Inn, Barrister-at-Law
Professor of Law,
University College, Cardiff

Tenth Edition

LONDON
PROFESSIONAL BOOKS LIMITED
1974

First edition 1934   *Seventh edition* 1957
Second edition 1937   *Reprinted* 1959
Reprinted 1938   *Eighth edition* 1963
Third edition 1939   *Reprinted* 1964, 1966
Fourth edition 1947   *Ninth edition* 1968
Fifth edition 1950   *Reprinted* 1971
Sixth edition 1954   *Tenth edition* 1974

Published in 1974
by Professional Books Limited
of 6½ Suffolk Street, London
and printed in Great Britain
by The Eastern Press Limited
London and Reading

ISBN: 0 903486 04 0

PREFACE
TO THE TENTH EDITION

IN the six years which have elapsed since the appearance of the ninth edition
there have been no major statutory changes in the law of trusts, apart from the
steadily increasing impact of taxation, and it would seem that, in spite of
the recommendations of a representative committee, the decision has now been
taken to retain the Public Trustee Office, at any rate for some years to come.
Had the recommendation been followed, English practice would have shown
an important variation from that of other Commonwealth nations. It may
be hoped that the abandonment of this proposal does not involve also the
abandonment of another one in the report, that professional trustees and trust
corporations should have a statutory power to charge. Times have changed,
and so has the general outlook on voluntary service, and the task of the
trustee today is frequently more onerous than it was in earlier times.

There have been a number of decisions of general importance in the Law
of Trusts since the ninth edition appeared. *Holder* v. *Holder*, [1968] Ch. 353,
has aroused misgivings among some; the full implications of *McPhail* v.
Doulton, [1971] A.C. 424, have yet to be investigated; and the repercussions
of *Vandervell* v. *Inland Revenue Commissioners*, [1967] 2 A.C. 291, and of
Re Vandervell's Trusts (No. 2), [1973] 3 W.L.R. 744, [1974] 3 W.L.R. 256,
upon the uncertainties of the law of implied and resulting trusts will ultimately
be considerable. Two other points should be mentioned. The Goodman Committee on Charities may have important changes to recommend; whilst the
introduction of a wealth tax and a capital transfer tax would produce new
problems both for draftsmen and for trustees.

The Trustee Act 1925 has now been in operation for half a century, and it
has been frequently amended, sometimes by statutory instrument. The amended
text, as it existed in August 1974, is printed in Part IV. We are of opinion:
(1) that it would be valuable for trustees and all who are concerned with the
law of trusts if this Act, as amended, could be republished at regular intervals;
(2) that it is time that some thought should be given to the preparation of a
new Trustee Act, taking into account recent developments in the law of trusts
in some of the nations of the Commonwealth; and (3) that when this is done,
consideration should be given to the consolidation of the law of trusts into a
single trusts code.

*   *   *

The White Paper on a capital transfer tax (Cmnd. 5705) and the Green
Paper on a wealth tax (Cmnd. 5704) were published on August 9, 1974, too
late for consideration in Chapter XXI. These taxes are intended to replace
estate duty.

A capital transfer tax is proposed for introduction, with effect from March
26, 1974, by a Finance Act to be enacted in late 1974. It is to be a tax on the
donor of gifts (including transfers for a consideration which is significantly
below market value), beginning when the taxable gifts he has made total

£15,000. The proposed rates of tax are from 10 per cent. on the first £5,000 (*i.e.* on non-exempt gifts totalling between £15,000 and £20,000), rising to 75 per cent. when the donor has made taxable gifts to a cumulative value of more than £2,000,000. Exemptions will include gifts between husband and wife, gifts totalling £1,000 or less in any year, wedding presents within limits varying with the relationship of the donor to the donee and gifts to charity up to a limit, yet to be fixed, of at least £50,000. There will be exemption for gifts to national heritage bodies, and works of art will be treated no less favourably than under estate duty law. There will be no tax on gifts out of income.

The tax will apply to gifts made on trust, capital taken out of a settlement (*e.g.* under the Trustee Act 1925, s. 32) and on any change in beneficial interests in possession under a trust (not only, as under estate duty law, on the death of a beneficiary). There will be a periodic charge to tax on the capital of discretionary trusts and trusts for accumulation, but this charge will not operate from a date before the autumn 1974 budget day. Paragraphs 17–23 of the White Paper, which relate to trusts, are as follows—

17. The broad principle to be applied to settled property is that in general the charge to tax should be neither greater nor smaller than the charge on property held absolutely. Accordingly, the Government intend to bring settled property within the scope of the Capital Transfer Tax to the extent that the settled funds were provided directly or indirectly by a person who at the time the funds were provided was domiciled in the United Kingdom (or had been brought within the scope of the tax by reason of a long-standing connection with this country). Where this test is satisfied there will, subject to the exemptions mentioned below, be a potential liability on any distribution of capital out of a trust and on the termination or transfer of the whole or part of an interest in possession under such a trust (*i.e.* the right to the income, if any, from or the enjoy-ment of the settled property). The charge will normally relate to the full value of the property in which the terminated or transferred interest in possession subsisted. Any distribution of trust capital which necessarily follows from the termination of an interest will not be a separate occasion of charge.

18. Where Estate Duty is chargeable on a death in the interim period (see paragraphs 6 and 10), or earlier, and the property ceases to be settled on the death, then no further liability to the transfer tax will arise on the formal transfer of the property to the person(s) who then become absolutely entitled to it.

19. Trustees will be liable for any tax chargeable, but there will also be rights of recovery from beneficiaries and, if the trustees are resident outside the United Kingdom, from settlors.

20. The tax payable by trustees in respect of a termination of, or change in, an interest in possession will be calculated as if the amount charge-able were a gift by the former beneficiary entering into his cumulative total of chargeable transfers. The amount chargeable will also be taken

into account in determining *subsequent* liabilities of the former beneficiary (including liabilities on his death).

21. The tax on a distribution of capital out of settled property where there is no interest in possession (*e.g.* a discretionary trust) will be calculated by rules which will be different for property settled on or after March 26, 1974, and for property settled before that date. For " pre-26 March trusts " the liability will be that which would be due from an individual who had made chargeable transfers equal to the capital distributed by the trust after March 25 (whether on one or more occasions). For property settled after March 25, distributions will be taxed at a rate which takes into account, inter alia, the settlor's liability to the Capital Transfer Tax at the time of his gift in settlement. There will also be a periodic charge on the capital of discretionary and accumulation trusts, but this will not be imposed from a date before the autumn Budget day.

22. There will be certain situations in which the distribution of trust capital will be treated as no more than the completion of the settlor's original gift and so exempted from charge. This treatment will usually be appropriate should a life tenant who has the right to the income from settled property become absolutely entitled to that property; in particular, exemption from tax will be provided where trust funds settled for the benefit of an infant or infants are transferred to these former infants on the expiration of the trust. This exemption will extend to funds which provide for discretion to accumulate or provide for maintenance not extending beyond the age of 25.

23. It would be outside the scope of this White Paper to give a detailed account of the provisions which the Government propose to introduce to govern the liabilities of trustees in respect of settled property. The Government recognise, however, that there are a number of cases where, under the terms of trust deeds executed before the Chancellor of the Exchequer's announcement on March 26, distributions of capital to beneficiaries have already become due, and that in such cases trustees are put in difficulty by the need to await publication of the legislation before the likely tax liability can be ascertained. To ease this situation they will introduce a provision which for property settled before March 26, 1974, will set a maximum liability in respect of chargeable events during the period between March 25 and a future date which will be fixed later—whatever the character of the trust. The tax will be no more than that which would be due if the trust were an individual who had made chargeable gifts equal to the capital of the trust becoming chargeable, whether on a distribution or on the termination of, or change in, an interest in possession. But this overriding limitation on liability in the interim period will not extend to cases where the chargeable event arises because of a death (to which the existing Estate Duty will apply). Nor will it in any way affect the subsequent liability of former beneficiaries (see paragraph 20).

Example

Under a settlement set up before March 26, 1974, A is life tenant of the trust investments which have a capital value of £25,000. On his death his son B will become entitled to the capital. In July 1974, *i.e.* before the date to be prescribed, A gives up his life interest so that B can enjoy the capital at once.

Under the special arrangement set out in this paragraph, Capital Transfer Tax will not exceed a charge calculated as follows:

On first £15,000		Nil
On next £5,000	at 10%	£500
On next £5,000	at 15%	£750
	Total Tax	£1250

If however A were to die during the interim period, the trust fund would be liable to Estate Duty under the existing law and the Capital Transfer Tax would not be charged.

A wealth tax is proposed for introduction in the tax year 1976–77. This would be a tax on the world-wide assets of individuals resident in the United Kingdom, and possibly on non-residents in respect of some types of United Kingdom assets. The tax would be levied annually on chargeable wealth exceeding £100,000, two rates of tax being suggested for discussion. Tax A would be at 1 per cent. on the first £400,000 (*i.e.* on wealth between £100,000 and £500,000), rising to $2\frac{1}{2}$ per cent. on wealth exceeding £5,000,000; while Tax B would be at 1 per cent. on the first £200,000 (*i.e.* on wealth between £100,000 and £300,000), rising to 5 per cent. on wealth exceeding £5,000,000. The Green Paper suggests that the wealth of infant children should be aggregated for purposes of the tax with that of the parent from whose side of the family the infant's wealth is derived, but leaves open the question of aggregation of the wealth of husband and wife.

In principle, wealth is regarded by the Green Paper as consisting of all assets with a realisable value. In addition to the exemption of the first £100,000, there may be a secondary exemption for personal and domestic property (not including dwellings) held primarily for current use and enjoyment. Other possible exemptions or adjustments include: (a) relief to take account of the investment income surcharge; (b) allowances for businessmen's and farmers' working capital; (c) relief for works of art, historic houses and other parts of the national heritage in private ownership but accessible to the public; (d) adjustments for copyrights and patents so that they are not overtaxed (as wealth while retained, and the proceeds as income when later sold); and (e) pension rights and similar arrangements for retirement.

Property held on trust or by personal representatives in the administration of an estate, other than property held on a charitable trust, would be subject to the tax. Paragraphs 16–25 of the Green Paper, relating to such property, are as follows—

16. So far as possible, no tax advantage or disadvantage should follow from holding assets in trust rather than absolutely. Hence there can be no

question of treating each trust as if it were a separate individual and allowing it the same exemptions limit and rate bands, for if this were done, substantial tax advantages could be obtained by fragmenting wealth between a number of trusts.

17. The Government therefore consider that all property held in trust should be prima facie liable to wealth tax at the top rate or perhaps, if the top rate applied only to a small number of people, on the next highest rate. However, there will be provision for trusts to have their liability abated. The following paragraphs set out rules for abatement for the main types of trust. Their practical effect will be that many small trusts will from the outset clearly have no liability to the tax. Trusts for wholly charitable purposes will in general be exempt from tax as will pension funds and certain trusts for employees. The assets of a trust which is subject to revocation by the settlor will be treated as belonging to the settlor.

18. For straightforward trusts with one or more life tenants and remaindermen a possible approach might be to attribute the trust capital to the various beneficiaries of the trust according to the actuarial values of their respective interests in it; and then to tax the various amounts of capital at the rate they would bear if they formed the top slices of the beneficiaries' own wealth. However, there would be two difficulties in this: first, the values of the interests of the various beneficiaries in a trust generally add up to less than 100 per cent. of the value of the trust funds and rules would have to be made for attributing the balance; second, it may not be possible, even with a non-discretionary trust, to identify all the reversionary interests (which may, for example, include children yet unborn). The best practical solution may therefore be to ignore the reversionary interests and to attribute the whole of the value of the trust funds to the life tenant: the trustees would then be relieved from the full charge to tax in so far as that charge exceeded the liability which would have been due if the trust assets (together with the assets of any other trust of which he was life tenant) formed the top slice of the life tenant's wealth. The examples in Appendix 1 show how this rule might work. Similarly, where the trustees of a trust are required to accumulate the income for an identified beneficiary contingent on his reaching a stated age with power to make payments to him at their discretion, the assets could be attributed to the beneficiary so that the rate would be found, if he was a minor, by aggregating them with his parents' wealth (as explained in paragraph 10).

19. The approach to straightforward trusts cannot apply to the wholly discretionary trust in which the trustees have unfettered discretion as to the application of income and capital between what may be a very large number of discretionary objects. In such a case there are no beneficiaries by reference to whose circumstances the charge at the top rate of tax might be abated. The Government consider that while the settlor remains

alive the charge should be calculated primarily by reference to his circumstances, as if the trust and any other discretionary trust he had set up had never been made. This will usually be close to the realities of the situation in which the trustees may be expected to follow the settlor's wishes. It may however be possible to give a measure of relief by reference to the payments of income actually made to the discretionary objects of a trust, although it would be necessary to assume for this purpose that the capital used to produce the distributed income was no more than was required to produce the income from investments yielding a reasonable rate of return. Indeed, if the settlor were dead such a method might provide the only basis whereby relief could be given as the years passed: it would however need to be carefully drawn bearing in mind the possibilities of abuse.

20. There are many types of trust falling between the extremes of the straightforward trust with indefeasible life interests in possession and reversionary interests on the one hand and the out and out discretionary trust on the other. These will require consideration according to their circumstances on the general lines set out above. The rules for trusts will apply to other arrangements having similar effect.

21. **The normal rule will be that the trustees should pay** the wealth tax out of the capital of the trust fund: the burden will thus effectively be borne by the life tenant as well as by the remainderman since it will erode the amount of the trust capital and, therefore, the income that it can produce. Some life tenants may be unwilling to reveal to the trustees the amount of their wealth in order that the latter may calculate the relief due, or even to allow the Revenue to calculate the relief and inform the trustees. In such a case the trustees would have to pay tax at the top rate, but it could be provided that the payment would then so far as possible be made out of income and that the life tenant could claim direct from the Revenue an appropriate repayment of the tax paid by the trustees.

22. Trusts where the trustees are not resident in the United Kingdom and the administration of the trust is ordinarily carried on outside this country fall into two broad categories.

23. The first category includes all those trusts set up with non-resident trustees by settlors who have little or no connection with this country. In such a case, even if there are one or more beneficiaries or discretionary objects resident in this country, there are no grounds on which it would be right to bring the trustees or the whole of the trust assets within the charge to the tax. But a United Kingdom resident individual with an interest in such a trust, whether in possession or reversion, has a realisable asset which should be included in his personal wealth at its actuarial value. If such a trust is discretionary, however, its objects generally have no interests in the trust assets on which they should be assessed.

24. The second category includes those trusts where a United Kingdom settlor arranges for the trustees to be non-resident or where the administration of an existing resident trust passes overseas. The legal ownership of the settled property is thus vested in persons outside United Kingdom jurisdiction and the arrangement is very frequently prompted by tax avoidance considerations. Accordingly, where settled funds were provided directly or indirectly by a person who at the time the funds were provided was domiciled or ordinarily resident in the United Kingdom, the trustees will be liable to the same extent as if the trust had been resident. This will apply whenever the the trust was set up. While the settlor remains alive there will be power to recover the tax from him if the trustees do not pay it; alternatively it will be recoverable out of any assets of the trust which are within the United Kingdom or from any residents to the extent that, after August 8, 1974, they receive benefits from the settlement whether directly or indirectly or whether of capital or income.

25. Special rules will be needed to deal with property passing under a deceased's will (or an intestacy) for the period while the estate is in course of administration. The eventual recipient of such property will be liable in respect of the total amount he receives as if it had formed part of his wealth at each valuation day (see paragraph 66) between the date of death and the date of receipt. Trustees will similarly be liable on the lines set out in paragraphs 16 to 24. Neither beneficiaries nor trustees will be required to pay tax until the property in question has been transferred to them, but interest at a commercial rate will run on deferred payments perhaps from a date 12 months after the date of death. As an alternative the Government will consider allowing a 12-month period from the date of death before the wealth tax liabilities begin to accrue. To deal with the possibility of very long delays in completing the administration of an estate it will also be necessary to have power to require personal representatives to make provisional payments of wealth tax on behalf of absolute beneficiaries or trustees.

Examples 2 and 3 given at the end of the Green Paper illustrate the possible application of the wealth tax to trusts—

Example 2

Y . . . has net wealth amounting to £1,000,000 but in addition he has a life interest in trust T which has assets amounting to £1,500,000.

The wealth tax payable by Y is the same as that payable by [any person with wealth amounting to £1,000,000]. The wealth tax payable by the trustees of T is found by attributing the whole of the trust assets to Y to see if there is any relief available against the charge at the top rate which would otherwise be due (paragraph 18). The calculation is as follows:

Wealth tax A

		£
First £100,000		Exempt
Next £400,000	at 1%	4,000
Next £1,500,000	at 1½%	22,500
Next £500,000	at 2%	10,000
		36,500
Tax payable by Y		11,500
Top slice attributable to T		25,000
Trust liability at top rate (£1,500,000 at 2½%)		37,500
Less top slice of Y's assumed liability		25,000
Relief available to trustees		£12,500

Wealth tax B

		£
First £100,000		Exempt
Next £200,000	at 1%	2,000
Next £200,000	at 2%	4,000
Next £1,500,000	at 3%	45,000
Next £500,000	at 4%	20,000
		71,000
Tax payable by Y		21,000
Top slice attributable to T		50,000
Trust liability at top rate (£1,500,000 at 5%)		75,000
Less top slice of Y's assumed liability		50,000
Relief available to trustees		£25,000

Example 3

The circumstances are identical to those in the previous example but Z is the life tenant of two trusts—U with assets of £600,000 and V with assets of £900,000. The calculation of Z's assumed wealth is made in the same way as that of Y and the top slice of his liability is then apportioned rateably, *i.e.* in the proportion of 2: 3, between U and V. The trustees can thus obtain relief as follows:

Wealth Tax A

	Trust U	Trust V
	£	£
Trust liability at top rate	15,000	22,500
Less top slice of Z's assumed liability	10,000	15,000
Relief available to trustees	£5,000	£7,500

Wealth Tax B

	Trust U	Trust V
	£	£
Trust liability at top rate	30,000	45,000
Less top slice of Z's assumed liability	20,000	30,000
Relief available to trustees	£10,000	£15,000

*   *   *

Every possible effort has been made to ensure that the book is up to date, but no account could be taken of legislation enacted but not published during the last few months.

We should like to express our thanks to Mr. O. P. Wylie, LL.B., Lecturer in Law at University College, Cardiff, who has prepared the index and who advised us on the taxation chapter; and to the publishers and printers, whose assistance in the preparation of this edition has greatly facilitated its speedy appearance.

September 1, 1974.   G. W. KEETON

L. A. SHERIDAN

CONTENTS

PART I—THE FORMATION OF A TRUST

CHAPTER I

CHAPTER II

CHAPTER III

CHAPTER IV

CHAPTER V

CHAPTER VI

CHAPTER XIX

CHAPTER XX

CHAPTER XXI

CHAPTER XXII

CHAPTER XXIII

PART III—BREACH OF TRUST

CHAPTER XXIV

CHAPTER XXV

CHAPTER XXVI

CHAPTER XXVII

PART IV

TABLE OF STATUTES

xxi

RULES AND ORDERS

TABLE OF CASES

TABLE OF REPORTS CITED
AND ABBREVIATIONS

England (excluding The Law Reports)

A.T.C.	Annotated (Accountant) Tax Cases	1922–current
Aleyn	Aleyn's Reports, King's Bench	1646–9
All E.R.	All England Law Reports	1936–current
[preceded by date]		
All E.R. Rep.	All England Law Reports Reprint	1558–1935
[preceded by date]		
Amb.	Ambler's Reports, Chancery	1737–84
And.	Anderson's Reports, Common Pleas	1534–1605
Anst.	Anstruther's Reports, Exchequer	1792–7
Asp. M.L.C.	Aspinall's Maritime Law Cases	1870–1940
Atk.	Atkyns's Reports, Chancery	1736–55
B. & C.R.	Reports of Bankruptcy and Companies Winding Up Cases	1918–41
[preceded by date]		
B. & P.	Bosanquet and Puller's Reports, Common Pleas	1796–1804
B. & P.N.R.	Bosanquet and Puller's New Reports, Common Pleas	1804–7
Barn. C.	Barnadiston's Reports, Chancery	1740–1
Barn. K.B.	Barnadiston's Reports, King's Bench	1726–34
Beav.	Beavan's Reports, Rolls Court	1838–66
Bing.	Bingham's Reports, Common Pleas	1822–34
Black. W.	William Blackstone's Reports	1746–80
Bligh	Bligh's Reports, House of Lords	1819–21
Bli. N.S.	Bligh's Reports, House of Lords, New Series	1827–37
Bridg. J.	J. Bridgman's Reports, Common Pleas	1613–21
Bro. C.C.	Brown's Chancery Cases	1778–94
Bro. P.C.	Brown's Parliament Cases	1702–1800
Brownl.	Brownlow and Goldesborough's Reports, Common Pleas	1569–1624
—	Burn's Ecclesiastical Law	
Burr.	Burrow's Reports, King's Bench	1756–72
C.B.N.S.	Common Bench Reports, New Series	1856–65
C.L.R.	Common Law Reports	1853–5
Cary	Cary's Reports, Chancery	1557–1604
Cas. t. Hard.	Cases *temp.* Hardwicke, King's Bench	1733–8
Cas. t. Talb.	Cases in Equity *temp.* Talbot	1733–8
Ch. Cas.	Cases in Chancery	1660–98
Ch. Rep.	Reports in Chancery	1615–1710
Char. Pr. Cas.	Charley's New Practice Reports	1875–6
Cl. & Fin.	Clark and Finnelly's Reports, House of Lords	1831–46
Co. Rep.	Coke's Reports	1572–1616
Coll.	Collyer's Reports, Vice-Chancellor's Court	1844–5
Com. Cas.	Reports of Commercial Cases	1895–1941
Coop. t. Brough.	C.P. Cooper's Cases *temp.* Brougham, Chancery	1833–4
Cowp.	Cowper's Reports, King's Bench	1774–8
Cox	Cox's Equity Cases	1745–97
Cr. & Ph.	Craig and Phillips's Reports, Chancery	1840–1
Cro. Car.	Croke's Reports *temp.* Charles I, King's Bench and Common Pleas	1625–41
Cro. Eliz.	Croke's Reports *temp.* Elizabeth I, King's Bench and Common Pleas	1582–1603
De G. & J.	De Gex and Jones's Reports, Chancery	1857–9
De G. & Sm.	De Gex and Smale's Reports, Vice-Chancellor's Court	1846–52
De G.F. & J.	De Gex, Fisher and Jones's Reports, Chancery	1859–62
De G.J. & S.	De Gex, Jones and Smith's Reports, Chancery	1862–6
De G.M. & G.	De Gex, M'Naghten and Gordon's Reports, Chancery	1851–7
Deac.	Deacon's Reports, Bankruptcy	1834–40
Deac. & Ch.	Deacon and Chitty's Reports, Bankruptcy	1832–5
Dick.	Dicken's Reports, Chancery	1559–1798
Donnelly	Donnelly's Reports, Chancery	1836–7
Dow	Dow's Reports, House of Lords	1812–18
Dow & Cl.	Dow and Clark's Reports, House of Lords	1827–32
Drew.	Drewry's Reports, Vice-Chancellor's Court	1852–9
Dr. & Sm.	Drewry's and Smale's Reports, Vice-Chancellor's Court	1860–5
Duke	Duke's Law of Charitable Uses	
Dyer	Dyer's Reports, King's Bench	1513–82
E.R.	English Reports	1220–1873

England (excluding The Law Reports) *(contd.)*

E. & E.	Ellis and Ellis's Reports, Queen's Bench	1858–61
East	East's Reports, King's Bench	1800–12
Eden	Eden's Reports, Chancery	1757–66
El. & Bl.	Ellis and Blackburn's Reports, Queen's Bench	1851–8
Eq. Cas. Abr.	Equity Cases Abridged	1667–1744
Eq. Rep.	Equity Reports	1853–5
Est. Gaz.	Estates Gazette	1858–current
Ex.	Exchequer Reports (Welsby, Hurlstone and Gordon)	1847–56
Freem. Ch.	Freeman's Reports, Chancery	1660–1706
G. Coop.	G. Cooper's Reports, Chancery	1792–1815
Gale	Gale's Reports, Exchequer	1835–6
Giff.	Giffard's Reports, Vice-Chancellor's Court	1857–65
H.B.R.	Hansell's Reports of Bankruptcy and Companies Winding Up Cases	1915–17

[preceded by date]

H.Bl.	H. Blackstone's Reports, Common Pleas and Exchequer Chamber	1788–96
H.L.C.	House of Lords Cases (Clark)	1847–66
H. & M.	Hemming and Miller's Reports, Vice-Chancellor's Court ...	1862–5
H. & Tw.	Hall and Twell's Reports, Chancery	1849–50
H. & W.	Hurlstone and Walmsley's Reports, Exchequer	1840–1
Hardr.	Hardres's Reports, Exchequer	1655–69
Hare	Hare's Reports, Vice-Chancellor's Court	1841–53
Hop. & Colt.	Hopwood and Coltman's Registration Cases	1868–78
Hop. & Ph.	Hopwood and Philbrick's Registration Cases	1863–7
Inst.	Coke's Institutes	
J.P.	Justice of the Peace	1837–current
J. & H.	Johnson and Hemming's Reports, Vice-Chancellor's Court...	1860–2
Jac.	Jacob's Reports, Chancery	1821–2
Jac. & W.	Jacob and Walker's Reports, Chancery	1819–21
Jur.	Jurist Reports	1837–54
Jur. N.S.	Jurist Reports, New Series	1855–67
K.I.R.	Knight's Industrial Reports	1966–current
K. & J.	Kay and Johnson's Reports, Vice-Chancellor's Court	1854–8
Kay	Kay's Reports, Vice-Chancellor's Court	1853–4
Keb.	Keble's Reports, King's Bench	1661–79
Keen	Keen's Reports, Rolls Court	1836–8
L.G.R.	Local Government Reports	1902–current
L.J.Bcy.	Law Journal Reports, Bankruptcy	1832–80
L.J.C.P.	Law Journal Reports, Common Pleas	1831–75
L.J. Ch.	Law Journal Reports, Chancery	1831–1946
L.J.Ex.	Law Journal Reports, Exchequer	1831–75
L.J.Ex.Eq.	Law Journal Reports, Exchequer in Equity	1835–41
L.J.K.B. (or Q.B.)...	Law Journal Reports, King's (or Queen's) Bench	1831–1946
L.J.O.S.Ch.	Law Journal Reports, Chancery, Old Series	1822–31
L.J.P.	Law Journal Reports, Probate, Divorce and Admiralty Division	1875–1946
L.J.P.C.	Law Journal, Privy Council	1865–1946
L.J.Q.B. (or K.B.)...	Law Journal Reports, Queen's (or King's) Bench	1831–1946
L.J.R.	Law Journal Reports	1947–9

[preceded by date]

L.Jo.	Law Journal Newpaper	1866–1965
L.T.	Law Times Reports	1859–1947
L.T.Jo.	Law Times Newpaper	1843–current
L.T.O.S.	Law Times Reports, Old Series	1843–59
Lev.	Levinz's Reports, King's Bench and Common Pleas	1660–97
Lloyd's Rep.	Lloyd's [List] Law Reports	1919–current

[preceded by date]

Lofft	Lofft's Reports, King's Bench	1772–4
M. & S.	Maule and Selwyn's Reports, King's Bench	1813–17
M. & W.	Meeson and Welsby's Reports, Exchequer	1836–47
Mac. & G.	M'Naghten and Gordon's Reports, Chancery	1849–51
Madd.	Maddock's Reports, Vice-Chancellor's Court	1815–22
Mans.	Manson's Bankruptcy and Company Cases	1893–1914
Meg.	Megone's Companies Acts Cases	1889–91
Mer.	Merivale's Reports, Chancery	1815–17
Mod.	Modern Reports	1669–1732
Mont.	Montagu's Reports, Bankruptcy	1829–32
Mont. & A.	Montagu and Ayrton's Reports, Bankruptcy	1832–8
Mont. & Ch.	Montagu and Chitty's Reports	1838–40
Moo. P.C.	Moore's Privy Council Cases	1836–62
Moo. P.C.N.S.	Moore's Privy Council Cases, New Series	1862–73

England (*excluding* The Law Reports) (*contd.*)

Moo. & S.	Moore and Scott's Reports, Common Pleas	1831–4
Moore K.B.	Moore's Reports, King's Bench	1485–1620
Morr.	Morrell's Reports, Bankruptcy	1884–93
Mos.	Mosely's Reports, Chancery	1726–31
My. & Cr.	Mylne and Craig's Reports, Chancery	1835–40
My. & K.	Mylne and Keen's Reports, Chancery	1832–5
Nels.	Nelson's Reports, Chancery	1625–93
New Rep.	New Reports	1862–5
—	Nottingham's Chancery Cases	
P. Wms.	Peere Williams's Reports, Chancery and King's Bench	1695–1735
P. & C.R.	Property (or Planning) and Compensation Reports	1950–current
Ph.	Phillips's Reports, Chancery	1841–9
Poll.	Pollexfen's Reports, King's Bench	1670–82
Poph.	Popham's Reports, King's Bench	1592–1627
Prec. Ch.	Precedents in Chancery	1689–1722
Price	Price's Reports, Exchequer	1814–24
Q.B.	Queen's Bench Reports (Adolphus and Ellis, New Series)	1841–52
R.	The Reports	1893–5
R.R.	Revised Reports	1785–1865
R. & I.T.	Rating and Income Tax Reports	1924–60
Rep. t. Finch	Reports *temp.* Finch	1673–80
Roll. Abr.	Rolle's Abridgment of the Common Law	
Rose	Rose's Reports, Bankruptcy	1810–16
Russ.	Russell's Reports, Chancery	1823–9
Russ. & M.	Russell and Mylne's Reports, Chancery	1829–31
S.J.	Solicitors' Journal	1856–current
Sel.cas.t.King	Select Cases *temp.* King	1724–34
Sim.	Simons's Reports, Vice-Chancellor's Court	1826–49
Sim. N.S.	Simons's Reports, Vice-Chancellor's Court, New Series	1850–2
Sm. & Giff.	Smale and Giffard's Reports, Vice-Chancellor's Court	1852–7
Smith K.B.	J.P. Smith's Reports, King's Bench	1803–6
St. Tr.	State Trials	1163–1820
St. Tr. N.S.	State Trials, New Series	1820–58
Sty.	Style's Reports, King's Bench	1646–55
Swanst.	Swanston's Reports, Chancery	1818–19
T.C.	Tax Cases	1875–current
T. Jo.	T. Jones's Reports, King's Bench and Common Pleas	1667–85
T.L.R.	Times Law Reports	1884–1952
[preceded by date 1951–2]		
T.R.	Taxation Reports	1939–current
[preceded by date]		
T.R.	Term Reports (Durnford and East)	1785–1800
T. Raym.	T. Raymond's Reports, King's Bench	1660–84
Taml.	Tamlyn's Reports, Rolls Court	1829–30
Toth.	Tothill's Transactions in Chancery	1559–1646
Turn. & R.	Turner and Russell's Reports, Chancery	1822–4
V. & B.	Vesey and Beames's Reports, Chancery	1812–14
Vent.	Ventris's Reports, King's Bench and Common Pleas	1668–91
Vern.	Vernon's Reports, Chancery	1681–1719
Ves. or Ves. Jun.	Vesey Junior's Reports, Chancery	1789–1817
Ves. Sen.	Vesey Senior's Reports, Chancery	1746–56
Vin. Abr.	Viner's Abridgment of Law and Equity	
W. Jo.	W. Jones's Reports, King's Bench and Common Pleas	1620–41
W.L.R.	Weekly Law Reports	1953–current
[preceded by date]		
W.N.	Weekly Notes	1866–1952
[preceded by date]		
W.R.	Weekly Reporter	1852–1906
West t. Hard.	West's Reports *temp.* Hardwicke	1736–9
Wilm.	Wilmot's Notes of Opinions and Judgments	1757–70
Wils. Ch.	Wilson's Reports, Chancery	1818–19
Y.B.	Year Books	
Y. & C.C.C.	Younge and Collyer's Chancery Cases	1841–3
Y. & C. Ex.	Young and Collyer's Reports, Exchequer in Equity	1833–41
Y. & J.	Younge and Jervis's Reports, Exchequer	1826–30

England: The Law Reports

L.R.C.P.	Court of Common Pleas	
L.R.Ch. App.	Court of Appeal in Chancery	
L.R.Eq.	Court of Chancery	
L.R.Ex.	Court of Exchequer	1865–75
L.R.H.L.	House of Lords (English and Irish Appeals)	
L.R.P.C.	Privy Council	
L.R.Q.B.	Court of Queen's Bench	

App. Cas.	House of Lords and Privy Council	1875–90
C.P.D.	Common Pleas Division	1875–80
Ch. D.	Chancery Division	1875–90
Ex. D.	Exchequer Division	1875–80
Q.B.D.	Queen's Bench Division	1875–90
P.D.	Probate, Divorce and Admiralty Division	1875–90

A.C. [preceded by date]	House of Lords and Privy Council	1891–current
Ch. [preceded by date]	Chancery Division	1891–current
Fam. [preceded by date]	Family Division	1972–current
K.B. or Q.B. [preceded by date]	King's (or Queen's) Bench Division	1891–current
P. [preceded by date]	Probate, Divorce and Admiralty Division	1891–1971
Q.B. or K.B. [preceded by date]	Queen's (or King's) Bench Division	1891–current
W.L.R. [preceded by date]	Weekly Law Reports	1953–current
W.N. [preceded by date]	Weekly Notes	1866–1952

Ireland

B. & B.	Ball and Beatty's Reports, Chancery	1807–14
Con. & L.	Connor and Lawson's Reports, Chancery	1841–3
Dr. & Wal.	Drury and Walsh's Reports, Chancery	1837–41
Dr. & War.	Drury and Warren's Reports, Chancery	1841–3
I.L.T.R.	Irish Law Times Reports	1867–current
I.R. [preceded by date]	Irish Reports	1894–current
I. R. Eq.	Irish Reports, Equity Series	1866–77
Ir. Ch. Rep.	Irish Chancery Reports	1850–66
Ir. Eq. Rep.	Irish Equity Reports	1838–50
Ir. Jur. N.S.	Irish Jurist Reports, New Series	1855–66
Jo. & Lat.	Jones and La Touche's Reports, Chancery	1844–6
L.R. Ir.	Law Reports (Ireland)	1877–93
Ll. & G.t.Plunk.	Lloyd and Goold's Reports *temp.* Plunkett, Chancery	1834–6
Mol.	Molloy's Reports, Chancery	1808–31
Ridg. P.C.	Ridgway's Parliamentary Reports	1784–96
Sch. & Lef.	Schoales and Lefroy's Reports, Chancery	1802–6

Scotland

D. (H.L.)	Dunlop, House of Lords Cases	1832–62
J.	Scottish Jurist	1829–73
Macq.	Macqueen's Scotch Appeals, House of Lords	1849–65
R.	Rettie's Court of Session Cases	1873–98
S.C. [preceded by date]	Session Cases	1906–current
S.C. (H.L.) [preceded by date]	Session Cases, on appeal to the House of Lords	1906–current
S.L.T.	Scots Law Times	1893–current

Australia

A.L.J.R.	Australian Law Journal Reports	1958–current
A.L.R.	Argus Law Reports	1895–1973
F.L.R.	Federal Law Reports	1956–current

Canada

D.L.R.	Dominion Law Reports	1912–current
Man. R.	Manitoba Reports	1883–1962

Canada (contd.)

O.R.	Ontario Reports	1931–current
[preceded by date]		
O.W.N.	Ontario Weekly Notes	1909–62
S.C.R.	Supreme Court Reports	1876–current
W.W.R.	Western Weekly Reports	1912–50 and 1971–current

United States of America

| L. Ed. .... | Supreme Court Reports, Lawyer's Edition .... | 1754–current |
| U.S. .... | Reports of Cases in the Supreme Court .... | 1754–current |

PART I

THE FORMATION OF A TRUST

Chapter I

THE NATURE OF A TRUST

THE trust is one of the most important, and flexible, institutions of modern English law, being rivalled in this respect only by the modern limited liability company. To some extent, moreover, the functions of these two great institutions may overlap. Many associations and organisations (including schools outside the state system) exist under trust deeds, but their objects could be carried out as effectively if some of the more active members of the governing body were incorporated under the Companies Acts, and indeed, this sometimes occurs.

In one sense, the modern trust is an offshoot from the medieval use of lands, but since the Restoration it has developed a considerable number of distinctive qualities, not possessed by the earlier use, and it has been applied to property of all kinds. Basically, a trust is a convenient method whereby a limited number of persons may hold property on behalf of other persons, who may be a large or fluctuating body, or who may include persons not yet born. For example, as soon as any voluntary association is called upon to face the problem of owning property it will usually solve it by appointing trustees to hold that property on behalf of its members. The body of members may be fairly small, as in a village club, or it may be very large, as in the case of a great union, but the trust is a device which is equally convenient for both. Once the property has been vested in trustees, the latter own the property, but they are compelled by law to exercise their ownership for the benefit of the members.

Another very large, and important, group of trusts are established by the wills of testators. A will is a formal act, by virtue of which a person directs how his property shall be disposed of at his death. A will is always revocable until death, and a number of legal rules govern its form. These, for the most part, are contained in the Wills Act 1837 with amendments which have been made by later Acts. A will may be very brief, and it may direct that the testator's property shall be given outright to one or more persons. In such a case, the duties of the executors of the will (who are appointed by the testator in his will) are confined to paying the death duties, funeral and other expenses of the deceased, and his debts, and finally, to distributing the estate in accordance with the testator's directions. Many wills, however, attempt to make further provision for the testator's family and relatives than this, and some may also contain legacies for charities or strangers. Where the testator leaves substantial property, it frequently happens that he wishes to leave the income of his property to his widow for life, and only on her death does he contemplate that his estate shall be distributed amongst his children. If, therefore,

1

the testator decides to leave his estate to his wife for life, and afterwards for his children in equal shares, it will be necessary, either to constitute his executors trustees for this purpose, or to appoint special trustees. Once the trustees have accepted the trust, they will carry out the testator's directions, in accordance with the rules which the courts of equity, and now statute, have evolved to govern the conduct of trustees.

One other example of the very wide scope of the modern law of trusts may be given. An increasingly common, and important, method by which a person may make investments is in the units of what is called a unit trust. Such a trust is a trust in the true sense of the word. A very considerable number of investors may subscribe varying sums to form the capital of the trust, which is then invested in a wide variety of securities. These are placed in the names of the trustees, who thenceforth hold them on behalf of the subscribers, in proportion to the capital which each has subscribed. The investments are managed by managers, who are responsible to the trustees, and subject to the costs of management, the profits accrue proportionally to the subscribers, all of whom are the beneficiaries of the trust. The interests of these beneficiaries, as indeed, of the beneficiaries of all trusts, may be assigned to other persons.

The unit trust is a useful example of the flexibility of the trust concept, and it may be contrasted with the investment trust, which, in a number of ways, has similar objects and functions to the unit trust, but the investment trust is not, technically, a trust at all, but a limited liability company, whose business is the purchase and sale of shares and securities in other companies. In such a case, therefore, the investor is purchasing the shares or stock of a limited liability company. He does not become a beneficiary under a trust.[1]

In a unit trust the assets, normally stocks and shares, are purchased by, and vested in, trustees who exercise the powers of management. The investors, or unit holders, as beneficiaries, are thus enabled to participate in the holding of a wide range of securities assembled by experts in stock-exchange practice. The adoption of the trust mechanism also allows the trustees to buy in units, thus avoiding the rule which prevents a company (including an investment trust) from buying its own shares.

A. THE DEFINITION OF A TRUST

The exact definition of a trust has always offered special difficulties to legal writers. As Maitland observes at the beginning of his Third Lecture, " Of all the exploits of Equity the largest and the most important is the invention and development of the Trust "[2] and, therefore, it is almost impossible to explain the nature of a trust without discussing the nature of equitable intervention, and the historical reasons for the extension of what was in essence an obligation depending upon personal confidence into a wide interest in property which, however, has always stopped short of turning into a right *in rem*, at all events until the legislature intervened in 1925.

---

[1] See also Wortley, " Le ' Trust ' et ses Applications Modernes en Droit Anglais " (1962) 14 *Revue Internationale de Droit Comparé* 699.
[2] *Equity*, p. 23. See also the symposium on trusts (1967) 39 *University of Colorado Law Review* 177.

Coke[3] defines a use of lands as " a trust or confidence reposed in some other, not issuing out of the land, but as a thing collateral, annexed in privity to the estate of the land, and to the person touching the land, . . . So that *cestui que use* . . . has no remedy . . . but by *subpoena* in chancery . . ." What Coke means when he speaks of a trust as not issuing out of the land, but as a thing collateral to it, is that it differs from such a thing as a legal interest (for example a rent) which, inasmuch as it issues out of the land itself, binds every person who takes the land. A trust on the other hand is regarded by Coke as an incident accompanying the land only so long as certain conditions continue to exist. This point is amplified in the next part of the definition. The fact that the trust is " annexed in privity to the estate " means that the existence of the trust requires the continued existence of the estate itself, on which the interest of the beneficiary depends. The trust is also " annexed in privity " to the person, which has the consequence that if a trust is to be enforced against the person who holds the legal estate, it must be shown that he is a volunteer or is in some way affected by notice of the beneficiary's equity. Thus, a bona fide purchaser for value takes free of it.

Coke's definition has been accepted by some eminent authorities, and formerly by Lewin,[4] as the model for a general definition of a trust. Maitland, however, objects to it on two grounds: that to call a trust a confidence does not materially assist in elucidating its meaning, and he doubts if it is true that wherever a trust exists there is, in fact, some reliance reposed by one person in another. Although this may be true of most trusts, it is not true of all. Where the *cestui que trust* is unborn, or is ignorant of the existence of the trust, he places no confidence in the trustee, in the ordinary sense of the word, at any rate.[5] Nor would it seem that either the creator of the trust or the beneficiaries repose confidence where the trust arises by implication of law. Underhill[6] objects to Coke's definition on other grounds. Where a trust of a chose in action exists, the equities attaching to it are generally not merely collateral. Further, the use of the phrase, " some other " implies that the trustee must be a person distinct either from the creator of the trust or from the beneficiary; but the trustee may be either of these. Finally, since the Judicature Acts, any division of the High Court may take cognisance of equitable rights.

There are, however, other and more fundamental objections to Coke's definition. Dr. Yale says of it: ". . . though a milestone in its day, [it] was a millstone round the neck of later generations."[7] This was primarily because Coke, regarding the beneficiary's interest as no more than a chose in action, appeared to have closed the door firmly upon the possibility of assigning it. Even before the Civil War, however, judicial opinion was turning against such a restricted view of the beneficiary's interest,[8] and Lord Nottingham finally achieved a transition, so that this interest progressively came to be regarded as a proprietary interest. Coincidently, the emphasis upon the obligation binding the conscience of the feoffee or trustee, so important in

---

[3] Co.Lit. 272*b*.
[4] *Law of Trusts* (15th ed.), p. 11.
[5] *Equity*, Lecture IV, pp. 43–44.
[6] *Law of Trusts and Trustees* (12th ed.), p. 4.
[7] *Lord Nottingham's Chancery Cases*, Vol. II, p. 89.
[8] *e.g.* Rolle, J., in *R.* v. *Holland* (1648), Aleyn 14 (Yale, *ibid.*, p. 90).

the earlier treatment of uses, declined, with the result that both the King and corporations came to be regarded as capable of trusteeship. "Though a corporation could not stand seised to an use, yet they may stand seised to a trust, for the old reason fails and there are other ways to enforce the execution of a trust besides the imprisonment of the trustee . . ." [9] Today, therefore, Coke's definition inadequately reflects the extent of the beneficiary's interest, where a trust has been created.

Another type of definition is furnished by Spence.[10] In his view, a trust is a beneficial interest in, or beneficial ownership of real or personal property, unattended with the possessory or legal ownership thereof. Mr. Justice Story's definition [11] is very similar—

> A trust . . . may be defined to be an equitable right, title, or interest in property, real or personal, distinct from the legal ownership thereof.

The definitions contained in Judge Josiah Smith's *Equity* and in early editions of Snell's *Equity* were almost identical, and another definition by Mr. Justice Story appears in *Wilson* v. *Lord Bury* [12]—

> A trustee is a person holding the legal title to property under an express or implied agreement to apply it, and the income arising from it, to the use and for the benefit of another person, who is called the cestui que trust.

Underhill objects, however, that this class of definition does not define a trust at all, but merely the beneficial interest arising under it. His own definition [13] of a trust is—

> . . . an equitable obligation, binding a person (who is called a trustee) to deal with property over which he has control (which is called the trust property), for the benefit of persons (who are called the beneficiaries or *cestuis que trust*), of whom he may himself be one, and any one of whom may enforce the obligation.

This definition was accepted without qualification by Romer, L.J., in *Green* v. *Russell*.[14] The only objections to this definition are that it will not include charitable trusts, nor again trusts which, though good, are unenforceable, *e.g.* a trust for the maintenance of a tomb in a churchyard or for the support of dogs and horses, provided it is limited to the period permitted by the perpetuity rule.[15]

It should also be observed that it is incorrect to speak of a trust as the

---

[9] *Sterling* v. *Wilford* (1676), Yale, *ibid.*, Case 579.

[10] *The Equitable Jurisdiction of the Court of Chancery*, Vol. I, p. 496.

[11] *Commentaries on Equity Jurisprudence* (3rd English ed., 1920), p. 394.

[12] (1880), 5 Q.B.D. 518, 530–531. See also *Re Williams*, [1897] 2 Ch. 12, 19, *per* Lindley, L.J.

[13] As given in his *Law Relating to Trusts and Trustees* (12th ed., 1930), p. 3.

[14] [1959] 2 Q.B. 226, 241. See also Cohen, J., in *Re Marshall's Will Trusts*, [1945] Ch. 217, 219.

[15] See *Re Dean* (1889), 41 Ch.D. 552, 557; *Mitford* v. *Reynolds* (1848), 16 Sim. 105; *Re Wood*, [1949] Ch. 498; *Re Wightwick's Will Trusts*, [1950] Ch. 260. It has been doubted whether unenforceable trusts can properly be regarded as trusts at all. See Kiralfy, "'Purpose Trusts,' Powers and Conditions" (1950) 14 *Conveyancer* (N.S.) 374; and *Re Astor's Settlement Trusts*, [1952] Ch. 534 (Keeton and Sheridan, *Case-Book on Equity and Trusts* (2nd ed.), p. 252). (Hereafter, this case-book is simply referred to as "Cases.") See also Chap. XI, ss. A-C, *post*.

relationship which arises when the legal ownership of property is vested in one person, and the beneficial ownership in another, for there may be a trust of an equitable interest, *e.g.* where a beneficiary under a settlement gives his beneficial interest on trust for another; and, moreover, in the case of settlements of land, the Settled Land Act 1925 secures that the legal estate shall be vested in the tenant for life, and the trustees of the settlement do not necessarily hold any property at all. In such a case the tenant for life is constituted an express trustee of the legal estate.[16] All that can be said of a trust, therefore, is that it is the relationship which arises wherever a person called the trustee is compelled in equity to hold property, whether real or personal, and whether by legal or equitable title, for the benefit of some persons (of whom he may be one [17] and who are termed beneficiaries) or for some object permitted by law, in such a way that the real benefit of the property accrues, not to the trustees, but to the beneficiaries or other objects of the trust.

The trustee, it may be noticed, may himself be a beneficiary; and, once the trust has been created, it is enforceable by the beneficiaries, and not by the person who has created the trust.

The American Law Institute, in its *Restatement of the Law of Trusts*, adopts a substantially similar definition. It states—

> A trust . . . when not qualified by the word " charitable," " resulting " or " constructive," is a fiduciary relationship with respect to property, subjecting the person by whom the title to the property is held to equitable duties to deal with the property for the benefit of another person, which arises as a result of a manifestation of an intention to create it.[18]

It will be noticed that three important types of trust are excluded from this definition, whilst the definition given above attempted to include them. In the United States, however, the conception of a constructive trust has been developed much further than it has been in England, and in consequence it requires separate treatment. Charitable trusts also are treated separately by the American Law Institute, although there seems to be no reason why a charitable trust should not be included within the definition offered by them.

Maitland's observation that Gierke was not familiar with the implications of an English trust [19] is no longer true of eminent continental lawyers, some of whom have devoted considerable attention to this particular institution of English law, and M. Pierre Lepaulle has done much to explain the trust to continental critics.[20] He observes that it is impossible to regard the characteristic of a trust as a right *in personam* of the *cestui que trust* against the trustee, or as a division of rights of property between them. If the essential element of a trust is discoverable, it is something which is common to all trusts, express, implied, constructive, public and private. There is, he maintains, no single essential right or duty common to all trusts. The only necessity is that property (in its widest sense, *res*) should exist, and that it

---

[16] Settled Land Act 1925, s. 16 (1).
[17] But not a secret trustee: *Re Rees*, [1950] Ch. 204.
[18] 2d, p. 6, s. 2.
[19] *Equity*, p. 23.
[20] *Traité Théorique et Pratique des Trusts*, esp. pp. 23–51. See also " Trusts and the Civil Law " (1933) 15 *Journal of Comparative Legislation* 18.

should be appropriated to the fulfilment of some object. A trustee is not an absolute necessity for a trust (" a trust shall never fail for want of a trustee "), though he is for its proper execution. Accordingly, "The rights and obligations of the trustee will vary according to only one thing, his mission. Such mission always consists in insuring that the *res* be properly appropriated to the aim to which it has been devoted, either by the settlor, by the court, or by operation of law. The rights that the trustee will have in each particular case depend on his obligations; they are tools given to him for the fulfilment of his duties, and such duties are determined by the appropriation to which the *res* has been devoted. Hence, it is apparent that: trustee, *cestui*, rights and obligations of either of them, are only means for reaching an end and ... that the essence of such legal institution can only be found in the *res* and its appropriation to some aim. Trusts appear to us, then, as a segregation of assets from the *patrimonium* of individuals, and a devotion of such assets to a certain function, a certain end." [21]

B. THE DISTINCTION BETWEEN A TRUST AND CERTAIN OTHER LEGAL INSTITUTIONS

1. Trust and Contract. It is essential to distinguish a trust from certain other relations which in some respects it may resemble. A trust has some of the characteristics of a contract, especially where it is the result of the act of the parties themselves. Sir Frederick Pollock,[22] indeed, suggests that in origin a trust is a form of contract, though it was treated distinctively in equity, and now possesses characteristics incompatible with the English theory of contracts. Thus, a trust, if completely constituted, may be enforced by a beneficiary who is not a party to it, whilst only the actual parties to a contract can, as a rule, sue upon it.[23] Further, a completely constituted voluntary trust is fully enforceable, whilst a contract not under seal, and lacking consideration, is not.

That there is a distinction between trust and contract will be evident from the existence of differing legal consequences attached to the two relations, as indicated in the preceding paragraph. It is also clear, however, that the determination of the question whether a given set of facts gives rise to a trust or a contract simply is not easy to determine. This point, as Professor Winfield justly observes,[24] has not hitherto received adequate attention from English textbook writers, notwithstanding the fact that difficulties arising out of it have been considered on several occasions by the court, and notwithstanding also that American writers have paid considerable attention to it.[25]

---

[21] " An Outsider's View Point of the Nature of Trusts " (1928) 14 *Cornell Law Quarterly* 52, 55.
[22] *Principles of Contract* (13th ed.), pp. 166–167. And see Maitland, *Equity*, p. 28, who points out that in the fourteenth century the common law courts had not yet begun to enforce simple contracts, so that an implied contract between feoffor and feoffee was still more beyond their jurisdiction.
[23] *Dunlop Pneumatic Tyre Co. Ltd.* v. *Selfridge & Co. Ltd.*, [1915] A.C. 847; *Scruttons Ltd.* v. *Midland Silicones Ltd.*, [1962] A.C. 446; *Snelling* v. *John G. Snelling Ltd.*, [1973] 1 Q.B. 87. But see the observations of Denning, L.J., in *Smith and Snipes Hall Farm Ltd.* v. *River Douglas Catchment Board*, [1949] 2 K.B. 500, 514 *et seq.*, and *Beswick* v. *Beswick*, pp. 11–12, *post*. [24] *The Province of the Law of Tort*, pp. 104–108.
[25] e.g. Corbin, " Contracts for the Benefit of Third Persons " (1930) 46 *Law Quarterly Review* 12, 33–36; Chafee, " Equitable Servitudes on Chattels " (1928) 41 *Harvard Law Review* 945.

Thus, in *Les Affréteurs Réunis Société Anonyme* v. *Leopold Walford (London) Ltd.*,[26] a charter-party provided that " A commission of three per cent. on the estimated gross amount of hire is due to Leopold Walford (London) Ld., on signing this charter (ship lost or not lost)." The House of Lords, following the decision in *Robertson* v. *Wait*,[27] held that the broker could join the charterers to sue under the charter as trustees for the broker. Here, however, there was an agreement between the parties enabling the broker to be joined. Again, in *Lord Strathcona S.S. Co. Ltd.* v. *Dominion Coal Co. Ltd.*,[28] the Lord Strathcona Company bought a ship from X, with notice of a charter-party made between X and the Dominion Coal Company. The Dominion Coal Company asked for a declaration that the Lord Strath-cona Company were bound to carry out the charter party, and also for an injunction against using the ship in a manner inconsistent with the charter-party. The Judicial Committee of the Privy Council upheld this claim of the Dominion Coal Company, holding that, as the Lord Strathcona Company had acquired the ship with notice of the fact that the ship was to be used for a particular purpose, they were in the position of constructive trustees, and were compelled to give effect to the charter-party. In reaching this decision, they purported to follow a dictum of Knight-Bruce, L.J., in *De Mattos* v. *Gibson*,[29] but, as Professor Winfield emphasises, there must necessarily be limits to this doctrine, otherwise the further doctrine of privity in contract has been demolished. The limits, he observed, " are that it applies only to *user* of the article transferred and that an interest in it must remain with the person who seeks to enforce the injunction."

In *Lord Strathcona SS. Co. Ltd* v. *Dominion Coal Co. Ltd.*,[30] the Privy Council were only incidentally concerned with the question of enforcing third party rights by way of trust. The main question to be decided was whether the purchasers of a ship could use it inconsistently with a pre-existing contract, made with the vendor, and known to the purchaser. The correctness of the decision reached by the Privy Council has frequently been doubted, and in *Port Line Ltd.* v. *Ben Line Steamers Ltd.*,[31] Diplock, J., reviewed the growth of the doctrine expounded in this case from the time of its birth in the observations of Knight-Bruce, L.J., in *De Mattos* v. *Gibson*.[32] In that case an injunction was granted to restrain a mortgagee of a ship, who had acquired his mortgage with knowledge of the plaintiff's charter-party, from interfering with the performance of a subsisting voyage charter. The decision, in the words of Knight-Bruce, L.J., was based on reason and justice, and was regarded by him as an application of the principle that equity will restrain a man who acquires property from another, with knowledge of a pre-existing contract affecting the property, from dealing with the property inconsistently with the rights of the third party under that contract. This, in 1858, was new law but it was apparently regarded as an extension of the principle in *Tulk* v. *Moxhay*,[33] which had been decided ten years earlier.

26 [1919] A.C. 801.
27 (1853), 8 Ex. 299.
28 [1926] A.C. 108.
29 (1859), 4 De G. & J. 276.
30 [1926] A.C. 108.
31 [1958] 2 Q.B. 146.
32 (1859), 4 De G. & J. 276.   33 (1848), 2 Ph. 774.

The observations of Knight-Bruce, L.J., in *De Mattos* v. *Gibson*,[34] were made in the course of an interlocutory appeal in which Turner, L.J., who concurred, expressed his view in different terms, as did Lord Chelmsford, L.C., who did not grant an injunction in the actual action. He based the right to an injunction on the fact that it is a tort knowingly to procure a breach of contract by another person.

The principle laid down by Knight-Bruce, L.J., was apparently capable of application to all kinds of property. Nevertheless in subsequent cases, this was doubted, and Scrutton, L.J., in *Barker* v. *Stickney*,[35] gave a list of decisions in which the courts had refused to apply it to various classes of property. The decision of the Privy Council in *Lord Strathcona S.S. Co. Ltd.* v. *Dominion Coal Co. Ltd.*,[36] in so far as it is based on the dictum of Knight-Bruce, L.J., was therefore a return to a doctrine which had long been discredited, and in *Port Line Ltd.* v. *Ben Line Steamers Ltd.*,[37] Diplock, J., regarded it as wrongly decided, and refused to follow it, although in doing so, he did not in any way challenge the proposition that if it could be found that either party had accepted obligations as trustee for the charterers these would be fully enforceable. This, once again, leaves open the question of the circumstances in which the courts may recognise and enforce a trust.

It has always been clear that a party to a contract can enter into it expressly as trustee for another. Thus, Jessel, M.R., in *Re Empress Engineering Co.*,[38] says—

> So, again, it is quite possible that one of the parties to the agreement may be the nominee or trustee of the third person. As Lord Justice *James* suggested to me in the course of the argument, a married woman may nominate somebody to contract on her behalf, but then the person makes the contract really as trustee for somebody else, and it is because he contracts in that character that the *cestui que trust* can take the benefit of the contract.

Such cases are simply normal applications of the trust-concept to contractual rights. It is when there is no express declaration of a trust that difficulties arise. A survey of the cases will show that the courts will not imply a trust where an intention to create one cannot be discovered in the surrounding circumstances. Thus Lord Greene, M.R., said in *Re Schebsman* [39]—

> It is not legitimate to import into the contract the idea of a trust when the parties have given no indication that such was their intention.

and in the same case, du Parcq, L.J., said [40]—

> It is true that, by the use possibly of unguarded language, a person may create a trust, as Monsieur Jourdain talked prose, without knowing

---

[34] (1859), 4 De G. & J. 276.
[35] [1919] 1 K.B. 121, 132.
[36] [1926] A.C. 108.
[37] [1958] 2 Q.B. 146.
[38] (1880), 16 Ch.D. 125, 129.
[39] [1944] Ch. 83, 89; and see Glanville Williams, "Contracts for the Benefit of Third Parties" (1944) 7 *Modern Law Review* 123; *Aschkenasy* v. *Midland Bank Ltd.* (1934), 50 T.L.R. 209, 51 T.L.R. 34; *Re Rose*, [1952] Ch. 499 (Cases, p. 225).
[40] [1944] Ch. 104.

it, but unless an intention to create a trust is clearly to be collected from the language used and the circumstances of the case, I think the court ought not to be astute to discover indications of such an intention.

In *Re Schebsman*, Mr. Schebsman, in retiring from his employment with a foreign company and its English subsidiary, had entered into an agreement with the companies whereby his employment ended upon payment of a fixed sum to him. The agreement also provided that if Schebsman should die within a specified period, the company should pay a sum to his widow, or if she were dead, to their daughter. Before the payments from the company to him were completed, Schebsman was adjudicated bankrupt, and died shortly afterwards. His trustee in bankruptcy claimed payment to him of all moneys payable, either to Schebsman, or his wife and daughter under the agreement, on the ground that the moneys formed part of the estate of Schebsman. The Court of Appeal rejected this contention, and in doing so, considered at length whether Schebsman could be regarded as trustee for his wife and daughter for the benefits to which they were entitled under the agreement. All three members of the Court of Appeal held that he was not. Whilst this decision freed the wife and daughter from possible claims by the trustee in bankruptcy it also (in the view of the Court of Appeal) had the consequence that neither Mrs. Schebsman nor the daughter could enforce their benefits under the contract, which, as regards them, were gratuitous payments by the company.

In reaching their decision in *Re Schebsman*,[41] the Court of Appeal were influenced by the decision of Simonds, J., in *Re Stapleton-Bretherton*,[42] three years earlier. Two brothers, Frederick and Edmund, executed a deed of covenant in which (1) Frederick covenanted with Edmund that if Frederick succeeded as tenant for life to an estate, he would during his life pay to Edmund and, after Edmund's death, to Edmund's widow, £1,000 a year; (2) Edmund covenanted with Frederick that in certain events, if he, Edmund, succeeded to the settled property, he would pay annual sums to the widow and daughter of Frederick. Edmund succeeded to the settled property, but when the widow and daughters of Frederick claimed payment of the sums under the covenant, Simonds, J., held that no trust had risen under the covenant in their favour. " They are not parties to the deed, and there is not to be found in it one word which suggests that either Frederick or Edmund was a trustee for any third party of the benefit of any covenant or of any sum of money that might be paid thereunder." [43]

A case of very considerable interest is *Harmer* v. *Armstrong*.[44] A agreed to purchase the copyright in certain periodicals from V, H, and L. The plaintiff, X, alleged that this agreement was entered into by A as agent and trustee of X, and although A denied it, this circumstance was proved to the satisfaction of the court. Eventually, the agreement between A and V, H, and L was rescinded, and the copyrights were sold, with notice of X's claim, to S. The plaintiff, X, thereupon brought an action against A, V, H, L and

41 [1944] Ch. 83.
42 [1941] Ch. 482.
43 [1941] Ch. 485.
44 [1934] Ch. 65.

S claiming a declaration that the defendant A had entered into the contract as agent and trustee for X, and claiming also specific performance of that agreement. The Court of Appeal accepted both these contentions, and granted X specific performance of the contract against S, the assignee of the contract with notice of the trust.

In *Harmer* v. *Armstrong*,[44] one of the parties to the contract had expressly contracted as agent and trustee for a third person. On the other hand, in *Re Miller's Agreement*,[45] A, on retiring from a partnership, sold his share in the partnership to the two other partners. They agreed under seal to pay annuities to A's three daughters from the date of his death, by quarterly payments, and the partners charged all their interests in the profits and assets of the partnership with the payment of the annuities. A died fifteen months after the execution of the deed, and estate duty was claimed on the value of the daughters' annuities, as being interests purchased or provided by the deceased within section 2 (1) of the Finance Act 1894. It was held that no legally enforceable interest arose on A's death, so that no duty could be levied. The daughters were not parties to the deed, and therefore could not sue on it, and the court decided that no trust in their favour had been created by the deed. Accordingly, they were not beneficiaries under a trust in equity.

Wynn-Parry, J.'s, decision in *Re Miller's Agreement*, it will be seen, is founded upon the same assumption as the decision in *Re Stapleton-Bretherton*, i.e. that as a matter of construction, there was no indication of any intention to create a trust discoverable in the agreement. In recent years, however, a more liberal principle has been accepted by some judges, and notably by Lord Denning. In *Smith and Snipes Hall Farm Ltd.* v. *River Douglas Catchment Board* [46] Denning, L.J. (as he then was), explained that the rule that no one could sue on a contract unless he was a party to it was not nearly so fundamental as was sometimes supposed, and that it had never entirely supplanted another, i.e. ". . . that a man who makes a deliberate promise which is intended to be binding, that is to say, under seal or for good consideration, must keep his promise; and the court will hold him to it, not only at the suit of the party who gave the consideration, but also at the suit of one who was not a party to the contract, provided that it was made for his benefit and that he has a sufficient interest to entitle him to enforce it, subject always, of course, to any defences that may be open on the merits."

Slightly later, he discussed the problem of a " sufficient " interest—

> It has sometimes been supposed that there must always be something in the nature of a " trust " for his benefit. (See *Vandepitte's* case.) [47] But this is an elusive test which does not explain all the cases, and it involves the trustee being made a nominal party to the action either as plaintiff or defendant, unless that formality is dispensed with, as it was in *Les Affréteurs Réunis Société Anonyme* v. *Leopold Walford Ld.*[48] The truth is that the principle is not so limited. It may be difficult to define what is a sufficient interest. Whilst it does not include the maintenance of prices to the public disadvantage, it does cover the protection

45 [1947] Ch. 615.
46 [1949] 2 K.B. 500, 514–516.
47 [1933] A.C. 70, 79.
48 [1919] A.C. 801.

of the legitimate property, rights and interests of the third person, although no agency or trust for him can be inferred. It covers, therefore, rights such as these which cannot justly be denied; the right of a seller to enforce a commercial credit issued in his favour by a bank, under contract with the buyer; the right of a widow to sue for a pension which her husband's employers promised to pay her under contract with him; (See *Dutton* v. *Poole* [49] and cf. *In re Schebsman* [50]); or the right of a man's servants and guests to claim on an insurance policy, taken out by him against loss by burglary which is expressed to cover them; cf. *Prudential Staff Union* v. *Hall*.[51] In some cases the legislature itself has intervened, as, for instance, to give the driver of a motor car the right to sue on an insurance policy taken out by the owner which is expressed to cover the driver. But this does not mean that the common law would not have reached the same result by itself.

Lord Denning also referred to section 56 of the Law of Property Act 1925 which provides that a person may take the benefit of any covenant or agreement respecting land *or other* property, although he may not be named as a party to it, and he pointed out: (1) that this was a statutory recognition of the principle; and (2) that the principle, and section 56 would have been sufficient in *Re Miller's Agreement* [52] to enable the daughters to sue on the covenant made for their benefit.

In *Drive Yourself Hire Co. (London) Ltd.* v. *Strutt* [53] he reaffirmed his belief that the effect of *Tweddle* v. *Atkinson* [54] was limited by the principle he had formulated, and also that section 56 of the Law of Property Act 1925 was wider than had commonly been supposed. It provoked strong dissent from other judges; for example, in *Green* v. *Russell*,[55] Romer, L.J., rejected it completely, and returned to the doctrine of *Tweddle* v. *Atkinson* [54] and *Dunlop* v. *Selfridge* [56] without qualification, at the same time confining the superimposition of trusts on contracts to cases where the trust was either express or where it arose from the construction of the instrument conferring the benefit. Even stronger repudiation came from Lord Simonds in *Scruttons Ltd.* v. *Midland Silicones Ltd.*,[57] where the House of Lords refused to allow a third party to a bill of lading to enforce some of its terms, which were inserted for his benefit. " For to me," said Lord Simmonds, " heterodoxy, or, as some might say, heresy, is not the more attractive because it is dignified by the name of reform " and he added that if it were desired to give a general right to a third party to sue on a contract for his benefit, this must be done by Parliament.

A further stage in this controversy was reached in *Beswick* v. *Beswick*.[58] Peter Beswick, a coal-dealer, made an agreement with his nephew, John

[49] (1678), 2 Lev. 210.
[50] [1944] Ch. 83, 103, 104.
[51] [1947] K.B. 685, 689, 690.
[52] [1947] Ch. 615.
[53] [1954] 1 Q.B. 250.
[54] (1861), 1 B. & S. 393.
[55] [1959] 2 Q.B. 226.
[56] [1915] A.C. 847.
[57] [1962] A.C. 446.
[58] [1966] Ch. 538.

Beswick, whereby in consideration of the transfer of his coal-dealing business to his nephew, the nephew would pay him £6 10s. a week for life and, on his death, £5 a week to his widow. All three members of the Court of Appeal held that the widow (suing as administratrix and in her own right) was entitled to enforce this agreement against the nephew, by specific performance of the agreement, even though no trust of the widow's interest under the agreement could be established. In his judgment, Lord Denning again affirmed that the rule in *Tweddle* v. *Atkinson*[54] was limited by the principle which he had already enunciated, and he added that the rule was simply one of procedure, affecting form, and not the underlying right. He also reaffirmed that section 56 of the Law of Property Act 1925 applied to all forms of property, real and personal, including things in action.[59] The widow's right was a thing in action, and accordingly, by virtue of section 56, the widow could enforce it, even though she was not a party to the original agreement. With this view the other two members of the Court of Appeal were in full agreement, but the House of Lords took a different view.[60] They did affirm the decision of the Court of Appeal that the widow could get specific performance, but only on the ground that she was the vendor's administratrix. They did not think (though Lord Upjohn was doubtful) that section 56 was anything more than a procedural provision: they thought it conferred no rights on third parties and that the context of the section excluded the application to it of section 205 (1) (xx).

To sum up, therefore: contractual rights in favour of third parties may be enforced by third parties where a contracting party, either expressly or by construction of the agreement, is established to be a trustee of those benefits for him.[61]

2. Trust and Bailment. Further, a trust must be distinguished from a bailment. This is not made any easier by the fact that the treatment of bailments in English law has been somewhat uncertain. Thus, Blackstone[62] defines a bailment as ". . . a delivery of goods in trust, upon a contract expressed or implied, that the trust shall be faithfully executed on the part of the bailee." Is a bailment, therefore, a trust or a contract? On the second point, it should be noticed that, although bailments are usually considered with contracts, and although many bailments are unquestionably contracts (*e.g.* carriage), yet not all bailments are contracts. Thus, an infant can make a valid bailment, whilst his capacity to enter into contracts is very restricted. Further, Blackstone's use of the word " trust " is misleading, for, in English law, that term has been appropriated to denote a relation which is only recognised and enforced in equity, whilst a bailment creates a binding legal obligation, enforceable at common law. It is submitted, therefore, that a better definition of a bailment would be: a delivery of goods to another for a limited purpose, *upon a condition*, express or implied, that they shall be redelivered to the bailor, or delivered to another at his order, when the limited

---

[59] See also s. 205 (1) (xx).
[60] [1968] A.C. 58.
[61] See, further, Samuels, " Contracts for the Benefit of Third Parties " (1968) 8 *University of Western Australia Law Review* 378; Wylie, " Contracts and Third Parties " (1966) 17 *Northern Ireland Legal Quarterly* 351.
[62] 2 *Commentaries*, Chap. 30, s. 2.

purpose is completely fulfilled. In a bailment, the bailor does not divest himself of ownership. He merely curtails his rights of enjoyment of the thing bailed in favour of the bailee. Further, the rights which the bailee acquires in virtue of the bailment may be enjoyed by him without reference to the bailor. He is in no sense given those rights simply to carry out some further purpose of the bailor's. This should not be misunderstood. In carriage, the bailee receives goods in order to transport them at the order of the bailor, but his rights as bailee do not arise in consequence of that purpose. They arise because of the bailment. The agreement to carry is a collateral undertaking which distinguishes this bailment from others. Under a trust, however, the trustee acquires full ownership of the property subject to it, and therefore the creator as such of the trust ceases to have any rights in the property at all, yet, at the same time, the trustee becomes owner only because he has undertaken to carry out the purpose of the trust and the fulfilment of that purpose conditions his ownership. Lastly it should be noticed (although the distinction is hardly fundamental) that whilst there may be a trust of all kinds of property, bailment extends only to chattels.[63]

3. Trust and the Office of Personal Representative. Again, the relationship of an executor or administrator to the beneficiaries under a will or towards those benefiting on intestacy is not necessarily that of trustee and *cestui que trust*. As Maitland points out,[64] the legatee's action for his legacy is older than the doctrine of trusts, and has never been brought entirely within it. Originally, the duties of personal representatives were enforced in the ecclesiastical courts, later in the common law courts, and (from the eighteenth century onwards) in the Court of Chancery. Yet an executor or administrator may very easily be a trustee, either as a consequence of the terms of the will,[65] or by operation of law, or some special circumstance. Thus, under the Administration of Estates Act 1925, s. 33, the personal representatives of a deceased intestate hold his real and personal estate upon trust for sale and conversion. Again, a personal representative who clears the estate becomes at that point a trustee if he holds on trust for an infant [66] or for persons in succession. Furthermore, most of the powers of trustees under the Trustee Act 1925 may also be exercised by personal representatives. Indeed a trust for the purposes of that Act is defined to include the duties incident to the office of a personal representative.[67] Nevertheless, the two offices still remain distinct. It will be shown later that different periods of limitation are applicable to them,[68] and the personal representative still possesses one or two powers not possessed by a trustee, *e.g.* a power to appropriate part of the estate in satisfaction of a beneficiary's interest. Moreover, a sole executor, acting alone, may dispose of the deceased's real property, whilst two trustees or a trust corporation would generally be required in the case of a trust.[69]

[63] For a juristic discussion of bailment, see Paton, *Jurisprudence*, Chap. XXII.
[64] *Equity*, p. 48.
[65] *Re Davis*, [1891] 3 Ch. 119; *Re Swain*, [1891] 3 Ch. 233; *Re Mackay*, [1906] 1 Ch. 25.
[66] *Re Cockburn's Will Trusts*, [1957] Ch. 438.
[67] Section 68 (17).
[68] *Post*, Chap. XXVI, s. C.
[69] As to when an administrator becomes a trustee *simpliciter*, see *Harvell* v. *Foster*, [1954] 2 Q.B. 367, where the observations of Sargant, J., in *Re Ponder*, [1921] 2 Ch. 59, were reconsidered. In *Re Cockburn's Will Trusts*, [1957] Ch. 438 Danckwerts, J., accepted the

4. Trust and Power of Appointment. A trust must also be distinguished from a power, more especially from a power of appointment. A power, said the learned authors of Goodeve and Potter's *Law of Real Property*, is " an authority to dispose of some interest in the land, but confers no right to enjoyment of the land. A power is the right to dispose of an estate or interest in property rather than ownership of an estate or interest." [70] A power is discretionary, whereas a trust is imperative; the trustee, if he accepts, must necessarily do as the settlor directs. [71] Furthermore, under a power, the persons amongst whom the appointment is to be made have no action against the appointor, in the absence of fraud, if he does not appoint, [72] whilst if property is left on trust to divide, the court will compel its division. In the last resort, the court will itself divide. Again, the objects of a power need not necessarily be capable of exact ascertainment whilst the objects of a trust must be certain. [73] Thus, when property is held on trust for the members of a class, the trust is void for uncertainty unless the class is described with sufficient precision to enable the trustees (without undue trouble and expense) to compile a list of all its members at the inception of the trust and to keep the list complete so long as the trust lasts. On the other hand, a power (including a discretionary trust) is valid even if no such list can be made; the only requirement of certainty is that a sufficient criterion of class membership be provided to enable the court to say of any person whether he is an object of the power or not. There are also certain powers which are termed " powers in the nature of trusts," and it may be that if the instrument purports to give a power, a trust is really intended, but the distinction rests upon the settlor's true intention. Thus, in *Burrough* v. *Philcox* [74] a testator gave property to trustees on trust for his two children for their lives, remainder to their issue, and, in default of issue, the survivor of them was to have power to dispose of the property by will " amongst my nephews and nieces or their children, either all to one of them, or to as many of them as my surviving child shall think proper." The testator's children having died without issue, and without any appointment having been made by the survivor, it was held that a trust in favour of the testator's nephews and nieces and their children had been created subject to a power of selection and distribution. Lord Cottenham observed [75] in that case: " . . . when there appears a general intention in favour of a class, and a particular intention in favour of individuals of a class to be selected by another person, and the particular intention fails, from that selection not being made, the Court will carry into effect the general intention in favour of the class."

---

contention of Sargant, J., in *Re Ponder*, [1921] 2 Ch. 59, that personal representatives who have completed administration, but who then execute the trusts of the will, become trustees in the full sense. They have the power under s. 36 of the Trustee Act 1925 to appoint trustees to act in their place.

[70] P. 344.

[71] By s. 25 (4) of the Law of Property Act 1925 a trust to retain or sell is now a trust to sell with power to postpone.

[72] The objects of a *bare* power may not have an action against the appointor even if there is fraud. The fraud would be upon the person entitled in default of appointment.

[73] See *Whishaw* v. *Stephens*, [1970] A.C. 508 ; *McPhail* v. *Doulton*, [1971] A.C. 424 (Cases, p. 84) ; *Re Baden's Deed Trusts (No. 2)*, [1973] Ch. 9 ; Keeton and Sheridan, *Equity*, p. 362, and 1974 Supplement, pp. 28–29. See also Chap. VIII, s. 3, *post*.

[74] (1840), 5 My. & Cr. 72. See also *Re Llewellyn's Settlement*, [1921] 2 Ch. 281.

[75] 5 My. & Cr. 92.

In the important case of *Brown* v. *Higgs*,[76] twice decided by Lord Alvanley, and then affirmed successively by Lord Eldon and by the House of Lords, Lord Eldon said, on the same point—

> . . . if the power is a power, which it is the duty of the party to execute, made his duty by the requisition of the Will, put upon him as such by the testator, who has given him an interest extensive enough to enable him to discharge it, he is a trustee for the exercise of the power, and not as having a discretion, whether he will exercise it, or not; and the Court adopts the principle as to trusts; and will not permit his negligence, accident, or other circumstances, to disappoint the interests of those, for whose benefit he is called upon to execute it.[77]

Where there is a power, with a gift over to other persons in default of appointment, however, this is sufficient to negative the presumption that there is a trust in favour of the persons who are the objects of the power. Even if there is no gift over, it does not necessarily follow that the court will execute the power as a trust. The test is whether the settlor has demonstrated an intention to benefit the class in any event. This was clearly emphasised in *Re Weekes' Settlement*.[78] There a woman gave property by will to her husband for life, with power to dispose of it by will amongst their children. The court held that there was no gift to such of the class as the husband might appoint (thus confining the husband's duties to a selection within the class), but a mere power to appoint with no general intention to benefit the class in any event. It is obvious from this decision that the actual intention of the testator finally governs the matter. This point is also well illustrated by *Re Combe*.[79] A testator devised and bequeathed residuary realty and personalty on certain trusts and then in trust for his only son for life, and from and after his death " In trust for such person or persons as my said son . . . shall by will appoint but I direct that such appointment must be confined to any relation or relations of mine of the whole blood." There was no gift over in default of appointment. Tomlin, J., observed [80]—

> Am I to approach this will governed by an inflexible and artificial rule of construction to the effect that where I find a power of appointment to a class not followed by any gift in default of appointment, I am bound to imply a gift to that class in default of the exercise of the power? Or ought I to approach this will for the purpose of construction in the same spirit as I approach any other will and endeavour to construe it and arrive at the testator's meaning by examining the words expressly used, only implying those things which are necessarily and reasonably to be implied?

Tomlin, J., held the latter was the correct principle, and decided that in this case a trust had not been intended, and had not been created.

These cases were followed in *Re Perowne*,[81] in which a testatrix gave all

76 (1799), 4 Ves. 708; (1800), 5 Ves. 495; (1803), 8 Ves. 561; (1813), 18 Ves. 192 (Cases, p. 77).
77 (1803), 8 Ves. 574.
78 [1897] 1 Ch. 289.
79 [1925] Ch. 210 (Cases, p. 80). See also *Tempest* v. *Lord Camoys* (1882), 21 Ch.D. 571; *Re Arnold*, [1947] Ch. 131.
80 [1925] Ch. 216.
81 [1951] Ch. 785.

her property to her husband for life, "Knowing that he will make arrangements for the disposal of my estate, according to my wishes, for the benefit
of my family. . . ." There was no gift over in default of appointment. The
husband died without having validly exercised the power to appoint. Harman,
J., held that there was no sufficient intention expressed in the will to impress
the power with the character of a trust.[82]

5. Trust and Agency. A trust must also be distinguished from agency. A
trustee has full title to the trust property in law; an agent employed to deal
with his principal's property does not have title to it, although he may have
special statutory powers of disposition. Moreover, an agent acts on behalf of
his principal and subject to his control. A trustee is not subject to the control
of a beneficiary, beyond his obligation to deal with the trust property in
accordance with the terms of the trust. Again, agency is based on agreement
between principal and agent, but there is not necessarily any agreement
between trustee and beneficiary. The American *Restatement of the Law of
Trusts* further notices that an agent can subject his principal to liabilities
towards third persons, whilst a trustee cannot involve his beneficiary in such
liabilities; further, agency arises as a result of consent between principal and
agent, whilst a trust can arise without the consent of trustee or of beneficiary
and, finally, agency may be terminated on the death or at the will of either
party, whilst a trust may not. Nevertheless, it must be added that trust and
agency sometimes coincide. This is considered later.[83]

C. THE PROPERTY THAT MAY BE HELD IN TRUST

Generally speaking, all property which may be privately owned, whether real
or personal, legal or equitable, may be held in trust, unless some special rule
of law prevents it, although in practice it will be found that the property most
frequently held on trust includes land, stock, and shares. Thus, in *Gilbert* v.
Overton,[84] A held an agreement for a lease, and assigned all his interest in it
to trustees upon certain trusts. It was held that, though this was a settlement
of an equitable interest only, it was perfectly good. The settlement of a
reversion is entirely valid.[85] The position of expectancies, however, is a little
different. There may be what purports to be an assignment in equity, which is
construed as an agreement to assign when the expectancy becomes a certainty.
From that date only is the assignment complete, so that if in the interval
the assignor becomes bankrupt, the assignment of the expectancy fails.[86]

Lord Shaw observed in *Lord Strathcona S.S. Co. Ltd.* v. *Dominion Coal
Co. Ltd.*[87]—

---

[82] As to powers of appointment, see Keeton and Sheridan, *Equity*, Chap. X, and 1974
Supplement, pp. 28–31.
[83] *Post*, Chap. XIV, s. H. On the position of the agent as trustee, see Brodhurst, " Following
Property in the Hands of an Agent " (1898) 14 *Law Quarterly Review* 272 ; Powell, *Law of
Agency*, 2nd ed., pp. 25–26 ; Hanbury, *Principles of Agency*, 2nd ed., pp. 3–10 ; Fridman,
Law of Agency, 3rd ed., pp. 15–18 ; Stoljar, *Law of Agency*, pp. 10–11. On the director as
trustee, see Keeton, " The Director as Trustee " (1952) 5 *Current Legal Problems* 11.
[84] (1864), 2 H. & M. 110.
[85] *Shafto* v. *Adams* (1864), 4 Giff. 492.
[86] *Tailby* v. *Official Receiver* (1888), 13 App.Cas. 523. Cf. *Re Lind*, [1915] 2 Ch. 345.
where an assignee of an expectancy failed to prove in the assignor's bankruptcy. The bankrupt received his discharge, and the Court of Appeal held that the assignment remained in
force. See also *Re Gillott's Settlement*, [1934] Ch. 97.   [87] [1926] A.C. 108, 124.

The scope of the trusts recognized in equity is unlimited. There can be a trust of a chattel or of a chose in action, or of a right or obligation under an ordinary legal contract, just as much as a trust of land. A ship-owner might declare himself a trustee of his obligations under a charter-party, and if there were such a trust an assignee, although he could not enforce specific performance of the obligation, he would fail to do so only on the broad ground that the Court of equity had no machinery by means of which to enforce the contract. Subject to this an assignee of the charterer could enforce his title to the chose in action in equity, even though he could not have done so at law.

Some types of property are made inalienable by statute. In this class are pensions to officers in the Crown's forces, or to the widow of an officer. The position of officers on half-pay is considered in *Grenfell* v. *Dean and Canons of Windsor*,[88] where it was held that half-pay is ". . . a sort of retainer, . . . the means by which they, being liable to be called into public service, are enabled to keep themselves in a state of preparation for performing their duties." In *Davis* v. *Duke of Marlborough*,[89] the duke's estate, having been granted as a reward, was held to be alienable, but his pension to support the object was not.

In *Earl Nelson* v. *Lord Bridport*[90] it was held that there could not be a trust of real estate, when the tenure under which it was held was inconsistent with the trust to be created.

The position of trusts of foreign property calls for special consideration. The rule of private international law is that moveables follow the person. Thus, if a person is within the jurisdiction, so is all his moveable estate, and accordingly an enforceable trust of it may be created.

As regards foreign lands, a long succession of cases has established the rule that the court will enforce natural equities, and compel the specific perform-ance of contracts if: (1) the parties are within the jurisdiction, and (2) there is no insuperable obstacle to the execution of the decree. This question is more fully discussed in Chapter XXVII.

Trusts of Insurance Policies. A particular problem has arisen where A takes out a policy of insurance, which is on the life of B, and which is expres-sed to be for the benefit of B. The cases have established: (1) the mere fact that A takes out a policy which is expressed to be for the benefit of B, does not establish a trust of which B is the beneficiary; (2) the mere fact that the policy provides that the policy moneys are to be payable to B does not create a trust in favour of B. Nevertheless, the true construction of the policy may establish that a trust is intended, and this may be when the person who takes out the policy ceases to have any beneficial interest in it, the trust being for the person for whose benefit the policy is expressed to have been taken out, and to whose personal representatives payment is to be made.[91]

---

[88] (1840), 2 Beav. 544, 549. See also *Davis* v. *Duke of Marlborough* (1818), 1 Swanst. 74.
[89] (1818), 1 Swanst. 74.
[90] (1846), 8 Beav. 547. See also *Allen* v. *Bewsey* (1877), 7 Ch.D. 453.
[91] *Cleaver* v. *Mutual Reserve Fund Life Association*, [1892] 1 Q.B. 147; *Re Engelbach's Estate*, [1924] 2 Ch. 348; *Re Sinclair's Life Policy*, [1938] Ch. 799; *Re Clay's Policy of Assurance*, [1937] 2 All E.R. 548; *Re Foster*, [1938] 3 All E.R. 357; *Re Webb*, [1941] Ch. 225; *Re Foster's Policy*, [1966] 1 W.L.R. 222.

CHAPTER II

THE DEVELOPMENT OF THE LAW OF TRUSTS

THE modern trust grew out of the medieval custom of putting land and other forms of property to use. It should be observed, however, that the ultimate origin of the conception of the use is still one of the controversial topics of jurisprudence. The view current in the early part of the nineteenth century, before the rise of the modern school of legal historians, was that the English use was the counterpart of the Roman *usus usufructus* or of the *fideicommissum*, but this theory may now be regarded as finally exploded, more especially since Maitland has demonstrated that the term itself is derived, not from *ad usus*, but from *ad opus*.

In *Abdul Hameed Sitti Kadija* v. *De Saram*,[1] the Privy Council examined the differences between a *fideicommissum* as it exists in the modern law of Ceylon (Sri Lanka), and a trust. Adopting the analysis of Professor R. W. Lee [2] they pointed out that—

(1) the distinction between the legal and equitable estate is the essence of a trust but not of a *fideicommissum*;

(2) in a trust the legal ownership of the trustee and the equitable ownership of the beneficiary are concurrent and often coextensive, whilst in a *fideicommissum* the ownership of the fideicommissary begins where that of the fiduciary ends; and

(3) " In the trust, the interest of the beneficiary, though not described as equitable ownership, is properly ' jus neque in re neque ad rem,' against the bona fide alienee of the legal estate it is paralysed and ineffectual; in the fidei commissum the fidei commissary, once his interest has vested, has a right which he can make good against all the world, a right which the fiduciary cannot destroy or burden by alienation or by charge."

Maitland himself held the view that the use arose out of the common law rules of agency, and was an informal agency applied originally to chattels, the relationship crystallising only when the practice was applied to land.[3] Mr. Justice Holmes held another view,[4] which at one time received very considerable support, and some of the implications of which have been accepted by Sir William Holdsworth. Holmes found the forerunner of the feoffee to uses in the *treuhand* or *salman* of early Teutonic law. The *salman* was the primitive executor, to whom property was transferred for certain purposes, and who administered the personal property of the deceased. The property was transferred to the *salman* in the lifetime of the owner of the land, to be applied for specified purposes after the owner's death. In this custom some may perhaps discern the origin of the English will to uses.

---

[1] [1946] A.C. 208, 217 (Cases, p. 192). See also *Abeyawardene* v. *West*, [1957] A.C. 176; Cooray, *Reception in Ceylon of the English Trust*.
[2] *Introduction to Roman-Dutch Law* (3rd ed., 1931), p. 372.
[3] See Maitland: *Collected Papers*, Vol. III, pp. 321–404.
[4] " Early English Equity," *Select Essays in Anglo-American Legal History*, Vol. II, p. 705.

Holmes also suggested that since jurisdiction with regard to the administration of the goods of a deceased passed to the ecclesiastical courts after the Conquest, the origin of the use in English law may therefore be ascribed in some measure to them. Holdsworth [5] carried this view a step further and regarded the old Teutonic institution as a characteristic of English land law shortly after the Conquest, but during the latter part of the fourteenth century the common law finally rejected the use as applicable to land, having by that time developed its own more rigid rules; although in respect of chattels the use received a species of recognition in the actions of detinue and account. The Chancellor, therefore, in protecting the beneficiary, was in reality giving effect to a relationship which was common, ancient, and well-understood.

Another view has been advanced by Professor Ames,[6] who held that the use was a product of the English legal system, and the logical consequence of the maxim that equity acts on the conscience. Furthermore, he was of the opinion that the Chancellor, in enforcing uses, was to some extent guided by the existence of the actions of account and detinue, applicable to the situation arising where chattels had been given for the use of third persons. This view has encountered considerable criticism, and Sir William Holdsworth stressed the point that the common law could never have evolved a satisfactory protection for the beneficiary from assumpsit.

All these theories, except in so far as they correct a false interpretation of the facts of legal history, are somewhat beside the point. Modern English law has very closely assimilated the position of the executor and the administrator to that of the trustee, but it would be as false to derive the modern office of personal representative from trusteeship as it is unnecessary to derive the office of trustee from that of the primitive executor. It is submitted that the basic conception of a use is fundamental, and appears in several systems of law, though the working out of its legal incidents eventually exhibits considerable differences. Where certain persons cannot hold the more important forms of property at all, and others can only hold it with difficulty or disadvantageously, then the lawyer must find a way out. The Roman lawyer in the time of Augustus evolved the *fidei commissum*, the medieval landowner, or his legal adviser, evolved the use, and then looked to some official to protect him. Holdsworth has shown that the common law judges only finally turned their backs on the use with regret.[7] Their loss was the Chancery's gain, and Potter rightly emphasises the fact that the ecclesiastical Chancellor of the Middle Ages was the proper person to prevent a serious breach of faith such as was involved in undertaking the execution of a use.[8]

Once the use obtained recognition in equity, its employment became exceedingly common. The medieval property-owner put his lands to use for one of several purposes—either for a lawful object, which for its fulfilment

---

[5] *History of English Law*, Vol. IV, pp. 410–417.

[6] " The Origin of Uses and Trusts," *Select Essays in Anglo-American Legal History*, Vol. II, p. 737 *et seq.*

[7] Possibly it was because juries were unable to declare whether uses existed or not, on account of the privacy which accompanied their creation: Holdsworth, *History of English Law*, Vol. IV, p. 415.

[8] *Historical Introduction to English Law* (4th ed.), p. 606.

required the interposition of someone other than the donor and the beneficiary, or for fraudulent purposes. In the first class of objects may be included the practice of making a will by way of use, since the medieval land law, regarding feudal tenure as a personal relationship, declined to permit alienation by will, and the position at common law remained unaltered until the Statute of Wills 1540; again, since at common law a man could not convey either to himself or his wife, he made a settlement of land by enfeoffing others, with the intent that they should re-enfeoff the feoffor and his wife to hold to them and the heirs of their bodies. Among fraudulent practices may be mentioned the granting of lands to uses to defraud creditors, and to delay actions for the recovery of the lands granted. Both these objects were from time to time prohibited by statutes,[9] which were nevertheless evaded. A third class of objects occupied an intermediate position. It became possible to evade the prohibition imposed by the Statutes of Mortmain upon the gifts of land to ecclesiastical foundations, some of whom, and especially the Franciscans, were bound to poverty, and so declined the legal ownership of land, but not its beneficial enjoyment. This evasion was attacked by the Statute 15 Ric. II, c. 5 but not completely abolished, for the statute did not prevent the grant of land by way of use to unincorporated bodies, such as parishes.

Finally, from the time of Edward I onwards, landowners adopted the practice of enfeoffing, not one person, but several, more especially where the object was to create a will by way of use. The advantages of this practice were two. In the first place, the beneficiary relied upon the faith, not of one person, but of several, and therefore when the use was enforced in the Chancery, he had recourse against all the feoffees; and, furthermore, it was possible to postpone, and ultimately to evade, many of the incidents of feudal tenure, for as between the feoffees the rule of survivorship applied, and if the feoffees or the beneficiaries had the power of appointing new feoffees in place of those who died, relief, wardship, marriage, forfeiture for treason or felony, and the wife's right to dower might all be successfully avoided. This was naturally disliked by the great feudal overlords, and more particularly by the King, who lost by the practice and secured no compensating gains. It is therefore not surprising to find that, by a statute of 1487, it was provided that where the *cestui que use* of lands who held in knight service died intestate, his heir was liable to wardship and relief. A much more comprehensive statute was, however, about to be passed.

The common law (it has been observed) declined to enforce the use in favour of the beneficiary, and therefore for some time the beneficiary had no real remedy. It seems, however, that there was a practice whereby persons, enfeoffed for a special purpose, plighted their faith to do the feoffor's will. As a result of this, if the feoffee failed to discharge his trust, a suit *laesio fidei* lay in the ecclesiastical courts. From the time of Henry II onwards, such suits, where they concerned a lay fee or involved chattels or debts other than those involved in a testamentary or matrimonial action, were prohibited. The creators of uses then attempted to secure the fulfilment of their wishes by means of conditions and covenants, but these only afforded an imperfect protection. At length, in the reign of Richard II, the Chancellor

---

[9] *e.g.* 50 Edw. III, c. 6; 1 Ric. II, c. 9; 2 Ric. II, st. 2, c. 3.

interfered to protect the beneficiary, either because, being ecclesiastics, the Chancellors were accustomed to regard breach of a solemnly undertaken obligation as actionable, or simply on the general equitable ground that the conscience of a dishonest feoffee ought to be purged.

Although the Chancery eventually gave the widest possible orbit to the use, the view of the common law courts was that the feoffee was the unencumbered owner of the property, and the beneficiary was simply a tenant at will. Accordingly, the beneficiary was deemed to have no *estate* in the land, and since, as Maitland has put it, equity comes not to destroy but to fulfil, this was a position which the Chancellor could not upset.[10] The beneficiary's remedy was therefore a personal one against the feoffee; but to allow the remedy to prevail against the feoffee alone was obviously only to open the door to fraud, and therefore the remedy was rapidly made available against the feoffee's heir, and even against a person to whom the feoffee sold the land, provided that the purchaser took the land with notice of the trust.[11] On the other hand, if the purchaser of the legal estate took in good faith and for value, without notice of the trust, the purchaser could retain the land as against the beneficiary, who was restricted to his personal action for breach of trust against the feoffee. These extensions of the beneficiary's rights were only conceded over a lengthy period, but at the close of the Middle Ages there had been developed the most striking characteristic of the equitable estate. It should be observed that, unlike the modern trust, a use of land could only arise out of a fee simple, and not out of a fee tail or a life estate. It would seem that there was no objection to a use of a term of years, which was regarded primarily as a chattel, and not as an estate in the land. Uses and trusts of chattels did not become common until the growth of capital permitted the accumulation of semi-permanent funds, *i.e.* until after the Renaissance.[12]

The relationship between feoffee and *cestui que use* was also subject to equitable regulation, for the Chancellor required feoffees to discharge the obligations they had undertaken. In this way some of the cardinal rules applying to modern trusts were anticipated. The feoffee was compelled to establish in the land those interests that the grantor declared. Furthermore, he was obliged to permit the *cestui que use* to take the profits of the land, and to maintain actions for the recovery of the land at the request of the beneficiary; and, again, he must dispose of the land in accordance with his beneficiary's instructions. The feoffee could, however, recover his out-of-pocket expenses from the estate.

---

[10] This point is brought out very clearly in a case in Y.B. 15 Hen. VII Mich., pl. 1, for a reference to which we are indebted to Mr. A. S. Gilbert—

Le primer cas que Thomas Frowike argue apres que il fuit fait chiefe Justice fuit, que si le feffour sur confidence priste bestes damages fesans en la terre les feoffes, queux teignount a son use, et de quel il doit occupier a lour sufferaunce; s'il poet avower le prisel de ceux en son nosme, et de son droit demesne, ou non ; et toutz les Justices del dit banke disoient que il no poet avower le prise pour damages fesauntz en la terre en son droit demesne, mes il poet faire conusance en droit les feoffes come servant a eux. Et la cause est pour ceo que il nad riens en la terre, ne interest en la terre, mes solement un confidens demourt enter eux etc. mes les feoffes poient punissher luy pour son occupacion par course del comune ley, que prove que il nad interest. Et sil poet prender eux pur damages fesantz, et aver amendes pur ceo donques cestuy que doit les bestes serra deux foitz punys, quar les feoffes purra luy punisher.

[11] Y.B. 5 Edw. IV, 7, pl. 16.

[12] Holdsworth, *History of English Law*, Vol. IV, p. 421.

It has been shown that the interest of the *cestui que use* was in origin a personal remedy against his feoffee. This was greatly extended when the interest became enforceable against all except a limited class of persons— bona fide purchasers for value of the legal estate, taking with no notice of the trust. It was therefore natural that in equity the beneficiary's interest should be treated as an estate in the land; and the Chancellor allowed similar interests to be carved out of it to those existing at common law. The common law system was not applied in its entirety, however, and a number of the technical rules relating to seisin (for example, that the seisin must never be in abeyance) were not introduced into equity. Notwithstanding this limitation, the beneficiary's interest came to be regarded more and more, in the view of equity, as an estate in the land. From the standpoint of alienation, the estate of the *cestui que use* was much easier to handle than the legal estate, for it could be disposed of without any of the formalities necessary for a common law conveyance. The *cestui que use* declared his will to his feoffee, and the feoffee was bound to fulfil it.

Apart from uses which were expressly declared, the Chancellor also recognised certain implied uses. Where, for example, A enfeoffed B, and B gave consideration, no matter how small, B was deemed to have the use of the land also; but if A enfeoffed B and there was no consideration, then it was held that B was enfeoffed to the use of A. Furthermore, where A bargained and sold land to B, then B was considered to have the use (or equitable estate) in the land as soon as the contract was completed, and before conveyance. Out of these rules eventually developed the modern law relating to implied and constructive trusts, although with important modifications.

The full protection given by the Court of Chancery to landowners who put their lands to use greatly extended their powers over their land. " They could use their land to pay their debts; they could charge it with annuities in favour of their relatives or dependants, or with portions to their wives or younger children; they could order it to be sold and the proceeds devoted to charity; and they could found charitable institutions and provide for their management. In other directions also the machinery of the use proved to be serviceable. Provision could be made for a family by a marriage settlement far more easily than by the cumbersome machinery of the common law. Finally by their means, gilds, chantries, and unincorporated bodies were in substance enabled to enjoy proprietary rights." [13] In the eighteenth and nineteenth centuries the trust was used as a substitute for incorporation for numerous local government bodies, and as a convenient device for property-holding by clubs and many kinds of unincorporated associations.[14]

It will be remembered that the Crown was the chief loser, where lands were put to use, through loss of the feudal dues; and the statute of 1487 only slightly modified the position. Henry VIII, however, considered that the time had arrived for a much more comprehensive statute, and conceived the possibility of drastically curtailing the employment of uses, if not of abolishing them altogether. A bill with the latter object was, indeed, drafted,

---

13 Holdsworth, *History of English Law*, Vol. IV, pp. 438-439.
14 *Ibid.*, pp. 477-479. Lloyd, *Unincorporated Associations*, p. 19 *et seq.*

but it proved so unpopular that a more modified proposal was substituted, and was enacted as the Statute of Uses (1535).[15] The objects of the statute are set forth in an elaborate preamble, which emphasises the fact that, through the establishment of the use, feudal dues have been largely evaded.[16]

The immunity of the *cestui que use* from the common law rules governing freehold estates, and the possibility of creating uses for purposes which conflicted with public policy, brought about (as might have been expected) legislative intervention. More especially was this considered to be desirable since so many medieval uses were passive, *i.e.* the feoffees to uses were mere repositories of the legal title, the actual enjoyment and administration of the property being in the hands of the *cestui que use*. A succession of statutes sought to prevent the creation of uses for fraudulent purposes; and a statute of 1483 [17] was designed to protect those who had acquired through an original purchase from the *cestui que use*. It provided that such dispositions by a *cestui que use* should be valid as against the *cestui que use* himself, against his heirs, and also as against all persons who had title or interest only to the use at the time when the disposition was made by the *cestui que use*, *i.e.* against the feoffee who held only to the use of the *cestui que use* who alienated. These statutes, and especially that of 1483, are interesting, for they show a desire on the part of the legislature to pierce the veil which the estate of the feoffee to uses interposed between the *cestui que use* and the outside world, and they foreshadow the wider provisions of the Statute of Uses, aimed to vest the full legal ownership and power of disposition in the *cestui que use*. The real defect of the statute of 1483 was that it left untouched the powers of disposition of the feoffee to uses, so increasing uncertainties of title—a situation which was ended by the Statute of Uses.

The statute therefore provided that where any person or persons stood *seised* of lands or other hereditaments to the *use, confidence* or *trust* of any other person, persons, or body politic, then such person, persons, or body politic should be deemed to have lawful seisin and possession of such lands for such estate as they have in the use; and the estate of the feoffee should be deemed to be executed in the beneficiaries. Section 2 also provided that a like result should follow where (as was then common) several persons were seised to the use of one of them.

It is apparent that the statute was very curiously worded, and that it did not completely abolish uses, nor was it intended to do so. For the statute to operate, it was necessary that one person should be " seised " to the use of another. There was therefore no difficulty in holding that it did not apply to uses of leaseholds, copyholds and chattels. Furthermore, whilst a grant of land to A to the use of a corporation was within the statute, a grant of land to a corporation to the use of A was outside it. More important, however, was the principle that the statute did not apply to active uses, *i.e.* those where the feoffee had some positive duty to perform, such as the collection of rents and profits. Trusts for sale were therefore outside the statute. Lastly, the statute did not apply where A was seised to the use of

---

[15] 27 Hen. VIII, c. 10.
[16] Holdsworth points out, however, that the preamble is rather an accusation than a statement of sober fact (*History of English Law*, Vol. IV, p. 460).
[17] Ric. III, c. 1.

himself; it was essential that he should be seised to the use of another. On this point Denman, J. (citing a note of Butler's to Co.Litt., 272*a*), observed in *Orme's Case* [18]—

> With respect to the mode by which conveyances to uses operate—It is to be observed that to raise an use under the statute, the possession or seisin to serve the use must be in some person distinct from the cestui que use; as the statute requires that the person seised to the use and the person to whom the use is limited should be different persons; so that, if the possession is conveyed, and the use limited to the same person, at least if the use is limited in fee-simple, that is not an use executed by the statute, but the party is in by the common law: for the statute of uses mentions those cases only where " any person or persons stand seised to the use of any other person or persons."

The fact that for nearly a century after the statute uses were comparatively rare may serve as an indication that the great majority of uses before the statute were passive, and served as a means of evading obsolescent feudal burdens upon land-tenure and the technicalities of common law conveyancing. The vast majority of modern trusts are, of course, active. This distinction between the medieval use and the modern trust (which has been sometimes ignored) was present in the minds of Tudor lawyers, for in *Chudleigh's Case* [19] it is observed—

> ... for the better apprehension of the mischiefs which were before this Act, certain former statutes made against the abuses of uses in particular cases (for the treatise shall be only of uses) are to be considered. And thereby the abuses of such uses will fully appear, and that fraud was the principal cause of the invention of them, in subversion of law and justice.

After reciting various early statutes, passed with the intention of suppressing particular classes of fraudulent uses, the report continues—

> The statute of 1 Rich. 3, c. 1, which is more general than the other statutes, intends to remedy four great mischiefs by reason of secret feoffments to uses: (1) danger to purchasers and other the King's subjects; (2) trouble; (3) costs; (4) grievous vexations: so that it was not only danger, but danger with trouble; and not danger with trouble only, but danger with trouble and costs; and not danger with trouble and costs only, but with great vexation. Also, examples thereof are expressed in the preamble of the Act, no purchaser of lands in perfect surety, no wife of dower, no lessee of his lease, no servant of any annuity granted to him for his service, etc. by reason of these privy and unknown uses; this statute intended to provide for these mischiefs in establishing all feoffments, grants, etc. made by *cestuy que use, etc.* But so mischievous and sinister is the invention and continuance of uses, that they also overreached the policy and providence of the makers of this Act also: for, for example, the purchaser was not in a better case than he was before,

---

[18] (1872), L.R. 8 C.P. 281, 290. See also *Jenkins* v. *Young* (1631), Cro.Car. 230; *Meredith* v. *Joans* (1631), Cro.Car. 244; *Doe* v. *Prestwidge* (1815), 4 M. & S. 178; *Savill Brothers Ltd.* v. *Bethell*, [1902] 2 Ch. 523.
[19] (1589), 1 Co.Rep. 113*b*, 123*a*.

for if the feoffor limit to himself but an estate for life, or in tail, or to his wife, or to his son, etc. or if the feoffees made secret leases or estates, the purchaser could not have a sure estate by any estate that *cestuy que use* could make, so that danger, trouble, costs, and great vexation remained in the realm by these covinous and fraudulent uses, notwithstanding the said stat. of 1 Rich. 3. For the remedy of which and many other mischiefs, was the stat. of 27 Hen. 8, c. 10 made. . . .

It must be emphasised that where the statute operated, the estate of the feoffee was entirely destroyed and the *cestui que use* obtained a legal estate exactly corresponding to that which he would have enjoyed in equity under the use before the statute. At law the erstwhile *cestui que use* was, after 1535, deemed to be in possession of the land, and this even though he had never entered upon it. This gave rise to some difficulty. It was held, for example, that the possession conferred by the statute was not sufficient for the *cestui que trust* on whom the legal estate had been conferred by the statute to maintain an action of trespass, as this is founded upon a disturbance of actual possession. The nature of the statutory possession was considered in *Heelis* v. *Blain* [20] and again in *Hadfield's Case*.[21] In the latter case Hadfield was seised in possession of a rentcharge in consequence of a conveyance operating under the statute. It was held, following *Heelis* v. *Blain*,[20] that Hadfield enjoyed " actual possession " so as to entitle him to be placed upon the register of voters for 1872. Bovill, C.J., said [22]—

If we were to go through and attempt to reconcile the subtleties of this branch of the law, we should be embarking on a task which is manifestly hopeless. For some purposes the statute does, and for others it does not, give the actual possession. No case has been found which shews distinctly what is the effect of the statute for conveyancing purposes or the vesting of estates. Under these circumstances, the question arises whether we can clearly arrive at the conclusion that the Court in *Heelis* v. *Blain* [23] were wrong in holding that the Statute of Uses did give the grantee the " actual possession " of the rent-charge within the meaning of s. 26 of the Reform Act of 1832. Probably, if the matter had been res nova, I should have held that actual possession meant what the words import. But, under the circumstances, I do not find sufficient reasons for saying that a decision which has been acted upon and has regulated the franchise for so many years, and which has not been interfered with by the legislature who have had the subject before them, and have legislated upon it since that decision, ought now to be departed from.

The operation of the statute was not confined to uses which were expressly declared. It applied also to implied uses. Therefore, if a feoffment was made without consideration, equity implied a resulting use to the feoffor, which the statute executed, and the attempted conveyance thus became a nullity.

[20] (1864), 18 C.B.N.S. 90.
[21] (1873), L.R. 8 C.P. 306.
[22] L.R. 8 C.P. 317. *Cf. Orme's Case* (1872), L.R. 8 C.P. 281 ; *Savill Brothers Ltd.* v. *Bethell,* [1902] 2 Ch. 523.
[23] (1864), 18 C.B.N.S. 90.

Hence, where it was desired to make a voluntary feoffment between 1535 and 1925, it was essential to insert the phrase " to the use of " in order to negative the possibility of a resulting use. Now, by the Law of Property Act 1925, s. 60 (3), it is provided that " In a voluntary conveyance a resulting trust for the grantor shall not be implied merely by reason that the property is not expressed to be conveyed for the use or benefit of the grantee." A further point of considerable importance (but lying outside the scope of this work) is that by virtue of the statute secret conveyances of land became possible, and, moreover, it became possible to create a number of new forms of future interests in land in consequence of the operation of the statute upon what had formerly been equitable future interests created by way of use.

For a period, the extent of which would appear to be very uncertain, the primary object of the statute was fulfilled, and wherever a use was declared to exist, under the conditions prescribed in the statute, the legal estate was executed in the beneficiary. Twenty-two years after the statute, however, an old question received reconsideration, in the light of the statute, in *Jane Tyrrel's Case.*[24]

The point at issue was this. If, before the Statutes of Uses, A bargained and sold land to B to the use of A, or of some third person, then two uses arose. There was the *declared* use in favour of A or of the third person, and there was also the use in favour of B implied from the bargain and sale; and in such a situation the Court of Chancery held the declared use void, as repugnant, and enforced that which was implied. After the statute, the question arose in a new form, for the courts had to decide to which use the legal estate should now be attached. In *Tyrrel's Case*, the old rule was followed to the extent that the legal estate was declared to be executed in B, and the declared use, which was void for repugnancy before 1535, was also inoperative to pass any legal estate under the statute, for, as Dyer's report puts it, " an use cannot be ingendered of an use." It was also decided that where there was a conflict between two expressly declared uses, the second use was also void for repugnancy and was destitute of all legal effect.

The establishment of trusts (other than active trusts which escaped the Statute of Uses) was of slow growth. For some time, the rule established in *Jane Tyrrel's Case*[25] that a second use, repugnant to an earlier one, was repugnant and destitute of legal effect, held the field. Gradually, however, it was perceived that to apply this doctrine in its full rigour to inexpertly drawn documents was producing new hardships. Thus, in *Girland* v. *Sharp*[26] A enfeoffed his sons to the use of himself for life, and after to the use of his sons and their heirs for the performance of his will. The grant operated to enfeoff the sons in fee simple, but the further provision was void. In other cases, there was a similar feoffment by the statute on trust to convey, and the trust similarly failed. At length, Chancery intervened to enforce such trusts, " according to the intent," and similar action was taken in respect of trusts for the payment of the debts of the feoffor.[27] Both these were regarded as active trusts, however, which equity would compel the trustee to

24 (1557), 2 Dyer 155a.
25 (1557), 2 Dyer 155a (Cases, p. 185).
26 (1595), Cro.Eliz. 382.
27 *Sir Moyle Finch's Case* (1600), 4 Inst. 86.

fulfil. Only where charitable trusts were concerned was the Chancery prepared to enforce a second use which was passive in the period between the Statute of Uses and the Civil War.

It is in this connection that *Sambach* v. *Dalston* [28] constitutes a milestone along the road. In that case there was a bargain and sale of lands by A to B to the use of C. From the record it appears that B was content to allow C the rents and profits of the land, *i.e.* to recognise a trust. The Court of Chancery refused, however, to accept this solution, and ordered that B should convey to C, " according to the intent." The case, therefore, is not an early anticipation of the modern trust, but an affirmation of the Chancery's determination to see that conveyances were carried out in accordance with the settlor's manifest intent. Thus the trust remained comparatively an exceptional instrument until after the Restoration.

Substantially, the modern law of trusts was made possible by the enlightened development initiated by Lord Nottingham. The trust owed its inspiration to the medieval use, but in Nottingham's hands it acquired a distinct and different character. As Lord Mansfield acknowledged in *Burgess* v. *Wheate*,[29] " . . . trusts were not on a true foundation till Lord *Nottingham* held the great seal. By steadily pursuing from plain principles, trusts in all their consequences, and by some assistance from the legislature, a noble, rational, and uniform system of law has since been raised. Trusts are made to answer all the exigencies of families, and all purposes, without producing one inconvenience, fraud, or private mischief, which the statute of *H*. 8 meant to avoid."

The successive steps by which Lord Nottingham achieved this great advance have been traced by Dr. Yale.[30] Initially, Lord Nottingham turned to the older rules applicable to the use, and gradually adapted them to the newer trust which arose on the enforcement of the second use. Thus, for a time, at the Restoration, the doctrine of privity between feoffee and beneficiary, which had been the foundation of Coke's definition of a use, produced some anomalies. For example, the assignee or heir of a beneficiary was in privity with the feoffee, and could therefore enforce the use, but a wife or judgment creditor could not, and both of them were therefore excluded from equitable relief. The same doctrine also prevented the use from being enforced against a tenant by the courtesy, a tenant in dower, a lord entering by escheat, and a number of others (including, of course, the bona fide purchaser without notice of the trust).

On the other hand, from the outset, Nottingham accepted the assignability of trust interests, freeing them from the cramping limitations at law which persisted in respect of choses in action. Even as early as 1648, Rolle, J., had stated [31] that a trust " is not a thing in action, but may be an inheritance or a chattel as the case falls out." This was Nottingham's view

---

[28] (1634), Tothill 188 (Cases, p. 185), also reported as *Morris* v. *Darston* (1635), Nels. 30. See further Strathdene, " Sambach *v.* Dalston: An Unnoticed Report " (1958) 74 *Law Quarterly Review* 550.
[29] (1759), 1 Eden 177, 223 (Cases, p. 185).
[30] Nottingham's Chancery Cases, Vol. II, p. 87 *et seq.*; " The Revival of Equitable Estates in the Seventeenth Century: An Explanation by Lord Nottingham " [1957] *Cambridge Law Journal* 72.
[31] *R.* v. *Holland*: see Nottingham's Chancery Cases, Vol. II, p. 90.

also, and on it he built, by a succession of decisions, the conception of the
beneficiary's estate in equity in which there could exist interests with many
of the characteristics of legal estates. With this development, the notion of
personal confidence, reposing in the trustee, progressively declined. The
beneficiary, as Lord Nottingham pointed out, has other means of redress
than the threat of personal coercion by the Court of Chancery. Of these,
the principal was the right of the beneficiary to proceed against the trust
property itself, and it therefore followed that Nottingham would be concerned
to disentangle the trust estate from the trustee's own property, and to ensure
that the trust estate would be free from liabilities attaching to the trustee's
own property. Thus even as early as 1673,[32] he protected the beneficiary's
interest against a judgment creditor of the trustee, and in 1725, Jekyll, M.R.,
completed this development by granting similar protection in the bankruptcy
of the trustee.[33]

The problem of escheat was not disposed of so quickly. It was not until
1759 that the Court of Chancery decided (Lord Mansfield dissenting) in
Burgess v. *Wheate*[34] that a trust estate did not escheat for want of heirs
of the *cestui que trust*. The problem of possible escheat on failure of the
trustee's heirs long remained unsettled, although the predominant opinion
was in favour of escheat in such a case. In 1834, the matter was at last
settled by statute,[35] and it was then provided that the estate of the trustee
should not escheat, either for felony or for failure of heirs.

These developments were paralleled by other decisions, making the
beneficiary's interest available by an equitable *fieri facias*, whilst section 10
of the Statute of Frauds provided that the sheriff could seize in execution
trust property in satisfaction of the claims of beneficiaries' judgment creditors.
Other decisions of Lord Nottingham's time extended the availability of the
beneficiary's interest to satisfy his creditors.

Perhaps the most fundamental question answered by Lord Nottingham
was the establishment of the true foundations of the law of trusts. These
were defined in historic terms in 1676 in *Cook* v. *Fountain*.[36] In his judgment
in that case, he divides trusts into express trusts " which are raised and
created by acts of the parties " and implied trusts " which are raised or
created by act or construction of law." Implied trusts, it will be seen, in
this definition include those trusts which today are classified as implied,
resulting and constructive trusts. Express trusts, he explains, are declared
either by word or writing, and " these declarations appear either by direct
and manifest proof, or violent and necessary presumption," and then he
adds, in relation to both presumptive and implied trusts—

> There is one good, general, and infallible rule that goes to both these
> kinds of trusts; it is such a general rule as never deceives; a general rule
> to which there is no exception, and that is this; the law never implies,
> the Court never presumes a trust, but in case of absolute necessity. The
> reason of this rule is sacred; for if the Chancery do once take liberty to

[32] *Medley* v. *Martin* (1673), Rept.t. Finch 63.
[33] *Bennet* v. *Davis* (1725), 2 P.Wms. 316.
[34] 1 Eden 177 (Cases, p. 185).
[35] 4 & 5 Will. IV, c. 23.
[36] 3 Swanst. 585 (Cases, p. 194).

construe a trust by implication of law, or to presume a trust, unnecessarily, a way is opened to the *Lord Chancellor* to construe or presume any man in *England* out of his estate; and so at last every case in court will become *casus pro amico*.[37]

This was a matter of considerable importance in Lord Nottingham's times, for many titles had been shaken, and many arrangements affecting property had been entered into, during the Civil War and the Commonwealth. In *Cook* v. *Fountain*[36] itself Lord Nottingham held that an implied trust of certain leases had been established, but not of a rentcharge, where the evidence was not clear.

Even under the old law of uses a feoffment without consideration raised a use in favour of the feoffor. Lord Nottingham applied this rule to trusts also, although in *Grey* v. *Grey*,[38] he also accepted a further branch of the rules governing uses, by deciding that where a father transferred property to the name of his son, the court would presume (in the absence of evidence to the contrary) that an advancement of the son was intended. His judgment contains an elaborate analysis of the circumstances in which the presumption of advancement may be displaced by an implied trust for the father. In *Elliot* v. *Elliot*,[39] in the same year, he returned to this question, and once again discussed the circumstances in which the presumption of advancement could be rebutted. In other decisions, he refused to extend the presumption of advancement to other relationships, *e.g.* that of uncle and nephew.

The cases collected by Dr. Yale show that Lord Nottingham exercised from the first the discretion of the court to transfer trusts to other trustees, where the conduct of the trustee fell short of what equity required. There are also other cases illustrating Lord Nottingham's willingness to modify the terms of a trust in the interests of efficient administration. These have a historic importance, for they were discussed and approved, with similar cases in the following century, by Denning, L.J., in *Re Downshire Settled Estates*,[40] and although the majority of members of the Court of Appeal and the House of Lords[41] were not at that time disposed to concede that the jurisdiction in modern times was so extensive, the Variation of Trusts Act 1958 has now conferred a statutory jurisdiction in terms which Lord Nottingham would have regarded as appropriate.

Although Lord Nottingham classed constructive trusts along with implied and resulting trusts, the nature of a constructive trust was well known to him, even at the outset of his career as Chancellor. In *Holt* v. *Holt*,[42] fifty-six years before Lord Keeper King's decision in *Keech* v. *Sandford*,[43] the principle was plainly declared that where an executor secured the renewal of a trust lease for his own benefit, the lease nevertheless accrued for the benefit of the *cestui que trust*. There were numerous similar decisions in Lord Nottingham's time.

---

[37] 3 Swanst. 591–592.
[38] (1677), 2 Swanst. 594.
[39] (1677), 2 Ch.Cas. 231.
[40] [1953] Ch. 218, 270–273.
[41] In *Chapman* v. *Chapman*, [1954] A.C. 429.
[42] (1670), 1 Ch.Cas. 190.
[43] (1726), Sel.Cas.t.King 61 (Cases, p. 195).

Dr. Yale also points out [44] that the problem of precatory words was considered by Lord Nottingham, and that his inclination was not to construe words recommendatory as raising a trust, unless the context made it clear that a binding obligation in equity was intended. Even if the word " trust " was actually used, he did not necessarily regard this as conclusive, for " the word ' trust ' does not always imply so much but may be a declaration of his mind what should be done in a discretionary way." In all these cases, he emphasised, the problem was to discover the settlor's true intention.

One important branch of Lord Nottingham's work in the recreation of the law of trusts was concerned with the delimitation of the powers and duties of the trustee, and with the rights of the beneficiary against him. In an early case before the Civil War, *Townley* v. *Chalenor*,[45] Lord Keeper Coventry had already decided that a trustee was not generally liable for the acts of a co-trustee, but only for his own acts and defaults, unless he had been guilty of fraud, and had thereby participated in the co-trustee's breach of trust. This decision remained an isolated landmark until after the Restoration, when a body of equitable principles was progressively established. A trustee was not to be penalised for an honest mistake. Several decisions, and notably *How* v. *Godfrey*,[46] made it plain that a trustee was entitled to his out-of-pocket expenses in managing the trust, but was not to be paid for acting as trustee, unless the settlor expressly prescribed that he should. Moreover, a trustee, unlike an executor, had no right to prefer his own claim, in priority to other creditors, where the settlor was indebted to him.[47]

In a number of cases, Lord Nottingham developed the principle that trustees were bound to show reasonable skill and care. In fact, they were not liable, unless they were guilty of wilful default, although in *Jevon* v. *Bush*[48] he was inclined to impose strict liability. This tendency continued during the eighteenth century, and it was only in the nineteenth century that the courts returned to Nottingham's standard of care in determining a trustee's liability.

It has already been noticed that there are decisions of Lord Nottingham and his immediate predecessors that establish the principle that if a trustee renews a lease in his own name, he nevertheless holds it on behalf of the trust. As far as trustees were concerned, the rule was generalised so far as to establish the principle that " a trustee shall not profit from his trust." Nevertheless, the application of the rule was complicated by two factors: (1) the limited and uncertain range of trustee investments; and (2) the special position of executors who, although often treated as quasi-trustees, were nevertheless subject to special rules.

In Lord Nottingham's time, land was regarded as a fit subject for trustee investment, whether by purchase, or by mortgage, but the supply was limited. Until the establishment of more modern conceptions of national finance after the Revolution, government securities were distinctly hazardous. Some trustees invested money in commerce, but the losses which followed

---

[44] Nottingham's Chancery Cases, Vol. II, pp. 128–131.
[45] (1634), Cro.Car. 312.
[46] (1678), Rep.t. Finch 361.
[47] *Gell* v. *Adderley* (1681), 2 Ch.Cas. 54.
[48] (1685), 1 Vern. 342.

the South Sea Bubble brought this type of investment to an abrupt close, and they were responsible for stricter rules applicable to the responsibilities of trustees generally. A cautious trustee might ask for the directions of the court upon investments, but the entire question remained in a state of uncertainty until, in the eighteenth century, investment in government stocks became the rule, since this was the policy in investing funds under the control of the court, and the court would not penalise a trustee for following a policy which it would itself authorise.

On the other hand, it was undoubtedly the case that a number of trustees themselves invested trust money, and made a profit from it. Here the rule developed by Lord Nottingham was that the trustees bore the loss, and accounted for the profit. It was in cases like this that the position of executors for a time differed from that of trustees. At this period, it was the regular practice for executors to use the estate for their own purposes, and to retain the profit. A little later a distinction was drawn between executors who were solvent, and those who were not. A solvent executor could retain his profits; an insolvent executor could not. The distinction was founded on the fact that a solvent executor was in a position to repay the principal, while an insolvent executor was not. This distinction disappeared however after Lord Hardwicke's Chancellorship in the middle of the next century. All through the eighteenth century, the practice was common for the executor to use the estate of the deceased for his own benefit, and it was only in the nineteenth that the position of the executor was, in this respect, assimilated to that of the trustee,[49] even though Lord Nottingham had viewed the situation with concern, and (where the executor was also a trustee) had sought to apply to him the rule which he had developed in respect of express trustees.

It has already been noticed that the protection afforded to the beneficiary by Lord Nottingham made it necessary to define the circumstances in which the beneficiary's estate would not prevail against a purchaser. By successive decisions there were evolved the proposition that only the bona fide purchaser for value without notice of the trust was able to take free of it. This principle was established as early as 1673, in the leading case of *Bassett* v. *Nosworthy*,[50] and in later decisions Lord Nottingham laid the foundations of the doctrine of notice in equity. Thus, in *Salsbury* v. *Bagott*[51] he held that " a purchaser with notice from him that had no notice, or a purchaser without notice from him that had notice, are equally free." In the same case there was an examination of what constituted notice. It must be more than mere rumour; but notice would be imputed where it was the logical deduction from facts known to the purchaser. Thus, in *Moor* v. *Simon Bennett*[52] " The bill was to have an annuity out of certain lands purchased by the defendant. He pleaded himself to be a purchaser without notice of the plaintiff's title, but because he purchased from the heir in tail whose estate was subject to a revocation by the will of the father, it follows that the purchaser must be

---

[49] Yale, *Lord Nottingham's Cases*, Vol. II, p. 147.
[50] (1673), Rep.t. Finch 102.
[51] (1677), 2 Swanst. 603, 608.
[52] Yale, *Lord Nottingham's Cases*, Vol. II, p. 147; (1678), 2 Ch.Cas. 246, *sub nom. Moore* v. *Bennett*.

presumed to be knowing of the will and consequently could not be ignorant of the charge created by it."

Finally, it should be mentioned that the rule was firmly established in Lord Nottingham's time that a trustee could not purchase the trust property, even by means of a fine.[53]

Trusts in Other Legal Systems

During the present century, the trust has not only demonstrated once again its almost unlimited capacity to adapt itself to new situations, but it has also been progressively adopted in other legal systems. It is, in fact, no longer a characteristically English institution; it has become international.

From one point of view, this has long been the case, for the trust appears in all those legal systems which have developed from the common law. It has an exceedingly vigorous life in the United States, where it has developed in close correspondence with its development in England; it has been retained and developed in the Irish Republic; and in addition, it appears substantially in the English form, in the laws of Canada, Australia, New Zealand, Malaysia, the West Indies, Ghana, Nigeria, and all other parts of the Commonwealth where English settlers have taken the common law with them. For some time, however, countries where legal systems are derived from the civil law proved hesitant as to any reception of the trust, especially as the civil law possesses in the *fideicommissum* a separate institution, which in some ways has proved capable of adaptation to a number of purposes which, in English law, are fulfilled by the trust. Today, however, the trust is to be found in a number of civil law countries, and notably in Quebec, Lichtenstein, Panama, Puerto Rico, Mexico, Venezuela, Louisiana, Scotland and Ceylon. This is by no means the full extent of the modern influence of the trust concept, which has more or less directly influenced many other legal systems.[54]

One consequence of this reception of the trust in a number of civil law countries has been the elaboration of theories concerning the nature of the trust, which seem somewhat strange to the Anglo-American equity lawyer. Of these theories, that of Lepaulle, already mentioned, is possibly the most widely known, and it has directly influenced trusts legislation in several countries, and particularly that of Mexico. Even where the trust has not been introduced, *e.g.* in France and Switzerland, there has been considerable discussion of its juristic nature and functions.[55]

Professor T. B. Smith [56] has also shown that the law of trusts in Scotland has a long and interesting history. Trusts were enforced before the close of the seventeenth century and originated independently of the English law of trusts, possibly as a result of the exercise of the ecclesiastical jurisdiction prior

[53] *Bovy* v. *Smith* (1682), 2 Ch.Cas. 124.

[54] See Ryan, "The Reception of the Trust" (1961) 10 *International and Comparative Law Quarterly* 265; Fratcher, "Trust" (Chap. 11 of Vol. VI, "Property and Trust," of the *International Encyclopedia of Comparative Law*), p. 84 *et seq.*

[55] *e.g.* Le Trust et le Droit Suisse by Claude Raymond, Basle, 1954 (in which a number of other works on trust, published in Switzerland, France and Germany are cited); Motulsky, " De l'impossibilité juridique de constituer un 'Trust' anglo-saxon sous l'empire de la loi française " (1948) 37 *Revue Critique de Droit International Privé* 451.

[56] *Scotland*: in the *United Kingdom* volume of the *British Commonwealth Series*, Chaps. 34 and 35.

to the Reformation, or possibly as an attempt to preserve property from the uncertainties arising during the Civil War. Since 1800, however, the Scottish law of trusts has been extensively influenced by English practice. The two systems have been brought even closer together by modern legislation, and especially by the Trusts (Scotland) Act 1921. The entire question of the relation of the English to the Scottish law of trusts is one which merits further exploration.

CHAPTER III

THE CLASSIFICATION OF TRUSTS

NUMEROUS methods of classification of trusts exist, some of which do not require extended discussion. A very common mode of classification is into *simple* and *special* trusts. The simple trust is nothing more or less than the old passive use, for the abolition of which the Statute of Uses was designed. This, it has been seen, became possible again in the seventeenth century, and now, since the Statute of Uses was repealed by the Law of Property Act 1925, it may be created directly, without circumlocution. Where a simple trust exists, the beneficiary, provided that he is *sui juris* and absolutely entitled, has a right to be put into actual possession of the property (*jus habendi*), and he enjoys the further right of compelling the trustees to dispose of the legal estate in accordance with his (the beneficiary's) instructions (*jus disponendi*). This device is frequently used today in respect of shares in companies, the trustee in whose name they are placed being usually termed a *nominee*. On the other hand, in a special trust, the trustee has some, and it may be many, duties to perform, the most common of which are the collection of the rents and profits of the property, and the transfer of them to the beneficiary; or, again, it may be that the trustees are directed by the settlor to sell the property and pay his debts out of the proceeds. Special trusts again, are divided into *ministerial*, or *instrumental*, trusts, and *discretionary* trusts, the point of distinction being that whilst in both the trustee has positive duties to perform, in a ministerial trust the duties are such that any person of normal competence could satisfactorily discharge them (as the distribution of an estate among named persons in specified shares), whilst in a discretionary trust the trustee is called upon to exercise personal choice as to the extent of the beneficial interests. Examples of a discretionary trust are one where the trustee is directed to distribute a fund amongst such charities as he shall consider most suitable, a trust in which the trustees are given a discretion to distribute a fund amongst the settlor's children or other relatives, and trusts of pensions funds where employees are judged according to their needs.

The distinction between lawful and unlawful trusts only requires passing mention, since it is perfectly clear that a trust, just as much as a contract, which contravenes the law, is not enforceable. This is particularly important in considering trusts to defraud creditors, although these have now, for the most part, been made the subject of special statutes.

The main division is between trusts which arise as a result of the act of parties, and trusts arising by operation of law.

In *Cook* v. *Fountain*,[1] Lord Nottingham attempted a classification of trusts in the following terms—

All trusts are either, first, express trusts, which are raised and created

---

[1] (1676), 3 Swanst. 585, 591 (Cases, p. 194).

by act of the parties, or implied trusts, which are raised or created by act or construction of law; again, express trusts are declared either by word or writing; and these declarations appear either by direct and manifest proof, or violent and necessary presumption. These last are commonly called presumptive trusts; and that is, when the Court, upon consideration of all circumstances presumes there was a declaration, either by word or writing, though the plain and direct proof thereof be not extant. In the case in question there is no pretence of any proof that there was a trust declared either by word or in writing; so the trust, if there be any, must either be implied by the law, or presumed by the Court.

It has already been seen that Lord Nottingham was of opinion that implied trusts should be raised only in cases of absolute necessity, and in *Cook* v. *Fountain* he gave examples; but he was more willing to imply a trust where the facts pointed to underhand dealing. What Lord Nottingham calls a presumptive trust is today called an implied trust, and his " trust implied by law " is the modern constructive trust.

The distinction between trusts arising by act of parties and trusts arising by operation of law is not by any means the same distinction as between express trusts and others, and it is therefore more than a little unfortunate that the courts, and following them, several writers, have grouped together all trusts, other than express trusts, and have termed them constructive, implied, or resulting trusts, as if these terms were synonymous. Lewin adverts to this difficulty when he writes [2]—

" Trusts arising by operation of law may be further divided into implied or presumptive, constructive and resulting trusts. A *resulting trust* arises where S transfers property to, or buys property in the name of, a stranger, T, without declaring any trusts, or declaring trusts which do not exhaust the whole beneficial interest. T is in those circumstances said to hold in a resulting trust for S, so far as no trusts are effectively declared. There is no generally agreed usage for *implied trusts*, which in previous editions was used to mean precatory trusts, but is in modern parlance generally used to include resulting trusts [3] and other trusts arising from a presumed intention on the part of the settlor. Nor is there any agreed meaning for *constructive trusts*, which in its narrower meaning includes only trusts imposed by law against the trustee's will, for instance where a trustee renews a trust lease in his own name, but which is sometimes used to include all trusts other than express trusts."

Commenting on Lewin's classification, Maitland observes—

> Lewin and other text writers divide trusts thus created into express and implied. It is difficult to draw the line, for since no formal words are necessary for the creation of a trust and since whenever the trust is created by the act of a party there almost of necessity will be some words used—even if a deaf-mute created a trust by " talking on his fingers " there would be words used—the distinction comes to be one between clear and less clear words, and clearness is a matter of degree. Thus Lewin, under the head of " Implied Trusts," treats of cases in which

[2] *Law of Trusts*, 16th ed., p. 8.
[3] *Re Llanover Settled Estates*, [1926] Ch. 626.

a testator creates a trust by such words as " I desire," " I request,"
" I hope." No firm line can be drawn—" I desire " is nearly as strong
as " I trust," and " I trust that he will do this " is almost the same as
" Upon trust that he will do this." I do not therefore think that the
distinction is an important one. . . .[4]

An express trust is one which has been intentionally created by the settlor
himself. It may be created by deed or will, or by unsealed writing *inter vivos*,
or even by word of mouth. In the terminology of this book, an implied trust
is one which the court deduces from the conduct of the parties and the
circumstances of the transaction. It is important to notice that here the
function of the court is to discover what the presumed intention of the parties
was, and to give effect to it. A good example arises where a person for
valuable consideration agrees to settle property for the benefit of another.
Here he immediately becomes a trustee of it.[5] This is quite a different type of
trust from the constructive trust, which arises where a person who is the
legal owner of property, but has some fiduciary position as regards another
person in respect of that property, obtains some personal advantage from that
position. Equity compels him to hold that advantage for the benefit of the
person for whom the fiduciary character is sustained.[6] Another type of
constructive trust arises where a person, with notice of the existence of an
express trust, intermeddles with trust property. In respect of it he becomes
a constructive trustee for the beneficiary under the express trust. It is
obvious here that the trust is imposed by law altogether apart from the will
of the parties, actually manifested or presumed, and that it may even be
imposed in spite of the fact that the will of the parties is directed to the end
that a trust shall not be created. Thus, in the leading case on constructive
trusts, *Keech* v. *Sandford*,[7] a trustee sought to secure the renewal of the
lease of a market on behalf of his *cestui que trust*. The owner of the market
declined to renew it for the beneficiary, and the trustee, having done all
he could for the beneficiary, asked for it to be renewed for himself personally,
and to this the owner agreed. Lord King held, nevertheless, that the trustee
held the renewed lease on trust for his beneficiary.

The distinction between implied and constructive trusts is thus a clear
one, but it is more difficult to classify resulting trusts. One example of a
resulting trust is where a settlor gives property to trustees for objects which
fail. Here the trustees hold for the settlor.[8] Another example is where the
settlor allocates specific annual interests to beneficiaries under the trust, and
in some years the income from the property increases so that the interests
do not exhaust it. Here the surplus is held also for the settlor. This latter
type of resulting trust was considered by Astbury, J., in *Re Llanover Settled
Estates*,[9] wherein he observes—

It is true no doubt, as the trustees contend, that a resulting trust in

---

[4] *Equity*, pp. 75–76.
[5] For another example, see *Bannister* v. *Bannister*, [1948] 2 All E.R. 133.
[6] *Williams* v. *Barton*, [1927] 2 Ch. 9.
[7] (1726), Sel.Cas.t.King 61 ; 2 Eq.Cas.Abr. 741, pl. 7 (Cases, p. 195). See also *Re Knowles'
Will Trusts*, [1948] 1 All E.R. 866 (C.A.).
[8] See *Bankes* v. *Salisbury Diocesan Council of Education Inc.*, [1960] Ch. 631.
[9] [1926] Ch. 626, 637-638.

ordinary circumstances is in one sense not really a trust at all. Where property is settled or devised upon limitations which do not exhaust it, a resulting use or trust of the unexhausted part is left in the settlor or devisor. But where, as in the present case, property is devised as a whole to trustees and the trusts declared do not exhaust the income during some particular period, although there is a resulting trust so called to the settlor or her heir at law, it is really a trust construed by the Court in the trustees of the income which they so hold, and which they cannot apply in accordance with any expressed trust in the settlement and which in the present case they hold on trust to pay to the person entitled thereto by reason of this so-called resulting trust. That, I think, is within the general meaning of implied or constructive trust.

In other words, though a resulting trust which arises from the fact that the dispositions expressly declared do not exhaust the whole of the property is not in strictness a trust at all, yet, where the declared trusts do not, during some period, exhaust the whole of the income, and the income is held by the trustees on a resulting trust for the settlor, that is really a resulting trust of income, which cannot be applied in conformity with any express trust, and is within the general meaning of an implied or constructive trust.

It is submitted that the antithesis of the terms " implied " and " constructive " in the last sentence is undesirable logically; but it is exceedingly difficult to see whether the court, in directing that the property should be held for the settlor, is to be considered as fulfilling his presumed intention, in which case the resulting trust would be properly grouped with implied trusts, or whether it is giving further effect to the maxim that a trustee shall not profit by his trust, and directs that the property should revert to the settlor as he has the best claim to it when the objects of the trust are fulfilled or have failed. If this is so, then the resulting trust of this type is more correctly classed as constructive.

The classic division of trusts which first appears in Lord Nottingham's judgment in *Cook* v. *Fountain* [10] is today not completely exhaustive, however, for the property legislation of 1925 created a new class of *statutory trusts, i.e.* trusts which the legislation declares wherever a certain relationship exists.[11] There are several examples of such trusts in the present law of property. Thus, under section 34 of the Law of Property Act 1925, wherever land is now held in undivided shares, the first four grantees hold the legal estate in the land on a statutory trust for sale for all the grantees as tenants in common in equity; and under section 36, where land is now conveyed to joint tenants, then usually the first four named joint tenants hold the land on a statutory trust for sale for all the grantees as joint tenants in equity. By section 35,[12] the statutory trust for sale for the purposes of sections 34 and 36 is defined as a trust to sell the land—

> . . . and to stand possessed of the net proceeds of sale, after payment of costs, and of the net rents and profits until sale after payment of rates, taxes, costs of insurance, repairs, and other outgoings, upon such trusts,

10 (1676), 3 Swanst. 585, 591 (Cases, p. 194).
11 See Lewis, " Statutory Trusts for Sale " (1940) 56 *Law Quarterly Review* 255.
12 As amended by the Law of Property (Entailed Interests) Act 1932, s. 1.

and subject to such powers and provisions, as may be requisite for giving effect to the rights of the persons (including an incumbrancer of a former undivided share or whose incumbrance is not secured by a legal mortgage) interested in the land, and the right of a person, who, if the land had not been made subject to a trust for sale by virtue of this Act, would have been entitled to an entailed interest in an undivided share in the land, shall be deemed to be a right to a corresponding entailed interest in the net proceeds of sale attributable to that share.

A similar statutory trust for sale arises under section 36 of the Settled Land Act 1925 where settled land is held for persons entitled in possession in undivided shares. The trustees of the settlement will become the joint tenants of the legal estate holding on a statutory trust for the benefit of the persons entitled in undivided shares.

Another statutory trust for sale arises under section 33 of the Administration of Estates Act 1925 where a person dies intestate. The personal representatives then hold the estate on statutory trusts for issue and certain other classes of relatives of the deceased. In such a case, by section 47 (1) (ii) the statutory powers of maintenance and advancement under sections 31 and 32 of the Trustee Act are applicable.

Still a further statutory trust arises under section 19 of the Law of Property Act 1925, where there is a conveyance of a legal estate in land to an infant jointly with one or more persons of full age. The conveyance operates to vest the legal estate in the other person or persons on the statutory trusts described in section 35 of the Law of Property Act 1925, but not so as to sever any joint tenancy in the net proceeds of sale or in the rents and profits until sale.[13]

Express trusts may be divided into executed and executory trusts. The importance of this distinction will be considered later; but an executed trust may be defined as one in which the intentions of the settlor (whether by deed, will, or other document) have been completely set forth, so that the trustee's primary duty is to act in accordance with the terms of the instrument. In an executory trust, some further act or instrument is necessary before the beneficial interests are accurately delimited, but the estate or interest of the trustee is nevertheless completely vested. This division of express trusts is quite distinct from that between completely and incompletely constituted trusts, which will be considered later. Thus, a testator may by his will direct that his property shall be held upon trust for sale, the proceeds to be held upon such trusts for his children as the trustees shall in their discretion determine. Here a valid trust arises immediately, but it is executory, in that a further instrument is necessary to complete the dispositions under it. In an executed trust, no further instrument is required. It is important to notice that the two terms most clearly relate to the manner in which the trust is created, and not to its duration, since in the second sense all trusts are executory until they are ended.

One final division should be noticed, and that is the division between public and private trusts. A public trust is one which benefits the public at

---

[13] For a further example, see the Law of Property Act 1925, s. 32.

large, or some considerable portion of it. The most clearly defined class of public trusts is charitable trusts, but owing to the technical meaning attributable to " charitable " by the courts there is a large and increasingly important class of public non-charitable trusts. Thus a trust for a political society would be a public, non-charitable trust.[14] A charitable trust is normally permanent, or at least indefinite, in duration, and its beneficiaries may be a fluctuating and uncertain body. A private trust is one for the benefit of specific individuals (even though these are not *immediately* ascertainable) and the interests therein delimited fail if they do not vest within the perpetuity period. Private trusts are enforceable at the suit of any of the beneficiaries, whilst a public trust may be enforced by any of the beneficiaries or (if the trust is charitable) by the Attorney-General.

[14] On such public non-charitable trusts, see Benas, " Quasi-charities " (1944) 9 *Conveyancer* (N.S.) 67.

CHAPTER IV

TRUSTS FOR SALE AND STRICT SETTLEMENTS OF LAND

IN the modern law of land there are two distinct types of trust of land—strict settlement and the trust for sale, each with its distinctive attributes.[1] The statutory rules governing strict settlements are mainly to be found in the Settled Land Act 1925; those governing trusts for sale are contained in the Law of Property Act 1925, together with the Trustee Act 1925 and the Administration of Estates Act 1925.

A. STRICT SETTLEMENTS

Historically, the strict settlement is the older legal institution. Basically it is a disposition of a series of interests, and it may be made either by deed or will. It may be made in contemplation of the settlor's death, or on the occasion of the marriage of an intended beneficiary. It may be voluntary, *i.e.* the beneficiaries give no consideration, or it may be made for valuable consideration, *e.g.* in contemplation of the marriage of a party, and where such a settlement occurs, the issue of that marriage are said to be " within the marriage consideration," and are therefore not treated as volunteers.

Originally, a strict settlement of land was a disposition of a number of limited interests in the settlor's land, intended to preserve it as an undivided whole within the eldest male line of descent, whilst at the same time providing interests for younger children, and possibly for widows of sons or grandsons, each of which would be charged on the land. As the land descended successively to male heirs, each of them would assume the obligation to raise the capital sums necessary to discharge these interests. Frequently, too, trustees of the settlement would be appointed, whose primary duty was to ensure that such interests were satisfied. Often the trustees would be given special powers for this purpose, *e.g.* to raise money by way of mortgage.

Since at an early date it became impossible to give each successive eldest son a life estate, because of the development of various rules against remoteness, the usual practice, on creating the settlement, was to give a life interest to the eldest son, followed by an estate in tail male (now termed an entailed interest) to his eldest son. Such an estate tail could be barred when the grandson came of age, but until that time, the estate was inalienable (except for the life of the eldest son), and when the grandson came of age, financial inducements to him, such as a substantial income, would normally be sufficient to secure his assent to a resettlement of the estate for a further period. In this way, land could be retained in the family for many generations. Before 1925, strict settlements could be of two kinds, according to their mode of creation. They could be created directly, so that the successive holders of the land obtained life interests and entailed interests *at law*, *i.e.* as legal estates; or they

[1] See Keeton, *Modern Developments in the Law of Trusts*, pp. 180–189.

40

could take effect behind a trust, in which case the successive beneficiaries obtained only equitable interests.

Whilst strict settlements normally achieved the desired object of keeping the land in the family, they had many serious disadvantages. Of these, the most important was that, so long as the settlement was in existence, there was no one who could transfer the land in fee simple. Further, the person in possession (who is usually termed the tenant for life) was unable to grant leases for a period longer than his life, or to undertake many other activities in relation to the land which would be beneficial. These drawbacks were found to be increasingly irksome in the changing social conditions of the nineteenth century.

In order to minimise them, it became customary for draftsmen to insert into settlements an increasingly wide range of powers, exercisable by the tenant for life, not only on his own behalf, but on behalf of all other beneficiaries. Amongst them were powers to grant binding leases for long periods. These were powers of administration. In addition, a settlement might also empower the tenant for life to sell the settled land or part of it, free of the interests under the settlement, usually with the consent of the trustees. Where a sale occurred, the purchaser (in order to be free of the interests under the settlement) was compelled to pay the purchase money to the trustees of the settlement, and it thereby became a fund out of which the various interests under the settlement were satisfied.

As the nineteenth century progressed, a succession of statutes gave additional specific powers, many of them to undertake improvements, to limited owners under settlements; and a number of Settled Land Acts extended the tenant for life's powers of administration. In some cases, however, these could only be exercised with the consent of the trustees; in others, an application to the court was necessary. A great step forward was taken by the Settled Land Act of 1882, particularly from the standpoint that the tenant for life should increasingly be regarded as the owner of the land, subject to the obligation to exercise his powers on behalf of all the beneficiaries. Ultimately, the Settled Land Act 1925 went much further in the same direction.

One important change was that trusts for sale were separated from strict settlements. If a trust for sale exists, it cannot now be governed by the Settled Land Act, as was the case with some trusts for sale under the Settled Land Act 1882. Secondly, strict settlements were reduced to a single general form. In all of them, the legal estate will now be vested normally in the tenant for life, as trustee for himself and all the other beneficiaries, and all beneficial interests under the settlement will take effect in equity. Thus a tenant for life will normally have two interests—the legal estate in fee simple which he holds as trustee and his own beneficial interest. Accordingly, he will be able to transfer the fee simple to a purchaser, who, so long as he pays the purchase-money to the trustees of the settlement, is not concerned with the equitable interests under the settlement. After the sale of the land, these take effect against the purchase money, which it is the duty of the trustees to invest, either in securities or in other land.

Although the powers of administration of the tenant for life have been extended by the Act of 1925, they are still limited in a number of ways. For this reason, it is usual for settlors to secure the insertion into their settlement of additional or wider powers than those specified in the Act.

The Act has detailed provisions for the transmission of the legal estate vested in the tenant for life. He is always deemed to have appointed the trustees of the settlement as his special personal representatives, in whom the settled land vests at his death, and it is the duty of the trustees to transfer the legal estate in the land to the person next entitled under the settlement to possession.

Since a legal estate cannot be vested in an infant after 1925, then so long as the infancy subsists, the legal estate vests in the trustees of the settlement (except where the settlement has been made by the will of the person who has just died, and the land had vested in the personal representatives of the settlor). Again, if for the time being there is no tenant for life, the trustees will have the legal estate vested in them, and will act as statutory owner.

These are by no means the only functions of trustees under a modern settlement. Their power to hold and invest capital money has already been mentioned. Capital money may include other sums than the proceeds of sale of land, and whenever this arises, the trustees have a duty to invest it, and for this purpose, in addition to their powers under the Settled Land Act, they have all the powers of trustees under the Trustee Act 1925. In making an investment the trustees must act under the direction of the tenant for life. By virtue of section 75 (5) of the Settled Land Act 1925 capital money and investments bought with it are regarded as land for all purposes of disposition and devolution.

Land held under a settlement is " settled land," and the term " settlement," as defined by section 1 of the Settled Land Act 1925 is very comprehensive. Section 1 (1) provides—

> Any deed, will, agreement for a settlement or other agreement, Act of Parliament, or other instrument, or any number of instruments, whether made or passed before or after, or partly before and partly after, the commencement of this Act, under or by virtue of which instrument or instruments any land, after the commencement of this Act, stands for the time being—
>
> > (i) limited in trust for any persons by way of succession; or
> > (ii) limited in trust for any person in possession—
> >
> > > (a) for an entailed interest whether or not capable of being barred or defeated;
> > > (b) for an estate in fee simple or for a term of years absolute subject to an executory limitation, gift or disposition over on failure of his issue or in any other event;
> > > (c) for a base or determinable fee or any corresponding interest in leasehold land;
> > > (d) being an infant, for an estate in fee simple or for a term of years absolute; or
> >
> > (iii) limited in trust for any person for an estate in fee simple or for a term of years absolute contingently on the happening of any event; or

(iv) [2]

(v) charged, whether voluntarily or in consideration of marriage or by way of family arrangement, and whether immediately or after an interval, with the payment of any rentcharge for the life of any person, or any less period, or of any capital, annual, or periodical sums for the portions, advancement, maintenance, or otherwise for the benefit of any persons, with or without any term of years for securing or raising the same;

creates or is for the purposes of this Act a settlement . . .

The phrase " limited in trust " deserves explanation, for if there is no trust, the land is not settled land. However, in all these cases none of the beneficial interests can exist as a legal estate. The interests are either limited in extent or are not at the time of the settlement in possession or are held by an infant. Accordingly all of them are cases in which the legal estate and the beneficial interest are separated, and hence a trust automatically comes into existence.

B. THE POSITION OF THE TENANT FOR LIFE

The term " tenant for life," under the Settled Land Act 1925 has an extended meaning. It includes not only a person who has a life interest, but also, in general terms, every limited owner of full age who is beneficially entitled in possession. This could, in appropriate circumstances, include a limited company.[3] Accordingly, whenever there is a person who is of full age and capacity, who is beneficially entitled to either the possession of the settled land or to the whole of the income from it, that person is the tenant for life, and may exercise the powers enumerated in the Settled Land Act. The settlement may give him additional powers, but they may not be alienated or curtailed.

It has already been mentioned above that the tenant for life, under the Act of 1925, and also under the Act of 1882, acts as a trustee. This might raise a difficulty if the tenant for life should wish to acquire part or the whole of the settled land for himself. In such a case, section 68 provides that the trustees of the settlement may exercise all the powers of the tenant for life.[4] A similar situation would arise if the tenant for life should wish to sell land to the settlement.

Since the tenant for life has a double interest in the land—the legal fee simple and his own beneficial interest—his trusteeship has been said to be a " highly interested " one.[5] Nevertheless, in exercising his powers, he is a trustee for all parties, and he must exercise his discretion as a fair, honest and careful trustee would do, and the court has frequently intervened at the suit of another beneficiary, where it has been shown that the trustee is departing from that standard, e.g. to restrain a sale at an undervalue, or an undesirable investment.

The powers of the tenant for life in his control of the settled land are

[2] para. (iv) was repealed by the Married Women (Restraint upon Anticipation) Act 1949, s. 1 (4) and Sched. 2.

[3] Re Earl of Carnarvon's Chesterfield Settled Estates, [1927] 1 Ch. 138.

[4] See Re Pennant's Will Trusts, [1970] Ch. 75.

[5] Per Younger, J., in Re Earl of Stamford and Warrington, [1916] 1 Ch. 404, 420. See also Re 90 Thornhill Road, Tolworth, Surrey, [1970] Ch. 261.

set out in Part II of the Settled Land Act 1925. They may be exercisable in different ways. For example, where the tenant for life wishes to sell, exchange, lease, mortgage or charge the land, or to grant an option, he must give written notice to the trustees of the settlement, and if he is known, to the solicitor of the trustees.[6] Some other powers can be exercised only with the consent of the trustees or under an order of the court, *e.g.* the power to sell the principal mansion house or settled chattels, the power to cut timber, and finally, the power to compromise claims. The majority of the powers may, however, be exercised without any notice being given or consent obtained.

C. TRUSTS FOR SALE

The origin of the practice of settling land on trust for sale has not yet been fully investigated, but it was a very common device in private Acts of Parliament (especially in the eighteenth century) passed, usually on the death of the legal owner, to facilitate the discharge of his debts by the sale of land. Towards the end of the eighteenth century, it came to be employed with increasing frequency by settlors of a type quite distinct from the older landed proprietors, who wished to confer benefits upon the whole of their families out of a fund derived from the realisation of their property at their death. One great advantage of such a settlement (sometimes known as a " traders' settlement ") was that the same trusts could govern the fund which had been created by the sale of all kinds of property, whether real or personal. By the operation of the doctrine of conversion, the fund was deemed to be converted into money from the moment when the trust became operative. Before 1926 the consequences of this were of great importance. From the time when the trust for sale was operative, the property, irrespective of its actual nature, was treated as personal property, and would devolve as personalty. That meant that on intestacy, it would pass to the next of kin, and not to the heir-at-law. With the introduction of a common order of devolution for real and personal property, however, conversion has lost much of its importance.[7]

In a trust for sale, the legal estate is vested in the trustees, and the interests of the beneficiaries are always equitable. Usually, the trustees were given a power to postpone sale, and to manage the land until sale. Often their powers were only exercisable with the consent of the beneficiaries entitled in possession to the income of the property, and sometimes it was possible for the trustees to delegate their power of managing the property to the tenant for life. Since the trust for sale was as convenient a device as the strict settlement for the provision of interests of many kinds (*e.g.* portions and annuities) and since also a sale of the land might be postponed almost indefinitely, the trust for sale steadily developed as a second mode of settlement of land. Some important differences remained. For example, before 1926 there could not be an entailed interest in personalty, and since all the beneficial interests under a will were, in equity, personalty, it followed that there could not be an entailed interest in the trust for sale. Like strict settlements, trusts for sale could be created either by deed or will, and very many wills included one.

[6] Settled Land Act, 1925, s. 101 (1).
[7] But compare *Irani Finance Ltd.* v. *Singh*, [1971] Ch. 59 with *National Westminster Bank Ltd.* v. *Allen*, [1971] 2 Q.B. 718.

Since 1925, a trust for sale is the only type of settlement which is excluded from the Settled Land Act,[8] and a trust for sale is defined, both in the Law of Property Act,[9] and in the Settled Land Act [10] as " an immediate binding trust for sale." This means that there must be a trust to sell, and not merely a *power* of sale. If a power only is included in a series of dispositions of land, the effect is to create a strict settlement. The trust for sale does not imply now, any more than it did before 1926, that the trustees will sell the land immediately, and it is now provided [11] that, in the absence of a contrary intention,[12] every trust for sale created after 1925 contains a power to postpone the sale.

Difficulties have arisen over the meaning of the phrase " immediate binding trust for sale." The term " immediate " implies that the trust can be immediately exercised. If it is specified that the trust shall only arise at some future date, then the land will be settled until that date. However, the Act also provides that a trust for sale does not cease to be " immediate " simply because the trustees can only exercise it on the request or with the consent of some person [13] (usually the tenant for life).

" Binding trust for sale " has unfortunately developed a technical meaning. It has been held that a trust for sale is not " binding " if there are prior equitable or legal interests which cannot be " overreached " on sale by the trustees. If such interests cannot be overreached, then the land is settled land. Accordingly, a " binding " trust for sale is one which binds the whole of the land subject to it, and in which there are no outstanding interests which the trustees cannot overreach on sale. The real source of the difficulty has been the determination to preserve the line of distinction between strict settlements and trusts for sale, and, as a consequence, the courts have decided that wherever there are interests prior to the trust for sale, outstanding from an earlier strict settlement, and therefore not overreachable, the trust for sale is not an " immediate binding trust for sale," and therefore the Settled Land Act is still applicable. As Romer, J., explained in *Re Norton*,[14] the trustees of a strict settlement are not to be discharged so long as there is outstanding an equitable interest which it is their duty to protect, and so long as that situation exists, the strict settlement remains in existence.

Trusts for sale are created either by deed or will, or by statute (*e.g.* in cases of co-ownership), or by implication of law, as (*a*) where partners acquire land for the purposes of the partnership, or (*b*) under the rule in *Howe* v. *Lord Dartmouth*,[15] which is discussed later. Such implied trusts for sale may not satisfy the statutory requirements, and in such a case it may be necessary to take steps to ensure conformity (*e.g.* by the appointment of an additional trustee) before a conveyance of the land may be made.[16]

---

[8] Settled Land Act 1925, s. 1 (7), added by the Law of Property (Amendment) Act 1926, s. 7 and Sched.

[9] s. 205 (1) (xxix).

[10] s. 117 (1) (xxx).

[11] Law of Property Act 1925, s. 25 (1).

[12] For an example of a contrary intention see *Re Atkins' Will Trusts*, [1974] 1 W.L.R. 761, 766–767.

[13] Law of Property Act 1925, s. 205 (1) (xxix).

[14] [1929] 1 Ch. 84. See also *Re Leigh's Settled Estates (No. 1)*, [1926] Ch. 852; *Re Parker's Settled Estates*, [1928] Ch. 247.

[15] (1802), 7 Ves. 137.

[16] See Garner, " A Single Trustee for Sale " (1969) 33 *Conveyancer* 240.

Once created, so far as a purchaser is concerned the trust for sale continues in existence until the land has been conveyed either to the beneficiaries or to some other person at their direction, or a sole surviving joint tenant has become beneficially entitled.[17]

A number of powers of management have been conferred on trustees by the Law of Property Act 1925. One of these is the power to postpone the sale, which has already been mentioned. The court will not normally interfere with the decision of trustees who have exercised their discretion, whether in favour of sale or retention, but if the trustees cannot agree, then the land must be sold, even though the majority wish to retain it, and the court will make an order directing a sale on the application of the trustee who wishes to sell [18] unless it exercises its discretion to deal with special cases under the Law of Property Act 1925, s. 30.

Before 1926, trustees for sale had no statutory powers of leasing, mortgaging or other dealings with the land, other than sale (except when the trust was within the Settled Lands Acts 1882 and 1884), although such powers were frequently inserted in the trust instrument. Now, however, they have all the powers of the tenant for life of settled land, and of Settled Land Act trustees, including the powers of management during a minority, even though there is no minority.[19] Provided they have not parted with all the land, so ceasing to be trustees for sale,[20] they may purchase other land with the proceeds of sale, and land so bought is also held on trust for sale. These statutory powers are exercisable only with the consent of any person whose consent to a sale is needed.[21] Finally, the powers of leasing and management of trustees for sale may be revocably delegated to a tenant for life of full age who is entitled to the profits of the land.[22]

---

[17] Law of Property Act 1925, s. 23; Law of Property (Joint Tenants) Act 1964.
[18] *Re Hilton*, [1909] 2 Ch. 548; *Re Roth* (1896), 74 L.T. 50; *Re Mayo*, [1943] Ch. 302. See also Miller, " Trusts for Sale and the Matrimonial Home " (1972) 36 *Conveyancer* 99.
[19] Law of Property Act 1925, s. 28 (1); *Re Gray*, [1927] 1 Ch. 242.
[20] *Re Wakeman*, [1945] Ch. 177.
[21] Law of Property Act 1925, s. 26 (2).
[22] Law of Property Act 1925, s. 29.

CHAPTER V

PARTIES TO A TRUST

A. AS SETTLOR

IN general, any person who is competent to deal with either the legal estate or the equitable interest in property may create a trust; but the capacity of one or two persons requires special consideration.

1. The Crown. The Queen may, by letters patent, declare a trust of her private property.[1] The grant by letters patent, if unrestricted by words indicating a trust, purports to be an act of bounty, and, therefore, it is not open to a third person to attempt to prove a parol trust operating upon property conveyed by letters patent. The trust must be expressed in the letters patent.[2] The Crown may also by will dispose of its private personal property to one person in trust for another. The will must be in writing and under the sign manual.[3]

2. Corporations. In general, any corporation, unless expressly restrained by law, can create a trust for purposes within the objects for which it is incorporated. In view of their general importance, however, the two following types of corporation require special consideration—

(a) **Local Authorities.** These are governed by the Local Government Act 1972. They have general power to hold property (section 111) and to dispose of it for the purposes of the corporation, subject to certain restrictions, in the case of land, set out in sections 123 (principal councils) and 127 (parish and community councils).

(b) **Companies.** Trading companies, incorporated under the Companies Acts, have implied power to borrow for the purposes of the company's business.[4] Very commonly, this power of borrowing is exercised by the issue of debentures, and for the purpose of supporting the issue the company has power (which is frequently exercised) of executing a trust deed, by which the company, after covenanting to repay the loan, with interest until payment, assigns to trustees real property or leaseholds belonging to the company, to constitute security for the repayment of the loan, and the trustees undertake to hold the property upon certain trusts in favour of the debenture holders.

3. Married Women. A married woman may create a trust of her property as if she were a *feme sole*.[5]

The progressive emancipation of the married woman from the restrictions imposed by the common law upon her capacity to hold and to deal with real

---

[1] Lewin on *Trusts*, Chap. 2. See also Bacon on *Uses*, p. 66.
[2] *Fordyce* v. *Willis* (1792), 3 Bro.C.C. 577.
[3] Crown Private Estate Act 1800, s. 10.
[4] *General Auction Estate and Monetary Co.* v. *Smith*, [1891] 3 Ch. 432.
[5] Married Women's Property Act 1882, as amended by the Law Reform (Married Women and Tortfeasors) Act 1935.

and personal property was, until the second part of the nineteenth century, almost exclusively the result of equitable intervention. At common law a wife's chattels became the absolute property of the husband. He possessed also the power to reduce her choses in action into possession; whilst upon the birth of issue, he enjoyed the seisin for life of such present estates of inheritance as his wife might have possessed, as " tenant by the curtesy." From the reign of Elizabeth I onwards,[6] however, the Court of Chancery steadily evolved the doctrine of the separate estate of the married woman, although it does not seem that this doctrine was applied to real property before the Restoration. In pursuance of this object, the Court of Chancery established that wherever property was given to trustees for the separate use of a married woman, she could hold and dispose of it in equity free from her husband's interference, and such property was protected effectually against the husband's debts or other obligations. Eventually it was decided that wherever the donor had expressed a plain intention that the property was for the separate use of the married woman, this should be effective whether trustees had been appointed or not, the trust being, in the last resort, imposed on the husband himself. As a further development, Lord Thurlow, at the end of the eighteenth century, evolved the " restraint on anticipation " clause, the object of which was to protect the wife against the solicitations of her husband (or her natural inclination) to surrender her beneficial enjoyment of the property to him. Such a clause made either the capital or the income of property (or both) incapable of alienation or anticipation, so long as she was subject to coverture, and the effectiveness of the clause was finally established before Lord Eldon in *Jackson* v. *Hobhouse*.[7] Nineteenth-century statutes, whose purpose was carried a stage further in the property legislation of 1925, have now permitted the enjoyment of full proprietary rights by a married woman at law, and have therefore greatly minimised the importance of a very characteristic product of equity, which only became possible through the evolution of the modern law of trusts. Under modern social conditions, however, the necessity for protecting a married woman against the designs of her husband has practically disappeared, and in spite of statutory provisions for lifting the restraint on anticipation on various occasions, it nevertheless remained a serious obstacle to the enforcement of the claims of the married woman's creditors. The Law Reform (Married Women and Tortfeasors) Act 1935 therefore abolished the " separate property " of a married woman, putting her in the position of a *feme sole*, and virtually prohibited the imposition of restraints on anticipation in the future. By the Married Women (Restraint upon Anticipation) Act 1949 all existing restraints were abolished. Section 1 (1) of that Act provides: " No restriction upon anticipation or alienation attached, or purported to be attached, to the enjoyment of any property by a woman which could not have been attached to the enjoyment of that property by a man shall be of any effect after the passing of this Act."

4. Infants. An infant cannot now hold a legal estate in land, so that no settlement or trust of a legal estate by him is now possible. He may settle an

---

[6] *Sanky* v. *Golding* (1579), Cary 87; *Gorge* v. *Chansey* (1639), 1 Ch. Rep. 125; *Darcy* v. *Chute* (1663), 1 Ch. Cas. 21; *Cotton* v. *Cotton* (1690), 2 Vern. 290. See, further, Keeton and Sheridan, *Equity*, Chap. XV.
[7] (1817), 2 Mer. 483.

equitable interest or personalty, but the settlement is voidable by him within a reasonable time after attaining full age; and it has been suggested that a voluntary conveyance, necessarily for the infant's prejudice, is void, not voidable.[8] Where the settlement is voidable, it is binding if it has been observed during infancy, and is affirmed on attaining the age of eighteen. An infant (other than a soldier on actual military service or a seaman at sea) cannot make a will.

5. Persons suffering from Mental Disorder. The law relating to mental disorder was radically changed and codified by the Mental Health Act 1959. By section 102 of the Act, a judge has wide powers in respect of the property of a patient for the benefit of the patient himself, and for his family. By section 103 (1) (*d*) (replacing section 171 of the Law of Property Act 1925) the judge may direct the settlement of any property of the patient for these purposes.

6. Convicts. Until 1948, a convict, as defined by the Forfeiture Act 1870, could not alienate or charge his property, and therefore he could not declare a trust of it. These disabilities, however, were removed by the Criminal Justice Act 1948, s. 70.

B. AS TRUSTEE

" A person to be a trustee," observes Lewin,[9] " must be capable of taking or holding the property of which the trust is declared: he should be competent to deal with the estate as required by the trust or as directed by the beneficiaries [10] and should not be under any disability by nature or by law. He should be capable of applying judgment and should have a knowledge of business; and he should be amenable to the jurisdiction of the court which administers the trust." The capacity of the following, therefore, requires special consideration, as deviating from the normal—

1. The Crown unquestionably has the capacity to hold all kinds of property, including a legal estate in land, but it is doubtful whether the obligations of a trustee can be fully enforced against it. As was pointed out by counsel in *Pawlett* v. *Attorney-General*,[11] a court of equity has no jurisdiction over the King's conscience, since the Chancellor's jurisdiction is simply the result of a delegation by the King of the power to exercise the Crown's equitable jurisdiction between subject and subject. In *Rustomjee* v. *The Queen* [12] the Court of Appeal held that in the discharge of sovereign acts, such as the making or performing of a treaty with another sovereign, the Crown could not be a trustee for a subject. Again, in *Kinloch* v. *Secretary of State for India*,[13] the Queen, by royal warrant, granted booty of war to the Secretary of State for India in trust to distribute it amongst the persons declared by the Court of Admiralty to share it. It was held that this did not operate as a declaration of

---

[8] See Goodeve and Potter, *Modern Law of Real Property*, p. 473, n. (*g*).
[9] *Trusts*, 16th ed., pp. 12–13.
[10] But see *Re Brockbank*, [1948] Ch. 206.
[11] (1667), Hardr. 465, 468. See also the discussion of this point in *Burgess* v. *Wheate* (1759), 1 Eden 177, 255 (Cases, p. 185); *Earl of Kildare* v. *Eustace* (1686), 1 Vern. 437.
[12] (1876), 2 Q.B.D. 69.
[13] (1880), 15 Ch.D. 1 ; (1882), 7 App.Cas. 619.

trust in favour of those persons, but that it merely constituted the Secretary of State the agent of the Crown for purposes of distribution.

In *Civilian War Claimants Association* v. *The King* [14] the suppliants, by petition of right, claimed compensation on behalf of civilians who had suffered loss as a result of German aggression during the war, alleging that the Crown had invited them to submit their losses to the Reparation Claims Department, which had included them in the sum total of reparations which Germany had agreed to pay under Article 232 of the Treaty of Versailles. The House of Lords held that the Crown, in so acting, had not constituted itself an agent or trustee for the claimants in respect of any money received by it from Germany on account of reparations. The facts of the case were very similar to those of *Rustomjee* v. *The Queen*,[12] and once again the fact that the Crown was discharging a sovereign act proved fatal to the claimants.

It is clear that the subject cannot raise a trust against the Crown where the Crown is performing a sovereign act, such as the negotiation of a treaty. Apart from this, however, there seems to be no reason why the Crown should not be a trustee, if it has assented to the trust.[15] The question then arises, what remedies has the subject against the Crown as trustee?

It was at one time thought that, although the subject might have no remedy against the Crown as trustee in the Court of Chancery, there might be a remedy in the Court of Exchequer, which had a special superintendence over the royal property. Thus, in *Penn* v. *Lord Baltimore*,[16] Lord Hardwicke said: " I will not decree [the King to be a trustee] in this court . . . but it is a notion established in courts of revenue by modern decisions, that the King may be a royal trustee . . ." Lord Northington (Lord Keeper Henley) was doubtful about this in *Burgess* v. *Wheate*,[17] however. Professor Holdsworth points out [18] that whilst in the fifteenth century it was settled that the King could not be a feoffee to uses, and whilst also it had been held at the beginning of the seventeenth that he could not be a trustee, in the eighteenth century the attitude of the courts had changed. The King could be a trustee, but the question still remained unsettled how his obligations as a trustee could be enforced against him. In the eighteenth century the Chancery might give relief against the Crown on a petition of right, whilst the Court of Exchequer might grant redress on a bill filed against the Attorney-General. These two remedies survived into the nineteenth century, and it is now settled that any court with equitable jurisdiction can grant relief by way of a bill filed against the Attorney-General.[19] The procedure is now regulated by the Crown Proceedings Act 1947.

2. Corporations. A corporation always has capacity to be a trustee of personalty, and it may also be a trustee of land if it has authority by statute to hold land. Mortmain was abolished by the Charities Act 1960, s. 38. Any local

---

14 [1932] A.C. 14 (Cases, p. 202), followed in *Administrator of German Property* v. *Knoop*, [1933] Ch. 439.
15 The courts, however, are reluctant to impose a constructive trust upon the Crown: *Re Mason*, [1929] 1 Ch. 1; *Re Blake*, [1932] 1 Ch. 54.
16 (1750), 1 Ves.Sen. 444, 453. See also *Reeve* v. *Attorney-General* (1741), 2 Atk. 223.
17 (1759), 1 Eden 177.
18 *History of English Law*, Vol. IX, p. 31.
19 See further, Holdsworth, *History of English Law*, Vol. IX, pp. 31–32; *Dyson* v. *Attorney-General*, [1911] 1 K.B. 410; Glanville Williams, *Crown Proceedings*, pp. 15, 87.

authority may accept gifts of real or personal property, except property which would be held in trust for an ecclesiastical charity or for a charity for the relief of poverty.[20] Moreover, a local authority may accept property on non-charitable trusts, provided they are for purposes for which the local authority is constituted.[21]

By the Bodies Corporate (Joint Tenancy) Act 1899, a body corporate is capable of acquiring and holding real or personal property in joint tenancy with an individual or another body corporate in the same way as an individual[22]; but this statute does not remove any of the restrictions otherwise regulating the holding of property by corporate bodies. A corporation sole may be a trustee.[23]

3. The Bank of England. The Bank of England may not be made a trustee of stock. It manages the accounts of public funds, and pays dividends, but only to those legal owners in whose names the stock is registered.[24]

4. Married Women. Before 1907 a married woman might be a trustee, but she required the concurrence of her husband to pass the legal estate of real property subject to the trust, and certain expensive formalities were also necessary. Now, however, the Law of Property Act 1925, s. 170, provides—

(1) A married woman is able to acquire as well from her husband as from any other person, and hold, any interest in property real or personal either solely or jointly with any other person (whether or not including her husband) as a trustee or personal representative, in like manner as if she were a feme sole; and no interest in such property shall vest or be deemed to have vested in the husband by reason only of the acquisition by his wife.

(2) A married woman is able, without her husband, to dispose of, or to join in disposing of, any interest in real or personal property held by her solely or jointly with any other person (whether or not including her husband) as trustee or personal representative, in like manner as if she were a feme sole.

5. Infants. It has been judicially held on several occasions that, as regards judgment and discretion, an infant lacks capacity.[25] Before 1926, therefore, the appointment of an infant as trustee was possible, but the effect of it varied, and was not by any means free from doubt.[26] Now, however, the Law of Property Act 1925, s. 20, provides: " The appointment of an infant to be a trustee in relation to any settlement or trust shall be void, but without prejudice to the power to appoint a new trustee to fill the vacancy." This would seem to relate to express trusts only, for an infant has been held capable of taking as trustee under an implied or resulting trust.[27] By section 19 (4), (5), a con-

[20] Local Government Act 1972, s. 139.
[21] See *Re Endacott*, [1960] Ch. 232.
[22] See *Re Thompson's Settlement Trusts*, [1905] 1 Ch. 229.
[23] *Bankes* v. *Salisbury Diocesan Council of Education*, [1960] Ch. 631.
[24] *Law Guarantee and Trust Society* v. *Governor of the Bank of England* (1890), 24 Q.B.D. 406.
[25] *e.g. per* Lord Hardwicke in *Hearle* v. *Greenbank* (1749), 3 Atk. 695.
[26] See Lewin on *Trusts*, 15th ed., pp. 30–31.
[27] *Re Vinogradoff*, [1935] W.N. 68.

veyance of a legal estate to an infant alone or to two or more persons jointly,
both or all of whom are infants, on any trust, operates as declaration of trust,
and does not pass any legal estate [28]; but if the conveyance of a legal estate is to
an infant jointly with one or more persons of full age on trust, it operates as
if the infant had not been named, so that the estate vests in the other person
alone, but without prejudice to any beneficial interest in the land intended to
be thereby provided for the infant. Moreover, the Trustee Act 1925, s. 36 (1),
states that where a person who is named as a trustee is an infant, then, subject
to the restrictions on the number of trustees contained in the Act, one or more
other persons may be appointed a trustee or trustees in his place. The point
of this subsection is that, under earlier legislation (which s. 36 (1) of the
Trustee Act of 1925 replaced), an infant trustee could not be displaced, so
that even if the court appointed another trustee in his place, the infant could
be restored when he came of age.[29] It would seem that this right of an infant
under the earlier Acts has not survived the Act of 1925.

6. Aliens. Before 1870, an alien could not be a trustee of freeholds or of
chattels real. By the Naturalisation Act 1870, s. 1,[30] however, an alien may
hold and dispose of all kinds of real and personal property, and may therefore
be a trustee. If the alien is domiciled abroad, objection to his fitness may be
lodged, since he is not within the jurisdiction of the court.[31]

7. Bankrupts. A bankrupt may be appointed a trustee, and if a trustee
becomes bankrupt, the trust estate does not vest in his trustee in bankruptcy.[32]
The bankruptcy of a trustee, however, may be a ground for removing him,
and appointing another trustee in his place, if the trustees are called upon to
handle money or stocks, under the Trustee Act 1925, s. 36; and the court may
make an order under s. 41 of the Trustee Act 1925 appointing a new trustee
in place of a trustee who is bankrupt.

8. Cestuis que trust are not legally incapable of being trustees, but it has
been pointed out in *Forster* v. *Abraham*,[33] that such appointments are in general undesirable, since there may be a conflict between the beneficiary's
interest and the trustee's duty. In *Re Paine's Trusts* [34] the court added two
trustees to the sole remainderman-trustee where there was an infant tenant for
life. In practice, however, it is frequently found convenient to appoint beneficiaries, and also difficult to find non-beneficiaries who are willing to act, and
it is clear that there is nothing legally improper in this; whilst even the court
has upon occasion, been reluctantly compelled to appoint beneficiaries. Moreover, in a considerable number of trusts which are either created or governed
by statute, the *cestuis que trust* are often expressly made trustees.[35]

---

[28] The effect is that there is an agreement for valuable consideration to execute a settlement (Settled Land Act 1925, s. 27). On conveyances to infants, see further Potter, " Dispositions of Land in favour of an Infant " (1933) 19 *Conveyancer* 1.

[29] *Re Shelmerdine* (1864), 33 L.J.Ch. 474.

[30] Re-enacted in the Status of Aliens Act, 1914, s. 17, as amended by the British Nationality
Act 1948, s. 34 (3) and Sched. 4.

[31] *Meinertzhagen* v. *Davis* (1844), 1 Coll. 335; *Re Harrison's Trusts* (1852), 22 L.J.Ch. 69.

[32] Bankruptcy Act 1914, s. 38.

[33] (1874), L.R. 17 Eq. 351.

[34] (1885), 28 Ch.D. 725.

[35] In the statutory trusts created by the Law of Property Act 1925, ss. 34–36, the beneficiaries have been created statutory trustees. See also the Settled Land Act 1925, s. 16.

9. Solicitors to the Trust. Such an appointment is also not legally invalid, but the court would not make, nor would it sanction, such an appointment.[36]

This is the rule of practice, but it does not mean that appointments of solicitors to the trust by the persons properly qualified to make the appointment, are invalid, and they are often made in practice, whilst even the court has, upon occasion, departed from the rule,[37] although only, as Stirling, J., pointed out in *Re Earl of Stamford*,[38] when it is assured " not only that no disadvantage is likely to occur from the appointment, but that advantages are to be gained by reason of the appointment."

As regards appointments by the donee of the power of appointment, Pearson, J., said in *Re Norris* [39]—

> I am very far from saying, and I must not be understood to say, that, if there was a trust which was not being administered by the Court, and the person who had the power of appointing new trustees had *bonâ fide* appointed as trustees a father and his son who were solicitors in partnership, it would be a bad appointment, so as to render any deed executed by the trustees so appointed null and void. I should be very sorry to hold that such an appointment outside the Court would be invalid. If such a case came before me, and I found that the appointment had been made *bonâ fide* outside the Court, I should certainly hold that the trustees were validly appointed.

On the question of the court's practice with regard to such appointments, he observed,[40] however—

> It is admitted that, according to the ordinary practice, the Court would not appoint as trustee the solicitor of the existing trustee, and I think that the Court would certainly not appoint as a co-trustee with that solicitor his partner, whether he was his son or some other person. The Court does not look at the competency of the particular person; it looks at the position which he fills, and, according to the ordinary rule of the Court, the solicitor of a trustee is not a person who should be appointed a trustee. I think it is of the greatest importance that the Court should adhere to the general rule, and for this, if for no other, reason, that it prevents the necessity of considering in any particular case whether the solicitor is or is not a person of respectability and trustworthy. The Court always declines to go into any question of that kind, and says, assuming that you are the very person who would be most fit to be a trustee, we object to you simply on the ground of the position which you hold.

In *Re Earl of Stamford* [41] the solicitor of the tenant for life of a settlement had been appointed trustee by the person nominated to appoint, and the court held that, although it would not itself have appointed him, yet since the beneficiaries had not objected, and the appointment was otherwise unexceptionable, it would not interfere.

---

[36] See *Re Norris* (1884), 27 Ch.D. 333 ; *Re Earl of Stamford*, [1896] 1 Ch. 288.
[37] *Re Marquis of Ailesbury*, [1893] 2 Ch. 345, 360.
[38] [1896] 1 Ch. 288, 299.
[39] (1884), 27 Ch.D. 333, 341.
[40] 27 Ch.D. 340.
[41] [1896] 1 Ch. 288. See also *Re Kemp's Settled Estates* (1883), 24 Ch.D. 485.

10. Relatives of Beneficiaries. In *Wilding* v. *Bolder*,[42] Sir John Romilly, M.R., held that he would not appoint as a trustee any relative, since frequent breaches of trust in practice resulted, at the instance of the beneficiaries related to the trustees. To avoid appointing a relative, or even a beneficiary himself, is often very difficult, and there is nothing which legally invalidates such an appointment. Indeed, in several instances, the court itself has appointed a relative, who was also himself a beneficiary,[43] whilst in *Re Lightbody's Trusts*,[44] Kay, J., appointed two persons, one of whom was a beneficiary, and the other the husband of a beneficiary, upon an understanding by both of them that if either was left as sole trustee, that person would endeavour to obtain the appointment of a new trustee.

C. AS CESTUI QUE TRUST

The general rule is that persons who are capable of holding the legal estate of property may also take an equitable interest under a trust. One or two persons, however require a word of additional explanation—

1. The Crown may be a beneficiary.

2. An Infant can be a beneficiary, and can, moreover, hold an equitable interest in land, although debarred from holding a legal estate.

3. Corporations. It has already been noticed that uses originally owed some of their popularity to the fact that it was possible to leave land to religious corporations by way of use. It was also observed that before long, the Statutes of Mortmain were extended to prohibit grants of land to religious corporations in this way, and the old restrictions, dating from earlier times, survived until the Charities Act 1960 abolished them. A trading company incorporated under the Companies Act 1948 may be the beneficiary of a trust of land, held for the purposes for which it was incorporated.

4. Aliens. Before 1870, a trust of lands might have been declared in favour of an alien, but the Crown might at any time have declared his interest forfeit.[45] In *Calvin's Case*,[46] however, it was decided that an alien could take neither a legal nor an equitable estate by operation of law, *e.g.* by descent. These disabilities were removed by the Naturalisation Act of 1870.[47] An alien was never disqualified from holding either a legal or an equitable interest in chattels, except that he could not, and still cannot, either directly or through the intervention of a trustee, be the owner of a British ship.

5. Persons Resident Outside the Sterling Area may not benefit under any trust involving the transfer of currency to persons resident outside the sterling area.[48]

---

[42] (1855), 21 Beav. 222.
[43] *e.g. ex parte Clutton* (1853), 17 Jur. 988.
[44] (1884), 52 L.T. 40.
[45] *Attorney-General* v. *Sands* (1669), Hardr. 488, 495.
[46] (1609), 7 Co.Rep. 1a.
[47] s. 2. Now the Status of Aliens Act 1914, s. 17, as amended by the British Nationality Act 1948, s. 34 (3) and Sched. 4.
[48] Exchange Control Act 1947, s. 29.

CHAPTER VI

SOME SPECIAL KINDS OF TRUSTEES

A. CUSTODIAN AND MANAGING TRUSTEES

IN recent commercial practice, it frequently occurs that trust property is vested in custodian and managing trustees, and the practice is reflected in the Public Trustee (Custodian Trustee) Rules 1971. In *Inland Revenue Commissioners* v. *Silverts Ltd.*[1] Evershed, M.R., remarked—

> Counsel for the Crown point out with force that a trust with custodian and managing trustees is in a class by itself, since it involves a statutory severance, with no counterpart elsewhere, of the functions normally combined in the office of trustee; so that the legal right to the trust property, including the legal right to exercise voting power in respect of shares subject to the trust, is vested in the custodian, whereas all powers of management, including the direction of any exercise of such voting power, are reserved to the managing trustees.

The powers and duties of custodian trustees are defined in section 4 (2) of the Public Trustee Act 1906. Where a custodian trustee is appointed, the trust property must be transferred to the custodian trustee. The remaining trustees thereupon become the managing trustees, and exercise the powers and discretions vested in the trustees. The custodian trustee has the custody of all securities and documents of title, although the managing trustees may have access to them. All sums payable in respect of the income or capital of the trust property are payable to the custodian trustee, although he may allow income to be paid to, or at the direction of, the managing trustees. The power to appoint new trustees is exercised by the managing trustees, although the custodian trustee has the same power of applying to the court for the appointment of a new trustee as any other trustee. Under the Trustee Act 1925 there is a limit to the number of trustees,[2] but for this purpose the custodian trustee is not included in the number.

The section also specifies the liability of the custodian trustee. If he acts in good faith, he is not liable for accepting as correct, and acting upon, any written statement by the managing trustees as to any birth, death, marriage or other matter of relationship of a beneficiary, or any other matter of fact upon which title to trust property depends, nor is he liable if he acts upon any legal advice obtained by the managing trustees independently of the custodian trustee.

The Public Trustee Act, s. 4 (1) provides that the Public Trustee may be appointed custodian trustee of any trust, by the settlor, or by a person having power to appoint new trustees, or by the court. The Act, and the rules made under it, provide that there may also be appointed as custodian trustee any

---

[1] [1951] Ch. 521, 530.
[2] s. 34.

trust corporation, and if such appointment is made, the trust corporation may then, independently of any provision in the trust instrument, make such charges for services as do not exceed those charged by the Public Trustee, when acting as custodian trustee.[3] The scale charges of the Public Trustee, and therefore of trust corporations when acting as custodian trustee, are lower than the scale charges of the Public Trustee for ordinary trust business.

In several cases, discussed later,[4] the court has refused to accept appointments of trust corporations, as both managing trustee and custodian trustee, made in order to circumvent the rule that a trustee may not profit from his trust.[5] It has regarded an appointment as a nullity, and accordingly, if the Public Trustee is acting as custodian trustee, and it is desired that he should act as an ordinary trustee, he must first be discharged from the custodian trusteeship, before the appointment of him as ordinary trustee is made.[6]

Apart from the statutory power to charge, a custodian trustee is just as much subject to the rule that a trustee may not profit from his trust as any other trustee.[7]

B. THE PUBLIC TRUSTEE

The office of Public Trustee was created by the Public Trustee Act 1906. He is a corporation sole, and may sue and be sued under the corporate name. He may act as ordinary trustee, or as custodian trustee, or as a judicial trustee, but he may only accept an English trust,[8] and he may not accept a trust exclusively for religious or charitable purposes.[9]

By section 5, the court has power to appoint the Public Trustee to be a new or additional trustee or beneficiary, even though the instrument directs that he shall not be appointed. Any losses to the trust estate resulting from his appointment are made good by the state.[10] It is also provided that he may not decline the administration of an estate because it is of small value. He may act either alone, or jointly with other trustees, and may have the same powers, rights, discretions and duties as an ordinary trustee.

Where the Public Trustee acts as an ordinary trustee, he may be appointed by will, settlement or other instrument, or as a new or additional trustee, in the same manner as if he was a private trustee, except that the Public Trustee may be appointed sole trustee. Where the Public Trustee has been appointed, a co-trustee may retire under the Trustee Act 1925, s. 39, notwithstanding that there are not more than two trustees, and without the consents required in section 39.

Wherever it is practicable, notice of the appointment of the Public Trustee must be given to the beneficiaries (or if they are infants, to their guardians) and a person to whom notice has been given may apply within twenty-one days for an order prohibiting the appointment. Failure to give notice does not

3 Public Trustee (Custodian Trustee) Rules 1971.
4 Post, Chap. XIX, s. C, 3.
5 Forster v. Williams Deacon's Bank Ltd., [1935] Ch. 359; Arning v. James, [1936] Ch. 158.
6 Re Squire's Settlement (1946), 174 L.T. 150.
7 Re Brooke Bond & Co. Ltd.'s Trust Deed, [1963] Ch. 357.
8 s. 17 (2); Re Hewitt's Settlement, [1915] 1 Ch. 228.
9 s. 2 (5); Re Hampton (1918), 88 L.J.Ch. 103.
10 s. 7.

affect the appointment.[11] In considering whether the desired order shall be made, the court must have regard to the interests of all the beneficiaries. The question whether the expense involved in the appointment would be a good reason for granting an order prohibiting the appointment was considered in *Re Firth*,[12] when Eve, J., said—

> . . . the Legislature cannot have intended that, in ordinary cases not involving any exceptional or disproportionate expenditure, the mere fact that the appointment would involve expense should be treated as a material element in determining the question whether it is " expedient " or not to make an order prohibiting the appointment.

Section 6 of the Public Trustee Act authorises the Public Trustee to act as administrator or executor, and any executor who has proved, or any administrator, notwithstanding the fact that he has acted, may, with the sanction of the court, and after notice to such beneficiaries as the court may direct, transfer the estate to the Public Trustee to administer either alone or with any other personal representatives. After transfer the retiring personal representative is in no way liable for any act done in relation to the estate after the date of the order, except acts done by himself or his agents.

Unless specially authorised, the Public Trustee may not accept a trust which involves carrying on a business, except for winding up within eighteen months (although he may act as custodian trustee of a business on certain conditions),[13] nor any trust under a deed of arrangement, nor the administration of an estate known or believed to be insolvent.[14]

The Public Trustee may be appointed a custodian trustee (1) by order of the court, on the application of any person who has the right to apply to the court for the appointment of a new trustee; (2) by the creator of the trust; (3) by the person having power to appoint new trustees. The trust property must be transferred to the custodian trustee as if he were sole trustee, and vesting orders for that purpose may be made where necessary, but the management of the property remains in the other trustees, as already described.

Section 3 of the Act gives power to persons who would be entitled to apply for administration to apply to the court for the appointment of the Public Trustee, where the estate is proved to be less than £1,000 in value, and the persons beneficially entitled are of small means. On the Public Trustee undertaking by deed to administer, the trust property other than stock vests in him, as well as the right to call for transfer of the stock, and the person otherwise entitled to administer is discharged from all future liability.

Section 13 provides that the accounts of a trust administered by the Public Trustee shall be audited annually, if required by a trustee or beneficiary, whilst by section 10 it is provided that a person aggrieved by any act or omission or decision of the Public Trustee in relation to any trust may apply to the

[11] Public Trustee Act 1906, s. 5 (4).
[12] [1912] 1 Ch. 806, 815. See also *Re Drake's Settlement* (1926), 42 T.L.R. 467. For the fees chargeable, see Public Trustee (Fees) Orders, 1969, 1970, 1970 (No. 2), 1971, 1973 and 1974 made under s. 9 of the Public Trustee Act 1906, as amended by Public Trustee (Fees) Act 1957, s. 1. On the payment of income fees to the Public Trustee, see *Re Evans' Will Trusts*, [1948] Ch. 185.
[13] Public Trustee Rules 1912, r. 7.
[14] Public Trustee Act 1906, s. 2 (4).

court, and the court may make such order as it thinks fit.[15] The same section also contains provisions for the audit of the accounts of any trust by the Public Trustee or a person appointed by him. These are described elsewhere.[16]

After several years of debate and uncertainty, the government announced at the end of July 1974 that the office of Public Trustee was to continue.[17]

C. TRUST COMPANIES

Various types of companies (including banks and insurance companies) undertake the duties of trustees and executors for a remuneration varying with the size of the estate which is administered. Usually the department which deals with this work is separately incorporated. There are a number of advantages in appointing such an institution, the principal ones being (1) continuity of administration, (2) the resources of the corporation are available to make good any breach of trust, (3) the review of investments at regular intervals by persons familiar with this business, and (4) the fact that a trust corporation alone may give receipts for capital moneys, whereas under the Settled Land Act 1925 and the Law of Property Act 1925 such receipts may not otherwise be given by a sole trustee. A trust corporation may therefore act alone in the trust or, if it is desired, in association with another trustee, or other trustees.

The term " trust corporation " is defined in the Law of Property Act 1925, s. 205 (1) (xxviii) as the Public Trustee or a corporation either appointed by the court in any particular case to be a trustee, or entitled by rule 30 [18] of the Public Trustee Rules 1912 to act as a custodian trustee. Rule 30 provides—

> The following corporations shall be entitled to act as custodian
> trustees:—
> (a) The Solicitor for the affairs of Her Majesty's Treasury;
> (b) Any corporation which is constituted under the law of the United
> Kingdom or any part thereof and having a place of business there
> and which is empowered by its constitution to undertake trust
> business (which for the purpose of this rule means the business of
> acting as trustee under wills and settlements and as executor and
> administrator), and which is:—
>> (i) a company incorporated by special Act or Royal Charter,
>> or
>> (ii) a company registered (whether with or without limited
>> liability) under the Companies Act 1948 and having a capital (in
>> stock or shares) for the time being issued of not less than
>> £250,000, of which not less than £100,000 shall have been paid
>> up in cash, or
>> (iii) a company registered without limited liability under the
>> Companies Act 1948 of which one of the members is a company
>> within any of the classes hereinbefore defined;

---

[15] See Re Oddy, [1911] 1 Ch. 532; Re Wilson, [1964] 1 W.L.R. 214.

[16] Post, Chap. XIX, s. E.

[17] The work of the Public Trustee was reviewed by a committee of inquiry set up in 1971, following whose report the government in office in 1972 had decided to run the department down with a view to winding it up.

[18] Substituted by the Public Trustee (Custodian Trustee) Rules 1971, r. 3. As to paras. (e) and (g), see, respectively, the National Health Service Reorganisation Act 1973, s. 24, and the Local Government Act 1972, s. 251 (1) and Sched. 29, Part I.

(c) Any corporation which is incorporated by special Act or Royal Charter or under the Charitable Trustees Incorporation Act 1872 which is empowered by its constitution to act as a trustee for any charitable purposes, but only in relation to trusts in which its constitution empowers it to act;

(d) Any corporation which is constituted under the law of the United Kingdom or of any part thereof and having its place of business there, and which is either:—

(i) established for the purpose of undertaking trust business for the benefit of Her Majesty's Navy, Army, Air Force or Civil Service or of any unit, department, member or association of members thereof, and having among its directors or members any persons appointed or nominated by the Defence Council or any Department of State or any one or more of those Departments, or

(ii) authorised by the Lord Chancellor to act in relation to any charitable ecclesiastical or public trusts as a trust corporation, but only in connection with any such trust as is so authorised;

(e) Any Regional Hospital Board, Board of Governors of a teaching hospital or Hospital Management Committee constituted under the National Health Service Acts 1946 to 1968, but only in relation to any trust which such a Board or Committee is authorised to accept by virtue of section 59 of the said Act of 1946;

(f) Any Area Gas Board and the Gas Council established under the Gas Act 1948, or any two or more of them jointly, but only in relation to a pension scheme or pension fund established or maintained by any such Board or that Council, or any two or more of them jointly, by virtue of the powers conferred on them by that Act;

(g) Any of the following, namely:—

(i) the Greater London Council,

(ii) the corporation of any borough (including a borough included in a rural district) acting by the council,

(iii) a county council, urban district council, rural district council or parish council, or

(iv) the Council of the Isles of Scilly,

but only in relation to charitable or public trusts (and not ecclesiastical or eleemosynary trusts) for the benefit of the inhabitants of the area of the local authority concerned and its neighbourhood, or any part of that area.

By the Law of Property (Amendment) Act 1926, s. 3, the term " ' trust corporation ' includes—the Treasury Solicitor, the Official Solicitor and any person holding any other official position prescribed by the Lord Chancellor, and, in relation to the property of a bankrupt and property subject to a deed of arrangement, includes the trustee in bankruptcy and the trustee under the deed respectively, and, in relation to charitable ecclesiastical and public trusts, also includes any local or public authority so prescribed, and any other corporation constituted under the laws of the United Kingdom or any part thereof which satisfies the Lord Chancellor that it undertakes the administration of any such trusts without remuneration, or that by its constitution it is required to apply the whole of its net income after payment of outgoings for charitable, ecclesiastical or public purposes, and is prohibited from distributing, directly or indirectly, any part thereof by way of profits amongst any of its members, and is authorised by him to act in relation to such trusts as a trust corporation."

Usually, however, where reference is made to a trust corporation, the term implies a corporation which undertakes trust business for profit. In *Re Skinner's Estate* [19] Grindlays Bank Ltd. had been appointed executors of a will. Subsequently, under a scheme of arrangement and amalgamation, Grindlays merged with the National Bank of India. The scheme provided that all the assets of Grindlays should be transferred to the National Bank, but this should not include property vested in Grindlays as personal representatives, and it also provided that Grindlays should, for the time being, remain in existence. Sachs, J., held that Grindlays as executors could not assign their trust, unless in the ordinary course of administration, and that as the bank remained in existence, with the required capital, although it had transferred all its assets, it was still competent to act as executor.

Where a trust corporation, other than the Public Trustee, is appointed a trustee or executor in the ordinary way, it has no power to charge for its services, although if the court appoints a trust corporation, it may, in doing so, permit it to charge.[20] If, however, a trust corporation is appointed a custodian trustee, it may then (as has been maintained) charge for its services as custodian trustee, but it may not avail itself of this possibility to charge, where a document purports to appoint the trust corporation as (a) custodian trustee and (b) as managing trustee.[21] Such a purported appointment is without legal effect.

By virtue of s. 138 of the Law of Property Act 1925, a trust corporation may be nominated by trustees to receive notices of dealings with equitable interests for the purpose of retaining priority under the rule in *Dearle* v. *Hall*,[22] the priority being effective from the date when the corporation receives the notice.

D. JUDICIAL TRUSTEES

By virtue of section 1 of the Judicial Trustees Act 1896 and the Judicial Trustee Rules 1972, the court may, on the application of the settlor, a trustee or a beneficiary, appoint any fit and proper person nominated in the application, or an official of the court, to be a judicial trustee, to act either alone or jointly with another, or, on proof of sufficient cause, in place of all or any existing trustees.[23] The Official Solicitor is often appointed, and a bank may also be

---

[19] [1958] 1 W.L.R. 1043.

[20] Trustee Act 1925, s. 42. The court also has an inherent jurisdiction to authorise remuneration for a trustee, whether appointed by the court or not: *Re Masters*, [1953] 1 W.L.R. 81.

[21] *Forster* v. *Williams Deacon's Bank Ltd.*, [1935] Ch. 359; *Arning* v. *James*, [1936] Ch. 158.

[22] (1823), 3 Russ. 1; (1828), 3 Russ. 48.

[23] A judicial trustee may be a Settled Land Act trustee: *Re Marshall's Will Trusts*, [1945] Ch. 217.

selected by the court to undertake the trust as a judicial trustee. The court may also appoint a judicial trustee to administer the estate of a deceased person instead of the executor or administrator. Such appointments are entirely discretionary,[24] and the judicial trustee so appointed is an officer of the court, and subject to its control and supervision. He may, therefore, at any time obtain the court's direction as to the way in which he is to act, without a formal application by summons. His accounts are audited annually, and he is entitled to such remuneration as the court allows. The office of judicial trustee corresponds with that of the " Judicial Factor " under Scottish law.

In *Re Ratcliff*[25] a testator appointed his wife sole executrix, giving her control of the property, of which she was tenant for life, and the court declined to appoint a judicial trustee at the instance of a reversioner, no allegation of misconduct having been made. In *Re Chisholm*[26] the court declined to appoint a judicial trustee where the person having the power of appointing under the instrument had appointed persons willing to act, and in *Re Martin*[27] the court expressed its disinclination to appoint a judicial trustee to act with one privately appointed.

By rule 6 of the Judicial Trustee Rules 1972 the court is not precluded by any existing practice from appointing as a judicial trustee a person who is a beneficiary, a solicitor to the trust or any person standing in any special position with regard to the trust.

A retiring judicial trustee has no statutory power to nominate his successor.[28]

---

[24] *Re Ratcliff*, [1898] 2 Ch. 352. See also *Re Wells*, [1968] 1 W.L.R. 44.
[25] [1898] 2 Ch. 352.
[26] (1898), 43 S.J. 43.
[27] [1900] W.N. 129.
[28] *Re Johnston* (1911), 105 L.T. 701. As to the various special kinds of trustee generally, see Keeton, *Modern Developments in the Law of Trusts*, pp. 16–27.

CHAPTER VII

THE CREATION OF AN EXPRESS TRUST

A. UNDER THE STATUTE OF FRAUDS 1677 AND THE LAW OF PROPERTY ACT 1925

ORIGINALLY in equity, no special form was required for the creation of the trust, and therefore a trust of any kind might be created by word of mouth, or even, according to the preamble of the Statute of Uses, by signs. By the Statute of Frauds, 1677, s. 7, it was provided that any declaration of trust must be evidenced by a memorandum in writing signed by the party creating the trust. This is now replaced by the Law of Property Act 1925, s. 53 (1) (b), which provides—

> . . . a declaration of trust respecting any land or any interest therein must be manifested and proved by some writing signed by some person who is able to declare such trust or by his will . . .

" Land " in the Law of Property Act 1925 [1] means land of any tenure, mines and minerals and other corporeal hereditaments, also all incorporeal hereditaments and any easements, rights, or privileges derived from the land. The effect of section 53 (1) (b) of the Act of 1925 is to make verbal changes in the earlier enactment only. The substance of the law is unaltered.

The meaning of the phrase " land or any interest therein " has provoked very extensive litigation. Leasehold interests, even before 1926, were clearly within the statute.[2] Chattels personal were just as clearly outside the statute, and thus, in *M'Fadden* v. *Jenkyns*,[3] a creditor desired his debtor to hold the debt in trust for A. The debtor did so, and eventually paid over part of it to A. It was held that a good trust had been created, with the debtor as trustee.

At one time it was thought the statute did not extend to charitable trusts, but Lord Talbot, Lord Hardwicke and Lord Northington successively declared that the asserted exception did not exist.[4]

In *Forster* v. *Hale*,[5] Arden, M.R., said—

> It is not required by the *Statute*, that a trust should be created by a writing . . . but that [trusts] shall be manifested and proved by writing; plainly meaning, that there should be evidence in writing, proving there was such a trust.

The terms of this section of the statute should be distinguished from those of section 53 (1) (c) of the Law of Property Act 1925 which provides that " a disposition of an equitable interest or trust subsisting at the time of the disposition, *must be in writing* signed by the person disposing of the same, or by

---

[1] s. 205 (1) (ix).
[2] *Skett* v. *Whitmore* (1705), Freem.Ch. 280; *Forster* v. *Hale* (1798), 3 Ves. 696.
[3] (1842), 1 Ph. 153, affirming 1 Hare 458.
[4] *Loyd* v. *Spillett* (1734), 3 P.Wms. 344; 2 Atk. 148; *Boson* v. *Statham* (1760), 1 Eden 508.
[5] (1798), 3 Ves. 696, 707.

62

his agent thereunto lawfully authorised in writing or by will." [6] Like section 4 of the Statute of Frauds, section 7 (now the Law of Property Act 1925, s. 53 (i) (*b*)) is a rule of evidence, and therefore it is sufficient if the necessary writing comes into existence at any time before action is brought upon the trust. A defendant relying upon these sections as a defence must expressly plead them, or the benefit of them will be forfeited.[7] A defendant may rely on the statute as a defence to proceedings here, even if they relate to the enforcement of a trust having as its object land situated abroad.[8]

The application of the statute is subject to one very important equitable rule. It may not be used as an instrument of fraud. This is illustrated by the leading case of *Rochefoucauld* v. *Boustead*.[9] A acquired the legal title to certain estates in Ceylon, and worked them for several years, during which time he conducted correspondence with B, which acknowledged certain beneficial rights of B in the property. B then claimed that A held the estates as trustee for her, and whilst admitting that the correspondence was probably insufficient to satisfy section 7 of the Statute of Frauds, offered to bring forward further evidence that would conclusively prove A's fraud in attempting to withhold the estates from her. The Court of Appeal allowed this evidence to be brought, and in consequence held that A could not claim the estates beneficially, but must hold them on trust for B. Another example is *Booth* v. *Turle*.[10] The plaintiff purported to assign to the defendant an agreement for a lease absolutely, but there was a collateral parol understanding that the defendant should hold part of the premises in trust for the plaintiff. It was held that the trust could be proved by parol evidence, since the effect of excluding it would be to facilitate a fraud.

The writing required need not take any particular form. It may be by memorandum or letter, and a recital of the trust in a defence to a Chancery suit has been held to be sufficient.[11] Where the trust is evidenced by correspondence, it must be shown that the letters relate to the subject-matter of the trust, which must be identified with reasonable precision. Parol evidence may not be introduced to supplement the correspondence, but it may be used to show the position of the writer, the circumstances surrounding the transaction and the degree of weight which ought to be attached to the correspondence.[12] Whilst all the terms of the trust must be validated by the signature, the rules of construction applicable to section 4 of the Statute of Frauds are also applicable to section 7, and now to section 53 (1) (*b*) of the Law of Property

[6] On which, see *Grey* v. *I.R.C.*, [1960] A.C. 1; *Oughtred* v. *I.R.C.*, [1960] A.C. 206; *Vandervell* v. *I.R.C.*, [1967] 2 A.C. 291; *Re Tyler*, [1967] 1 W.L.R. 1269; *Re Danish Bacon Co. Ltd. Staff Pension Fund Trusts*, [1971] 1 W.L.R. 248. See also *Re Paradise Motor Co. Ltd.*, [1968] 1 W.L.R. 1125, 1143 (C.A.), on s. 53 (1) (*c*), not s. 53 (2) as there stated. This provision does not require writing when the settlor, having vested property in trustees, later declares the trusts, thus creating express beneficial interests in place of his own beneficial interest under a resulting trust: *Re Vandervell's Trusts (No. 2)*, [1974] 3 W.L.R. 256.

[7] R.S.C., O. 18, r. 8. The same rule applies to other sections of the statute.

[8] *Rochefoucauld* v. *Boustead*, [1897] 1 Ch. 196, 207 (C.A.).

[9] [1897] 1 Ch. 196 (Cases, p. 205). See also *Bannister* v. *Bannister*, [1948] 2 All E.R. 133 (C.A.); *Hodgson* v. *Marks*, [1971] Ch. 892 (C.A.). Section 53 (2) of the Law of Property Act 1925 provides that subs. (1) does not affect the creation or operation of resulting, implied or constructive trusts (Chaps. XIII–XIV, *post*).

[10] (1873), L.R. 16 Eq. 182. See also *Lincoln* v. *Wright* (1859), 4 De G. & J. 16; *Re Duke of Marlborough*, [1894] 2 Ch. 133; *Bannister* v. *Bannister*, [1948] 2 All E.R. 133 (C.A.).

[11] *Hampton* v. *Spencer* (1693), 2 Vern. 287.

[12] *Morton* v. *Tewart* (1842), 2 Y. & C.C.C. 67.

Act 1925, so that documents unsigned, if clearly referable to documents which are signed, may be connected to form one complete memorandum.[13]

B. THE CREATION OF TRUSTS BY WILL: SECRET TRUSTS

By virtue of the Wills Act 1837, s. 9, together with section 53 (1) (c) of the Law of Property Act 1925 (formerly the Statute of Frauds, 1677, ss. 5 and 9), all trusts created by testamentary disposition must be executed and attested in accordance with the formalities therein prescribed. These are (1) that the will shall be in writing; (2) that it shall be signed at the foot or end thereof by the testator, or by some other person in his presence and by his direction; (3) that the signature be acknowledged by the testator in the presence of two or more witnesses present at the same time, the witnesses attesting in the presence of the testator. Furthermore, it must not be overlooked that, before 1926, a will was revoked by the subsequent marriage of the testator, but now, by the Law of Property Act 1925, s. 177, if a will is expressed to be made in contemplation of a marriage, it is not revoked by the solemnisation of *that contemplated marriage*.[14]

Exactly as equity will not permit the Statute of Frauds to be used as an instrument of fraud, so also it will not permit the Wills Act to be used for such a purpose; and this has been responsible for the growth of the equitable principles relating to secret trusts. These principles seem to date from the second half of the seventeenth century, for the earliest decided case upon the doctrine appears to be *Crook* v. *Brooking*,[15] decided by Lord Chancellor Jeffreys in 1688. There the testator bequeathed £1,500 to Simon and Joseph Snow to be disposed of by them on a secret trust which he communicated to Simon. After the testator's death, Simon revealed the secret trust to Joseph, the object of the trust being that if the testator's daughter died in the lifetime of her husband, the £1,500 should go to the children of another daughter, as the first daughter should direct. The first daughter died in her husband's lifetime, and the children of the other daughter claimed as beneficiaries under the verbal secret trust. It was held that, since the testator had declared the terms of the trust to Simon in his lifetime, there was a good secret trust, although the actual method of distribution among the beneficiaries was uncertain. This decision was upheld by the Lords Commissioners.

This rule was followed in *Pring* v. *Pring in* 1689,[16] wherein a man gave property to his executors, and directed that it should be held in trust, and the testator's wife brought a bill declaring that the trust was in her favour. The court held that as the will had declared that the executors only held in trust, with no declaration for whom, it was open to the wife to prove that the testator communicated, by words or conduct in his lifetime, his intention to benefit the wife to his executors, and the claim was therefore admitted.

The doctrine so established was applied in *Smith* v. *Attersoll*,[17] where the

---

[13] *Forster* v. *Hale* (1798), 3 Ves. 696.
[14] See *Pilot* v. *Gainfort*, [1931] P. 103, and *Sallis* v. *Jones*, [1936] P. 43.
[15] 2 Vern. 50.
[16] 2 Vern. 99. See also *Thynn* v. *Thynn* (1684), 1 Vern. 296.
[17] (1826), 1 Russ. 266.

gift was to executors in trust for purposes previously communicated; and in *Podmore* v. *Gunning*,[18] although in this case the trust was not proved. These cases turned on the provision of the Statute of Frauds which required writing, although, in the case of wills of personalty, no attested signature of the testator was then necessary. After the Wills Act 1837 the cases upon the requirements of that Act were similarly decided.

It will be seen that the essence of a secret trust is an equitable obligation engrafted upon a gift in a will and communicated to the intended trustee in the testator's lifetime. In permitting such obligations to be regarded as binding, it would seem at first sight that equity is interfering very directly with statutory requirements, and it therefore becomes necessary to appreciate the nature of equitable intervention in these cases. Equity cannot nullify the requirements of a statute; it can merely ensure that a statute is not permitted to operate in an inequitable manner. If the trust were regarded as part of the will, then equity could not permit the trust to be effective unless it were created in accordance with the requirements of the Wills Act. Equity, however, regards the trust as something outside the testamentary dispositions. In the words of Lord Sumner in *Blackwell* v. *Blackwell* [19]—

> In itself the doctrine of equity, by which parol evidence is admissible to prove what is called " fraud " in connection with secret trusts, and effect is given to such trusts when established, would not seem to conflict with any of the Acts under which from time to time the Legislature has regulated the right of testamentary disposition. A Court of conscience finds a man in the position of an absolute legal owner of a sum of money, which has been bequeathed to him under a valid will, and it declares that, on proof of certain facts relating to the motives and actions of the testator, it will not allow the legal owner to exercise his legal right to do what he will with his own. This seems to be a perfectly normal exercise of general equitable jurisdiction. The facts commonly but not necessarily involve some immoral and selfish conduct on the part of the legal owner. The necessary elements, on which the question turns, are intention, communication, and acquiescence. The testator intends his absolute gift to be employed as he and not as the donee desires; he tells the proposed donee of this intention and, either by express promise or by the tacit promise, which is signified by acquiescence, the proposed donee encourages him to bequeath the money in the faith that his intentions will be carried out. The special circumstance, that the gift is by bequest only makes this rule a special case of the exercise of a general jurisdiction, but in its application to a bequest the doctrine must in principle rest on the assumption that the will has first operated according to its terms. It is because there is no one to whom the law can give relief in the premises, that relief, if any, must be sought in equity. So far, and in the bare case of a legacy absolute on the face of it, I do not see how the statute-law relating to the form of a valid will is concerned at all, and the expressions, in which the doctrine has been habitually described, seem to bear this out. For the

---

[18] (1836), 7 Sim. 644.
[19] [1929] A.C. 318, 334–345 (Cases, p. 210). See also *Ottaway* v. *Norman*, [1972] Ch. 698, 711, *per* Brightman, J.; Burgess, " Secret Trust Property " (1972) 36 *Conveyancer* 113; Bandali (1973) 36 *Modern Law Review* 210.

prevention of fraud equity fastens on the conscience of the legatee a trust, a trust, that is, which otherwise would be inoperative; in other words it makes him do what the will in itself has nothing to do with; it lets him take what the will gives him and then makes him apply it, as the Court of conscience directs, and it does so in order to give effect to wishes of the testator, which would not otherwise be effectual.

The same point of view is also adopted by Lord Cairns in *Jones* v. *Badley*,[20] where he observes that when a devisee seeks to apply what has been devised to him otherwise than in accordance with the testator's intentions, communicated by him and accepted by the devisee—

> . . . it is in effect a case of trust, and in such case the Court will not allow the devisee to set up the *Statute of Frauds,* or, rather, the *Statute of Wills.* . . . But in this the Court does not violate the spirit of the statutes; but for the . . . prevention of fraud, it engrafts the trusts on the devise by admitting evidence which the statute would in terms exclude, in order to prevent a devisee from applying property to a purpose foreign to that for which he undertook to hold it.

Another test, which has been founded on the same principles, and which has sometimes been applied, is to consider the case as unaffected by the Statutes of Frauds or Wills, and then to inquire whether a trust has been imposed by the testator, and accepted by the devisee in such a way that a court of equity would enforce it as binding on the conscience of the devisee. One peculiarity of a secret trust is that the secret trustee, unlike other trustees, cannot himself be a beneficiary.[21]

How ought secret trusts to be classified—as express or as constructive trusts? Most writers have regarded them as constructive trusts, based upon the fraud of the promisor, if he fails to carry out the obligation he has assumed. This view is held in a qualified way by one of us,[22] taking the view that half-secret trusts are express trusts. The language of the courts in dealing with these cases is ambiguous, and although there are frequent references to the fraud which would ensue if the secret trust were not enforced, and although the observations of Lord Sumner, in *Blackwell* v. *Blackwell,*[23] which have been cited above, also stress the element of fraud (which indeed was the original basis for the enforcement of trusts in equity), they are also not inconsistent with the view that the legatee, even in a fully secret trust, undertakes a trust in the lifetime of the testator, and that it becomes operative when the property rests in him at the testator's death. As Waters points out,[24] " . . . the courts have always been anxious to enforce the promise which the recipient made or led the transferor to believe he made." This is, in fact, exactly what Lord Cairns said in *Jones* v. *Badley.*[25]

In discussing the cases which have been decided upon the doctrine, it is necessary to distinguish carefully between those cases in which the person

---

[20] (1868), L.R. 3 Ch.App. 362, 364.
[21] *Re Rees*, [1950] Ch. 204.
[22] Sheridan, " English and Irish Secret Trusts " (1951) 67 *Law Quarterly Review* 314.
[23] [1929] A.C. 318, 334, 334–335 (Cases, p. 210).
[24] *Constructive Trusts,* p. 58. See also Burgess, " The Juridical Nature of Secret Trusts " (1972) 23 *Northern Ireland Legal Quarterly* 263.
[25] (1868), L.R. 3 Ch.App. 362, 364.

intended to act as trustee takes the property under the will apparently beneficially, and those cases in which he is designated in the will as trustee.

1. Cases in which the Trustee takes Beneficially upon the Face of the Will.
If the person designated is given the property apparently beneficially, and
then subsequently to the testator's death some document is found purporting
to be a direction of the testator to him to hold on certain trusts, the legatee is
not bound by the document and he takes beneficially. In such a case, his conscience is not affected by any trust, and equity will not interfere.[26]

If, however, the trusts are communicated in the testator's lifetime to a person who on the face of the will takes beneficially, another rule becomes operative. Equity will never allow a man to profit by his own fraud, and the court
says that since the person to whom the trusts have been communicated before
death and to whom the property has been bequeathed by will, or to which he
has succeeded on intestacy has, in effect, induced the testator to retain his will
in that form, or has induced him not to make a will at all, the person so benefiting will be bound by the trusts, and this notwithstanding that they are not
expressed in writing. As Lord Westbury observed in *McCormick* v.
Grogan[27]—

> The Court of Equity has, from a very early period, decided that even
> an Act of Parliament shall not be used as an instrument of fraud; and if
> in the machinery of perpetrating a fraud an Act of Parliament intervenes,
> the Court of Equity, it is true, does not set aside the Act of Parliament,
> but it fastens on the individual who gets a title under that Act, and im-
> poses upon him a personal obligation, because he applies the Act as an
> instrument for accomplishing a fraud. In this way the Court of Equity
> has dealt with the *Statute of Frauds,* and in this manner, also, it deals with
> the *Statute of Wills.* And if an individual on his deathbed, or at any other
> time, is persuaded by his heir-at-law, or his next of kin, to abstain from
> making a will, or if the same individual, having made a will, communi-
> cates the disposition to the person on the face of the will benefited by
> that disposition, but, at the same time, says to that individual that he has
> a purpose to answer which he has not expressed in the will, but which he
> depends on the disponee to carry into effect, and the disponee assents to
> it, either expressly, or by any mode of action which the disponee knows
> must give to the testator the impression and belief that he fully assents to
> the request, then, undoubtedly, the heir-at-law in the one case, and the
> disponee in the other, will be converted into trustees, simply on the prin-
> ciple that an individual shall not be benefited by his own personal fraud.

There is an additional point which should be mentioned. If the testator
communicates the trust to the legatee or devisee in the testator's lifetime, the
latter has an opportunity to disclaim. If he does not, he deprives the testator
of the chance of selecting other trustees.

In *Stickland* v. *Aldridge*,[28] it was pointed out that if a father devised his

---

[26] *Re Stirling*, [1954] 1 W.L.R. 763 ; *Re Falkiner*, [1924] 1 Ch. 88.
[27] (1869), L.R. 4 H.L. 82, 97. See the comments by Brightman, J., in *Ottaway* v. *Norman*,
[1972] Ch. 698, 711–712.
[28] (1804), 9 Ves. 516.

property to his youngest son, who promised the father in his lifetime that he would pay £10,000 to the eldest son, the court would compel the youngest son to declare what had passed between the testator and himself, and then constitute him a trustee for the eldest son for £10,000.

Again, in *Sellack* v. *Harris*,[29] a father was induced by his eldest son not to make a will, on the ground that the son himself would hold certain freehold land (which the father had bought with a younger son's money) for the younger son's enjoyment, and the court compelled the heir to make the provision contemplated, for by agreeing to do so, he had induced the owner of the property to refrain from making a will.

Difficulty sometimes arises in applying these principles where a testator leaves property to two or more persons, apparently beneficially, and relies on the promise of one of them to undertake certain trusts. Where the gift is made to *joint tenants* on the strength of a promise by one of them to execute the trust, the secret trust binds both; but this is not so where a will is simply left unrevoked on the faith of a later promise by one of them, or where the gift is made to them *as tenants in common*. In either of these two last cases, only the person actually promising is bound. This is explained by Farwell, J., in *Re Stead*[30] (remembering that legal tenancy in common of land cannot exist since 1925)—

> If A induces B, either to make, or leave unrevoked, a will leaving property to A and C as tenants in common, by expressly promising, or tacitly consenting, that he and C will carry out the testator's wishes, and C knows nothing of the matter until after [B's] death, A is bound, but C is not . . . ; the reason stated being, that to hold otherwise would enable one beneficiary to deprive the rest of their benefits by setting up a secret trust. If, however, the gift were to A and C as joint-tenants, the authorities have established a distinction between those cases in which the will is made on the faith of an antecedent promise by A and those in which the will is left unrevoked on the faith of a subsequent promise. In the former case, the trust binds both A and C . . . the reason stated being that no person can claim an interest under a fraud committed by another; in the latter case A and not C is bound . . . the reason stated being that the gift is not tainted with any fraud in procuring the execution of the will.[31]

As an illustration of these observations with regard to joint tenants, a good example is afforded by an Irish case, *Turner* v. *Attorney-General*.[32] Property was left to four persons as joint tenants, and they took beneficially. In the will of one of them, certain observations were made which pointed to the existence of a secret trust, but it was held that these observations could not affect the right of the survivor of the joint tenants to take beneficially.

2. Cases in which the Trustee Takes as Trustee upon the Face of the Will. The cases in which the trustee takes apparently beneficially upon the face

---

[29] (1708), 5 Vin.Abr. 521, pl. 31.
[30] [1900] 1 Ch. 237, 241. See Perrins, " Can You Keep Half a Secret?" (1972) 88 *Law Quarterly Review* 225.
[31] See also *Tee* v. *Ferris* (1856), 2 K. & J. 357; *Russell* v. *Jackson* (1852), 10 Hare 204; *Jones* v. *Badley* (1868), L.R. 3 Ch. 362; *Burney* v. *Macdonald* (1845), 15 Sim. 6; *Moss* v. *Cooper* (1861), 1 J. & H. 352; on which these observations are founded.
[32] (1876), I.R. 10 Eq. 386.

of the will are logical and unambiguous. Unfortunately the same cannot be said about the cases which now fall to be considered.

Where property is bequeathed to a person *as trustee*, it is perfectly clear that the testator never intended him to take beneficially, and equity respects the intention. For example, where a testator devised the whole of his estate after payment of his debts and testamentary expenses " unto my trustees absolutely they well knowing my wishes concerning the same " the Court of Appeal held that the whole of the gift to the trustees was a fiduciary one, and the trustees could not claim it beneficially. Moreover, evidence was not admissible to show that such a gift was what the testator intended.[33] The distinction between a conditional gift and a trust may sometimes be a fine one, but it exists. In Lord Eldon's words,[34] " If I give to A and his Heirs all my real Estate, charged with my Debts, that is a Devise to him for a particular Purpose, but not for that Purpose only. If the Devise is upon Trust to pay my Debts, that is a Devise for a particular Purpose, and nothing more; and the Effect of those Two Modes admits just this Difference. The former is a Devise of an Estate of Inheritance for the Purpose of giving the Devisee the beneficial Interest, subject to a particular Purpose: the latter is a Devise for a particular Purpose; with no Intention to give him any beneficial Interest." If, after the will is proved a document is found in a form other than that prescribed by the Wills Act, directing that the property be held on certain trusts, this is void, as being a document which can only take effect as a testamentary disposition and which must, therefore, conform to the requirements of the Act; but the testator's intention prevails so far as to prevent the intended trustee from taking beneficially, and a resulting trust arises in favour of the testator's residuary legatee or devisee, or if there be no such person, or if the trust is imposed upon the residuary legatee, then in favour of the testator's intestate successors. Any other construction would have the effect of permitting the testator to make testamentary dispositions in a form other than that prescribed by the Wills Act.

Precisely the same principles apply where, although the intended trustee takes apparently beneficially in the will, nevertheless he has accepted the capacity of a trustee in respect of the property in the testator's lifetime, but the testator has omitted to communicate to him the beneficiaries of the trust prior to his death. Thus, in *Re Boyes*,[35] the testator made a will bequeathing all his property to Mr. Carritt, and appointing him sole executor. Mr. Carritt was the testator's solicitor and had drawn the will, and in evidence he stated that the testator had intended him to hold the property as trustee for objects to be subsequently indicated by him. The testator, however, had never indicated these objects during his lifetime, but after his death Mr. Carritt found two letters in which the testator expressed his desire that with the exception of a trinket, valued at £25, all the rest of the testator's property should go to a Mrs. Brown. It was clear from the first that Mr. Carritt could not take beneficially, and the question was whether Mrs. Brown or the next-of-kin was the beneficiary. Kay, J., held that for the trust in favour of Mrs. Brown to be valid, it

---

[33] *Re Rees*, [1950] Ch. 204. See also *Re Pugh's Will Trusts*, [1967] 1 W.L.R. 1262.
[34] *King* v. *Denison* (1813), 1 V. & B. 260, 272–273.
[35] (1884), 26 Ch.D. 531.

was essential that it should be communicated to the legatee-trustee in the testator's lifetime, and that he should accept this trust. As this had not been done, Mr. Carritt was a trustee for the next-of-kin.

It remains to consider the cases in which the testator designated the trustee in the will specifying no beneficiaries, and in his lifetime communicates the objects of the trust to the trustee, who assents. Here it is necessary to distinguish cases in which the communication of the objects is made at or before the making of the will, and cases in which such communication is only made *after* the will has been made, but still in the testator's lifetime.

(a) Where the communication of the objects takes place at or before the making of the will, it is not questioned that the trust so declared is binding on the trustee.

In *Irvine* v. *Sullivan*,[36] a testator devised and bequeathed all his real and personal estate to trustees to sell, and he directed that all moneys arising from the sale, after payment of funeral, testamentary and other expenses, should be paid by the trustees to D absolutely, " trusting that she will carry out my wishes with regard to the same, with which she is fully acquainted." The testator, shortly before the date of the will, had expressed his wish to D that she should, out of the property he left her, make various gifts to several persons. On leaving the testator, D wrote down the testator's wishes, but the paper was never seen or signed by the testator. James, V.-C., held that D took the residue of the estate beneficially, subject to the performance of the testator's communicated wishes, in respect of which D had bound herself.

Again, in *Riordan* v. *Banon*,[37] the testator by will directed that a pecuniary legacy should be disposed of in accordance with instructions in a memorandum which the testator would leave the legatee. It was proved that before the execution of the will, the testator had informed the legatee that he intended to bequeath the legacy in trust for a person whom he then named, and that the legatee had consented to accept the legacy for this purpose, and had promised the testator that he would carry out his wishes. The residuary legatees claimed the legacy, but the court held there was a valid secret trust for the person named by the testator. Parol evidence was admissible to prove that a legacy had been bequeathed upon trust entirely or partially undisclosed upon the face of the will when, at or before the execution of the will, the trust had been communicated by the testator to the legatee, and had been accepted by the legatee. The learned Vice-Chancellor in that case observed [38]—

> The result of the cases appears to me to be that a testator cannot by his will reserve to himself the right of disposing subsequently of property by an instrument not executed as required by statute, or by parol; but that when, at the time of making his will, he has formed the intention that a legacy thereby given shall be disposed of by the legatee in a particular manner, not thereby disclosed, but communicated to the legatee and assented to by him, at or before the making of the will, or probably, according to *Moss* v. *Cooper*,[39] subsequently to the making of it, the Court

[36] (1869), L.R. 8 Eq. 673.
[37] (1876), I.R. 10 Eq. 469.
[38] I.R. 10 Eq. 477–478.
[39] (1861), 1 J. & H. 352, 367.

will allow such trust to be proved by admission of the legatee, or other parol evidence, and will, if it be legal, give effect to it. The same principle which led this Court, whether wisely or not, to hold that the Statute of Frauds and the Statute of Wills were not to be used as instruments of fraud, appears to me to apply to cases where the will shows that some trust was intended, as well as to those where this does not appear upon it. The testator, at least when his purpose is communicated to and accepted by the proposed legatee, makes the disposition to him on the faith of his carrying out his promise, and it would be a fraud in him to refuse to perform that promise. No doubt the fraud would be of a different kind if he could by means of it retain the benefit of the legacy for himself; but it appears that it would also be a fraud though the result would be to defeat the expressed intention for the benefit of the heir, next-of-kin, or residuary donees.[40]

In another Irish case, *Cullen* v. *Attorney-General for Ireland*,[41] Lord Westbury emphasised the attitude of the court, which was expounded in *Riordan* v. *Banon*,[42] and which was adopted expressly in the later cases (and particularly in *Blackwell* v. *Blackwell*[43]). He said—

. . . where there is a secret trust, or where there is a right created by a personal confidence reposed by a testator in any individual, the breach of which confidence would amount to a fraud, the title of the party claiming under the secret trust, or claiming by virtue of that personal confidence is a title *dehors* the will, and which cannot be correctly termed testamentary.

There was an illustration of the application of this principle in the case of *Re Young*,[44] where it was held that a beneficiary under a secret trust was not prevented from taking, although he was an attesting witness to the will of the settlor, for the interest arose, not under the will, but under the trust, which was *dehors* the will.

This line of reasoning is undoubtedly a correct reflection of equitable principle in operation upon the Wills Act, but it must not be pressed too far. In *Re Maddock*[45] the testatrix left her residuary personalty by will to W, whom she appointed one of her executors. By a subsequent memorandum, communicated to W in the lifetime of the testatrix, she directed W to hold a specified part of the residue in trust for other persons. The Court of Appeal held that the residuary estate outside the scope of the memorandum was primarily liable for the payment of the testatrix's debts, and that the position was not, as Kekewich, J., had thought, that the debts were paid out of the residue as a whole, before the trust attached. In other words, as far as payment of debts was concerned, the part of the residue bound by the secret trust must be treated as if it was specifically bequeathed.

[40] See also *Attorney-General* v. *Dillon* (1862), 13 Ir.Ch.Rep. 127, 133; *McCormick* v. *Grogan* (1869), L.R. 4 H.L. 82.
[41] (1866), L.R. 1 H.L. 190, 198.
[42] (1876), I.R. 10 Eq. 469.
[43] [1929] A.C. 318 (Cases, p. 210).
[44] [1951] Ch. 344.
[45] [1902] 2 Ch. 220.

The principles established by the earlier authorities were reviewed and restated in *Re Fleetwood*.[46] In that case the testatrix left to a named person all her personalty " to be applied as I have requested him to do." The request was made out, and the named trustee jotted down in the presence of the testatrix the names of the persons and the amounts which the testatrix desired to give and, after this, the codicil was executed, declaring the existence of the trust, but not the person for whom it was established. Hall, V.-C., held that parol evidence was admissible to prove communication of the terms of the trust to the trustee. This decision was criticised adversely in *Le Page* v. *Gardom*[47] and again in *Re Gardner*,[48] apparently because the communication to the trustee was verbal and not by memorandum. It is a little difficult to see why such criticisms should have been made, in view of the earlier and similar decision in *Irvine* v. *Sullivan*.[49] In any event, *Re Fleetwood* was followed in *Re Huxtable*,[50] where a testatrix bequeathed £4,000 to X " for the charitable purposes agreed upon between us." The testatrix verbally communicated to the legatee the fact that it was her intention to provide out of the income of that sum for the relief of sick and necessitous members of the Church of England, whilst the legatee was to dispose of the principal as his own property. Farwell, J., admitted the evidence, including that which conferred on the trustee the power of disposing of the principal on his death. The Court of Appeal held that the evidence was admissible as to the trusts of the £4,000 which, upon the face of the will, was wholly given for charitable purposes, but was not admissible for the purpose of providing for the £4,000 on the trustee's death, since the will purported to give the whole £4,000, and to admit such evidence would be to contradict the will.

The doctrine embodied in *Re Fleetwood* was regarded as of doubtful authority until the decision of the House of Lords in *Blackwell* v. *Blackwell*.[51] Thus, in *Re Gardner*,[52] a testatrix gave by will all her property to her husband for his use and benefit during his life, " knowing that he will carry out my wishes." Four days after making her will, the testatrix had signed an unattested memorandum, in which she desired that all the money she left to her husband should be divided by him among named beneficiaries. The testatrix left only personalty and made no disposition of the corpus. Five days after her death the husband also died, whereupon the will and memorandum of the wife were found in the husband's safe. There was also evidence that, shortly after the execution of the will, the testatrix had said in the presence of her husband that her property after her husband's death was to be divided among the beneficiaries named in the memorandum, and that the husband had assented. It should be noticed that on the wife's death, as there was no disposition of the corpus of the property under the will, the husband took it *jure mariti*. The Court of Appeal held that the words " knowing that he will carry out my wishes " related only to the husband's life interest, and that those wishes did not appear; but that as to the corpus of the estate, the husband,

---

[46] (1880), 15 Ch.D. 594.
[47] (1915), 84 L.J.Ch. 749, 752–753.
[48] [1920] 2 Ch. 523, 532.
[49] (1869), L.R. 8 Eq. 673.
[50] [1902] 2 Ch. 793.
[51] [1929] A.C. 318 (Cases, p. 210).
[52] [1920] 2 Ch. 523, followed in *Re Young*, [1951] Ch. 344.

though taking apparently beneficially *jure mariti*, in fact took it fettered by a secret trust contained in the memorandum communicated in the testatrix's lifetime, and also in the oral conversations to the same effect. Warrington, L.J., said [53]—

> *Johnson* v. *Ball*,[54] and *In re Gardom* [55] appear to me to have no reference to a case such as the present. Those were cases in which the person on whom it was sought to impose the trust did not take under the terms of the will for his own benefit; he took expressly under the terms of the will as trustee. In such cases as that the trusts upon which the trustee is to hold the property must be contained in the will itself, or in some document in existence at the date of the will, or it may be, if *In re Fleetwood* was properly decided, declared by parol and accepted by the trustee at or before the execution of the will. But that limitation " at or before the execution of the will " has no application, as was pointed out by Lord Davey in *French* v. *French*,[56] to such a case as that with which we have to deal.

It should be added that *Re Gardner* was further elucidated in a second decision,[57] in which it was held that, since the beneficiaries were named in the memorandum, the trust arose from the date when the memorandum was communicated to the husband and of his assent thereto, so that the interest of a beneficiary who survived the memorandum, but died before the testatrix, did not lapse, but passed to the deceased beneficiary's personal representatives.

In *Blackwell* v. *Blackwell*,[58] a last determined effort was made to shake the effect of *Re Fleetwood*,[59] but Eve, J. (following *Re Fleetwood* and also the view expressed by him in *Re Gardom* [60]), the Court of Appeal and the House of Lords were at one in holding the case rightly decided, and the doctrine of secret trusts, as considered above, is at length finally established. In *Blackwell* v. *Blackwell*,[58] a testator, by a codicil, gave £12,000 to five persons to apply the yearly income " for the purposes indicated by me to them," with power to pay the capital sum of £8,000 to persons indicated to them by the testator, whilst the remaining £4,000 was to fall into the residuary estate. Detailed parol instructions were given by the testator to one of the trustees, C, and the object of the trust was known in outline and accepted by all before the codicil was executed. On the same day that the codicil was executed, C wrote out a memorandum of the instructions which the testator had given him. It was held that there was a binding trust for the objects which the testator had indicated. Even so late as 1929, however, the doctrine was accepted by the House of Lords with some hesitation, for Lord Warrington observed [61]—

> I confess to having felt considerable doubt during the argument whether to apply the principle in such a case as the present would not be to give validity to a parol will in spite of the provisions first of the Statute of

[53] [1920] 2 Ch. 532.
[54] (1851), 5 De G. & Sm. 85.
[55] (1915), 84 L.J.Ch. 749.
[56] [1902] 1 I.R. 172, 230.
[57] [1923] 2 Ch. 230.
[58] [1929] A.C. 318 (Cases, p. 210).
[59] (1880), 15 Ch.D. 594.
[60] [1914] 1 Ch. 662, 669.
[61] [1929] A.C. 342.

Frauds and secondly of the Wills Act. Subsequent reflection however and a careful perusal of the judgment of Hall V.-C. in *In re Fleetwood*, wherein the earlier authorities under both statutes are cited and discussed, have satisfied me that that case and, in consequence, the present case in the Courts below were rightly decided. I think the solution is to be found by bearing in mind that what is enforced is not a trust imposed by the will, but one arising from the acceptance by the legatee of a trust, communicated to him by the testator, on the faith of which acceptance the will was made or left unrevoked, as the case might be. If the evidence had merely established who were the persons and what were the purposes indicated it would in my opinion have been inadmissible, as to admit it would be to allow the making of a will by parol. It is the fact of the acceptance of the personal obligation which is the essential feature, and the rest of the evidence is merely for the purpose of ascertaining the nature of that obligation.

In *Re Hawkesley's Settlement*,[62] a testatrix appointed by her will her husband and two other persons " to be my executors and residuary legatees to carry out instructions that I may leave in writing or verbally which I have not yet fully completed." The court held that the residuary legatees took as trustees, and since the purposes intended by the testatrix could not be ascertained, they held as trustees for the next-of-kin.

A further problem affecting this type of secret trust was decided in *Re Colin Cooper*.[63] A testator bequeathed the sum of £5,000 to two trustees upon trusts " already communicated to them." Just before his death, he executed a later will, revoking the earlier one, cancelling the bequest of £5,000, but giving the same trustees the sum of £10,000, " they knowing my wishes regarding this sum." The testator never told the trustees of the revocation and new bequest, and the Court of Appeal held that, whilst the trust operated against the original £5,000, which had been specifically mentioned to the trustees, the trust failed against the additional sum, for lack of communication. The report simply says that the added gift of £5,000 failed, so that presumably the trustees held it for the residuary legatee.

(b) There remains for consideration that type of case in which the trustee is so designated on the face of the will, but no objects are indicated, but these are communicated to the trustee, either by memorandum or verbally, in the testator's lifetime, but *after* the will is made. It might be objected at first sight that there should be no difference on principle between these cases and those in which the trustee takes apparently beneficially on the face of the will. In each case, communication of the trusts in the testator's lifetime should be sufficient to take them outside the Wills Act. This is indeed the view expressed in the American *Restatement of the Law of Trusts*,[64] but there exist judicial pronouncements of weight against it. Thus, in *Re Keen*,[65] Lord Wright said—

In *Blackwell* v. *Blackwell*[66]; *In re Fleetwood*[67] and *In re Huxtable*,[68]

---

62 [1934] Ch. 384.
63 [1939] Ch. 811.
64 *Trusts*, 2d, § 55, comments *c* and *h*.
65 [1937] Ch. 236, 246–247 (Cases, p. 216).
66 [1929] A.C. 318 (Cases, p. 210).
67 (1880), 15 Ch.D. 594.
68 [1902] 2 Ch. 793.

the trusts had been specifically declared to some or all of the trustees at or before the execution of the will and the language of the will was consistent with that fact. There was in these cases no reservation of a future power to change the trusts, in whole or in part. Such a power would involve a power to change a testamentary disposition by an unexecuted codicil and would violate s. 9 of the Wills Act. . . . The trusts referred to but undefined in the will must be described in the will as established prior to or at least contemporaneously with its execution.

It will be seen that the substance of this view is that the prior declaration of trust in fact completes the trust which is partially declared in the will. If this is in fact so, it is hard to see why, apart from another doctrine to be mentioned in a moment, this type of trust could ever be held to be good, even though the communication is prior to the will, for it seems quite clearly to involve the incorporation into the will of something which is not executed in accordance with the terms of the Wills Act.

There exists, however, in the law of wills, a doctrine known as the doctrine of incorporation by reference, which saves *written* memoranda not executed in accordance with the requirements of the Wills Act, under certain conditions. The conditions are that the memoranda must be written, they must be in existence before the will is made, or at the latest at the time when the will is made, and they must be referred to in the will, as matter to be incorporated in it. This is established by a long line of cases, and is excellently illustrated by the case of *In the goods of Smart*.[69] A will contained the following clause: " I direct my trustees to give such of my friends as I may designate in a book or memorandum that will be found with this will " the different articles specified for such friends in such book or memorandum," and subsequently the testatrix did write up such book or memorandum, and after she had done so, she executed a codicil which did not refer in any way to such book or memorandum, but confirmed the will with various alterations. The court held that, although the will was republished by the codicil and must be taken to speak from the date of such codicil, the allusion in the will to the " book or memorandum " was still to a future, and not to an existing, document, so that it could not be regarded as incorporated into the will. Gorell Barnes, J., said [70]—

It seems to me that it has been established that if a testator, in a testamentary paper duly executed, refers to an existing unattested testamentary paper, the instrument so referred to becomes part of his will; in other words, it is incorporated into it; but it is clear that, in order that the informal document should be incorporated in the validly executed document, the latter must refer to the former as a written instrument then existing—that is, at the time of execution—in such terms that it may be ascertained. . . . If the document is not existing at the time of the will, but comes into existence afterwards, and then, after that again, there is a codicil confirming the will, the question arises, as it has done in a number of these cases, whether that document is incorporated. It appears to me that, following out the principle which I have already referred to, the

69 [1902] P. 238. See also *Allen* v. *Maddock* (1858), 11 Moo.P.C. 427.
70 [1902] P. 238, 240–241.

will may be treated, by the confirmation given by the codicil, as executed again, and as speaking from the date of the codicil, and if the informal document is existing then, and is referred to in the will as existing, so as to identify it, there will be incorporation; but if the will, treated as being re-executed at the date of the codicil, still speaks in terms which shew that it is referring to a future document, then it appears to me there is no incorporation.

The principle upon which *In the goods of Smart* was decided was directly applied in *Re Jones*.[71] In that case a testator bequeathed a legacy to trustees under a special declaration of trust made on the date of the will, adding that the trustees should be governed by the terms of the special declaration or any substitution therefor, or modification or addition, which the testator might execute after making his will. Simonds, J., deciding this case on the doctrine of incorporation by reference, held that there could not be a valid incorporation of documents not yet executed. The terms of the Wills Act 1837 were therefore not satisfied, and the gift failed. A somewhat similar clause was also held invalid in *Re Edward's Will Trusts*.[72]

This doctrine is logical, and the decided cases relating to it are free from ambiguity. It is submitted, however, that this doctrine is distinct from the doctrine of secret trusts, although it is quite clear that some of the judgments upon the type of secret trusts we are now considering have confused them. This is the only possible explanation for the curious and ill-founded view that *Re Fleetwood*[73] was wrongly decided because the communication prior to the will was verbal and not by memorandum. Where such prior verbal communication takes place, it quite clearly cannot be identified as a memorandum can; and it seems quite consistent with principle to hold that a communication may fail to be incorporated by reference because it fails to satisfy the conditions set out above, but that it may nevertheless take effect as a secret trust. The two principles have different origins—one is an equitable principle, the other a rule of probate—different orbits, and different effects (for in the one case a trust operates *dehors* the will, and in the other certain matter is added to the will itself).

It remains to consider the cases which have been regarded as relating to this type of secret trust.

In *Johnson* v. *Ball*,[74] a testator gave a policy of assurance to two trustees " to hold . . . upon the uses appointed by letter signed by them and myself." No such letter existed, though it would appear that the trustees had previously agreed to accept the bequest for the benefit of persons mentioned by the testator. Such a communication, however, would be ineffective in this case, as it did not conform to the terms of the will. Some time after making the will, the testator wrote a letter to his executors, saying that he had left the policy in his will to the two trustees for purposes they had agreed to carry out. At the same time the testator signed an unattested memorandum

---

[71] [1942] Ch. 328.
[72] [1947] 2 All E.R. 521, reversed on other grounds, [1948] Ch. 440, *sub nom. Re Edwards' Will Trusts*. See also *Re Schintz' Will Trusts*, [1951] Ch. 870.
[73] (1880), 15 Ch.D. 594.
[74] (1851), 5 De G. & Sm. 85. See also *Re Tyler*, [1967] 1 W.L.R. 1269; *Re Bateman's Will Trusts*, [1970] 1 W.L.R. 1463.

declaring the trusts on which the trustees were to hold the policy. The trustees retained both the letter and the memorandum until after the testator's death, when one of the beneficiaries under the memorandum sought to enforce his claim against the executors and trustees. Parker, V.-C., held that the testator could not prospectively create for himself a power to dispose of property by an instrument not duly executed as a will, and that the letter did not operate as a gift *inter vivos*. The trustees accordingly held the proceeds of the policy in trust for the residuary legatee. It would seem that this case was considered purely upon the footing of incorporation by reference—a supposition which is strengthened by the following observations [75] from the learned Vice-Chancellor's judgment—

> Cases in which there is no trust appearing on the will, and where the Court establishes a trust on the confession of the legatee, have no application to the present; nor, as it appears to me, have those cases cited in the argument, in which the will refers to a trust created by the testator by communication with the legatee antecedently to or contemporaneously with the will.

Nevertheless, both Lord Buckmaster in *Blackwell* v. *Blackwell* [76] and Lord Wright in *Re Keen* [77] appear to have regarded them as authority for the proposition that where a trust is partially declared on the face of the will, it cannot be completed by a communication of objects posterior to the execution of the will, but prior to the testator's death; although, as Sir William Holdsworth points out, [78] of the two authorities relied on by Parker, V.-C., in *Johnson* v. *Ball*, [74] the first, *Croker* v. *Marquis of Hertford*, [79] was purely a case of incorporation by reference, and the second, *Briggs* v. *Penny* [80] was a case where the communication of the testator's intention only took place after his death. On the other hand, in *Moss* v. *Cooper*, [81] Page Wood, V.-C., was of opinion that in trusts of this type it was immaterial whether communication occurred before or after the making of the will.

In *Re Keen*, [82] a testator made a will, giving a sum of money to his executors " to be held upon trust and disposed of by them among such person, persons or charities as may be notified by me to them or either of them during my lifetime." Failing such notification, the money was to fall into residue. He had earlier told one of his executors that he wished the money to be held for the benefit of an unidentified person, whose name was contained in a sealed envelope which he handed to the executor, to be opened after the testator's death. The Court of Appeal, adopting an opinion of Kay, J., in *Re Boyes*, [83] decided that handing over a sealed envelope was sufficient communication. The court also held that the words of the will necessarily implied that the communication must be made after the will was made, and as the notification was, in fact, anterior to the will, the terms of the will were unsatisfied, and the

---

75 5 De G. & Sm. 91.
76 [1929] A.C. 318, 331 (Cases, p. 210).
77 [1937] 1 Ch. 236 (Cases, p. 216).
78 " Secret Trusts " (1937) 53 *Law Quarterly Review* 501, 502.
79 (1844), 4 Moo.P.C. 339.
80 (1849), 3 De G. & Sm. 525.
81 (1861), 1 J. & H. 352, 367.
82 [1937] 1 Ch. 236 (Cases, p. 216).
83 (1884), 26 Ch.D. 531, 536.

gift therefore failed.[84] With this narrow point of construction, issue cannot be joined, and if this be regarded as the *ratio decidendi* of *Re Keen*, the broad question whether communications posterior to the execution of the will are effective in this type of case is still open for decision. Lord Wright, however, discussed the problem on a broader basis, and, regarding *Johnson* v. *Ball* [85] as an authority on secret trusts, expressed the view that, even if the communication had satisfied the terms of the will, it would still have been ineffective as a reservation of a future power to change the trust. Such an argument draws a distinction between fully secret trusts, where the contest is between the donee on the face of the will and the beneficiary under the alleged trust, and half secret trusts, where the trustee on the face of the will cannot take and the contest is between the secret beneficiary and the beneficiary under a resulting trust. The contrary view is that both types of secret trust operate outside the will and should be treated alike.[86]

C. THE DISTINCTION BETWEEN AN EXECUTED AND AN EXECUTORY TRUST

The distinction between these two types of trust has already been noticed. In an executed trust, the limitations of the beneficial interest are clear and complete; in an executory trust, though the proposed limitations are unambiguous, something more must be done, or some other document executed, before the settlement is complete. In both cases, the transfer of the legal or other estate to the trustees is complete. At one time it was doubted whether any consequences of importance followed from this distinction,[87] but it has been long established, and Sir George Jessel, M.R., stated it clearly in *Miles* v. *Harford*,[88] when he observed—

> . . . it is called an executory trust, . . . where [the testator], instead of expressing exactly what he means, that is, filling up the terms of the trust, . . . tells the trustees to do their best to carry out his intention. In that way it is executory, that if he has not put into words the precise nature of the limitations, he has said in effect: " Now there are my intentions, do your best to carry them out. . . ."

As Lord St. Leonards put it, in *Egerton* v. *Earl Brownlow*,[89] the test is whether the settlor has been his own conveyancer, or whether he has left it to the court to make out from general expressions what his intention is.

In practice, executory trusts are only met with in two types of instrument: (i) in " marriage articles "; and (ii) in wills. Marriage articles are the preliminary agreement drawn up for the purpose of establishing in general terms the provision which is being made for the parties to the marriage and their

---

[84] See also *Re Spence*, [1949] W.N. 237.
[85] (1851), 5 De G. & Sm. 85.
[86] See, in addition to articles already cited, Fleming, " Secret Trusts " (1947) 12 *Conveyancer* (N.S.) 28; Scamell, " Secret Trusts " (1949) 16 *The Solicitor* 224; Delany, " Equity and the Law Reform Committee " (1961) 24 *Modern Law Review* 116, 120–121; Kaye, " The Problems of Secret Trusts " (1970) 2 *Kingston Law Review* 30. *Cf. Re Spence*, [1949] W.N. 237, where communication was to one trustee only, when communication to all was necessary.
[87] On this, see Lord Northington's observations in *Austen* v. *Taylor* (1759), 1 Eden 361, 368.
[88] (1879), 12 Ch.D. 691, 699.
[89] (1853), 4 H.L.C. 1, 210.

issue. This is usually drawn up before the marriage, and it is followed (either before or after the marriage) by a full marriage settlement. Difficulties of construction might arise, however, either where no formal marriage settlement was executed, or where the formal marriage settlement differed in some particular from the intention of the settlor as expressed in the marriage articles. An executory trust would arise in a will which, for example, bequeathed personal property to a single man to be settled on his marriage.[90]

The first important consequence of the distinction is that, whereas in an executed trust equity will follow the law in respect of the terms used, and if technical terms are used, they are construed according to their technical meaning (although equity, unlike the common law, would always give effect to informal words with a clear meaning, so that a limitation in equity of an interest to A " absolutely " would be regarded as creating an equitable fee simple),[91] in an executory trust, the court will temper this strict rule, and seek to follow the true intention of the settlor, provided that this can be ascertained. Thus, in *Lord Glenorchy* v. *Bosville*,[92] the settlor devised real estate to trustees upon trust, on the occurrence of the marriage of his granddaughter, to convey the estate to the use of her for life, remainder to the use of her husband for life, remainder to the issue of her body, with remainders over. It was held that though the granddaughter would, under the rule in *Shelley's Case*, have taken an estate tail had the trust been an executed trust, yet since the trust was executory, and as the testator's intention was to provide for the children of the marriage, that intention would be best carried out by a conveyance to the granddaughter for life, remainder to her husband for her life, remainder to her first and other sons in tail, with remainder to her daughters.

The Construction of Executory Trusts before 1926

It is necessary, however, to draw still a further distinction between executory trusts in marriage articles and executory trusts in wills. In the former the very nature of the contract gives a clear indication of the intention of the settlor, which is wanting in the case of a will,[93] so that in the case of marriage articles the court is able to carry out the primary purpose of the settlor in providing for the parties and issue of the marriage, whereas in a will the court usually has no such clue to the testator's primary intention, and is therefore compelled to look elsewhere for it. Thus, in *Sackville-West* v. *Viscount Holmesdale*,[94] Lord Chelmsford said—

> In considering a question of this description the Court is not confined to the language of the will itself in order to discover the intention of a testator; it may not only refer to the motives which led to the will, and to its general object and purpose, to be collected from other instruments to which the will itself refers, but also to any circumstances which may have

---

[90] *Re Gowan* (1880), 17 Ch.D. 778. See also *Re Parrott* (1886), 33 Ch.D. 274.

[91] *Re Bostock's Settlement*, [1921] 2 Ch. 469. *Cf. Re Arden*, [1935] Ch. 326, where the operative clause was not in strict conveyancing language, and a different construction was therefore placed upon the instrument.

[92] (1733), Cas.t.Talb. 3.

[93] See the observations of Sir W. Grant in *Blackburn* v. *Stables* (1814), 2 V. & B. 367.

[94] (1870), L.R. 4 H.L. 543, 561 (Cases, p. 219).

influenced the mind of the maker towards the provisions it contains. The best illustration of the object and purpose of an instrument furnishing an indication of intention in the case of executory trusts, is to be found in the instance of marriage articles, where the object of the settlement being to make a provision for the issue of the marriage, no words, however strong, which in the case of an executed trust would place the issue in the power of the father, will be allowed to prevail against the implied intention.

Earlier,[95] Lord Hatherley, L.C., after reviewing the authorities, had said—

These examples will suffice to shew:—(1) That the intent must be so manifested on the face of the instrument directing the settlement to be made that the technical words used cannot be followed in the perfect instrument without defeating the manifest intent of the parties. (2) That in articles made before marriage there will be an assumed intent, assumed from the nature of the case, that the settlement should not be liable to immediate destruction by the act of the settlor, and the Court will alter the words so as to prevent the settlor taking an immediate estate tail. (3) That even in such a case the intent is not sufficiently strong to prevent the very words of the articles being used, though an estate be directed to be given to the husband (the settlor) for life, with a limitation to the heirs of his body, if that limitation is so framed as to prevent his destroying the estate without the concurrence of the intended wife. (4) That in the case of a will, or deed of gift, the intention that the very words mentioned in the instrument as proper for the more complete conveyance are not to be used must be plainly manifested by the first instrument, and will not be assumed merely because the trust is executory.[96]

It was the problem mentioned in the concluding part of Lord Chelmsford's observations and in the second of Lord Hatherley's propositions that caused the real difficulty in the construction of marriage articles. If, in marriage articles, real property of one of the parties was limited to the " heirs " of the contracting parties, or alternatively to the " heirs of the body " or the " issue " of such parties, immediately after the grant of a life estate to the parent, then if these expressions were given their strict technical significance the rule in *Shelley's Case* would apply, and the expressions used would be regarded as words of limitation, and not of purchase. The practical result would be that the father would get, in the one case, a fee simple which he could alienate at once to defeat the expectations of the issue of the marriage, and in the other case, a fee tail, of which the father, being of full age and in possession, could bar the entail, so creating a fee simple which again he could alienate with like results. To avoid this latter consequence, the words " heirs of the body " were construed in marriage articles, where the context allowed, to create a life interest in the father, and entailed interests in the first and other sons of the marriage successively. In wills, however, there was no dominating motive to provide for the issue of the devisee. On the other hand, in wills, the presumption that the words " heirs of the body " were used to invoke the operation of

[95] L.R. 4 H.L. 555.
[96] On the construction of informal expressions in instruments since 1925, see the Law of Property Act 1925, s. 130 (2), pp. 81–82, *post*.

the rule in *Shelley's Case* could be excluded by evidence, both from the will itself and from surrounding circumstances, that the testator had no such intention. Thus, a direction that property should be settled on a devisee and " his issue in tail male " " as counsel shall advise " is strong evidence that the testator did not intend a simple estate tail to be created in favour of the devisee.[97]

Other problems of intent sometimes arose in the construction of marriage articles. For example, joint tenancy between the children of the marriage was disliked, as no severance could occur during the minority of the children. Consequently, where possible, the court would construe words as creating a tenancy in common where otherwise a joint tenancy might have been expected.

Many of the questions of construction arising upon executory trusts in wills are extremely technical, especially where, before 1926, chattels such as heirlooms were settled. A modern example of another difficulty which may arise, however, is afforded by *Re Potter's Will Trusts*.[98] A testator by his will made provision for his infant daughter " and any children she may have," such provision to be secured by a settlement; with other provisions in the event of the daughter marrying under twenty-five without the consent of her guardian or of her dying unmarried. The daughter married twice, the second time after the death of her first husband, and the question to be decided was whether the children of the second marriage should be included in the provision to be made in the settlement. Bennett, J., thought that only the children of the first marriage were included in the words of the will, but the Court of Appeal unanimously decided that the children of the second marriage were entitled to share in the provision.

The Construction of Executory Trusts after 1925

Important changes in the construction of trusts were introduced by the Law of Property Act 1925. In the first place, section 131 abolished the rule in *Shelley's Case*, so that if in an instrument today a gift is made to A and after his death to his " heirs," or " to A and after his death to the heirs of his body," then A will take a life interest, and his heir will take an absolute interest, and he will take that interest by way of purchase. This rule will now apply, therefore, both to executed and to executory trusts. Accordingly, one of the main differences between the construction of executory and executed trusts has now gone.

Two other points must be noticed. The Law of Property Act 1925, s. 130 (1), permits entailed interests to be created in personalty as well as in realty (in both cases behind a settlement). Before 1926 entails in personalty could not be created. Such entailed interests, however, can only be created by the like expressions as those by which before 1926 a similar estate tail could have been created by deed in freehold land. This means that such entails can only be created by the use of the expressions " to A and the heirs of his body " or " to A in tail."

Section 130 (2), however, provides—

[97] *White* v. *Carter* (1766), 2 Eden 366; (1768), Amb. 670. See also *Read* v. *Snell* (1743), 2 Atk. 642.
[98] [1944] Ch. 70.

Expressions . . . which, in a will, or executory instrument coming into operation before [1926], would have created an entailed interest in freehold land, but would not have been effectual for that purpose in a deed not being an executory instrument, shall (save as provided by [s. 131]) operate in equity, in regard to property real or personal, to create absolute, fee simple or other interests corresponding to those which, if the property affected had been personal estate, would have been created therein by similar expressions before [1926].

Since, before 1926, estates tail in personalty could not be created, then it would appear that entailed interests cannot be created by the use of informal expressions. Whether, however, section 130 (1) applies to executory trusts or not is by no means clear. Lewin [99] thinks that it does not, and this would appear to be the better opinion, since an executory trust is not intended to express technical limitations, for which a second instrument is necessary.

D. COMPLETELY AND INCOMPLETELY CONSTITUTED TRUSTS

The distinction between executed and executory trusts is quite different from that between completely and incompletely constituted trusts. A trust which is completely constituted is one in which the trust property has been finally and completely vested in the trustees; when and so long as this is not done, the trust is incompletely constituted. For example, if a person simply declares his intention to create a trust, this is insufficient to constitute it. All trusts arising under wills are completely constituted, though they may be either executed or executory.

The distinction between completely and incompletely constituted trusts is of importance principally with regard to the question of consideration. If valuable consideration is given in exchange for the creation of the trust, it does not matter whether the trust is completely constituted or not, for equity regards as done that which ought to be done, and will perfect the imperfect conveyance; but equity will not perfect an imperfect voluntary trust. So Lord Eldon observed in *Ellison* v. *Ellison* [1]—

I take the distinction to be, that if you want the assistance of the Court to constitute you *cestuy que trust*, and the instrument is voluntary, you shall not have that assistance, for the purpose of constituting you *cestuy que trust*; as upon a covenant to transfer stock, etc., if it rests in covenant, and is purely voluntary, this Court will not execute that voluntary covenant: but if the party has completely transferred stock, etc., though it is voluntary, yet the legal conveyance being effectually made, the equitable interest will be enforced by this Court.

The general principle applicable has been enunciated by Turner, L.J., in *Milroy* v. *Lord*,[2] as follows—

. . . in order to render a voluntary settlement valid and effectual, the settler

[99] 16th ed., p. 57. See also Cheshire, *Real Property*, 11th ed., pp. 196–198.
[1] (1802), 6 Ves. 656, 662. See also the similar observations of Romilly, M.R., in *Pearson* v. *Amicable Assurance Office* (1859), 27 Beav. 229. *Cf. Meek* v. *Kettlewell* (1842), 1 Hare 464.
[2] (1862), 4 De G.F. & J. 264, 274.

must have done everything which, according to the nature of the property comprised in the settlement, was necessary to be done in order to transfer the property and render the settlement binding upon him. He may of course do this by actually transferring the property to the persons for whom he intends to provide, and the provision will then be effectual, and will be equally effectual if he transfers the property to a trustee for the purposes of the settlement, or declares that he himself holds it in trust for those purposes; . . . but, in order to render the settlement binding, one or other of these modes must, as I understand the law of this Court, be resorted to, for there is no equity in this Court to perfect an imperfect gift.

On the same point, Romer, L.J., said in *Timpson's Executors* v. *Yerbury* [3]—

Now the equitable interest in property in the hands of a trustee can be disposed of by the person entitled to it in favour of a third party in any one of four different ways. The person entitled to it (1) can assign it to the third party directly; (2) can direct the trustees to hold the property in trust for the third party . . . ; (3) can contract for valuable consideration to assign the equitable interest to him; or (4) can declare himself to be a trustee for him of such interest.

The principle embodied in Turner, L.J.'s judgment in *Milroy* v. *Lord* [4] must be accepted with the qualifications mentioned by the Court of Appeal in *Re Rose*. [5] In that case the deceased, by two transfers dated March 30, 1943, (1) transferred to his wife 10,000 shares in an unlimited company, and (2) transferred a further 10,000 shares in the same company to trustees to hold upon the trusts of a voluntary settlement. The transfers were in the form required by the company's articles, but these articles also gave the directors power to decline to register any transfer. The transfers were duly stamped on April 12, 1943, and registered in the books of the company on June 30, 1943. When the deceased died on February 16, 1947, it became necessary to determine for estate duty purposes the effect of these transactions. The Court of Appeal held that, since the deceased had done everything in his power by executing the transfer to transfer his legal and beneficial interest in the shares to the transferees, the transferees had become beneficial owners of the shares from March 30, when the transfers were executed, until registration was complete. During that time, therefore, the transferor was a trustee of the legal title for the transferees. The Court of Appeal reached this conclusion after consideration of the fact that, having regard to the form and operation of the transfers, the nature of the property transferred and the necessity for registration to perfect legal title, and finally the discretionary power of the directors to withhold registration, there was no further step that the transferor could take to divest himself of title. Commenting on the observations of Turner, L.J., in *Milroy* v. *Lord*, [4] Evershed, M.R., said [6]—

I agree that if a man purporting to transfer property executes documents which are not apt to effect that purpose, the court cannot then

[3] [1936] 1 K.B. 645, 664.
[4] (1862), 4 De G.F. & J. 264.
[5] [1952] Ch. 499 (Cases, p. 225). See also *Re Rose*, [1949] Ch. 78.
[6] [1952] Ch. 510.

extract from those documents some quite different transaction and say that they were intended merely to operate as a declaration of trust, which ex facie they were not; but if a document is apt and proper to transfer the property—is in truth the appropriate way in which the property must be transferred—then it does not seem to me to follow from the statement of Turner L.J. that, as a result, either during some limited period or otherwise, a trust may not arise, for the purpose of giving effect to the transfer.

In *Re King* [7] a settlor wrote a letter to an intending trustee, purporting to assign six policies of assurance upon trusts for his children, sending the three policies which were then in his possession. He stated that he intended to execute a trust deed and appoint another trustee. Hall, V.-C., treated this as a valid assignment of the policies to the trustee, and since the settlor had done all in his power to make an effective settlement, it was completely constituted, notwithstanding the non-execution of the contemplated deed.

An example of a transaction in which no effective transfer of the property voluntarily settled occurred is afforded by *Jefferys* v. *Jefferys*. [8] A father voluntarily conveyed freeholds to trustees upon trusts for the benefit of his daughters; he also covenanted to surrender copyholds to the trustees upon the same trusts. He died without surrendering the copyholds, and by his will he devised parts of both the freeholds and the copyholds to his wife. His daughters sought to enforce the trust, and the court held that, as far as the freeholds were concerned, the trust was completely constituted, and the daughters' title was complete; but as far as the copyholds were concerned, the court would not decree their surrender, for the trust was incompletely constituted. The settlor had not transferred them to the trustees, nor had he declared himself a trustee of them. He had merely made a voluntary agreement to transfer them, which was *nudum pactum* both at law and in equity. [9]

From a consideration of this case, it will appear that a trust is completely constituted: (1) if the property is conveyed to trustees, or (2) if the settlor declares himself a trustee of it. Where either of these things has been done, a beneficiary may enforce the trust, even if he is only a volunteer. [10]

1. WHERE THE SETTLOR CONVEYS TO ANOTHER

If the settlor is both the legal and the equitable owner of the property, he must take all due steps to do all that it is in his power to do to vest the property in the trustee. The position is the same where a person intends to make a direct gift to another. The appropriate modes of transfer must always be used. In *Antrobus* v. *Smith*, [11] the owner of shares in a company endorsed on the certificate a memorandum that he had assigned it to his daughter, but it was held there was no valid gift, as the purported assignment did not pass the legal interest, and did not amount to a declaration of trust. On the other hand, in *Re Rose*, [12] the settlor had taken all the steps which were in his power to

---

[7] (1879), 14 Ch.D. 179.
[8] (1841), Cr. & Ph. 138. See also *Paul* v. *Paul* (1882), 20 Ch.D. 742.
[9] See also *Dillon* v. *Coppin* (1839), 4 My. & Cr. 647.
[10] *Re Adlard*, [1954] Ch. 29.
[11] (1805), 12 Ves. 39. See also *Richards* v. *Delbridge* (1874), L.R. 18 Eq. 11; *Re Williams*, [1917] 1 Ch. 1; *Re Swinburne*, [1926] Ch. 38.
[12] [1952] Ch. 499 (Cases, p. 225).

take to transfer the shares, and the court accepted the position that, until registration was complete, there was a trust in favour of the transferee.

Where the intending donor or settlor himself only possesses an equitable interest in the property, it is sufficient if he transfers that. It is not necessary that he should procure a conveyance of the legal estate.[13] In *Kekewich* v. *Manning*,[14] a testator bequeathed residuary personalty to his wife for life, remainder to his daughter absolutely. The daughter assigned the whole of her interest to trustees for the benefit of her nieces. It was held that the trust was good, as the daughter had done all in her power to divest herself of her interest, which was equitable. If she had been legal owner, she would have had to transfer it by the use of the appropriate legal forms. In *Re Bowden*[15] a settlor, by a voluntary settlement made in 1868, settled any property to which she might become entitled upon her father's death, and gave the trustees full power to give receipts for the property in her name. Her father died in 1869, and between 1871 and 1874 the executors of the father's will transferred the settlor's share to the trustees of the voluntary settlement. In 1935, the settlor requested that the trustees should transfer the property to her. The court held that the trustees had received the settlor's share impressed with the trusts of the voluntary settlement, and since the settlement was completely constituted, the settlor was bound by it, and could not revoke it.[16]

2. WHERE THE SETTLOR MAKES A DECLARATION OF TRUST

Instead of conveying to trustees, the settlor himself may declare that he holds on trust for others, whether the interest he holds is legal or equitable. If the trust relates to land, it must be evidenced by writing, but otherwise the declaration may be oral, or it may be inferred from conduct. Any words clearly expressing intention are sufficient, and provided that the declaration of trust is unconditional, the settlor is thereafter bound.[17] However, an ineffectual attempt to transfer property to another is not construed as a declaration of trust.[18] But when everything which the settlor can do to transfer the property has been done, but some outstanding formality outside the settlor's control remains, *e.g.* registration of a transfer of shares, or of a transfer of registered land in the Land Registry, then, pending that formality, the transferor is a trustee.[19]

Since, therefore, an incompletely constituted trust which is also voluntary cannot be enforced, the question of what is a voluntary trust, and what is a trust for valuable consideration, must next be considered. Valuable consideration in the law of trusts, as in the law of contract, is some valuable thing assessable in terms of money, with the proviso that marriage, and also a forbearance to sue, are so considered; and therefore wherever consideration of this type is present, the trust is not voluntary. The phrase " good consider-

[13] *Gilbert* v. *Overton* (1864), 2 H. & M. 110.
[14] (1851), 1 De G.M. & G. 176.
[15] [1936] Ch. 71.
[16] See also *Re Fry*, [1946] Ch. 312 ; *Re Rose*, [1949] Ch. 78.
[17] *Lady Naas* v. *Westminster Bank Ltd.*, [1940] A.C. 366.
[18] See pp. 82–83, *ante*. See also the observations of Jessel, M.R., in *Richards* v. *Delbridge* (1874), L.R. 18 Eq. 11. An apparent exception occurs in the case of attempts to create informal settlements of land : Settled Land Act 1925, s. 9 (1) (iii). *Cf. Bannister* v. *Bannister*, [1948] 2 All E.R. 133.
[19] *Re Rose*, [1952] Ch. 499 (Cases, p. 225).

ation " is sometimes used, as applied to natural love and affection, but this consideration, though good, is not " valuable," and was only used for the purpose of rebutting a resulting use or trust. It therefore does not make an incompletely constituted settlement enforceable at the instance of a volunteer.
— The question of marriage as consideration must be considered further. If the settlement is made before and in consideration of marriage, it is made for valuable consideration. So it is, also, if made after marriage, but in fulfilment of an ante-nuptial agreement to settle, but if the settlement is made after marriage, and not in pursuance of an ante-nuptial agreement, it is voluntary. By section 4 of the Statute of Frauds 1677 an agreement in consideration of marriage had to be evidenced by writing under the hand of the party to be charged; evidenced, that is, sometime before action is brought, and therefore, if a post-nuptial settlement recited an ante-nuptial agreement to settle, two consequences followed: (1) the requirements of the statute were satisfied; and (2) the settlement was not voluntary.[20] Since the Law Reform (Enforcement of Contracts) Act 1954, however, the need for writing has been abolished.

In these circumstances, the question, who is within the scope of the marriage consideration, becomes one of great importance, and it has now been settled, after a good deal of uncertainty, that the only persons within the marriage consideration are the actual parties, the husband, the wife and the issue of that marriage.[21] All other persons, therefore, are volunteers and cannot enforce the provisions of a settlement as *against the settlor,* so far as the transfer of the property is still incomplete, *e.g.* an agreement to settle after-acquired property on them. In *Re Plumptre's Marriage Settlement,*[22] the husband and wife, on their marriage in 1878, covenanted with their trustees to settle the wife's after-acquired property for the benefit of herself and her husband successively for life, then for the issue of the marriage, and then for the wife's next-of-kin. In 1884, the husband bought certain stock in his wife's name, and the wife afterwards sold it, investing the proceeds in other stock. In 1909 the wife died without issue, leaving her husband her administrator. It was held that the next-of-kin, being volunteers, could not enforce the wife's covenant to settle the stock against her husband as her administrator; nor could the trustees sue for damages for breach of the covenant, for the claim was statute-barred.

Even where the claim under the covenant is not statute-barred, the trustees are under no duty to enforce the covenant at the suit of volunteers only, nor will the court direct them to do so, for to do so would be to give the volunteers indirect relief which they could not obtain by direct procedure.[23] Where, however, a beneficiary, though a volunteer, is a party to the covenant, then he can sue, not as a beneficiary in equity, but as a covenantee at common law.[24]

On the other hand, in *Pullan* v. *Koe,*[25] in 1879, a wife was given a sum of money which was bound by a covenant executed by herself and her husband in their marriage settlement to settle her after-acquired property. The money

---

[20] *Re Holland,* [1902] 2 Ch. 360.
[21] *De Mestre* v. *West,* [1891] A.C. 264.
[22] [1910] 1 Ch. 609 (Cases, p. 222).
[23] *Re Pryce,* [1917] 1 Ch. 234; *Re Kay's Settlement,* [1939] Ch. 329; *Re Ames' Settlement,* [1946] Ch. 217.
[24] *Cannon* v. *Hartley,* [1949] Ch. 213.
[25] [1913] 1 Ch. 9.

was paid into the husband's account, on which the wife had power to draw, and shortly afterwards part of it was invested in bonds, which remained at the bank, the interest on them being credited to the account. When the husband died in 1909, the bonds came into the hands of his executors. There were several children of the marriage, and the court held that, since they were within the marriage consideration, they could enforce the transfer of the bonds to the trustees of the marriage settlement.

Another illustration of strangers to the consideration (not marriage) is *Colyear* v. *Lady Mulgrave*.[26] A father, who had a legitimate son and four illegitimate daughters, covenanted with the son whereby the father agreed to transfer £20,000 to a trustee for the four daughters, and the son agreed to pay the father's debts. The son paid some of the debts, but died before his father had discharged his part of the undertaking. The son, by his will, left his father as his sole legatee and executor, and it was held that the daughters could not compel the father to perform the covenant to settle, for although the son had given value, the daughters were strangers to the consideration.

A case with closely similar facts is *Fletcher* v. *Fletcher*.[27] A father covenanted with five trustees that if his two infant illegitimate sons should survive him, his personal representatives would pay to the trustees the sum of £60,000 on trust for each of these sons who survived him. The father retained this deed, which was discovered on his death. The trustees declined to take any steps to enforce the deed in favour of the surviving son. Wigram, V.-C., however, decided, rather strangely, that the court was not called upon to render any assistance to enforce the deed, since the trust in this case, though voluntary, was completely constituted. It would seem that Wigram, V.-C., regarded the trust as being of a chose in action—the right to recover money under the covenant.

In *Re Cook's Settlement Trusts*[28] Buckley, J., described the covenant in *Fletcher* v. *Fletcher* as creating a debt enforceable at law, *i.e.* a property right which, although to bear fruit only in the future and upon a contingency, was capable of being the subject of an immediate trust. For that reason, he did not regard the decision in *Fletcher* v. *Fletcher* as applicable to the covenant with which he had to deal. This was made between a father and his son, and provided that the son should exchange a reversionary interest under a will for certain other property, and that the son should settle part of that property on trust for certain beneficiaries, who were members of the son's family. The rest of the property which the son received (consisting principally of valuable pictures) was subject to an agreement with the father that, if any pictures were sold in the son's lifetime, the proceeds of sale were to be paid to the trustees of the settlement for the same beneficiaries. Subsequently the son covenanted with the trustees of the settlement in similar terms. Buckley, J., held that the covenant was an executory contract to settle property which, so far as the proceeds of sale of the pictures were concerned, might never come into existence. It therefore did not create a debt enforceable at law, as in *Fletcher* v. *Fletcher*. Alternatively, it could be regarded as a promise for valuable con-

[26] (1836), 2 Keen 81.
[27] (1844), 4 Hare 67.
[28] [1965] Ch. 902, 913-914. See also Lee, " The Public Policy of Re Cook's Settlement Trusts " (1969), 85 *Law Quarterly Review* 213.

sideration between father and son, which the beneficiaries, being volunteers,
could not enforce either directly or by requiring the trustees to bring proceedings.

It has been suggested that where a settlement is made by a widow in contemplation of a second marriage, and the settlement provides for her children
by the first marriage, then such children, though technically volunteers from
the standpoint of the second marriage settlement, may nevertheless enforce it.
This, however, has been doubted, and cannot be regarded as settled.[29]

It is sometimes said that to the rule that equity will not assist a volunteer
there are certain exceptions. (1) The rule does not apply to a *donatio mortis
causa*. If the requisites of a valid *donatio mortis causa* have been fulfilled, the
gift will take effect, even though the actual transfer before death is incomplete.[30] Such gifts, however, are on a special footing: they are governed by
special rules and cannot properly be considered with ordinary gifts *inter vivos*.
(2) The rule that equity will not assist a volunteer has no application to wills.
An executor must carry out the provisions of a will in favour of beneficiaries
who are volunteers, but here again, the property vests, by the death of the
testator, in the executor on trust to carry out the dispositions of the will. (3)
A further case requiring consideration is where a person makes an imperfect
gift to A, and subsequently appoints A his executor. Here, on the death of the
donor, the property vests fully in A, and the equity of the beneficiary under
the will is displaced by A's prior equity, and A may therefore retain the property, notwithstanding the fact that, until the donor's death, A's title was
imperfect.[31]

In *Re James*[32] the same rule was applied where the donee had not been
appointed executor, but had taken out letters of administration to the estate
of the donor. Again, it was applied to the personal representatives of a person
who had covenanted in favour of volunteers, and had subsequently been appointed a trustee of the settlement in favour of the volunteers.[33] For the
exception to apply, however, the gift must have been perfect in all respects,
save for the legal formalities necessary for the proper transfer of title. In *Re
Freeland*,[34] a testatrix promised to give the plaintiff a motor car at a future
date, but never did so. The plaintiff, on the death of the testatrix, became her
executrix, and claimed that the imperfect gift had been thereby perfected. The
Court of Appeal declined to apply the rule in *Strong* v. *Bird,* since there had
been no intention to make the plaintiff the owner of the car there and then.

Whenever the rule in *Strong* v. *Bird* is invoked, there must be a continuing
intention on the part of the donor up to the time of his death. Failure to prove
this was fatal to the claim of the donee in *Re Wale*.[35] Certain investments
(described as the A investments), of which the settlor was absolute owner,
were settled by her voluntarily in 1939 for the benefit of her daughter. The
settlor took no steps to transfer these investments to the trustees who, how-

[29] See *Gale* v. *Gale* (1877), 6 Ch.D. 144 ; *Attorney-General* v. *Jacobs Smith*, [1895] 2 Q.B. 341.
See also *Re Cameron and Wells* (1887), 37 Ch.D. 32.
[30] *Re Wasserberg*, [1915] 1 Ch. 195 ; *Wilkes* v. *Allington*, [1931] 2 Ch. 104.
[31] *Strong* v. *Bird* (1874), L.R. 18 Eq. 315 ; *Re Innes*, [1910] 1 Ch. 188. For an ingenious, but
unsuccessful, attempt to extend this principle, see *Re Greene*, [1949] Ch. 333.
[32] [1935] Ch. 449.
[33] *Re Ralli's Will Trusts*, [1964] Ch. 288.
[34] [1952] Ch. 110.
[35] [1956] 1 W.L.R. 1346.

ever, were appointed executors of the settlor's will. The will was altered from time to time, and it eventually disposed of all her estate to other beneficiaries. An incompletely constituted trust in favour of a volunteer had been created by the settlement of 1939, but Upjohn, J., held that the settlor had not shown any continuing intention to benefit the daughter, but that she had in fact forgotten the existence of the settlement which therefore failed.

There are also certain statutory exceptions. Thus, by section 27 (1) of the Settled Land Act 1925, a conveyance of a legal estate in land to an infant does not vest a legal estate in him, but operates as " an agreement for valuable consideration to execute a settlement." Further, by section 4 of the same Act, it is not now possible to create a proper settlement of the legal estate in land without two documents—a trust instrument and vesting deed or assent. But an informal attempt to create a settlement creates an enforceable trust (section 9). The explanation of both these exceptions is that the Settled Land Act was concerned with machinery, and cannot be used to deprive beneficiaries of their interests.

CHAPTER VIII

THE CREATION OF AN EXPRESS TRUST—(*continued*)

THE CONSTRUCTION OF LANGUAGE USED TO CREATE AN EXPRESS TRUST

In *Knight* v. *Knight,*[1] Lord Langdale declared that for a trust to be validly created three things were necessary: (1) the words employed must be so couched that, taken as a whole, they ought to be construed as imperative; (2) the subject-matter of the trust must be certain; (3) the objects, or persons intended to be benefited, must also be certain. These three requirements have often been termed the " three certainties " of a trust, and although this hard and fast distinction may be a little misleading, for a trustee is always necessary for the execution of a trust, it will be convenient to consider each in turn.[2]

1. CERTAINTY OF WORDS

Since equity looks at the intent rather than at the form, no special form of words is necessary for the creation of a valid trust, and if an intention to create a trust may unmistakably be construed from the expressions which the settlor has used, the court will give effect to that intention. The really difficult question in these cases is, what did the settlor really intend? For example, if he used words *precatory, recommendatory* or *expressing a belief,* did he intend to create a binding trust or not? The court has not always given the same answer to this question. In the past, the following words have been held to raise a binding trust, though for reasons that will appear below, it is not considered that all such expressions would now, of themselves, be held to raise a binding trust—

Desire, will, request, will and desire, will and declare, wish and request, wish and desire, entreat, most heartily beseech, order and direct, authorise and empower, recommend, beg, hope, do not doubt, be well assured, confide, have the fullest confidence, trust, trust and confide, have full assurance and confident hope, be under the firm conviction, in full belief, well know, the legatee will give, she will at her death dispose, etc.

At one time, the courts regarded practically any intimation of desire on the part of the testator as imperative, and thus binding upon persons benefited by him, and whilst there is no rule of law limiting the rules relating to precatory trusts to trusts arising by will, practically all the cases have turned upon trusts created by will. The rule that the testator's desire was to be construed as a command was an old equitable rule which was applied in the first instance to executors. Indeed, where a testator used precatory words in relation to a bequest, Dr. Yale has shown that Lord Nottingham did not readily construe them as creating a binding trust. Thus in *Chamond* v. *Carter* [3] the testator

---

[1] (1840), 3 Beav. 148, 172–173.
[2] See also Williams, " The Three Certainties " (1940) 4 *Modern Law Review* 20.
[3] (1673), Nottingham's Cases, Case 3.

bequeathed his residuary estate to his wife, adding: " I desire her and my will and meaning is that when she dies she should leave the moiety of all the estate she hath at the time of her death " to a number of persons. Lord Nottingham rejected the contention that these words should be construed as a trust, and gave effect to the widow's will, which disposed of the whole of the property to other beneficiaries. On the other hand, in *Brest* v. *Offley,*[4] the testator " desired " that his executor should give the plaintiff £200, and this was held to be binding. Five years later, in *Pary* v. *Juxon,*[5] the executor of Archbishop Juxon was directed by the Archbishop in his lifetime to give the next presentation of the Mastership of St. Cross to Dr. Pary. This was held to be a binding trust on the executor. Accordingly in *Eales* v. *England,*[6] the general principle was laid down that—

> . . . words of recommendation and desire in a will are always expounded a devise. . . .

The reason for this rule was that when, in the seventeenth and early eighteenth centuries, the Court of Chancery took over the administration of the estates of deceased persons from the Church courts, it found that the executor was permitted to take the undisposed-of residue in wills. It therefore sought, wherever circumstances permitted, to make him a trustee of this undisposed-of residue, and even so early as the time of Lord Chancellor Jeffreys it was decided [7] that a legacy given to an executor was to compensate him for his trouble, so that in these circumstances the executor became a trustee of the residue for the next-of-kin. A new set of problems arose, however, where there were several executors. If a legacy was given to them jointly, they became trustees for the next-of-kin again. Moreover, if one of the executors, through receiving a legacy, was a trustee, then they were all trustees, because they took jointly.[8] If, however, the testator gave the executors unequal legacies, they were apparently in this case not receiving them in the character of executors, and so, paradoxically, they could claim the residue beneficially.[9] In the nineteenth century, the tide finally set against this claim of the executor, the Executors Act 1830 providing that thereafter an executor should hold undisposed-of residue for the next-of-kin, unless the testator had shown an intention that the executor should take beneficially.

Before this desirable change had been achieved, however, one well-established doctrine of equity had been thrown into confusion as a result of the influence of equitable practice in respect of executors. No special difficulties had existed in the law of trusts concerning certainty of words, so long as the property and the objects of the trust were defined with certainty. If a testator leaves £500 to X " in full confidence that X will use it for the benefit of Y," the opinions of laymen and lawyers would coincide that the testator intended to make X a trustee for Y. It is much less clear that a trust is intended if the testator leaves £10,000 to X, " in full confidence that he will use as much as need be for the benefit of Y "; and if for " Y " there is substituted " my

---

[4] (1664), 1 Ch.Rep. 246.
[5] (1669), 3 Ch.Rep. 38.
[6] (1702), Prec.Ch. 200, 202.
[7] *Foster* v. *Munt* (1687), 1 Vern. 473.
[8] *White* v. *Evans* (1798), 4 Ves. 21.
[9] *Griffiths* v. *Hamilton* (1806), 12 Ves. 298.

relations," the intention becomes vague indeed. Problems such as these occur in the eighteenth century reports, and there is a tendency at first to say that, if the property and objects are certain, then this raises an inference that the words expressing the hope or desire were intended to be imperative, and so a trust was created. This is a clear enough principle, but it became completely confused when the same Chancery judges, in other cases, were called upon to deal with executors (whose office they were fast assimilating to that of trustee) who claimed the undisposed-of residue under wills. Here, the court seized on *any* expression of hope or desire to negative the presumption that the executor was intended to take beneficially, and to establish the fact that he took as trustee for the next-of-kin. In these cases, the problem of certainty of objects and property did not arise. Then, in turn, the equity judges applied this later rule to words in wills *not* relating to the executor's claim to undisposed-of residue. Lord Redesdale did what he could to clear up this muddle, but he was not completely successful. Thus, in *Cary* v. *Cary* [10] he said—

> When a testator, having in his power to dispose of property, expresses a desire as to the disposition of the property, and the objects to which he refers are certain, the desire so expressed amounts to a command; and if he shows his desire, he, in fact, expresses his intention, provided the objects to which he refers are so defined, that a court can act upon the desire so expressed. If he is sufficiently explicit in that respect, words expressing desire, words simply intimating that he has no doubt such and such things will be done, will operate as imperative on the person to whom they are directed. The cases are clear on this subject, that where the property and the objects are certain, any words intimating a wish or desire, raise a trust: if the objects be not certain, a trust can no more be raised upon words of desire or request, than upon words of actual devise.

The repeated emphasis on certainty of property and objects in words not relating to the executor's claim to undisposed-of residue is noteworthy. Similarly, in the earlier case of *Harding* v. *Glyn*,[11] a testator gave property to his wife by will " but did desire her at or before her death, to give such leases, house, furniture, goods and chattels, plate and jewels, unto and amongst such of his own relations, as she should think most deserving and approve of." This was held to be a trust, but Verney, M.R., observed [12]—

> Where the uncertainty is such, that it is impossible for the court to determine what persons are meant, it is very strong for the court to construe it only as a recommendation to the first devisee, and make it absolute as to him; but here the word *relations* is a legal description, and this is a devise to such *relations*, and operates as a trust in the wife, by way of power of naming and apportioning, and her non-performance of the power shall not make the devise void, but the power shall devolve on the court . . .

Thus, if there had been uncertainty of objects, the court would not have con-

---

[10] (1804), 2 Sch. & Lef. 173, 189. See also *Richardson* v. *Chapman* (1760), 1 Burn's *Ecclesiastical Law*, 245.

[11] (1739), 1 Atk. 469.

[12] 1 Atk. 470.

strued the desire as a trust. In *Bland* v. *Bland*,[13] there was uncertainty of property. In that case the Manor of Withington was devised to Sir John Bland, with other real and personal estate, and the testatrix added: ". . . it is my earnest request to my son Sir John Bland, that on failure of issue of his body, he will some time in his lifetime . . . settle the said premises, or so much thereof as he shall stand seized of at . . . his decease," on the testatrix's daughter. Lord Hardwicke held that there was no trust, inasmuch as *so much as he shall die seised of* gave the son absolute ownership, the other expressions amounting to nothing more than words of recommendation, leaving it to the discretion of the party whether he would comply with the request or not. Obviously the amount of property which the son might have at his death was in the highest degree uncertain.[14] Following *Bland* v. *Bland*,[13] a succession of eighteenth-century cases held words of recommendation inoperative on account of uncertainty of objects or property. Thus, in *Cunliffe* v. *Cunliffe*,[15] the testator recommended his son and heir to give and devise all his property on the son's death to the testator's other son. This was exactly covered by *Bland* v. *Bland,* and it was held that there was no trust. Similarly, no trust arose in *Le Maitre* v. *Bannister*,[16] where a testatrix gave her fortune to Captain Roach, and if he should die without issue, she recommended to him that he should do justice to A and her children if he should think them worthy. On precisely the same lines were decided *Harland* v. *Trigg*,[17] wherein Philip Harland bequeathed certain leasehold estates to " my brother John Harland for ever, hoping he will continue them in the family "; *Wynne* v. *Hawkins*,[18] which concerned a devise to the testator's wife " not doubting but that she will dispose of what shall be left at her death, to our two grandchildren "; and *Sprange* v. *Barnard*.[19] In none of these cases was the property delimited with sufficient clarity to raise a trust.

The line of distinction in these late eighteenth-century cases between what was a sufficiently clear delimitation of property and objects to create a trust, and what was not, was obviously a fine one, for in *Nowlan* v. *Nelligan*[20] a testator gave all his real estate to his wife, and said: " I make no provision expressly for my dear daughter, knowing that it is my dear wife's happiness, as well as mine, to see her comfortably provided for; but in case of death happening to my said wife, in that case, I hereby request my friends Stables and Hunter, to take care of, and manage to the best advantage, for my lovely daughter Harriot Nowlan, all . . . I may die possessed of." It was held that this raised a binding trust, so that the wife received a life estate, and subject to that, the " lovely daughter " was entitled to the property absolutely.

Pierson v. *Garnet*,[21] was decided in the same way. Property was left by the testator to P. Pierson, " and it is my dying request to the said Peter Pierson, that, if he shall die without leaving issue, living at his death, that the said

[13] (1745), 2 Cox 349.
[14] This view of Lord Hardwicke's decision is adopted in *Pierson* v. *Garnet* (1786), 2 Bro. C.C. 38, 46.
[15] (1770), Amb. 686.
[16] (1770), Prec.Ch. 201n.
[17] (1782), 1 Bro.C.C. 142.
[18] (1782), 1 Bro.C.C. 179.
[19] (1789), 2 Bro.C.C. 585.
[20] (1785), 1 Bro.C.C. 489.
[21] (1786), 2 Bro.C.C. 38.

Peter Pierson do dispose of what fortune he shall receive under this my will, to and among the descendants of . . . Ann Coppinger, . . . in such manner and proportion as he shall think proper." This might seem to be exactly covered by *Cunliffe* v. *Cunliffe*,[22] but the court gave full consideration to the earlier case, and then refused to follow it. From this point in the history of the Court of Chancery until the fourth decade of the nineteenth century, the older rules relating to certainty of property and objects were relaxed, and very few expressions of desire on the part of a testator failed for uncertainty. In *Paul* v. *Compton*[23] Lord Eldon observed—

> The cases upon words of recommendation have, I take it, now settled this rule: whether the terms are those of recommendation, or precatory, or expressing hope, or, that the testator has no doubt, if the objects, with regard to whom such terms are used, are certain, and the subjects of property to be given are also certain, the words are considered imperative; and create a trust. But the questions are very different, whether the words of a will create a trust or a power. If the words are imperative, they do not create a power; but they execute themselves by the force of the terms.

That certainty of property was essential is also shown by Lord Redesdale's observations in *Cary* v. *Cary*.[24] At the same time, certainty of property at the turn of the century seems to have meant little more than the possibility of identifying some property (not infrequently the whole of the testator's property) with the trust. In this respect the eighteenth-century test for certainty of property was more precise than Lord Eldon's, and approaches the modern test without being identical with it.

About midway through the nineteenth century the attitude of the courts changed. They came to the conclusion that, in treating the wish of the testator as a command, they were in danger of defeating his true intention, which in many cases was obviously to leave the donee some discretion to decide whether to give effect to the testator's wish or not. Moreover, the claim of the executor to the undisposed-of residue was now abolished. In *Shaw* v. *Lawless*,[25] there was a positive direction to the trustees of a will to employ an individual and to allow him a salary. Lord St. Leonards held that this constituted a trust for the individual, but the House of Lords reversed his decision, being obviously of the opinion that in many of the older cases the court had probably gone beyond the testator's true intention, and had really supplemented his will. Following this decision, many of the older phrases, such as " will," " wish," " desire," " hope and desire," " in full confidence " and many others received fresh consideration.

By 1840 the current of the decisions was plainly changing. Already in *Heneage* v. *Lord Andover*[26] Richards, L.C.B., had remarked—

> . . . I hope to be forgiven if I entertain a strong doubt whether, in

---

[22] (1770), Amb. 686, p. 93, *ante*.
[23] (1803), 8 Ves. 375, 380.
[24] (1804), 2 Sch. & Lef. 173, 189: see p. 92, *ante*.
[25] (1838), 5 Cl. & Fin. 129.
[26] (1822), 10 Price 230, 265.

many, or perhaps in most, of the cases the construction was not adverse to the real intention of the testator.

And in *Sale* v. *Moore* [27] Sir Antony Hart observed—

> The first case that construed words of recommendation into a command, made a will for the testator; for everyone knows the distinction between them. The current of decisions has, of late years, been against converting the legatee into a trustee.

In *Ford* v. *Fowler*, [28] a testator bequeathed £10,000 to his daughter, adding " and I recommend to my said daughter and her said husband, that they do forthwith settle and assure the said sum . . . for the benefit of my said daughter . . . and her children." Lord Langdale, M.R., held that the word " recommend " was imperative, and since the wife was dead, her children were entitled to claim. The case next following in Beavan's Reports was *Knight* v. *Knight*, [29] where the effect of precatory words was more fully discussed. In this case a testator, R. P. Knight, who died in 1824, left all his estates, real and personal, to his brother, Thomas Andrew Knight, and failing him, to his nephew, Thomas Andrew Knight the younger. The will provided—

> . . . I do hereby constitute and appoint the person who shall inherit my said estates under this my will my sole executor and trustee, to carry the same and every thing contained therein duly into execution; confiding in the approved honour and integrity of my family, to take no advantage of any technical inaccuracies, but to admit all the comparatively small reservations which I make out of so large a property, according to the plain and obvious meaning of my words. . . .

The will also stated that it was his intention that the estates should be settled upon the next descendant in the direct male line of the testator's grandfather, Richard Knight of Downton. When the testator died, Thomas Andrew Knight the elder succeeded to the estates. Thomas Andrew Knight the younger died intestate without issue in 1827, and subsequently Thomas Andrew Knight the elder by his will settled the estate upon persons who were not the next descendants in the direct male line of Richard Knight. The question therefore was whether the words in the will of R. P. Knight created a trust binding upon Thomas Andrew Knight the elder. Lord Langdale, M.R., held that the words were not sufficiently imperative, and that no trust binding upon Thomas Andrew Knight the elder had been created. The state of the law, as it then existed, was described by Lord Langdale as follows [30]—

> . . . it is not every wish or expectation which a testator may express, nor every act which he may wish his successors to do, that can or ought to be executed or enforced as a trust in this Court; and in the infinite variety of expressions which are employed, and of cases which thereupon arise, there is often the greatest difficulty in determining, whether the act desired or recommended is an act which the testator intended to be executed as a trust, or which this Court ought to deem fit to be, or cap-

[27] (1827), 1 Sim. 534, 540.
[28] (1840), 3 Beav. 146.
[29] (1840), 3 Beav. 148.
[30] 3 Beav. 172–175.

able of being enforced as such. In the construction and execution of wills, it is undoubtedly the duty of this Court to give effect to the intention of the testator whenever it can be ascertained: but in cases of this nature, and in the examination of the authorities which are to be consulted in relation to them, it is, unfortunately, necessary to make some distinction between the intention of the testator and that which the Court has deemed it to be its duty to perform; for of late years it has frequently been admitted by Judges of great eminence that, by interfering in such cases, the Court has sometimes rather made a will for the testator, than executed the testator's will according to his intention; and the observation shews the necessity of being extremely cautious in admitting any, the least, extension of the principle to be extracted from a long series of authorities, in respect of which such admissions have been made.

As a general rule, it has been laid down, that when property is given absolutely to any person, and the same person is, by the giver who has power to command, recommended, or entreated, or wished, to dispose of that property in favour of another, the recommendation, entreaty, or wish shall be held to create a trust.

First, if the words were so used, that upon the whole, they ought to be construed as imperative;

Secondly, if the subject of the recommendation or wish be certain; and,

Thirdly, if the objects or persons intended to have the benefit of the recommendation or wish be also certain.

In simple cases there is no difficulty in the application of the rule thus stated.

If a testator gives £1,000 to AB, desiring, wishing, recommending, or hoping that AB will, at his death, give the same sum or any certain part of it to CD, it is considered that CD is an object of the testator's bounty, and AB is a trustee for him. No question arises upon the intention of the testator, upon the sum or subject intended to be given, or upon the person or object of the wish.

So, if a testator gives the residue of his estate, after certain purposes are answered, to AB, recommending AB, after his death, to give it to his own relations, or such of his own relations as he shall think most deserving, or as he shall choose, it has been considered that the residue of the property, though a subject to be ascertained, and that the relations to be selected, though persons or objects to be ascertained, are nevertheless so clearly and certainly ascertainable—so capable of being made certain, that the rule is applicable to such cases.

On the other hand, if the giver accompanies his expression of wish, or request by other words, from which it is to be collected, that he did not intend the wish to be imperative: or if it appears from the context that the first taker was intended to have a discretionary power to withdraw any part of the subject from the object of the wish or request; or if the objects are not such as may be ascertained with sufficient certainty, it has been held that no trust is created. Thus the words " free and unfettered," accompanying the strongest expression of request, were held to prevent the words of request being imperative. Any words by which it is expressed or from which it may be implied, that the first taker may apply any part of the subject to his own use, are held to prevent the subject of the gift from being considered certain; and a vague description of the object, that is, a description by which the giver neither clearly defines the object himself nor names a distinct class out of which the first taker is to select, or which leaves it doubtful what interest the object or class of objects is to take, will prevent the objects from being certain within the meaning of the rule; and in such cases we are told [31] that the question " never turns upon the grammatical import of words—they may be imperative, but not necessarily so; the subject-matter, the situation of the parties, and the probable intent must be considered." And [32] " Wherever the subject, to be administered as trust-property, and the objects, for whose benefit it is to be administered, are to be found in a Will, not expressly creating trust, the indefinite nature and *quantum* of the subject, and the indefinite nature of the objects, are always used by the Court as evidence, that the mind of the testator was not to create a trust; and the difficulty, that would be imposed upon the Court to say, what should be so applied, or to what objects, has been the foundation of the argument, that no trust was intended;" or, as Lord Eldon expresses it in another case,[33] " where a trust is to be raised characterized by certainty, the very difficulty of doing it is an argument, which goes to a certain extent, . . . towards inducing the Court to say, it is not sufficiently clear what the testator intended."

Eventually, in *Mussoorie Bank Ltd.* v. *Raynor,*[34] the Privy Council held that where a testator left all his property to his widow " feeling confident that she will act justly to our children in dividing the same when no longer required by her," there was no trust for the children (in contrast with the decision in *Nowlan* v. *Nelligan* [35] a century earlier), and Sir A. Hobhouse observed [36]—

> . . . their Lordships are of opinion that the current of decisions now prevalent for many years in the Court of Chancery shews that the doctrine of precatory trusts is not to be extended . . .

A similar decision was given in *Re Adams and the Kensington Vestry,*[37] where the testator gave his property—

> . . . to the absolute use of my wife, . . . her heirs, executors, administrators, and assigns, in full confidence that she will do what is right as to the disposal thereof between my children, either in her lifetime or by will after her decease.

These decisions have been followed, with slight variations of fact, in *Hill* v. *Hill,*[38] *Re Williams,*[39] *Re Conolly* [40] and *Re Hill.*[41]

[31] *Meggison* v. *Moore* (1795), 2 Ves.Jun. 630, 633.
[32] *Morice* v. *Bishop of Durham* (1805), 10 Ves. 522, 536–537.
[33] *Wright* v. *Atkyns* (1823), Turn. & R. 143, 159.
[34] (1882), 7 App.Cas. 321.
[35] (1785), 1 Bro.C.C. 489.
[36] 7 App.Cas. 330.
[37] (1884), 27 Ch.D. 394.
[38] [1897] 1 Q.B. 483.
[39] [1897] 2 Ch. 12.
[40] [1910] 1 Ch. 219.
[41] [1923] 2 Ch. 259.

In all these cases, the testator did not intend finally to bind the donee, but meant to leave him some freedom of judgment in the ultimate disposition of the property. As Lindley, L.J., observed in *Re Hamilton* [42]—

> You must take the will which you have to construe and see what it means, and if you come to the conclusion that no trust was intended, you say so, although previous judges have said the contrary on some wills more or less similar to the one which you have to construe.

From these and similar observations it is clear that precatory words may still raise a trust in a proper case.[43] The question is, what is a proper case? Some light is thrown upon this question by *Re Diggles*.[44] In that case the testatrix left all her property to her daughter, adding, " and it is my desire that she allows to . . . Anne Gregory . . . an annuity of £25 during her life . . ." There was also a similar intimation that Anne Gregory ought to have the use of the testatrix's furniture that the daughter did not wish to retain. The daughter paid the annuity for several years, and then discontinued it, and the Court of Appeal held that the testator's words raised no trust for Anne Gregory. It might seem that here at any rate it was intended to impose a binding obligation on the daughter, but the learned Lords Justices gave very careful consideration to the words and to the circumstances. Cotton, L.J., referred to his judgment in *Re Adams and the Kensington Vestry*,[45] and saw no reason for applying a different rule to these facts. Fry, L.J., pointed out that in ordinary parlance " that she allows " would imply some element of discretion to the daughter. The mind reverts naturally to a son's " allowance," although the verb is derived from the French *allouer*, which is less discretionary, and the nearest equivalent to which is " grant." If the statement were therefore paraphrased " I desire that she grant," the element of discretion would practically disappear. The learned Lord Justice made what is undoubtedly a stronger point when he observed that the effect of construing the desire as a trust would be to impose a trust upon the entire estate to satisfy an annuity of £25—

> No fund is directed to be set apart, so if there be a trust, it is a trust affecting the whole property. If so, the residuary legatee could not sell a bedstead or give away a ring without committing a breach of trust.[46]

In *Re Williams* [47] the Court of Appeal considered a will in which the testator left all his real and personal property to his widow " absolutely in the fullest confidence " that she would carry out his wishes. Amongst them was a direction that she would pay premiums on her insurance policy for £1,000 on her own life, and that by will, she would leave the money payable under this policy, together with the proceeds of one on the testator's life, to their daughter. The Court of Appeal by a majority held that the language of the will was insufficient to impose trusts of the policies upon the widow, or to put her to her election to carry out the testator's wishes or compensate the daughter. In the judgment of Lindley, L.J., and in the dissenting judgment

[42] [1895] 2 Ch. 370, 373.
[43] See *Comiskey* v. *Bowring-Hanbury*, [1905] A.C. 84.
[44] (1888), 39 Ch.D. 253.
[45] (1884), 27 Ch.D. 394.
[46] 39 Ch.D. 258.   [47] [1897] 2 Ch. 12.

of Rigby, L.J., the earlier authorities are reviewed, and Lindley, L.J., pointed out that in wills, as in daily life, an expression may be imperative in its real meaning, although couched in language which is not imperative in form. The continuing difficulty, however, is to establish that real meaning; in the same case, Rigby, L.J.'s examination of the will led him to the opposite conclusion.

Since no technical words are required to constitute a trust, precatory words may constitute one, if the intention is sufficiently clearly expressed. The testator's intention is therefore the paramount consideration, and the court must discover it. It will not presume he intended to create a trust. That must be proved. If any element of discretion is left to the donee, there is no trust. Furthermore, if it is not clear (as it was not in *Re Diggles*) whether a discretion is in fact left to the donee, the effect of construing the gift as a trust must be considered. There must always be certainty of property and objects (as was pointed out, even in the day of the older decisions, in *Cary* v. *Cary* [48]), and certainty of property means that the property specifically appropriated to the trust must be clearly indicated. The court will be reluctant to construe an expression as creating a trust which has the effect of making the whole or the bulk of the property trust property to satisfy a comparatively trifling beneficial interest. If it does so, it is because the expression used eliminates the element of discretion completely. Finally, the object of a trust, where precatory words are used, must also be defined with clarity. Any such expressions as " to do what is right ... between my children " [49] or " for division among charities " [50] or " for the benefit of themselves and their respective families " [51] do not at the present time constitute a trust unless, in addition to clearly indicated property, the words of grant are unambiguously imperative, and not precatory.[52]

In a later case, *Re Barton*,[53] a testatrix bequeathed her residuary estate to Cardinal Bourne, or the person who for the time being should discharge the administrative duties of Ordinary of the Roman Catholic Diocese of Westminster at the date of her death, adding, " it being my wish that the same should be dealt with in such manner as I shall by a separate memorandum or letter direct." No such memorandum or letter ever existed, so that there could be no question of a valid secret trust. The testator's next-of-kin therefore contended that the words of desire raised a good precatory trust, and, therefore, since Cardinal Bourne held as trustee, with no objects declared, he held in trust for the next-of-kin. Reliance was placed upon the word " direct " as indicating that an enforceable trust was intended. Farwell,

---

[48] (1804), 2 Sch. & Lef. 173.
[49] *Re Adams and the Kensington Vestry* (1884), 27 Ch.D. 394.
[50] See *Re Conolly*, [1910] 1 Ch. 219.
[51] *Re Hill*, [1923] 2 Ch. 259.
[52] Where the words of grant are unambiguous, the court is not deterred by difficulties of construction in giving effect to the gift. In *Re Bridgen*, [1938] Ch. 205, an unmarried testatrix directed: " In case of my immediate decease I wish [E.] and [H.] to take possession of all my possessions to be held in trust after my death and divided equally amongst all my relations." At her death she had no parents living and no brothers. Her four sisters had predeceased her, but issue of the four sisters survived. The court held that the estate should be divided in equal shares *per capita* amongst the persons who would have been entitled under the Administration of Estates Act 1925 if the testatrix had died intestate.
[53] (1932), 48 T.L.R. 205.

J., held, however, that, upon the true construction of the will, there was no trust, but only a wish with no binding legal consequence. In actual fact, Cardinal Bourne wished to employ the whole of the residue for the benefit of the Roman Catholic Diocese of Westminster, and thus the object of an intended secret trust which was never completed was indirectly fulfilled.

In *Re Williams*,[54] there was an example of a precatory trust that was also regarded as having some of the characteristics of a secret trust. A wife gave all her property to her husband absolutely, " knowing that he is fully aware of my intention that at his death all my possessions are to be sold and given to All Souls' Church, Hastings." The testatrix added: " I am aware of my husband's intention to bestow his possessions at his death on the same All Souls Church . . ." The wife died, and the husband took the property, following which the husband died intestate. The Parochial Church Council claimed the wife's property, whilst the husband's next-of-kin claimed that he had taken the property absolutely, and free from any trust. Farwell, J., held that the husband knew of the contents of his wife's will, and by his silence had agreed to carry out her wishes. Accordingly, an equitable obligation to carry out the wife's wishes arose, and this obligation the court, following *McCormick* v. *Grogan*[55] and *Re Gardner*,[56] would enforce.[57] The learned judge observed[58]—

> Mr. Potts [for the next-of-kin] has laid great stress on the fact that the property is given to the husband absolutely, and he says that the mere expression of a belief that the husband will give effect to her wishes is insufficient to impose a trust. That argument would have much force if the latter part of the will had been omitted, but I find in the latter part of the will that the testatrix expresses herself in these most emphatic words: " I charge my dear husband to pay £20 free of legacy duty to my dear friend Mrs. Adelaide Francis Shoesmith." Now, the words " I charge my husband to pay the sum " are wholly inconsistent with the mere expression of a wish. That in itself must, in my judgment, create a trust, which could be enforced if the husband failed to pay to the lady her legacy. If that be the true effect of those words, they largely discount the effect of the word " absolutely " in the gift to the husband, because, although the husband is given the property in terms absolutely, he is charged to do something with a portion of it. In my judgment, those words alone are sufficient to indicate that the word " absolutely " cannot be read without some qualification, and this, coupled with the proviso in the last part of the will, that in the event of her husband not being able to carry out her wishes to benefit the defendant Council, then someone else is to take up the burden, and to see that the property goes as she desires, seems to me to point very strongly to the conclusion that the true effect of the testator's will is not an absolute gift to her husband subject to a mere expression of desire as to how the property is to go after his death, but

54 [1933] Ch. 244 (Cases, p. 231).
55 (1869), L.R. 4 H.L. 82.
56 [1920] 2 Ch. 523.
57 See also *French* v. *French*, [1902] 1 I.R. 172, 230 (House of Lords). In *Re Falkiner*, [1924] 1 Ch. 88, there was an express direction that no trust should arise.
58 [1933] Ch. 253.

that it is a gift to the husband for life, with a trust to dispose of the property after his death in the way she has indicated.

In this part of the judgment the learned judge addressed himself to the interpretation of the precatory words. A little earlier [59] he considered the effect of the husband's acquiescence in his wife's intention, expressed at the time when she made her will—

> . . . if the evidence establishes that there was a promise or an agreement by the husband that the property when he got it should go at his death to the defendant Council, then in my judgment he took the property burdened with that obligation, and it is an obligation which the Court will enforce, and since, in my judgment, the evidence does establish the existence of such a promise, it follows that, the husband having died without having taken steps to ensure that his promise should be carried out, this Court will now give effect to that promise by declaring that the property of the wife to which the husband was entitled under the will belongs to the Parochial Council in question.

It would therefore appear that the court would now recognise and enforce a trust created by precatory words provided that the subject-matter and objects of the trust were indicated with clarity, and also provided that the court was of opinion, from the general context of the words employed, that these were intended to govern the conduct of the trustee.[60] Thus, in *Re Steele's Will Trusts* [61] the testatrix left a diamond necklace to her son " to go and be held as an heirloom by him and by his eldest son on his decease and to go and descend to the eldest son of such eldest son and so on to the eldest son of his descendants as far as the rules of law and equity will permit (and I request my said son to do all in his power by his will or otherwise to give effect to this my wish)." Wynn-Parry, J., held that a precatory trust had been created, so that the eldest son, the grandson, and the great-grandson (all of whom were in existence at the testator's death) took the necklace successively for life. On the other hand, in *Re Perowne*,[62] the words: " Knowing that he will make arrangements for the disposal of my estate " did not create any trust.

A number of cases raising questions of precatory words have been concerned with the maintenance of children. The gift may have been expressed simply in the form that a motive for it has been expressed, and in such a case no trust arises.[63] On the other hand, it may be possible to construe the words to show that a trust was intended. In *Re Booth* [64] the testator left the income of his estate to his widow for life, for her own use and benefit " and for the maintenance and education of my children." North, J., held that there was a trust for the children, and although in general such a trust would cease at the end of their minority, in this case the trust was not limited to those children who were under twenty-one or unmarried.

[59] [1933] Ch. 252.
[60] As to the effect of the words: " I particularly desire " in a will, see *Re Green*, [1935] W.N. 151.
[61] [1948] Ch. 603, following *Shelley* v. *Shelley* (1868), L.R. 6 Eq. 540.
[62] [1951] Ch. 785.
[63] *e.g. Re Hill*, [1923] 2 Ch. 259.
[64] [1894] 2 Ch. 282.

In such cases, the recipient of the fund is entitled to the surplus for his own benefit, and he also has a discretion as to the mode in which he applies it.

2. CERTAINTY OF SUBJECT-MATTER

It was observed in *Re Diggles* [65] that uncertainty of subject-matter will adversely affect the creation of a trust. Another example is *Curtis* v. *Rippon*,[66] wherein the testator appointed his wife guardian of his children, and then left all his property to her, " trusting that she will, in fear of God and in love to the children committed to her care, make such use of it as shall be for her own and their spiritual and temporal good, remembering always, according to circumstances, the Church of God and the poor." The court held that the wife was absolutely entitled to the property, since no specific part of it had been appropriated for the children, the Church, or the poor. Other examples of trusts held to be invalid for the same reason are: a direction to " remember " certain persons,[67] a direction " to reward . . . my old servants and tenants according to their deserts," [68] and a gift to a wife absolutely, followed by a direction that, " as to such parts of my . . . estate as she shall not have sold or disposed of," it should be held in trust for certain persons.[69]

3. CERTAINTY OF OBJECTS

Certainty of objects implies two things: (1) that the recipients or purposes of the gift should be identifiable with certainty; (2) that the interest they take should be discoverable. Gifts such as those for " charitable or philanthropic " purposes fail. So where leasehold lands were given to A with the hope " that he will continue them in the family," [70] it was held that the objects of the bounty were too uncertain for the trust to be enforced. Again, in *Meredith* v. *Heneage*,[71] real and personal estate were together given to A, in full confidence that she would devise the whole of the estate to " such of my . . . father's heirs as she may think best deserves her preference." The court was unable to determine whether heirs, or next-of-kin, or both, were intended, and the trust was not enforced; whilst in *Sale* v. *Moore*,[72] A was recommended to " consider my near relations," and the court experienced difficulty in discovering how the relations were to be ascertained, so that no binding trust arose. In *Re Wood* [73] the provision of a sum of £2 per week for " The Week's Good Cause " of the B.B.C. was held to have no *cestui que trust* which was certain, or which could be made certain by following the directions of the testatrix, since seven good causes were advocated one week in each month by speakers from different stations.

It was established in *Whishaw* v. *Stephens* [74] that a bare power of appointment among a class was valid if it could be said with certainty whether any

[65] (1888), 39 Ch.D. 253. See p. 98, *ante*.
[66] (1820), 5 Madd. 434.
[67] *Bardswell* v. *Bardswell* (1838), 9 Sim. 319.
[68] *Knight* v. *Knight* (1840), 3 Beav. 148.
[69] *Re Jones*, [1898] 1 Ch. 438. *Cf. Re Sanford*, [1901] 1 Ch. 939.
[70] *Harland* v. *Trigg* (1782), 1 Bro.C.C. 142.
[71] (1824), 1 Sim. 542.
[72] (1827), 1 Sim. 534.
[73] [1949] Ch. 498. See also *Re Astor's Settlement Trusts*, [1952] Ch. 534 (Cases, p. 252).
[74] [1970] A.C. 508. See also p. 14, *ante*.

given individual was a member of the class or not, even if it was impossible to ascertain every member of the class. In *McPhail* v. *Doulton* [75] there was a gift to trustees of a fund which they were to apply " in making at their absolute discretion grants to or for the benefit of any of the officers and employees or ex-officers or ex-employees of the company or to any relatives or dependants of any such persons in such amounts at such times and on such conditions (if any) as they think fit. . . ." The House of Lords held unanimously that the disposition created a discretionary trust, not a bare power. The majority held that such a " trust power " was governed by the same criterion of certainty as that which the House had laid down for bare powers in *Whishaw* v. *Stephens*,[74] and remitted the case to the Chancery Division for determination whether, on that basis, the clause was valid. From that later determination there was again an appeal. The Court of Appeal, affirming the decision [76] of Brightman, J., upheld it.[77] These decisions do not mean that there has been any relaxation in the requirement of certainty of objects where the trust does not involve any discretion by the trustees in selecting recipients of the gift.

The objects of a charitable trust need not be definite,[78] but uncertainty of objects may be a problem in determining whether a charitable trust has been established. If the fund has been appropriated *exclusively* to charitable purposes, then it does not matter if the objects are uncertain: the trust will be applied to charitable purposes. But if the fund is to be applied partly to charitable and partly to non-charitable purposes (*e.g.* " to charitable or benevolent purposes "), the entire gift will fail for uncertainty.[78]

To sum up the effect of the modern decisions, it should first be stated that mere expressions of benevolence, such as " deal justly with " are insufficient to raise any trust. Secondly, if the donor makes the gift in absolute terms (*e.g.* by using the words " unfettered " or " unlimited " in respect of the gift) it will be difficult, if not impossible, to construe subsequent precatory words as creating a trust.[79] Thirdly, although in some cases uncertainty of objects can be considered apart from uncertainty of words which may create a trust, in numerous cases the two appear together, and uncertainty of objects will raise a doubt whether the words used were intended to be construed imperatively, or were inserted solely to guide the donee in his use of the property. In modern trusts when such expressions of desire are used, it is not unusual to find it stated that the words are not intended to create a trust.

4. EFFECT OF UNCERTAINTY

The effect of uncertainty in respect of one of the three essentials of a trust is not always the same. Where the *words* of a trust are too uncertain, then no intention to create a trust at all has been established, and the donee, therefore, takes the property beneficially. Similarly, the donee takes beneficially where the trust fails for *uncertainty of property*, since, although it may have been

---

[75] [1971] A.C. 424. See also Keeton, *Modern Developments in the Law of Trusts*, pp. 321–330.
[76] [1972] Ch. 607.
[77] *Re Baden's Deed Trusts* (*No. 2*), [1973] Ch. 9.
[78] See Chap. XII, s. C, *post*; Keeton and Sheridan, *The Modern Law of Charities*, 2nd ed., pp. 38–46.
[79] *Meredith* v. *Heneage* (1824), 1 Sim. 542.

clear in this case that there was an intention to create a trust, there is no **property** to which it can be annexed.[80] For example, in *Re Jones* [81] there was an absolute gift of property by will to a wife, followed by a direction that " such parts of my real and personal estate as she shall not have sold or disposed of " should be held in trust for other persons. Byrne, J., held that no trust was created, and the wife took an absolute interest. In the third case, *uncertainty of objects*, assuming that the other two requisites are fulfilled, the donee holds on trust for the settlor, residuary legatee or devisee, or intestate successor.

---

[80] See *Curtis* v. *Rippon* (1820), 5 Madd. 434, p. 102, *ante*. If the amount of property which is to pass to the intended trustee is uncertain, the entire transaction fails, *e.g.* a gift of " some part of my property to A on trust for B."

[81] [1898] 1 Ch. 438.

CHAPTER IX

TRUSTS TO PAY CREDITORS

TRUSTS to pay creditors may raise a question of construction. Did the settlor really mean to make his creditors beneficiaries of the trust deed, or was he simply establishing machinery for the payment of his debts for his own convenience? This distinction is not always easy to establish, and in *Smith* v. *Hurst*,[1] Turner, V.-C., after reviewing the authorities, said that they appeared to establish—

> that in cases of deeds vesting property in trustees upon trust for the benefit of particular persons the deed cannot be revoked, altered or modified by the party who has created the trust; but that in cases of deeds purporting to be executed for the benefit of creditors the question whether the trusts can be revoked, altered or modified depends upon the circumstances of each particular case. It is difficult, at first sight, to see the distinction between the two classes of cases; for in each of the classes a trust is purported to be created, and the property is vested in the trustees; but I think the distinction lies in this: In cases of trusts for the benefit of particular persons the party creating the trust can have no other object than to benefit the persons in whose favour the trust is being created, and, the trust being well created, the property in equity belongs to the *cestui que trust* as much as it would belong to them at law if the legal interest had been transferred to them; but in cases of deeds purporting to be executed for the benefit of creditors, and to which no creditor is a party, the motive of the party executing the deed may have been either to benefit his creditors or to promote his own convenience; and the Court has to examine into the circumstances, for the purpose of ascertaining what was the true purpose of the deed; and this examination does not stop with the deed itself, but must be carried on to what has subsequently occurred, because the party who has created the trust may, by his own conduct, or by the obligations which he has permitted his trustees to contract, have created an equity against himself.

Such deeds, it is apparent, if executed without the concurrence of the settlor's creditors, may substantially prejudice their rights, and therefore (subject to the qualifications set out below) may be set aside by the court at the suit of a creditor who has been prejudiced. Moreover, once it is established that the trust is not executed with the intention of conferring benefits on individual creditors, they are unable to sue upon it as beneficiaries.

If the effect of the deed is simply to constitute the trustees agents for the payment of the settlor's debts, then (again subject to the qualifications set out below) the settlor himself may revoke it at any time, and the trustees are trustees of the property conveyed, not for the creditors, but for him.

If the debtor has merely entered into the deed because he was going abroad,

[1] (1852), 10 Hare 30, 47.

105

the trustees are mere mandatories to pay the settlor's debts, and the creditors may not sue on the deed.[2] Further, the debtor may at any time revoke or vary the trusts, or call for a reconveyance of the property. This position, however, is dependent upon the circumstance that the execution of the trust has not been communicated to the creditor, for if it has been so communicated, and the creditor has refrained from proceeding against the debtor, on the faith of the deed, then it becomes irrevocable.

Such deeds, establishing trusts for the payment of creditors, are often known as deeds of arrangement. They were of very considerable importance before the passing of the modern bankruptcy laws, for prior to that date, only a trader could be made bankrupt, and a deed of arrangement to which the creditors assented was therefore the only means by which the debtor could be relieved of his liabilities and escape a debtors' prison. Thus, the question whether the creditors had been parties to or had assented to the deed was of great importance in considering the rights which they could exercise.

The leading case upon this type of trust is *Garrard* v. *Lord Lauderdale*.[3] The Duke of York, by an indenture between himself of the first part, trustees of the second part, and the creditors of the third part, transferred property to trustees for the creditors, and when the deed was executed, a circular giving notice of it was sent to all the creditors. It was contended for the creditors that, in consequence of the circular, they had forborne to sue, but the court held that receipt of the circular was not admitted, and, even if received, the creditors had not refrained from suing, as they had proved in an administration suit against the Duke's estate. Accordingly, the creditors could not enforce the trust. This view was upheld on appeal, and Brougham, L.C., observed [4]—

> . . . I take the real nature of this deed to be . . . not so much a convey-
> ance vesting a trust in A for the benefit of the creditors of the grantor,
> but rather that it may be likened to an arrangement made by a debtor for
> his own personal convenience and accommodation—for the payment of
> his own debts in an order prescribed by himself—over which he retains
> power and control, and with respect to which the creditors can have no
> right to complain, inasmuch as they are not injured by it, they waive no
> right of action, and are not executing parties to it.

Whilst the effect of this case has sometimes been discussed,[5] its authority is unquestioned, although it has been held several times since that where the property is assigned to a trustee, and the trustee communicates the trust to certain creditors, who express their approval of the arrangement, the trust may not be revoked, for the creditors are relying on the deed rather than upon their ordinary rights of recourse against their debtor.[6] Furthermore, the courts have declared that the doctrine under which trusts of this type may be revocable has been carried far enough, and will not now be extended.[7]

[2] *Cornthwaite* v. *Frith* (1851), 4 De G. & Sm. 552.
[3] (1830), 3 Sim. 1; (1831), 2 Russ. & M. 451. See also Sheridan, " Trusts for Paying Debts " (1957) 21 *The Conveyancer* 280.
[4] 2 Russ. & M. 455.
[5] See *Browne* v. *Cavendish* (1844), 7 Ir.Eq.Rep. 369, 388–389, *per* Sir Edward Sugden, L.C.
[6] *Harland* v. *Binks* (1850), 15 Q.B. 713.
[7] *Wilding* v. *Richards* (1845), 1 Coll. 655.

Certain specific instances of irrevocable trusts in favour of creditors must now be added—

1. Where the settlor provides that the provisions in favour of creditors are to come into operation only after his death, the trust is irrevocable, for revocability belongs to the settlor alone, and the beneficiaries under his will may not claim it.[8]

2. Where a creditor is a party to the deed and executes it, it is now clear that the deed is irrevocable *as regards him*.[9]

3. If the deed is communicated to any creditors, who assent to the deed, and are thereby induced to some forbearance in respect of their claims which they would not otherwise have exercised, the deed cannot be revoked against them.[10] Mere communication alone is not sufficient. The creditors must have placed reliance on the document, and must either have acted on it, or have forborne to sue in consequence of it.

4. If, from the conduct of the settlor and the language of the instrument, it appears that the settlor intended to create a true trust, then it is irrevocable, and enforceable by the creditors.[11]

The importance of the question of revocability of trusts for creditors has been much diminished by the provisions of several statutes. By the Deeds of Arrangement Act 1914, ss. 1–4 (amended by the Administration of Justice Act 1925, s. 22), an assignment for the benefit of creditors generally, or (where the debtor is insolvent) in favour of any three or more of them, is void, unless registered within seven days at the Department of Trade and Industry; and further, if the assignment is for the benefit of creditors generally, it is also void unless it is agreed to by a majority in number and value of creditors within twenty-one days of registration. If the assignment is not made for the benefit of creditors generally, it may amount to a fraudulent preference.

Furthermore, a deed of arrangement affecting *land* for the benefit of creditors must also be registered at the Land Registry under the Land Charges Act 1972, ss. 1 (1) (*d*), 7, 8; otherwise it is void against a purchaser for value.

Further, even if the deed is registered, if it comprises the whole (or substantially the whole) of the debtor's property, and is for the benefit of creditors generally, it constitutes an act of bankruptcy, and may be used to support a bankruptcy petition by a person who has not assented to or acquiesced in it (Bankruptcy Act 1914, s. 1 (1) (*a*)), or it could be so used by an assenting creditor, if the deed became void under the Deeds of Arrangement Act.[12] Finally, if the debtor is adjudicated bankrupt on a petition presented within three months of the execution of the deed, it is void against the trustee in bankruptcy; so that the trustee of the deed cannot safely act upon it before that time, unless all the creditors have assented, or are debarred from presenting a petition.[13]

---

[8] *Synnot* v. *Simpson* (1845), 5 H.L.C. 121; *Re FitzGerald's Settlement* (1887), 37 Ch.D. 18.
[9] *Mackinnon* v. *Stewart* (1850), 1 Sim. N.S. 76.
[10] See *Acton* v. *Woodgate* (1833), 2 My. & K. 492; *Harland* v. *Binks* (1850), 15 Q.B. 713.
[11] *Sharp* v. *Jackson*, [1897] 2 Q.B. 19; [1899] A.C. 419.
[12] See the Deeds of Arrangement Act 1914, s. 24; Bankruptcy Act 1914, s. 4.
[13] Bankruptcy Act, 1914, s. 44.

Where, under a trust for creditors, there is a surplus after all debts and expenses are paid, the destination of the surplus is usually the settlor, or his personal representative; but where the property was assigned *absolutely* to the trustees the creditors in this case are entitled to the surplus.[14] The question is exclusively one of the settlor's intention, as demonstrated in the instrument.

14 *Smith* v. *Cooke*, [1891] A.C. 297.

CHAPTER X

TRUSTS WHICH ARE VOID OR VOIDABLE

A. ILLEGAL TRUSTS

1. TRUSTS FOR ILLEGITIMATE CHILDREN

Direct Gifts

No trust which infringes the law or violates the principles of public policy, including the rules of morality, which the courts have evolved, is valid. It is absolutely void. Thus, in *Medworth* v. *Pope*,[1] a settlement of property upon illegitimate children to be thereafter born was held void. If, however, the settlor creates a trust in favour of illegitimate children begotten but not then born, the trust is good, for the immorality is past.[2] The whole question was exhaustively reviewed by the Lord Chancellor and the Lords Justices of Appeal in *Occleston* v. *Fullalove*,[3] where a testator, *by his will*, gave property to his trustees for the benefit of three of his illegitimate children, two being born at the date of the will, and the third, at the time *en ventre sa mère*, being born before the testator's death. The court held (Lord Selborne dissenting) that all three children were entitled to benefit under the will. In the course of his judgment, James, L.J., pointed out that to limit the benefit to children in existence when the will was made might be equivalent to sentencing those born afterwards (themselves innocent) to destitution. He then added [4]—

> . . . if there be any inducement to do wrong, the law can and does deal with it. If there be any covenant for a *turpis causa*, the covenant is void. If there be an illicit condition precedent or subsequent to a gift, it either avoids the gift or becomes itself void. If the gift requires or implies the continuation of wrong-doing, that is in substance a condition of the gift, and falls within the rule as to conditions. But how can that apply to an instrument like a will, with reference to gifts taking effect at the death in favour of persons then in existence?

Where, however, there is a provision in the will for illegitimate children of a particular person, pre-1969 cases decided that only those may take who are in existence at the testator's death, otherwise the bequest would operate as an inducement to continue a course of immoral conduct.[5] If the gift is to the illegitimate children of a woman, according to the older cases, this will include all her children who are in existence at the testator's death. If they are described as being her children by a particular man, those children will take

---

[1] (1859), 27 Beav. 71.
[2] *Ebbern* v. *Fowler*, [1909] 1 Ch. 578.
[3] (1874), L.R. 9 Ch.App. 147. See also *Re Bolton* (1886), 31 Ch.D. 542.
[4] L.R. 9 Ch.App. 161–162.
[5] *Occleston* v. *Fullalove, supra*; *Crook* v. *Hill* (1876), 3 Ch.D. 773; *Re Harrison*, [1894] 1 Ch. 561. It remains to be seen whether these cases have survived s. 15 of the Family Law Reform Act 1969 (p. 112, *post*), which draws no express distinction between illegitimate children in existence and those born afterwards.

who have acquired the reputation of being the children of those parents (*e.g.* through acknowledgment by the father).[6] For this reason, where a testator makes provision for the illegitimate children of a male without reference to the mother (even though that male is himself) only those illegitimate children can take who are in existence *at the date of the will*. Illegitimate children born subsequently, even though acknowledged by him before his death, cannot take.[7] (In view of changed ideas of public policy, the courts may have to review their attitude to " immorality.")

The Problem of Construction

Prima facie, in dispositions taking effect before section 15 of the Family Law Reform Act 1969 came into force, the words child, son or issue, when employed in a will, mean legitimate child, son or issue.[8] However, where upon the true construction of a will it appears that the testator used the term, not with its prima facie meaning, but to include illegitimate children, the court will give effect to that intention.[9] The question is always, what was the testator's real intention? Thus, if the testator mentions a child of that name, the child benefits.[10] In *Re Fish*[10] the testator left property to my " niece Eliza Water-house." The testator had no niece of that name, but his wife had two grandnieces of that name, one of whom was legitimate, the other illegitimate. The Court of Appeal decided that the testator, in using the word " niece," really meant grandniece, and since there was a legitimate grandniece named " Eliza Waterhouse," she took to the exclusion of the illegitimate grandniece of the same name, even though there was reason to suppose that, in reality, the illegitimate grandniece was intended. In this case, no extrinsic evidence of the testator's intention was admissible to rebut the rule of construction.

In one case, however, extrinsic evidence of intention may be admissible. This occurs where there are two *legitimate* persons, each of whom satisfies the testator's description. Thus, in *Doe d. Gord* v. *Needs*,[11] a testator, who owned three houses, devised one to " John Gord, the son of George Gord," another to " George Gord, the son of George Gord," and the third to " George Gord, the son of Gord." The will left the destination of the third gift ambiguous, as a legacy was also given to " George Gord, the son of John Gord," so there were two Georges, son of Gord. This constituted what is technically known as an equivocation, permitting the admission of extrinsic evidence of the testator's intention. When this was admitted, it showed that the testator intended the third house to be taken by the son of George Gord.

It was the existence of a similar equivocation which permitted the courts to reach the right answer in a modern case, in which the existence of an illegitimate person satisfying the testator's description was a further complication in a problem where there was also an equivocation. In *Re Jackson*[12]

---

[6] *Re Hastie's Trusts* (1887), 35 Ch.D. 728; *Re Loveland*, [1906] 1 Ch. 542.
[7] *Re Bolton* (1886), 31 Ch.D. 542; *Re Du Bochet*, [1901] 2 Ch. 441.
[8] *Wilkinson* v. *Adam* (1813), 1 V. & B., 422, 462; *Hill* v. *Crook* (1873), L.R. 6 H.L. 265; *Re Wohlgemuth's Will Trusts*, [1949] Ch. 12. Similar principles are applicable to adopted children. *Re Fletcher*, [1949] Ch. 473. See now the Adoption Act 1958, s. 16 (2) (*a*).
[9] *Re Hastie's Trusts* (1887), 35 Ch.D. 728; *Re Horner* (1887), 37 Ch.D. 695.
[10] *Re Fish*, [1894] 2 Ch. 83.
[11] (1836), 2 M. & W. 129.
[12] [1933] Ch. 237.

the testatrix devised and bequeathed all her property to her trustees on trust for sale for the benefit of her two brothers, two sisters, and " my nephew Arthur Murphy " in equal shares. Actually, the testatrix had three nephews of that name, two of whom were legitimate sons of testatrix's brothers, and the third was an illegitimate son of a sister, who had married a legitimate niece of the testatrix. Farwell, J., held that if there had been only two legitimate nephews it would have been, in the circumstances, impossible to tell which was intended—

> . . . and had the matter ended there I must have found that there was an intestacy on the ground of uncertainty. But the matter does not end there, because the evidence shows that one of the testatrix's sisters had a son born out of wedlock, who was also named Arthur Murphy, and that he was in close relationship with the testatrix, and had married one of her nieces, and therefore in some sense may be called a nephew. Now in the circumstances what course ought I to adopt? If there had been one legitimate nephew only named Arthur Murphy that nephew would undoubtedly have been entitled to the legacy, and no evidence at all as to the existence of the illegitimate nephew would have been admissible . . . But as soon as it appears from the evidence that there is more than one nephew who exactly answers the description in the will, the Court is entitled to have evidence of the state of the family generally, and to be put to some extent in the position of the testatrix in order to ascertain not what the testatrix intended but what the words which she has used were intended to mean. Now if from that evidence it appears that neither of the legitimate nephews was intended by the words which the testatrix has used, but that the words were used to describe the illegitimate nephew, I am, I think, bound to give effect to that evidence as a whole. I cannot disregard it, and if it convinces me that the testatrix intended by the words " my nephew Arthur Murphy " her illegitimate nephew, in my judgment I must give effect to it.[13]

Where the testator excepts an illegitimate child from his bounty, and there are several illegitimate children, the inference is that with this exception the testator intended to benefit both legitimate and illegitimate children.[14] Again, if there is a gift to *children* of a deceased person, and there is only one legitimate child, illegitimate children are held to be included,[15] but this implication does not arise if the gift is to the children of a *living* person, for the testator may have been contemplating the birth of other legitimate children.[16] Furthermore, it follows, from the principles already enunciated, that if it appears that the testator was referring simply to children in existence at the date of the will, and at this time there are illegitimate children only, these will take.[17] At the same time, it must always be remembered that if, upon the construction of the will, it appears that the testator intended to benefit his

---

13 [1933] Ch. 242.
14 *Re Lowe* (1892), 61 L.J.Ch. 415.
15 *Re Embury (No. 2)* (1914), 111 L.T. 275.
16 *Re Yearwood's Trusts* (1877), 5 Ch.D. 545.
17 *Re Haseldine* (1886), 31 Ch.D. 511; *Re Deakin*, [1894] 3 Ch. 565.

legitimate children only, the fact that there are no legitimate children who may benefit will not of itself admit illegitimate children.[18]

By section 15 (1) of the Family Law Reform Act 1969—

In any disposition made after the coming into force of this section—

(a) any reference (whether express or implied) to the child or children of any person shall, unless the contrary intention appears, be construed as, or as including, a reference to any illegitimate child of that person; and

(b) any reference (whether express or implied) to a person or persons related in some other manner to any person shall, unless the contrary intention appears, be construed as, or as including, a reference to anyone who would be so related if he, or some other person through whom the relationship is deduced, had been born legitimate.

Section 17 protects trustees and personal representatives who distribute property in ignorance of the existence of a claim created by section 15 (1).

2. TRUSTS VIOLATING EXCHANGE CONTROL REGULATIONS

By the Exchange Control Act 1947 no person resident in the United Kingdom may settle property, otherwise than by will (except with the permission of the Treasury), so as to confer an interest in that property on a person who, at the time of the settlement, is resident outside the sterling area. Offences against the Act are punishable by fine and imprisonment; but the prohibition contained in the Act does not render a settlement invalid except so far as it purports to confer any interest on a person resident outside the sterling area.

3. OTHER UNLAWFUL PURPOSES

Amongst other dispositions held void have been a trust with a condition inserted with the object of separating parent or child, or of depriving a father of his parental duties,[19] and trusts subversive of religion and morality.[20] Again, a trust which takes effect upon the separation of husband and wife *in the future* is void,[21] but not one which contemplates an immediate separation which has already been decided upon as inevitable.[22] If no separation in fact occurs, the trust is completely void, the consideration having wholly failed.[23] Furthermore, although it is not a condition precedent to the enjoyment of benefits under a separation deed that the beneficiary should not commit adultery, yet if the deed is, in fact, drawn for the purpose of facilitating adultery it is on that account void.[24] It may be that a separation deed includes

---

[18] *Godfrey* v. *Davis* (1801), 6 Ves. 43; *Kenebel* v. *Scrafton* (1802), 2 East 530; *Dorin* v. *Dorin* (1875), L.R. 7 H.L. 568; *Re Brown* (1890), 63 L.T. 159; *Re Pearce*, [1914] 1 Ch. 254.

[19] *Re Sandbrook*, [1912] 2 Ch. 471. See also *Re Piper*, [1946] 2 All E.R. 503.

[20] See *De Themmines* v. *De Bonneval* (1828), 5 Russ. 288; *Thornton* v. *Howe* (1862), 31 Beav. 14; *Bowman* v. *Secular Society Ltd.*, [1917] A.C. 406.

[21] *Marquis of Westmeath* v. *Marchioness of Westmeath* (1830), 1 Dow & Cl. 519; *Re Moore* (1888), 39 Ch.D. 116.

[22] *Wilson* v. *Wilson* (1848), 1 H.L.C. 538; (1854), 5 H.L.C. 40.

[23] *Bindley* v. *Mulloney* (1869), L.R. 7 Eq. 343.

[24] *Evans* v. *Carrington* (1860), 2 De G.F. & J. 481; *Fearon* v. *Earl of Aylesford* (1884), 14 Q.B.D. 792; *Wasteneys* v. *Wasteneys*, [1900] A.C. 446.

some covenants which are good, and others which are illegal. If this is so, and they are separable, the court will enforce those which are valid and ignore the rest.[25] Finally, a trust for a wife, to last so long as she remains deserted by her husband, has been held valid,[26] and in *Re Hope Johnstone*,[27] a trust in favour of a wife to last only so long as she lived with her husband, with a gift over to the husband if she ceased to do so, was held good. In *Egerton* v. *Egerton* [28] Denning, L.J., remarked: " . . . a settlement which contains provisions as to what should happen in the case of divorce is not contrary to public policy." Such provisions are void if they offer an incentive to break up the marriage.[29]

Trusts in total restraint of marriage are void, and this is so even where the object of the clause is not apparently to impose a total restraint, if in fact that is the probable result.[30] A prohibition on marriage with a particular person is, however, valid, and so is a restriction preventing a second marriage.[31] Again, if the gift is expressed to last until marriage, this is good, for here the interest is not divested by way of penalty on the happening of the event; it merely reaches its logical conclusion under conditions which are not in any way affected with illegality.[32] Furthermore, a gift with a condition attached requiring the consent of some person to a marriage is also good.[33]

One class of trusts which is void as contrary to public policy is that class which contemplates immoral relations. Where the benefit is given in consideration of future immoral association, the trust is void,[34] but a trust where the parties contemplate future immoral connection, but this is not the consideration, is valid.[35]

A trust to procure a peerage [36] is void, and an unreasonable trust, such as a trust for the purpose of blocking up the windows of a house for twenty years, has also been held void.[37] Furthermore, trusts having as their object the restraint of the beneficiary from alienating his interest are void. Nevertheless, if the restraint would be valid in the country where the trust was created, it will be enforced.[38]

Some years ago, the courts had a period of concern with the question whether the " name and arms " clause is contrary to public policy, or whether it should still be upheld. The position up to the beginning of 1961 is summarised by Wilberforce, J., in *Re Howard's Will Trusts* [39]—

> Name and arms clauses have been in use, and examples of them can be found in books of conveyancing precedents, for a century at least, and,

[25] *Merryweather* v. *Jones* (1864), 4 Giff. 509; *Hamilton* v. *Hector* (1871), L.R. 6 Ch.App. 701.
[26] *Re Charleton*, [1911] W.N. 54.
[27] [1904] 1 Ch. 470.
[28] [1949] 2 All E.R. 238, 242.
[29] *Re Johnson's Will Trusts*, [1967] Ch. 387.
[30] *Lloyd* v. *Lloyd* (1852), 2 Sim. N.S. 255.
[31] *Allen* v. *Jackson* (1875), 1 Ch.D. 399. *Cf. Leong* v. *Lim Beng Chye*, [1955] A.C. 648.
[32] *Morley* v. *Rennoldson* (1843), 2 Hare 570, 579–581, *per* Wigram, V.-C.
[33] *Re Whiting's Settlement*, [1905] 1 Ch. 96.
[34] *Gray* v. *Mathias* (1800), 5 Ves. 286; *Hall* v. *Palmer* (1844), 3 Hare 532; *Re Vallance* (1884), 26 Ch.D. 353.
[35] *Re Wootton Isaacson* (1904), 21 T.L.R. 89.
[36] *Earl of Kingston* v. *Lady Elizabeth Pierepont* (1681), 1 Vern. 5. *Cf. Egerton* v. *Earl Brownlow* (1853), 4 H.L.C. 1.
[37] *Brown* v. *Burdett* (1882), 21 Ch.D. 667.
[38] *Re Fitzgerald*, [1904] 1 Ch. 573.
[39] [1961] Ch. 507, 516–517.

so far as reported cases go, no general objection was raised to them until after the World War of 1939–45, although, undoubtedly, opportunities for such objection arose. From 1945 onwards a wind of change of increasing force developed against them. Vaisey J. held such a clause void in 1945 [40] on grounds, inter alia, of public policy, and followed this with two further decisions in 1951 [41] and 1952, [42] the latter followed immediately by a decision of Wynn Parry J., [43] in which the invalidity was based on uncertainty. Later in 1952 Danckwerts J. held [44] that a clause almost identical with that with which I am concerned was void for uncertainty, and also as being contrary to public policy, and described it as out of date and inconsistent with the spirit of the time. It is not surprising that the editors of Key and Elphinstone's Precedents in Conveyancing [45] should, with some degree of defeatism, have recommended to their readers to abandon the attempt to construct a binding clause and to limit themselves to a provision having only precatory force.

So far the tide flows strongly in one direction, but in 1960 Cross J., again on a clause very similar to the present, held [46] that it was not void for uncertainty, and, although expressing his willingness to follow Danckwerts J. on the issue of public policy in similar circumstances, found that the particular clause in that case, being almost exclusively directed towards male persons, was not contrary to public policy. Finally, in the course of this year, Plowman J. followed Danckwerts J. in holding a shorter clause contrary to public policy, but stated that he would not have rejected it on grounds of uncertainty alone. [47]

To this brief summary of the cases I should add that in 1955, after Upjohn J. had upheld a clause not unlike the present, [48] the Court of Appeal [49] rejected it on account of certain special difficulties inherent in its drafting, but did not express or indicate favour or disfavour of the trend of decisions given at first instance.

In *Re Howard's Will Trusts* [50] Wilberforce, J., said that where the clause was applicable to a married woman, it was now contrary to public policy, but the Court of Appeal in *Re Neeld* [51] took a different view, holding a clause in the usual form valid, overruling the earlier decisions on which Wilberforce, J., had relied, and reviewing the principles.

It remains now to consider the effect of creating a trust for an illegal purpose. The first rule is that the court will not assist anyone who seeks to obtain any benefit under the instrument, nor will it assist the settlor to obtain his property back if it has been transferred, for the maxim is: *melior est*

[40] *Re Fry*, [1945] Ch. 348.
[41] *Re Lewis' Will Trust*, [1951] 2 T.L.R. 1032.
[42] *Re Bouverie*, [1952] Ch. 400.
[43] *Re Wood's Will Trusts*, [1952] Ch. 406.
[44] *Re Kersey*, [1952] W.N. 541.
[45] 15th ed. (1953), Vol. 2, p. 784.
[46] *Re Neeld*, [1960] Ch. 455.
[47] *Re Harris' Will Trusts* (1961), *The Times* newspaper, March 1.
[48] *Re Murray*, unreported.
[49] *Re Murray*, [1955] Ch. 69.
[50] [1961] Ch. 507.
[51] [1962] Ch. 643.

conditio possidentis. In *Re Great Berlin Steamboat Co.,*[52] X placed money
to the credit of a company, for the purpose of giving the company a fictitious
credit, with the understanding that the company was to hold the money on
trust for him. Some of the money was withdrawn with the consent of X, and
then the company was wound up. The Court of Appeal held that they would
offer no assistance to X for the purpose of recovering the balance of his money.
Cotton, L.J., said [53]—

> . . . the Appellant says that the company were to hold this sum in trust
> for him, and the resolution no doubt says that they shall. But that
> declaration of trust is coupled with a statement that the advance is made
> in order that the company may appear to have a creditable balance at
> their bankers if inquiries are made—a purpose which is admitted to be
> fraudulent. The money was to be represented to be the money of the com-
> pany, but by a private arrangement it was not to be their money. Then it is
> said that a person who parts with his property for a fraudulent purpose
> may repudiate the bargain and get his property back. I give no opinion
> whether in November last the Appellant could have done so. He did not
> attempt to do so, but waited till the event happened which put an end to
> the purpose for which the money was deposited. He left the money at the
> bank as long as the possibility of carrying out the illegal purpose con-
> tinued, and it is now too late for him to reclaim it. Assuming that he had
> the right to repudiate the bargain, he has, in my opinion, lost that right.

The concluding observations in this judgment point to an important
qualification to the general rule. It is clear that when the illegal purpose has
been fulfilled, the court will not assist the settlor to recover his money,[54] for
the parties are *in pari delicto*; but if the illegal purpose is still executory, and
the property has been transferred, the court will assist the settlor to recover it,
if the illegal purpose has been abandoned, for the consequences of refusing
to aid him might be to ensure that the illegal purpose will be carried out.[55]
Further, if the parties are not *in pari delicto*, the court may assist that person
who is not tainted with illegality. Knight Bruce, L.J., observed in *Reynell*
v. *Sprye* [56]—

> . . . where the parties to a contract against public policy, or illegal, are not
> in *pari delicto* (and they are not always so), and where public policy is
> considered as advanced by allowing either, or at least the more excusable
> of the two, to sue for relief against the transaction, relief is given to
> him. . . .[57]

A second exception arises from a distinction noticed by Lord Eldon, and
based upon the same fact that the parties are not *in pari delicto*, that if the

[52] (1884), 26 Ch.D. 616. See also *Palaniappa Chettiar* v. *Arunasalam Chettiar*, [1962] A.C.
294.
[53] 26 Ch.D. 619–620.
[54] *Sykes* v. *Beadon* (1879), 11 Ch.D. 170; *Kearley* v. *Thomson* (1890), 24 Q.B.D. 742;
Thwaites v. *Coulthwaite*, [1896] 1 Ch. 496.
[55] *Birch* v. *Blagrave* (1755), Amb. 264; *Ayerst* v. *Jenkins* (1873), L.R. 16 Eq. 275, 283.
[56] (1852), 1 De G.M. & G. 660, 679.
[57] See also *Osborne* v. *Williams* (1811), 18 Ves. 379; *Consolidated Exploration and Finance
Co.* v. *Musgrave*, [1900] 1 Ch. 37.

person who is claiming relief is not the fraudulent party himself, but a person claiming through him, who is no party to the fraud, he may obtain relief, "for there is a great difference between the case of an heir coming to be relieved against the act of his ancestor in fraud of the law, and of a man coming upon his own act under such circumstances." [58]

If a person has obtained money as agent or trustee of another, he cannot set up the fact that the money has arisen out of an illegal transaction as an excuse for its retention by him,[59] and the same rule applies to an executor whose testator has obtained the money illegally.[60]

4. TOTAL FAILURE OF OBJECTS OF SETTLEMENT

Where there is a total failure of the objects the trust will be cancelled. In *Essery* v. *Cowlard*,[61] a settlement entered into in consideration of an intended marriage between A and B provided that stock, transferred to the trustees by B, should be held by them on trust for the benefit of A and B, and for the issue of the marriage. The marriage was never celebrated, but the parties cohabited and there were three children. In 1883 A and B brought an action for the trust to be set aside, and this was done.[62]

Cases in which a marriage settlement is established, and the marriage actually occurs, but is afterwards declared void following a decree of nullity, require special treatment. Where a father made a settlement upon trusts for himself until his son's intended marriage, and then for the son, and the son married, so that he enjoyed the interest, and afterwards the marriage was declared null on the grounds of the son's impotence, it was held that the settlor continued always to be entitled to the interests in the settlement which were specified to continue until the marriage.[63] In *Re Eaves* [64] a testator gave property by his will to his widow during widowhood, and thereafter to his son absolutely. He appointed his widow and his son to be his executors and trustees. The widow remarried, and the property was transferred to the son absolutely. Some years later, the widow's second marriage was pronounced null and void, not having been consummated, and the wife claimed from the son the income of the property. Farwell, J., held that the nullity decree restored the widow's interest from the moment when it had ceased on her remarriage, but he also held that since she had accepted the position for a number of years, during which the marriage could have been avoided, it was too late to claim the property back from the son. Similarly, in *Re Ames'* *Settlement*,[65] where there was a settlement in contemplation of a marriage subsequently declared null and void, it was held that the trusts failed and the property was held on a resulting trust for the settlor's executors.

---

[58] *Muckleston* v. *Brown* (1801), 6 Ves. 52, 68.

[59] *Farmer* v. *Russell* (1798), 1 B. & P. 296; *De Mattos* v. *Benjamin* (1894), 63 L.J.Q.B. 248.

[60] *Joy* v. *Campbell* (1804), 1 Sch. & Lef. 328, 339.

[61] (1884), 26 Ch.D. 191.

[62] See also *Bond* v. *Walford* (1886), 32 Ch.D. 238, where the contract to marry was broken off, and the property was restored.

[63] *Re Wombwell's Settlement*, [1922] 2 Ch. 298, following *Chapman* v. *Bradley* (1863), 4 De G.J. & S. 71, and *Re Garnett* (1905), 74 L.J.Ch. 570.

[64] [1939] Ch. 1000, affirmed, [1940] Ch. 109, partly on other grounds. *Cf. Re Dewhirst*, [1948] Ch. 198.

[65] [1946] Ch. 217.

B. TRUSTS VOIDABLE THROUGH MISTAKE, MISREPRESENTATION, DURESS, FRAUD, OR UNDUE INFLUENCE

Where a trust has been established as a result of mistake, fraud, undue influence, misrepresentation, or duress, it may be set aside altogether, or in some cases rectified, provided that the settlor has not acquiesced after the impairment of consent has ceased to exist, or after he was aware of the legal effect of it. Settlements which are cancelled on this ground are usually voluntary, but it would appear that the remedy is not confined to voluntary settlements, although the court will resort to it more readily in such cases than if valuable consideration has been given. Where the settlor asks for relief on one of these grounds, the onus of proof is on him, except where the settlement itself is so absurd that no sane person would knowingly have entered into it, or where the beneficiary occupied a fiduciary position as regards the settlor, in which case there is a presumption of undue influence.[66]

1. DURESS

There are very few reported cases relating to duress as a ground for avoiding a trust, but in *Ayliffe* v. *Murray*,[67] the court set aside a deed that had been obtained by two executors and trustees of a will, after the issuing of threats to a beneficiary under it; whilst in *Barrett* v. *Hartley*,[68] Sir J. Stuart, V.-C., laid down the general principle—

> In order to render a contract, or an agreement of any kind, binding, there must be the assent of both parties to the agreement under such circumstances as to shew that there was no pressure—no influence existing of a kind to make the assent an imperfect assent, or an assent which, under other circumstances, would have been refused. If the assent to the agreement is not an assent given under such circumstances as that both parties are on an equal footing, and the agreement one perfectly free from any influence or pressure, in the eye of this Court, it is not an assent sufficient to constitute an agreement.

2. MISTAKE

Mistake may vitiate consent, or make it inequitable to enforce a trust, and generally gives rise to a right to have the whole instrument cancelled.[69]

In *Forshaw* v. *Welsby*,[70] a person, apparently at the point of death, executed a voluntary settlement, which was never read to him, of which he understood nothing, and from which the solicitor purposely omitted a power of revocation, since he knew the settlor's changeable character. The settlement was cancelled when the settlor recovered. Similarly, deeds have frequently been set aside when they have been signed without sufficient explanation, so that their purport

---

[66] *Allcard* v. *Skinner* (1887), 36 Ch.D. 145 (Cases, p. 234).
[67] (1740), 2 Atk. 58.
[68] (1866), L.R. 2 Eq. 789, 794–795.
[69] As to the general equitable principles relating to mistake, see Keeton and Sheridan, *Equity*, pp. 547–550 (rescission), 530–542 (rectification) and 333–336 (inequitable and unconscientious bargains); 1974 Supplement, pp. 57–58, 56 and 26.
[70] (1860), 30 Beav. 243.

is misunderstood.[71] In *Baker* v. *Monk*,[72] an infirm and ignorant woman executed a conveyance *for valuable consideration*, without comprehending its nature, and it was set aside. Sir J. Romilly, M.R., observing that the only ground on which such a transaction could be supported would be the fact that the purchaser had given full value.

In *Dutton* v. *Thompson*,[73] a testator left a one twenty-seventh share of his estate to X (a person of less than ordinary intelligence), with power to his trustees to withhold the transfer of the share until X attained the age of twenty-five, which he did in January 1882. The stepmother of X and his uncle (who was also a trustee) persuaded X, after an initial refusal, and in view of the well-known improvident habits of X, to convey his share to A and B on trust for such persons and generally in such manner as X should with the consent of his trustees, A and B, by any deed appoint, the granting of consent to be in the absolute discretion of A and B; and, subject to the power of appointment, in trust to pay the income to the plaintiff during his life, and after his death to his children and other issue; with other trusts in default of issue. A year after the execution of this settlement, X sought to have it set aside, and the Court of Appeal held that he was entitled to this relief since, although the settlement was read over to X, it was quite clear that he did not understand its effect. *Dutton* v. *Thompson* appears to have been decided on the ground of mistake, although it would seem from the facts that a claim to set aside the settlement on the ground of undue influence would also have been successful. *Strauss* v. *Sutro*[74] is a similar case. The plaintiffs were just over twenty-one years of age when they executed a settlement by which they tied up very strictly the funds of a marriage settlement to which they were entitled. In this case they never read the settlement, the terms of which were never explained to them. The court excluded the possibility of undue influence on the part of the father of the settlors, but held that the settlements must be set aside, as the settlors were ignorant of what they were doing.

In the cases mentioned above, the mistake affected the very nature of the transaction undertaken.

In certain circumstances, however, which will be considered together later, relating to voluntary settlements, and to those made in contemplation of marriage, the court will order the instrument to be rectified. In *James* v. *Couchman*,[75] a settlor assigned property to his trustees for himself for life, remainder to his wife, remainder to his issue, and in default of issue to his *paternal* next of kin. It was proved that the settlor's attention was not called to the last, rather unusual, limitation, and that he did not understand the effect of it. North, J., declined to cancel the whole settlement, but allowed it to be rectified so as to give the settlor a power of appointment in default of issue.

In *Fowler* v. *Fowler*,[76] Lord Chelmsford, L.C., said—

> It is clear that a person who seeks to rectify a deed upon the ground of mistake must be required to establish, in the clearest and most satisfactory

---

[71] *Proctor* v. *Robinson* (1866), 35 Beav. 329; *Price* v. *Price* (1852), 1 De G.M. & G. 308; *Anderson* v. *Elsworth* (1861), 3 Giff. 154.
[72] (1864), 33 Beav. 419.
[73] (1883), 23 Ch.D. 278.
[74] [1948] L.J.R. 33.
[75] (1885), 29 Ch.D. 212.
[76] (1859), 4 De G. & J. 250, 265.

manner, that the alleged intention to which he desires it to be made conformable continued concurrently in the minds of all parties down to the time of its execution, and also must be able to shew exactly and precisely the form to which the deed ought to be brought. For there is a material difference between setting aside an instrument and rectifying it on the ground of mistake. In the latter case you can only act upon the mutual and concurrent intention of all parties for whom the Court is virtually making a new written instrument.

Where the settlement is voluntary, moreover, the court will exercise its power to rectify with greater caution than in the case of a contract *inter partes*. So the court refused rectification to a settlor who had entered into a deed of covenant with the object of reducing the tax payable on his income, when the deed of covenant failed to produce the desired result.[77]

In *Banks* v. *Ripley*[78] a marriage settlement was rectified, when it appeared that a life interest had been given to the children of the marriage where a gift of the fee simple had been intended.

3. INNOCENT MISREPRESENTATION

A good illustration of this ground of invalidity is *Re Glubb*,[79] wherein a charitable institution innocently misstated that it was in a position to obtain a large legacy, if other people would subscribe other sums before a specified date. Actually, the date on which the legacy could have been obtained had passed, and the Court of Appeal held that there was a duty cast upon the committee to return the sums so obtained.

4. FRAUD

The type of fraud here considered as invalidating settlements is that by an intending beneficiary upon the settlor. The position where the settlor himself makes a settlement with a fraudulent object has already been considered,[80] whilst trusts in fraud of the settlor's creditors will be considered later,[81] since they have been made the subject of special legislation.

Fraud in equity is much wider than fraud at common law, and, in fact, in equity, duress, fraud, and undue influence shade off into one another, whilst it is also clear that some types of fraud may create such a mistake in the mind of the settlor as to give rise to cancellation on that ground.[82] " Fraud is infinite, and were a Court of Equity once to lay down rules, how far they would go, and no farther, in extending their relief against it, . . . the jurisdiction would be cramped, and perpetually eluded by new schemes, which the fertility of man's invention would contrive." [83] The same point was considered

---

[77] *Van der Linde* v. *Van der Linde*, [1947] Ch. 306. See also *Whiteside* v. *Whiteside*, [1949] Ch. 448.

[78] [1940] Ch. 719.

[79] [1900] 1 Ch. 354. As to the general principles relating to innocent misrepresentation, see Keeton and Sheridan, *Equity*, pp. 544–547.

[80] pp. 115–116, *ante*.

[81] Chap. XI, s. D, *post*.

[82] See Keeton and Sheridan, *Equity*, pp. 329–356, 543–544; 1974 Supplement, pp. 26–27, 57; Sheridan, *Fraud in Equity*.

[83] Lord Hardwicke, in a letter to Lord Kames: see Parkes, *History of the Court of Chancery*, p. 508.

by Lord Haldane in *Nocton* v. *Lord Ashburton*,[84] where the Lord Chancellor observed—

> . . . when fraud is referred to in the wider sense in which the books are full of the expression, used in Chancery in describing cases which were within its exclusive jurisdiction, it is a mistake to suppose that an actual intention to cheat must always be proved. A man may misconceive the extent of the obligation which a Court of Equity imposes on him. His fault is that he has violated, however innocently because of his ignorance, an obligation which he must be taken by the Court to have known, and his conduct has in that sense always been called fraudulent, even in such a case as a technical fraud on a power. It was thus that the expression " constructive fraud " came into existence. The trustee who purchases the trust estate, the solicitor who makes a bargain with his client that cannot stand, have all for several centuries run the risk of the word fraudulent being applied to them. What it really means in this connection is, not moral fraud in the ordinary sense, but breach of the sort of obligation which is enforced by a Court that from the beginning regarded itself as a Court of conscience.

It is plain, therefore, that precise rules regulating the occasions when the court will set aside a settlement on the ground of fraud cannot be formulated, but the case of *Baker* v. *Monk*,[85] where mistake was induced by fraud, may serve as an illustration. It is clear, however, that the court will only set aside settlements on the ground of fraud, or on any of the grounds now under consideration, where there can be *restitutio in integrum*. Thus, in *Johnston* v. *Johnston*,[86] a settlor had married a woman who had represented that she had divorced her first husband for adultery and cruelty. In fact, he had divorced her for adultery. When the settlor discovered this, he sought to have the settlement cancelled, but the Court of Appeal held that since the consideration for it was marriage, which the settlor could not return, the settlement could not in consequence be set aside.

5. UNDUE INFLUENCE

The jurisdiction exercised by Courts of equity over the dealings of persons standing in certain fiduciary relations has always been regarded as one of a most salutary description. The principles . . . have been long settled . . . , but the Courts have always been careful not to fetter this useful jurisdiction by defining the exact limits of its exercise. Wherever two persons stand in such a relation that, while it continues, confidence is necessarily reposed by one, and the influence which naturally grows out of that confidence is possessed by the other, and this confidence is abused, or the influence is exerted to obtain an advantage at the expense of the confiding party, the person so availing himself of his position will not be permitted to retain the advantage, although the transaction could not have been impeached if no such confidential relation had existed.[87]

---

[84] [1914] A.C. 932, 954.   [85] (1864), 33 Beav. 419, p. 118, *ante*.   [86] (1884), 52 L.T. 76.
[87] These remarks by Lord Chelmsford, L.C., in *Tate* v. *Williamson* (1866), L.R. 2 Ch.App 55, 60, were adopted by Sir Raymond Evershed, M.R., in the Court of Appeal in *Tufton* v *Sperni*, [1952] 2 T.L.R. 516, 521–522. As to undue influence generally, see Keeton and Sheridan, *Equity*, pp. 337–352; 1974 Supplement, pp. 26–27; Sheridan, *Fraud in Equity*, pp. 87–106.

The application of this principle to the relation of trustee and beneficiary accounts for one great class of constructive trusts. The principle, however, applies to many other relations, and wherever undue influence is established, the party adversely affected by it may, subject to certain conditions, claim to have the settlement set aside.

Where the confidential relationship has been shown to exist, equity imposes upon the beneficiary (who is also the stronger party) the task of showing, if the transaction is to stand, that no undue influence in fact existed, that the settlor had the opportunity of taking outside advice, and that he thoroughly understood the nature and extent of the disposition he was making. In the words of Bowen, L.J., in *Allcard* v. *Skinner* [88]—

> . . . it is plain that equity will not allow a person who exercises or enjoys a dominant religious influence over another to benefit directly or indirectly by the gifts which the donor makes under or in consequence of such influence, unless it is shewn that the donor, at the time of making the gift, was allowed full and free opportunity for counsel and advice outside—the means of considering his or her worldly position and exercising an independent will about it. This is not a limitation placed on the action of the donor; it is a fetter placed upon the conscience of the recipient of the gift, and one which arises out of public policy and fair play.

Transactions between various classes of persons, where one is clearly in a dominating position in respect of the other, and that dominating person derives a benefit out of that relation, are said to raise a presumption of undue influence, which the beneficiary must disprove if he can, before he may enjoy the benefit he has gained. It has already been pointed out that uncle and nephew, where the nephew has no nearer relation to look to for guidance and protection, is one instance of such a relation. *A fortiori,* such a presumption exists where a child confers a benefit on his parent. The real reason for equity's intervention in these cases is the inexperience of the party who has surrendered his property. For this reason, a person of mature age and experience can make a gift to his father and mother without the presumption arising, whilst a younger person cannot,[89] and a person who has just come into possession of considerable property on attaining the age of majority is particularly exposed to it.[90] When a daughter, shortly after attaining her majority, made over her property to her father, without consideration, the father was called upon to show that the daughter had acted as a free agent, and had enjoyed independent advice.[91] However, in such cases it may be that the child is genuinely prompted by natural love and affection to make a settlement in favour of the parent, and, if this is so, it may be allowed to stand, even though the child in fact did not have independent advice.[92] The rule just stated does not extend to the ordinary resettlement of family estates when an

[88] (1887), 36 Ch.D. 145, 190 (Cases, p. 234).
[89] *Per* Farwell J., *Powell* v. *Powell*, [1900] 1 Ch. 243, 246.
[90] *Re Pauling's Settlement Trusts*, [1964] Ch. 303.
[91] *Bainbrigge* v. *Browne* (1881), 18 Ch.D. 188.
[92] *Re Coomber*, [1911] 1 Ch. 174. See also *Inche Noriah* v. *Shaik Allie Bin Omar*, [1929] A.C. 127.

eldest son attains his majority,[93] unless the father obtains an unduly large advantage thereby.[94] In *Powell* v. *Powell*,[95] a young woman was induced by her stepmother to execute a settlement by which she shared her property with the children of that stepmother. She had enjoyed the advice of a solicitor, who in fact was acting for the other parties, and although he had expressed disapproval, he had gone no further. It was held that the settlement must be set aside.

In *Lancashire Loans Ltd.* v. *Black*[96] a young married woman, who had separated from her husband, and had then returned home to live with her mother, was induced by the mother to mortgage certain property to a money-lender to secure debts owing by the mother to the moneylender. The Court of Appeal held that whilst there was no presumption of undue influence in such a case, it might be established as a fact, and being established, the transaction must be set aside.[97]

There is no presumption of undue influence where a wife settles her property upon her husband,[98] although it may still be established as a fact in a particular instance.[99] But it would seem that a presumption exists where a woman makes a gift to her fiancé.[1]

In transactions between guardian and ward, the same presumption arises while the relationship subsists, and, further, if the transaction occurs shortly after the guardianship has ended,[2] but this does not prevent a ward from giving the guardian a reasonable gift.[3] Exactly the same principles apply between an individual and his religious adviser[4] or his medical adviser,[5] " spiritualists "[6] and similar persons. Not all fiduciary relationships give rise to the presumption; the relationship must be of such a kind as suggests undue influence.[7]

Transactions between solicitor and client, whereby the solicitor himself, or his wife,[8] or some near relation,[9] obtains a benefit are, however, clearly within the rule. In this case it is almost a positive rule that the client cannot make a gift to his solicitor[10] which cannot be set aside by the client, if he chooses. It is certainly essential to show that when the gift was made the client actually enjoyed independent advice, and that the fiduciary relation did not then

[93] *Hoblyn* v. *Hoblyn* (1889), 41 Ch.D. 200.
[94] *Hoghton* v. *Hoghton* (1852), 15 Beav. 278.
[95] [1900] 1 Ch. 243.
[96] [1934] 1 K.B. 380.
[97] See also *Bullock* v. *Lloyds Bank Ltd.*, [1955] Ch. 317.
[98] *Howes* v. *Bishop*, [1909] 2 K.B. 390.
[99] *Bank of Montreal* v. *Stuart*, [1911] A.C. 120, explained in *Brydon* v. *Hawkins*, [1949] 3 D.L.R. 252, 274–275. See also *Ginter* v. *Ginter* (*No. 2*), [1953] O.W.N. 750; *Luchak* v. *Sitko* (1956), 3 D.L.R. (2d) 682; *Domenco* v. *Domenco* (1963), 41 D.L.R. (2d) 267; *First Independent Bank* v. *Proby* (1966), 57 W.W.R. 360. And see *Chaplin & Co. Ltd.* v. *Brammall*, [1908] 1 K.B. 233.
[1] *Re Lloyds Bank Ltd.*, [1931] 1 Ch. 289.
[2] *Pierse* v. *Waring* (1745), 1 P.Wms. 121n.
[3] *Hatch* v. *Hatch* (1804), 9 Ves. 292.
[4] *Huguenin* v. *Baseley* (1807), 14 Ves. 273; *Allcard* v. *Skinner* (1887), 36 Ch.D. 145, p. 124, *post* (Cases, p. 234).
[5] *Dent* v. *Bennett* (1839), 4 My. & Cr. 269; *Radcliffe* v. *Price* (1902), 18 T.L.R. 466. See also *Re C.M.G.*, [1970] Ch. 574.
[6] *Lyon* v. *Home* (1868), L.R. 6 Eq. 655.
[7] *Re Coomber*, [1911] 1 Ch. 723.
[8] *Liles* v. *Terry*, [1895] 2 Q.B. 679.
[9] *Willis* v. *Barron*, [1902] A.C. 271.
[10] *Tomson* v. *Judge* (1855), 3 Drew. 306; *Wintle* v. *Nye*, [1959] 1 W.L.R. 284.

exist.[11] In *Demerara Bauxite Co. Ltd.* v. *Hubbard*,[12] a solicitor held an option on his client's property, which he exercised, the client taking no independent advice. The court held that the transaction could not stand unless the purchaser fully disclosed all the information he possessed concerning the transaction, and it was entirely fair and as advantageous as if the purchaser had been a stranger. Furthermore, even though in fact the relationship of solicitor and client had terminated, the rule still applied so long as the confidence arising out of that relation could be presumed to exist. This was a sale, and not a gift. The same rule also extends to purchases by a solicitor from his client's trustee in bankruptcy[13] and to sales by a solicitor, either beneficially or as trustee, to his client.[14]

Besides those relationships in which undue influence is presumed, there are also many cases in which undue influence has been proved, in fact, to have existed. Thus, in *Smith* v. *Kay*,[15] a young man had incurred very extensive debts through association with an older man, who had acquired great influence over him, encouraging him to a course of extravagance. The House of Lords held that the young man was entitled to relief, and Lord Kingsdown observed[16]—

> The principle applies to every case where influence is acquired and abused, where confidence is reposed and betrayed. The relations with which the Court of Equity most ordinarily deals, are those of trustee and *cestui que trust*, and such like. It applies specially to those cases, for this reason and this reason only, that from those relations the Court presumes confidence put and influence exerted. Whereas in all other cases where those relations do not subsist, the confidence and the influence must be proved extrinsically; but where they are proved extrinsically, the rules of reason and common sense and the technical rules of a Court of Equity, are just as applicable in the one case as in the other.

For this reason contracts and settlements of an improvident nature made by poor and ignorant persons, acting without independent advice, have frequently been set aside, unless fair and reasonable,[17] and so have catching bargains with persons expecting to benefit under the will of a person still alive.[18] Section 174 of the Law of Property Act 1925 (re-enacting the Sales of Reversions Act 1867) provides that no acquisition made in good faith, without fraud or unfair dealing, of any reversionary interest, including an expectancy or possibility, in real and personal property, for money or money's worth, shall be set aside merely on the ground of undervalue, but the section does not affect the jurisdiction of the court to set aside or modify unconscionable bargains.

Where undue influence is presumed or established, the settlement is void-

---

[11] *Re Haslam and Hier-Evans*, [1902] 1 Ch. 765; *Wright* v. *Carter*, [1903] 1 Ch. 27 (Cases, p. 238).

[12] [1923] A.C. 673.

[13] *Luddy's Trustee* v. *Peard* (1886), 33 Ch.D. 500.

[14] *Moody* v. *Cox & Hatt*, [1917] 2 Ch. 71.

[15] (1859), 7 H.L.C. 750. See also *Lancashire Loans Ltd.* v. *Black*, [1934] 1 K.B. 380; *Re Craig*, [1971] Ch. 95.

[16] 7 H.L.C. 779. See also *Lloyds Bank Ltd.* v. *Bundy* [1974] *The Times*, August 1, 1974.

[17] *How* v. *Weldon* (1754), 2 Ves.Sen. 516; *Fry* v. *Lane* (1888), 40 Ch.D. 312.

[18] See *Shelly* v. *Nash* (1818), 3 Madd. 232; *Perfect* v. *Lane* (1861), 3 De G.F. & J. 369.

able. If, however, the settlor, knowing the whole circumstances of the transaction, and enjoying the opportunity for independent advice, does not choose to set it aside promptly, he may be held to have acquiesced in it, if he seeks to set aside at some later period. In *Mitchell* v. *Homfray*,[19] a patient made a gift to her medical adviser, and decided to abide by it after that relationship had ceased. It was held by the Court of Appeal that her executors could not have the gift set aside. A similar position arose in *Turner* v. *Collins*,[20] where a son, under his father's influence, settled property on his stepmother and stepsister, and then raised no objection for several years. In *Allcard* v. *Skinner*,[21] the plaintiff sought to recover property which she had transferred to a sisterhood under the undue influence of the mother-superior. She had left the sisterhood in 1879, but she did not seek to recover her property until 1885, and the Court of Appeal held that it was too late for her to recover her property.

Bowen, L.J., said [22] on this point—

> . . . if her delay has been so long as reasonably to induce the recipient to think, and to act upon the belief that the gift is to lie where it has been laid, then, by estoppel, . . . the donor of the gift would be prevented from revoking it. But I do not base my decision here upon the ground of estoppel. Yet a long time has elapsed. Five years is a long time in the life of anybody, and is a long time in the life of a person who has passed her life in seclusion like the Plaintiff. Every day and every hour during those five years she has had the opportunity of reflecting upon her past life and upon what she has done. She has had that opportunity since she passed away from the influence of the Defendant . . . She was surrounded by persons perfectly competent to give her proper advice. . . . I draw unhesitatingly the inference . . . that she did, in or shortly after 1879, consider this matter and determine not to interfere with her previous disposition. Was she aware of her rights at the time she formed this resolution? . . . I . . . think that she must have been, having regard to the character of the advisers who surrounded her; but . . . It is enough if she was aware that she might have rights and deliberately determined not to . . . act upon them.

There is no presumption of undue influence between testator and legatee whatever their relationship, although in any particular case it may be established as a fact.

C. TRUSTS WHICH ARE VOID AS CONTRAVENING
THE RULES RELATING TO PERPETUITIES
OR ACCUMULATIONS

1. PERPETUITIES

It has always been the policy of English landowners to seek to tie up their

---

[19] (1881), 8 Q.B.D. 587. In this case it was not clear that the donor had ever intended to abandon a possible equitable remedy, as it was not proved that she was aware that the gift was voidable.
[20] (1871), L.R. 7 Ch.App. 329.
[21] (1887), 36 Ch.D. 145 (Cases, p. 234).
[22] 36 Ch.D. 192.

land, so as to make it descend inalienably in the family as far as the rules of law permit; whilst the general policy of English law, and of the English courts, has been in favour of the free disposition of land. In furtherance of this policy, the common law judges developed the rule relating to perpetuities, to which the legislature added at a later date the rule relating to accumulations. Equity was always bound by the latter rule, and applied also the former, so that, except where the interest is enjoyed under a trust for charitable purposes, it must not violate the rules relating to perpetuities and accumulations, for as Lord Guildford observed in *Duke of Norfolk* v. *Howard* [23]—

> If in equity you should come nearer to a perpetuity, than the rules of common law would admit, all men, being desirous to continue their estates in their families, would settle their estates by way of trust; which might indeed make well for the jurisdiction of the court, but would be destructive to the commonwealth.

This rule, as it existed before 1964, may be defined as follows: The vesting of real or personal property must not be postponed for a period longer than a life or lives in being, or for twenty-one years after the cesser of such life, with the addition, in necessary cases, of the period of gestation.[24] The remoteness against which the rule operates relates to the vesting of interests in property, and not to their duration or determination, which may occur at any period of time, no matter how remote.[25] Before 1964, also, the court considered possible events, and not those which occurred or were probable, no judicial notice being taken, for example, of the period at which a woman ceased to be capable of child-bearing.[26] *Physical* incapacity was in fact completely disregarded.[27] Where the settlor did not mention a life or lives which could be taken as a standard of measurement of the vesting period, he was restricted to a period of twenty-one years.

This traditional formulation of the rule against perpetuities was modified in a number of ways by the Perpetuities and Accumulations Act 1964. Section 1 provides that although a settlor may still select as the perpetuity period a life or lives in being plus twenty-one years, he may now select as an alternative a fixed period of not more than eighty years. This possibility extends to settlements except exercises of powers of appointment and discretionary trusts, to which special rules are applicable. By section 2 certain presumptions of law have been introduced in respect of capacity for childbearing. When a question of perpetuity arises, there is a presumption that a male under fourteen years of age and a woman under twelve or over fifty-five are incapable of producing children. Provision is made in section 2 (2) for the admission of evidence in the rare case in which a younger person or a woman over fifty-five actually does have a child.

Section 3 (1) abolishes the rule that possible, and not actual events, must

---

[23] (1683), 1 Vern. 163, 164. See also Keeton, *Modern Developments in the Law of Trusts,* pp. 201–214.

[24] *Cadell* v. *Palmer* (1833), 1 Cl. & Fin. 372; *Re Wilmer's Trusts,* [1903] 2 Ch. 411. On the subject generally, see Morris and Leach, *The Rule Against Perpetuities,* 2nd ed.

[25] *Wainwright* v. *Miller,* [1897] 2 Ch. 255; *Re Chardon,* [1928] Ch. 464 (Cases, p. 284).

[26] *Re Wood,* [1894] 3 Ch. 381; *Re Wilmer's Trusts* [1903] 2 Ch. 411.

[27] *Re Gaite's Will Trusts,* [1949] 1 All E.R. 459. But an infringement of the rule against perpetuities does not arise merely because distribution may be delayed by a breach of trust: *Re Atkins' Will Trusts,* [1974] 1 W.L.R. 761.

be considered, together with the rule that an interest which might by any possibility vest too remotely is void, even though it actually vests within the perpetuity period. In place of these rules, there is now substituted a new principle
—that of "wait and see," that is to say, the disposition is regarded as valid
until events happen which make it clear that the interest cannot vest within
the perpetuity period.[28]

The law relating to perpetuities was amended by the property legislation of
1925, with a view to clarifying various points in relation to it, and modifying
the effect of some of the older decisions. The Law of Property Act 1925, section 161, provides—

> (1) The rule of law prohibiting the limitation, after a life interest to an
> unborn person, of an interest in land to the unborn child or other issue of
> an unborn person is hereby abolished, but without prejudice to any other
> rule relating to perpetuities.
>
> (2) This section only applies to limitations or trusts created by an
> instrument coming into operation after the commencement of this Act.

The purpose of this section is to abolish what has been variously termed
the rule against double possibilities and the rule in *Whitby* v. *Mitchell*,[29] although, as Farwell, L.J., pointed out in *Re Nash*,[30] the rule is older than that
case, and "was due to Lord Coke's love of scholastic logic . . ." The rule
invalidated such a remainder to an unborn person, whether it infringed any
other rule against perpetuities or not.

Section 163 of the Law of Property Act 1925 has now been repealed by
section 4 of the Perpetuities and Accumulations Act 1964. Section 4 (1) (which
applies to gifts over as well as to direct gifts) provides that where there is a
gift to an unborn person to vest at an age greater than twenty-one, and the
gift is not saved as a result of the procedure introduced by section 3 of the
Perpetuities and Accumulations Act 1964, then the specified age must be
reduced to the age nearest the specified age which will permit the gift to take
effect. Section 4 (2) makes similar provision for the saving of gifts where there
are two or more specified ages (a case which was not provided for in section
163 of the Law of Property Act 1925).

Before the passing of the Act of 1964 problems frequently arose from the
application of the perpetuity rule to "class gifts," *e.g.* "to the children of A."
Where there was a gift to a class, the whole gift failed if one member or the
size of his share might not be ascertained within the perpetuity period, even
though some of the members were bound to fulfil the conditions (if they did
so at all) within the perpetuity period. This has now been changed. Section 4
(4) provides that if it is apparent, either at the time when the disposition is
made or subsequently, that the inclusion of any persons, whether potential
members of a class or unborn persons who at birth would become actual or
potential members of the class, would make the disposition void for remoteness, all such members shall be excluded from the disposition to the class for
all purposes. Section 4 (3) is a complementary provision which is applicable

---

[28] For an application of this section to a power of distribution under a trust of a pension
fund, see *Re Thomas Meadows & Co. Ltd. and Subsidiary Companies (1960) Staff Pension
Scheme Rules,* [1971] Ch. 278.
[29] (1889), 42 Ch.D. 494; (1890), 44 Ch.D. 85.
[30] [1910] 1 Ch. 1, 10.

to cases not covered by section 4 (1) and (4), for example, where there is a gift to a mixed class of children and grandchildren with a provision that the vesting age for the children, and also the grandchildren, is an age greater than twenty-one.[31]

The Law of Property Act does not affect the position reached in prior decisions [32] that a trust for sale, or a power of sale, must be limited within the period of the perpetuity rule to be valid. Nevertheless, if the trust is invalid, it is regarded as machinery which has become inoperative, and this does not affect the interests of the beneficiaries, provided that these vest within the permitted period,[33] but if any of the beneficiaries have died, the property will pass to their personal representatives, as the trust or power has failed.[34]

Thus in *Re Daveron* [35] there was a trust for sale of freeholds at the end of forty-nine years, and a gift of the proceeds to a class ascertainable within the limits of the rule against perpetuities. Chitty, J., held that the gift was good; but, the trust for sale being void, the beneficiaries took the property as realty.

When it is necessary to wait and see, if a fixed period is not chosen as the perpetuity period, the lives in being are specified in section 3 (4), (5), of the Act of 1964. But in determining validity *ab initio,* any life in being may be selected, and it has been the practice to select all the issue of Queen Victoria living at the time when the instrument comes into operation. This practice is not now generally followed owing to difficulty of proof, but if an example arises at the present time, the inquiry will be undertaken, and the limitation is valid.[36] Issue of George V may be preferred, since if it is in fact impracticable to discover when the selected life ended, the trust is void. Thus, in *Re Moore,*[37] the settlor selected the survivor of all persons then living.

Another important change in the rules governing remoteness is introduced by section 6 of the Perpetuities and Accumulations Act 1964. Prior to this Act, a succession of cases had decided that where there were later interests in a settlement, dependent upon prior interests which were void for remoteness, such ulterior interests were also void for remoteness, because they were dependent upon void limitations, even though they were otherwise valid. Section 6 provides that if the ulterior limitation is otherwise valid, it will take effect and be accelerated, even though dependent upon dispositions which failed for remoteness.

Two other provisions of the Act of 1964 are of importance from the standpoint of the law of trusts. Section 8 provides that the administrative powers of trustees (*e.g.* to lease, sell or exchange trust property) and also provisions for the payment of trustees or others are not subject to the rule against perpetuities. Sections 1 (2), 3 (3) and 7 deal with the application of the Act to special powers of appointment (which by section 15 (2) also include discretionary trusts). Where there is a special power, then the donor of the power

---

[31] On the Act of 1964, see Ryder, " The Perpetuities and Accumulations Act, 1964 " (1965) 18 *Current Legal Problems* 39.

[32] *Goodier* v. *Edmunds (No. 2),* [1893] 3 Ch. 455; *Re Wood,* [1894] 3 Ch. 381; *Re Bewick,* [1911] 1 Ch. 116.

[33] *Re Daveron,* [1893] 3 Ch. 421; *Goodier* v. *Johnson* (1881), 18 Ch.D. 441.

[34] *Goodier* v. *Edmunds (No. 2),* [1893] 3 Ch. 455.

[35] [1893] 3 Ch. 421.

[36] *Re Warren's Will Trusts* (1961), 105 S.J. 511. See also *Re Villar,* [1929] 1 Ch. 243; *Re Leverhulme (No. 2),* [1943] 2 All E.R. 274.

[37] [1901] 1 Ch. 936.

may specify a fixed period of years, not exceeding eighty, within which the power may be exercised, and this will govern the validity of any appointment under it; but the donee of the power may not specify such a period : otherwise the period would be prolonged, after it had begun. Section 7 defines a special power, by providing that a power of appointment is to be treated as a special power unless—

(a) in the instrument creating the power it is expressed to be exercisable by one person only, and

(b) it could, at all times during its currency when that person is of full age and capacity, be exercised by him so as immediately to transfer to himself the whole of the interest governed by the power without the consent of any other person or compliance with any other condition, not being a formal condition relating only to the mode of exercise of the power . . .

The position of charitable trusts with reference to the rule relating to perpetuities deserves special consideration. It is sometimes suggested that the rule does not apply to charitable trusts,[38] but actually this is too wide. In addition to the rule relating to perpetuities, there is another principle of English law that real property shall not be limited in such a way that it becomes inalienable. It has been said that the effect of bestowing real property in fee upon a charitable organisation capable of holding it is that it becomes practically inalienable.[39] Notwithstanding this, however, English law encourages such gifts, although were property given to a private individual with the intention of creating similar consequences the gift would be void. As a further concession, English law also permits dispositions to one charitable body, with a gift over upon the occurrence of a contingency to another charitable body, and the contingency may occur at any time, however remote.[40] On the other hand, a gift to charitable uses by way of executory limitation, if it is one which might by possibility not vest within the perpetuity period, is void, like any other executory limitation.[41]

2. ACCUMULATIONS

It was discovered that, even within the limits of the perpetuity rule, accumulations of *income* could be directed by settlors so as to deprive their children of the enjoyment of property in favour of remoter issue. In *Thellusson* v. *Woodford*,[42] Mr. Thellusson directed that his property, real and personal, should be accumulated during the lives of all his sons and grandsons born in his lifetime or living at his death, for the benefit of those of his issue who, at the expiration of that period, should be within the class of heirs male of his sons. This postponed the vesting of the property and its income for about

[38] *Thomson* v. *Shakespear* (1860), 1 De G.F. & J. 399, 407 ; *Yeap Cheah Neo* v. *Ong Cheng Neo* (1875), L.R. 6 P.C. 381, 394.
[39] *Re Dutton's Will Trusts* (1878), 4 Ex.D. 54
[40] *Christ's Hospital* v. *Grainger* (1849), 1 Mac. & G. 460; *Re Tyler*, [1891] 3 Ch. 252.
[41] *Chamberlayne* v. *Brockett* (1872), L.R. 8 Ch.App. 206, 211 ; *Re Mander*, [1950] Ch. 547 ; *Re Wightwick's Will Trusts*, [1950] Ch. 260. See also Keeton and Sheridan, *The Modern Law of Charities*, 2nd ed., pp. 202–206.
[42] (1799), 4 Ves. 227 (Cases, p. 250). See also Keeton, *Modern Developments in the Law of Trusts*, pp. 215–275 ; " The Thellusson Case and Trusts for Accumulations " (1970) 21 *Northern Ireland Legal Quarterly* 131.

seventy or eighty years, but the disposition was within the perpetuity period. This particular will was upheld, but in 1800 the Thellusson Act was passed to prevent such dispositions in the future, by restricting accumulations within a reasonable period.[43]

Accumulations are now dealt with in sections 164–166 of the Law of Property Act 1925 which provide [44]—

164—(1) No person may by any instrument or otherwise settle or dispose of any property in such manner that the income thereof shall, save as hereinafter mentioned, be wholly or partially accumulated [45] for any longer period than one of the following, namely:

(a) the life of the grantor or settlor; or

(b) a term of twenty-one years from the death of the grantor, settlor or testator; or

(c) the duration of the minority or respective minorities of any person or persons living or en ventre sa mere at the death of the grantor, settlor or testator; or

(d) the duration of the minority or respective minorities only of any person or persons who under the limitations of the instrument directing the accumulations would, for the time being, if of full age, be entitled to the income directed to be accumulated.

In every case where any accumulation is directed otherwise than as aforesaid, the direction shall (save as hereinafter mentioned) be void; and the income of the property directed to be accumulated shall, so long as the same is directed to be accumulated contrary to this section, go to and be received by the person or persons who would have been entitled thereto if such accumulation had not been directed.

(2) This section does not extend to any provision—

(i) for payment of the debts of any grantor, settlor, testator or other person;

(ii) for raising portions for—

(a) any child, children or remoter issue of any grantor, settlor or testator [46]; or

(b) any child, children or remoter issue of a person taking any interest under any settlement or other disposition directing the accumulations or to whom any interest is thereby limited;

(iii) respecting the accumulation of the produce of timber or wood; and accordingly such provisions may be made as if no statutory restrictions on accumulation of income had been imposed.

(3) The restrictions imposed by this section apply to instruments made on or after the twenty-eighth day of July, eighteen hundred, but in the

---

[43] Readers of Galsworthy's *Forsyte Saga* will recall Timothy Forsyte's will, and the comments of Soames Forsyte on it. For a discussion of the objects of the Thellusson Act, see *Bassil* v. *Lister* (1851), 9 Hare 177, 183. It is not normally applicable to accumulations by unit trusts: *Re A.E.G. Unit Trust (Managers) Ltd.'s Deed*, [1957] Ch. 415.

[44] The reduction in the age of majority from 21 to 18 years does not invalidate a direction for accumulation made before the change: Family Law Reform Act 1969, s. 1 (4) and Sched. 3, para. 7.

[45] As to what constitutes accumulation under this subsection, see *Re Earl of Berkeley*, [1968] Ch. 744. See also Pearce, " Retention of Income by Trustees " (1972) 36 *Conveyancer* 38.

[46] As to what constitutes a portion under this subsection, see *Re Bourne's Settlement Trusts*, [1946] 1 All E.R. 411.

case of wills only where the testator was living and of testamentary capacity after the end of one year from that date.

165. Where accumulations of surplus income are made during a minority under any statutory power or under the general law, the period for which such accumulations are made is not (whether the trust was created or the accumulations were made before or after the commencement of this Act) to be taken into account in determining the periods for which accumulations are permitted to be made by the last preceding section, and accordingly an express trust for accumulation for any other permitted period shall not be deemed to have been invalidated or become invalid, by reason of accumulations also having been made as aforesaid during such minority.

166—(1) No person may settle or dispose of any property in such manner that the income thereof shall be wholly or partially accumulated for the purchase of land only,[47] for any longer period than the duration of the minority or respective minorities of any person or persons who, under the limitations of the instrument directing the accumulation, would for the time being, if of full age, be entitled to the income so directed to be accumulated.

(2) This section does not, nor do the enactments which it replaces, apply to accumulations to be held as capital money for the purposes of the Settled Land Act, 1925, or the enactments replaced by that Act, whether or not the accumulations are primarily liable to be laid out in the purchase of land.

(3) This section applies to settlements and dispositions made after the twenty-seventh day of June, eighteen hundred and ninety-two.

Two further periods were added by the Perpetuities and Accumulations Act 1964, s. 13 (1). They are—

(e) a term of twenty-one years from the date of the making of the disposition, and

(f) the duration of the minority or respective minorities of any person or persons in being at that date.

One or two points arising out of these sections require further explanation.

Subject to any qualification imposed by section 165, the restrictions imposed in section 164 extend to directions which are implied, as well as those which are express.[48] Whether such a direction is implied is a question of construction. The implication is possible, for example, where the disposition cannot be carried into effect without accumulation.[49]

As regards the periods from which a selection of the accumulations period may be made, the determination of the appropriate period is a question of construction.[50] The first period is the one which would be prima facie adopted where the accumulation is directed by deed, unless some other is expressly indicated; and the second period of twenty-one years from the death is the

---

[47] This includes a direction to accumulate for the purchase of " real estate ": *Re Clutterbuck*, [1901] 2 Ch. 285.
[48] *Tench* v. *Cheese* (1855), 6 De G.M. & G. 453.
[49] *Mathews* v. *Keble* (1868), L.R. 3 Ch.App. 691.
[50] *Jagger* v. *Jagger* (1883), 25 Ch.D. 729.

one prima facie applying where the accumulation is directed by will, and no period is indicated.[51] The second period is reckoned from the death of the settlor, even if there is a direction that the accumulation is not to begin until some future time, as for example the death of an annuitant.[52] The distinction between the third and fourth periods is that, whereas under the third period, the person whose minority is selected must be in existence at the death of the settlor, and the period begins from that death, the fourth period contemplates the minorities of persons who need not necessarily be born in the testator's lifetime, and it does not necessarily begin on the death of the testator, for it may obviously extend to successive minorities of persons who, if of full age, would be entitled to the income,[53] but in this case, unless there is another beneficiary during whose minority an accumulation is directed, there may not be any accumulation before the birth of that person who is unborn at the death of the testator.[54]

If there is a direction to accumulate for a period longer than is permitted, the direction is invalid only as to the excess over the permitted period, and the excess goes to those entitled as if such accumulation had not been directed.[55] Where it is void, the section provides for a resulting trust, but such a trust does not take effect in one case, *i.e.* where the direction to accumulate is accompanied by a general charitable intention. In such a case, the *cy-près* rule applies.[56]

The restrictions upon accumulation imposed in section 164 and section 13 (1) of the Perpetuities and Accumulations Act 1964 apply in respect of a power to accumulate income, whether or not there is a duty to exercise the power, and they apply whether or not the power to accumulate extends to income produced by the investment of income previously accumulated.[57]

The Perpetuities and Accumulations Act 1964 contains one other new provision. Section 14 provides that section 2, dealing with presumptions affecting child-bearing in respect of perpetuities, shall also be applicable where beneficiaries seek to put an end to accumulations. Under the rule in *Saunders* v. *Vautier*,[58] where all the beneficiaries solely entitled to an accumulation of income are of full age and capacity, they can agree to terminate the accumulation and divide the capital among themselves. They will be unable to do this where there is a possibility, however remote, of another beneficiary coming into existence, and for this purpose, the possibility of a child being born to an elderly woman past the age of child-bearing was accepted.[59] Now, under section 2, if the age of the woman is greater than fifty-five, this possibility will be ignored.

---

[51] *Griffiths* v. *Vere* (1803), 9 Ves. 127; *Oddie* v. *Brown* (1859), 4 De G. & J. 179.
[52] *Webb* v. *Webb* (1840), 2 Beav. 493.
[53] *Re Cattell*, [1914] 1 Ch. 177.
[54] *Ellis* v. *Maxwell* (1841), 3 Beav. 587, 596.
[55] *Griffiths* v. *Vere* (1803), 9 Ves. 127; *Re Jefferies*, [1936] 2 All E.R. 626; *Re Robb*, [1953] Ch. 459. See also *Re Watt's Will Trusts*, [1936] 2 All E.R. 1555; *Re Ransome*, [1957] Ch. 348.
[56] *Re Bradwell*, [1952] Ch. 575. Prior to 1964, a direction to accumulate was totally void if the accumulation might last longer than the perpetuity period. It is uncertain whether that rule has survived the " wait and see " provision of section 3 of the Act of that year. See Megarry and Wade, *The Law of Real Property*, 3rd ed., pp. 280–281.
[57] Perpetuities and Accumulations Act 1964, s. 13 (2).
[58] (1841), 4 Beav. 115. See also *Wharton* v. *Masterman*, [1895] A.C. 186.
[59] *Re Deloitte*, [1926] Ch. 56.

The effect of section 165 is that if a testator directs income to be accumulated for twenty-one years from his death, and after this period terminates, it happens that the fund is held in trust for an infant, the accumulations during the twenty-one years' period and the further accumulations during the minority of the infant (*e.g.* under the Trustee Act 1925, s. 31) are both valid. This point was considered by Astbury, J., in *Re Maber*,[60] where he observed—

> It may be that the section is difficult to construe, but in my view the first portion effects the following result—namely, that if during a minority income is accumulated under a statutory power, e.g., s. 43 of the Conveyancing Act, 1881, the period of that minority accumulation is not to be taken into account in ascertaining the allowable Thellusson period in the particular case. In other words the years of minority accumulation are not to be reckoned in that period.

One final point should be noticed. If there is an express provision to accumulate income, this excludes the power of maintenance conferred on trustees by section 31 of the Trustee Act 1925.[61]

---

60 [1928] Ch. 88, 92.
61 *Re Reade-Revell*, [1930] 1 Ch. 52; *Re Stapleton*, [1946] 1 All E.R. 323.

CHAPTER XI

TRUSTS FOR NON-CHARITABLE
INSTITUTIONS AND OTHER PURPOSES

A. INSTITUTIONS

A TRUST for a non-charitable institution may be valid, provided it complies with the conditions discussed below.

In the first place, the institution must be one which does not contravene either law or public policy.[1] Secondly, the beneficiaries and the nature of the interests which they are to take must both be certain. Thirdly, the trust must take effect in such a form that it cannot exist beyond a limited period, usually stated to be the perpetuity period. What this means in this context must be discussed more fully.

No question of perpetuity will arise if the disposition contemplates an out and out unconditional gift to the institution, for in that case the gift can be used at once and retained entirely as the governing body of the institution may direct, and it is regarded as a gift to the existing members. Sports clubs, libraries, voluntary societies and innumerable other institutions regularly receive gifts of this type. On the other hand, if the gift is fettered by a trust, or by conditions, a question of perpetuity may arise, and if the fetter extends beyond the permissible period, the whole gift will fail. The distinction between the two types of gifts is sometimes a fine one, but it turns upon the determination of the questions (1) whether the society or institution can freely dispose of the subject-matter of the gift or not; and (2) whether the gift is a gift to the institution or to the individual members of it. In the latter case, no question of perpetuity can arise, but when the gift is to the institution, this question must also be considered.[2]

In *Leahy* v. *Attorney-General for New South Wales*[3] the Privy Council examined the earlier decisions. Viscount Simonds, in delivering their opinion, pointed out that in *Cocks* v. *Manners*,[4] where there was a gift to a religious order which was not (in the technical sense) charitable, this had been construed as a gift to the members individually, and on that account had been held valid. There was greater difficulty where the gift was made in terms that, although it was not contemplated that the individual members would divide it among themselves, there was nothing in the constitution of the association which prevented the members from disposing of it; and he pointed out that in such a case, a prudent testator would add a clause providing that the receipt of the treasurer or other official should be a good discharge to the trustees of the will.

Thus, in *Re Clarke*[5] there was a gift to the Corps of Commissionaires in

---

[1] *Bowman* v. *Secular Society Ltd.*, [1917] A.C. 406.
[2] See Hogg, " Testamentary Dispositions to Unincorporated Associations " (1971) 8 *Melbourne University Law Review* 1.
[3] [1959] A.C. 457.
[4] (1871), L.R. 12 Eq. 574.
[5] [1901] 2 Ch. 110.

London, to aid in the purchase of their barracks, or to be used in any other way beneficial to the Corps. Byrne, J., held this to be a valid gift, on the ground that all the members could join together to dispose of it. This decision was followed in *Re Drummond* [6] where there was a gift to the old Brad-fordians Club in London, with a provision that the receipt of the treasurer should be a sufficient discharge to the trustees of the will. Eve, J., held that although he could not hold (as in *Re Clarke* [7]) that this was a gift to the members individually, it was nevertheless a gift of money which the committee of the Club could spend as they wished at any time, and it was therefore valid. Similarly, in *Re Price* [8] Cohen, J., held that a gift of a share of residue to the Anthroposophical Society in Great Britain " to be used at the discretion of the Chairman and Executive Council of the Society for carrying on the teachings of the founder, Dr. Rudolf Steiner," was a valid gift. He therefore treated the gift as freely disposable at any time; as also did Eve, J., in *Re Prevost*.[9] Pennycuick, J., in *Re Wootton*,[10] held valid a *power* to distribute the testatrix's residuary estate to an " organisation or body not being registered as a charity but in the opinion of my trustees as having charitable objects " (these not necessarily *being* charitable, as the *opinion* of the trustees might be erroneous).

Clearly on the other side of the line is *Re Wightwick's Will Trusts*,[11] in which the testatrix bequeathed property to trustees to pay the income to an anti-vivisection society, the income to be paid to the treasurer, and to be at the disposal of the society's committee for the purposes of the society. It was held that the gift was invalid, since the income was appropriated in perpetuity to a non-charitable object. In this case the non-charitable appropriation of the gift fettered the power of the members to dispose of the money.

The leading authority for decisions in this sense has long been that of the House of Lords in *Carne* v. *Long*.[12] In that case a testator devised his house to the trustees of the Penzance Public Library for ever for the benefit and maintenance of the library. The library was not a charity and was maintained by gifts and subscriptions from members. Lord Campbell, L.C., held that the gift could not be construed as a gift to the existing individual members, and it therefore failed for perpetuity. In *Re Macaulay's Estate* [13] (reported only in a footnote to *Re Price*,[8] but discussed in *Leahy* v. *Attorney-General for New South Wales* [14]) the House of Lords came to a similar conclusion in respect of a gift for the maintenance and improvement of the Theosophical Lodge at Folkestone. In the Court of Appeal in that case, Lord Hanworth, M.R., said [15]—

> The problem may be stated in this way. If the gift is in truth to the
> present members of the society described by their society name so that

6 [1914] 2 Ch. 90.
7 [1901] 2 Ch. 110.
8 [1943] Ch. 422.
9 [1930] 2 Ch. 383. *Cf. Re Recher's Will Trusts*, [1972] Ch. 526, where Brightman, J., did so construe a gift to an anti-vivisection society but held that the gift failed because the society mentioned by the testatrix had ceased to exist on amalgamation with another society.
10 [1968] 1 W.L.R. 681.
11 [1950] Ch. 260.
12 (1860), 2 De G.F. & J. 75.
13 [1943] Ch. 435.
14 [1959] A.C. 457.
15 See [1959] A.C. 483–484.

they have the beneficial use of the property and can, if they please, alienate and put the proceeds in their own pocket, then there is a present gift to individuals which is good: but if the gift is intended for the good not only of the present but of future members so that the present members are in the position of trustees and have no right to appropriate the property or its proceeds for their personal benefit then the gift is invalid.

This distinction proved fatal to the gift, as a direct gift, in *Leahy's* case. The residuary estate of the testator had been bequeathed on trust for an order of nuns, which was not, in the circumstances of the gift, necessarily charitable. The Privy Council decided that it could not be construed as a direct gift to the existing members of the order, and it would therefore have failed for perpetuity but for the saving provisions of section 37D of the Conveyancing Act 1919–1954 of New South Wales.[16]

If, therefore, gifts to such non-charitable institutions are to be effective, they should be made in such terms that the use of the income and capital is not fettered beyond what is often termed " the perpetuity period," which in the decisions has been regarded, in the absence of directions from the testator, as approximately twenty-one years. A learned writer [17] has suggested that, under the provisions of the Perpetuities Act, a trust for an institution to endure for a period not exceeding eighty years might be valid, provided it were stated that the gift during that period was for the members of the institution; and he adds that in view of the decisions which have been discussed, a gift for a similar period " for the purposes of the institution " would not be valid. In the past, however, the courts have not shown any disposition to construe " the perpetuity period " in the context as extending for more than twenty-one years. Sect. 15 (4) of the Perpetuities and Accumulations Act 1964 provides that nothing in the Act is to affect the operation of the rule of law rendering void for remoteness certain dispositions under which property is limited to be applied for purposes other than the benefit of any person or class of persons in cases where the property may be so applied after the end of the perpetuity period, so the " wait and see " provision in Sect. 3 is inapplicable.

B. ANIMALS AND NON-HUMAN OBJECTS

There exists a group of decisions in which the courts have accepted the validity of trusts for animals of various kinds, usually domestic animals of the testator, and also for some inanimate objects, usually memorials. Such trusts present unusual difficulties from the standpoint of theory, in that the objects benefited cannot enforce them. Hence, such trusts have sometimes been called imperfect, or unenforceable trusts. Thus, a trust by will for the maintenance of the testator's horses or dogs is valid.[18] So also is a direction to an executor to apply a certain sum for the erection of a tombstone in memory of someone already deceased.[19] In trusts of this kind, the direction

[16] As to such legislation saving imperfect trust provisions, see Keeton and Sheridan, *The Modern Law of Charities*, 2nd ed., pp. 179–201.

[17] Andrews, " Gifts to Purposes and Institutions " (1965) 29 *Conveyancer* 165, 170.

[18] *Re Dean* (1889), 41 Ch.D. 552. In *Re Wood*, [1949] Ch. 498, " This Week's Good Cause " was held to be too indefinite, since there were many of them.

[19] *Mussett* v. *Bingle*, [1876] W.N. 170.

may be made indirectly enforceable by the addition of a *gift over* on failure to comply with the direction but the gift over must necessarily take effect within the perpetuity period.[20] Where a surplus remains in the hands of the trustee after the purpose has been fulfilled, there is a resulting trust of it for the settlor, unless it appears that the trustee is to take beneficially.

Since in several other cases relating to non-charitable trusts, valid though unenforceable for lack of human beneficiaries, the question has been raised whether these trusts are not merely unenforceable, but void, it is necessary to consider them a little more closely. In *Pettingall* v. *Pettingall*,[21] the testator bequeathed £50 a year for the maintenance of a favourite black mare, the executor to be bound in honour to fulfil the request. The court held that £50 a year should be paid to the executor during the life of the mare, on his giving an undertaking to maintain her properly. If there was any surplus, then, on the construction of the will, it was to be enjoyed by the executor beneficially; and if the mare was not properly attended to, any of the residuary legatees was at liberty to apply to the court. This case will illustrate the methods by which such a trust may become indirectly enforceable. Again, in *Re Haines*,[22] Danckwerts, J., held that a trust for the maintenance of the testator's cats was good, judicial notice being taken of the fact that the maximum life of a cat is approximately sixteen years.

In *Gott* v. *Nairne*,[23] the testator gave £12,000 to his trustees to invest either wholly or partially in the purchase of an advowson, and until the occurrence of a specified event, they were to present some fit person to the living, but subject thereto, the advowson was to be held in trust for A. Until purchase, the fund was to be accumulated with the income for twenty-one years, following which, if the advowson had not then been purchased, the whole of it was to belong to A. Similarly, if the event contemplated occurred before the advowson was purchased, or if a balance remained after purchase, the whole, or the remainder of the fund was to be given to A. In view of these facts, A claimed the transfer of the fund with accumulations, as a beneficiary absolutely entitled, under the rule in *Saunders* v. *Vautier*,[24] but the court held that A was not a sole beneficiary absolutely entitled, since the trustees could buy an advowson, and present any person they thought fit. Again, in *Re Gibbons*,[25] a testator gave his residuary estate to his executors " to dispose of [it] to my best spiritual advantage, as conscience and sense of duty may direct." When the effectuation of this purpose was opposed, the court held that the purpose was one which the executors could fulfil, if they chose.

In *Pirbright* v. *Salwey*,[26] the testator gave £800 to the rector and church-wardens of a parish with a direction that the income should be applied, so long as the law permitted, in keeping up his grave, and decorating it with flowers. The court thought the trust was not charitable, but held it valid for twenty-one years. Similarly, in *Re Hooper*,[27] the testator directed that his

20 *Re Chardon*, [1928] Ch. 464 (Cases, p. 284); *Re Chambers' Will Trusts*, [1950] Ch. 267; *Re Wightwick's Will Trusts*, [1950] Ch. 260.
21 (1842), 11 L.J.Ch. 176. See also *Re Thompson*, [1934] Ch. 342.
22 (1952), *The Times* newspaper, Nov. 7.
23 (1876), 3 Ch.D. 278.
24 (1841), 4 Beav. 115.
25 [1917] 1 I.R. 448.
26 [1896] W.N. 86.
27 [1932] 1 Ch. 38.

trustees should hold a certain sum to devote the income "so far as they legally can do so" for the care of certain graves and monuments in certain cemeteries, and a tablet and window in a church, with a gift over to certain other persons. Since some of this was manifestly not charitable, the question was whether the trust was good in whole or in part, and Maugham, J., following *Pirbright* v. *Salwey*,[28] held that, as regards the tablet and window this was a valid charitable trust, and as regards the graves, this was not charitable, but good for a period of twenty-one years.

The decision in *Pirbright* v. *Salwey*,[28] and consequently the other cases similarly decided, have been criticised on the ground that all trusts which are not charitable must have a *cestui que trust*. In support of this the following observations of Grant, M.R., in *Morice* v. *Bishop of Durham*[29] have been advanced—

> There can be no trust, over the exercise of which this Court will not assume a control; for an uncontrollable power of disposition would be ownership, and not trust. If there be a clear trust, but for uncertain objects, the property, that is the subject of the trust, is undisposed of, and the benefit of such trust must result to those, to whom the law gives the ownership in default of disposition by the former owner. But this doctrine does not hold good with regard to trusts for charity. Every other trust must have a definite object. There must be somebody, in whose favour the Court can decree performance.

It would appear, however, that the Master of the Rolls is here adverting to one of what have been termed "the three certainties of a trust," and is saying no more than that, if the objects are uncertain, the trust fails. In all the cases cited the objects have been sufficiently definite, and, therefore, although the trusts have not been directly enforceable, they have been regarded as valid.

Nevertheless, there has been a disposition in the modern cases to regard the observations of Grant, M.R., as meaning that a trust must have definite human or charitable objects, and by construing them in this sense, they have been effectively employed, as will be shown, to prevent the development of purpose trusts.

A further point that arises out of the cases of *Pirbright* v. *Salwey*[28] and *Re Hooper*[30] is that in them the expressions "so long as the law for the time being permits" and "so far as they legally can do so" were used. It is settled that phrases such as these do not save dispositions which otherwise infringe the rules relating to perpetuities or accumulations where the trust is executed,[31] but if the trust is executory, that is to say if the testator indicates the objects, and leaves to his trustees the task of deciding upon the appropriate scheme for fulfilling them, then the court will give effect to the testator's wishes so far as the law permits.[32] Apparently therefore the trusts in *Pirbright* v. *Salwey* and in *Re Hooper* were regarded as executory.

The general result of the cases therefore seems to be that trusts for non-

[28] [1896] W.N. 86.
[29] (1804), 9 Ves. 399, 404–405 (affirmed (1805), 10 Ves. 522).
[30] [1932] 1 Ch. 38.
[31] *Re Harcourt*, [1921] 1 Ch. 187; *sub nom. Portman* v. *Viscount Portman*, [1922] 2 A.C. 473.
[32] *Re Beresford-Hope*, [1917] 1 Ch. 287.

human beneficiaries are lawful and the trustees act properly if they carry them out, but the non-human object may not enjoy the benefit of the trust for a period longer than the perpetuity period. Where a life is selected, it must be a human life and not the life of an animal which may be the object of the trust. Where the settlor selects no human life, he is confined to the absolute period of twenty-one years.

The best judicial exposition of the principle linking these decisions is still that of North, J., in *Re Dean.*[33] In that case a testator had devised his freehold estates, subject to an annuity of £750 and a term of fifty years in favour of his trustees, to the use of the plaintiff for life. He also gave his horses, ponies and hounds to his trustees, directing them to apply the annuity for the period of fifty years, if the horses and hounds should so long live, for the maintenance of the horses and hounds, and the stables and kennels in which they lived. North, J., held that the trust was good during the lives of the animals, and to the objection that there was no *cestui que trust* who could enforce the trust, he said [34]—

> There is not the least doubt that a man may if he pleases, give a legacy to trustees, upon trust to apply it in erecting a monument to himself, either in a church or in a churchyard, or even in unconsecrated ground, and I am not aware that such a trust is in any way invalid, although it is difficult to say who would be a *cestui que trust* of the monument. In the same way I know of nothing to prevent a gift of a sum of money to trustees, upon trust to apply it for the repair of such a monument. In my opinion such a trust would be good, although the testator must be careful to limit the time for which it is to last, because, as it is not a charitable trust, unless it is to come to an end within the limits fixed by the rule against perpetuities, it would be illegal. But a trust to lay out a certain sum in building a monument, and the gift of another sum in trust to apply the same to keeping that monument in repair, say, for ten years, is, in my opinion, a perfectly good trust, although I do not see who could ask the Court to enforce it. If persons beneficially interested in the estate could do so, then the present Plaintiff can do so; but, if such persons could not enforce the trust, still it cannot be said that the trust must fail because there is no one who can actively enforce it.

However, the decision in *Re Astor's Settlement Trusts* [35] has made it clear that where no person is entitled in default, a trust for non-human and non-charitable objects may be held invalid. In that case Roxburgh, J., reviewed all the earlier authorities on purpose trusts (other than charitable trusts), and after pointing out that the general principle was that " a gift on trust must have a *cestui que trust*," he referred to the " group of cases relating to horses and dogs, graves and monuments—matters arising under wills and intimately connected with the deceased—in which the courts have found means of

---

[33] (1889), 41 Ch.D. 552.

[34] 41 Ch.D. 556–557.

[35] [1952] Ch. 534, 547 (Cases, p. 252). See further, Marshall, " The Failure of the Astor Trust " (1953) 6 *Current Legal Problems* 151 ; Sheridan, " Trusts for Non-Charitable Purposes " (1953) 17 *Conveyancer* 46 ; Morris and Leach, *The Rule Against Perpetuities*, 2nd ed., pp. 307–327 and literature mentioned on p. 307, n. 1 ; McKay, " Trusts for Purposes— Another View " (1973), 37 *Conveyancer* 420.

escape from these general propositions . . . ." These, he suggested (adopting Underhill's view) [36] could be regarded as concessions to human weakness or sentiment, and they could not be used to justify the conclusion that a court of equity would recognise as an equitable obligation affecting the income of large funds in the hands of trustees a direction to apply it in furtherance of enumerated non-charitable purposes in a manner which no court or department could control or enforce. It would seem, therefore, that there is little scope for widening the class of purposes which achieve this limited recognition.[37] Some legal writers have argued that trusts of this kind should more properly be regarded as powers,[38] but in *Re Endacott*,[39] the Court of Appeal did not regard this with favour.

A rather different kind of unenforceable trust arises where a settlor grants property to trustees to apply money at their absolute discretion for the benefit of a particular person. Here the beneficiary cannot enforce the payment of any part of the money, and the persons interested in the remainder are only entitled to whatever unapplied surplus exists when the primary purpose has been fulfilled.[40] Such a trust is also only valid for the perpetuity period.[41]

These trusts were considered by the Law Revision Committee in connection with other problems of perpetuity, and they reported in favour of their validity, subject to the existing limitations, and they added a further suggestion that it should be made possible to devote a limited sum (they suggested £1,000) *in perpetuity* to the upkeep of a grave, tomb or monument. This recommendation was not incorporated in the Act, which has therefore left the position of trusts for non-human objects unaltered.[42]

C. PURPOSES

Re Astor's Settlement Trusts [43] directly raised a problem distinct from that of the anomalous (and now limited) class of trusts for non-human objects. This was the major question whether trusts could be established and enforced for the effectuation of abstract purposes. Prior to the *Astor* case the fact that the testator had named an abstract purpose does not appear to have been regarded as a difficulty. Thus, in *Re Thompson* [44] the testator bequeathed £1,000 to a friend to be applied by him for the promotion of foxhunting; and he bequeathed his residuary estate to Trinity Hall, Cambridge. Clauson, J., held that the gift was valid. Following the procedure of Knight Bruce, V.-C., in *Pettingall* v. *Pettingall*,[45] Clauson, J., ordered that, upon the defendant, the friend to whom the £1,000 had been bequeathed, giving an undertaking to apply the legacy for the advancement of foxhunting, the legacy should be paid

---

[36] *Law of Trusts*, 8th ed., p. 79.
[37] See also *Re Rank* (1955), *The Times* newspaper, Feb. 23; *Re Shaw*, [1957] 1 W.L.R. 729; [1958] 1 All E.R. 245.
[38] *e.g.* Sheridan, "Purpose Trusts and Powers" (1958) 4 *University of Western Australia Annual Law Review* 235.
[39] [1960] Ch. 232. See also *Leahy* v. *Attorney-General for New South Wales*, [1959] A.C. 457, p. 135, *ante*.
[40] *Re Bullock* (1891), 60 L.J.Ch. 341.
[41] *Re Blew*, [1906] 1 Ch. 624; *Re De Sommery*, [1912] 2 Ch. 622; *Re Coleman*, [1936] Ch. 528. See further on discretionary trusts, pp. 151-155, *post*.
[42] Perpetuities and Accumulations Act, 1964, s. 15 (4), p. 135, *ante*.
[43] [1952] Ch. 534 (Cases, p. 252).
[44] [1934] Ch. 342.
[45] (1842), 11 L.J.Ch. 176.

to him. In case the legacy were not so applied by him, the residuary legatees
would be at liberty to apply to have it paid over to them. The basic assumption of Clauson, J., in deciding this case was, therefore, that it was governed by
the same principles as those applicable to cases of gifts for the benefit of
animals or for the creation and maintenance of monuments. It was this basic
assumption which was considered and rejected by Roxburgh, J., in the *Astor*
case. In that case, there was a settlement of substantially the whole of the
issued shares of *The Observer* newspaper for twenty years from the death of
the survivor of the issue of Viscount Astor and of George V actually born
before the date of the settlement upon trust to further a number of objects
relating primarily to the independence and freedom of the Press. Roxburgh,
J., disposed of the animals and monuments cases in the manner already
mentioned, and then explained that Clauson, J., in *Re Thompson* [46] had been
able to hold the foxhunting trust good because there was a residuary legatee
who could secure its enforcement, so that he was able to make an order in
the form in which it had been made in *Pettingall* v. *Pettingall*. He then held
the trust void on two distinct grounds: (1) there was no justification in the
earlier decisions for holding that a trust could be created in respect of large
funds for the furtherance of non-charitable purposes, in a manner which no
court or department could control or enforce; and (2) on the ground that the
purposes were not defined with sufficient precision. " The purposes," he
said,[47] " must be so defined that if the trustees surrendered their discretion, the
court could carry out the purposes declared, not a selection of them arrived at
by eliminating those which are too uncertain to be carried out."

A similar problem was considered by Harman, J., in *Re Shaw*.[48] By his will,
George Bernard Shaw left the residue of his estate (which amounted to several
hundred thousand pounds) to trustees to initiate enquiries into the establishment of an alphabet of at least 40 letters, in which the English language
could be best expressed, and then to publish and distribute an edition of
Androcles and the Lion written in this alphabet. Harman, J., held that this
was not a charitable trust, and then considered it as a purpose trust. After
recalling Roxburgh, J.'s judgment in *Re Astor,* he pointed out that both
Greene, M.R., in *Re Diplock* [49] and Jenkins, L.J., in *I.R.C.* v. *Broadway
Cottages Trust* [50] had recently affirmed that non-charitable purpose trusts
were invalid, and that, in any event, they would frequently fail for uncertainty.
He then pointed out that, in the United States, the American Restatement
and a number of writers had treated purpose trusts as a species of power. This
way out, however, had been rejected by Jenkins, L.J., in *I.R.C.* v. *Broadway
Cottages Trust* and Harman, J., followed him in that rejection. Accordingly,
the alphabet trusts were invalid.

In *Re Endacott* [51] the Court of Appeal again considered the problem
created by attempts to create trusts of this kind. In this case the testator had

---

[46] [1934] Ch. 342.
[47] [1952] Ch. 548.
[48] [1957] 1 W.L.R. 729. See further, Keeton, " Bernard Shaw's Will and the Advancement
of Education " (1963) 2 *Solicitor Quarterly* 348.
[49] [1941] Ch. 253, 259.
[50] [1955] Ch. 20, 30.
[51] [1960] Ch. 232. See further, Sheridan, " Power to Appoint for a Non-Charitable Purpose: A Duologue or Endacott's Ghost " (1964) 13 *De Paul Law Review* 210.

left his residuary estate to the North Tawton Parish Council " for the purpose of providing some useful memorial to myself . . ." The Court of Appeal held: (1) that this was not an out and out gift to the parish council, but an attempt to create a trust; and (2) that the trust was not charitable. They also held that the trust did not come within the anomalous class of trusts for animals and monuments, which, Lord Evershed observed, ought not to be extended. In *Re Endacott*, the trust was too wide and uncertain to be included within the class; and Harman, L.J., added the caution that at some time, it might be necessary to consider whether the anomalous cases where trusts for animals and monuments had been accepted as valid had been wrongly decided.

More recently, in *Re Denley's Trust Deed*,[52] Goff, J., said that the objection was not that the trust was for a purpose or object *per se*, but the absence of a beneficiary; and that where the trust, though expressed as being for a purpose, was directly or indirectly for the benefit of individuals, it was outside the mischief of that objection. Accordingly he held valid a trust (expressed with certainty and complying with the rule against perpetuities) to maintain a sports ground for the benefit of employees of a company.

D. TRUSTS VOID AS AGAINST THE SETTLOR'S CREDITORS

1. UNDER THE LAW OF PROPERTY ACT 1925, s. 172

Whenever a creditor seeks to recover property which was once owned by his debtor, but which the debtor has attempted to place beyond his reach by transferring it to another (often the debtor's wife or children), there are two statutory provisions which may be of assistance to him. The first is section 44 of the Bankruptcy Act 1914, which allows the trustee in bankruptcy to set aside alienations of property made by the debtor otherwise than for value, under certain conditions. The other is section 172 of the Law of Property Act 1925. Although these two sections overlap in their application to a debtor's property, and are therefore often invoked together, they are based on different principles and are different in effect. For example, section 44 of the Bankruptcy Act 1914 is only applicable if bankruptcy proceedings are in progress, the initiative to set aside the settlement being taken by the trustee in bankruptcy. Moreover, under this section it is impossible to set aside transactions entered into by the debtor more than ten years before the bankruptcy. Finally, section 44 only applies to transactions entered into by the debtor without consideration. When section 172 of the Law of Property Act 1925 is relied upon, there need be no bankruptcy proceedings, there is no time limit in respect of the debtor's past transactions, and in certain circumstances, the section may apply to settlements for value.

Section 172 of the Law of Property Act 1925 is a section which is rather curiously drafted, and which has a lengthy history. It reads as follows—

> (1) Save as provided in this section, every conveyance of property, made whether before or after the commencement of this Act, with intent to defraud creditors, shall be voidable, at the instance of any person thereby prejudiced.

[52] [1969] 1 Ch. 373.

(2) This section does not affect the operation of a disentailing assurance, or the law of bankruptcy for the time being in force.

(3) This section does not extend to any estate or interest in property conveyed for valuable consideration and in good faith or upon good consideration and in good faith to any person not having, at the time of the conveyance, notice of the intent to defraud creditors.

As might be anticipated, the section (and its predecessors) have attracted a very extensive case law, but even so, it cannot be said that all problems arising out of it have been disposed of. It replaces the statute of 13 Eliz. I, c. 5, sometimes known as the Act against Fraudulent Deeds and Alienations, which was drafted in more elaborate terms. These terms are, however, not without importance in considering the extent of the application of the present section which, like the statute which it has replaced, has been given an extremely wide application, and which, it has been suggested, was itself declaratory of the common law. The Act of 1570 declares that it has been enacted " for the avoiding and abolishing of feigned, covinous and fraudulent feoffments, gifts, grants, alienations, conveyances, bonds, suits, judgments and executions, as well of lands and tenements as of goods and chattels ... which feoffments, gifts, grants, alienations, conveyances, bonds, suits, judgments and executions, have been and are devised and contrived of malice, fraud, covin, collusion or guile, to the end, purpose and intent, to delay, hinder or defraud creditors and others . . ."

Section 2 therefore provides that all transactions made for the " intent or purpose . . . declared . . . shall be . . . clearly and utterly void, frustrate and of none effect; any pretence, colour, feigned consideration, expressing of use, or any other matter or thing to the contrary notwithstanding."

Section 4 covers much of the ground now covered by section 172 (2), and section 6 deals with the saving proviso contained in section 172 (3) in the following way—

. . . this Act, or any thing therein contained, shall not extend to any estate or interest in lands, tenements, hereditaments, leases, rents, commons, profits, goods or chattels had, made, conveyed or assured, or hereafter to be had, made, conveyed or assured, which estate or interest is or shall be upon good consideration and *bona fide* lawfully conveyed or assured to any person or persons, or bodies politic or corporate, not having at the time of such conveyance or assurance to them made, any manner of notice or knowledge of such covin, fraud or collusion as is aforesaid; any thing before mentioned to the contrary hereof notwithstanding.

It is worth while remembering that, although the language of the Elizabethan statute is more prolix than that of section 172, it is freer from ambiguity. For example, the insertion, in section 172 (3) of " and in good faith " at the point at which it appears has puzzled a number of people. Obviously the transferor could not give in good faith, and the good faith of the recipient is covered by the first words of the subsection. The subsection would have been less ambiguous if it had read: " This section does not extend to any estate or interest in property conveyed for valuable consideration or upon good consideration to any person taking in good faith and not having, at the time of the conveyance, notice of the intent to defraud creditors." In fact it is in this sense that the courts have always construed it. Moreover, the courts, remembering the language of the earlier statute, have always treated it, and its modern successor, as applicable to all types of transfer of property of every kind. In *Cadogan* v. *Kennett*[53] Lord Mansfield had observed that the Elizabethan statute " cannot receive too liberal a construction, or be too much extended in suppression of fraud," and in expressing this view, he was doing no more than express what had already been said in *Twyne's Case* in 1601,[54] where it was declared that all statutes against fraud should be liberally expounded in order to secure its suppression.

The principle which the statute embodies is not peculiar to English law. Justinian's *Digest*[55] states that all acts done by debtors to defraud their creditors should be revoked, and this has been incorporated into numerous modern legal systems, including Scottish law. In Scotland, however, a statute of 1621, closely following the Elizabethan statute, placed this branch of the law on a statutory basis.

Although there is considerable difference between the wording of the Elizabethan statute and section 172, the general tendency has been to regard the bulk of the pre-1925 decisions as equally applicable to section 172. Harman, J., dealt with this question in *Re Eichholz*[56] and referred to the judgment of du Parcq, L.J., in *Westminster Bank Ltd.* v. *Riches.*[57] He was there considering the Law Reform Act 1934, which repealed and replaced part of the Civil Procedure Act 1833, and he remarked[58]—

> Citations from cases referring to sections 28 and 29 of the Civil Procedure Act, 1833, are, in my opinion, of doubtful assistance. Indeed, I am of opinion that when the legislature has repealed a statute and has not re-enacted it, but replaced it with a new enactment in different terms, it is in general a salutary rule that such case law as has accumulated round the repealed statute should be regarded as having expired with it.

A different course, however, has been followed in respect of section 172. The Law of Property Act has been regarded as a consolidating statute, and the earlier decisions on the Elizabethan statute have been treated as generally applicable. This, for example, has been particularly the case in respect of the transactions affected by the section. The Elizabethan statute spoke of transactions " by writing or otherwise," whilst section 172 speaks of " conveyances " (which suggests writing). However, Harman, J., in *Re Eichholz*[59] pointed out that in *Kerr on Fraud and Mistake*[60] it is stated that section 172 " applies to every conveyance of property. 13 Elizabeth, Chapter 4, employed several words more or less synonymous with conveyance and several words more or less synonymous with property. There is no reason to suppose that the new section is in any respect narrower or wider than the old statute.

---

[53] (1776), 2 Cowp. 432, 434.
[54] 3 Co.Rep. 80b.
[55] Book 42, tit. 8, para. 1.
[56] [1959] Ch. 708, 726.
[57] [1945] Ch. 381.
[58] [1945] Ch. 388.
[59] [1959] Ch. 728.
[60] 7th ed., p. 304.

Early decisions under the statute limited its application to property which could be taken to satisfy debts, and the long historical development by which almost all property can now be taken in satisfaction of its owner's debts is traced in the preceding edition of this book. It is now safe to say that the section applies to any property." Section 172, however, contains a further change from the language of the Elizabethan statute, the effect of which is by no means clear. The Elizabethan statute excepted from its operation conveyances to persons who took in good faith upon *good* consideration. To these section 172 has added persons who take in good faith for *valuable* consideration. Once again it may be asked whether this change has any deep significance. Before doing so, however, it is first necessary to discover what meaning has been placed upon the phrase " good consideration " in the Elizabethan Act. The courts have consistently held in recent times that this meant " valuable consideration " only, even though there were early indications that a settlement made in favour of a wife and children, and made in consideration of natural love and affection (*i.e.* " good " consideration), was upon the same footing as a settlement made for valuable consideration.[61] This view, however, was not maintained, and throughout the nineteenth century the decisions proceeded undeviatingly upon the principle that a settlement in favour of a wife and children was treated in exactly the same way as a voluntary settlement and, if made with intent to defeat or delay creditors, was voidable at the instance of the creditors, irrespective of the good faith of the beneficiaries. So also were settlements made upon entirely inadequate consideration.[62]

Section 172 of the Law of Property Act 1925, however, expressly included " good consideration " as well as " valuable consideration," and the plain inference from such inclusion would seem to be that settlements made in favour of a wife and children, in consideration of natural love and affection, have now been placed upon the same footing as settlements for valuable consideration. This, at any rate, is the view of the learned editors of the seventh edition of *Kerr on Fraud and Mistake*, for they observe [63]—

> Conveyances grounded on meritorious consideration alone, or on a consideration entirely inadequate, which were formerly looked on as voluntary, will not now so be treated.

In view of this plain statement, the absence of any discussion of this question in the report of Harman, J.'s judgment in *Re Eichholz* [64] is the harder to understand. In that case, the deceased married Mrs. Eichholz as his second wife on 18 January 1955. By a contract dated 14 February 1955, he agreed to buy a house for £15,500, and by a letter to his bank, of the same date, he requested a loan for the purchase which, he stated, was for his wife's benefit. On 15 March 1955, the house was conveyed to the wife in fee simple. The husband died on 17 November 1957, heavily insolvent, and it was found that he had also been insolvent at the date when the house was purchased. Accordingly, the creditors claimed the house from the widow, claiming either

---

[61] *Tyre* v. *Littleton* (1612), 2 Brownl. 187; *Lord Townshend* v. *Windham* (1750), 2 Ves. Sen. 1.
[62] *Strong* v. *Strong* (1854), 18 Beav. 408.
[63] p. 341.
[64] [1959] Ch. 708.

that she was a trustee of it for her husband or, alternatively, that they were entitled to recover the house under section 172 of the Law of Property Act 1925. On the first ground the creditors obviously could not succeed. Where a husband puts property in the name of his wife, there is a presumption that he intends to confer a benefit on her, thus negativing the usual presumption of an implied trust for the husband. Altogether apart from the presumption of advancement, however, there was clear evidence, in the husband's letter to the bank, written on the same day as the contract, that the husband intended the wife to take the house beneficially, and not as trustee. The creditors were therefore compelled to rely on section 172.

From this point of view, the questions of consideration and the good faith of the wife were all important. Harman, J., in his judgment, expressly found that the widow took in good faith, and without any knowledge of the husband's insolvency. He then went on to deal with the argument advanced on behalf of the wife that the gift of the house was made in consideration of marriage, and he found that there was no evidence that, before marriage, Mr. Eichholz had undertaken to provide a house for her, and he concluded this part of his judgment by saying: " Accordingly, I reject the argument that there was any consideration for the gift." Valuable consideration there certainly was not, but the question of good consideration does not appear to have been argued, nor does the question of law, or the extent of the change of the law which may have been introduced by the changed wording of section 172. This is the more remarkable, as Harman, J., quoted at length the language of the Elizabethan statute in order to compare it with section 172 of the Law of Property Act 1925. Indeed, he discussed at length the effect of the difference in wording on another point, and concluded on that point that the observations of Scrutton, L.J., in *Gilbert* v. *Gilbert* [65] and of Romer, L.J., in *Re Turner's Will Trusts*,[66] that, in construing a consolidating Act, one starts from the principle that the Act is not intended to alter the law, were applicable. This, however, is merely a presumption, and it cannot be pressed too far, more especially as the Law of Property Act *did* change the law on a very considerable number of points.[67] We are therefore left with the fact that Harman, J., in *Re Eichholz* [68] reached his decision upon the question of consideration on the basis that there was no valuable consideration, and the question of " good consideration," *i.e.* natural love and affection, was not discussed. Since decisions upon section 172 tend to arise with some frequency, this is a matter which will no doubt be discussed at some future date.

It should be noticed that the facts given in the report of *Re Eichholz* [68] not only established that the wife took in good faith, but also suggest that she enjoyed the real benefit of the transaction. This differentiates the case from *Gascoigne* v. *Gascoigne*,[69] a case in which a husband again placed property in his wife's name for the purpose of defeating creditors, and to the knowledge of the wife, but in subsequent proceedings by him the wife sought

---

[65] [1928] P. 1, 8.
[66] [1937] Ch. 15, 24 (Cases, p. 331).
[67] Actually, the 1925 Act did not change the law, but consolidated a series of Acts passed from 1922-24 which themselves changed the law (in so far as they came into force) or would have changed the law if they had not been repealed before they came into force.
[68] [1959] Ch. 708.
[69] [1918] 1 K.B. 223.

to establish that the transaction was really one of advancement. The Divisional Court held that, *as between husband and wife,* the husband could not set up his own intended fraud on creditors to defeat the presumption of advancement. Of course, nothing in this decision adversely affects the right of the creditors to set aside such a transaction, should they seek to do so.

Where the court holds that a settlement is made with the intent of defeating or defrauding creditors, it can always be set aside as regards a volunteer, but in respect of settlements made for good or valuable consideration, the transferee can successfully resist this if he can show, not only that there was consideration, but also good faith on his part. A substantial consideration may itself be evidence of good faith, but Lord Mansfield pointed out in *Cadogan* v. *Kennett* [70] that there had been several cases in which a debtor had transferred goods for a full and fair price, but since the debtor had intended to defraud creditors, the transaction had been set aside. In such cases, of course, the purchasers had been aware of the transferor's intention, and were willing to become parties to it. In *Lloyds Bank Ltd.* v. *Marcan,* [71] too, where a lease by a husband to his wife at a rack rent was set aside under section 172, the wife had actual notice of the husband's intention to defraud a creditor.

Twyne's Case [72] itself is an excellent illustration of the same point. Pierce was indebted to Twyne for £400, and to Chamberlain for £200. Chamberlain sued Pierce upon the debt, whereupon Pierce transferred his assets, which amounted to about £300, to Twyne in satisfaction of his debt of £400. Chamberlain, having obtained judgment upon his debt, then sought to recover the £300 from Twyne, and the Court of Star Chamber held that the transfer of the assets was within 13 Eliz. I, c. 5, and although made for valuable consideration, the transferee, Twyne, was a party to Pierce's fraudulent intent, and the transfer should therefore be set aside.

Even marriage settlements have been set aside on this ground, although in the ordinary case, the wife and, *a fortiori,* the children of the marriage, will take in good faith. However, in *Colombine* v. *Penhall* [73] Stuart, V.-C., pointed out that if there were evidence that the marriage was part of a scheme to protect property against creditors, and the wife was aware of it, the settlement founded upon the marriage could not stand, if the creditors attacked it. In that case, a man married his mistress within two months of his bankruptcy, and before doing so he transferred all his property upon trust for his wife and children, although it remained under the husband's control until the bankruptcy. Stuart, V.-C., held that the settlement must be set aside. *Bulmer* v. *Hunter* [74] was a similar case, in which the principle laid down in *Colombine* v. *Penhall* was approved and applied, but it should be emphasised that, in such cases, the creditors will have to produce evidence that the wife was actually a party to the fraud. It is not sufficient to show simply that the wife knew the husband was indebted, even heavily indebted. The court in such cases will have to decide what the wife's dominating motive was.

[70] (1776), 2 Cowp. 432, 434.
[71] [1973] 1 W.L.R. 1387 (C.A.).
[72] (1601), 3 Co.Rep. 80b.
[73] (1853), 1 Sm. & Giff. 228, 256.
[74] (1869), L.R. 8 Eq. 46.

The cases have established the principle that if there is any intent to defeat or defraud *any* creditors, then the settlement may subsequently be set aside, subject to the exception in favour of a transferee taking in good faith when the settlement in transfer is for value. This is well illustrated by the case of *Re Butterworth* [75] in which a person who had prospered as a baker, on the eve of purchasing a grocery business, which he intended to undertake in addition to his bakery, made a voluntary settlement of most of his property upon his wife and children. He did this because, although he was not at the time indebted, he wished to minimise the risk of loss as a result of conducting the grocery business. After conducting the grocery business for six months, and being somewhat disappointed at the result of his efforts, he sold the grocery business for as much as he gave for it. He continued in the bakery business for another three years, when he became insolvent, and the creditors sought to set aside the settlement. This was resisted on the grounds: (1) that at the time of the settlement, the baker was fully solvent, and any debts which might then have existed had been paid; and (2) although the object of making the settlement might have been to defeat the creditors of the grocery business, this situation had not arisen, as the grocery business had been sold. The court held, however, that the intention to defeat or defraud *any* creditors was sufficient to cause the settlement to be set aside.

Although the word " defraud " is frequently used to describe the debtor's conduct, it is not necessary that he should have been guilty of fraud, in any common usage of that term. It is sufficient to show that his motive at the time of the transfer was to defeat or delay his creditors, *i.e.* to attempt to put property beyond their reach.[76] It is not always easy to do this, especially when a considerable interval of time has elapsed since the transfer, and accordingly, it is not surprising to find that, in most cases, the actual financial position of the debtor at the time of transfer has been considered to be a matter of direct relevance. As long ago as Lord Hardwicke's decision in *Lord Townshend* v. *Windham* [77] it was established that if a person who was substantially indebted executed a transfer, the settlement or conveyance might be set aside by his creditors, and following that decision, it was occasionally suggested that *any* indebtedness might give the creditors ground for invoking the statute. This, however, was to give the statute too wide a sphere of operation, and the suggestion was disposed of by Lord Langdale, M.R., in *Townsend* v. *Westacott* [78] when he said—

> There has been a little exaggeration in the arguments on both sides as to the principle on which the Court acts in such cases as these : on one side it has been assumed that the existence of any debts at the time of the execution of the deed would be such evidence of a fraudulent intention as to induce the Court to set aside a voluntary conveyance, and oblige the Court to do so under the Statute of Elizabeth. I cannot think the real and just construction of the statute warrants that proposition, because there is scarcely any man who can avoid being indebted to some amount : he may intend to pay every debt as soon as it is contracted, and constantly

75 (1882), 19 Ch.D. 588.
76 See *Lloyds Bank Ltd.* v. *Marcan*, [1973] 1 W.L.R. 339, 344, *per* Pennycuick, V.-C.
77 (1750), 2 Ves.Sen. 1.
78 (1840), 2 Beav. 340, 344–345.

use his best endeavours, and have ample means to do so, and yet may be frequently, if not always, indebted in some small sum: there may be a withholding of claims, contrary to his intention, by which he is kept indebted in spite of himself; it would be idle to allege this as the least foundation for assuming fraud or any base intention. On the other hand, it is said that something amounting to insolvency must be proved to set aside a voluntary conveyance: this too, is inconsistent with the principle of the Act, and with the judgments of the most eminent Judges.

This principle has been consistently acted upon, and one extremely good example is to be found in *Freeman* v. *Pope*,[79] a case in which a clergyman, who was being pressed by his creditors, transferred his only considerable asset, a policy of insurance upon his life, to his god-daughter, Mrs. Pope. There was no suggestion whatever that the transferor had any fraudulent intent, but the Lord Chancellor and Gifford, L.J., on appeal, decided that since the transaction had the effect of delaying creditors, that, coupled with the transferor's indebtedness, was sufficient to permit the settlement to be set aside, and Lord Hatherley, L.C., in the course of an illuminating judgment explained the principle upon which the court acts with some fullness [80]—

> The principle on which the statute ... proceeds is this, that persons must be just before they are generous, and that debts must be paid before gifts can be made.
>
> The difficulty the Vice-Chancellor seems to have felt in this case was, that if he, as a special juryman, had been asked whether there was actually any intention on the part of the settlor in this case to defeat, hinder, or delay his creditors, he should have come to the conclusion that he had no such intention. With great deference to the view of the Vice-Chancellor, and with all the respect which I most unfeignedly entertain for his judgment, it appears to me this does not put the question exactly on the right ground; for it would never be left to a special jury to find, *simpliciter,* whether the settlor intended to defeat, hinder, or delay his creditors without a direction from the Judge that if the necessary effect of the instrument was to defeat, hinder, or delay the creditors, that necessary effect was to be considered as evidencing an intention to do so. A jury would undoubtedly be so directed, lest they should fall into the error of speculating as to what was actually passing in the mind of the settlor, which can hardly ever be satisfactorily ascertained, instead of judging of his intention by the necessary consequences of his act, which consequences can always be estimated from the facts of the case. Of course there may be cases—of which *Spirett* v. *Willows* [81] is an instance—in which there is direct and positive evidence of an intention to defraud, independently of the consequences which may have followed, or which might have been expected to follow, from the act. In *Spirett* v. *Willows* the settlor, being solvent at the time, but having contracted a considerable debt, which would fall due in the course of a few weeks, made a voluntary settlement by which he withdrew a large portion of his property

---

[79] (1870), L.R. 5 Ch.App. 538.
[80] L.R. 5 Ch.App. 540–541.
[81] (1865), 3 De G.J. & S. 293.

from the payment of debts, after which he collected the rest of his assets and (apparently in the most reckless and profligate manner) spent them, thus depriving the expectant creditor of the means of being paid. In that case there was clear and plain evidence of an actual intention to defeat creditors. But it is established by the authorities that in the absence of any such direct proof of intention, if a person owing debts makes a settlement which subtracts from the property which is the proper fund for the payment of those debts, an amount without which the debts cannot be paid, then, since it is the necessary consequence of the settlement (supposing it effectual) that some creditors must remain unpaid, it would be the duty of the Judge to direct the jury that they must infer the intent of the settlor to have been to defeat or delay his creditors, and that the case is within the statute.

It is not necessary, therefore, that at the time of the settlement the settlor should be, in the strict sense, insolvent, although this has occasionally been suggested.[82] It is sufficient if the settlor is so heavily indebted that the execution of the settlement will tip the scale against his solvency. In these cases, it has been said that the burden of proving solvency at the date of the settlement is upon the settlor himself,[83] and as a necessary consequence he must furnish a statement of his assets at that time. The process of determining their true value may sometimes be difficult, and the decisions have settled a large number of particular questions. For example, if one of the assets is a business, its goodwill should not be included. On the other hand, a contingent liability, such as a guarantee, should be taken into account.

One point must also be made. Quite apart from the question of indebtedness, a settlement is void under section 172 against subsequent creditors, if it is made with the actual intention of defeating, delaying, or defrauding creditors, even though at the time of settlement there were, in fact, no creditors. There are a considerable number of decisions establishing this proposition, but it will be sufficient to recall the facts of *Re Butterworth*.[84]

2. UNDER THE LAW OF PROPERTY ACT 1925, s. 173

By 27 Eliz. I, c. 4, as interpreted by the courts, a voluntary settlement of *land* was formerly liable to be upset by a subsequent conveyance by the settlor to a purchaser for value. There was a presumed intention to defraud the purchaser here. The position was modified by the Voluntary Conveyances Act 1893, but both statutes have now been repealed and replaced by section 173 of the Law of Property Act 1925, which provides that every voluntary disposition of land made with intent to defraud a subsequent purchaser is voidable at the instance of that purchaser; but for the purposes of the section, no voluntary disposition, whenever made, is to be deemed to have been made with intent to defraud by reason only that a subsequent conveyance for valuable consideration was made.

---

[82] *e.g. Lush* v. *Wilkinson* (1800), 5 Ves. 384.
[83] *Townsend* v. *Westacott* (1840), 2 Beav. 340; *Crossley* v. *Elworthy* (1871), L.R. 12 Eq. 158.
[84] (1882), 19 Ch.D. 588: see p. 147, *ante*.

3. UNDER THE BANKRUPTCY ACT 1914, s. 42 (1)

The Bankruptcy Act 1914, s. 42 (1), provides that a voluntary settlement [85] of property may, under certain conditions, be avoided by the subsequent bankruptcy of the settlor, although it is not fraudulent. Such a settlement is void as against the trustee in bankruptcy if the settlor becomes bankrupt within two years after the date of the settlement, even though the bankrupt was solvent at the time when the settlement was made. Furthermore, the settlement, if made more than two years before bankruptcy, but within ten years thereof, is void (which is judicially interpreted as voidable) against the trustee in bankruptcy unless the persons claiming under the settlement can prove (i) that the settlor was, at the date when the settlement was made, able to pay all his debts without the aid of the property settled [86]; and (ii) that his interest in that property passed to the trustee of the settlement.

This subsection does not apply to settlements made before or in consideration of marriage, nor in favour of a purchaser in good faith and for value (neither of which are voluntary), nor to those made on or for the wife or children of the settlor of property which has accrued to the settlor after marriage in right of his wife. *Re Mathieson,*[87] however, rules that the section applies only to settlements of the settlor's own property, or property in which he has a beneficial interest, and does not apply to settlements made in exercise of a general power of appointment.

It applies, however, where the debtor supplies the purchase-money for the sale of a house to a wife, and subsequently becomes bankrupt.[88]

The section says the settlements are " void," but actually it has been held that they are voidable, from which it follows—

1. The trustee in bankruptcy has to make an application to the court to have the settlement set aside.[89]

2. If a third party has bona fide and for value acquired the beneficiary's interest, the settlement cannot be set aside, if he had no notice of the act of bankruptcy.[90]

3. The effect of avoiding the settlement is only to set it aside to the extent necessary for satisfying the settlor's debts and the bankruptcy costs.[91]

Further, by section 42 (2), where an ante-nuptial settlement includes a covenant to pay money in the future for the benefit of the settlor's wife or husband or children, or for the settlement of future acquired property in which the settlor on marriage had no interest for those purposes (and not being property acquired in right of husband or wife) then if that settlement or covenant has not been executed at the date of bankruptcy, it is void against the trustee in bankruptcy, except that the beneficiaries may prove their claim in the bankruptcy, although these claims will be postponed to those of other creditors for valuable consideration in money. A good illustration

---

85 See *Re Schebsman,* [1943] Ch. 366; [1944] Ch. 83 (C.A.); *Re Macadam,* [1950] 1 All E.R. 303. See also the Matrimonial Causes Act 1973, s. 39.
86 This means without the aid of the property which by the settlement passes to other persons: *Re Lowndes* (1887), 18 Q.B.D. 677; *Re Baker,* [1936] Ch. 61.
87 [1927] 1 Ch. 283.
88 *Re A Debtor,* [1965] 1 W.L.R. 1498.
89 *Re Brall,* [1893] 2 Q.B. 381.
90 *Re Carter and Kenderdine's Contract,* [1897] 1 Ch. 776.
91 *Re Parry,* [1904] 1 K.B. 129.

of the effect of this subsection is afforded by *Re Cumming and West.*[92] In 1910, A married X, and executed an ante-nuptial settlement which included a covenant to keep up a policy of insurance on his life and to pay premiums. He then entered into business in partnership with B, and in 1927 both partners were adjudicated bankrupt. On their bankruptcy, the trustees of the settlement lodged a proof in A's bankruptcy, for a sum which was equivalent to the single payment which would be necessary to convert the policy into a fully-paid policy. The court held that the claim of the settlement trustees must be postponed until not only A's creditors, but also the partnership creditors of A and B, had been paid in full.

Moreover, even where such property has actually been transferred, the trustee in bankruptcy can avoid the transfer unless the beneficiary can prove: (a) that it was made more than two years before the commencement of the bankruptcy, or (b) that at the date of the transfer the settlor was able to pay all his debts without the aid of that property; or (c) that the payment or transfer was made in pursuance of a covenant or contract to pay or transfer money or property expected to come to the settlor from or on the death of a specified person, and was made within three months after the money or property came within the settlor's control. If the payment or transfer under this subsection (s. 42 (3)) is declared void, the beneficiary can also claim a dividend under the covenant in like manner as if it had not been executed at the commencement of the bankruptcy, *i.e.* after the other creditors have been paid in full.

The term " settlement " as used in section 42 includes any conveyance or transfer of property,[93] but it is not necessary that the property should be transferred by the settlor to a trustee or beneficiary. It is enough if the settlor declares himself a trustee for the beneficiary.[94] However, the term extends only to property in the hands of the beneficiary when bankruptcy supervened, or else which is invested in forms which are traceable, or which has been changed into other identifiable property.[95] The beneficiary is liable to account for any property in its original or changed form which remains under his control, but he is not liable to restore property which he has disposed of before the date of the bankruptcy.[96]

E. DISCRETIONARY, PROTECTIVE AND OTHER SIMILAR TRUSTS

It is impossible to create a trust with a stipulation that the beneficiary's interest may not be alienated, if the property has been given absolutely.[97] Furthermore, a trust must not contain a stipulation that the beneficiary's interest shall not be subject to the claims of creditors. The fact to be established is whether the beneficiary was intended to take a vested interest. If he was, though the trustees had a discretion with regard to the time and

---

92 [1929] 1 Ch. 534. Followed in *Re A Debtor*, [1947] Ch. 313. See also *Re Howes*, [1934] Ch. 49.
93 *Ex parte Todd* (1887), 19 Q.B.D. 186.
94 *Shrager* v. *March*, [1908] A.C. 402.
95 *Re Player* (1885), 15 Q.B.D. 682 ; *Re Plummer*, [1900] 2 Q.B. 790.
96 *Re Tankard*, [1899] 2 Q.B. 57 ; *Re Plummer*, [1900] 2 Q.B. 790.
97 *Re Dugdale* (1888), 38 Ch.D. 176.

mode of payment, then the interest is available for satisfaction of the beneficiary's creditors. In *Snowdon* v. *Dales*,[98] the trustees were directed to pay the interest of a sum of money to A for life, or during such part thereof as the trustees should think proper, and at their will and pleasure, but not otherwise, and so that A should not have any right, title, claim or demand, other than the trustees should think proper; after A's death, to pay the interest to his widow for life; and after her death to assign principal and " all savings or accumulations of interest, if any," to the children. The court held that upon the construction of the whole of the instrument, the trustees had no power to withhold and accumulate any portion of the interest during A's lifetime, and, accordingly, on his bankruptcy, A's creditors became absolutely entitled. (Here the trustees were directed to apply the whole income at their discretion.)

Where, however, the trust is not exclusively for the benefit of the bankrupt, but is for the benefit of the bankrupt and another, the creditors may only take so much as was intended for the bankrupt. In *Page* v. *Way*,[99] trustees were directed to apply the annual profits of property " for the maintenance and support of F. Jones, his wife and children (if any); or otherwise, if they should so think proper, permit the same . . . to be received by the said F. Jones " for his life. Jones became bankrupt, with a wife, but no children, and the court held that the wife should be supported out of the property. Whilst the wife was maintained by Jones, the trustees had a discretion to give him the whole income, but it was their duty to see that the wife was maintained. When, as a result of his bankruptcy, Jones could no longer receive the whole income, the trustees must maintain the wife out of the property, and it must be referred to a Master to settle what a proper allowance was.

Again, in *Godden* v. *Crowhurst*,[1] trustees were directed to pay the proceeds of residuary personalty to the testator's son for life, with a direction that if he did any act whereby the interest vested in him would become forfeited to others, the trustees were to apply the annual income ' for the maintenance and support of [the son] and any wife and child or children he might have, . . . as [the trustees] . . . should, in their discretion, think fit. . . ." The court held that nothing was directed to be paid; it was to be applied, and, therefore, the persons named might be maintained without their receiving anything at all. Accordingly, on the son's bankruptcy, nothing passed to the trustee in bankruptcy.

A person may settle property on A for life, until alienation or bankruptcy, and when that happens, the interest shall pass to B, or with a proviso that when the event happens, the interest shall shift over to B. This is what is known as a protective trust, and its validity was recognised at the beginning of the nineteenth century.[2] During the intervening period such clauses have become very common, and they are now given statutory recognition in the Trustee Act, section 33, which provides that where *any income* (including

---

[98] (1834), 6 Sim. 524.
[99] (1840), 3 Beav. 20.
[1] (1842), 10 Sim. 642.
[2] *Brandon* v. *Robinson* (1811), 18 Ves. 429, 433–434. See also Keeton, *Modern Developments in the Law of Trusts*, pp. 190–200; Sheridan, " Protective Trusts " (1957) 21 *Conveyancer* 110.

an annuity or other periodical income payment) is directed to be held on protective trusts [3] for the benefit of a person (termed the principal beneficiary) for his life or a less period, the income shall, without prejudice to any prior interest, be held on the following trusts—

1. Upon trust for the principal beneficiary during the trust period or until he, whether before or after the termination of any prior interest, does or attempts to do anything whereby, if the said income were payable during the trust period to the principal beneficiary absolutely during that period, he would be deprived of the right to receive the same or a part thereof, in any of which cases, as well as on the termination of the trust period, whichever first happens, the trust of the income shall fail or determine;

2. If the trust does fail or determine during the trust period, then for the residue of that period, the income shall be held upon trust for the maintenance or support, or otherwise for the benefit of all or any one or more of the others of the following persons at the absolute discretion of the trustees—

(a) The principal beneficiary, the wife or husband of such, and the issue (including, under the Family Law Reform Act 1969, s. 15 (3), in respect of any disposition made after the section came into force, illegitimate issue and issue of illegitimate issue) of them;

(b) If there is no wife, husband or issue, then the principal beneficiary, and the persons who would, if he were actually dead, be entitled to the trust property or the income thereof.

The section does not apply to trusts coming into operation before the Act, and takes effect subject to any variation of the above interests which may be contained in the instrument.[4] Furthermore, the section does not make valid any trust otherwise invalid,[5] e.g. a settlement by a person upon himself until bankruptcy.[6]

Where a sequestration of the tenant for life's property occurs, this puts an end to the protected life interest, and the discretionary trust arises.[7] Similarly there is a forfeiture where the principal beneficiary resides in enemy-controlled territory.[8] In a specially drawn protective trust, however, this result may be avoided.[9] There is also forfeiture of the husband's protected life interest where an order of the Family Division is made, charging the husband's protected interest with payments to the wife.[10]

Before 1926 it was the custom to insert clauses into personalty settlements, made by husband and wife before marriage, creating such protective and

---

[3] On which, see *Re Isaacs* (1948), 92 S.J. 336.

[4] s. 33 (2).

[5] s. 33 (3).

[6] *Higinbotham* v. *Holme* (1812), 19 Ves. 88; *Re Burroughs-Fowler*, [1916] 2 Ch. 251.

[7] *Re Baring's Settlement Trusts*, [1940] Ch. 737. For a forfeiture of the life interest on settlement of a part of the income, see *Re Dennis's Settlement Trusts*, [1942] Ch. 283, and *Re Haynes Will Trusts*, [1949] Ch. 5. There is no forfeiture of the protected life interest on the appointment of a receiver in lunacy: *Re Westby's Settlement*, [1950] Ch. 296; Law Reform (Miscellaneous Provisions) Act 1949, s. 8.

[8] For the effect of such a forfeiture, see *Re Gourju's Will Trusts*, [1943] Ch. 24, and *Re Wittke*, [1944] Ch. 166, decided on s. 7 of the Trading with the Enemy Act 1939. For the present position, see Trading with the Enemy (Custodian) (Specified Persons) Order 1946 (S.R. & O. 1946, No. 1040).

[9] *Re Pozot's Settlement Trusts*, [1952] Ch. 427.

[10] *Re Richardson's Will Trusts*, [1958] Ch. 504. See also R.E.M. (1958) 74 *Law Quarterly Review* 182.

discretionary trusts in respect of the husband. This was achieved as follows: In respect of the *wife's* fortune, it was declared that the wife should enjoy it for life. This was followed by a protective trust, which recited that the income should be held on trust for the husband, if he survived his wife, until his death or until he did something whereby the interest passed from him. This prevented the interest from being lost in the event of the husband's bankruptcy, or if he attempted to alienate it to his creditors; and it was customary to insert a discretionary trust at this point, authorising the trustees to apply such part of the income as they thought fit, during the remainder of the husband's life, for the benefit of all or one or more of the members of a class of whom the husband was one, as the trustees should think fit. This would permit the trustees, if necessary, to apply the income for the benefit of the children.[11] There is, moreover, nothing to prevent the husband's property from being settled upon an *immediate* discretionary trust. Such clauses are still occasionally inserted in settlements, although they are implied in any settlement by which the income is directed to be held on protective trusts.

Where the settlement is for the benefit of a person until his bankruptcy, and it is desired that the interest should not pass to the trustee in bankruptcy, nothing must be paid to the beneficiary, or applied for his benefit, under the discretionary trust which arises after the life interest is forfeited, beyond what is absolutely necessary for his support, nor should it be paid to any other beneficiary with a secret trust for the benefit of the principal beneficiary who has become bankrupt.[12] The result is that the balance beyond this must be paid to or applied for the other objects designated in section 33, or by the instrument varying it.[13]

Purely discretionary trusts (*i.e.* not part of a protective trust mechanism) are often created,[14] and were even more popular before recent changes in estate duty law.[15]

Care must be taken in drafting a discretionary trust to ensure that the trusts do not fail for uncertainty,[16] and a discretionary trust is a kind of special power of appointment, so that the power of selection must be exercised within the perpetuity period. Each exercise of the trustees' discretion is regarded as a separate gift.[17] For this reason, it is a common practice to insert a provision that distributions shall not infringe the rule against perpetuities.[18] A superannuation fund may be registered under the Superannuation and other Trust Funds (Validation) Act 1927, under certain conditions,[19] and if it is, the application of the perpetuity rule is excluded.

It is of the essence of a discretionary trust that the trustees themselves

---

[11] For the effect of an order of the Family Division extinguishing the husband's interests under the settlement see *Re Allsopp's Marriage Settlement Trusts*, [1959] Ch. 81.

[12] *Holmes* v. *Penney* (1856), 3 K. & J. 90; *Re Ashby*, [1892] 1 Q.B. 872.

[13] See *Re Bullock* (1891), 60 L.J.Ch. 341; *Re Burroughs-Fowler*, [1916] 2 Ch. 251.

[14] See, generally, Sheridan, " Discretionary Trusts " (1957) 21 *Conveyancer* 55.

[15] See Chap. XXI, s. D, *post*, as to discretionary trusts and taxation.

[16] See pp. 102–103, *ante*.

[17] See *Re Coleman*, [1936] Ch. 528.

[18] On the construction of such clauses, see *I.R.C.* v. *Williams*, [1969] 1 W.L.R. 1197.

[19] See *Re Flavel's Will Trusts*, [1969] 1 W.L.R. 444. See also the Social Security Act 1973, s. 69.

should exercise the discretion.[20] Accordingly, if they cannot agree, they cannot surrender it to the court in advance, although they can apply to the courts for directions in respect of income which is actually available for distribution. They cannot retain the income for future distribution. If they decide to make a payment, and then disagree as to the remainder, the court will treat the discretion as at an end.[21]

In *Re Garside* [22] a testator, who died in 1893, devised freehold property on trust for sale, with a direction to apply the income, or any part of it, for the benefit of his eldest son for life, and on his death, he directed that it should pass to the residue. When the eldest son died in 1918, there was a fund comprising accumulated income, derived from income not applied for the son's benefit, in the hands of the trustees. The court held that there was a valid accumulation for 21 years, which was personalty under the trust for sale, and that the sums validly accumulated passed as capital residue under the bequest. Surplus accumulations beyond twenty-one years, however, could not pass as capital, and were distributed as income of the residue.

The object of a discretionary trust can release his right to be considered, thus ceasing to be an object.[23]

---

[20] See Hawkins, " The Exercise by Trustees of a Discretion " (1967) 31 *Conveyancer* 117, as to the position of the court when the trustees die or neglect or refuse to exercise their discretion. See also pp. 14–16, *ante*.
[21] *Re Allen-Meyrick's Will Trusts*, [1966] 1 W.L.R. 499. *Cf. Re Gulbenkian's Settlements* (*No. 2*), [1970] Ch. 408.
[22] [1919] 1 Ch. 132.
[23] *Re Gulbenkian's Settlements* (*No. 2*), [1970] Ch. 408.

CHAPTER XII

CHARITABLE TRUSTS

THE law of charitable trusts is a distinct branch of the law of charities, and it has contained until recently a number of rules not found elsewhere in the law of trusts. Some of these, such as the doctrine of mortmain, have at last been abolished by the Charities Act 1960, but others, such as the *cy-près* doctrine, have been retained, and the *cy-près* doctrine itself has been given an extended application. A full treatment of the law of charities would be inappropriate in a work dealing with trusts generally, and accordingly, the present chapter will consider only the evolution of the law of charities, the difficulties of definition, the problem of uncertainty and the *cy-près* doctrine.[1]

A. HISTORICAL INTRODUCTION

The law of charities had emerged as a distinct branch of equitable jurisdiction before Tudor times, the mediaeval law being primarily concerned with gifts, whether *inter vivos* or (more frequently) by will to pious uses. Very often such gifts were made to the Church, or to some priest, with a direction to apply them for the relief of poverty, either generally, or more particularly in some place, or for the benefit of some group, or for some other purpose of accepted public utility, such as the repair of churches, bridges or roads, or for the redemption of prisoners who might have been enslaved abroad. Indeed, it is apparent that the traditional branches of charitable activity, many of which were enumerated in the Statute of Charitable Uses 1601, are very ancient.

The Church was by no means the only charitable institution in the Middle Ages, however. Schools were established through the intervention of feoffees to uses, the colleges of Oxford and Cambridge existed as charitable corporations, whilst the guilds held much property for charitable purposes. Even before 1500, private benefaction had also been responsible for the creation of many small charitable trusts, administered by feoffees or trustees. Frequently, such small trusts were limited in their operation to a particular locality.

Before the close of the Middle Ages, two problems affecting charitable trusts had made their appearance. The first was the question of mortmain. Parliament, containing as it did extensive representation of landowners, disliked the accumulation of land in the hands of corporations (especially the Church) and trustees for charitable purposes, since this greatly reduced the value of the feudal dues payable in respect of land so held. The King shared this view, since, as the chief landowner, he was also the principal loser. Grants of land to corporations and charities were known as feoffments in

---

[1] For full treatment of the law of charities, see Keeton and Sheridan, *The Modern Law of Charities*, 2nd ed.; Tudor *on Charities*, 5th ed.; Keeton, *Modern Developments in the Law of Trusts*, pp. 276–313.

mortmain, the hand of the corporation being dead in the sense that it was no longer productive of benefits to the overlord. From the time of *Magna Carta* onwards, therefore, a succession of statutes prohibited the Church and other corporations from receiving grants of land without a licence from the Crown. Such a licence, which incidentally was an example of the royal dispensing power, was usually only obtained by payment of a fee; and in course of time the prohibition of alienation into mortmain was extended to charitable uses also. Although in the nineteenth century the old Statutes of Mortmain were repealed in the course of the reform of the law of real property which was then undertaken, their restrictive effect in relation to gifts to charities was retained in the Mortmain and Charitable Uses Acts of 1888, 1891 and 1892, and it was not until the passing of the Charities Act 1960 that the doctrine of mortmain ceased to have any application to charitable corporations and trusts.

The second problem in the law of charities which made its appearance at an early date was that of securing the proper administration of charitable trusts, and especially of ensuring that the funds were applied to the objects designated by the donor. This was a matter in which the church courts were originally interested, especially where gifts (of personalty) were made by wills, when the question would arise in the course of the administration of the testator's estate. However, from the fifteenth century onwards, the Chancellor and the Court of Chancery assumed and exercised this jurisdiction.

At this period resort to court was infrequent, and there could be no doubt that in respect of a very considerable number of small and local trusts, abuses in their administration existed unchecked. In some cases, no doubt, all knowledge of the original terms of the trust had been forgotten, and the trustees, possibly with the full approval of their neighbours, had deflected the funds to purposes which they considered socially desirable. In others, possibly, the trustees had misappropriated the funds. The primary difficulty in respect of enforcement was that, in many cases, no one suffered *directly* from misapplication of charitable funds. Moreover, even if someone did suffer, if he instituted proceedings in the Chancery, these would probably be lengthy and expensive, and the cost of them would fall primarily (and possibly ultimately) upon the complainant himself.

This problem is a recurrent one in the development of the law of charities, and it had become a problem of major importance by the close of the Tudor period. Professor Jordan [2] has shown that during the Tudor period there was a vastly-increased impetus towards charitable giving, mainly for secular purposes. Much of it was concerned with the aid of deserving poor (whose numbers had increased considerably as a consequence of the social changes of the sixteenth century), and with such matters as education and apprenticeship which (the successful Tudor merchant firmly believed) could enable the children of the deserving poor to achieve the same material success that the charitable donor himself had done. This growth of charitable giving for secular purposes coincided in time, and was linked, with the first efforts of the State to tackle the problem of poverty on a national scale. The first

---

[2] *Philanthropy in England* 1460–1660. See also Keeton and Sheridan, *The Modern Law of Charities*, 2nd ed., pp. 3–9.

national Poor Law Act was passed in 1601, the year in which the Statute of Charitable Uses was also passed.

The Statute of Charitable Uses was therefore legislation which sought to establish some system of control for the administration of charities, which was linked with the central government. It introduced commissions of enquiry, composed mainly of local magnates, usually magistrates, and sometimes accompanied by a judge, or an official of the Chancery. The commissions travelled the counties, enquiring into the existence of charitable donations and the manner in which they were administered. Where abuses were discovered, the commissioners had limited powers of correction, but cases of serious misappropriation were remitted to London for examination and determination by the Court of Chancery itself. Not all charitable gifts and foundations were subject to the jurisdiction of the commissioners. The Church, the colleges of Oxford and Cambridge, and some of the greater public schools were exempted from it, and this exemption, which seems to have made its first appearance in this Act, has been repeated in much of the later legislation where problems of administration have been tackled.

The system of commissions of enquiry worked well in the four decades which intervened between the death of Elizabeth I and the opening of the Civil War. They were resumed at the Restoration, but much of the impetus had been lost, and commissions ceased to conduct investigations in the early part of the eighteenth century. For the next century and a half, those who complained of abuses in the administration of charities were compelled to resort to the Court of Chancery. In view of the dilatory nature of Chancery proceedings at this period, and the steadily increasing expense of them, it is surprising that anyone did. From time to time, however, some body of charitable trustees was compelled to give satisfaction for long periods of maladministration, and in the early years of the nineteenth century, the machinery for the institution of enforcement proceedings was made rather more flexible.[3]

The next movement towards reform of the law of charities originated in the desire to improve the country's educational system, which was one of the early objectives of nineteenth-century liberalism. Before measures could be framed to achieve this, it was considered necessary to discover first what funds were actually in existence for providing education, or which could be applied to this object. It was with this specific object in view that Parliament, a few years after the close of the Napoleonic Wars, set up a fresh Commission of Enquiry, charged with the gigantic task of investigating and recording every charitable trust in the country, with some important exceptions. Once again, trusts for religious objects, the colleges at Oxford and Cambridge, and the public schools were expressly excepted from the work of the commission. The amount of evidence accumulated was immense, and once again the country learned with discomfort of the extent to which charitable funds had been misapplied or misappropriated. Some reformers therefore called for the creation of a strong Charity Commission with wide powers of supervision and control. Unfortunately, these desires were never satisfied. The

[3] For a full treatment of the developments prior to the second quarter of the nineteenth century, see Jones, *History of the Law of Charity* 1532–1827.

Charitable Trusts Act 1853 established the Charity Commission, it is true, but this new department was small, its powers were severely limited, its jurisdiction was concurrent with that of the High Court, and no Minister of State was charged with the duty of presenting to Parliament the proposals for the reform of the law of charities which the Commissioners from time to time prepared.[4]

The results of this timidity in the establishment of the Charity Commission were in the highest degree unfortunate. Many matters affecting the administration of charities were referred to the courts, which were ill-suited to deal with them, and the courts progressively resolved problems relating to the nature of a charitable gift in an atmosphere of rigid technicality which stands in striking contrast, for example, with the treatment of this question in Scottish courts. Although the Charities Act 1960 has introduced a number of overdue reforms in administration, has given the Charity Commissioners a number of additional powers, and for a limited number of purposes, has associated them with the Home Office, so that the Home Secretary will now be the main Minister responsible for charity matters in the House of Commons, that Act has done nothing to solve the extremely complex problem of definition, nor has it in any way altered the jurisdiction of the courts in this matter. The necessary consequence will be that the decisions will continue to accumulate, and they will probably continue to show the complete disregard for any unifying principles to determine what is, and what is not, a charitable gift that they have almost invariably shown in the past.

B. THE DEFINITION OF A CHARITY

The problem of defining what is a charitable gift or trust has always been, since the beginning of the seventeenth century, one of particular difficulty in English law, and the decisions have gradually made it one of very great (and possibly unnecessary) technicality. It might have been possible, for example, to define charitable gifts simply as gifts for public benefit, but the courts have consistently regarded this form of definition as too comprehensive, although in Scottish law (apart from questions of income tax, which will be mentioned later) this is the position which the courts have taken up. Historically, too, English law before 1600 tended to regard as charitable gifts for religion, almsgiving or public benefit. This is evidenced by the list of charitable purposes which was included in the Statute of Charitable Uses 1601. This list was as follows—

> The relief of aged, impotent and poor people; the maintenance of the sick, and maimed soldiers and mariners; schools of learning, free schools, and scholars in universities; the repair of bridges, ports, havens, causeways, churches, seabanks and highways; the education and preferment of orphans; the relief, stock or maintenance of houses of correction; the marriage of poor maids; the help of young tradesmen and persons decayed; the relief and redemption of prisoners or captives; and aid to poor inhabitants concerning payment of taxes.

[4] As to the origin and development of the law of charities, see Keeton and Sheridan, *The Modern Law of Charities*, 2nd ed., pp. 1-21.

Reference to the decisions upon charitable purposes at once shows that the courts have never regarded themselves as limited by this list, although in deciding whether the purpose which they were called upon to consider was charitable or not, they have frequently attempted to determine whether it was within the " spirit and intendment " of this list. Some of the decisions reached as a result of this enquiry have been surprising, and the list has proved a poor substitute for a general principle. Perhaps no other course was possible, for in any event, even in 1601, the list was not a complete enumeration of charitable objects, nor was it intended to be. It did no more than enumerate the types of gift which were to be within the scope of enquiries initiated by the Commissions of Enquiry, and it has already been mentioned that some of the most important charitable foundations in the country were excluded from the scope of their activities. Moreover, in one important respect, the sphere of charitable activity had been changed by the legislation which embodied the religious upheavals of the sixteenth century. Prior to the Reformation, a gift for religious purposes had necessarily been a gift to the Catholic Church and its institutions; and a great many gifts for the relief of poverty had also been entrusted to the Church for administration. At the Reformation, a prolonged effort was made to establish a national church, of which all subjects were deemed to be members. A gift for religious purposes to be valid was therefore necessarily a gift to the Anglican Church as established at the Reformation, and until the growth of toleration in the eighteenth century, a gift for any other church—even a nonconformist Protestant church —was not only not charitable, but invalid. In one instance, however, the State was prepared to go further. Some considerable time elapsed, and the Stuart dynasty had to be replaced by the Hanoverians, before the threat of a return to Rome ceased to haunt the minds of statesmen and legislators. The Reformation statutes for a time imposed heavy penalties upon those who celebrated mass or sought to propagate Roman Catholicism, and advantage was taken of the confiscatory language of two statutes, one of Henry VIII's reign, and the other of Edward VI, to develop the doctrine of " superstitious uses." As applied by the courts, this had the effect of deciding that gifts for the maintenance of certain distinctively Romish doctrines and practices were void. A fortiori, therefore, they were not charitable. Following the enactment of the Roman Catholic Relief Act 1829, any application of the doctrine of " superstitious uses " to the Roman Catholic faith generally was no longer possible, but there was a vestigial survival of the doctrine in the decision in West v. Shuttleworth in 1835 [5] that a bequest to Roman Catholic priests for the celebration of masses for the dead was still void as a superstitious use. It was therefore not until the decision of the House of Lords in Bourne v. Keane [6] that it was possible to reverse this anachronistic decision. After an exhaustive historical survey, the House of Lords decided in that case that a gift for the celebration of masses for the dead was not void as a superstitious use. The House of Lords did not decide, however, that such gifts were now valid as charitable gifts, although in Re Caus [7] a court of first instance took this

[5] 2 My. & K. 684.
[6] [1919] A.C. 815.
[7] [1934] Ch. 162.

further step. Even so, doubts have been thrown upon the correctness of this decision by members of the House of Lords in *Gilmour* v. *Coats*.[8]

A survey of the charity decisions will abundantly show (as many judges have recognised) that they conform to no general principle, or principles. The matter is complicated by the fact that legal charity includes a great many purposes which cannot be related to almsgiving, which is what the layman normally understands by the term. This was so even in Elizabethan times, as the list embodied in the Statute of 1601 shows. Some judges have stated that, although the term " public purposes " is wider than " charitable," nevertheless public benefit is a necessary element in charitable gifts. This, incidentally, assumes that what is for the public benefit can be determined, which in turn, prompts the question, who determines this, and according to what criterion? Broadly, however, this generalisation may be accepted, with one qualification. At the beginning of the nineteenth century, the courts accepted that gifts for the relief of poverty among poor relations were charitable gifts, and this view has been maintained in modern cases.[9] In recent discussions of these decisions,[10] it has been recognised that they are anomalous, and that they cannot be extended, for example, so as to permit gifts for the *education* of the donor's relations to be regarded as charitable. Nevertheless, the same principle has been applied to gifts for the relief of poverty (in the broad sense) among the employees, or ex-employees of a commercial company,[11] although had the trust been for the *education* of the employees or ex-employees of a firm, it would have failed to qualify as a charity.[12]

Since the Charities Act 1960 came into force, the problem of definition has been affected by another factor. The Act contains no definition of a charitable purpose, but it nevertheless repealed the preamble to the Statute of Charitable Uses. The assumption upon which this was based was that the case law nevertheless remained as binding as it was before repeal. Since, however, judges in deciding whether a gift was charitable or not, have repeatedly declared that the gift, to qualify, must be within the " spirit and intendment " of the Act of 1601, the obscurity which has always surrounded this question would appear to have been deepened by the Act of 1960.

It is frequently stated that the absence of any statutory attempt to define a charity is compensated by the classification of charities which is contained in certain observations of Lord Macnaghten in *Commissioners of Income Tax* v. *Pemsel*,[13] and these have been so frequently quoted by subsequent judges when faced with the necessity of determining whether a gift is charitable or not that the Nathan Report suggested that these observations should be given statutory force. This suggestion was not adopted, although the observations enjoy a

8 [1949] A.C. 426.

9 *Re Scarisbrick*, [1951] Ch. 622 (Cases, p. 267); *Re Cohen*, [1973] 1 W.L.R. 415.

10 *e.g.* in *Re Compton*, [1945] Ch. 123.

11 *Gibson* v. *South American Stores* (*Gath and Chaves*) *Ltd.*, [1950] Ch. 177; *Re Coulthurst*, [1951] Ch. 661; *Dingle* v. *Turner*, [1972] A.C. 601.

12 *Oppenheim* v. *Tobacco Securities Trust Co. Ltd.*, [1951] A.C. 297. See also *George Drexler Ofrex Foundation Trustees* v. *I.R.C.*, [1966] Ch. 675; *I.R.C.* v. *Educational Grants Association Ltd.*, [1967] Ch. 993.

13 [1891] A.C. 531, 583 (Cases, p. 261). As to the question of general principles governing the meaning of charity, see Keeton and Sheridan, *The Modern Law of Charities*, 2nd ed., pp. 22–51; Sheridan, " Charity versus Politics " (1973) 2 *Anglo-American Law Review* 47.

currency almost as wide as a statutory definition would have. They are as follows—

> " Charity " in its legal sense comprises four principal divisions: trusts for the relief of poverty; trusts for the advancement of education; trusts for the advancement of religion; and trusts for other purposes beneficial to the community, not falling under any of the preceding heads. The trusts last referred to are not the less charitable in the eye of the law, because incidentally they benefit the rich as well as the poor, as indeed, every charity that deserves the name must do either directly or indirectly.

Pemsel's case itself settled two extremely important questions. The first was that, in England, the scope of legal charity (however difficult it may be to define) is exactly the same for income-tax purposes as it is for the general law *i.e.* for gifts to charity. Secondly, it decided that, although the Scottish general law gives a wider significance to charity than English law does, nevertheless when questions of income-tax are being determined, the Scottish courts must apply the English law of charities. The consequence of this is that in Scotland, a gift may take effect as charitable, but it may still fail to qualify for the exemption from income-tax which, in English law, attaches to all charitable gifts. Not unnaturally, this conclusion has been productive of dissatisfaction in Scotland, but it was reaffirmed in *I.R.C.* v. *City of Glasgow Police Athletic Association.*[14]

It will be seen that in Lord Macnaghten's fourth, or residual, class, there is reference to " purposes beneficial to the community," and numerous judges have stated that all charitable trusts (with the exception of trusts for poor relations and poor employees) must include an element of public benefit. This may be so, although in some cases, this element is rather nebulous; nevertheless, the courts have also made it clear that not all gifts for the public benefit are charitable. The term " public benefit " is therefore wider than " charity " and in determining whether a gift for the public benefit is also charitable, it is therefore necessary to resort to some other test. If the gift is for the advancement of religion or education, or for the relief of poverty, the enquiry may well stop at that point. It is, however, when the question is whether the gift is within the fourth of Lord Macnaghten's classes that the problem becomes almost insoluble, and that the decisions sometimes appear arbitrary and unsatisfactory. A few points in connection with each of these four heads may, nevertheless, be usefully mentioned.

1. THE ADVANCEMENT OF RELIGION [15]

In the course of four centuries, the law of charities has moved from the extreme of exclusiveness, in which only gifts for the national church were recognised as charitable, to the position in which any religion, which is not subversive of public morality, is capable of being the object of a charitable gift. The court will not enter into any enquiry concerning the value of the religion, or even whether its followers are numerous, provided they exist.[16] Non-

---

[14] [1953] A.C. 380.
[15] Keeton and Sheridan, *The Modern Law of Charities*, 2nd ed., pp. 52–71.
[16] See the observations of Sir John Romilly, M.R., in *Thornton* v. *Howe* (1862), 31 Beav. 14, 19.

Christian religions qualify equally with the Christian religion, and equal treatment is given to all denominations of the Christian religion.

Nevertheless, the gift, to be valid as a charity, must be for the advancement of religion, and therefore a gift for a closed order of nuns is not charitable,[17] since the element of public benefit is lacking.

A gift for the advancement of religion in general terms is charitable; but so also are many gifts for specific religious purposes, *e.g.* for the increase of the stipends of the clergy,[18] for the improvement or upkeep of the fabric of the church,[19] or for the improvement of its services. A gift for the maintenance of a tomb in a church is charitable, since this is part of the fabric of the church,[19] and further, a gift for the maintenance of a churchyard, including the tombs in it, is also charitable,[20] but a gift for the erection or maintenance of a particular tomb in a churchyard is not.

2. THE ADVANCEMENT OF EDUCATION [21]

This branch of charity has also been given a liberal construction by the courts, provided that the necessary element of public benefit is reflected in the gift through the *advancement,* or furtherance, of some educational purpose.[22] Subject to this, education has been construed very widely indeed. It has even been held to include chess-playing among boys and youths,[23] the support of zoological gardens,[24] a gift for " finding " the Bacon-Shakespeare manuscripts,[25] and the publication of law reports.[26] On the other hand, a gift for the advancement of political education in association with a political party, and in furtherance of its aims, is not charitable.[27]

An educational trust must also benefit some cross-section of the community, considered in its public capacity, *e.g.* a gift for education within a locality, or within a profession. A gift for the education of the descendants of a particular person, or of the descendants of several persons, is not charitable, nor is a gift for the education of children of employees, or of ex-employees, of a firm.[28] It must be conceded that the distinction between gifts of this kind and gifts to establish " founder's kin " scholarships is a fine one; however, in " founder's kin " trusts, the element of public benefit is apparently satisfied by the provision that the scholarship may be competed for by persons generally, although a preference is expressed for the selection of persons having a blood relationship with the founder.

Modern legislation, such as the Education Acts and the National Health Service Act, by making universal free provision of many educational and

---

17 *Gilmour* v. *Coats*, [1949] A.C. 426.
18 *Middleton* v. *Clitherow* (1798), 3 Ves. 734.
19 *Hoare* v. *Osborne* (1866), L.R. 1 Eq. 585.
20 *Re Pardoe*, [1906] 2 Ch. 184. See also *Scottish Burial Reform and Cremation Society Ltd.* v. *Glasgow Corp.*, [1968] A.C. 138.
21 Keeton and Sheridan, *The Modern Law of Charities*, 2nd ed., pp. 72–86.
22 *Whicker* v. *Hume* (1858), 7 H.L.C. 124, 155.
23 *Re Dupree's Deed Trusts*, [1945] Ch. 16.
24 *Re Lopes*, [1931] 2 Ch. 130; *Re North of England Zoological Society*, [1959] 1 W.L.R. 773.
25 *Re Hopkins' Will Trusts*, [1965] Ch. 669.
26 *Incorporated Council of Law Reporting for England and Wales* v. *Attorney-General*, [1972] Ch. 73.
27 *Bonar Law Memorial Trust* v. *I.R.C.* (1933), 49 T.L.R. 220; *Re Hopkinson*, [1949] 1 All E.R. 346.
28 See p. 161, *ante.*

health services, may (as the Nathan Report noticed) have rendered obsolete various charitable trusts, and where a testator now seeks to set up a trust for such a service, the will must be given its natural construction, even though this may involve the failure of the trust.[29]

3. THE RELIEF OF POVERTY [30]

Gifts for the relief of poverty have always been regarded as charitable, whether such gifts are of sums of money for direct and immediate distribution, or whether they are directed to be applied for some more permanent end, such as the support of an organisation whose object is the relief of poverty, or the establishment of institutions, such as almshouses or homes for the aged. Here again, gifts must be, in general, for the relief of poverty amongst some class or section of the community, although it has already been noticed that, as exceptions to this general rule, gifts for the benefit of poor relations of the donor, and, more recently, gifts for the benefit of the widows and children of deceased ex-employees of a firm, have been regarded as charitable.[31]

Poverty is not an absolute concept, *i.e.* there is no condition that the recipients of gifts for the relief of poverty must be destitute. There can be, for example, perfectly good charitable gifts for the assistance of persons of limited means,[32] and where there is a gift for those members of a class or profession who are in need, the requirement of poverty is determined by reference to the general standard of the profession or class.

The statute of 1601 referred to the aged and the impotent separately from the poor. It has now been established [33] that the relief of old people's difficulties and similar purposes are charitable without proof that the objects of the charity are poor.

4. OTHER CHARITABLE PURPOSES

The innumerable charitable purposes which are collected together under Lord Macnaghten's fourth head are so miscellaneous that no principle links them, and decisions often appear to be quite arbitrary. Judges themselves frequently do not agree upon what should be included under this head, and it is apparent that reasoning by analogy is often no help, and may, indeed, be an obstacle, to a decision which on non-legal grounds may seem desirable.[34] They include: (1) the provision of relief for the aged,[33] bereaved persons, persons under disability, such as the blind or the maimed, and other persons in need of care, such as orphans, and this provision may be by building or maintaining homes, establishing a disaster fund, or otherwise [35]; (2) matters associated with health, such as the provision of hospitals, training of nurses, and some kinds of propaganda, *e.g.* in favour of temperance or against drugs or smoking cigarettes [36]; (3) care and treatment of animals [37]; (4) some—very

---

29 *Re Mackenzie*, [1962] 1 W.L.R. 880, where apparently no question of *cy-près* arose.
30 Keeton and Sheridan, *The Modern Law of Charities*, 2nd ed., pp. 99–106.
31 See p. 161, *ante.*
32 *Re Gardom*, [1914] 1 Ch. 662.
33 *e.g.* in *Re Robinson*, [1951] Ch. 198.
34 *e.g. Re Sahal's Will Trusts*, [1958] 1 W.L.R. 1243, distinguishing *Re Cole*, [1958] Ch. 877.
35 Keeton and Sheridan, *The Modern Law of Charities*, 2nd ed., pp. 107–113.
36 *Op. cit.*, pp. 114–118.
37 *Op. cit.*, pp. 87–90.

limited—recreational purposes [38]; (5) gifts for the general benefit of the country or of a locality, such as a parish or town [39]; (6) local public works and amenities [40]; (7) purposes connected with the armed forces [41]; and (8) the promotion of industry, commerce and agriculture.[42]

Little purpose would be served by collecting examples of gifts which have been held charitable or not charitable under this fourth category. Those which have been accepted include a very wide variety of socially useful purposes, but the degree of social utility affords no test of value. For example, a gift " for the welfare of cats and kittens " has been accepted as charitable [43] but a gift to establish a centre for Welsh culture in London has been rejected.[44] Sport as such, for some strange reason, is not charitable, although recreation within a locality or a class is. Even here, however, the decision of the House of Lords in *I.R.C.* v. *Baddeley* [45] raised a number of doubts, some of which were set at rest by the Recreational Charities Act 1958. In *I.R.C.* v. *Baddeley*,[45] the House of Lords held that trusts for the provision of facilities for social and physical training and recreation in the boroughs of West Ham and Leyton of persons who belonged to or were likely to belong to the Methodist Church were not charitable trusts, since the class to be benefited was not a " public " class of the community. However, it was also thought that the House of Lords, in their observations, had cast doubts upon the charitable status of other trusts for recreation and social welfare, such as those for women's institutes, youth clubs, village halls and community centres. The Recreational Charities Act 1958, s. 1, therefore makes it clear that such trusts, if established in the interests of social welfare and for the public benefit, are charitable.

C. UNCERTAINTY AND CHARITABLE TRUSTS

Over-technicality not only affects the determination of the question whether the purposes of a particular gift are charitable, but also the determination of the question whether it is given for charitable purposes *exclusively*. The courts have held, somewhat arbitrarily, that whilst it is possible to determine, in a particular case, whether a gift is charitable or not, if there is a possibility that the gift may be applied for non-charitable purposes, the gift fails for uncertainty. This is principally due to the fact that, although a gift for " charity," or for " religious charity," or for " the advancement of education," or for some other undoubted charitable purposes will not be allowed to fail for uncertainty, and the court will direct its application to some specific charitable purpose, the same favour will not be extended to gifts in general terms for general non-charitable objects, and where there is no means of determining which part of the gift is applicable for charitable, and which for non-charitable purposes, the court will not attempt to apportion the funds. Further, the courts have consistently held that gifts for " benevolent,"

---

[38] *Op. cit.*, pp. 91–98.
[39] *Op. cit.*, pp. 119–122.
[40] *Op. cit.*, pp. 123–128.
[41] *Op. cit.*, pp. 129–131.
[42] *Op. cit.*, pp. 132–133.
[43] *Re Moss*, [1949] 1 All E.R. 495.
[44] *Williams' Trustees* v. *I.R.C.*, [1947] A.C. 447.
[45] [1955] A.C. 572.

" public," " patriotic," " philanthropic " or similar purposes, are wider than gifts for " charitable " purposes, and may include a variety of non-charitable purposes. This, in turn, has been productive of frequent and serious difficulties where donors have made gifts, on the one hand for " charitable *and* benevolent," " charitable *and* public," purposes, and the like; and on the other, for " charitable *or* benevolent," " charitable *or* public " purposes, and the like.

The difficulty in these cases is a difficulty of construction, bearing in mind that the task of the court is to discover the donor's intention, as disclosed by the words which he has used, in the context of the particular gift. In a number of instances in which " charitable " has been linked by " and " with other objects, the courts have held that the gift is for charitable purposes only. As Pearson, J., put it in *Re Sutton* [46]—

> To my mind the words " charitable and deserving objects " mean only one class of objects, and the word " charitable " governs the whole sentence. It means objects which are at once charitable and deserving.

Where this method of construction is adopted, therefore, the words added to " charitable " are regarded as an additional test which must be satisfied by the gift—a conclusion which, incidentally, makes it necessary for the courts to assign some definite meaning to those additional words. Other judges, however, have pointed out that rather different formulations, in rather different contexts, may make it plain that the class of objects has been extended beyond what is *necessarily* charitable. For example, if the gift is for " charitable institutions and benevolent purposes " it appears likely that the class has been extended beyond the permissible limits. [47]

Similar difficulties have arisen from the use of the word " or." This has frequently been used disjunctively, but this is not always the case. As Lord Simonds pointed out in *Chichester Diocesan Fund and Board of Finance (Inc.)* v. *Simpson*, [48] " or " has a secondary meaning—

> . . . which may, perhaps, be called exegetical or explanatory . . . So used, it is equivalent to " alias " or " otherwise called." The dictionary examples of this use will generally be found to be topographical, as " Papua or New Guinea," but . . . this use of the word " or " is only possible if the words or phrases which it joins connote the same thing and are interchangeable the one with the other.

This, however, fails to resolve the problem now under consideration which is, ultimately, the sense intended by the donor in using the second phrase. Not unnaturally, therefore, judges, in deciding upon particular gifts, have not always reached the same conclusions. A testator who made gifts for " charitable institutions or benevolent purposes " might reasonably be assumed to mean by the second phrase something wider than the first, but the same conclusion cannot necessarily be reached if he speaks of " charitable or benevolent " purposes simply. In *Wilkinson* v. *Lindgren*, [49] *Re Sinclair's Trust*, [50]

[46] (1885), 28 Ch.D. 464, 465.
[47] *Williams* v. *Kershaw* (1835), 5 Cl. & Fin. 111; *Attorney-General* v. *National Provincial and Union Bank of England*, [1924] A.C. 262.
[48] [1944] A.C. 341, 369 (Cases, p. 274).
[49] (1870), L.R. 5 Ch.App. 570.
[50] (1884), 13 L.R.Ir. 150.

Re Allen,[51] and *Re Bennett,*[52] " charitable " or some class of charity was linked with some wider term by " or " and in each of these cases, the court decided that the gift was a valid gift for charity. On the other hand, in *Chichester Diocesan Fund and Board of Finance (Inc.)* v. *Simpson,*[53] the House of Lords held that a gift for " such charitable institution or institutions or other charitable or benevolent object or objects in England as my ... executors ... may ... select " failed for uncertainty. Clearly this decision by no means disposes of all the problems which may arise upon the effect of the use of " or " in these dispositions.

Precisely similar problems of construction have arisen in the law of charities in Australia and New Zealand, and in three Australian states—New South Wales, Victoria and Western Australia—as well as in New Zealand and some other jurisdictions (*e.g.* Manitoba and Northern Ireland), statutes have provided that a trust shall not be held invalid because some non-charitable and invalid purpose has been included with a charitable purpose in a disposition. In such cases, the gift or trust will take effect as if given for charitable purposes only.[54] A clause to have a similar effect in English law was rejected during the discussions in the House of Lords of the Charities Act 1960.

The unsatisfactory state of the law which was so strikingly illustrated by *Chichester Diocesan Fund and Board of Finance (Inc.)* v. *Simpson,*[53] together with uncertainties arising from two other decisions, *Oxford Group* v. *I.R.C.*[55] and *Ellis* v. *C.I.R.,*[56] led the Nathan Committee on Charities in their report to suggest a limited change in the law to remove some *existing* uncertainties. This was embodied in the Charitable Trusts (Validation) Act 1954, which is not only very limited in effect, but is also obscurely worded. It provides for the removal of uncertainties in imperfect trust provisions in instruments taking effect before December 16, 1952, and provides that where such uncertainties exist, the instrument shall take effect as if the disposition were exclusively charitable. The extent of the application of this Act is extremely uncertain. It did not save the appeal in *Re Gillingham Bus Disaster Fund,*[57] nor did it save a gift for institutions having for their main object the assistance and care of wounded and incapacitated members of the armed forces in *Re Harpur's Will Trusts.*[58] On the other hand, Buckley, J., held in *Re Wykes*[59] that a gift to the directors of a company " to be used at their discretion as a benevolent or welfare fund or for welfare purposes for the sole benefit of the past, present and future employees of " the company was an imperfect trust provision which was saved by section 1 (2) of the Charitable Trusts (Validation) Act 1954, it being a provision which, as the Act requires, took effect before December 16, 1952. The gift, in fact, was contained in the will of a testator who died in 1947, but it was subject to the life interest of the testator's widow, who died in 1954.

51 [1905] 2 Ch. 400.
52 [1920] 1 Ch. 305.
53 [1944] A.C. 341 (Cases, p. 274).
54 See Keeton and Sheridan, *The Modern Law of Charities,* 2nd ed., pp. 179–201.
55 [1949] 2 All E.R. 537.
56 (1949), 93 S.J. 678.
57 [1959] Ch. 62.
58 [1962] Ch. 78.
59 [1961] Ch. 229. See also *Re Chitty's Will Trusts,* [1970] Ch. 254.

In *Re Wykes*,[60] Buckley, J., reached his decision notwithstanding that the gift contained no reference to charity, or that the validation could only be effected by confining the purposes of the trust to a particular charitable purpose, *i.e.* the relief of poverty. In *Re Mead's Trust Deed* [61] the object of the trust was the provision of a sanatorium for consumptive members of a trade union, a convalescent home and a home for aged members of the union, who were no longer able to support themselves by working. Cross, J., held that the members of the union could not be regarded as a section of the public, and therefore the trust would fail, unless it was saved by the Act and the deletion of the first two purposes. He therefore followed the decision in *Re Wykes*,[60] and held the trust validated by the statute.

In *Re Saxone Shoe Co. Ltd.'s Trust Deed*,[62] the company in 1914 established a trust fund, the income of which was by clause 6 (*a*) to provide pensions for employees or former employees, and allowances for the maintenance, education or benefit of their dependants, at the discretion of the directors. Later subclauses enumerated other purposes for the benefit of employees or dependants, and subclause (*g*) gave the directors discretion to apply the income to " any other purpose whatsoever ... for the benefit of the employees or dependants."

Cross, J., decided that clause 6 imposed an imperative trust, and that the definition of " dependant " contained in the deed was a sufficiently clear description of a beneficiary under the trust. Nevertheless, since a complete list of beneficiaries could not have been compiled in 1914, the trust declared by clause 6 (which contained many other matters than the relief of poverty amongst employees, former employees and their dependants) failed unless saved by the Charitable Trusts (Validation) Act 1954. Cross, J., decided that the trust deed had created a private discretionary trust for a fluctuating class, to which the Act was not applicable. The line of distinction between this decision and that in *Re Wykes* [60] is a slender one, and is to be found in the observations of Cross, J., that in the phrase " welfare purposes," which appeared in the earlier trust deed, there was at least *some* flavour of charity, which was lacking in the trust deed before him.

D. THE *CY-PRÈS* DOCTRINE [63]

In one important respect the law of charities greatly favours gifts for charity, and saves a number of gifts for charitable purposes which would otherwise fail. This occurs where—

    (1)   the donor has made it clear that he wishes his property to go to charity, but has not selected a specific charity, or has omitted some essential details for carrying out his charitable purpose; or

    (2)   at the time the gift to charity is meant to take effect, it is impossible to carry out the precise charitable object indicated by the donor, or

---

60 [1961] Ch. 229.
61 [1961] 1 W.L.R. 1244.
62 [1962] 1 W.L.R. 943. See also *Re Flavel's Will Trusts*, [1969] 1 W.L.R. 444.
63 See, generally, Keeton and Sheridan, *The Modern Law of Charities*, 2nd ed., pp. 134–164; Sheridan and Delany, *The Cy-Près Doctrine*; Sheridan, " Cy-Près in the Sixties: Judicial Activity " (1968) 6 *Alberta Law Review* 16; Sheridan, " Cy-Près in Spate " (1972) 1 *Anglo-American Law Review* 101.

impossible to carry it out in some particular, and the donor can be shown to have had a general charitable intent, *i.e.* an intention to benefit charity in some wider way than the precise mode that is impossible; or

(3) after the property has become subject to a binding trust, it becomes wholly or partly impossible to continue to apply the property in the same way, and there is no provision for a gift over in that event.

Where such a situation arises, the court will direct the gift to be applied to a charitable object as close as possible to that indicated by the donor (if he indicated one).

The principal examples of the third class are changes in social conditions,[64] a surplus of funds after a charitable purpose has been completed [65] and the winding up of a charitable institution, often on its work being taken over by another organisation.

Further, the Charities Act 1960 has introduced some important statutory extensions of the *cy-près* doctrine.[66]

When it is required, whether a general charitable intent has been shown is a question of construction of the particular gift.[67] The decisions upon the existence or non-existence of a general charitable intent, where (as is usually the case) it is not expressly stated, have established some fine distinctions. This may be illustrated by the difficulties which have arisen in respect of gifts to institutions which have never existed, or which have existed but have come to an end before the death of the testator. Where an institution has existed, but has come to an end before the testator's death, there is a strong presumption that the testator intended simply to benefit the particular institution, and if the court finds this to be the case, then the gift lapses [68]; but if the institution named has never existed, the Court acts upon the assumption that the testator intended to benefit a purpose of the type named, and holds that there is a general charitable intent (unless the contrary can be shown),[69] directing that the gift should be applied *cy-près.*[70]

Still another type of problem may arise where a testator named a particular charity, but no existing organisation can be identified with it. In *Re Satterthwaite's Will Trusts* [71] the testatrix had bequeathed money to named organisations for the care and cure of animals. One of these was a private business carried on by an unqualified veterinary surgeon, which could not take as a charity. Another was " the London Animal Hospital," and the Blue Cross organisation claimed this in respect of an animal hospital which it maintained. The Court of Appeal held that this could not be identified with the institution named in the will, but it further held that the whole gift showed

---

[64] *Re Colonial Bishoprics Fund, 1841,* [1935] Ch. 148; *Re Dominion Students' Hall Trust,* [1947] Ch. 183.

[65] *Re Campden Charities* (1881), 18 Ch.D. 310; *Re Raine,* [1956] Ch. 417.

[66] See Keeton and Sheridan, *op. cit.,* pp. 165–178; pp. 170–172, *post.*

[67] *Per* Parker, J., in *Re Wilson,* [1913] 1 Ch. 314.

[68] *Re Slatter's Will Trusts,* [1964] Ch. 512; *Re Stemson's Will Trusts,* [1970] Ch. 16. *Cf. Re Roberts,* [1963] 1 W.L.R. 406; *Re Vernon's Will Trusts* (1962), [1972] Ch. 300; *Re Finger's Will Trusts,* [1972] Ch. 286. See also Martin, " The Construction of Charitable Gifts " (1974) 38 *Conveyancer* 187.

[69] See *Re Tharp,* [1942] 2 All E.R. 358.

[70] *Re Harwood,* [1936] Ch. 285; *Re Knox,* [1937] Ch. 109 (Cases, p. 276); but see *Re Bennett,* [1960] Ch. 18.

[71] [1966] 1 W.L.R. 277.

an intention to benefit the welfare of animals, and therefore showed a general charitable intent, so that the bequest could be applied *cy-près*.

In *Re Lysaght* [72] Buckley, J., discussed the meaning of " general charitable intent," and concluded that it may be regarded as being present where it can be established that the donor had a paramount intention to effect a charitable purpose, which the court can find a method of putting into effect, even though it is impracticable to give effect to a direction by the donor, which is not an essential part of his paramount intention. In this case, the donor had bequeathed money for the establishment of medical studentships, to be awarded by the Royal College of Surgeons, with the provision that beneficiaries should be British born subjects " not of the Jewish or Roman Catholic faith." The College informed the trustees of the will that they could not accept the bequest with the condition attached, and raised the question of its validity. Having rejected the view that it was void for uncertainty or conflict with public policy, the learned judge agreed that a trust could not be modified merely because of the opinions of the trustee. But he decided that administration of the trust by the Royal College of Surgeons was of the essence of the trust, so that if the College refused the gift, it became impracticable to carry out the charitable purpose in the manner decided by the testatrix. Buckley, J., said that the impracticability of a minor condition could not defeat the general, paramount, intention. Accordingly he was able to direct the *cy-près* application of the fund by the deletion of the discriminating clause.

Where there is an absolute gift by will to a charity which comes to an end *after* the testator's death, then the property is applicable *cy-près*.[73]

Impossibility need not be absolute. It is sufficient if the purpose to be achieved is one which, in the circumstances, cannot reasonably be undertaken. In *Re Whittaker*,[74] a testator, who died in 1914, had left money, subject to a number of annuities, for erecting and maintaining a hospital for the poor at Broadstairs. In 1943, when the last annuitant had died, the erection of a hospital was impossible, and after the war, as a result of the passing of the National Health Service Act 1946, it was highly impracticable. Harman, J., held that a general charitable intent to benefit the poor of Broadstairs had been shown, and the money should be applied *cy-près*. On the other hand, in *Re Good's Will Trusts* [75] a testator had described the objects which he wished to achieve with such particularity, that when the object became impracticable, because increasing costs made its achievement impossible, Wynn-Parry, J., was unable to find any general charitable intent, so that there could be no *cy-près* application, and the gift failed.

E. THE CHARITIES ACT 1960

The Charities Act 1960 contains two important sections which extend the powers of the court to direct *cy-près* applications of charitable funds. Section 13 specifies a number of occasions, falling short of complete failure of the trust, in which *cy-près* application may now be directed, provided [76] a general

---

[72] [1966] Ch. 191.
[73] *Re Slevin*, [1891] 2 Ch. 236.
[74] [1951] 2 T.L.R. 955.
[75] [1950] 2 All E.R. 653.
[76] S. 13 (2).

charitable intent is shown in cases where that was necessary when there was impossibility before the Act. Prior to the passing of this Act, the general rule applicable was, that if the trust could be carried out, even under considerable difficulties, according to the settlor's expressed intentions, it must be so carried out.[77] Section 13 has relaxed the strictness of the rule, so as to permit *cy-près* application—

(*a*) Where the original purposes, in whole or in part, have been fulfilled, or cannot be carried out, either at all, or according to the directions and to the spirit of the original gift.

This provision gives statutory force to the decisions of the courts in one or two earlier cases, and is illustrated by *Re Dominion Students' Hall Trust*,[78] where the court directed the *cy-près* modification of a memorandum of association, which restricted the use of a students' hostel to white students, so as to delete the racial discrimination.

(*b*) Where the original purposes are satisfied by the use of part only of the property available.

Thus, in *Re King*[79] a testatrix directed that property should be applied for the installation and maintenance of a stained-glass window in a church in memory of her son. When this purpose had been completed, there was a substantial surplus, and the court directed that this should be applied *cy-près* to the installation and maintenance of other stained-glass windows in the same church.

(*c*) Where the property given and other property applicable for similar purposes can be more effectively used in conjunction, and to that end can be suitably made applicable to common purposes, having regard to the spirit of the gift.

This provision has the effect of reversing the decision of the Court of Appeal in *Re Weir Hospital*.[80]

(*d*) Where the original purposes were laid down by reference to an area which was then, but has since ceased to be, a unit for some other purpose, or by reference to a class of persons or to an area which has for any reason since ceased to be suitable, regard being had to the spirit of the gift, or to be practical in administering the gift.

This also is a new statutory power.

(*e*) Where the original purposes, either in whole or in part, have, since they were laid down—

(i) been adequately provided for by other means (as was the case in *Re Welsh Hospital* (*Netley*) *Fund*[81]); or

(ii) ceased, as being useless or harmful to the community, or for other reasons, to be in law charitable (an instance being *National Anti-Vivisection Society* v. *I.R.C.*[82]); or

(iii) ceased in any other way to provide a suitable and effective method of using the property available, regard being had to the spirit of the gift.

This is a new power.

---

[77] *Re Weir Hospital*, [1910] 2 Ch. 124.
[78] [1947] Ch. 183 (Cases, p. 278).
[79] [1923] 1 Ch. 243.
[80] [1910] 2 Ch. 124, *supra*.
[81] [1921] 1 Ch. 655.
[82] [1948] A.C. 31.

Subsection (5) of the same section now imposes on charity trustees a duty to secure the effective use of charity property for charitable purposes by securing a *cy-près* scheme where circumstances require it.

Section 14 was added whilst the Charities Act 1960 was before Parliament, and is designed to solve a conundrum which had been frequently before the courts, and to which the courts had found no satisfactory answer. It arose wherever funds were raised by public appeal, and in a variety of ways, *e.g.* street collections, whist drives, concerts and, possibly, direct subscriptions, for an admittedly charitable object, the achievement of which became impossible or impracticable,[83] or in which, after the object had been achieved, there was a surplus.[84] If the court could have decided in all these cases that the contributors to public appeals had manifested a general charitable intent, then there could have been a *cy-près* application of the funds. In some cases, this decision was reached. In others, however, the opposite decision was reached, and then there arose for decision the question whether unclaimed surpluses passed to the Crown as *bona vacantia* or reverted by way of a resulting trust to the donors. The courts decided that in such cases there was a resulting trust for the donors, leaving unsolved the problems how, in a particular case, the donors were discoverable, and also how, if the donors were discovered, the remaining sums should be distributed.

Section 14 solves this problem by directing that if property is given for specific charitable purposes which fail, it shall be applicable *cy-près*, as if given for charitable purposes generally, provided either that the donor has disclaimed in writing, or the donor cannot be discovered after reasonable advertisements and inquiries have been made.[85] Moreover, section 14 (2) provides that property shall be conclusively presumed (without advertisement or inquiry) to belong to unidentifiable donors if the property consists of the proceeds of cash collections by means of collecting boxes, or similar means, or is the proceeds of lotteries, competitions, entertainments or similar money-raising activities. It is important to appreciate that the section (which is retrospective in operation) only applies where the original appeal was for a charitable purpose, and therefore it can have no application to a situation such as that which arose in *Re Gillingham Bus Disaster Fund*,[86] where the court eventually decided that the original purposes were not exclusively charitable.[87]

---

[83] *Re Hillier's Trusts,* [1954] 1 W.L.R. 700; *Re Ulverston and District New Hospital Building Trusts,* [1956] Ch. 622.

[84] *Re Wokingham Fire Brigade Trusts,* [1951] Ch. 373; *Re North Devon and West Somerset Relief Fund Trusts,* [1953] 1 W.L.R. 1260.

[85] What advertisements and inquiries may be regarded as reasonable is discussed in *Re Henry Wood National Memorial Trust,* [1966] 1 W.L.R. 1601.

[86] [1959] Ch. 62.

[87] As to charities and the rule against perpetuities, see p. 128, *ante*; as to the Charity Commissioners, see Keeton and Sheridan, *The Modern Law of Charities*, 2nd ed., pp. 207–230; as to the special duties of charity trustees, see *ibid.*, pp. 231–241; as to relief from rates for charities, see *ibid.*, pp. 249–260; as to exemption of charities from income tax, see *ibid.*, pp. 242–247; as to relief for charities from estate duty and capital gains tax, see Chap. XXI, *post.*

CHAPTER XIII

IMPLIED AND RESULTING TRUSTS

THE function of the court in enforcing implied and resulting trusts is to carry out the presumed intention of the settlor, whereas in a constructive trust the court imposes a trust upon the parties irrespective of their intentions, actual or presumed, and sometimes even in opposition to those intentions, as in *Keech* v. *Sandford*.[1]

The distinction between an implied trust and an express trust is one of degree. As Maitland said, it is hard to draw a strict line of demarcation between them, and in any event the division is not usually of importance. The important dividing line is between trusts arising by act of parties and trusts arising by operation of law. Lewin regards a precatory trust as an implied trust, but inasmuch as the court does not consider that the trust is enforceable at all unless, after a consideration of the whole facts, it comes to the conclusion that the words were used imperatively, and since no particular form of words is required to create an express trust, it would rather seem that precatory trusts are examples of express trusts. On the other hand, in both an implied trust and a resulting trust, the court is seeking to give effect to the presumed intention of the settlor, and therefore no really useful purpose is served by attempting to distinguish between them. An infant, it has been decided, may be an implied trustee.[2]

A. PURCHASE IN THE NAME OF ANOTHER

The best example of a trust implied by law is where property is purchased by A in the name of B; that is to say, A supplies the purchase-money, and B takes the conveyance. Here, in the absence of any explanatory facts, such as an intention to give the property to B, equity presumes that A intended B to hold the property in trust for him. This point was incidentally elucidated in *Rochefoucauld* v. *Boustead*.[3] Eyre, L.C.B., stated the general rule as long ago as 1788 in the leading case of *Dyer* v. *Dyer*,[4] as follows—

> The clear result of all the cases, without a single exception, is, that the trust of a legal estate, whether freehold, copyhold, or leasehold; whether taken in the names of the purchasers and others jointly, or in the name of others without that of the purchaser; whether in one name or several whether jointly, or *successive,* results to the man who advances the purchase-money . . . and it goes on a strict analogy to the rule of the common law, that where a feoffment is made without consideration, the use results to the feoffor.

Although the Lord Chief Baron only refers here expressly to trusts of real

---

[1] (1726), Sel.Cas.t.King 61 (Cases, p. 195).
[2] *Re Vinogradoff,* [1935] W.N. 68.
[3] [1897] 1 Ch. 196 (Cases, p. 205).
[4] 2 Cox 92, 93 (Cases, p. 287).

property, the principle has been consistently applied to personalty,[5] and it applies also where two or more persons advance purchase-money jointly and the conveyance is taken in the name of a third.[6] In such a case the third person holds in trust for the purchasers to an extent proportionate to the amount of the purchase-money which each has advanced. The same rule applies where the conveyance is taken in the name of one of the purchasers only. Thus, in *Gravesend Corporation* v. *Kent County Council,*[7] the Gravesend Corporation, being in 1893 the local authority for higher education, borrowed money to build a technical school. The money was to be repaid by instalments, terminating in 1931. By the Education Act 1902 the Kent County Council became the higher education authority, and since the county council had agreed to pay a fraction of the annual instalments, the Gravesend Corporation, after 1902, let the technical school to the county council at a nominal rent. When in 1931 the instalments were paid off, the Gravesend Corporation claimed the right to let the school to the county council for an economic rent. The court decided that the corporation was entitled to do this, but that in doing so, it must have regard to the fact that in equity the county council and the corporation were entitled to the school in proportion to the purchase-money supplied by each. The position where the conveyance is taken in the name of all the purchasers is treated differently, but it does not fall under the present rule, and is therefore considered separately below.

A common case in modern law is where two persons (usually husband and wife), or more, advance money for the purchase of a house, and the conveyance is taken in the name of one. In *Bull* v. *Bull,*[8] a mother and son contributed, the conveyance being taken in the son's name. In *Cook* v. *Cook*[9] the contributors were husband and wife. In *Cooke* v. *Head*[10] they were a man and his mistress. In all these cases, there is an implied trust, in the absence of any indication of an intention to confer a benefit, for the contributories as equitable tenants in common, in proportion to their respective contributions, the legal owner holding on trust for sale. In cases of husband and wife, the principle has been applied, so as to give the wife an equitable interest in the house, where her contribution to its acquisition has been indirect, as where the husband is only enabled to pay for the house because the wife bears other family expenses which would otherwise have fallen on the husband.[11] On the other hand, the mere sharing of household expenses will not give the wife an interest under an implied or resulting trust of the house if the cost of buying it and other family expenses could have been borne by the husband without

---

[5] *Ebrand* v. *Dancer* (1680), 2 Ch.Cas. 26; *Ex parte Houghton* (1810), 17 Ves. 251; *Re Policy No. 6402 of the Scottish Equitable Assurance Society,* [1902] 1 Ch. 282.

[6] *Wray* v. *Steele* (1814), 2 V. & B. 388. (The point had been doubted by Lord Hardwicke in *Crop* v. *Norton* (1740), 9 Mod. 233.)

[7] [1935] 1 K.B. 339.

[8] [1955] 1 Q.B. 234.

[9] [1962] P. 235. See also *Brown* v. *Brown,* [1959] P. 86; *Heseltine* v. *Heseltine,* [1971] 1 W.L.R. 342; *Davis* v. *Vale,* [1971] 1 W.L.R. 1022; *Cowcher* v. *Cowcher,* [1972] 1 W.L.R. 425; *Re Nicholson,* [1974] 1 W.L.R. 476; Lesser, "The Acquisition of Inter Vivos Matrimonial Property Rights in English Law: A Doctrinal Melting Pot" (1973) 23 *University of Toronto Law Journal* 148.

[10] [1972] 1 W.L.R. 518. The headnote suggests that the equitable shares of the parties were not quantified by reference to their contributions to the acquisition of the house, but the better view of what the Court of Appeal decided is that they were so quantified, taking into account indirect as well as direct contributions, as in the cases of husband and wife cited below. *Cf.* *Richards* v. *Dove,* [1974] 1 All E.R. 888.

[11] *Hargrave* v. *Newton,* [1971] 1 W.L.R. 1611; *Hazell* v. *Hazell,* [1972] 1 W.L.R. 301.

the wife's contribution. In *Gissing* v. *Gissing*,[12] there being no agreement between the parties, the House of Lords held that the wife had no equitable interest in a house paid for by the husband, and of which he was the legal owner, where all the wife had done was pay a small sum for some furniture and the laying of a lawn and to pay for her own clothes and those of her son and for some extras.

In *Hussey* v. *Palmer* [13] the plaintiff paid for an extension, for her own occupation, to a house already belonging to her son-in-law. When she left after a period of discord, she was held entitled to an equitable interest in the house. The basis of the decision is not clear, except that their Lordships thought the plaintiff should get her money back. Phillimore, L.J., " thought it was more appropriate to regard it as an example of a resulting trust " [14]; Lord Denning, M.R., " thought that the trust in this case, if there was one, was more in the nature of a constructive trust " [15] : Cairns, L.J., dissented.

In *Savage* v. *Dunningham*,[16] Plowman, J., declined to extend the doctrine of implied or resulting trusts to a lease, taken in the name of one of three tenants all of whom shared for a time in the rent and other expenses, since rent was paid for the use of property, not for the acquisition of a capital asset. It might be otherwise, he thought, if all the tenants had shared in a premium for the acquisition of a lease.

Neither the Statute of Frauds nor the Law of Property Act 1925 applies to the creation of or operation of implied, resulting or constructive trusts, and therefore it is not necessary that there should be any evidence in writing of the intention of the persons supplying the purchase-money, so that they may prove the fact of their payment by parol, even though the deed states that the purchase-money is supplied by the person in whose name the conveyance is taken, the court holding, where the latter is stated, that the apparent purchaser was really the agent of the true purchaser.[17] The parol evidence, however, must clearly prove the fact of payment by the person for whom it is attempted to establish the trust, although circumstantial evidence (*e.g.* that the means of the nominal purchaser were so small that he would have been unable to supply the money himself) will be accepted as sufficient.[18] Furthermore, the evidence must show that the purported beneficiary, claiming as the real purchaser, advanced the money *as purchaser,* for if the money was intended to be advanced by way of loan to the person in whose name the conveyance was taken, there is no implied trust, and the legal owner will merely be the debtor of the other.[19] Again, if it can be proved that at the time of the purchase it was the intention that the person who took the conveyance should have the beneficial interest, the person who advanced the purchase-money cannot subsequently change his mind and seek to establish a trust [20]; while if

---

[12] [1971] A.C. 886. See also *Pettitt* v. *Pettitt*, [1970] A.C. 777 (Cases, p. 291); *Kowalczuk* v. *Kowalczuk*, [1973] 1 W.L.R. 930, where the husband was already the legal owner of the house before the marriage.

[13] [1972] 1 W.L.R. 1286. See also (1973) 89 *Law Quarterly Review* 2; Hayton (1973) 37 *Conveyancer* 65; Fairest, (1973) 32 *Cambridge Law Journal* 41; Strathy, " The Constructive Trust as a Restitutionary Remedy " (1974) *University of Toronto Faculty of Law Review* 83. *Cf. Dodsworth* v. *Dodsworth* (1973), 228 Est.Gaz. 1115 (C.A.).　　　[14] [1972] 1 W.L.R. 1291.

[15] [1972] 1 W.L.R. 1289.　　　　　　　　　　　　　　　　[16] [1973] 3 W.L.R. 471.

[17] *Bartlett* v. *Pickersgill* (1760), 1 Eden 515; *Heard* v. *Pilley* (1869), L.R. 4 Ch.App. 548.

[18] *Willis* v. *Willis* (1740), 2 Atk. 71.

[19] *Bartlett* v. *Pickersgill* (1760), 1 Eden 515. See also *Hussey* v. *Palmer*, [1972] 1 W.L.R. 1286.　　　　　　　　　　　　　　[20] *Groves* v. *Groves* (1829), 3 Y. & J. 163, 172.

the conveyance sets out an express trust, a resulting trust cannot be appealed to (in the absence of fraud or mistake) for the purpose of establishing equitable interests different from those of the express trust.[21]

In cases of this type, the true purchaser should seek to establish the trust as soon as possible, for the presumption is weakened by lapse of time, more especially if the legal owner is in actual possession of the property. It has been suggested, indeed, that after the death of the legal owner, the presumption can never be established, at any rate by parol evidence only, but it would appear that this is not correct: the death of the nominal purchaser may detract from the weight of the parol evidence, but does not affect its admissibility.[22]

Furthermore, the presumption of a trust does not operate where the consequence would be contrary to public policy, *e.g.* where it would enable the purchaser to defeat his creditors.[23] In such cases, the legal owner holds beneficially.

The presumption of a trust only arises where there are no other circumstances to explain the transaction and remove the presumption. In *Young* v. *Sealey*[24] a Miss J. had a banking account and certain shares in the joint names of herself and her nephew, she having provided the money and the shares. Oral evidence and evidence of the surrounding circumstances was admitted to rebut the presumption of a resulting trust to her estate. One example of such explanatory circumstances arises where the real and apparent purchasers are closely related, for here another presumption of equity, the presumption of advancement, may operate. The typical example of the operation of this second presumption, defeating the first, is where a father purchases in the name of his child or children. Eyre, L.C.B., observed in *Dyer* v. *Dyer*[25]—

> . . . the circumstances of one or more of the nominees, being *a child or children* of the purchaser, is to operate by rebutting the resulting trust; and it has been determined in so many cases that the nominee being a child shall have such operation as *a circumstance of evidence,* that we should be disturbing land-marks if we suffered either of these propositions to be called into question, namely, that such circumstance shall rebut the resulting trust, and that it shall do so as a *circumstance of evidence.* I think it would have been a more simple doctrine, if the children had been considered as purchasers for valuable consideration. . . . This way of considering it would have shut out all the circumstances of evidence which have found their way into many of the cases, and would have prevented some very nice distinctions, and not very easy to be understood. Considering it as a circumstance of evidence, there must be of course evidence admitted on the other side. Thus, it was resolved into a question of intent, which was getting into very wide sea, without very certain guides.

In view of the older case-law, much of which is now of historical importance only, the Lord Chief Baron's observations are no overstatement, but it

---

[21] *Re Johns' Assignment Trusts,* [1970] 1 W.L.R. 955 ; *Leake* v. *Bruzzi,* [1974] 2 All E.R. 1196.

[22] Lewin, *Trusts,* 16th ed., p. 132.

[23] *Gascoigne* v. *Gascoigne,* [1918] 1 K.B. 223.

[24] [1949] Ch. 278.   [25] (1788), 2 Cox 92, 93–94 (Cases, p. 287).

is submitted that the question of an implied or resulting trust in the circumstances now under consideration is purely one of intent, and it is therefore difficult to see how any other procedure could have been adopted. The difficulties are no greater than those in discovering the true intent of a testator, and from these the Court of Chancery, from the time when it first assumed testamentary jurisdiction, has never had any possibility of escape.

As examples of some of the earlier distinctions, based upon conflicting evidence, and which have now been abandoned, it may be noticed that at one time it was considered that, if the child were an infant, the father would have the beneficial interest. The modern view, however, is that infancy is a factor which peculiarly supposes an intention to benefit the child.[26] Conversely, it has been suggested that, where the son is an adult, and the conveyance is taken in his name, but the father enjoys the possession of the property, the presumption of advancement would be rebutted, but, as Lord Nottingham pointed out in *Lord Grey* v. *Lady Grey*,[27] this was insufficient, unless the father had in fact previously and amply made provision for his son, for example by making a settlement upon him on his marriage. In *Grey* v. *Grey*,[27] the father had advanced the money, and after the conveyance had received the profits for twenty years, made leases, taken fines, enclosed part of a park on the estate, embarked upon building, and had entered into negotiations for the sale of the land, yet notwithstanding this the son was deemed to hold beneficially. Further, where the father had previously settled a reversionary estate upon the son, this was not considered to be such a provision as would negative the presumption of advancement, since, as the court observed, the son might starve before his reversionary estate fell into possession.[26]

Where a conveyance was taken in the joint names of son and father, Lord Hardwicke thought this did not fulfil the purpose of an advancement (in respect of the son's share of the joint tenancy), since if the son died his beneficial share passed to his father by survivorship, and if he was an infant he would not be able to effect a severance.[28] This, however, is at variance with the weight of authority.[29] In a modern Canadian case a father bought a house in the name of his son. The father and his family lived in the house rent-free, and both the father and the mother spent money improving it. The Manitoba Court of Appeal held that these facts did not displace the presumption of advancement.[30] In *Warren* v. *Gurney*,[31] however, a father bought a house in 1929 in the name of his daughter Catherine, retaining the title deeds. By a document written in 1943 he expressed the desire that the house should belong to his three daughters. On the father's death in 1944, Catherine claimed the house. The Court of Appeal rejected the document written in 1943 as not being contemporaneous with the purchase of the house, but held there was other contemporaneous evidence rebutting the presumption of advancement.

The presumption of advancement also exists where a husband supplies the

---

[26] *Lamplugh* v. *Lamplugh* (1709), 1 P.Wms. 111.
[27] (1677), 2 Swanst. 594.
[28] *Stileman* v. *Ashdown* (1742), 2 Atk. 477.
[29] *Back* v. *Andrews* (1690), 2 Vern. 120, and cases cited in *Grey* v. *Grey*, 2 Swanst. 599–600.
[30] *Northern Canadian Trust Co.* v. *Smith*, [1947] 3 D.L.R. 135.
[31] [1944] 2 All E.R. 472.

purchase-money and the conveyance is taken in the name of the wife.[32] For example, when a husband purchases a dwelling-house in the name of his wife, and pays the instalments of the purchase-price, the presumption is applicable.[33] If the conveyance is taken in the names of himself and his wife, the wife is still entitled to a half-share.[34]

The presumption continues to be applied nowadays,[35] despite some judicial pronouncements that it has little application to disputes over the matrimonial home. In *Falconer* v. *Falconer*[36] the house in which a married couple lived before they separated was vested in the wife, having been acquired by the financial efforts of both of them. Holding that the wife was a trustee of the house for herself and her husband in equal shares, members of the Court of Appeal said—

> If this case had come up for decision 20 years ago, there would undoubtedly have been a presumption of advancement: because at that time whenever a husband made financial contributions towards a house in his wife's name, there was a presumption that he was making a gift to her. That presumption found its place in the law in Victorian days when a wife was utterly subordinate to her husband. It has no place, or, at any rate, very little place, in our law today: see *Pettitt* v. *Pettitt*.[37] We have decided these cases for some years without much regard to a presumption of advancement, and I think we should continue so to do.[38]

> I think that the presumption of advancement in cases of this sort can rarely apply now. I would refer to a passage in the speech of Lord Diplock in the recent decision in *Gissing* v. *Gissing*.[39] Lord Diplock, having referred to the decision of the House of Lords in *Pettitt* v. *Pettitt*,[40] said that as he understood the speeches of four members of the House of Lords in that case they took the view that, even if the presumption of advancement as between husband and wife still survived today:

> > it could seldom have any decisive part to play in disputes between living spouses in which some evidence would be available in addition to the mere fact that the husband had provided part of the purchase price of property conveyed into the name of the wife.[41]

With respect, the presumption of advancement is not, or not solely, a manifestation of the Victorian subordination of women. It is a realistic presumption that when a spouse gives a present to the other spouse the donor intends

---

[32] The presumption is even stronger where the parties are about to marry: *Moate* v. *Moate*, [1948] 2 All E.R. 486, 487, *per* Jenkins, J. As to the property of engaged couples when the engagement is terminated without marriage, see also the Law Reform (Miscellaneous Provisions) Act 1970, ss. 2-3.

[33] *Silver* v. *Silver*, [1958] 1 W.L.R. 259.

[34] *Kingdon* v. *Bridges* (1688), 2 Vern. 67; *Re Condrin*, [1914] 1 I.R. 89; *Smith* v. *Smith*, [1945] 1 All E.R. 584.

[35] See *Re Figgis*, [1969] 1 Ch. 123 (joint bank account); *Tinker* v. *Tinker*, [1970] P. 136 (family house).

[36] [1970] 1 W.L.R. 1333.

[37] [1970] A.C. 777, *per* Lord Reid at p. 793, *per* Lord Hodson at p. 811 and *per* Lord Diplock at p. 824 (Cases, p. 291).

[38] *Per* Lord Denning, M.R., [1970] 1 W.L.R. 1335-1336.

[39] [1971] A.C. 886, 907.

[40] [1970] A.C. 777 (Cases, p. 291).

[41] *Per* Megaw, L.J., [1970] 1 W.L.R. 1337.

the donee to keep it. What is *wrong* is that the presumption does not apply to purchase by a wife in her husband's name. What has *changed* is that the presumption can be rebutted more easily nowadays in the light of the greater frequency of contribution by both spouses to the family income and outgoings. The passage Megaw, L.J., quoted from Lord Diplock's judgment in *Gissing* v. *Gissing*, in referring to the availability of evidence, is directed towards the rebuttal of the presumption, not its failure to arise.

The rights of husband and wife may now be affected by section 1 of the Married Women's Property Act 1964, which provides—

> If any question arises as to the right of a husband or wife to money derived from any allowance made by the husband for the expenses of the matrimonial home or for similar purposes, or to any property acquired out of such money, the money or property shall, in the absence of any agreement between them to the contrary, be treated as belonging to the husband and the wife in equal shares.

When the presumption of advancement exists in favour of the wife, the husband will not be allowed to rebut it by bringing forward evidence to show that the sole purpose of the transaction was to enable the husband to avoid either English law or the payment of foreign income tax, for equity will not assist a person who seeks to contravene revenue laws, whether English or foreign. In either case, to establish such a position would be for the husband to seek to commit a fraud.[42] There is, however, no presumption in favour of a reputed wife, who has not been through a valid ceremony of marriage with the reputed husband.[43] On the other hand, if the parties are in fact married, and the marriage is subsequently declared null in consequence of a canonical disability which makes the marriage not void *ab initio,* but voidable only, the presumption exists.[44] There is no such presumption, however, where the parties cohabit without being married at all.[45] Furthermore, the presumption does not operate when a wife buys property in the name of her husband,[46] and it should also be observed that when a mother buys property in the name of her child, then, whether the father is alive or not, there is no presumption of advancement, since equity does not impose upon the mother an obligation to provide for the child. In *Sayre* v. *Hughes* [47] and *Garrett* v. *Wilkinson,*[48] it was thought that such a presumption did exist, but the point was later settled in a contrary sense.[49] However, since the Married Women's Property Act 1882, s. 21, and the National Assistance Act 1948, s. 42, impose on a woman an obligation to maintain her children, it may be that today the point would be decided differently.

Besides the instances just considered, the presumption of advancement will also be regarded as existing in certain cases where the true purchaser stands *in loco parentis* to the nominal purchaser. Thus, the presumption has been

---

[42] *Gascoigne* v. *Gascoigne,* [1918] 1 K.B. 223 ; *Re Emery's Investment Trusts,* [1959] Ch. 410 ; *Tinker* v. *Tinker,* [1970] P. 136.
[43] *Soar* v. *Foster* (1858), 4 K. & J. 152.
[44] *Dunbar* v. *Dunbar,* [1909] 2 Ch. 639.
[45] *Rider* v. *Kidder* (1805), 10 Ves. 360.
[46] *Mercier* v. *Mercier,* [1903] 2 Ch. 98.
[47] (1868), L.R. 5 Eq. 376.
[48] (1848), 2 De G. & Sm. 244.
[49] *Re De Visme* (1863), 2 De G. J. & S. 17 ; *Bennet* v. *Bennet* (1879), 10 Ch.D. 474.

held to exist where a grandfather, being *in loco parentis* through the death of the father, purchased in the name of the grandson[50]; where a nephew had been adopted as a son[51]; and where a stepson had been treated as a son.[52] Furthermore, it has been held that, since there is a moral obligation upon the father to provide for his illegitimate child, the presumption will here exist,[53] but it will not operate in favour of the illegitimate son of a legitimate daughter, to whom the grandfather has placed himself *in loco parentis*.[54] It may be, however, that in this case, the court was not satisfied that the grandfather really had put himself *in loco parentis*. He had taken care of the boy, and had sent him to school, and Page Wood, V.-C., observed[55] that it would be going too far to—

> . . . hold that the testator was under the obligation of making provision for an illegitimate child, whom he was not under any liability, moral or legal, to support, and whose father was alive, merely on the ground that he had voluntarily brought up and educated him.

Furthermore, it would seem that there is no such presumption in favour of a distant relation or of a stranger towards whom the person who pays the purchase-money stands *in loco parentis*.[56]

The operation of the presumption is, as was pointed out in *Grey* v. *Grey*,[57] evidential, and since the presumption is rebuttable, it can be rebutted by evidence of the real purchaser's actual intention. The best evidence is, of course, a declaration by the person who supplies the purchase-money at the time of the purchase, and it has been noticed that subsequent declarations cannot rebut the intention to advance if it really was present at the time of the purchase. Moreover, it was also established in *Grey* v. *Grey*,[57] that, even if the father subsequently remains in control of the property, that will not rebut the presumption, although the father still remains in control when the son comes of age. Where the son is also the father's solicitor, this is sufficient to rebut the presumption, unless it can be shown from the remaining evidence that the father really did intend to provide for the son.[58]

The effect of the declaration by the person supplying the purchase-money at the time of the purchase, should be noticed. This is not a declaration of trust. If it were, and it were made simply by parol, it would be subject to the requirement of the Statute of Frauds, now section 53 (1) (*b*) of the Law of Property Act 1925, that to be enforceable it must be in writing if the property bought is land. The effect of the declaration is evidential. It furnishes material from which the court may conclude that the presumption was not intended to operate.[59]

Again, although the subsequent acts and statements of the purchaser may not be used by him to negative the presumption and prove a trust, they may

---

[50] *Ebrand* v. *Dancer* (1680), 2 Ch.Cas. 26.
[51] *Currant* v. *Jago* (1844), 1 Coll. 261.
[52] *Re Paradise Motor Co. Ltd.*, [1968] 1 W.L.R. 1125.
[53] *Beckford* v. *Beckford* (1774), Lofft 490.
[54] *Tucker* v. *Burrow* (1865), 2 H. & M. 515.
[55] 2 H. & M. 527.
[56] *Tucker* v. *Burrow, supra*; *Re Policy No. 6402 of the Scottish Equitable Assurance Society*, [1902] 1 Ch. 282.
[57] (1677), 2 Swanst. 594.
[58] *Garrett* v. *Wilkinson* (1848), 2 De G. & Sm. 244.
[59] *Williams* v. *Williams* (1863), 32 Beav. 370.

be used against him by the donee to support the presumption.[60] On the other hand, if the donee was a party to the transaction, the donee's subsequent acts and statements may be used against him by the purchaser, as an indication, through the donee's view of the transaction, what the purchaser's intention at the time of the transaction really was. This point is illustrated by *Pole* v. *Pole*,[61] wherein a father, on his son's marriage, gave him a large advancement, there being several younger children not provided for. Later he sold property, and received only £500 of the purchase price, taking a mortgage for the remainder jointly in the names of himself and his son. The interest, however, was always paid, together with the principal that was repaid, to the father alone, although the son joined in the receipts. It was held that the presumption of advancement was here rebutted, and Lord Chancellor Hardwicke observed—

> . . . where a father takes an estate in the name of his son, it is to be considered as an advancement, but that is liable to be rebutted by subsequent acts: so if the estate be taken jointly, so as the son may be intitled by survivorship; that is weaker than the former case, and still depends on the circumstances. The son knew here, that his name was used in the mortgage deed, and must have known, whether it was for his own interest, or only as a trustee for the father, and instead of making any claim, his acts are very strong evidence of the latter: nor is there any colour why the father should make him any farther advancement, when he had so many children unprovided for. . . .

It should be observed that when Lord Hardwicke is talking of the subsequent acts, he must necessarily refer to the son's subsequent acts, for the father's are only admissible against him. The court, therefore, is here using the son's subsequent acts (*e.g.* his acquiescence in the father's control and sole receipt of interest and principal) as evidence that the son knew that his father, at the time of the transaction, had not intended to confer any benefit on him.

B. MUTUAL WILLS

Another example of an implied or resulting trust arises where two persons (the examples are nearly all of husband and wife, but the relationship does not seem essential) make an agreement for the disposal of their property, and execute mutual wills in pursuance of that agreement, to regulate the devolution of the property after their deaths, so that the survivor will have a life interest in the other's property, whilst a third person will take the property of both testators on the death of the survivor. It has been held that where mutual wills are made in pursuance of an independent antecedent agreement, then if the survivor takes the benefit given by the other will, and then alters his own, his personal representative holds on trust for the person who would have taken under the mutual arrangement. There is not a great deal of authority upon the topic.[62] The first reported case is *Dufour* v. *Pereira*.[63] In that case,

---

[60] *Redington* v. *Redington* (1794), 3 Ridg. P.C. 106.
[61] (1748), 1 Ves.Sen. 76.
[62] But mutual wills are discussed by Mitchell, " Some Aspects of Mutual Wills " (1951) 14 *Modern Law Review* 136; Burgess, " A Fresh Look at Mutual Wills " (1970) 34 *Conveyancer* 230; O'Donell, " Contracts to Make Joint or Mutual Wills " (1972) 55 *Marquette Law Review* 103; and Waters, *The Constructive Trust*, pp. 62–65.
[63] (1769), Dick. 419; 2 Hargr. Jurid. Arg. 304.

a husband and a wife, who had power to bequeath some personal property secured to her separate use, made mutual wills of November 21, 1745. The residuary estate of each was pooled into one common fund and bequeathed to the survivor for life with limitations over. The wife survived, and, having enjoyed the property for her life, died, leaving a will which disregarded the trusts of the mutual will. The beneficiaries under the mutual will filed a bill, and Lord Camden made a decree declaring that the surviving wife had bound herself to make good all the bequests in the mutual will, and made an order based on that declaration. The judgment was founded on the fact that the two parties had agreed to pool their estates and, in consideration of the agreed benefits that the survivor was to take, to give effect to the agreement which Lord Camden held they made with regard to the disposition of the capital. Lord Camden observed [64]—

> The instrument itself is the evidence of the agreement and he, that dies first, does by his death carry the agreement on his part into execution. If the other then refuses, he is guilty of a fraud, can never unbind himself, and becomes a trustee of course. For no man shall deceive another to his prejudice. By engaging to do something that is in his power, he is made a trustee for the performance, and transmits that trust to those that claim under him.

In *Lord Walpole* v. *Lord Orford*,[65] Lord Loughborough came to the conclusion that an agreement had been made, but he was unable to ascertain its terms with certainty and precision. He therefore did not enforce the agreement as a trust, as too uncertain, although he assented to Lord Camden's decision above. The effect of Lord Loughborough's decision has been discussed several times in the later cases, but this view of the case is taken by Sir Robert Collier in *Denyssen* v. *Mostert*,[66] and by Astbury, J., in *Re Oldham*.[67] *Dufour* v. *Pereira* [63] was approved in *Stone* v. *Hoskins*.[68] In that case there was a prior arrangement, and mutual wills made in pursuance of that arrangement. It was held that the survivor could not object if the first to die departed from the arrangement in a subsequent will: the survivor is free to change his own will. In *Re Oldham*,[69] the earlier authorities were reviewed. As in the other cases, a husband and wife made mutual wills, but there was no proof that these were made in pursuance of a prior agreement. Moreover, each gave the other an absolute interest in the whole of the property if he or she survived, but if either of the parties did not survive the other, then the property of the survivor was to pass to third parties. The husband died first, and the wife married again, making a fresh will, ignoring the provisions of her mutual will. Astbury, J., held there was no implied trust preventing the wife from disposing of her property as she pleased, observing [70]—

> ... a very great difference between *Dufour* v. *Pereira* [71] and the present case is that in *Dufour* v. *Pereira* [71] the capital of the trust property was

[64] 2 Hargr. Jurid. Arg. 310.
[65] (1797), 3 Ves. 402.
[66] (1872), L.R. 4 P.C. 236, 253.
[67] [1925] Ch. 75, 85 (Cases, p. 296).
[68] [1905] P. 194.
[69] [1925] Ch. 75 (Cases, p. 296). See also *Re Green*, [1951] Ch. 148.
[70] [1925] Ch. 88.
[71] (1769), Dick 419.

secured in fact by the life interest only being given to the survivor, whereas in the present case the survivor is given the whole estate absolutely, and could, if so minded, dispose of the whole property inter vivos.

In *Gray* v. *Perpetual Trustee Co. Ltd.*,[72] the decision in *Re Oldham*[73] was approved by the Privy Council, who held that the fact that a husband and wife have simultaneously made mutual wills, giving each other a life interest with similar provisions in remainder, is not in itself evidence of an agreement not to revoke; and in the absence of a definite agreement to that effect, there is no implied trust preventing the wife from making a fresh will, inconsistent with the earlier one, even though the husband has died and the wife has benefited under his will. Lord Haldane explained the earlier decisions as follows [74]—

In *Dufour* v. *Pereira*[71] the conclusion reached was that if there was in point of fact an agreement come to that the wills should not be revoked after the death of one of the parties without mutual consent, they were binding. That they were mutual wills to the same effect was at least treated as a relevant circumstance, to be taken into account in determining whether there was such an agreement. But the mere simultaneity of the wills and the similarity of their terms do not appear, taken by themselves, to have been looked on as more than some evidence of an agreement not to revoke. The agreement, which does not restrain the legal right to revoke, was the foundation of the right in equity which might emerge, although it was a fact which had in itself to be established by evidence, and in such cases the whole of the evidence must be looked at. It was upon this ground that Lord Loughborough, in the later case of *Lord Walpole* v. *Lord Orford*,[75] dismissed the claim founded on the principle of Lord Camden's judgment, holding that no sufficiently definite agreement had been proved.

The most recent judgment on the effect of mutual wills made by husband and wife, without independent evidence of any contract, is that of Astbury J. in *In re Oldham*.[73] That learned judge subjected the authorities to a careful examination, and came to the conclusion that the mere fact that two wills were made in identical terms does not of necessity imply any agreement beyond that so to make them. In the case before him he found that there was not sufficient evidence of any further agreement, and that there was nothing in the authorities referred to in the argument that constrained him to decide otherwise.

Their Lordships agree with the view taken by Astbury J. The case before them is one in which the evidence of an agreement, apart from that of making the wills in question, is so lacking that they are unable to come to the conclusion that an agreement to constitute equitable interests has been shown to have been made. As they have already said, the mere fact of making wills mutually is not, at least by the law of England,

72 [1928] A.C. 391.
73 [1925] Ch. 75.
74 [1928] A.C. 399–400.
75 (1797) 3 Ves. 402.

evidence of such an agreement having been come to. And without such a
definite agreement there can no more be a trust in equity than a right
to damages at law.

Thus, the prior agreement is an essential condition of the trust, and it will
not be implied from the fact that mutual wills are in fact made. In *Re
Hagger*,[76] such an agreement was satisfactorily proved. Husband and wife
executed a joint will by which they gave everything they possessed at the
death of the first dying to the survivor for life, with remainders over. They
also agreed that the will should not be altered or revoked except by mutual
agreement. The wife died first, and the husband received the income of the
whole estate till his death. Three of the beneficiaries of the joint will survived
the wife, but predeceased the husband. The court held that from the death of
the wife the property of which the husband was then possessed was subject to
a trust under which the beneficiaries took vested interests in remainder, and
accordingly the death of the three beneficiaries before the husband's death did
not cause a lapse of their shares.[77]

C. JOINT PURCHASE AND JOINT MORTGAGE

A third case of an implied trust arises where two or more persons advance
the purchase price of property, or jointly lend money on mortgage and the
conveyance is taken in all their names (thus distinguishing the case of sale
here considered from the first example of an implied trust discussed in this
chapter). Prima facie the common law rule of survivorship applies in both
cases, so that the survivor may claim the whole interest, but equity leans
against joint tenancies, and may attach a different consequence to the transaction from that which follows at law. Here, however, it is necessary to
distinguish between joint purchases and joint mortgages. In a joint purchase,
if the two purchasers supply the purchase-money in *unequal* shares, and they
then take the conveyance jointly, courts of equity have held that, although on
the death of one the survivor or survivors hold the entirety of the legal
estate, yet in equity, the survivor or survivors will be considered as trustees
for the personal representatives of the deceased purchaser, to the extent of his
share of the purchase-money. If, on the other hand, the purchase-money was
advanced in *equal* shares, equity considers there is no justification for the
presumption of a resulting or implied trust in favour of the deceased's
personal representatives, holding that persons making equal contributions of
the purchase-money might very consistently wish to take an estate in joint
tenancy, since each before 1926 had power to compel a partition in his lifetime, or by conveyance could pass a moiety of the estate.[78] By the Law of
Property Act 1925, s. 36, however, such land would always be held by the
joint purchasers on trust for sale, for the benefit of themselves as joint
tenants in equity. Nevertheless, it is open to the personal representatives of
the deceased purchaser to prove circumstances collateral to the purchase,

---

[76] [1930] 2 Ch. 190. See also *Re Green*, [1951] Ch. 148. As to the exercise of a power of
appointment by a joint will, see *Re Duddell*, [1932] 1 Ch. 585.

[77] See further, Jarman on *Wills*, Chap. II.

[78] *Robinson* v. *Preston* (1858), 4 K. & J. 505; *Lake* v. *Gibson* (1729), 1 Eq.Cas.Abr. 290,
pl. 3, and on appeal (*sub nom. Lake* v. *Craddock*) (1732), 3 P.Wms. 158.

from which the court may infer that a tenancy in common, now necessarily equitable and held under a trust for sale,[79] was really intended,[80] and so wherever the purchasers are partners there is a trust for the deceased, since the rule of survivorship has no place in mercantile law.

Where money is jointly advanced on mortgage, however, it makes no difference whether the money is advanced in equal or in unequal shares. In both cases the survivor holds as trustee for the deceased mortgagee's estate to the extent of the deceased's share of the loan, for equity holds that in such a transaction it could not have been the intention of the lenders that there should be survivorship, but rather that each should receive back his own money, though for convenience a joint security was taken.[81] Moreover, the insertion of a joint-account clause is not conclusive evidence of an intention that the rule of survivorship should operate, for such a clause was usually inserted in a joint mortgage before the Conveyancing Act 1881, s. 61 of which (now replaced by the Law of Property Act 1925, s. 111) permitted the surviving mortgagee to give the mortgagor a receipt for the whole of the mortgage money. This, however, is simply a conveyancing device, and does not prevent a further investigation into the question whether he was really intended to take the whole of the money beneficially, or whether it was intended that he should hold a part of it for the personal representatives of the deceased joint mortgagee.[82]

D. JOINT ACCOUNTS OF HUSBAND AND WIFE

The interesting case of *Jones* v. *Maynard*[83] raised questions of a special character affecting joint accounts. In 1941, a husband about to go overseas authorised his wife to draw on his account, which was thereafter operated as a joint account, upon which both husband and wife drew, and into which both paid their earnings. The husband from time to time withdrew money to pay for investments which were made in his name. No special agreement governed the account, and the parties were divorced in 1948. The former wife brought an action against her former husband, claiming the balance of the account, and half the investments. The husband claimed that the balance and the investments should be divided proportionately to the payments in, which had been made by the parties. Vaisey, J., held that the wife was entitled to half the final balance and one half of the investments existing at the time when the account was closed. The learned judge decided that where there was a joint account between husband wife, and a common pool into which they put all their resources, it was not equitable that it should be subsequently picked apart to establish the proportionate shares of each, the husband being credited with his earnings and the wife with hers. This would be quite inconsistent with the original fundamental purpose of a joint purse or common pool—

That being my view (he continued)[84], it follows that investments paid

[79] Law of Property Act 1925, ss. 34–35.
[80] *Robinson* v. *Preston* (1858), 4 K. & J. 505.
[81] *Per* Arden, M.R., *Morley* v. *Bird* (1798), 3 Ves. 629, 631.
[82] *Re Jackson* (1887), 34 Ch.D. 732.
[83] [1951] Ch. 572.
[84] [1951] Ch. 575.

for out of the joint account, although made in the name of the husband, were in fact made by him in his own name as a trustee as to a moiety for his wife. If the investments out of the joint account had been made in the name of the wife alone, there is no doubt that the ordinary presumption of law would have applied and she would have been entitled to the investments; but as they were made in the name of the husband, it seems to me that the assumption of half and half is the one which I ought to apply.

The basis of this principle, added Vaisey, J., is the maxim that "Equality is Equity." [85] It has been evolved to determine the rights of the parties on the break-up of the marriage and it is not necessarily applicable whilst the marriage subsists.[86]

E. WHERE THE BENEFICIAL INTEREST IS NOT COMPLETELY DISPOSED OF

A clear case of a resulting trust arises where the settlor gives property to trustees on certain trusts which do not exhaust the whole beneficial interest, or where the beneficial interests wholly or partially fail. In such a case there is a resulting trust for the settlor, or if he is dead for his residuary legatee or devisee, or his intestate successor. A possible example of this type of resulting trust is provided by *Re Vandervell's Trusts (No. 2)*.[87] The settlor had given shares to the Royal College of Surgeons, and had given an option to a Vandervell family trust company to buy the shares from the College after the College had accumulated sufficient in dividends to found a Chair of Pharmacology. Later, the company exercised the option, but (according to the judge of first instance) there was nothing in the terms of the grant of the option to indicate whether the company were to hold the shares on trust and, if on trust, for whom. Megarry, J., held that the company were not intended to take beneficially and, since no trusts had been declared, they therefore held on a resulting trust. In the course of a careful judgment, the learned judge reviewed the authorities on resulting trusts and offered a classification.[88] This type of case he referred to as "automatic resulting trusts." The Court of Appeal [89] reversed the decision on the ground that express trusts had been validly declared, but leave was given to appeal to the House of Lords. A special kind of resulting trust also arises where trusts of income are declared which in ordinary years are sufficient to exhaust the whole of the income, but in certain years there is a surplus which is unprovided for. Here again there is a resulting trust of the surplus in favour of the settlor.[90]

A common case of a resulting trust of the type now under consideration

[85] See also *Rimmer* v. *Rimmer*, [1953] 1 Q.B. 63; *Cobb* v. *Cobb*, [1955] 1 W.L.R. 731; *Fribance* v. *Fribance (No. 2)*, [1957] 1 W.L.R. 384; *Hine* v. *Hine*, [1962] 1 W.L.R. 1124; *Ulrich* v. *Ulrich*, [1968] 1 W.L.R. 180; *Chapman* v. *Chapman*, [1969] 1 W.L.R. 1367; pp. 174–175, *ante*, and cases cited there. *Cf. Re Bishop*, [1965] Ch. 450; *Cracknell* v. *Cracknell*, [1971] P. 356. On the position of husband and wife as trustees for sale of the matrimonial home, see *Jones* v. *Challenger*, [1961] 1 Q.B. 176; *Rawlings* v. *Rawlings*, [1964] P. 398; *Re Solomon*, [1967] Ch. 573; *Jackson* v. *Jackson*, [1971] 1 W.L.R. 1539.
[86] *Gage* v. *King*, [1961] 1 Q.B. 188.
[87] [1973] 3 W.L.R. 744 (Cases, p. 300).
[88] [1973] 3 W.L.R. 766–7 (the passage is given in Cases, pp. 300–301).
[89] [1974] 3 W.L.R. 256.
[90] *Re Llanover Settled Estates*, [1926] Ch. 626.

arises where the settlor gives property to A, with an instruction to pay the income to B for life, with no direction what is to happen on B's death. In such a case the fact that the resulting trust is based upon the settlor's presumed intention is most clearly demonstrated, for, apart from the fact that the settlor may have expressed an intention that A should not take beneficially (which would, of course, be conclusive), it may be either that the settlor wished the beneficial interest to result to himself on B's death, or that he then wished A to take beneficially. What was his true intention may be gathered from a consideration of the whole document, and if this is a will the fact that the grant is made " upon trust " or that the donee is designated as " trustee " is not conclusive. The function of the court is to discover the settlor's true intention, and it is open to the donee to prove, if he can, from the instrument that the settlor really intended him to take beneficially at the expiration of the specified interest. Furthermore, the absence of the words " trust " and " trustee " does not imply that the donee then takes beneficially. But, where a testator gave the whole of his property to his sister *absolutely* on trust to pay his wife an annuity, and the income was more than sufficient for this, it was held that the sister was entitled to the surplus.[91] In such cases it should be noticed that the true intention of the settlor is ultimately gathered from the written instrument itself, and, accordingly, parol evidence is not admissible to prove an intention contrary to that which the court has established.[92]

It is in this last respect that the resulting trusts just considered differ from a very similar class which will now be mentioned. It has been seen that where A purchases property in the name of B, or in the names of himself and B, there is a presumption of law that the beneficial interest should result to A, unless the contrary presumption of advancement replaces it. The courts have also had to consider what the intention of the donor really was where property was given directly *inter vivos* without consideration, or for nominal consideration, and without any reference to the beneficial interest. It was mentioned when discussing the effect of the Statute of Uses that before 1535, where A enfeoffed B, simply without consideration and without any reference to the beneficial interest, the Court of Chancery held that there was a resulting *use* to the grantor. This could be negatived by a declaration of a use, either to a third person or to the feoffee himself. After 1535, where A enfeoffed B without consideration, and without declaring a use, the use resulted to the grantor and the Statute of Uses annexed the legal estate to it, and the conveyance became a nullity. As the Statute of Uses was repealed by the Law of Property Act 1925, s. 207 and Sched. 7, this particular conveyancing consequence no longer follows, so that it is no longer necessary for the grantor to use the formula " unto and to the use of B " in order to pass the legal estate. However, with the rise of the modern trust, courts of equity once more had to solve the problem created by a voluntary grant *inter vivos*, but here the answer has been rather uncertain. Where the grantor transfers property to himself and another, it would appear that in all cases there is a presumption that the whole beneficial interest is to be enjoyed by the grantor. Thus, in

[91] *Re Foord*, [1922] 2 Ch. 519.
[92] *Langham* v. *Sanford* (1811), 17 Ves. 435; on appeal (1816), 19 Ves. 641; *Irvine* v. *Sullivan* (1869), L.R. 8 Eq. 673; *Re Rees*, [1950] Ch. 204.

Standing v. *Bowring*,[93] a widow placed £6,000 Consols in the joint names of herself and her godson with the express intention that she should have the whole of the dividends for her life; and her godson was to take them at her death. Cotton, L.J., observed [94]—

> ... the rule is well settled that where there is a transfer by a person into his own name jointly with that of a person who is not his child, or his adopted child, then there is *primâ facie* a resulting trust for the transferor. But that is a presumption capable of being rebutted by shewing that at the time the transferor intended a benefit to the transferee, and in the present case there is ample evidence that at the time of the transfer, and for some time previously, the Plaintiff intended to confer a benefit by this transfer on her late husband's godson.

In *Lloyd* v. *Spillit*,[95] Lord Hardwicke said that, although this presumption might exist in respect of pure personalty, it had no application where a transfer of interests in land was made in similar circumstances, since the Statute of Frauds 1677, s. 7, required trusts of land to be manifested and proved by writing. Such reasoning, however, would seem to be fallacious, for, altogether apart from the fact that equity has never allowed the statute to be used to effect a fraud, section 8 excepts all trusts arising by implication of law from the requirements of section 7. Moreover, the presumption has been frequently applied to transfers of land to strangers, where no intention of giving the beneficial interest appears.[96] This is illustrated by a consideration of three cases: *Leman* v. *Whitley*,[97] *Haigh* v. *Kaye* [98] and *Rochefoucauld* v. *Boustead*.[99] In the first case, a son conveyed a valuable estate to his father for £400. Later, he brought an action against the devisees of his father for its reconveyance, arguing that he never intended to part with the beneficial interest in the property, his true intention being to facilitate the raising of money by means of mortgage. Sir John Leach held that because of the requirement of section 7 of the Statute of Frauds, parol evidence could not be admitted to prove the trust, the true intention being that the father should appear to be the beneficial owner. No implied trust was therefore raised in this case. In *Haigh* v. *Kaye*,[98] however, it was held, on similar facts, that since the statute could not be used to facilitate fraud, parol evidence could be admitted, and a trust raised, whilst in *Re Duke of Marlborough*,[1] Stirling, J., said that *Leman* v. *Whitley* [97] had virtually been overruled by *Haigh* v. *Kaye*,[98] the principle of which was admitted in most general terms in *Rochefoucauld* v. *Boustead*,[99] where A granted estates in Ceylon to B, and B subsequently sought to deny A's beneficial interest in them.

Where there is a direct transfer of property without consideration to a person who is not related to the donor, there is a presumption that the trans-

---

[93] (1885), 31 Ch.D. 282.
[94] 31 Ch.D. 287. See also *Fowkes* v. *Pascoe* (1875), L.R. 10 Ch.App. 343; *Re Vinogradoff*, [1935] W.N. 68; *Young* v. *Sealey*, [1949] Ch. 278.
[95] (1740), Barn.C. 384.
[96] *Duke of Norfolk* v. *Browne* (1697), Prec.Ch. 80; *Elliot* v. *Elliot* (1677), 2 Ch.Cas. 231 (*per* Lord Nottingham); *Attorney-General* v. *Wilson* (1840), Cr. & Ph. 1.
[97] (1828), 4 Russ. 423.
[98] (1872), L.R. 7 Ch.App. 469.
[99] [1897] 1 Ch. 196 (Cases, p. 205).
[1] [1894] 2 Ch. 133, 146.

feree is a trustee for the donor; but this presumption may be rebutted by evidence of an intention to confer a benefit on the transferee.[2]

It may be, however, that if property is transferred directly to another, a presumption of advancement will arise if there is near relationship and a duty on the part of the grantor to provide for the grantee, this presumption replacing that of a resulting trust. In *Crabb* v. *Crabb*,[3] a father transferred stock from his own name to the joint names of the son and a banker, telling the latter to place the dividends to his son's account. By a codicil to his will, executed after the transfer, he gave the stock to another. It was held that the son took absolutely, an advancement being plainly intended. Everything depends, however, on the intention of the donor, although the categories of evidence admissible to establish this intention are not settled.[4]

Again, in *O'Brien* v. *Sheil*,[5] A lodged securities at the bank in the names of himself and his daughter jointly. After his death, a memorandum dated fifteen months later was discovered in which he directed that the securities should be applied for other purposes. It was held that the memorandum was not admissible to rebut the presumption of advancement.

The same presumption exists in favour of a wife [6] and is not destroyed by the fact that the marriage is subsequently avoided by a decree of nullity.[7]

Sometimes it happens that property is held upon trust absolutely for a person who is living when the trust instrument comes into operation, but who has died intestate without any successors subsequently. Here, if it is clear that the settlor intended to part with his whole beneficial interest, the trustee is not allowed to take beneficially, but will hold the equitable interest for the Crown as *bona vacantia*.[8] The same rule applies where the beneficiary was a corporation which has been dissolved without the equitable interest being assigned.[9] This rule, which now applies to all kinds of property, previously applied only to personalty, for in *Burgess* v. *Wheate*,[10] it was decided that where a beneficiary under a trust of land died intestate, without leaving anyone who could claim through him, his interest did not escheat to the overlord, escheat being a feudal doctrine, and inapplicable to estates created by equity. It was formerly held that in such a case, the trustee could claim beneficially, although in *Re Sir Thomas Spencer Wells* [11] it was suggested that if the Crown, in *Burgess* v. *Wheate*,[10] had claimed the estate as *bona vacantia,* the claim would have been successful. However, by the Intestates' Estates Act 1884 the law of escheat was extended to equitable interests in real property. Thus, in *Re Wood*,[12] a testatrix devised real property on trust for sale, and the executors had a balance in hand after the objects of the trust had been carried out. There was no residuary gift and, as the testatrix had no heirs or next of kin, it was held that the property escheated to the Crown. By the Adminis-

---

[2] *Per* Lord Upjohn, *Vandervell* v. *I.R.C.,* [1967] 2 A.C. 291, 312.
[3] (1834), 1 My. & K. 511.
[4] *Shephard* v. *Cartwright,* [1955] A.C. 431 (Cases, p. 289).
[5] (1873), I.R. 7 Eq. 255. See also *Williams* v. *Williams* (1863), 32 Beav. 370.
[6] *Christ's Hospital* v. *Budgin* (1712), 2 Vern. 683.
[7] *Dunbar* v. *Dunbar,* [1909] 2 Ch. 639.
[8] *Middleton* v. *Spicer* (1783), 1 Bro.C.C. 201 ; *Re Bond,* [1901] 1 Ch. 15.
[9] *Re Higginson and Dean,* [1899] 1 Q.B. 325. For a consideration of some of Wright, J.'s observations in this case, see *Re Wells,* [1933] Ch. 29. See also p. 308, *post.*
[10] (1759), 1 Eden 177 (Cases, p. 185).
[11] [1933] Ch. 29.
[12] [1896] 2 Ch. 596.

tration of Estates Act 1925, s. 45, all existing modes and canons of descent (except so far as related to the descent of an entailed interest) and escheat are abolished, and now, where there are no intestate successors, the interest passes to the Crown (or to the Duchy of Lancaster or Duke of Cornwall), as *bona vacantia.*

The position of an executor who was not also a trustee was formerly rather different. Prior to the Executors Act 1830 where there was an undisposed-of surplus after full administration, the executor could claim it, so far as it was personalty (including leaseholds), unless it appeared to have been the testator's intention to exclude him. In such a case the executor would hold on trust for the next-of-kin. By the Executors Act 1830 it was provided that the executor should hold on trust for such persons, unless it appeared from the testator's disposition that he intended the executor to take beneficially. By the Administration of Estates Act 1925, s. 49, the present position is that where there is any property undisposed of after administration is complete, it is to be distributed or held in trust for the intestate successors specified in section 46, unless it appears from the will that the personal representative was intended to take the property beneficially. The persons who take the residue, if issue of the testator, but not otherwise, must bring into account any beneficial interest taken by them under the will. If there are no intestate successors, or if there is none within the degrees specified in section 46, the property passes to the Crown as *bona vacantia.* The result is that in spite of the repeal of the Executors Act 1830, by the Administration of Estates Act 1925, the executor can never take beneficially unless an intention that he should do so is shown.[13]

A resulting trust may arise out of a commercial transaction, where, for example, money is handed over for a purpose which cannot be carried out. In *Barclays Bank Ltd.* v. *Quistclose Investments Ltd.*[14] a company borrowed just over £200,000 from the respondents for the purpose of paying a dividend, and a cheque for the amount was paid into a special account opened for the purpose with the appellants. Before any drawing on the special account, the company went into liquidation, so it could not pay a dividend. The House of Lords held that the amount in the special account was held on a resulting trust for the respondents, and was therefore not available for other creditors in the liquidation.

13 *Re Skeats*, [1936] Ch. 683.
14 [1970] A.C. 567.

CHAPTER XIV

CONSTRUCTIVE TRUSTS

THE term *constructive trust* covers a variety of different relationships, having very few features in common. Moreover, the rights and liabilities of constructive trustees vary widely, so that it is necessary to consider each relationship separately in order to discover exactly what is implied in it. Generally, it may be said that a constructive trust is a relationship created by equity in the interests of good conscience and without reference to any express or implied intention of the parties. Wherever a person clothed with a fiduciary character avails himself of it to obtain some personal advantage, such a person becomes a constructive trustee of all profits for the person at whose expense the profit has been made.[1]

There is also another type of constructive trust defined as follows by Bowen, L.J., in *Soar* v. *Ashwell* [2]—

> A constructive trust is one which arises when a stranger to a trust already constituted is held by the Court to be bound in good faith and in conscience by the trust in consequence of his conduct and behaviour. Such conduct and behaviour the Court construes as involving him in the duties and responsibilities of a trustee, although but for such conduct and behaviour he would be a stranger to the trust. A constructive trust is therefore, as has been said, " a trust to be made out by circumstances."

Of this type of constructive trustee Lord Selborne said in *Barnes* v. *Addy* [3]—

> ... strangers are not to be made constructive trustees merely because they act as the agents of trustees in transactions within their legal powers, transactions, perhaps of which a Court of Equity may disapprove, unless those agents receive and become chargeable with some part of the trust property, or unless they assist with knowledge in a dishonest or fraudulent design on the part of the trustees.

Both Bowen, L.J., and Lord Selborne, as well as all other equity judges, treat the constructive trust as an *institution, i.e.* as one class of the *genus* trust. It is true that, in doing so, several questions are left unanswered. For example, for a constructive trust to exist, must there be a fiduciary relationship, as has been suggested above, or are there other circumstances from which it can be inferred? Or again, are there any criteria by virtue of which the extent of the constructive trustee's rights and liabilities may be deter-

---

[1] For a discussion of constructive trusts from the standpoint of American law, see Scott, "Constructive Trusts" (1955) 71 *Law Quarterly Review* 39. For English law, see Waters, *The Constructive Trust* and "The English Constructive Trust: A Look into the Future" (1966) 19 *Vanderbilt Law Review* 1215; Maudsley, "Restitution in England," *ibid.*, p. 1123; Oakley, "Has the Constructive Trust become a General Equitable Remedy?" (1973) *Current Legal Problems* 17.

[2] [1893] 2 Q.B. 390, 396.

[3] (1874), L.R. 9 Ch.App. 244, 251–252. See also *Williams-Ashman* v. *Price and Williams*, [1942] Ch. 219; pp. 212–213, *post.*

mined? Again (and most important of all), is the constructive trust properly described as an institution? May it not be simply a form of remedial process?

Each of these questions requires separate treatment, but something must first be said of the history of the constructive trust, an institution which Professor Waters has described as " a well of enigmas, of contradictions and of deluding seeming simplicities." [4] Although the decision of Lord King, L.C., in *Keech* v. *Sandford* [5] is usually regarded as the starting-point for the development of the law of constructive trusts, there are decisions even earlier in date than Lord Nottingham's Chancellorship, and in one of them *Keech* v. *Sandford* is almost exactly anticipated. In *Holt* v. *Holt,* [6] executors obtained the renewal of a lease, and claimed that the renewal did not accrue to the trust estate, but the whole court (Lord Keeper Bridgman and Twisden, Wyld, Rainsford and Windham JJ.) held " that in case of an Executorship in Trust, the Renewal of such a Lease shall go to the Benefit of *Cestuy que Trust.*" Dr. Yale [7] gives a number of examples of constructive trusts from Lord Nottingham's decisions, and concludes that they were well established in his time.

Waters [8] has acutely discussed the emphasis which is placed upon the fiduciary relationship between the parties in English discussions of the constructive trust. Some writers, indeed (and some judges), have regarded constructive trusts simply as a development of the rule in *Keech* v. *Sandford.* Even where writers have taken a wider view, they have still usually regarded this rule as of greatest importance. Waters has pointed out, however, that equity was often asked to help a litigant by providing a better remedy against a party who had failed in his obligations than the common law did. One of these cases was where a binding contract for the sale of land existed, and it was necessary to protect the purchaser's interests in the interval between contract and conveyance. At another time, equity was asked to rectify the situation where property had been acquired by fraud. In these cases, and in numerous others in which the Court of Chancery intervened, the Chancery judges habitually used the language of a trust to describe the consequences of its intervention. These cases often had no real connection with each other, and in some of them there was no fiduciary relationship. Waters therefore concludes [9]—

> The truth of the matter is that the constructive trust was coined as a term because Chancery was invited to adjudicate in disputes where the relationship of the parties was rooted in the common law, and upon which Chancery imposed the language of trust. The language of trust came naturally, moreover, when Chancery was invited to impose the rudiments of trust obligation upon persons who were not trustees by express or implied creation. But, unlike the doctrine of *Moses* v. *Macferlan,* [10] there was never a theme behind the use of constructive trust by Chancery. It was never any more than a convenient and available language medium through which for the Chancery mind the obligations

4 *The Constructive Trust,* p. 7.
5 (1726), Sel.Cas.t.King 61 (Cases, p. 195).
6 (1670), 1 Ch.Cas. 190.
7 *Lord Nottingham's Chancery Cases,* Vol. II, p. 125 *et seq.*
8 *Op. cit.,* pp. 33–35.
9 *Op. cit.,* p. 39.
10 (1760), 2 Burr. 1005.

of parties might be expressed or determined. Whereas the divided jurisdictions of law and Equity gave rise to the ready use of trust language where common law language might equally well have served, the dominance of the trust in all Chancery thinking after the seventeenth century brought about the process of ready thinking by analogy. In short, a separated Court of Chancery gave us the term constructive trust, and the application by analogy with the express trust was Chancery's practice from the beginning.

It is possible to accept Waters' major hypothesis without accepting his initial supposition. Yale has shown that the constructive trust, as a device to control erring trustees, was already firmly established in Lord Nottingham's day, and when, in *Cook* v. *Fountain*,[11] he speaks of the constructive trust it is of this kind of relationship and not of one " rooted in the common law " of which he is thinking. Waters is quite right, however, to emphasise the great importance of the development of the rule in *Keech* v. *Sandford*[12] during the eighteenth and nineteenth centuries, and the part which it has played in linking the constructive trust with a fiduciary relationship.

It was pointed out at the beginning of this chapter that the rights and liabilities of the various classes of constructive trustee might vary widely, as the constructive trusts themselves do. In some cases, as where a person acquires trust property from the trustee, knowing the sale is in breach of trust, or where a trustee profits from his trust, the constructive trustee is subject to the full obligations of an express trustee. Even so, however, it would not be correct to regard the trust which exists as the complete equivalent of an express trust. If it were, as Waters points out, the constructive trustee would be bound to carry out the duties of management of the trust property and of the investment of trust funds, and sale with notice of the trust might become simply another method of appointing trustees to an express trust.[13]

In other cases, the constructive trust is much more limited in its consequences. Of constructive trustees of this type, the vendor and the mortgagee are in modern law the best examples, and the limited nature of their trusteeship will be explained later.

English law, therefore, has classified the constructive trust as an institution and as one variety of trusts, though of an anomalous kind, linking a number of situations not possessing any unifying thread, and some of them of doubtful utility in modern law. It has sought to remedy this defect in part by stressing the importance of the *Keech* v. *Sandford* cases, and by extending the principle which they embody to all situations where a fiduciary relationship exists, and by making the principle of tracing applicable. In the United States, however, as Professor Waters, Professor Maudsley and other writers have pointed out,[14] the constructive trust has been regarded as a remedial process, extending to a wide variety of cases of unjust enrichment, many of which do not depend upon the existence of a fiduciary relationship. It is a remedy which is involved wherever legal remedies prove inadequate.[15] This approach is unfamiliar to

---

[11] (1676), 3 Swanst. 585.
[12] (1726), Sel.Cas.t.King 61.
[13] *Op. cit.*, p. 16.
[14] See p. 191, *ante*, n. 1.
[15] Waters, *op. cit.*, p. 10.

English lawyers, Waters suggests, because of the long and historic separation of law and equity in England prior to the Judicature Acts. In the view of English equity, a constructive trust arises by operation of law, independently of the will of the parties; but the courts have failed, in many cases of constructive trusts, to indicate what purpose they are intended to serve. American law, on the other hand, by treating the concept as a remedy, has clearly indicated the uses to which it may be put. " It is a means whereby a person may recover or gain title to that which is unfairly withheld from him to the benefit of the withholder. Because of the unfair enrichment the deprived person is entitled to preference over the withholder's creditors and, if the withholder is insolvent, to follow against the third party to whom transfer has been made and whose transferor is insolvent." [16] Of course, that still leaves the question of when enrichment is unfair.

American law would have made light of the difficulties which English courts encountered in *Sinclair* v. *Brougham*,[17] *Re Diplock* [18] and *Reading* v. *Attorney-General*.[19] In each of these cases an equitable restitutionary remedy would have been readily available. It is Waters' contention that the way is still open for English courts to develop the constructive trust in a manner similar to that which has occurred in the United States.

A. THE VENDOR AS CONSTRUCTIVE TRUSTEE [20]

Where a binding contract for the sale of land exists, it is frequently stated that the vendor is, until completion, a constructive trustee of the property for the purchaser. This is an expression which should only be used with caution. Without qualification, it may very well lead to misleading results. It is certainly true that, from the date of the contract, the purchaser takes the benefits and bears the losses.[21] This, however, does not necessarily make the vendor a constructive trustee. The general proposition was enunciated and fully discussed by Jessel, M.R., in *Lysaght* v. *Edwards*,[22] wherein the Master of the Rolls observes that the doctrine was settled before Lord Hardwicke's time—

> What is that doctrine? It is that the moment you have a valid contract for sale the vendor becomes in equity a trustee for the purchaser of the estate sold, and the beneficial ownership passes to the purchaser, the vendor having a right to the purchase-money, a charge or lien on the estate for the security of that purchase-money, and a right to retain possession of the estate until the purchase-money is paid, in the absence of express contract as to the time of delivering possession. In other words, the position of the vendor is something between what has been called a naked or bare trustee, or a mere trustee (that is, a person without beneficial interest), and a mortgagee who is not, in equity (any more than

16 Waters, *op. cit.*, p. 12.
17 [1914] A.C. 398.
18 [1948] Ch. 465 (C.A.); *Ministry of Health* v. *Simpson*, [1951] A.C. 251 (H.L.).
19 [1951] A.C. 507.
20 See further Waters, " Constructive Trust—Vendor and Purchaser " (1961) 14 *Current Legal Problems* 76.
21 *Paine* v. *Meller* (1801), 6 Ves. 349.
22 (1876), 2 Ch.D. 499, 506–508 (Cases, p. 302).

a vendor), the owner of the estate, but is, in certain events, entitled to what the unpaid vendor is, viz., possession of the estate and a charge upon the estate for his purchase-money.... If anything happens to the estate between the time of sale and the time of completion of the purchase it is at the risk of the purchaser. If it is a house that is sold, and the house is burned down, the purchaser loses the house. He must insure it himself if he wants to provide against such an accident. If it is a garden, and a river overflows its banks without any fault of the vendor, the garden will be ruined, but the loss will be the purchaser's. In the same way there is a correlative liability on the part of the vendor in possession. He is not entitled to treat the estate as his own. If he wilfully damages or injures it, he is liable to the purchaser; and more than that, he is liable if he does not take reasonable care of it. So far he is treated in all respects as a trustee, subject of course to his right to being paid the purchase-money, and his right to enforce his security against the estate. With these exceptions, and his right to rents till the day for completion, he appears to me to have no other rights.

The same view was expressed by Lord Westbury in *Holroyd* v. *Marshall*,[23] where he pointed out that the doctrine is also applicable to those contracts for the sale of personal property which will be specifically performed. The availability of specific performance is the determining factor whether or not a constructive trust is imposed on the vendor, whether the property be realty or personalty.[24] Where specific performance is available, the position of the vendor as constructive trustee for the purchaser precludes him from declaring an express trust of the property for anyone else;[25] and if he sells the property to someone else, the vendor is a trustee of the purchase-money for the first purchaser.[26]

The remarks of Jessel, M.R., in *Lysaght* v. *Edwards* marked an important stage in the nineteenth century controversy upon the nature of this troublesome constructive trust. Already at the beginning of the eighteenth century it was accepted equitable doctrine that, from the time the contract of sale was signed, there was conversion, in consequence of which the purchaser acquired an equitable estate. This doctrine concealed a number of problems. One of them was that conversion depended upon the availability of specific performance, and this will not be available to a vendor until he has proved a good title. Waters points out that Lord Hardwicke would not accept the existence of a constructive trust until title had been accepted, and the money paid into court. During Lord Eldon's Chancellorship, however, there was a return to the earlier view that the trust arose at the moment of the execution of the contract, and the purchaser was therefore to be regarded as the equitable owner.[27]

A further problem was discussed by Plumer, V.-C., in *Acland* v. *Gaisford*.[28] Until the purchase-money was paid, the vendor was entitled to retain possession. It might be that he was never under a duty to convey at all. Accordingly,

[23] (1862), 10 H.L.C. 191, 209. See also Atkin, L.J.'s judgment in *Re Wait*, [1927] 1 Ch. 606.
[24] *Per* Lord Parker in *Central Trust and Safe Deposit Co.* v. *Snider*, [1916] 1 A.C. 266, 271–272.   [25] *McCarthy & Stone Ltd.* v. *Julian S. Hodge & Co. Ltd.*, [1971] 1 W.L.R. 1547.
[26] *Lake* v. *Bayliss*, [1974] 1 W.L.R. 1073.
[27] *Op. cit.*, pp. 76–77.   [28] (1816), 2 Madd. 28.

in his view in *Wall* v. *Bright*,[29] a constructive trust would only arise when the uncertainties had been resolved, and the duty to convey unqualifiedly existed. Before that date, the vendor was merely a trustee *sub modo*, a term which apparently was intended to mean that the vendor, though not yet a trustee, was on his way to becoming one. *Dowson* v. *Solomon*[30] advanced yet a third view, *i.e.* that the vendor only became a trustee for the purchaser at the date fixed for completion. Whether, in these circumstances, Plumer, M.R., and Kindersley, V.-C., would have agreed that conversion operated from the moment of the contract, having regard to the shadowy nature of trusteeship until the resolution of uncertainties in the one case, or of the date fixed for completion in the other, does not appear.

It was between these varying views that the members of the House of Lords were called upon to decide in *Shaw* v. *Foster*.[31] Three members (Lords Chelmsford, Cairns and O'Hagan) accepted the traditional view that a constructive trust arose when the contract of sale was signed, subject to the overriding right of the vendor-trustee to protect his interest as vendor. With this Lord Hatherley, L.C. (who had already expressed a different view in the court below), reluctantly concurred.

Four years later, Sir George Jessel, M.R., faced the same problem in *Lysaght* v. *Edwards*.[32] Following a contract of sale and acceptance of title by the purchaser, the vendor died, having devised all his real estate which he held as trustee to X subject to the trusts governing it. The question was whether the land within the contract of sale passed to X or to the heir-at-law. Jessel, M.R., held that the trust arose, not at the time when the contract was made, but when it was fully binding on both parties, *i.e.* when the vendor had made out his title, which the purchaser accepted. When this situation arose, the constructive trust related back to the moment when the contract was entered into. This, he thought, was what Plumer, M.R., meant when he stated that a trust *sub modo* arose at the time when the parties contracted, which became a constructive trust when the title was made out and accepted. At this point there was conversion, whether or not the purchase-money was then paid.[33]

The doctrine that the vendor, as constructive trustee, must use reasonable care in respect of the property is illustrated by *Phillips* v. *Silvester*,[34] in which a vendor allowed property to deteriorate after the contract of sale had been signed, and the purchase-money was proportionately reduced. Again, in *Royal Bristol Permanent Building Society* v. *Bomash*,[35] and in *Earl of Egmont* v. *Smith*,[36] it was held that where the vendors sold businesses as going concerns, they must carry them on to prevent the destruction of the goodwill or the purchaser would be entitled to repudiate. The business so carried on is at the purchaser's risk. In one case, *Dakin* v. *Cope*,[37] where a contract existed for the sale of a public-house, the purchaser declined to complete, and the vendors remained in possession and carried on the business.

---

[29] (1820), 1 Jac. & W. 494.
[30] (1859), 1 Dr. & Sm. 1.
[31] (1872), L.R. 5 H.L. 321.
[32] (1876), 2 Ch.D. 499 (Cases, p. 302).
[33] For a discussion of this case, see Waters, *op. cit.*, pp. 83–85.
[34] (1872), L.R. 8 Ch.App. 173. Followed in *Clarke* v. *Ramuz*, [1891] 2 Q.B. 456.
[35] (1887), 35 Ch.D. 390.
[36] (1877), 6 Ch.D. 469, 475.
[37] (1827), 2 Russ. 170.

In this case, although the vendors could not have discontinued business without materially diminishing the goodwill, Lord Eldon held that, since they carried on the business for their own benefit, it was continued at their risk. This is not necessarily in conflict with the cases mentioned above, for no notice had been given to the purchaser that the business was being carried on at his risk.

> Lord Eldon therefore did not think it just to impose on the purchaser the loss sustained by the vendor. . . . it stands on its own facts and does not go to the extent of deciding that, when the goodwill of a business has been sold, the vendor is not entitled to throw on the purchaser losses incurred by him in carrying on the business after the date fixed for completion, when he has acted reasonably and told the purchaser of the loss that is being incurred and given him an opportunity of saying what course should be pursued . . .[38]

This, however, does not mean that if the purchaser tells the vendor to close down, the vendor must comply, for he has his own position to consider.[38]

The limitations of the constructive trust in the vendor-purchaser relationship were strongly emphasised in *Rayner* v. *Preston*.[39] In that case, the vendor agreed to sell a house, which he had insured against fire. The contract contained no reference to the insurance; the house was damaged by fire, after the conclusion of the contract but before completion; and the vendor received payment from the insurance company. Following completion the Court of Appeal (Brett and Cotton, L.JJ., James, L.J., dissenting) upheld the decision of Jessel, M.R., that the purchaser was not entitled to claim the proceeds from the vendor. It should be observed that the position is now otherwise, for the Law of Property Act 1925, s. 47 (1), provides that where, after a contract of sale, money becomes payable under the policy of insurance maintained by the vendor in respect of the property, such money, on completion of the contract, is to be paid by the vendor to the purchaser. The subsection is subject to any stipulation to the contrary in the contract, any requisite consents of insurers, and the payment by the purchaser of the proportionate part of the premium from the date of the contract.[40] (Money could not become payable to the vendor by the insurance company, except ex gratia, as the risk has passed to the purchaser.)

This, however, does not affect the general position of the parties, and the observations of the Court of Appeal in 1881 still hold good. Cotton, L.J., observed [41]—

> An unpaid vendor is a trustee in a qualified sense only, and is so only because he has made a contract which a Court of Equity will give effect to by transferring the property sold to the purchaser, and so far as he is a trustee he is so only in respect of the property contracted to be sold. Of this the policy is not a part. A vendor is in no way a trustee for the

---

[38] *Per* Sargant, J., in *Golden Bread Co. Ltd.* v. *Hemmings*, [1922] 1 Ch. 162, 173–174, in which the purchaser was held liable to bear the loss incurred, the general principle in *Shaw* v. *Foster* (1872), L.R. 5 H.L. 321, being applied.

[39] (1881), 18 Ch.D. 1.

[40] s. 47 (2).

[41] 18 Ch.D. 6–7.

purchaser of rents accruing before the time fixed for completion, and here the fire occurred and the right to recover the money accrued before the day fixed for completion. The argument that the money is received in respect of property which is trust property is, in my opinion, fallacious.

This may be described as the middle view. Brett, L.J., was of opinion that the relation between the parties is not that of trustee and *cestui que trust* at all. He said [42]—

> With the greatest deference, it seems wrong to say that the one is a trustee for the other. The contract is one which a Court of Equity will enforce by means of a decree for specific performance. But if the vendor were a trustee of the property for the vendee, it would seem to me to follow that all the product, all the value of the property received by the vendor from the time of the making of the contract ought, under all circumstances, to belong to the vendee. What is the relation between them, and what is the result of the contract? Whether there shall ever be a conveyance depends on two conditions; first of all, whether the title is made out, and, secondly, whether the money is ready; and unless those two things coincide at the time when the contract ought to be completed, then the contract never will be completed and the property never will be conveyed. But suppose at the time when the contract should be completed, the title should be made out and the money is ready, then the conveyance takes place. Now it has been suggested that when that takes place, or when a Court of Equity decrees specific performance of the contract, and the conveyance is made in pursuance of that decree, then by relation back the vendor has been trustee for the vendee from the time of the making of the contract. But, again, with deference, it appears to me that if that were so, then the vendor would in all cases be trustee for the vendee of all the rents which have accrued due and which have been received by the vendor between the time of the making of the contract and the time of completion; but it seems to me that that is not the law. Therefore, I venture to say that I doubt whether it is a true description of the relation between the parties to say that from the time of the making of the contract, or at any time, one is ever trustee for the other.

This is, as Waters has remarked, " the simple *exposé* of the incompatibility of the trust to the vendor-purchaser relationship." [43]

Still a third view was advanced in the dissenting judgment by James, L.J.[44]—

> I am of opinion that the relation between the parties was truly and strictly that of trustee and *cestui que trust*. I agree that it is not accurate to call the relation between the vendor and purchaser of an estate under a contract while the contract is *in fieri* the relation of trustee and *cestui que trust*. But that is because it is uncertain whether the contract will or will not be performed, and the character in which the parties stand to

[42] 18 Ch.D. 10–11.
[43] *Op. cit.*, p. 86.
[44] 18 Ch.D. 13.

one another remains in suspense as long as the contract is in *fieri*. But when the contract is performed by actual conveyance, or performed in everything but the mere formal act of sealing the engrossed deeds, then that completion relates back to the contract, and it is thereby ascertained that the relation was throughout that of trustee and *cestui que trust*. That is to say, it is ascertained that while the legal estate was in the vendor, the beneficial or equitable interest was wholly in the purchaser. And that, in my opinion, is the correct definition of a trust estate.

In *Shaw* v. *Foster*,[45] Lord Hatherley substantially anticipated the view of James, L.J., adding (by way of citation from his own earlier decision)—

It is quite true that authorities may be cited as establishing the proposition that the relation of trustee and *cestui que trust* does, in a certain sense, exist between vendor and purchaser; that is to say, when a man agrees to sell his estate he is trustee of the legal estate for the person who has purchased it, as soon as the contract is completed, but not before.

Farwell, J., followed Lord Hatherley and James, L.J., in *Ridout* v. *Fowler*.[46] In that case the contract never was completed, and therefore the learned judge observed that—

. . . it is quite clear that the relationship of trustee and cestui que trust never was created by the completion of the contract. . . .

Equally clear is the opinion of Lord Cairns in *Shaw* v. *Foster*.[47] He says—

Under these circumstances I apprehend there cannot be the slightest doubt of the relation subsisting in the eye of a Court of Equity between the vendor and the purchaser. The vendor was a trustee of the property for the purchaser; the purchaser was the real beneficial owner in the eye of a Court of Equity of the property, subject only to this observation, that the vendor, whom I have called the trustee, was not a mere dormant trustee, he was a trustee having a personal and substantial interest in the property, a right to protect that interest, and an active right to assert that interest if anything should be done in derogation of it. The relation, therefore, of trustee and *cestui que trust* subsisted, but subsisted subject to the paramount right of the vendor and trustee to protect his own interest as vendor of the property.

In the same case Lord Chelmsford and Lord O'Hagan expressed themselves in similar terms.

This view of Lord Cairns is based on the assumption that the contract is ultimately completed. Lord Parker, in *Howard* v. *Miller*,[48] and again in *Central Trust and Safe Deposit Co.* v. *Snider*,[49] bases the trust between vendor and purchaser upon the fact that the contract is one which a court of equity will implement by specific performance.

The decision of the Court of Appeal in *Rayner* v. *Preston*[50] has been

45 (1872), L.R. 5 H.L. 321, 356.
46 [1904] 1 Ch. 658, 662, affirmed, [1904] 2 Ch. 93 (C.A.).
47 (1872), L.R. 5 H.L. 321, 338.
48 [1915] A.C. 318, 326.
49 [1916] 1 A.C. 266, 272.
50 (1881), 18 Ch.D. 1.

followed in two later cases. In *Re Lyne-Stephens and Scott-Miller's Contract*,[51] there was a contract for the sale of a house with vacant possession. There was at the time of the contract a lease of the house which came to an end between the date of the contract and the date fixed for completion. Sargant, J., and the Court of Appeal held that the vendor, although a trustee of the property sold, was not a trustee for the purchaser of ancillary rights in respect of the house. More recently in *Re Hamilton-Snowball's Conveyance*,[52] Upjohn, J., reached the same conclusion with regard to compensation money which became payable after contract on the derequisitioning of a house which was the subject of the sale.

The limitations of the rule that the vendor is a constructive trustee are apparent from the observations of Kekewich, J., in *Plews* v. *Samuel*,[53] in which it is pointed out that if the contract is not performed, even though the vendor was for months or years the trustee of the purchaser, until the contract was finally discharged the vendor could obviously not be proceeded against for neglect or even for malfeasance. As Knight Bruce, L.J., observed in *Sherwin* v. *Shakspear*,[54] if there is an analogy between the vendor and a trustee it is " an imperfect analogy." This is illustrated by the case of *Re Colling*,[55] in which persons authorised to sell property on behalf of A C, a person of unsound mind, sold it in May 1885, completion to follow in November. A C died in June, and the persons selling sought to establish ;that, after the contract has been concluded. A C was a trustee for the purchaser within the meaning of the Trustee Act 1850. This was not accepted by the Court of Appeal, following *Re Carpenter*.[56]

In *Re Earl of Carnarvon's Chesterfield Settled Estates*,[57] the matter again arose, and though it did not receive extended consideration this case illustrates the importance of defining exactly what is implied in the relationship of vendor and purchaser. By an agreement of August 10, 1925, the Earl of Carnarvon agreed to sell his life interest in the estates to a company. In argument it was assumed that this agreement constituted the Earl a trustee for the company. This was impliedly accepted by Romer, J., but nothing was said as to whether the title was accepted by the company, or whether the Earl had received any part of the purchase-price. It has already been observed that the nature of the trust subsisting differs upon this point. If the consideration had not passed, the nature of the company's interest in the estate would have been merely the limited beneficial interest, dependent upon completion, which has been described. Romer, J., regarded it, however, as the full trust estate, and, therefore, it would seem that the only thing remaining to be done in respect of the Earl's contract was the formal conveyance.

It will be remembered that in the course of his judgment in *Shaw* v. *Foster*,[58] Lord Cairns observed that the vendor is not a dormant trustee,

51 [1920] 1 Ch. 472.
52 [1959] Ch. 308.
53 [1904] 1 Ch. 464, 468.
54 (1854), 5 De G.M. & G. 517, 531.
55 (1886), 32 Ch.D. 333.
56 (1854), Kay 418.
57 [1927] 1 Ch. 138.
58 *Ante*, p. 199.

but one who has a personal and substantial interest of his own in the property to protect. This interest of the vendor is his right to the purchase-money, and in many cases that interest is protected by a lien, which arises immediately upon the execution of the contract of sale.[59] It may be exercised not only before the vendor has conveyed, but afterwards, although in this last case the relationship of the parties will be reversed as a result of the transfer of the legal estate, so that the purchaser will now become a trustee *pro tanto* for the vendor for what is unpaid, unless the vendor by his words or conduct plainly shows an intention to renounce his lien, and intends to rely upon some other security, or upon the personal credit of the purchaser.[60] The mere taking of a collateral security is not, in itself, however, sufficient evidence that the vendor has renounced his lien.[61]

Where the vendor's lien for the unpaid purchase-money exists, the vendor is entitled to retain the property until the money has been paid (whether there has been an agreement to this effect or not), and the lien operates not only in the sale of freeholds, but also in sales of leaseholds [62] and other personalty [63]; and the vendor is not prevented from exercising it against the purchaser by the circumstance that a receipt for the purchase-money is embodied in the deed, or has been endorsed upon it (though such a receipt can constitute an estoppel in favour of a third party).

It has been observed that merely taking collateral security does not destroy the lien; but it may be that the vendor has accepted such consideration with the object of renouncing the lien, and where this is so the lien is clearly lost. As Lord Eldon observed in *Mackreth* v. *Symmons*,[60] the question whether the lien has or has not been reserved depends upon the circumstances of each case. A lien is a charge upon the property, and it is therefore enforced by the issue of a writ, claiming a declaration that the vendor is entitled to it, and when such a declaration has been made, the vendor, in default of payment, is entitled to all the remedies he would have enjoyed under an express mortgage.[63] The lien is also enforceable, not only against the purchaser himself, but against his personal representatives, and all persons claiming through the purchaser as volunteers. It is also enforceable against the purchaser's trustee in bankruptcy.[64] Before 1926, a lien was also enforceable against a purchaser for value from the purchaser, unless the second purchaser took without notice of it. Thus, in *Rice* v. *Rice*,[65] an equitable mortgagee from the purchaser was held to take the property free from the lien, since the original vendor had endorsed a receipt for the purchase-money on the conveyance and had also delivered the title-deeds to the first purchaser, who thereupon deposited them with the mortgagee. Although vendor and equitable mortgagee both had equitable titles only, and the vendor's was earlier in point of time, he was postponed, since he had been negligent in endorsing the receipt upon the conveyance whilst the purchase-money remained unpaid. It should be noticed, however, that where the lien exists in respect of land,

59 *Re Birmingham*, [1959] Ch. 523.
60 *Mackreth* v. *Symmons* (1808), 15 Ves. 329.
61 *Collins* v. *Collins* (*No. 2*) (1862), 31 Beav. 346.
62 *Davies* v. *Thomas*, [1900] 2 Ch. 462.
63 *Re Stucley*, [1906] 1 Ch. 67.
64 *Ex parte Hanson* (1806), 12 Ves. 346, 349.
65 (1854), 2 Drew. 73.

it is a general equitable charge which, since 1925, should be registered (now under the Land Charges Act 1972, s. 2 (4)). Such registration constitutes actual notice to all claiming through the purchaser, but in the absence of registration, the lien is void against a subsequent purchaser for value, even though in fact he has notice of the existence of the lien. Apart from renunciation of the lien by the vendor, or from the alienation of the property by the purchaser to a person who has no notice of it (actual or constructive in the case of personalty, or by registration, where land is the subject of the contract), the lien may also in some cases become barred by lapse of time, for a constructive trustee may plead the Statutes of Limitation.

In the relationship of vendor and purchaser, that person is constructive trustee for the other who possesses the legal estate in the property, whilst he still owes duties to the other in respect of it. Accordingly, if the purchaser pays his purchase-money or a part of it before obtaining conveyance, the vendor is still a constructive trustee for him, and the purchaser will in this case have a lien on it for the return of his purchase-money. This lien seems to have exactly the same characteristics as the vendor's lien, and will operate against the same persons under the same conditions relating to notice,[66] and therefore, where it relates to land, it should now be registered as a land charge.

A lessee has also a lien for money spent where his lessor has contracted to grant him a lease, and the lessee has entered and has expended money upon the property, and the lessor then fails to grant the lease.[67]

B. THE MORTGAGEE AS CONSTRUCTIVE TRUSTEE

In concluding his analysis of the sterility of the constructive trust in the relationship of vendor and purchaser, Waters points out [68] that it has sometimes been linked by judges with the relationship of mortgagor and mortgagee. Indeed, in *Phillips* v. *Silvester* [69] Lord Selborne stated that, in principle, there was no reason why a vendor, under a contract of sale in which the equitable ownership had passed to the purchaser, should not be treated in exactly the same way, if he continued in possession, as a mortgagee who also remained in possession, *i.e.* as a constructive trustee.

It is Waters' thesis that the introduction of the constructive trust into both relationships has yielded little benefit, and has been productive of some error of principle; and further, that to regard such relationships as extensions of the trust concept as an institution has obstructed the development of the constructive trust as a remedy by the English courts. This is a topic upon which much has been, and could be, written. Inasmuch as the common law courts have not yet developed the quasi-contract as a general remedy for unjust enrichment, it is at least open to question whether these same judges, administering equity since the Judicature Acts, would have been willing to undertake a development, or rather transformation, of the constructive trust for a similar purpose. Moreover, it may perhaps be suggested that Waters

---

[66] *Rose* v. *Watson* (1864), 10 H.L.C. 672.
[67] *Middleton* v. *Magnay* (1864), 2 H. & M. 233.
[68] *The Constructive Trust*, pp. 142–143.
[69] (1872), L.R. 8 Ch.App. 173, 176.

underestimates the value of describing the situations in which a mortgagee is a trustee as a species of constructive trust. Against this must be set the fact that, at periods during the nineteenth century, there was a tendency for writers and Chancery judges to interpret an unduly large number of situations calling for equitable intervention in terms of the law of trusts. Particularly is this tendency apparent where the mortgagee in possession is liable to be called to account for all rents and profits received, and, as Waters points out, Turner's rejection of this interpretation is not convincing.[70]

The right of the mortgagor to enjoy the land, so long as he fulfilled his obligations, became established during the latter part of the sixteenth century, and although it was threatened for a time during the Civil War, and although a mortgagee can take possession, Lord Nottingham firmly reasserted the principle that the mortgagee's right was by way of security only, and was not a right, in ordinary circumstances, to beneficial occupation of the land itself. One potent factor which helped to establish this situation was the liability of the mortgagee to account for all rents and profits, and from this it was reasonable to conclude, as equity judges were doing as early as the beginning of the eighteenth century, that a mortgagee in possession was " in the nature of a trustee for the mortgagor." [71] As the century progressed, the courts were concerned to elucidate whether the equity of redemption was a mere chose in action or was an equitable estate in the land. In *Casburne* v. *Scarfe* [72] Lord Hardwicke emphatically affirmed that it was an estate in the land. Of the mortgagee, Lord Hardwicke said—

. . . he is a trustee for the mortgagor till the equity of redemption is foreclosed, either by decree or by such length of time as courts of equity allow to bar a redemption.

As Waters points out, a proposition so broadly affirmed raised many questions. How far did the extensive obligations of trustees apply to mortgagees? In particular, could they purchase the trust property?

Some of the consequences of Lord Hardwicke's formulation of the principle of trusteeship were apparent in *Quarrell* v. *Beckford*.[73] In that case a mortgagee had gone into possession under a decree of foreclosure which was not made absolute, and had paid off the loan and interest out of the profits. Thereafter, he retained the profits. Some years later, the assignees of the mortgagor claimed the subsequent profits with interest on them on the ground that a mortgagee who remained in possession after repayment of the debt was a trustee. Plumer, V.-C., held the mortgagee liable to account. Although Waters [74] finds difficulty in accepting Sir Thomas Plumer's argument, what the Vice-Chancellor said is clear enough. When a mortgagee is in possession, and receives rents, he is a trustee, at first with an interest to repay himself. Thereafter, he is " converted into the situation of a bare naked trustee " holding the legal estate and all profits from it for the mortgagor.

[70] Turner, *The Equity of Redemption*, p. 172. Waters, *op. cit.*, pp. 145–146. See also Keeton and Sheridan, *Equity*, pp. 257–262.
[71] *Per* Wright, L.K., *Amhurst* v. *Dawling* (1700), 2 Vern. 401. Waters, *op. cit.*, p. 149.
[72] (1738), 2 Jac. & W. 194, 196.
[73] (1816), 1 Madd. 269.
[74] *Op. cit.*, p. 154.

Nevertheless, four years later Plumer, M.R., in *Marquis Cholmondeley* v.
Lord Clinton,[75] substantially demolished the analogy between the mortgagee
and the constructive trustee. The case had already been considered by Grant,
M.R.,[76] and by the full court of King's Bench (both of whom accepted the
analogy) and it was also to be heard by the House of Lords,[77] who upheld
Sir Thomas Plumer's decree. Grant, M.R., had accepted the assumption that
the mortgagee was a trustee, but Plumer, M.R., pointed out in his judgment
that, although at various times the mortgagee-mortgagor relationship had
been compared with numerous others, it was really *sui generis.* The mortgagee
acquires a distinct and independent beneficial interest, which equity will
protect and enforce. He then considered in detail the extent of the mortgagee's
independent interest, and the rights which he has to enforce it. From this he
concluded that the mortgagee's primary character is not fiduciary, and he is
not concerned with the claims of those who seek to recover the equity of
redemption.

Plumer, M.R.'s decision was upheld by the House of Lords, but the
members of that court did not discuss at length the views upon the mortgagee
as trustee which the Master of the Rolls had put forward. It marked, as
Waters points out, an important stage in the progressive rejection by English
courts of the principle that a mortgagee is to be regarded as a special kind
of trustee, and acceptance that resemblances between the two relationships on
particular points were purely accidental. For example, it has long been
established that a mortgagee, like a trustee, cannot sell to himself.[78] On the
other hand, the rule that a trustee is presumed to have exercised undue
influence if he purchases his *cestui que trust's* property has never been applied
to the mortgagee buying the equity of redemption.

Waters has examined in detail the decisions relating to the exercise of
other powers by the mortgagee. Between 1820 and 1858, there was some
disposition to regard the mortgagee as a trustee of his power of sale, but in
Nash v. *Eads*[79] Jessel, M.R., firmly rejected this hypothesis, and so did Kay,
J., in *Warner* v. *Jacob*,[80] and since these decisions it has not been doubted
that a mortgagee is not a trustee of his power of sale. He must conduct a
proper sale, he must sell at a fair value, and he may not sell to himself, and
that is all.[81]

A further difficulty arose in the first quarter of the nineteenth century,
when the mortgage was made in the form of a trust, in order to give the
mortgagee the powers of a trustee for sale when exercising his power of sale.
Since at the same period there was a tendency to regard *any* mortgagee as a
constructive trustee, it was suggested that the only effect of expressing a
mortgage in the form of a trust was to make the mortgagee an express trustee.
Once again Jessel, M.R., this time in *Re Alison*,[82] ended doubts by firmly
asserting that the transaction remained a mortgage, and not an express trust.

75 (1820), 2 Jac. & W. 1.   76 (1817), 2 Mer. 171.
77 (1821), 4 Bligh 1.
78 See *Farrar* v. *Farrars Ltd.* (1888), 40 Ch.D. 395; *Henderson* v. *Astwood*, [1894] A.C. 150;
Williams v. *Wellingborough Corp.* (1974), *The Times* newspaper, Aug. 2; Keeton and Sheridan,
Equity, pp. 254–256.
79 (1880), 25 S.J. 95.
80 (1882), 20 Ch.D. 220.
81 See, further, Keeton and Sheridan, *Equity*, pp. 253–254; 1974 Supplement, pp. 20–21.
82 (1879), 11 Ch.D. 284.

A stronger case has been made at various times for the proposition that a mortgagee in possession becomes, by the fact of going into possession, a constructive trustee, and indeed, the latest edition of Lewin *on Trusts* asserts this in the plainest terms.[83] Waters considers this view.[84] It is not doubted that a mortgagee in possession must account for rents and profits which he receives (or, but for his wilful default, would have received), whilst in possession, but no additional duties are placed upon him as a consequence of going into possession. His position in this respect, however, is identical with that of the constructive trustee, although since 1860 judges have not been accustomed to describing him as one.

A further problem exists in respect of the position of a trustee who has sold the mortgaged property, and has received a price in excess of his mortgage debt. From the time of Lord Nottingham onwards, courts have said that the mortgagee is a trustee of such a surplus and must account to the mortgagor for it.[85] Now, by section 105 of the Law of Property Act 1925, mortgagees are statutory trustees of any surplus for the mortgagor or other person entitled to the equity of redemption.

Closely allied with this question is that of the position of the mortgagee in respect of later mortgagees. In so far as a later encumbrancer is within the terms of section 105 of the Law of Property Act 1925 (*i.e.* as a person entitled to be repaid from surplus moneys), the trusteeship of the mortgagee is now statutory, although " the statutory trust of the Conveyancing Act [1881] is not only the old constructive trust in statutory form, but decisions upon the Act and its re-enacted form in the Law of Property Act 1925 [s. 105], have been based upon the pre-1881 law." [86]

Besides this statutory trusteeship of proceeds of sale, and the liability to account when the mortgagee enters into possession, nothing of substance has survived the property legislation in respect of the constructive trusteeship of the mortgagee. It was fleetingly invoked by Lawrence, L.J., in *Re Wells* [87] as a possible explanation of why a mortgagor could not rely upon his legal title to resist a claim by the Crown to an equity of redemption as *bona vacantia.* Since the circumstances of that case were unusual, the observations of Lawrence, L.J., have not provoked subsequent judicial discussion, and Waters has suggested that they do little more than emphasise how valueless the analogy between mortgagee and constructive trustee has now become.

C. THE ACQUISITION OF PROPERTY BY FRAUD

Where one person has acquired property in consequence of his fraud upon another, equity converts him into a constructive trustee, for the benefit of the person who has been injured by the fraud. This is not always the person upon whom the fraud has operated. Thus, where a person is induced not to make a will because the person entitled on intestacy promises the intending

---

[83] 16th ed., p. 149.
[84] *Op. cit.*, pp. 189–197.
[85] *Banner* v. *Berridge* (1881), 18 Ch.D. 254; *Charles* v. *Jones* (1887), 35 Ch.D. 544.
[86] Waters, *op. cit.*, p. 216.
[87] [1933] Ch. 29.

testator that he will benefit X as the testator desires, this is a secret trust which equity will impose as a constructive trust upon the intestate successor.[88] The attitude of equity in cases of constructive trusts resulting from fraud was explained as follows by Lord Westbury in *McCormick* v. *Grogan* [89]—

> . . . the jurisdiction which is invoked here by the Appellant is founded altogether on personal fraud. It is a jurisdiction by which a Court of Equity, proceeding on the ground of fraud, converts the party who has committed it into a trustee for the party who is injured by that fraud. Now, being a jurisdiction founded on personal fraud, it is incumbent on the Court to see that a fraud, a *malus animus*, is proved by the clearest and most indisputable evidence. It is impossible to supply presumption in the place of proof, nor are you warranted in deriving those conclusions in the absence of direct proof, for the purpose of affixing the criminal character of fraud, which you might by possibility derive in a case of simple contract. The Court of Equity has, from a very early period, decided that even an Act of Parliament shall not be used as an instrument of fraud; and if in the machinery of perpetrating a fraud an Act of Parliament intervenes, the Court of Equity, it is true, does not set aside the Act of Parliament, but it fastens on the individual who gets a title under that Act, and imposes upon him a personal obligation, because he applies the Act as an instrument for accomplishing a fraud.

This principle has an exceedingly wide orbit. In *Bannister* v. *Bannister* [90] the plaintiff bought the defendant's cottage for less than its value, under an oral agreement that the defendant could live in it rent free as long as she liked. The Court of Appeal held that this created a life interest in the defendant's favour, and also that the plaintiff could not set up the absolute character of the conveyance so as to defeat the defendant's beneficial interest. The fraud in this case, therefore, consisted in setting up the absolute character of the conveyance. That decision was applied by the majority of the Court of Appeal in *Binions* v. *Evans*.[91] The owners of a cottage contracted to allow the defendant to live in it rent free for life. Later they sold the cottage to the plaintiffs, at a reduced price because the sale was expressed to be subject to the defendant's rights. It was held that the plaintiffs could not evict the defendant because they held on a constructive trust for her for life. Lord Denning, M.R., who agreed in the result, classed the defendant's right as a contractual licence protected in equity, not a life interest under a constructive trust. That avoids the peculiar consequence of the majority view, and of the unanimous decision in *Bannister* v. *Bannister*,[90] that the person with the right of residence, having an equitable life interest, is the tenant for life of the land within the meaning of the Settled Land Act 1925, s. 19, is entitled to have the legal estate vested in him, and has the power of sale; so that all that the plaintiffs in *Binions* v. *Evans* [91] bought was an equitable reversionary interest.

---

88 *Sellack* v. *Harris* (1708), 5 Vin.Abr. 521, pl. 31. See pp. 64–78, *ante*.
89 (1869), L.R. 4 H.L. 82, 97.
90 [1948] 2 All E.R. 133.
91 [1972] Ch. 359. See also Martin, " Contractual Licensee or Tenant for Life? " (1972) 36 *Conveyancer* 266 ; Smith, " Licences and Constructive Trusts—' The Law is What it Ought To Be ' " (1973), 32 *Cambridge Law Journal* 123. *Cf. Dodsworth* v. *Dodsworth* (1973), 228 Est. Gaz. 1115.

D. AN EXPRESS TRUSTEE AS A CONSTRUCTIVE TRUSTEE

A cardinal rule of equity is that a trustee shall not make a profit from his trust, nor even use his position as trustee to secure a personal advantage at the expense of his beneficiary. Certain exceptions to this rule now exist, and will be discussed later. For the present, it must be stated that if a trustee does secure such an unauthorised advantage or profit, he holds it as a constructive trustee for his beneficiary. The leading case upon this type of constructive trust is *Keech* v. *Sandford*.[92] A trustee held a lease of Romford Market upon trust for an infant. The lease expired, and the trustee sought to renew it on behalf of his beneficiary. This the lessor refused to do, but intimated that he had no objection to a renewal by the trustee on his own behalf; whereupon the trustee took a renewal for himself. Lord King, L.C., held that the lease must be held on trust for the infant, adding [93]—

> ... I very well see, if a trustee, on the refusal to renew, might have a lease to himself, few trust estates would be renewed to *cestui que use* ...

This is a principle which has received the very widest application, for it has been extended to all who occupy a fiduciary position, including executors and administrators,[94] an executor *de son tort*[95] (*i.e.* a person who interferes with the estate of a deceased, without possessing the necessary authority), and also agents of these persons[96] and to the husband or wife of a person in a fiduciary position,[97] whilst it applies equally where a person purchases the right to renew from the trustee, executor or tenant for life, and in this case the trust attaches to the purchase-money and not to the renewed lease.[98]

There is some doubt whether a distinction must be drawn between the trustee obtaining a renewal of the lease, as in *Keech* v. *Sandford*,[99] when the trustee holds the new lease on a constructive trust, and the trustee buying the landlord's freehold reversion. In *Bevan* v. *Webb*[1] Warrington, J., reviewed the authorities and concluded: (1) *Keech* v. *Sandford* applies if one partner obtains a personal renewal of the lease of the partnership premises; but (2) there is no constructive trust if the partner purchases the freehold reversion, at least in the absence of fraud, unless the partnership lease is renewable by custom or contract (or now, presumably, by statute). That was one of two grounds for the decision, Warrington, J., also holding that the partnership had a licence, not a lease, anyway, so that there was no property on to which the freehold could be grafted. In *Protheroe* v. *Protheroe*,[2] on the other hand, the Court of Appeal decided that a husband, who was trustee of the lease of the matrimonial home for himself and his wife, held the freehold on

---

92 (1726), Sel.Cas.t.King 61. (Cases, p. 195.) See also Paling, " The Pleadings in Keech *v.* Sandford " (1972), 36 *Conveyancer* 159; Jones, " Unjust Enrichment and the Fiduciary's Duty of Loyalty " (1968), 84 *Law Quarterly Review* 472; McClean, " The Theoretical Basis of the Trustee's Duty of Loyalty " (1969) 7 *Alberta Law Review* 218.

93 Sel.Cas.t.King 62.

94 *Walley* v. *Walley* (1687), 1 Vern. 484; *Re Jarvis*, [1958] 1 W.L.R. 815.

95 *Mulvany* v. *Dillon* (1810), 1 B. & B. 409.

96 *Griffin* v. *Griffin* (1804), 1 Sch. & Lef. 352; *Mulvany* v. *Dillon*, *supra*.

97 *Ex parte Grace* (1799), 1 B. & P. 376; *Re Biss*, [1903] 2 Ch. 40, 58.

98 *Owen* v. *Williams* (1773), Amb. 734.

99 (1726), Sel.Cas.t.King 61.

1 [1905] 1 Ch. 620, applied in *Brenner* v. *Rose*, [1973] 1 W.L.R. 443.

2 [1968] 1 W.L.R. 519.

a constructive trust when he bought it after separating from his wife. Neither *Bevan* v. *Webb* nor any other case was cited to the court. Lord Denning, M.R., said [3]—

> There is a long established rule of equity from *Keech* v. *Sandford*, downwards that if a trustee, who owns the leasehold, gets in the freehold, that freehold belongs to the trust and he cannot take the property for himself. On that principle when the husband got in the freehold, it attached to and became part of the trust property.

But the husband was also held entitled to be reimbursed the cost of buying the freehold, out of the proceeds when the house was sold. *Protheroe* v. *Protheroe* [2] was applied, and *Bevan* v. *Webb* [1] was again not cited, in *Thompson's Trustee in Bankruptcy* v. *Heaton*,[4] where, after a partnership had been dissolved without any disposition of the lease, a company formed by one of the ex-partners acquired the freehold reversion of the leasehold property. Pennycuick, V.-C., held that a fiduciary relation arose from the duty of good faith which each partner owed to the other, and that that relation continued after dissolution of the partnership so long as its affairs remained unsettled. The learned Vice-Chancellor said [5]—

> It necessarily follows, I think, that where the property of a dissolved partnership includes a leasehold interest, then subect to any other arrangement which may be made between the partners concerning that interest, each of the former partners owes the same obligation to the other former partner in respect of that interest as he did while the leasehold interest remained the partnership property and, accordingly, he is under the same limitations with regard to the purchase of the reversion as he would have been had the partnership still been subsisting.

Further extensions of the rule have imposed a constructive trust where a lease is renewed for himself by a tenant for life,[6] a partner,[7] a mortgagor or mortgagee,[8] a joint tenant (but not a tenant in common),[9] even though some of these persons do not necessarily occupy a fiduciary position towards the other persons interested. In *Holmes* v. *Williams*,[10] it was held that where a lease held by trustees for several beneficiaries was forfeited, and one of the beneficiaries secured its renewal, the rule did not apply, and he was not a constructive trustee for his co-beneficiaries.

The rule does not apply in as full a form to the persons just considered as to the first class. The constructive trust may, in the second class of cases, be rebutted by proof that the position occupied has not been in any way abused, but the difficulty of rebutting it varies, so that the clearest evidence would be required to free a partner, a mortgagor or a mortgagee from the trust. In *Re Biss*,[11] the whole question was fully discussed. A shopkeeper

---

[3] [1968] 1 W.L.R. 521.
[4] [1974] 1 W.L.R. 605.
[5] [1974] 1 W.L.R. 613.
[6] *Randall* v. *Russell* (1817), 3 Mer. 190; *Lloyd-Jones* v. *Clark-Lloyd*, [1919] 1 Ch. 424.
[7] *Featherstonhaugh* v. *Fenwick* (1810), 17 Ves. 298.
[8] *Rushworth's Case* (1676), Freem.Ch. 13; *Rakestraw* v. *Brewer* (1728), 2 P.Wms. 511.
[9] *Palmer* v. *Young* (1684), 1 Vern. 276; *Kennedy* v. *De Trafford*, [1897] A.C. 180.
[10] [1895] W.N. 116.
[11] [1903] 2 Ch. 40 (Cases, p. 196). See also *New Zealand Netherlands Society 'Oranje' Inc.* v. *Kuys*, [1973] 1 W.L.R. 1126.

holding under a yearly tenancy died intestate, leaving a widow and three children. The widow was appointed administratrix, and she continued the business with the assistance of one of the sons. Her application for a renewal of the lease was refused, whereupon the son applied and secured it. The Court of Appeal held that he could keep the lease for himself, since he did not stand in a fiduciary position to the other persons entitled on intestacy, whilst the position he had occupied in the business had not been abused.

Both Collins, M.R., and Romer, L.J., in the Court of Appeal, discussed at length the extent of the rule in *Keech* v. *Sandford*.[99] Collins, M.R., after pointing out that a party may not derive any advantage out of his fiduciary or quasi-fiduciary position, added that where such a position was found not to exist, it was a question of fact, or possibly a rebuttable presumption of law, whether the advantage must be surrendered to some other, or whether the connection between them was either ended, or too remote, when the acquisition occurred. Romer, L.J., approached the problem differently. He said that there were three distinct situations in which a person could not retain a benefit which he had secured: (1) where the acquirer occupied a fiduciary position; (2) where a person not in a fiduciary position acquired property by fraudulently representing that he was acting on behalf of others; and (3) where a person occupied a special position, and in virtue of it, owed a duty towards others interested in the benefit acquired. In the view of Waters, persons within Romer, L.J.'s third class corresponded with those non-fiduciary persons who were subject to a presumption of fact.[12]

Romer, L.J., in the course of a comprehensive judgment said [13]—

> . . . the cases shew that, with regard to a person obtaining a renewal who occupies a fiduciary position, it is contrary to public policy to allow him to rebut the presumption that in obtaining a renewal he acted in the interests of all persons interested in the old lease. I may also add that some of the decided cases, where persons not in a fiduciary position obtaining renewals have been held to be constructive trustees, depend upon the fact that those persons acted fraudulently in the matter; as, for instance, by representing to the lessors, or by inducing or allowing the lessors to believe, that they were acting in the interest of those entitled to the old lease. And of course, if a person has obtained a new lease by reason and in consideration of a surrender or attempted surrender of an old lease or rights belonging to third parties, he cannot, as against those third parties, pretend to hold the new lease as his own absolute property. But cases falling within the two last-mentioned classes stand apart, and need no further examination by me. . . .
>
> The cases which really demand full consideration are those where the person renewing the lease does not clearly occupy a fiduciary position. On inquiry into those cases it appears to me, as a result, that a person renewing is only held to be a constructive trustee of the renewed lease if, in respect of the old lease, he occupied some special position and owed, by virtue of that position, a duty towards the other persons interested.

---

[12] *The Constructive Trust*, pp. 31–33. See also Hart, "The Development of the Rule in *Keech* v. *Sandford*" (1905) 21 *Law Quarterly Review* 258.
[13] [1903] 2 Ch. 60–62.

Take, for example, the case of a tenant for life under a settlement of leaseholds. Although not a trustee for the remaindermen,[14] yet his position is not that of a stranger as regards them. He owes, by virtue of his position, certain duties towards them in respect of the settled property; and if, by virtue of his position, he is enabled to obtain a renewal of the lease, equity clearly demands that the new right obtained in virtue of the old should be regarded as a graft on the old, and be treated accordingly as settled property.

Take next the case of a partner obtaining a renewal of a partnership lease: here, apart from the fact that in ordinary cases concerning the carrying on of the partnership business he is an agent for the partners, he clearly owes a duty to his co-partners not to acquire any special advantage over them by reason of his position. And, therefore, as a rule, even if a partnership lease has come to an end, yet if that partner, by virtue of his position, obtains a renewed lease, he will be held to have acquired it on behalf of all the partners. . . .

I will next deal with the cases decided as between mortgagor and mortgagee. Each of these owes a duty to the other in respect of the mortgaged property; and in case of one being able, by virtue of his position, to obtain a renewal of a mortgaged lease, there are obvious grounds why it should be held against him, at any rate as a rule, that the renewed lease should be treated as engrafted on the old and as forming part of the mortgage security.

Re Biss,[15] therefore, stands in clear contrast with *Re Knowles' Will Trusts*,[16] where a son was residuary legatee and manager of the deceased's business, but he was also a trustee of the will. When he renewed the lease in his own name, therefore, the Court of Appeal held that the renewal accrued for the benefit of all the beneficiaries under the trust.

Where a trustee, executor or other person has incurred expense in renewing the lease, or has expended money in permanent improvements on the strength of it, he has a lien upon the property for his costs, with interest,[17] and he is also entitled to be indemnified for all personal covenants he may have entered into in renewing the lease,[18] whilst on his side, the trustee must account to his *cestui que trust* for all mesne rents and profits,[19] and he must free the property from all encumbrances which he has created, except underleases at a rack-rent.[20]

Another illustration of the misuse of a fiduciary capacity is afforded by a trustee, tenant for life or executor permitting a prejudicial act in relation to the trust property in return for valuable consideration. Here the consideration received is subject to a constructive trust. Thus, in *Pole* v. *Pole*,[21]

---

[14] But a tenant for life in whom the leasehold is vested under the Settled Land Act 1925 is made a trustee by s. 16 (1).

[15] [1903] 2 Ch. 40 (Cases, p. 196).

[16] [1948] 1 All E.R. 866.

[17] *Holt* v. *Holt* (1670), 1 Ch.Cas. 190; *Rowley* v. *Ginnever*, [1897] 2 Ch. 503.

[18] *Keech* v. *Sandford* (1726), Sel.Cas.t.King 61 (Cases, p. 195); *Re Jarvis*, [1958] 1 W.L.R. 815.

[19] *Keech* v. *Sandford, supra*; *Giddings* v. *Giddings* (1827), 3 Russ. 241.

[20] *Bowles* v. *Stewart* (1803), 1 Sch. & Lef. 209, 226.

[21] (1865), 2 Dr. & Sm. 420.

a tenant for life for valuable consideration permitted an Act of Parliament sanctioning a railway affecting his property to pass unopposed by him, and it was held that the money received was subject to a trust. In *Aberdeen Town Council* v. *Aberdeen University*,[22] yet another aspect of the doctrine was emphasised. The town council of Aberdeen held certain lands adjacent to the sea in trust for Aberdeen University and its professors. The council then obtained a grant of salmon-fishings in the sea opposite the land which they held in trust, and the House of Lords held that the grant must be held in trust for the university and its professors.

Again, if a tenant for life commits waste by felling timber, and he is impeachable for waste, the persons entitled to the first estate of inheritance under the settlement may claim the timber, or damages at law, and in equity the tenant for life is a constructive trustee, accountable for the proceeds, with interest at 4 per cent.[23] It may happen, however, that, at the time when the waste is committed, the tenant for life is himself entitled to the first estate of inheritance, and if that is so, he is a constructive trustee for all the persons interested according to their estates, since no one may take advantage of his own wrong.[24] Further, if the tenant for life and the person with the first vested estate of inheritance agree together to cut timber and share the proceeds, they are both constructive trustees for all the other persons interested in the estate.[25]

E. MISUSE OF A FIDUCIARY RELATIONSHIP

The constructive trust which arises when an express trustee makes a profit from his trust is simply an illustration of a still wider equitable principle, which was defined by Lord Herschell in *Bray* v. *Ford*[26] as follows—

> It is an inflexible rule of a Court of Equity that a person in a fiduciary position . . . is not, unless otherwise expressly provided, entitled to make a profit; he is not allowed to put himself in a position where his interest and duty conflict. It does not appear to me that this rule is, as has been said, founded upon principles of morality. I regard it rather as based on the consideration that, human nature being what it is, there is danger, in such circumstances, of the person holding a fiduciary position being swayed by interest rather than by duty, and thus prejudicing those whom he was bound to protect.

Discussing the same principle in *Regal (Hastings) Ltd.* v. *Gulliver*,[27] Lord Wright said—

> [The] question can be briefly stated to be whether an agent, a director, a trustee or other person in an analogous fiduciary position, when a demand is made upon him by the person to whom he stands in the

---

22 (1877), 2 App.Cas. 544.
23 *Garth* v. *Cotton* (1753), 3 Atk. 751. Certain acts committed by the tenant for life are now dealt with in the Settled Land Act 1925 but, except where such statutory provision has been made, it is conceived that the law relating to waste remains in force.
24 *Williams* v. *Duke of Bolton* (1784), 1 Cox 72.
25 *Garth* v. *Cotton, supra.*
26 [1896] A.C. 44, 51.
27 [1942] 1 All E.R. 378, 392.

fiduciary relationship to account for profits acquired by him by reason of his fiduciary position, and by reason of the opportunity and the knowledge, or either, resulting from it, is entitled to defeat the claim upon any ground save that he made the profits with the knowledge and assent of the other person. The most usual and typical case of this nature is that of principal and agent. The rule in such cases is compendiously expressed to be that an agent must account for net profits secretly (that is, without the knowledge of his principal) acquired by him in the course of his agency. The authorities show how manifold and various are the applications of the rule. It does not depend on fraud or corruption.

Boardman v. *Phipps* [28] furnished an illustration of the application of this rule to persons who had acted as agents, and had been so treated, although in fact they were not.

F. A STRANGER INTERMEDDLING WITH THE TRUST

Where a stranger to the trust receives trust property from the trustee, knowing it to be part of the trust estate, and knowing also that it is handed to him in breach of trust, he becomes a constructive trustee for the persons beneficially entitled.[29] His liability as a constructive trustee is unaltered even though he may have given value, or if he knowingly assists the trustees to commit a breach of trust without actually receiving the trust property. Again, where a volunteer receives trust property, whether with or without notice, he becomes a constructive trustee of it.[30] A stranger to the trust, however, does not become a constructive trustee simply because he acts as agent of the trustee in transactions within the legal powers of the trustees unless the agent receives and becomes chargeable with some part of the trust property, or unless he knowingly assists in a fraudulent purpose of the trustee.[31] This principle and the relevant authorities were considered fully by Ungoed-Thomas, J., in *Selangor United Rubber Estates Ltd.* v. *Cradock (No. 3).*[32] In that case, and in *Karak Rubber Co. Ltd.* v. *Burden (No. 2),*[33] a bank was held liable as constructive trustee on the basis that one " knowingly assists " in a fraudulent purpose if one has knowledge of circumstances which would indicate to an honest, reasonable man that there was such a purpose, or which would put one on inquiry as to whether there was a fraudulent purpose and one failed to make such inquiry A solicitor does not become a constructive trustee of money he receives from his client merely because he knows that another party *claims* that the client is a trustee of the funds out of which the solicitor is paid.[34] Furthermore, the Partnership Act 1890, s. 13, provides that a partner of a trustee who has improperly employed trust

[28] [1967] 2 A.C. 45.
[29] *Barnes* v. *Addy* (1874), L.R. 9 Ch.App. 244.
[30] *Re Eyre-Williams,* [1923] 2 Ch. 533.
[31] *Per* Lord Selborne in *Barnes* v. *Addy* (1874), L.R. 9 Ch.App. 244, 251 ; *Williams-Ashman* v. *Price and Williams,* [1942] Ch. 219.
[32] [1968] 1 W.L.R. 1555, 1578-91.
[33] [1972] 1 W.L.R. 602.
[34] *Carl Zeiss Stiftung* v. *Herbert Smith & Co. (No. 2),* [1969] 2 Ch. 276. See also p. 191, *ante.*

property in the partnership business does not become a constructive trustee unless he has notice of the breach of trust committed by the other; and the trust money may be recovered if still under the control of the partnership.

In *Bridgman* v. *Gill*,[35] a trust fund stood in the names of two trustees at a bank, the manager of which knew it was a trust fund. The bankers, at the request of the tenant for life only, paid the fund into the account of the tenant for life, who thereby repaid the bank a debt. It was held that the bankers were constructive trustees for the beneficiaries, and that the Statute of Limitations did not apply to protect the bank.

There are many examples of the principle that a person who acts as trustee without having authority to do so is held liable in exactly the same way as if he were in fact a trustee.[36] In *Lyell* v. *Kennedy*[37] the House of Lords held that a person who, without authority, collected the rents of property which he knew to belong to others, had assumed a fiduciary character in respect of the rents he had collected. Again, in *Boardman* v. *Phipps*,[38] Boardman, a solicitor to a trust, and Thomas Phipps, a principal beneficiary, assumed authority to act as agents to the estate, and in that capacity used their position to obtain knowledge of the affairs of a company in which the trust held shares, and in which Boardman and Thomas Phipps then acquired shares of their own. The House of Lords held that all profits derived from these transactions must be accounted for to the trust, exactly as if they had been properly appointed agents, but that, as the solicitor and the beneficiary had acted honestly and in a way that raised the value of the trust shares considerably, they were to be allowed payment on a liberal scale for their work.

G. OTHER CONSTRUCTIVE TRUSTS

Besides the groups of constructive trusts already discussed, a constructive trust may be an incident of many miscellaneous relationships.[39] There may be a constructive trust of sums of money recovered under a promissory note. Thus, in *Hirachand Punamchand* v. *Temple*,[40] a son owed a sum to a money-lender under a promissory note, and his father wrote to the money-lender, offering an amount less than that owing under the promissory note, and enclosing a draft for the smaller amount. The draft was cashed, and the money-lender then sued the son for the balance. The Court of Appeal held that he could not recover, and Farwell, L.J., observed[41]—

> . . . I have no hesitation in saying that a Court of Equity would have regarded the plaintiffs as disentitled to sue except as trustees for the father, and would have restrained them from suing under such circumstances as existed in the present case.

35 (1857), 24 Beav. 302. See also *Rolfe* v. *Gregory* (1865), 4 De G.J. & S. 576; *Imperial Bank of Canada* v. *Begley*, [1936] 2 All E.R. 367.
36 See, *e.g.*, *Rackham* v. *Siddall* (1850), 1 Mac. & G. 607.
37 (1889), 14 App.Cas. 437.
38 [1967] 2 A.C. 45, commented on by Poole, "The Honour of being a Constructive Trustee" (1967) 31 *Conveyancer* 352. See also Fridman, "Agency and Secret Profits" (1968) 3 *Manitoba Law Journal* 17; Marshall, "Conflict of Interest and Duty" (1955) 8 *Current Legal Problems* 91.
39 For a constructive trust arising out of an oral agreement, see *Oughtred* v. *I.R.C.*, [1960] A.C. 206.
40 [1911] 2 K.B. 330. See also *Re Richards* (1887), 36 Ch.D. 541.
41 [1911] 2 K.B. 342.

This was amplified by Vaughan Williams, L.J., who, after considering whether the promissory note had in the circumstances ceased to be a negotiable instrument, added [42]—

> ... alternatively, assuming that this was not so, and that the instrument did not cease to be a negotiable instrument, then, in my judgment, from the moment when the draft sent by Sir Richard Temple was cashed by the plaintiffs a trust was created as between Sir Richard Temple and the money-lenders in favour of the former, so that any money which the latter might receive upon the promissory note, if they did receive any, would be held by them in trust for him. ... In my judgment, if I am right in saying that any moneys received on the note by the plaintiffs would be held by them in trust for Sir Richard Temple, then, without any question of resort to a Court of Equity, there might have been a defence in a Court of law on the ground that any money recoverable on the note by the plaintiffs was recoverable by them merely as trustees for Sir Richard Temple, and that, under the circumstances disclosed by the correspondence, the relations between the father and son were such that it was impossible to suppose that the father wished to insist on payment of the note by the son.

An annuitant (when an annuity is given by will free of tax) who suffers business losses is a trustee not only of the sums he may recover in tax on account of such losses, but also of the right to make the necessary claim.[43]

Again, a director of a company is so far a constructive trustee that he cannot enter into profitable contracts with the company,[44] buy property and sell it to the company for a profit, receive commissions from persons buying from the company, or use information obtained as director for the purpose of securing himself private remuneration,[45] and if a director diverts company money and invests it in his own name, he will hold the investment on trust for the company[46]; but directors are not trustees for the creditors of the company,[47] nor are they trustees for individual shareholders, and therefore they may purchase shares from shareholders without disclosing existing negotiations for the sale of the company's business.[48] Promoters of a company also occupy a fiduciary position to the company, so that they may not retain secret commissions from persons who are selling property to the company which is being formed.[49] The secretary of a company is subject to a similar incapacity.[50] A solicitor who purchases property from a client must show not only that he gave full value for it, but also that the client benefited from

[42] [1911] 2 K.B. 337.
[43] Re Kingcome, [1936] Ch. 566; Re Lyons, [1952] Ch. 129.
[44] Great Luxembourg Railway Co. v. Magnay (No. 2) (1858), 25 Beav. 586.
[45] Industrial Development Consultants Ltd. v. Cooley, [1972] 1 W.L.R. 443.
[46] Rose v. Humbles, [1970] 1 W.L.R. 1061, 1072, per Buckley, J., a point that did not fall to be decided by the Court of Appeal when they varied the order made by the learned judge: [1972] 1 W.L.R. 33.
[47] Re A. M. Wood's Ships' Woodite Protection Co. Ltd. (1890), 62 L.T. 760.
[48] Percival v. Wright, [1902] 2 Ch. 421. See further, Keeton, " The Director as Trustee " (1952) 5 Current Legal Problems 11; Sealy, " The Director as Trustee " (1967) Cambridge Law Journal 83.
[49] Gluckstein v. Barnes, [1900] A.C. 240.
[50] McKay's Case (1875), 2 Ch.D. 1.

the sale. In *Spencer* v. *Topham*,[51] a client desired to sell property, but had been unable to find a purchaser. Ultimately the solicitor bought it, and on its being proved that the sale was entirely fair, that the client fully understood the transaction, and that the price exceeded what could have been obtained elsewhere, the sale was held to be good; but such sales should normally be conducted through a second solicitor[52]; and if the solicitor, after buying from a client, subsequently sells to a person who has notice of the voidability of the sale, the second sale is also liable to be impeached.[53]

Constructive trusts also arise out of contracts of assurance. For example, where a person with a limited interest in property (*e.g.* a carrier) insures the property so as to cover not only his own interest, but that of other persons, the insured becomes a trustee for the excess of the sum recovered over the amount of his own loss on behalf of the others interested. ". . . it is a trust clearly binding on the plaintiffs in equity, who will hold the amount which they now recover, in the first place for the satisfaction of their own claims, and in the next, as to the residue, in trust for the owners."[54]

H. THE AGENT AS TRUSTEE

The question whether an agent is a trustee for his principal has provoked considerable discussion. It is certainly clear that an agent cannot make a profit out of his position as agent, and if he does, he is accountable for that profit to his employer. Unless there is some evidence of a fiduciary relationship, however, the position of the parties in respect of the profit unlawfully made is that of debtor and creditor, and not that of trustee and *cestui que trust*.[55] It has been suggested also that an agent is always a constructive trustee of property of the principal, committed to his charge, but the better view would seem to be that he is only a trustee where there is some special, confidential relationship, *e.g.* where the principal gives the agent property for safe custody, sale or investment,[56] but where there is no such specially confidential relationship, there is no relationship of trustee and beneficiary, and the principal's remedy is at common law for money had and received.[57] Thus, a solicitor to whom money is handed for general investment,[58] a stockbroker[59] and a land agent are all constructive trustees of property committed to their charge. Some of the decisions have suggested that it is the degree of discretion which is given to the agent which determines whether he is also a fiduciary. So in *Re Hindmarsh*[60] Kindersley, V.-C., said in

---

51 (1856), 22 Beav. 573. See also *McMaster* v. *Byrne*, [1952] 1 All E.R. 1362—a sale of shares to a solicitor held liable to be set aside if the solicitor failed to disclose material facts.
52 *Cockburn* v. *Edwards* (1881), 18 Ch.D. 449, 455.
53 *Spencer* v. *Topham*, *supra*.
54 *Per* Wightman, J., in *London and North Western Railway Co.* v. *Glyn* (1859), 1 E. & E. 652, 661. See also *Waters* v. *Monarch Fire and Life Assurance Co.* (1856), 5 El. & Bl. 870, 881 ; *Re Bladon*, [1911] 2 Ch. 350, 354.
55 *Lister & Co.* v. *Stubbs* (1890), 45 Ch.D. 1, 13.
56 *North American Land and Timber Co. Ltd.* v. *Watkins*, [1904] 1 Ch. 242.
57 *Piddocke* v. *Burt*, [1894] 1 Ch. 343.
58 *Burdick* v. *Garrick* (1870), L.R. 5 Ch.App. 233.
59 *Re Strachan* (1876), 4 Ch.D. 123.
60 (1860), 1 Dr. & Sm. 129, 132. Waters' explanation of this, and similar cases (*The Constructive Trust*, p. 302 *et seq.*) does not affect the circumstance that, in these cases, agents acquired personal advantage by the direct use of their principal's property and no special, confidential relationship was held to exist (*cf. op. cit.*, p. 234).

respect of the agency of two solicitor partners, who were claiming the protection of the Statutes of Limitation, that they had received moneys " in the ordinary character of agents," and accordingly the relationship of trustee and beneficiary did not arise.

Further, if an agent was in a position of authority, to which he had been appointed by his principal, if he obtains a profit for himself, he is accountable for it to his principal [61]; and he is similarly accountable where he uses information or knowledge which he is employed by his principal to collect, or which he has acquired for the use of his principal.[62] This liability to account does not extend to profits obtained by an agent, but not on behalf of, or for the use of, his principal. If, however, the agent has used his principal's property or his position to obtain a profit, he is accountable for it, even though his principal has lost no profit, or has suffered no damage thereby, because the profit is an unjust benefit which the agent is not allowed to retain.

In his speech in *Boardman* v. *Phipps* [63] Lord Upjohn pointed out that the accountability of the agent depended upon a number of factors—

(a) The facts and circumstances must be examined to see whether a purported agent, or even a confidential agent, is in a fiduciary relationship to his principal. This may not be the case.[64]

(b) Once it is established that such a relationship exists, it must be examined to see what duties are thereby imposed upon the agent, in order to discover the scope and ambit of the duties charged upon him.

(c) Having defined the scope of those duties, it is necessary to see whether the agent has committed some breach of them, and by placing himself within the scope and ambit of those duties in a position where his duty and his interest may possibly conflict. Only at this stage does the question of accountability arise.

(d) Finally, having established accountability, this only goes so far as to render the agent accountable for profits made within the scope and ambit of his duty.

So far as confidential information is concerned, an injunction can be granted to restrain its transmission if this is in breach of a confidential relationship.

In *The Constructive Trust,* Waters discusses fully the position of the agent from the standpoint of trusteeship in his final chapter, extending to 110 pages. It is impossible in a short compass to do justice to the number and variety of the problems which he discusses, but it should be appreciated that the author's primary concern is to show that the constructive trust should not be regarded as an institution, as English lawyers have been accustomed to regard it since Lord Nottingham's celebrated classification, but as a remedial process. Regarded from this standpoint, Waters is able to show that judicial decisions and the views of legal writers alike show wide variations, even upon the occasions or the types of agency in which a fiduciary relationship can be established, and he concludes his own analysis with the observations—

> . . . what this chapter does aim to show is that it is meaningless to ask

[61] *Reading* v. *Attorney-General,* [1951] A.C. 507.
[62] *Lamb* v. *Evans,* [1893] 1 Ch. 218; *Regal (Hastings) Ltd.* v. *Gulliver,* [1942] 1 All E.R. 378; *Boardman* v. *Phipps,* [1967] 2 A.C. 45. See also p. 213, *ante.*
[63] [1967] 2 A.C. 45, 127.
[64] *Re Coomber,* [1911] 1 Ch. 723; *Re Diehl K.G.'s Application,* [1970] 2 W.L.R. 944.

the question whether an agent is a fiduciary. All agents, it is submitted, are by the nature of their function obligated to put self-interest aside when acting within the scope of their agency or otherwise utilizing their office in any particular. The concomitant of this obligation is that the principal is enabled to trace whenever this obligation is breached and proprietary advantage ensues. It is for the instant court to decide whether the particular principal has not imposed the full gamut of this obligation.[65]

In his final paragraph, Waters dismisses the use of the term " fiduciary " to describe certain types of agency as no more than a historic survival. It may be questioned, nevertheless, whether the adoption of so drastic an expedient will necessarily aid in the solution of the problems which Waters discusses. How, it may be asked, will a court decide in a particular case, whether a principal has, or has not, " imposed the full gamut of this obligation " (with the object of imposing the remedy of restitution by way of tracing)? If one says that in certain cases, " the full gamut of the obligation " has been imposed, is this so very different from saying that in such a case the agency has a fiduciary character? After all, the primary purpose of such an inquiry is to determine whether the equitable remedy of tracing is applicable.[66] A secondary one, with which the nineteenth century judges were much concerned, was whether an agent with a fiduciary character was to be treated on the footing of an express trustee, so that lapse of time would not bar claims against him. Two such cases, of outstanding importance, are *Burdick* v. *Garrick*[67] and *Soar* v. *Ashwell*.[68] In the former case, a solicitor, acting on behalf of a client who was in the United States, was authorised by his principal to sell real property, and to collect personal property, and then invest the proceeds in real property. As Waters points out,[69] such a general power of investment should of itself have been sufficient to constitute the solicitor a constructive trustee, and so to deprive him of the defence of lapse of time under the Statute of Limitations. However, he had also paid his client's money into his own account at the bank, and Lord Hatherley and Gifford, L.J., in holding that the statute was not applicable, based their decision on the proposition that such an agent was bound to keep his client's money distinct from his own, and accordingly a trust of it had been created, so that the sums belonging to the client could be traced, notwithstanding that the period of limitation had expired.

In *Soar* v. *Ashwell*[70] the agent, again a solicitor, received trust moneys on behalf of a trust for which he was acting, for the purposes of investment, and misapplied it. Once again, he was held to be in the position of an express trustee, and the Court of Appeal attempted a classification of the various kinds of constructive trustees, in order to distinguish those trustees who could claim the benefit of Statutes of Limitations from those who could not, and who were therefore in the same position as express trustees. Among the latter were fiduciaries who were such before they had committed the wrongful act.

[65] pp. 337–338.
[66] *Re Hallett's Estate* (1880), 13 Ch.D. 696 (Cases, p. 351); *Lister & Co.* v. *Stubbs* (1890), 45 Ch.D. 1.
[67] (1870), L.R. 5 Ch.App. 233.
[68] [1893] 2 Q.B. 390.
[69] p. 305.
[70] [1893] 2 Q.B. 390.

It is the view of Waters that English and American law have diverged in their treatment of the fiduciary element in agency. In English law, it has been treated as a question of fact, whilst in American law, it is a question of law.[71] So far as English law is concerned, Waters argues that this is not a satisfactory situation; and that it ought to be accepted for English, as for American, law that the question whether the relation of principal and agent is fiduciary is also a matter of law. If the agent is found to be a fiduciary, then the remedy of constructive trust is available to compel him to transfer to the principal property which is either the principal's, or which the principal asserts should be his, because the agent has used his position as agent to secure it for himself.[72] However, Waters' analysis of the cases leads him to the conclusion that, " far from the contention being exact that not all agents are fiduciaries, it is only by an accident of legal history that the fiduciary relationship was ever invoked at all as a pre-requirement before the principal might make the agent disgorge." [73] It nevertheless remains true that the fiduciary relationship was invoked by equity as a reason for intervention on behalf of the principal, and that in the nineteenth century, in spite of inconsistencies which Waters exposes, it played an important, and possibly decisive, part in determining the the extent of equitable relief where a principal was claiming property from the agent, which the agent was retaining in violation of his duty.

[71] p. 260.
[72] p. 264.
[73] p. 275.

PART II

THE ADMINISTRATION OF A TRUST

CHAPTER XV

THE APPOINTMENT, REMOVAL AND RETIREMENT OF TRUSTEES

THE capacity of a person to fill the office of trustee has already been considered. It remains to add that the appointment of two trustees is desirable to protect the beneficiaries and it is normally required in the case of trusts relating to land, unless the trustee appointed is a trust corporation, for a sole trustee (not being a trust corporation) cannot give a valid receipt for the proceeds of sale or other capital money arising out of a trust for sale of land,[1] nor for capital money arising out of a settlement governed by the Settled Land Act 1925.[2] At the same time, the Trustee Act 1925, s. 34, provides that the maximum number of trustees of a settlement of land (including a trust for sale) shall be four, and if more than four are named, then the first four named who are able and willing to act shall be the trustees.

This section only applies to trusts for sale and settlements of land, and it does not apply—

(a) To land vested in trustees for charitable, ecclesiastical or public purposes; or

(b) Where the net proceeds of the sale of land are held for those purposes; or

(c) To the trustees of a term of years absolute limited by a settlement on trusts for raising money, or of a like term created under the statutory remedies relating to annual sums charged on land.[3]

Furthermore, section 42 of the Administration of Estates Act 1925 provides that where personal representatives appoint trustees for the property of an infant, they must appoint either a trust corporation or not less than two and not more than four individual trustees.

The section does not apply if there is a surviving husband or wife who takes a life interest, or the infants are contingently entitled.[4]

Since the duties and obligations of trustees are many, no one may be compelled to undertake a trust.[5] This means that the office may be renounced before acceptance. Afterwards the trustee will only be released in the ways specified below. A trustee who does not propose to act, however, should disclaim as soon as possible, and in any case before he has interfered with the trust property. Neglect to disclaim may be treated as acquiescence, although it may not be too late to disclaim even after a number of years, provided that a satisfactory explanation of the delay may be furnished to rebut the pre-

---

[1] Trustee Act 1925, s. 14 (2).
[2] s. 94 (1).
[3] For an example, see the Law of Property Act 1925, s. 121 (4).
[4] *Re Yerburgh*, [1928] W.N. 208.
[5] *Per* Lord Talbot in *Robinson* v. *Pett* (1734), 3 P.Wms. 249, 251.

sumption of acceptance by acquiescence.[6] Disclaimer of the office of trustee of necessity involves also disclaimer of the estate of trustee,[7] and the entirety of the estate then devolves upon the acting trustees.

Disclaimer may be by deed or conduct, but it is desirable to disclaim by deed since this affords clear and unambiguous evidence of the act.[8] There may not be a partial disclaimer of the office, and so, if a trustee purports to disclaim the trust with relation to some part of the trust property, this is ineffectual to disclaim any part of the trust.[9] Where the trust property comprises personalty only, disclaimer may be by parol declaration.[10]

The position of a married woman who wishes to disclaim requires special consideration. By the Real Property Act, 1845, s. 7, a married woman could disclaim an estate in land by deed, but the concurrence of her husband was necessary. How far a woman could disclaim under the Married Women's Property Acts was not clear, but now the Law of Property Act 1925, ss. 167–168, provides that a married woman may disclaim a trust without the concurrence of her husband.[11]

In a will, a person is usually appointed executor and trustee of the will. If that person renounces probate, it has the effect of relieving him from his executorship, and although of itself it does not have the effect of a disclaimer of any trusts, it is nevertheless evidence from which, coupled with a failure to act, the court will presume that the person named has disclaimed.[12]

A trustee may accept office by becoming a party to the settlement and executing it,[13] or by making an express declaration of assent.[14] More frequently, however, if the trustee is not a party to the settlement, acceptance is presumed from the subsequent conduct of the trustee in relation to the trust. Acceptance will be presumed where the trustee performs acts in execution of the trust, and there is no difference whatever in the effects of an acceptance by deed and one by parol, or which is implied from conduct.[15] Comparatively slight acts in relation to the trust may be construed as acceptance. Thus, in *James* v. *Frearson*,[16] a person was named in a will as executor and trustee for sale, and when the property was sold by direction of the trustees he was present, and gave orders respecting the sale, and subsequently called on a co-executor to give him information concerning the testator's accounts. These acts were held to constitute acceptance.[17] Nevertheless, merely interfering with the trust property will not of itself necessarily constitute acceptance, for it may be explainable on some other ground,[18] but if the acts of the trustee are ambiguous, he cannot subsequently take advantage of that ambiguity and claim that he has not accepted. Thus, in *Conyngham* v. *Conyngham*,[19] X was

6 *Doe* d. *Chidgey* v. *Harris* (1847), 16 M. & W. 517. But see *Holder* v. *Holder*, [1968] Ch. 353 (Cases, p. 340).
7 *Re Birchall* (1889), 40 Ch.D. 436; *Re Clout and Frewer's Contract*, [1924] 2 Ch. 230.
8 *Stacey* v. *Elph* (1833), 1 My. & K. 195.
9 *Re Lord and Fullerton's Contract*, [1896] 1 Ch. 228.
10 *Doe* d. *Chidgey* v. *Harris* (1847), 16 M. & W. 517, 520-1, *per* Parke, B.
11 See also s. 170.
12 *Re Gordon* (1877), 6 Ch.D. 531.
13 *Buckeridge* v. *Glasse* (1841), Cr. & Ph. 126.
14 *Doe* d. *Chidgey* v. *Harris* (1847), 16 M. & W. 517.
15 *Lord Montford* v. *Lord Cadogan* (1816), 19 Ves. 635.
16 (1842), 1 Y. & C.C.C. 370.
17 *Cf. Orr* v. *Newton* (1791), 2 Cox 274. See also *Doyle* v. *Blake* (1804), 2 Sch. & Lef. 229.
18 *Stacey* v. *Elph* (1833), 1 My. & K. 195.
19 (1750), 1 Ves.Sen. 522. See also *Re Sharman's Will Trusts*, [1942] Ch. 311.

appointed trustee of a will, but never expressly accepted the trust, which related *inter alia* to the rents of a plantation leased to the son and heir-at-law of the testator. X acted as the son's agent, and received from him the rent of the plantation, and it was held that after receipt of the rents he could not repudiate the trust, for if he wished to refrain from acceptance, he ought to have disclaimed before.

These rules relating to the acceptance of a trust extend also to the acceptance of the office of executor,[20] but one or two special rules applying to executors should be noticed.

1. An executor of a sole or last surviving executor is also the executor of the original testator, and if the second executor accepts office with regard to the estate of the first, he cannot renounce office in relation to the estate of the original testator[21]; but this substitution of an executor of a first executor does not apply where the first executor has not proved the will, or where the original testator has appointed another executor, who afterwards proves. Wherever an administrator is appointed, the chain of representation is broken, so that neither an executor of an administrator nor an administrator of an executor can administer the estate of the original testator.[22]

2. Where the testator appoints X as executor and trustee of his will, and X either renounces probate or disclaims the trust, then if Y is appointed administrator *cum testamento annexo,* Y does not also become trustee of the will[23]; but under the Trustee Act 1925, s. 36 (5), where a sole or last surviving executor intends to renounce, or where all the executors intend to renounce, he or they may, before renouncing probate, and without thereby accepting the offer of executor, appoint one or more persons to act as trustees.

3. Where a person is appointed trustee of two distinct trusts by the same instrument, he cannot accept one and disclaim the other[24]; but this is an equitable doctrine, and, therefore, an executor may accept office and at the same time disclaim a devise of real estate under the will.[25] On the other hand, if a person is appointed executor and trustee of a will, by accepting the office of executor, he accepts also that of trustee.[26]

4. Under the Administration of Estates Act 1925, ss. 46–47,[27] certain statutory trusts now arise on intestacy. It was held in *Re Yerburgh,*[28] that the statutory trusts arise only when the administration is complete.

This is only a particular example of a more general rule, *i.e.* that personal representatives, whether executors or administrators, who have completed administration as personal representatives, then become trustees for those entitled, although they still remain personal representatives. As trustees, they

---

[20] *Cf. Re Coghlan,* [1948] 2 All E.R. 68.

[21] *Brooke* v. *Haymes* (1868), L.R. 6 Eq. 25.

[22] Administration of Estates Act, 1925, s. 7. See also the Administration of Estates Act 1971, s. 1 (3).

[23] *Wyman* v. *Carter* (1871), L.R. 12 Eq. 309. In *Re Robinson,* [1951] Ch. 198, the testator appointed certain persons to be his executors, but failed to name them as trustees. Vaisey, J., held that he had intended them also to act as trustees.

[24] *Re Lord and Fullerton's Contract,* [1896] 1 Ch. 228.

[25] *Lord Wellesley* v. *Withers* (1855), 4 El. & Bl. 750.

[26] *Ward* v. *Butler* (1824), 2 Mol. 533.

[27] Amended by the Intestates' Estates Act 1952, s. 1, Family Provision Act 1966, ss. 1, 9 and 10 (2) and Sched. 2, and the Family Law Reform Act 1969, s. 3 (2).

[28] [1928] W.N. 208.

will have the powers conferred on them by the Trustee Act 1925, in place of those exercisable under the Administration of Estates Act 1925.[29]

A cardinal principle of equity in relation to trusts is that " a trust shall not fail for want of a trustee." Accordingly, if a clear intention to create a trust is shown, the trust follows the legal estate wheresoever it goes, unless it comes into the hands of a purchaser for valuable consideration without notice of the trust.[30] Therefore, if a testator established a trust for specified purposes, the trust devolves upon the personal representatives. Again, if a settlor declares a trust without conveying the property to anyone, he himself holds as trustee; and if he appoints a sole trustee who disclaims, the property reverts to the settlor or his personal representatives, who are bound by the trust.[31] Moreover, on the death of a sole or last surviving trustee, the property passes to the personal representatives of that person,[32] who have the power of appointing new trustees in the absence of anyone else entitled under the settlement to appoint,[33] and " Until the appointment of new trustees, the personal representatives or representative for the time being of a sole trustee, or, where there were two or more trustees of the last surviving or continuing trustee, shall be capable of exercising or performing any power or trust which was given to, or capable of being exercised by, the sole or last surviving or continuing trustee, or other the trustees or trustee for the time being of the trust." [34]

The principle just enunciated is of importance also in relation to powers. The distinction between bare powers and powers coupled with a trust (or powers imperative) has already been noticed.[35] Where the power is coupled with a trust, it partakes so far of the attributes of a trust that if the donee dies without executing it, or refuses to act, the court ensures its execution.

The distinction and the attitude of the court towards it were clearly expressed by Lord Eldon in *Brown* v. *Higgs* [36]—

> It is perfectly clear, that, where there is a mere power of disposing, and that power is not executed, this Court cannot execute it. It is equally clear, that, wherever a trust is created, and the execution of that trust fails by the death of the trustee, or by accident, this Court will execute the trust. . . . But there are not only a mere trust and a mere power, but there is also known to this Court a power, which the party, to whom it is given, is intrusted and required to execute; and with regard to that species of power the Court consider it as partaking so much of the nature and qualities of a trust, that if the person, who has that duty imposed upon him, does not discharge it, the Court will, to a certain extent, discharge the duty in his room and place. . . .

[29] See further, *Re Cockburn's Will Trusts*, [1957] Ch. 438; *Re King's Will Trusts*, [1964] Ch. 542.

[30] *Per* Wilmot, L.C.J., *Attorney-General* v. *Lady Downing* (1767), Wilm. 1, 21, 22.

[31] *Mallott* v. *Wilson*, [1903] 2 Ch. 494. But if the trustee of a fully secret trust dies before the testator, the trust engrafted on the legacy fails, since the legacy lapses.

[32] Administration of Estates Act 1925, ss. 1 and 3.

[33] Trustee Act 1925, s. 36 (1).

[34] Trustee Act 1925, s. 18 (2).

[35] p. 14, *ante*.

[36] (1803), 8 Ves. 561, 570–4. See also the decisions of Arden, M.R. (1799), 4 Ves. 708; (1800), 5 Ves. 495. The decree was affirmed in the House of Lords (1813), 18 Ves. 192 (Cases, p. 77).

> . . . if the power is a power, which it is the duty of the party to execute, made his duty by the requisition of the Will, put upon him as such by the testator, who has given him an interest extensive enough to enable him to discharge it, he is a trustee for the exercise of the power, and not as having a discretion, whether he will exercise it, or not; and the Court adopts the principle as to trusts; and will not permit his negligence, accident, or other circumstances, to disappoint the interests of those, for whose benefit he is called upon to execute it.

Discussing this passage from Lord Eldon's judgment in *McPhail* v. *Doulton*,[37] Lord Hodson remarked that it shows " that where powers of a fiduciary character, as opposed to being mere powers not coupled with a duty, are concerned the court's position differs in no way from that which it occupies in the case of trusts generally."

Thus, a power coupled with a trust does not fail through the death of the donee in the testators' lifetime, or by disclaimer, disagreement of the donees, failure to execute it by them or other such circumstances; the court will take upon itself the duty to execute the power, and will do so, so long as it is possible, no matter what difficulties attend the execution of it.[38] How the court will execute the power depends upon the circumstances. Where the settlor has directly made some special provision for its exercise, the court will attempt to put itself in the place of the appointors, and be governed by the conditions which would have governed them. Thus, in *Gower* v. *Mainwaring*,[39] trustees were directed to divide residuary estate amongst the settlor's relations " where they should see most necessity, and as they should think most equitable and just." The court directed a division amongst those entitled under the Statute of Distributions according to their necessities. Where no rule is laid down by the testator, however, the court follows the maxim that " Equality is Equity." [40] In the application of this rule, two important points must be noticed:

1. Where the intention was to annex a trust to the power of appointment, and the donee was given power to select among members of a class, then, in the absence of special circumstances (considered in 2, below), the court will not attempt any selection, but will divide equally among the class from which selection was to have been made. Thus, in *Harding* v. *Glyn*,[41] where the principle was first discussed, the donee of the power was desired to distribute property " among such of the testator's relations as she should think most deserving and approve of." The court divided the property equally amongst all the testator's relations living at the time of the appointor's death.[42]

2. It may be that the testator has expressly stated that the whole of the property shall be given to that member of the class, or to only some members of the class, whom the trustees shall select. Here, notwithstanding the difficulty

---

[37] [1971] A.C. 424, 441 (Cases, p. 84).
[38] *Pierson* v. *Garnet* (1786), 2 Bro.C.C. 38.
[39] (1750), 2 Ves.Sen. 87.
[40] *Doyley* v. *Attorney-General* (1735), 2 Eq.Cas.Abr. 195, pl. 15 (*b*).
[41] (1739), 1 Atk. 469, discussed by Lord Wilberforce in *McPhail* v. *Doulton*, [1971] A.C. 452.
[42] See also *Brown* v. *Higgs*, p. 222, *ante*; *Burrough* v. *Philcox* (1840), 5 My. & Cr. 72.

of selection, the court will attempt it. Thus, in *Mosely* v. *Moseley*,[43] a testator left an estate to his trustees to settle upon such (one) of the sons of N as they should think fit. The trustees failed to select, and the court directed the trustees, within a fortnight of the order, to nominate such a son of N as they should think fit, failing which, the court would undertake the task of selection.[44]

The appointment of trustees is usually provided for in the trust instrument, but the following persons have power to appoint them—

1. The settlor, when the trust is created.

2. The beneficiaries, if all of them are *sui juris* and collectively entitled to the whole beneficial interest. The power of the beneficiaries to appoint collectively cannot be exercised, however, if some person possesses a power of appointment under the instrument, or under section 36 (1) (*b*) of the Trustee Act 1925. In such a case, however, the beneficiaries might put an end to the trust and establish a new settlement (which would attract *ad valorem* stamp duty).[45]

3. Some person nominated for the purpose in the trust instrument.[46]

4. Failing some person so nominated, then the surviving or continuing trustees or trustee for the time being, or the personal representatives of the last surviving or continuing trustee.[47]

Furthermore, section 36 (6) of the Trustee Act 1925, provides that where a sole trustee, other than a trust corporation, is originally appointed to act in a trust, or where, in the case of any trust, there are not more than three trustees (none of them being a trust corporation), then—

> (a) The person or persons nominated for the purpose of appointing new trustees by the instrument, if any, creating the trust; or
> (b) If there is no such person, or no such person able and willing to act, then the trustee or trustees for the time being;

may, by writing, appoint another person to be an additional trustee, subject, however, to the qualification that the total number of trustees must not exceed four.[48]

A person nominated to appoint trustees may not appoint himself as an *additional* trustee[49] although section 36 (1) permits him to appoint himself as a *replacement* trustee, to fill a vacancy, if there are not more than two continuing trustees.

Generally, the trust instrument gives a power to appoint new trustees to some person without specifying the events in which he can exercise it. Where this is the case that person is the " person nominated for the purpose " within the meaning of section 36.[50] If, however, the power is limited, and some only

---

[43] (1673), Rep. t. Finch 53.
[44] See further on powers and trusts, pp. 14–16, *ante*; Scott's *Abridgement of the Law of Trusts* (1960), s. 122.
[45] *Re Brockbank*, [1948] Ch. 206.
[46] Trustee Act 1925, s. 36 (1) (*a*).
[47] Trustee Act 1925, s. 36 (1) (*b*). An executor who has not yet proved the will cannot appoint a trustee under this provision: *Re Crowhurst Park*, [1974] 1 W.L.R. 583. See also Crane (1974) 38 *Conveyancer* 211.
[48] See also notes to section 36 in Wolstenholme & Cherry's *Conveyancing Statutes*, 13th ed., vol. 4, pp. 53–61.
[49] *Re Power's Settlement Trusts*, [1951] Ch. 1074.
[50] *Re Walker and Hughes' Contract* (1883), 24 Ch.D. 698.

of the occasions mentioned in the section are contemplated, then, as far as the other cases not specified in the trust instrument are concerned, the person to whom the power is given is not " the person nominated for the purpose " and the appointment must be made by the other persons specified in section 36, e.g. the surviving or continuing trustee.[51] Where the person to whom the power is given also takes an interest under the settlement, and he alienates that interest, his power to appoint new trustees remains in him,[52] and where the power is given to two or more to be exercised by them jointly, it cannot usually be exercised by the survivor or survivors in the absence of express provision.[53] If two or more persons nominated to appoint jointly fail to agree, an appointment may be made by the person who is entitled to do so when there is no person " able and willing to appoint." [54] In *Montefiore* v. *Guedalla*,[55] the donee of the power of appointment wanted to appoint himself, and Buckley, J., sanctioned it in the special circumstances, but in earlier decisions such appointments were held invalid [56] since the Trustee Act 1893, provided for the appointment of " another person," whilst under the Act of 1925 the donee may appoint himself under section 36 (1) which contains the words: " (whether or not being the persons exercising the power)," thus differing from section 10 of the Trustee Act 1893, but he cannot appoint himself under section 36 (6) which does not contain these words.[57]

The question is largely one of construction of the power of appointment. Thus it may be a power to appoint another person trustee or one to appoint any person (including the appointor) or one to appoint " any person." All except the first include power to appoint oneself.

Where an infant beneficiary is given a power to appoint new trustees, he is not bound by any act which is either imprudent or prejudicial to his interests, e.g. the appointment of the beneficiary's mother as sole trustee.[58] There is nothing in s. 36 (1) to prevent the appointment of trustees who are resident abroad. Accordingly where, under an English trust, the beneficiaries had long been resident in Jersey, and trustees resident in Jersey were appointed trustees, the court agreed to interfere.[59]

Trustees appointed under section 36 of the Trustee Act have exactly the same powers, authorities and discretions as if appointed under the original instrument.[60] If for any reason there is no person capable of appointing trustees under section 36, the court may appoint,[61] whenever it is found difficult, inexpedient or impracticable to appoint without the assistance of the court, and the court's order may have the effect of appointing either in substitution for, or in addition to, any existing trustee or trustees, or although there is no existing trustee. In particular, the court may make an order appointing a new

51 *Cecil* v. *Langdon* (1884), 28 Ch.D. 1 ; *Re Sichel's Settlements*, [1916] 1 Ch. 358.
52 *Hardaker* v. *Moorhouse* (1884), 26 Ch.D. 417 ; *Re Spencer* (1916), 33 T.L.R. 16.
53 *Re Harding*, [1923] 1 Ch. 182.
54 *Re Sheppard's Settlement Trusts*, [1888] W.N. 234.
55 [1903] 2 Ch. 723.
56 *Re Skeats' Settlement* (1889), 42 Ch.D. 522 ; *Re Newen*, [1894] 2 Ch. 297.
57 *Re Power's Settlement Trusts*, [1951] Ch. 1074.
58 *Re Parsons*, [1940] Ch. 973.
59 *Re Whitehead's Will Trusts*, [1971] 1 W.L.R. 833.
60 Trustee Act 1925, s. 36 (7).
61 Trustee Act 1925, ss. 41 and 43. Under ss. 44–56, the court has a wide power to make vesting orders *not only* when a new trustee is appointed, but on many other occasions.

trustee in substitution for a trustee who is insane or a defective, or is a bank-rupt,[62] or is a corporation which is in liquidation or has been dissolved. The court will remove a trustee under section 41 and appoint another trustee in his place, even against the will of the trustee, for good reason. The court will also appoint a new trustee under section 41 in place of an existing trustee, where there is friction between the trustees.[63] The court's order, and any conse-quential vesting order, do not operate further as a discharge to a former or a continuing trustee than an appointment of new trustees under any power given by the instrument would have done. Application for the appointment of a trustee may be made by any beneficiary or trustee [64] by originating summons.

The court, however, will not appoint where there is a person able and willing to do so.[65]

Although the occasions when it will be necessary to apply to the court under section 41 of the Trustee Act 1925 will be greatly reduced in number, owing to the wide powers of appointment conferred in section 36, situations still do arise where it is necessary to make application, and it will therefore be profitable to consider in what circumstances the court has, under similar powers conferred by older Acts, replaced a trustee. In *Re Dawson's Trusts*,[66] the court appointed new trustees in place of a trustee whose ill-health was so extreme that he was unable to undertake the exertion of signing the necessary papers; whilst in *Re Lemann's Trusts*,[67] the court replaced a trustee 79 years of age, who, through failure of memory and decay of intellect, was unable to attend to the trust business. In that case, Chitty, J., observed [68]—

> If a trustee is in such a condition that he cannot act properly in his trust, and is, in fact, incapable of acting, it is undoubtedly expedient for the court to appoint a new trustee in his place . . .

A similar case to *Re Lemann's Trusts* was *Re Phelps' Settlement Trusts*,[69] where the Court of Appeal replaced a trustee of 85 years of age, who was very deaf, and whose intellectual powers had decayed to such an extent that he was incapable of transacting the trust business. Lastly, in *Re Martin's Trusts*,[70] the court appointed a new trustee in place of one who suffered from softening of the brain, though he was neither a lunatic nor a person of unsound mind.

In addition to its powers of appointing trustees under the Trustee Act 1925, the court also possesses powers under two other statutes.

By virtue of section 1 of the Judicial Trustees Act 1896, and the Judicial Trustees Rules 1972, the court may, on the application of the settlor, a trustee or a beneficiary, appoint any fit and proper person nominated in the applica-tion, or an official of the court, to be a judicial trustee, to act either alone or jointly with another, or, on proof of sufficient cause, in place of all or any

[62] *Re A Solicitor*, [1952] Ch. 328.
[63] *Re Henderson*, [1940] Ch. 764.
[64] Trustee Act 1925, s. 58.
[65] *Re Higginbottom*, [1892] 3 Ch. 132.
[66] (1864), 3 New Rep. 397.
[67] (1883), 22 Ch.D. 633.
[68] 22 Ch.D. 635.
[69] (1885), 31 Ch.D. 351.
[70] (1887), 34 Ch.D. 618.

existing trustees,[71] and by the Public Trustee Act 1906, s. 5, the court has power to appoint the Public Trustee to be a new or additional trustee, on the application by originating summons of any trustee or beneficiary, notwithstanding the fact that the instrument directs that he shall not be appointed.

Finally, it must be added that, altogether apart from its power under these three statutes, the court has a jurisdiction to remove trustees and to appoint newcomers in their place, wherever it considers the interests of the beneficiaries require it. Thus, it may do so in any administration, notwithstanding that the removal of the trustee has not been asked for in the pleadings.[72] Moreover, in exercising the statutory powers of removal, the welfare of the beneficiaries is the paramount consideration, as in the case where a trustee becomes bankrupt, and, from the fact that he has to deal with trust funds, there is a possibility that he might misappropriate them.[73]

A. THE MODE OF APPOINTMENT OF TRUSTEES OUT OF COURT

The persons who can appoint new trustees have already been considered. It remains now to state the occasions when new trustees may be appointed. These are contained in section 36 of the Trustee Act 1925, subs. (1) of which provides that where a trustee is dead, or remains out of the United Kingdom for more than twelve months, or desires to be discharged from all or any of the trusts or powers reposed in or conferred on him, or refuses or is unfit to act therein, or is incapable of acting therein, or is an infant, then, subject to the restrictions imposed by this Act on the number of trustees—

(a) the person or persons nominated for the purpose of appointing new trustees by the instrument, if any, creating the trust; or

(b) if there is no such person, or no such person able and willing to act, then the surviving or continuing trustees or trustee for the time being, or the personal representatives of the last surviving or continuing trustee;

may, by writing, appoint one or more other persons to be a trustee or trustees in the place of the trustee so deceased, remaining out of the United Kingdom, desiring to be discharged, refusing, or being unfit or being incapable, or being an infant, as aforesaid. Nowadays the inclusion of a person with power to appoint new trustees is unusual. Even if such a person is nominated, the statutory power is not excluded.[74]

Subs. (2) provides that where a trustee is removed under a power contained in the instrument, the provisions of section 36 (1) shall apply to the new appointment.[75]

Appointments of new trustees are made in writing. A deed is desirable in

---

[71] A judicial trustee may be a Settled Land Act trustee: *Re Marshall's Will Trusts*, [1945] Ch. 217. The court will not appoint a judicial trustee of part of an estate, where the whole estate is being administered, nor will it appoint a judicial trustee to the whole of the estate, where the rights of the beneficiary are sufficiently protected: *Re Wells*, [1968] 1 W.L.R. 44. See also pp. 60–61, *ante*.

[72] *Re Wrightson*, [1908] 1 Ch. 789.

[73] *Re Barker's Trusts* (1875), 1 Ch.D. 43 ; *Re Adams' Trust* (1879), 12 Ch.D. 634.

[74] *Re Wheeler and De Rochow*, [1896] 1 Ch. 315.

[75] Appointment of trustees under the Settled Land Act 1925, is governed by ss. 30 and 34 of that Act.

order that the new trustees should obtain the benefit of section 40 of the Trustee Act 1925 but not essential. Where the appointment is made by the personal representatives, the concurrence of an executor who has renounced or has not proved is not required,[76] but as was stated before, a sole or last executor who intends to renounce (or all the executors if they propose to renounce) may appoint new trustees without thereby accepting the executorship.[77] Where the appointment is made to replace a mentally infirm trustee who is also entitled to some beneficial interest under the trust, leave of the authority under the Mental Health Act 1959 is required.[78]

It is to be observed that, although section 36 (1) of the Trustee Act 1925 gives a power to appoint in place of a trustee who remains abroad for more than twelve months, even against the will of the absent trustee,[79] merely going abroad does not make the trustee " incapable of acting." [80] Turner, V.-C., observed in *Re Watts* [81]—

> I think the terms " become incapable " . . . have reference to personal incapacity, and that the absence of [the trustee] and his situation with regard to his bankruptcy do not constitute personal incapacity.

At the same time, it must be remembered that when a trustee becomes bankrupt he is usually " unfit to act," [82] and the same is true if a trustee absconds.[83]

A lunatic is incapable of acting [84] (although this is now expressly covered by section 36) and a trustee who was suffering from a serious illness, so that he was unfit to transact any business for a lengthy period, would also appear to be incapable of acting, within the section.[85] Today, if a person becomes incapable of acting by reason of mental disorder within the meaning of the Mental Health Act 1959 and he is also entitled to a beneficial interest in the trust property, no appointment of a new trustee may be made under section 36 (1) (b) unless leave to make the appointment has been given by the authority with jurisdiction under Part VIII of the Mental Health Act 1959.[86]

It should also be noticed that whilst there may not be partial disclaimer of the trust, under section 36 a trustee may be relieved of part only of the trusts. Previously, it had been doubted whether this could be done without the intervention of the court.[87]

The phrase " more than twelve months " is strictly construed. The absence must have been continuous for the twelve months, and it has been held that a return for a week is sufficient to prevent the power coming into operation.[88]

Where new trustees are appointed, the number may be increased, but not beyond four (unless the trust is for a charitable object), except that a separate set of trustees (not exceeding four) may be appointed for any part of the trust

76 Trustee Act 1925, s. 36 (4).
77 Trustee Act 1925, s. 36 (5).
78 Mental Health Act 1959, s. 149 (1) and Sched. 7.
79 *Re Stoneham Settlement Trusts*, [1953] Ch. 59.
80 *Withington* v. *Withington* (1848), 16 Sim. 104; *Re Harrison's Trusts* (1852), 22 L.J.Ch. 69.
81 (1851), 20 L.J.Ch. 337.
82 *Re Roche* (1842), 2 Dr. & War. 287.
83 *Re Wheeler and De Rochow*, [1896] 1 Ch. 315, 322, *per* Kekewich, J.
84 *Re East* (1873), L.R. 8 Ch.App. 735; *Re Elizabeth Blake*, [1887] W.N. 173.
85 *Re Weston's Trusts*, [1898] W.N. 151.
86 Sect. 36 (9), as amended by the Mental Health Act 1959, s. 149 (1) and Sched. 7.
87 *Savile* v. *Couper* (1887), 36 Ch.D. 520; *Re Moss's Trusts* (1888), 37 Ch.D. 513, 516.
88 *Re Walker*, [1901] 1 Ch. 259.

property which is subject to distinct trusts. It is not obligatory (except as mentioned below) to appoint more than one trustee where one only was originally appointed, nor is it obligatory to fill up the original number where more than two were originally appointed. But, except in the case where only one trustee was originally appointed, and the sole trustee so appointed has power to give valid receipts for all capital money, a trustee is not to be discharged unless there are two trustees or a trust corporation left to perform the trust.[89] The exception made relates only to trusts of pure personalty, for a sole trustee cannot give a receipt for capital money arising under a trust for sale or a trust or strict settlement of land. Even if the instrument purported to give a sole trustee such power, it would be ineffective.[90] Where new trustees of a trust for sale of land are appointed, the same persons must also be appointed as are for the time being trustees of the settlement of the proceeds of sale.[91]

The provisions of the Trustee Act 1925 relating to the appointment of trustees apply also to the appointment of trustees for the purposes of the Settled Land Act 1925.

Formerly, unless the instrument otherwise provided, an additional trustee could only be appointed when there was a vacancy in the trust. It is now provided, however, that an additional trustee may be appointed, but only if a sole trustee, other than a trust corporation, has been originally appointed, or where there are not more than three trustees, none of whom is a trust corporation.[92] The position of a purchaser in relation to the appointment of new trustees is provided for in section 38. This section provides that statements that a trustee has been appointed in accordance with the provisions of section 36 (1) shall be conclusive evidence of the matter stated, and shall thus afford a full protection to the purchaser.

Formerly, when a new trustee was appointed, it was necessary to vest the property in him by special conveyance or assignment. Now, however, the position is greatly simplified by section 40 of the Trustee Act 1925 (replacing section 12 of the Trustee Act 1893), which provides that an express vesting declaration may be included in the instrument of appointment, or, in all appointments after 1925, a vesting declaration is implied (unless the contrary is expressed). *Appointments containing express or implied vesting declarations must be by deed,* and the section does not cover—

(a) Land conveyed by way of mortgage for securing money subject to the trust, except land conveyed on trust for securing debentures or debenture stock. This exception contemplates the position where, a trust having been created, trust money is invested in the mortgage of land, and a new trustee is appointed of the trust money, and the mortgage term has to be vested in the new trustee.[93]

(b) Land held under a lease (or an underlease) which contains a covenant not to assign without consent, unless before the execution of the deed the requisite consent has been obtained, or unless by virtue of any statute or rule

---

[89] Trustee Act 1925, s. 37 (1) (c).
[90] *Ibid.*, s. 14.
[91] *Ibid.*, s. 35 (1).
[92] *Ibid.*, s. 36 (6).
[93] *London and County Banking Co.* v. *Goddard*, [1897] 1 Ch. 642, 649, *per* North, J.

of law the vesting declaration, express or implied, would not operate as a breach of covenant or give rise to a forfeiture. But for this exception, the assignment under the vesting declaration, being without licence, might give rise to a forfeiture.

(c) Any share, stock, annuity, or property which is only transferable in books kept by a company or other body or in manner directed by or under an Act of Parliament.

It should be observed that (a) and (c) cover a considerable proportion of trust investments, which therefore must be separately transferred. One of us [94] has suggested that the Trustee Act should be amended so as to permit the existence of the trust to be disclosed, where trustees own shares.

The decision of Pennycuick, J., in *Re King's Will Trusts* [95] has shown that there are limits to the operation of section 40. In that case, an executor of a will, who also held certain properties specifically devised by the will as sole surviving trustee, executed a deed, appointing a second trustee, without first making a written assent as executor, vesting the estate in the trust property in himself. Pennycuick, J., held that section 40 of the Trustee Act 1925 only operated to vest the estate in the new trustee where the trust estate was already vested in the existing trustee making the appointment. In this case, the estate, at the time of the appointment, had been vested in him merely as personal representative.

If it is difficult or impossible to obtain a transfer of a legal interest in trust property, application must be made to the court for a vesting order. [96]

As far as registered land is concerned, the Land Registration Act 1925, s. 47, provides that on application, entries will be made on the register to give effect to vesting declarations.

B. THE DUTIES OF A TRUSTEE ON TAKING OFFICE

On appointment, there are duties which the prudent trustee should forthwith undertake. The first duty is that he should ensure either that the fund is in a proper state of investment, or is in the account of the trustees at a bank. He should also examine the documents relating to the trust, in order to inform himself of encumbrances and other relevant matters. [97] His duty in relation to trustee investments is a continuing one, and will be described in detail later, but there are certain steps which may have to be taken immediately. For example, if an authorised investment has depreciated, he will have to consider whether it is opportune to dispose of it, [98] and he must also consider whether an investment, originally authorised, which has now ceased to be authorised, should be sold; but he will not be liable *merely* for continuing to hold an investment which was originally authorised either by law or by the trust instrument. [99]

[94] Sheridan, " The Trustee Act, 1966 " (1965) 4 *Solicitor Quarterly* 196.
[95] [1964] Ch. 542.
[96] Trustee Act 1925, ss. 44–56; *Re Harrison's Settlement Trusts*, [1883] W.N. 31; *Re Keeley's Trusts* (1885), 53 L.T. 487.
[97] *Hallows* v. *Lloyd* (1888), 39 Ch.D. 686; *Tiger* v. *Barclays Bank Ltd.*, [1952] 1 All E.R. 85.
[98] *Rawsthorne* v. *Rowley*, [1909] 1 Ch. 409.
[99] Trustee Act 1925, s. 4; Trustee Investments Act 1961, s. 6.

C. THE APPOINTMENT OF TRUSTEES BY THE COURT

Section 41 of the Trustee Act 1925 gives the court jurisdiction to appoint new trustees whenever it is expedient, or when it is impracticable to do so otherwise. In particular, the court will appoint a new trustee in place of an existing trustee, where that trustee is suffering from mental disorder within the meaning of the Mental Health Act 1959. In that case, the Court of Protection must concur in the appointment.

The exercise of this discretion depends upon the circumstances of the case, but it may be exercised in spite of the opposition of an existing trustee.[1] It is impossible to enumerate all the occasions when it may be expedient for the court to act, but examples are the age and infirmity of a trustee, the bankruptcy of a trustee, or the fact that a trustee has not been traceable for some time.

As a general rule, if there is a person named in the trust instrument with the power of appointing new trustees, the court will not make an appointment, so long as that person is willing to appoint.

It has already been pointed out [2] that the court will be reluctant to appoint as a trustee a beneficiary, or a solicitor to the trust, although it will do so where no other suitable person is readily available. The court will also be reluctant to appoint a trustee who is resident out of the jurisdiction, although it will do so where there are special circumstances, and particularly when the trust property is situated abroad.

D. THE DEATH, RETIREMENT AND REMOVAL OF TRUSTEES

The rule of survivorship applies to trustees, and therefore, where there are two or more, and one dies, both the office and the estate devolve upon the survivor or survivors. Where a sole surviving trustee had died without making any new appointment, his personal representatives, as was stated above,[3] are capable of exercising or performing any power that could have been exercised by the sole surviving trustee, or other the trustees or trustee for the time being of the trust.[4]

Where a trustee wishes to retire from the trust, he must normally adopt one of the following courses—

(1) He must obtain the consent of all the beneficiaries, who must all be *sui juris* and must be collectively absolutely interested.

(2) If there is a special power conferred upon the trustee in the instrument, he may retire by taking advantage of it.

(3) He may take advantage of the power contained in the Trustee Act 1925.

(4) He may apply to the court.

(1) The limitations on the first mode of retirement are obvious. If there

---

[1] *Re Liddiard* (1880), 14 Ch.D. 310; *Re Henderson*, [1940] Ch. 764; *Re A Solicitor*, [1952] Ch. 328; *Re Seale's Marriage Settlement*, [1961] Ch. 574.
[2] pp. 52–53, *ante.*
[3] p. 224, *ante.*
[4] Trustee Act 1925, s. 18 (2).

are infants or unborn persons as beneficiaries then, since these cannot consent, no effective discharge may be obtained in this way. An adult married woman who is a beneficiary is *sui juris*.

(2) The provisions of the Trustee Act 1925 have made the insertion of a special power to permit the retirement of a trustee of little importance, but formerly, it was customary to insert a power, in terms resembling section 36 of the Trustee Act 1925, that if any or all the trustees should die, be abroad for a year, desired to be discharged from the trust, or refused it or became incapable of acting, it should be lawful for the surviving or continuing trustee or a beneficiary, by deed or in writing, to nominate some other person to be a trustee, and such a newly-appointed trustee was to be deemed capable of discharging all the functions of an original trustee. Such a clause is now unnecessary in view of the very wide terms of section 36 of the Trustee Act 1925.

(3) Before the Conveyancing Act 1881 unless the instrument permitted it, a trustee could not retire without ensuring that a new trustee was appointed in his place. Section 39 of the Trustee Act 1925, however, now provides that where a trustee wishes to retire from the trust, and after his retirement there will remain either two trustees or a trust corporation, the trustee may retire, with the consent of his co-trustees, without any new appointment being made.

If the trustee who retires does so in circumstances not contemplated in this section, he has not been effectively discharged, and will be liable for losses incurred by the beneficiaries.

(4) If the trustee is unable to obtain his discharge in any of the above ways, he may apply to the court. In such a case, if the trustee who wishes to retire is a sole trustee, and no suitable new trustee can be found, the court would not discharge the trustee; " The Court will, however, take care that the trustee shall not suffer thereby." [5] Where the trustee applies to the court, he will have to pay the costs, unless he can show that circumstances have arisen altering the nature of his duties.

Two special cases of retirement require mention. Under section 5 of the Public Trustee Act 1906 a trustee may retire, on or after the appointment of the Public Trustee as an ordinary trustee, without leaving two trustees, and without the consents required by s. 39 of the Trustee Act 1925. Secondly, under the Judicial Trustees Act 1896, s. 4, and the Judicial Trustees Rules 1972, rule 20, a judicial trustee may retire on giving notice of his desire to the court.

Trustees may be removed in the following ways—

(1) Under a power contained in the trust instrument.

(2) Under a statutory power.

(3) By the court.

(1) An example of such a power occurs where, in a mortgage, the mortgagor declares himself trustee of the property for the mortgagee, and then confers on the mortgagee powers to remove the mortgagor from the trust, and to appoint new trustees. Such a power is frequently included in mortgages to a

---

[5] *Per* Sugden, L.C., *Courtenay* v. *Courtenay* (1846), 3 Jo. & Lat. 519, 533. See also *Forshaw* v. *Higginson* (1857), 8 De G.M. & G. 827 ; *Re Chetwynd's Settlement*, [1902] 1 Ch. 692.

bank by deposit of title-deeds, together with a power enabling the mortgagee to vest the property in a purchaser free from the right of redemption.

(2) The statutory power to remove trustees is contained in section 36 of the Trustee Act 1925 and has already been discussed.

(3) The court has an inherent jurisdiction to control the activities of the trustee, and to ensure the proper execution of the trust, and for this purpose it may go to the length of removing a trustee on the application of a beneficiary. In discharging this function, the court does not follow any fixed principle, beyond that of ensuring the proper execution of the trusts.[6] Not every mistake of the trustee will be regarded by the court as a ground for removal, but where there is positive misconduct, the court will not hesitate to interpose. Moreover, a trustee will not be removed at the caprice of a beneficiary. Reasonable cause must be shown, and this must be more than an allegation that the trustee has declined to exercise a power at the request of a beneficiary or tenant for life.[7] The court formerly exercised its power of removal where the trustee refused to act, or became incapable of acting, but these grounds of removal have now become statutory, and the power of appointing new trustees in the place of such persons has been given to the appointor under the settlement, or a continuing trustee.

E. THE BANKRUPTCY OF A TRUSTEE

Bankruptcy does not inevitably involve a trustee's removal from the trust. Sir G. Jessel enunciated the general principle in *Re Barker's Trusts,*[8] when he observed—

> ... it is the duty of the Court to remove a bankrupt trustee who has trust money to receive or deal with, so that he can misappropriate it. There may be exceptions, under special circumstances, to that general rule; and it may also be that where a trustee has no money to receive he ought not to be removed merely because he has become bankrupt; but I consider the general rule to be as I have stated. The reason is obvious. A necessitous man is more likely to be tempted to misappropriate trust funds than one who is wealthy; and besides, a man who has not shewn prudence in managing his own affairs is not likely to be successful in managing those of other people.

An illustration of one of the exceptions is afforded by *Re Bridgman,*[9] where a trustee whose bankruptcy was due solely to misfortune, and was entirely free from any moral stigma, was permitted to retain his office.

By the Bankruptcy Act 1914, s. 38, the property which a bankrupt holds as trustee for any other person does not pass to his trustee in bankruptcy for division amongst his creditors, unless the trustee has a beneficial interest.[10] This applies not only to what is immediately identifiable as trust property, but to any property or money into which the trust property has been converted,

---

[6] *Letterstedt* v. *Broers* (1884), 9 App.Cas. 371, 386, *per* Lord Blackburn, giving the opinion of the Privy Council.

[7] *Lee* v. *Young* (1843), 2 Y. & C.C.C. 532.

[8] (1875), 1 Ch.D. 43–44.

[9] (1860), 1 Drew. & Sm. 164.

[10] See *Morgan* v. *Swansea Urban Sanitary Authority* (1878), 9 Ch.D. 582; *Governors of St. Thomas's Hospital* v. *Richardson,* [1910] 1 K.B. 271.

so long as the money remains identifiable.[11] The principle is well illustrated by *Taylor* v. *Plumer*,[12] wherein A handed money to a stockbroker for the purchase of stock. The broker purchased unauthorised stock and absconded. It was held that the stock purchased belonged to A and not to the broker's trustee in bankruptcy, for a broker is a constructive trustee for his principal; and, as Lord Ellenborough observed [13]—

> ... the property of a principal entrusted by him to his factor for any special purpose belongs to the principal, notwithstanding any change which that property may have undergone in point of form, so long as such property is capable of being identified, and distinguished from all other property.

It makes no difference that the trustee was committing a breach of trust in converting the property, for a trustee can confer no right upon those claiming through him in respect of an abuse of his trust. Accordingly, if money which represents the proceeds of a sale of trust property has been placed by the bankrupt in bags,[14] or has been changed into notes or negotiable instruments,[15] or has been placed in the bankrupt's account at the bank,[16] in all these cases the beneficiary may claim the money against the trustee in bankruptcy. If, however, the trust money has become so merged in the general property of the bankrupt trustee that it can no longer be identified, the beneficiary has no other course than to prove with the other creditors in bankruptcy, but if it has been merged in a mixed fund, which can be traced, the beneficiaries have an equitable charge upon the mixed fund.[17]

Where the bankrupt has vested in him both the legal estate, and a limited beneficial interest, then the legal estate remains vested in him, and the beneficial interest passes to the trustee in bankruptcy. This rule is applicable to trustees for sale.

The exemption conferred by section 38 applies not only to express trustees, but also to any person who holds title on behalf of some other beneficial owner,[18] *e.g.* a chose in action in a solicitor's client account; and to settled land vested in the estate owner.[19]

It must also be noticed that there pass to the trustee in bankruptcy for division among the bankrupt's creditors (under section 38 of the Bankruptcy Act 1914) all goods which at the commencement of the bankruptcy were " in the possession, order or disposition of the bankrupt, in his trade or business, by the consent and permission of the true owner, under such circumstances that the bankrupt is the reputed owner thereof ..." It was decided under the earlier Bankruptcy Acts (which did not confine the operation of this rule to property in the order and disposition of the bankrupt in his trade or business) that there did not pass to the bankrupt's trustee in bankruptcy under this

---

11 *Harris* v. *Truman* (1882), 9 Q.B.D. 264.
12 (1815), 3 M. & S. 562.
13 3 M. & S. 573–574.
14 *Tooke* v. *Hollingworth* (1793), 5 T.R. 215.
15 *Ex parte Dumas* (1754), 2 Ves.Sen. 582.
16 *Re Hallett's Estate* (1880), 13 Ch.D. 696 (Cases, p. 351).
17 *Re Hallett's Estate* (1880), 13 Ch.D. 696 (Cases, p. 351). See further, on following trust funds, Chap. XXV, s. C, *post.*
18 *Re A Solicitor*, [1952] Ch. 328, 332.
19 Settled Land Act 1925, s. 103.

section property in the control of the bankrupt in such circumstances that the bankrupt was holding it as trustee. Thus, where A was in possession of goods, in virtue of a life interest given to her by will, with a limitation on her death to B absolutely, and A became bankrupt, the goods did not pass to the trustee in bankruptcy.[20]

F. VESTING ORDERS IN RESPECT OF SOME TYPES OF TRUSTEE

Sections 44–56 of the Trustee Act 1925 confer upon the court powers to vest trust property in trustees on numerous occasions. Sections 44 and 51 are of special importance in relation to the office of trustee. Section 44 provides that when a trustee in whom land is vested, either solely or jointly with other persons—

(a) is under disability; or

(b) is out of the jurisdiction; or

(c) cannot be found; or

(d) being a corporation, has been dissolved,

and also in a number of other situations, the court may make an order vesting the land in any person and in such manner as the court may think fit.

Section 51 makes provision for the transfer of stocks and shares and things in action in somewhat similar terms.

Persons under disability are not infrequently mental patients, and in *Re Harrison's Settlement Trusts*,[21] two trustees asked that land subject to settlement should be vested in them alone, since the affairs of a third trustee had been placed under the control of the Court of Protection. Cross, J., whilst agreeing that the court had jurisdiction to make the order under section 44, held that where a vesting order was asked for without the removal of the trustee under disability, and the trust was continuing, the order would only be made in exceptional circumstances, and there were none in this case.

---

[20] *Ex parte Martin* (1815), 19 Ves. 491.
[21] [1965] 1 W.L.R. 1492.

Chapter XVI

THE TRUSTEE'S POWER TO DELEGATE HIS OFFICE

THE office of trustee is one of personal confidence, and can, therefore, only be delegated in consequence of an express power contained in the trust instrument or of the statutory power contained in the Trustee Act 1925 or in other Acts, and it will have the consequences therein specified. Apart from these provisions, if a trustee delegates his office, or any duty or right in connection with it, he will be liable exactly as if he had performed the acts himself,[1] and the rule applies equally if the persons to whom the discharge of the duties is committed is a co-trustee or a co-executor. Nevertheless, if the delegation occurs in consequence of the testator's directions, trustees will not be responsible if they do no more than was directed. So, in *Kilbee* v. *Sneyd*,[2] Hart, L.C., observed that if a testator pointed out an agent to be employed by his executor, and the agent received money in consequence and defaulted, the executor would be free from liability if he could show that the testator had indicated that person, and that the executor could not recover the money by the exercise of reasonable care.

Even before statutory intervention, it had been decided that a trustee could appoint agents to whom to delegate some of his duties where there was a legal or a physical necessity to do so. The test, as was pointed out in *Speight* v. *Gaunt*,[3] was always the reasonableness of the employment. As Lord Redesdale observed in *Joy* v. *Campbell*[4]—

> . . . he could not transact business without trusting some persons, and it would be impossible for him to discharge his duty if he is made responsible where he remitted to a person to whom he would have given credit, and would in his own business have remitted money in the same way.

The matter was very fairly put by Kekewich, J., in *Re Weall*[5]—

> A trustee is bound to exercise discretion in the choice of his agents, but so long as he selects persons properly qualified he cannot be made responsible for their intelligence or their honesty. He does not in any sense guarantee the performance of their duties. It does not, however, follow that he can intrust his agents with any duties which they are willing to undertake, or pay them or agree to pay them any remuneration which they see fit to demand. The trustee must consider these matters for himself, and the Court would be disposed to support any conclusion at which he arrives, however erroneous, provided it really is his conclusion—that is, the outcome of such consideration as might reasonably be expected to be given to a like matter by a man of ordinary prudence guided by such rules and arguments as generally guide such a man in his own affairs.

---

[1] *Per* Lord Langdale in *Turner* v. *Corney* (1841), 5 Beav. 515, 517.
[2] (1828), 2 Mol. 186, 200.
[3] (1883), 9 App.Cas. 1. See also *Re Weall* (1889), 42 Ch.D. 674.
[4] (1804), 1 Sch. & Lef. 328, 341–342.
[5] (1889), 42 Ch.D. 674, 678.

The Trustee Act 1925 has expressly recognised this doctrine, and has provided for various cases of delegation. One illustration of this appeared in section 25, which permitted a trustee who was going abroad for a period exceeding a month to appoint, by power of attorney, a person to execute the trust on his behalf during his absence. In such a case, the trustee remained fully liable for the acts of his attorney. Little use was made of this section, however, and it was replaced by section 9 of the Powers of Attorney Act 1971, which permits a trustee to delegate for a period not exceeding twelve months the execution of the trust by power of attorney. This power of delegation now exists whether the trustee is going abroad or is remaining in England, and once again the trustee remains fully responsible for the acts of his attorney. Further, the trustee must give within seven days of the execution of the power written notice to each person who, under the instrument, has power to appoint a new trustee and also to each of the other trustees. A trustee appointing an attorney under this section may not appoint a sole co-trustee.

The other sections in the Trustee Act 1925 reproduce and extend similar sections in the Act of 1893 or of the Settled Land Act 1882. Section 23 provides—

(1) Trustees or personal representatives may, instead of acting personally, employ and pay an agent, whether a solicitor, banker, stockbroker, or other person, to transact any business or do any act required to be transacted or done in the execution of the trust, or the administration of the testator's or intestate's estate, including the receipt and payment of money, and shall be entitled to be allowed and paid all charges and expenses so incurred, and shall not be responsible for the default of any such agent if employed in good faith.

(2) Trustees or personal representatives may appoint any person to act as their agent or attorney for the purpose of selling, converting, collecting, getting in, and executing and perfecting insurances of, or managing or cultivating, or otherwise administering any property, real or personal, moveable or immoveable, subject to the trust or forming part of the testator's or intestate's estate, in any place outside the United Kingdom or executing or exercising any discretion or trust or power vested in them in relation to any such property, with such ancillary powers, and with and subject to such provisions and restrictions as they may think fit, including a power to appoint substitutes, and shall not, by reason only of their having made such appointment, be responsible for any loss arising thereby.

(3) Without prejudice to such general power of appointing agents as aforesaid—

(a) A trustee may appoint a solicitor to be his agent to receive and give a discharge for any money or valuable consideration or property receivable by the trustee under the trust, by permitting the solicitor to have the custody of, and to produce, a deed having in the body thereof or endorsed thereon a receipt for such money or valuable consideration or property, the deed being executed, or the endorsed receipt being signed, by the person entitled to give a receipt for that consideration;

(b) A trustee shall not be chargeable with breach of trust by reason only of his having made or concurred in making any such appointment; and the production of any such deed by the solicitor shall have the same statutory validity and effect as if the person appointing the solicitor had not been a trustee;

(c) A trustee may appoint a banker or solicitor to be his agent to receive and give a discharge for any money payable to the trustee under or by virtue of a policy of insurance, by permitting the banker or solicitor to have the custody of and to produce the policy of insurance with a receipt signed by the trustee, and a trustee shall not be chargeable with a breach of trust by reason only of his having made or concurred in making any such appointment:

Provided that nothing in this subsection shall exempt a trustee from any liability which he would have incurred if this Act and any enactment replaced by this Act had not been passed, in case he permits any such money, valuable consideration, or property to remain in the hands or under the control of the banker or solicitor for a period longer than is reasonably necessary to enable the banker or solicitor, as the case may be, to pay or transfer the same to the trustee.

If the trustee knew or ought to have known of the receipt of such money by the agent, and fails to show reasonable diligence, he will be liable for any loss.[6] In their selection of agents, trustees must exercise common prudence, and so also in their subsequent supervision of those agents.[7] In particular, they should not employ agents outside their proper sphere, e.g. a solicitor as valuer. Where a trustee permitted a solicitor to appoint a valuer, it was held that the trustee had not used normal prudence in the selection of the agent,[8] although by this it is not intended to imply that a trustee may not consult a solicitor on these and other topics, provided that, after the receipt of such advice, he then exercises his own discretion in the matter. If money is allowed to remain in the hands of an agent for an unnecessarily long period, the trustee will usually be liable for any resulting loss.[9]

In *Re Vickery*,[10] an executor employed a solicitor to obtain payment of money due to the estate, and gave him documents for that purpose. The solicitor misappropriated the money and it was argued that, having regard to what the executor had learned of the solicitor's reputation, he ought to have cancelled the solicitor's authority before he had the opportunity to receive the money. Maugham, J., held that section 23 empowered the executor to appoint the solicitor to collect the money, and that, as section 30 provides that a trustee shall not be liable for the default of any person with whom trust money may be deposited, unless the same happens through the trustee's own default, the executor was not liable.

The exact scope of the decision in *Re Vickery*[10] would seem to be a matter of some uncertainty. In the course of his judgment, Maugham, J., said [11]—

6 *Wyman* v. *Paterson*, [1900] A.C. 271 ; *Re Sheppard*, [1911] 1 Ch. 50.
7 *Speight* v. *Gaunt* (1883), 9 App.Cas. 1 ; *Re Weall* (1889), 42 Ch.D. 674.
8 *Fry* v. *Tapson* (1884), 28 Ch.D. 268.
9 *Robinson* v. *Harkin*, [1896] 2 Ch. 415.
10 [1931] 1 Ch. 572 (Cases, p. 304).
11 [1931] 1 Ch. 581.

It is hardly too much to say that [section 23 (1)] revolutionizes the position of a trustee or an executor so far as regards the employment of agents. He is no longer required to do any actual work himself, but he may employ a solicitor or other agent to do it, whether there is any real necessity for the employment or not. No doubt he should use his discretion in selecting an agent, and should employ him only to do acts within the scope of the usual business of the agent; but, as will be seen, a question arises whether even in these respects he is personally liable for a loss due to the employment of the agent unless he has been guilty of wilful default.

The term "wilful default" is an exceedingly difficult one to define, and many judges have grappled with it. The most frequently quoted definition is that of Lord Alverstone in *Forder* v. *Great Western Railway Co.*[12] which in turn adopted and slightly modified the definition given in an Irish case.[13] Lord Alverstone says [14]—

"Wilful misconduct in such a special condition means misconduct to which the will is party as contradistinguished from accident, and is far beyond any negligence, even gross or culpable negligence, and involves that a person wilfully misconducts himself who knows and appreciates that it is wrong conduct on his part in the existing circumstances to do, or to fail or omit to do (as the case may be), a particular thing, and yet intentionally does, or fails or omits to do it, or persists in the act, failure, or omission regardless of consequences." The addition which I would suggest is, "or acts with reckless carelessness, not caring what the results of his carelessness may be."

Sir E. Pollock, M.R., also approved of this definition in *Re City Equitable Fire Insurance Co. Ltd.*[15] (where a number of other definitions are also considered) but in that case, it was one of the articles of the company which provided that the directors should only be liable for wilful default.

The effect of section 23 has been widely discussed, and varying views of its effect upon the pre-existing law have been expressed. Some have thought, especially in the light of Maugham, J.'s decision in *Re Vickery* that the section has altered the law in a drastic way: (1) by allowing trustees almost unrestricted freedom to appoint agents, and (2) by freeing the trustee from responsibility, except for "wilful default." To this, it has been objected that if so wide an interpretation is given to section 23 (1), it makes both section 23 (3) and section 30 (1) meaningless and unnecessary.[16] This, however, is something of an overstatement for, whilst authority may be given to an agent under section 23 (1) to receive money, section 23 (3) may be necessary to give the agent in advance a receipt and other documents.

Sir William Holdsworth, in accepting the implications of *Re Vickery*, thought that the legislation had gone too far, in section 23, in limiting the

---

12 [1905] 2 K.B. 532.
13 *Graham* v. *Belfast and Northern Counties Railway*, [1901] 2 I.R. 13, 19, *per* Johnson, J.
14 [1905] 2 K.B. 535–6.
15 [1925] Ch. 407.
16 See Potter (1931) 47 *Law Quarterly Review* 330; Jones, "Delegation by Trustees: A Reappraisal" (1959) 22 *Modern Law Review* 381; Sheridan, "The Trustee Act, 1966" (1965) *Solicitor Quarterly* 186.

liability of the trustee, so that in some cases the beneficiary is now insufficiently protected.[17] On the other hand, Dr Gareth Jones, after pointing out that section 23 (1) permitted a trustee to delegate, even though there is no legal or moral necessity to do so, adds [18]—

> In our submission the subsection does no more. A trustee should not, by means of an honest appointment, be able to ignore with complacency the activities of his agent; his liability for that agent's acts or defaults should still be determined by the rule in *Speight* v. *Gaunt* [19] and the norm of the reasonable man of business.

Finally, one or two commentators have suggested that section 23 (1) is no more than declaratory of pre-existing equitable principle. This is difficult to support, in view of the wide terms in which it is framed. It may also be suggested that section 23 (1) reflects, in some degree, the increasing reliance which the trustee, in his administration of the trust, must now place upon agents with special qualifications. If, as Maugham, J., suggested, the trustee can now appoint agents of all kinds, it would be unreasonable to expect him to exercise the continuing supervision over them which was formerly required, more especially in view of their specialist skills. He must appoint them in good faith, assuring himself that they possess normal skills, and are of good repute. Thereafter, he is only responsible for his own wilful default. Even today, however, the trustee cannot delegate his discretion; for example, if he delegates his power of selecting agents, as was done in *Fry* v. *Tapson*,[20] he incurs liability.

On this assumption, what meaning can be attached to section 23 (3)? It may be admitted that section 23, as a whole, is somewhat clumsily framed, and, whilst subsection (1) was new, subsection (3) reproduces section 17 (1), (2) of the Trustee Act 1893. The earlier enactment gave power to the trustee to appoint agents to perform trust work which it was beyond the strict scope of their professional duty to perform, and the incorporation of this possibility was presumably to remove doubts whether this was included within section 23 (1). Indeed, Maugham, J., may well have been contemplating this possibility in expressing the view in the wide terms which have been reproduced above.

It should be remembered that whereas under section 25 the trustee remains liable for his attorney, under section 23 the trustee's liability is limited to the extent stated above.

Some additional light on the problem has been shed by the decision of Cross, J., in *Re Lucking's Will Trusts*.[21] Lucking was the sole trustee of the will of his wife, in which the residuary estate, comprising the majority of the shares in a private company, was bequeathed to a number of persons. The remainder of the shares were owned by Lucking, who was also entitled to three-quarters of the trust estate. Later, a co-trustee was appointed.

Dewar was appointed managing director of the company, and he presented a number of cheques drawn on the company to Lucking, who signed them (some of these being blank cheques) without inquiry.

17 (1931) 47 *Law Quarterly Review* 463.
18 22 *Modern Law Review* 393.
19 (1883), 9 App.Cas. 1.
20 (1884), 28 Ch.D. 268.   21 [1968] 1 W.L.R. 866.

After Dewar's dismissal, it was found that he had overdrawn on the company's account to a total of £15,890, none of which was recoverable. A beneficiary under Mrs. Lucking's will sought to make Lucking and his co-trustee liable for the loss.

Cross, J., held him liable on the basis that he had failed to show the care of a reasonably prudent man of business. He said [22]—

> The conduct of the defendant trustees is, I think, to be judged by the standard applied in *Speight* v. *Gaunt*,[23] namely, that a trustee is only bound to conduct the business of the trust in such a way as an ordinary prudent man would conduct a business of his own.

Section 8 (1) of the Trustee Act gives a further power to employ agents. By virtue of this section, trustees are relieved from liability for lending money on the mortgage of real property, if they act on a report of a properly qualified surveyor or valuer, employed independently of the owner of the property, provided the valuer advises the loan, which does not exceed two-thirds of the value of the property.[24]

By section 6 of the the Trustee Investments Act 1961 a trustee must obtain advice before investing in wider range securities.

Finally, under section 29 of the Law of Property Act 1925 trustees for the sale of land may, until sale, revocably delegate by writing their powers of leasing, accepting surrenders of leases and management, to any person of full age (not being merely an annuitant) for the time being beneficially entitled in possession to the net rents and profits during his life or any less period. Where such delegation occurs, the trustees are not liable for the acts or defaults of the tenant for life.[25]

The fact that a trustee may not delegate his office except where permitted by equity or statute, and also the fact that trustees of statutory trusts for sale are in this respect in the position of ordinary trustees, are well illustrated by *Green* v. *Whitehead*.[26] In 1925, two partners, A and B, purchased Blackacre in fee simple. By virtue of section 36 of the Law of Property Act 1925 they held this on and after January 1, 1926, as statutory trustees for sale. During 1926 they entered into a contract to sell part of the freehold, but no steps were taken towards completion for two years. In 1928, A gave a general power of attorney to R, authorising him to sell and convey any property belonging to A, whether solely or jointly, and this power included a power to sell Blackacre. The vendors tendered a conveyance executed by B and R, which the purchasers declined to accept. Eve, J., held that the power of attorney amounted to a complete delegation of the trust, and as the vendors had contracted to sell as statutory trustees, the purported delegation of the power to convey was invalid. Complete delegation, observed Eve, J., was only possible under section 25 of the Trustee Act, which only became operative if the trustee who delegated was absent from the United Kingdom. Today, under section 9 of the Powers of Attorney Act 1971 such a delegation would be possible, provided it was limited to a period not exceeding twelve months.

---

[22] [1968] 1 W.L.R. 874.
[23] (1883), 22 Ch.D. 727.
[24] The effect of this section is considered on p. 251 *et seq.*, *post*.
[25] It should also be noticed that the Settled Land Act 1925, s. 102 (2), clearly implies the employment of agents by the trustees.   [26] [1930] 1 Ch. 38.

CHAPTER XVII

THE TRUSTEE'S POWERS AND DUTIES IN THE ADMINISTRATION OF A TRUST

A. THE REDUCTION OF THE TRUST PROPERTY INTO POSSESSION

THE first duty of a trustee on appointment is to ascertain what the trust property is, what are the directions of the trust instrument in regard to it, and then to discover whether the trust property has been properly and safely invested. He must also secure the transfer to him of any property which did not pass to him in virtue of the deed whereby he was appointed, as well as the transfer of all documents affecting the trust property, such as title-deeds and share certificates. As Kekewich, J., observed in *Hallows* v. *Lloyd* [1]—

> ... when persons are asked to become new trustees, they are bound to inquire of what the property consists that is proposed to be handed over to them, and what are the trusts. They ought also to look into the trust documents and papers to ascertain what notices appear among them of incumbrances and other matters affecting the trust.

Thus, where the trust fund includes an equitable interest, and the legal estate cannot be got in, it is the duty of the trustees to give notice as soon as possible to the persons in whom the legal estate is vested, so that the trustees shall obtain priority over any subsequent incumbrance.[2] Similarly, if the trust estate includes a *chose in action*, the trustee must get it in at the earliest moment which is expedient, for failure to do so will involve the trustee in liability.[3]

Several sections of the Trustee Act 1925 give to the trustees powers which would automatically be enjoyed by a beneficial owner, which the trustee has full discretion to exercise on behalf of the trust, so long as he does so honestly. Thus, section 22 (1) gives the trustee power to value reversionary property at the time when it is due to fall into possession, and also power to accept any authorised investments in lieu of the actual property to be transferred, together with a further power to give releases to any person bound to the trust estate.

By section 22 (2) it is provided that the trustees shall not be chargeable with any breach of trust because they have omitted to place any distringas notice [4] or to apply for any stop order on any securities or other property out of which the share or interest is derived; nor are they liable because they have omitted to take any proceedings on account of any act or default of the persons in whom such securities or other property are for the time being vested, unless and until required to take such steps by any person beneficially

---

[1] (1888), 39 Ch.D. 686, 691. See also Paling, " The Trustee's Duty to Reduce Assets into Possession " (1974) 4 *Kingston Law Review* 18.

[2] *Jacob* v. *Lucas* (1839), 1 Beav. 436.

[3] *Re Brogden* (1888), 38 Ch.D. 546; *Re Stevens,* [1898] 1 Ch. 162.

[4] A form of stop order, applicable to stocks and shares, prohibiting dealings without notice to the person obtaining the order.

interested under the trust, and unless due provision is made for the trustees' costs. But nothing in this subsection relieves " the trustees of the obligation to get in and obtain payment or transfer of such share or interest or other thing in action on the same falling into possession." In illustration of section 22 (2), if the trustees genuinely believe that the institution of proceedings would be fruitless, they are excused from the necessity of taking such proceedings to enforce payment.[5]

If the trust property includes chattels, the trustee should have a proper inventory made. Similarly, if a beneficiary under either a will or a trust is entitled to chattels for life, remainder to some third persons, he should sign an inventory, thus evidencing the nature and value of the property.[6] As a further illustration of this rule, if there is a covenant in a marriage settlement by a wife to settle after-acquired property, it is the duty of the trustees of the settlement, if they know, or have reasonable ground to believe that, property has come to her which should be settled, to ensure that it is so settled.[7]

The position of executors is in this respect very similar to that of trustees. It was pointed out in *Re Chapman* [8] that there is no absolute rule specifying a particular time within which a trustee or an executor must realise assets. The trustee or executor must use his own discretion, and the test of the trustee's liability is whether he has acted prudently and honestly, and in the belief that he was acting in the best interests of all the beneficiaries; and so, where the executors honestly exercised their discretion, postponing the sale of some foreign railway bonds which formed part of the assets of a trust, and which thereafter declined in value, they were not made responsible, although there had been an error of judgment. It would be very hard upon executors who have been saddled with property of this speculative kind, and have endeavoured to do their duty honestly, if they were to be fixed with a loss arising from their not having taken what, as it was proved by the result, would have been the best course.

Generally speaking, unless the executor has good reason to suppose that the property will materially appreciate, he should realise it within the executor's year, and if he fails to do so, the onus is on the executor to show some valid reason for the delay.[9] However, if the testator gives the executor an absolute discretion to postpone the sale and conversion of the estate, he is not compelled to convert within the year, and in the absence of bad faith he is not responsible for loss resulting from failure to convert.[10]

Where a trust investment has depreciated, so that the trust fund becomes jeopardised in consequence, the trustees ought to consider whether the time has not arrived to realise it. In *Re Medland*,[11] money was lent on the security of freehold mortgages, the proper margin being allowed, but the property subsequently depreciated so that the margin of safety was overstepped, and

---

5 *Clack* v. *Holland* (1854), 19 Beav. 262, 271–272 ; *Re Brogden* (1888), 38 Ch.D. 546.
6 *Temple* v. *Thring* (1887), 56 L.J.Ch. 767. It is not customary now to require security from the tenant for life, unless there is reason to anticipate loss. See Keeton and Sheridan, *Equity*, p. 557.
7 *Ex parte Geaves* (1856), 8 De G.M. & G. 291.
8 [1896] 2 Ch. 763, 782.
9 *Per* Page Wood, L.J., in *Grayburn* v. *Clarkson* (1868), L.R. 3 Ch.App. 605, 606.
10 *Re Norrington* (1879), 13 Ch.D. 654.
11 (1889), 41 Ch.D. 476.

the trustees failed to call in the mortgage. North, J., held, however, that there was no absolute duty upon the trustee in these circumstances to call in the mortgage at once, but there was a discretion, which they must exercise with due regard to all the circumstances, including the solvency of the mortgagor; and, furthermore, the Trustee Act 1925, s. 4, now provides that—

> A trustee shall not be liable for breach of trust by reason only of his continuing to hold an investment which has ceased to be an investment authorised by the trust instrument or by the general law.

It is scarcely necessary to add that this section in no way relieves from liability a trustee who, in such circumstances, fails to exercise his discretion.

A trustee or executor ought never to allow trust money to remain outstanding simply on the personal security of the debtor, even though the money had been lent by the testator himself, for the quality of the debtor may change from day to day; and if the executor or trustee fails to get in the debt within reasonable time, he becomes himself the debtor's surety.[12] Trustees must not, in general, lend trust money on personal security, even with a guarantor,[13] although if the trustee is expressly empowered to lend on personal security, he may do so,[14] even lending to the tenant for life if satisfied that there is a reasonable prospect of repayment.[15]

The Trustee Act 1925, s. 24, provides—

> Where an undivided share in the proceeds of sale of land directed to be sold, or in any other property, is subject to a trust, or forms part of the estate of a testator or intestate, the trustees or personal representatives may (without prejudice to the trust for sale affecting the entirety of the land and the powers of the trustees for sale in reference thereto) execute or exercise any trust or power vested in them in relation to such share in conjunction with the persons entitled to or having power in that behalf over the other share or shares, and notwithstanding that any one or more of the trustees or personal representatives may be entitled to or interested in any such other share, either in his or their own right or in a fiduciary capacity.

Where there are two or more trustees the trust property should be placed within the control of all the trustees, and not left in the sole control of one beyond what is reasonable in respect of time and circumstances.[16] Thus, in *Lewis* v. *Nobbs*,[17] trustees invested trust money in bearer bonds, which one trustee allowed to remain in the custody of the other, who misappropriated them. The one trustee was held liable for his negligence in permitting them to remain with the other, so that they could be so misappropriated. The position is now regulated by section 7 of the Trustee Act 1925 which provides that securities payable to bearer retained or taken as an investment by a

---

[12] *Lowson* v. *Copeland* (1787), 2 Bro.C.C. 156; *Powell* v. *Evans* (1801), 5 Ves. 839; *Re Tucker*, [1894] 1 Ch. 724, 734; *Khoo Tek Keong* v. *Ch'ng Joo Tuan Neoh*, [1934] A.C. 529 (Cases, p. 363).
[13] See *Holmes* v. *Dring* (1788), 2 Cox 1; *Styles* v. *Guy* (1849), 1 Mac. & G. 422.
[14] *Pickard* v. *Anderson* (1872), L.R. 13 Eq. 608.
[15] *Re Laing's Settlement*, [1899] 1 Ch. 593, where the power was to lend on " personal credit without security " subject to the consent of the tenant for life, who was also the settlor.
[16] See Chap. XVII, s. B, 3, and Chap. XXIV, s. E, *post*.
[17] (1878), 8 Ch.D. 591.

trustee (not being a trust corporation) shall, until sold, be deposited by him for safe custody and collection of income with a bank, and a trustee is not responsible for any loss incurred by reason of such deposit and any sum payable in respect of such deposit and collection shall be paid out of the income of the trust property.

It has already been noticed that section 23 (3) of the Trustee Act, apart from the general powers of delegation in section 23 (1), permits a trustee to employ a solicitor as his agent to receive and give a discharge for property under the trust, without being responsible for the defaults of the solicitor, if the trustee acts in good faith; but the trustee must then ensure that the money or other property does not remain under the control of the solicitor longer than is reasonably necessary. The same rule also applies where, under the same section, the trustee appoints a banker or a solicitor to be his agent to receive and give a discharge for any money payable to the trustee under a policy of insurance.

Where a person owes money to the trust estate, section 14 of the Trustee Act 1925 provides that the trustee's receipt for it, or for any other personal property due to be transferred, shall be a full discharge of the debtor's obligation.

An important power in respect of trust property is also given to the trustee by the next section (section 15). This section gives a personal representative or two or more trustees (or a trust corporation) power to accept property before the time when it is due to be transferred, power to give time for payment of a debt, power to enter into any composition with a debtor, or to compound with him, or enter into arbitration. These powers are intended to make the trustee the judge of the appropriate steps to be taken, whenever the debtor is in difficulties and cannot fulfil his obligations.[18]

In pursuance of these powers, since the trustee, when he is legal owner, bears all the burdens incident to ownership,[19] he may bring any action with regard to the trust property (in fact, in a court of law, he is the only person to bring such actions, for only equity regarded the beneficiary as possessing an interest entitling him to sue), and, in particular, where a debtor to the trust becomes bankrupt, it is the trustee's duty to prove in bankruptcy, and for this he does not need the concurrence of the beneficiary, unless the latter is *sui juris* and absolutely entitled, in which case the court may require the concurrence of the *cestui que trust*.[20] The trustee is also entitled to the custody of title-deeds, but the beneficiaries are entitled to inspect them at all reasonable times.[21]

If a trustee, in the execution of his trust, carries on a business on behalf of the beneficiaries, he is personally liable to the creditors and may be made bankrupt in respect of the debts.[22] Furthermore, if trustees hold shares in a company, even if the trust is noticed in the company's books, they are liable

---

[18] For an example of a compromise, see *Re Ezekiel's Settlement Trusts*, [1942] Ch. 230. A judicial trustee has the power to compromise: *Re Ridsdel*, [1947] Ch. 597.

[19] *Per* Lord Northington in *Burgess* v. *Wheate* (1759), 1 Eden 177, 251 (Cases, p. 185).

[20] *Ex parte Green* (1832), 2 Deac. & Ch. 113; *Ex parte Gray* (1835), 4 Deac. & Ch. 778.

[21] *Wynne* v. *Humberston* (1858), 27 Beav. 421.

[22] *Farhall* v. *Farhall* (1871), L.R. 7 Ch.App. 123; *Ex parte Garland* (1804), 10 Ves. 110, 119.

in full as if they were beneficial owners, and it is fruitless for them to allege that they are only liable to the extent of the trust estate.[23]

In *Schalit* v. *Nadler Ltd.*,[24] Nadler was trustee of a lease for Messrs. Nadler Ltd., Schalit being the sub-lessee. The company levied a distress for arrears of rent, and the plaintiff contended it was wrongful. The county court judge held that only the trustee as legal owner, and not the beneficiary, could recover arrears of rent of trust property, and the Divisional Court upheld this decision, pointing out that a beneficiary is not entitled to the actual rent of trust property, but only to an account from the trustee of the profits received from the demise.[25]

B. THE POWER OF INVESTMENT

1. Trustee Investments [26]

A glance at the Trustee Investments Act 1961 will show the range of trustee investments open to a trustee, apart from any further powers of investment conferred upon him by the trust instrument itself. This power of investment in securities set out in the Trustee Investments Act 1961 applies, unless otherwise expressly provided, to trusts, executorships and administratorships, arising either before or after the Act. The powers are available to the trustees only in so far as no contrary intention appears in the instrument and they are, by section 1 (3), subject to the provisions therein contained.

Before the modern Trustee Acts, the powers of trustees to invest trust money, apart from special powers in the instrument, or under orders of the court, were very limited. It has already been noticed that trustees ought not to lend on personal security; and it was also consistently held that they ought not to invest in the stock of any private company. Before the Law of Property Amendment Act 1859 trustees could not invest in Bank of England stock without express permission.

In the seventeenth century, the position of the trustee was ambiguous in the extreme, and in cases of doubt, the trustee often sought the advice of the court. Even the power to invest in mortgages with wide margins was doubted by Lord Thurlow,[27] though it was admitted by Lord Hardwicke [28] and Lord Alvanley,[29] who laid down the general principle " that, when an executor or trustee, instead of executing the trust, as he ought, by laying out the property either in well secured real estates or upon Government securities, takes upon him to dispose of it in another manner, the *Cestuys que trust* may call him to an account . . ."

At the beginning of the eighteenth century there was need for a wider field

---

[23] *Re Phoenix Life Assurance Co.* (1862), 2 J. & H. 229; *Re Cheshire Banking Co.* (1886), 32 Ch.D. 301, 309. On the position of trustees as directors, see *Barclays Bank Ltd.* v. *I.R.C.*, [1961] A.C. 509.

[24] [1933] 2 K.B. 79.

[25] *Cf. Baker* v. *Archer-Shee*, [1927] A.C. 844; *Archer-Shee* v. *Garland*, [1931] A.C. 212; Chap. XXI, *post*, as to income tax and the beneficiary's interest.

[26] See further, Keeton, " Trustee Investments and the National Investments Policy," *The Accountant*, 4th April 1953, pp. 390–393; Keeton, " The Changing Conception of Trusteeship " (1950) 3 *Current Legal Problems* 14; Keeton, *Modern Developments in the Law of Trusts*, pp. 45–80.

[27] *Ex parte Cathorpe* (1785), 1 Cox 182.

[28] *Knight* v. *Earl of Plymouth* (1747), Dick. 120, 126.

[29] *Pocock* v. *Reddington* (1801), 5 Ves. 794, 800.

of trustee investment, as the amount of land available for mortgages was small, and in the absence of any statutory rule the courts laid down principles for the guidance of trustees. The need for these was emphasised by the rash speculation of trustees in the South Sea Company and similar hazardous ventures. The successful wars of the eighteenth century progressively increased the national debt, and the Court of Chancery repeatedly decided that whilst commercial speculation was not a risk that could properly be incurred by a trustee unless the trust deed expressly authorised it, the trustee would be free from liability if he invested funds under his control in Government three per cent stock. As overseas trade extended, the number of trusts increased, and the funds therein settled were reinvested in Government stock. This accounts, to a considerable degree, for the steadiness of British credit, in the long-drawn-out struggle with Revolutionary France and the Napoleonic Empire.

The nineteenth century, with its rapid growth of industry and commerce, brought also a demand for a wider field of trustee investment. This was partially satisfied by the Law of Property Amendment Act 1859, permitting trustees to invest in stocks of the Banks of England and Ireland and in East India stock. The change was greatly disliked by property lawyers, who thought that it opened the way to jobbing in trust funds. Accordingly, the courts held that the Act applied only to trusts created after the passing of the Act. In 1860, however, a further Act was passed, making the provision retrospective, and at the same time giving the Lord Chancellor power to make general orders as to the securities in which cash under the control of the court, as well as ordinary trust funds, might be invested. There were further Acts slightly extending these powers in 1867, 1871, 1875, and 1882. Nevertheless, the field of permissible investment still excluded wide and important classes of stocks—for example, municipal and colonial loans.

In 1888, the National Debt Conversion Act was passed, reducing the rate of interest on Consols from three per cent. to two-and-a-half per cent. At once there arose an insistent demand that the field of trustee investment should be extended. This led to the Trust Investment Act of 1889, which allowed trustees to invest in the debentures and preference shares of railway companies, provided that the railways had paid a three per cent. dividend on their ordinary shares for two years previously. The result was a heavy investment by trustees in railways during the next decade, although the Trustee Act 1893 supplied a note of caution by insisting that the ordinary shares of railways should have paid a dividend for ten years previously.

The tide now flowed strongly in favour of greater freedom of investment, and the Trustee Act 1893 extended the freedom still further. Trustees were allowed to invest in British Government stocks, stocks of the Banks of England and Ireland, the stock of the London County Council, and of any county council or municipal borough having a population exceeding 50,000, as well as in Metropolitan Board of Works stock and that of English water supply companies, and certain classes of Indian Government and Indian railways stock. The most important additions included in this list were a few public utilities and local loans. These had been created under the National Debt and Local Loans Act of 1887 and they are Government-sanctioned borrowing by local authorities arising out of the new conception of local government established by the Municipal Corporations Act 1835. A further addition to the range of trustee stocks occurred in 1900, when the Colonial Stock Act of that year gave trustees power to invest in a number of colonial stocks registered in England.

Since that date, until 1961, there were no general legislative changes in the range of trustee investments, although the class was extensively modified in other ways. Thus, the Agricultural Credits Act of 1928 authorised trustees to invest in the debenture stock of the Agricultural Mortgage Corporation, formed to assist in the provision of credit for agriculture. The Housing Acts have permitted trustees to lend money for the provision of houses under these Acts. The Coal Act 1938 enabled them to invest money representing compensation for royalties in the debenture, preference or guaranteed stock of companies that had paid a dividend of at least three per cent per annum on their ordinary capital for at least five years previously, or in ordinary stock if dividends of four per cent. had been paid on this for ten years previously. Government stocks created under successive Nationalisation Acts have also been included in the list of trustee stocks.

The twentieth century has also furnished problems of a new type. When the Irish Free State was established in 1922, its stocks ceased to be included within those of the United Kingdom in the Act of 1893, and moreover, the Free State chose not to give the guarantees required under the Colonial Stock Act 1900. Consequently, Government, municipal and railway stocks of Southern Ireland ceased to be trustee stocks. The adoption of the Statute of Westminster 1931 by the Union of South Africa produced a somewhat similar problem there, which was solved by special agreement between the Governments of the United Kingdom and the Union of South Africa. When South Africa left the Commonwealth in 1961, South African Government stocks ceased to be trustee stocks. On the other hand, special clauses in the Acts creating new Commonwealth nations conferred trustee status on their Government stocks.

The mere fact that an investment is included by statute in the list of trustee investments does not absolve the trustees from the duty of care in making an investment. A trustee stock may be " gilt-edged," but it is not necessarily " cast-iron." In the 'thirties, when industrial depression and severe competition from road haulage companies greatly reduced railway earnings, the railway companies were compelled to strain their resources to the uttermost to continue to pay a dividend on their ordinary stock, and so retain trustee status for their preference stock and debentures. When the railways were nationalised, however, their stock was exchanged for Government stock, so that the problem cannot now arise. A still more serious situation arose with regard to Australian Government stocks. There had been very heavy borrowing by Australia in consequence of the ready grant of trustee status to such loans, so that in 1933, the trustee stocks of Australia were seven times the amount of those of Canada. Owing to the depression, there were defaults in the payment of interest on some of these loans. Nevertheless, it then appeared that a colonial stock which fulfils the necessary statutory requirements cannot be removed from the trustee list (except by legislation) simply because the interest is not paid. Such a situation therefore emphasises the need for prudence, even with regard to investment in trustee stocks.

At the time when the Trustee Act was passed in 1925, there was discussion of the question whether the range of trustee investments ought to be widened, and a Government Committee was appointed in 1925 to consider the position. The main recommendation was that there should be no change in policy, and this cautious conclusion was vindicated during the 'thirties, during which period trust funds in the United States, invested with greater freedom, suffered serious losses. Today, however, conditions have changed again very considerably from those which existed in 1925. Taxation has seriously diminished the yield from Government stocks which, unlike that of commercial shares, is of fixed amount. Moreover, the persistence of inflation has involved a continuous decline in the real capital value of all Government stocks; whilst the ordinary shares of large industrial enterprises have tended to show considerable " growth." To some extent, the difficulty has been met by giving trustees increasingly wider powers of investment in the trust instrument itself; a policy which is always open to the criticism that whilst those of substantial means may take steps to avoid or minimise present difficulties, the man of limited means has no such remedy; nor has the charitable foundation which works under trust deeds which were drafted many years ago. For these, the only possible remedy has been by new legislation. The demand that the field of trustee investment should be widened to include prior charges on some of our greatest industrial and commercial undertakings, and also the capital of building societies, accordingly grew steadily.

In the United States, there have in the past been very wide variations in the practice of individual states in respect of trustee investments. At one end of the scale, a group of states—usually the less developed states of the Union— have forbidden investment in commercial enterprises by trustees. At the other end of the scale, a large and influential group of states, which includes New York and most of the New England states, follow what is known as the " prudent man " rule. This permits trustees to invest in the same range of stocks and shares, and in the same manner, as a prudent man would do, when investing on behalf of others.[30] The tendency in the United States is for an increasing number of states to follow this rule.

The Nathan Committee, which reported on charitable trusts in 1952,[31] recommended the adoption in England of a modified Massachusetts rule, suggesting that trustees should be permitted to invest up to 50 per cent. of the funds under their control in the debentures and stocks and shares of financial, industrial and commercial companies quoted on the Stock Exchange.

After nation-wide discussion the Trustee Investments Act 1961 was placed on the statute-book. This makes an entirely fresh departure by completely repealing section 1 of the Trustee Act 1925. The first schedule to the Act introduces a new scheme of trustee investments. The first class (termed narrower range investments not requiring advice) comprises investments which the trustee can make at any time before consulting anyone. The class is a

[30] See further, Latham, " Trustee Investments and American Prac*ice " (1954) 7 *Current Legal Problems* 139.
[31] Cmd. 8710.

small one. It comprises Defence Bonds, National Savings Certificates, Ulster Saving Certificates, Ulster Development Bonds, National Development Bonds and British Savings Bonds, deposits in the National Savings Bank, and ordinary deposits in a trustee savings bank, and other bank deposits. Beyond these investments, however, there are two larger classes. For both of these, advice is needed before investment. In the first class, called " narrower range investments," are to be found the various classes of Government stock, local loans, stock of nationalised industries, and stocks of Commonwealth nations and colonies formerly appearing in section 1 of the Trustee Act 1925, with some interesting additions, such as European Investment Bank and European Coal and Steel Community stock, and some omissions made necessary by change of circumstances. In the second class (" wider range investments ") are securities and shares of commercial enterprises in the United Kingdom and units in unit trusts in the United Kingdom.

It is in this section of the schedule that the English trustee is for the first time empowered to invest in the stocks and shares of industrial and commercial enterprises normally quoted on the stock exchange. There are, however, important changes of procedure. The trustee, in making wider range investments, is required to divide the trust fund into two parts of equal value. One part only may then be invested in the wider range investments; the other must remain in the narrower range investments. Further, in making investments (except for those in the narrower range not requiring advice), or in changing them, the trustee must secure proper advice in writing on investments, from " a person who is reasonably believed by the trustee to be qualified by his ability in and practical experience of financial matters . . ."[32] Moreover, in making investments, the trustee must have regard to the need to diversify the trustee investments, and to their suitability for his trust.[33]

The settlor may, of course, exclude some of the investments specified in the Trustee Investments Act 1961 and if he does, the range of choice of the trustees is thereby limited. A direction to invest in certain specified types of securities is not, however, an implied exclusion of the Act of 1961.[34] Moreover, the court will not invest trust funds in securities prohibited by the settlor.[35] On the other hand, a direction by the settlor to invest in a prescribed investment does not prevent the trustees from placing trust money in other trustee investments if they choose,[36] and where a testator specifically bequeaths shares in a company to trustees upon trust to pay the income to beneficiaries, the trustees have power to sell those shares.[37]

Where the trustee is given power to vary investments " as he thinks fit," that does not permit him to go outside the range of trustee investments and those additional investments permitted by the instrument.[38]

In selecting securities for investment, the trustee must remember that the range of securities changes from time to time. Moreover, the statute does not

---

[32] Trustee Investment Act 1961, s. 6 (2)–(4).
[33] Section 6 (1).
[34] Re Warren, [1939] Ch. 684.
[35] Ovey v. Ovey, [1900] 2 Ch. 524, not following Re Wedderburn's Trusts (1878), 9 Ch.D 112.
[36] Re Burke, [1908] 2 Ch. 248.
[37] Re Pratt's Will Trusts, [1943] Ch. 326. (Decided on s. 1 of the Trustee Act 1925)
[38] Re Hazeldine, [1918] 1 Ch. 433.

confer an absolute authority upon the trustee to invest money in the permitted securities. He must still exercise his discretion, and, except for a few narrower range investments, he must act on competent advice. The power of investment includes a power of varying trust investments, by selling some authorised securities and purchasing others; and furthermore, where the instrument expressly authorises the trustees to invest in real securities, it entitles them to sell authorised investments for the purpose of laying out money on mortgage, notwithstanding the fact that the investments have depreciated, and the trustees sell out at a loss.

The general duty of the trustee in relation to investments was exhaustively considered, both by the Court of Appeal and by the House of Lords, in *Re Whiteley*,[39] wherein it was pointed out that whilst equity generally required from a trustee the same diligence as he showed in his own private affairs, yet he is not allowed the same discretion in regard to investment as he enjoys in his private affairs; for he may be prepared to take a hazard for his personal benefit to secure a greater immediate return. As a trustee, however, it is his duty to preserve the trust fund for the benefit of persons entitled in succession, and he must therefore avoid all hazardous enterprises, even though included within the list of trustee investments.

> The duty of a trustee is not to take such care only as a prudent man would take if he had only himself to consider; the duty rather is to take such care as an ordinary prudent man would take if he were minded to make an investment for the benefit of other people for whom he felt morally bound to provide.[40]

With regard to investments by trustees in mortgages, the Trustee Act 1925, s. 8, provides that trustees shall not be liable for loss to the beneficiaries, if, in making the loan on mortgage, they have complied with certain conditions. In the first place, the security must be one on which the trustees can properly lend money, *i.e.* it must be freehold property, or leaseholds within the limits allowed by the Trustee Investments Act 1961. Secondly, the loan must not exceed two-thirds of the value of the property. Thirdly, the valuation of the property must be undertaken by a person he reasonably believes to be " an able, practical surveyor or valuer instructed and employed independently of any owner " of the property, *and the valuer or surveyor, in his report, must advise that the loan should be made.*

A number of points in this section (which replaces section 8 of the Trustee Act 1893) require comment. In the first place, it was decided in *Re Somerset*,[41] with reference to subs. (1) (*a*), that the trustee must believe the surveyor or valuer to be able, whilst he must in fact be employed independently of the owner of the property. In selecting the surveyor or valuer, the trustee should use his own judgment, and that does not mean that he may leave the selection to his solicitor.[42] Whilst it is no longer necessary to select the valuer or surveyor from the locality where the property is, the possession of local knowledge may, nevertheless, be very material in determining his ability.[43]

---

[39] (1886), 33 Ch.D. 347; (1887), 12 App.Cas. 727, *sub nom. Learoyd* v. *Whiteley*.
[40] *Per* Lindley, L.J., 33 Ch.D. 355.
[41] [1894] 1 Ch. 231. See also *Re Dive*, [1909] 1 Ch. 328.
[42] *Re Walker* (1890), 59 L.J.Ch. 386, 391; *Fry* v. *Tapson* (1884), 28 Ch.D. 268.
[43] See *Fry* v. *Tapson, supra.*

A further point is that the report must be of such a nature that the loan can be regarded as having been made " under the advice of the surveyor or valuer." In consideration of the statutory requirements, therefore, Lewin suggests [44] that the following points should be borne in mind by the trustee—

(1) The instructions to the valuer should be in writing. (2) It should appear how the trustees became acquainted with the property. (3) The valuer should be informed that the loan is one of trust money; and (4) Generally of all material circumstances known to the trustees or their adviser in reference to the property and neighbourhood. (5) The report should be in writing. (6) It should particularly describe the character of the property, and should not extend to any property other than that on which the loan is to be made. (7) All matters connected with the property tending to decrease its value in reference to repairs, outgoings, and the like should be stated. (8) The means of knowledge and capacity of the valuer should be clearly made to appear, especially his experience, if any, in the locality, and his information as to actual recent sales in the district. (9) The valuer should expressly state what amount may be safely advanced, and advise such advance being made; and if any supplementary letter is written by him he should therein repeat or confirm such advice. (10) The report should be expressed in plain businesslike language, and not in inflated phraseology.

It should be emphasised that the object of the surveyor's report is to supply the trustees with adequate information concerning the property, and with the assistance of the report the trustees must exercise their judgment in deciding whether the investment is in fact a proper one.

Not more than two-thirds of the value of the property may be advanced on mortgage, and the money may be advanced not only on the security of land, but also on that of houses. Care must be exercised, however, to ascertain whether the value of the premises is increased in consequence of a business being carried on there, for if this is so, the amount of the advance ought to be less. In general, if the trustee is lending on the security of business premises, he ought to disregard the value of the business in making the advance, or confine his loan to not more than half the value of the premises as enhanced by the business carried on there.[45] Moreover, the trustee should also be careful to avoid investment in a wasting security, such as a freehold brickfield.[46] He is not debarred, however, from lending money on the security of freehold property which is let on weekly tenancies,[47] although he should not lend money on the security of unlet houses, more particularly if the mortgagor is a builder,[48] and cottage property in a town should be regarded with caution, since its value is subject to considerable fluctuation with the circumstances.[49]

It is provided by section 9 (1) of the Trustee Act 1925 that where a trustee improperly advances trust money on a mortgage security which would at the time of the investment be a proper investment in all respects for a smaller

44 *Trusts* (16th ed.), p. 364.
45 See *Re Olive* (1886), 34 Ch.D. 70 ; *Palmer* v. *Emerson*, [1911] 1 Ch. 758.
46 *Learoyd* v. *Whiteley* (1887), 12 App.Cas. 727. See also *Re Turner*, [1897] 1 Ch. 536.
47 *Re Solomon*, [1913] 1 Ch. 200.
48 *Fry* v. *Tapson* (1884), 28 Ch.D. 268.
49 *Re Salmon* (1889), 42 Ch.D. 351, 368.

sum than is actually advanced thereon, the security shall be deemed an authorised investment for the smaller sum, and the trustee shall only be liable to make good the sum advanced in excess thereof with interest. In *Shaw* v. *Cates* [50] the sum advanced was £4,440, and the security was held to have been a proper one for an advance of £3,400, so the trustee could not be liable for loss in excess of £1,040. But it is important to notice that this relief may only be claimed by the trustee where the security is otherwise unobjectionable. [51]

The disadvantages attaching to the loan of money by trustees on a second mortgage are so substantial that a trustee would only rarely be justified in adopting this form of investment, for a first mortgagee might sell under disadvantageous conditions, whilst the trustees might not have the funds available to redeem him and prevent the sale. Formerly, too, there was the added peril that a third mortgagee might tack the first mortgage against the trustee as second mortgagee, and although the dangers of this kind of tacking have been abolished since 1925, it is still possible for a first mortgagee to tack further advances. [52] Should the mortgagee, for any reason, decide to adopt this form of investment, he should in no circumstances fail to register, as there would otherwise be an obvious example of negligence. Again, since an equitable mortgagee by deposit of title-deeds runs the risk of being postponed to a purchaser for value of the legal estate without notice (which would be the case where the mortgagor could satisfactorily account for the absence of his title-deeds), courts of equity have usually regarded this also as an unsuitable investment for a trustee who has power to invest in real securities. [53] Trustees should also avoid joining in a contributory mortgage, for this would place the power to realise the security beyond their exclusive control. [54] There is, however, nothing to prevent trustees lending by way of sub-mortgage, since the trustees get a legal estate and the title-deeds, together with a covenant from the original mortgagor in addition. [55] The power of the ordinary trustee to invest in real securities does not extend to the purchase of land, but only to loans on mortgage. This rule is applicable to trustees for sale who have sold all the land subject to the trust [56]; but where some part of the land subject to the trust is retained, trustees for sale, possessing as they do the powers of a tenant for life under the Settled Land Act 1925, may now invest in the purchase of land. [57] Where trustees sell land, they must obtain the best price. [58]

The Trustee Act 1925 conferred on trustees only a very limited power to invest in mortgages on the security of leasehold property. This power was extended by the Trustee Investments Act 1961, [59] which makes mortgages of leaseholds with an unexpired term of not less than sixty years at the time of the investment a narrower range investment, for which, therefore, expert advice is needed before the investment can be made.

[50] [1909] 1 Ch. 389.
[51] *Re Somerset*, [1894] 1 Ch. 231 ; *Re Turner*, [1897] 1 Ch. 536.
[52] See Law of Property Act 1925, s. 94.
[53] *Norris* v. *Wright* (1851), 14 Beav. 291, 308 ; *Swaffield* v. *Nelson*, [1876] W.N. 255.
[54] *Webb* v. *Jonas* (1888), 39 Ch.D. 660 ; *Re Massingberd's Settlement* (1890), 63 L.T. 296 ; *Stokes* v. *Prance*, [1898] 1 Ch. 212.
[55] *Smethurst* v. *Hastings* (1885), 30 Ch.D. 490.
[56] *Re Wakeman*, [1945] Ch. 177.
[57] *Re Wellsted's Will Trusts*, [1949] Ch. 296.
[58] *Buttle* v. *Saunders*, [1950] 2 All E.R. 193.
[59] Sched. 1, Pt. II, para. 13.

Certain powers supplementary to the trustee's power of investment are given by section 10 of the Trustee Act 1925. Thus, subs. (1) permits the trustees, in lending on mortgage, to covenant that the mortgage shall not be called in for a period not exceeding seven years.

Subs. (2) provides that where the tenant for life or the trustees sell land, either in fee simple or for a term having at least five hundred years to run, two-thirds of the purchase price may be left on mortgage, either with or without a charge on other property, and the mortgagor must covenant to keep the property, if it includes buildings, insured against fire. In such a case, the trustees shall not be bound to obtain any report as to the value of the land or other property to be comprised in such a charge or mortgage, or any advice as to the making of the loan, and shall not be liable for any loss which may be incurred by reason only of the security being insufficient at the date of the charge or mortgage, and the trustees of the settlement shall be bound to give effect to such contract made by the tenant for life or statutory owner.

By subs. (3), where the securities of a company are the subject of a trust, the trustees have power to concur in any scheme (*a*) for the reconstruction of the company; (*b*) for the sale of all or any part of the property of the company to another company; (*c*) for the acquisition of the securities of the company, or of control thereof, by another company; (*d*) for the amalgamation of the company with another company; (*e*) for the release, modification or variation of any rights, privileges or liabilities attached to the securities or any of them, exactly as if the trustees were beneficially entitled, and the trustees have power to accept securities of any kind in the reconstructed, new or purchasing company in exchange for the original securities. The trustee is not responsible for any ensuing loss if he has acted in good faith. If any conditional or preferential right to subscribe for any securities in any company is offered to trustees in respect of any holding in such company, they may, as to all or any of such securities, either exercise such right and apply capital money subject to the trust in payment of the consideration, or renounce such right, or assign for the best consideration that can be reasonably obtained the benefit of such right or the title thereto to any person, including any beneficiary under the trust, without being responsible for any loss occasioned by any act or thing so done by them in good faith.[60] The powers exercised under section 10 are subject to any consents which the instrument may require[61]; and if a loan under section 10 (1) or a sale under section 10 (2) is made under the order of the court, the powers conferred apply only so far as the court may direct.[62]

By section 11, trustees may deposit money at a bank whilst a mortgage is being prepared or an investment sought. Any interest that may be payable is regarded as income. Furthermore, trustees may apply capital money of the trust towards paying calls on the shares subject to the trust.

2. Investment Clauses

It has been pointed out that the trust instrument may narrow or broaden the field of trustee investments, and one or two examples of such variations

---

[60] Trustee Act 1925, s. 10 (4).
[61] Trustee Act 1925, s. 10 (5).
[62] Trustee Act 1925, s. 10 (6).

must be considered. The general rule applicable to all investment clauses is that they are a deviation from the law laid down in the Trustee Acts, and as such, investment clauses are always construed strictly; that is to say, the onus is on the trustee to show that he has acted within the very words of the clause.

One problem which has arisen in respect of such clauses has been the effect of phrases designed to exclude, from the field of permissible investments, those specified in section 1 of the Trustee Act 1925, or now in the Trustee Investments Act 1961. Such exclusion, to be effective, must always be in express words; it is never implied.[63] In *Re Hill*,[64] however, a power was given to invest in certain specified investments, and in no other investments whatsoever. In this case, the investments in section 1 of the Act of 1925 were held to be excluded. More recently in *Re Rider's Will Trusts*,[65] a clause in a will directed that moneys should be invested " in or upon any stocks funds or securities of or guaranteed by the government of the United Kingdom or of any British colony or dependency . . . or upon real securities in England but not otherwise." Two questions were raised by summons: (1) whether the clause authorised all trustee investments, or whether some were excluded; and (2) whether stocks of a colony or dependency were permissible investments, if such a possession at the date of the testator's death in 1908 had since become a self-governing dominion. Harman, J., held that the phrase " but not otherwise " governed the entire clause, and therefore excluded any class of investments but those stated. However, dominion stocks were within the general class stated in the will, so that it was unnecessary to consider whether dominion stocks were within the words " any British colony or dependency." This is not the only decision in which these words have caused difficulty. In *Re Maryon-Wilson's Estate*,[66] the court thought that the transformation of a colony into a dominion did not adversely affect the status of the stock; but in *Re Brassey's Settlement*,[67] the question of the status of Canadian stock was in issue, the settlement having been made after Canada had adopted the Statute of Westminster. The court then held that it is now not appropriate to include a dominion within the phrase " colony or dependency." Obviously, in the rapid transformations in colonial status which have recently been occurring, it may be safer to avoid the phrase altogether.

In *Re Kolb's Will Trusts*,[68] a settlor directed his trustees to invest in " blue chip " securities, at the same time excluding Government securities from the range of investments. Cross, J., decided that " blue chip " was too uncertain a description, and since the exclusion of Government securities depended upon the power to invest in " blue chips," the exclusion was ineffective.

Where the trust instrument authorises the trustees to lend money at their discretion, or " on such good security as the trustees can obtain," this does not permit them to lend money on personal security,[69] nor in an ordinary trading concern.[70] Where the consents of various persons are required for an

[63] *Re Burke*, [1908] 2 Ch. 248.
[64] [1914] W.N. 132.
[65] [1958] 1 W.L.R. 974.
[66] [1912] 1 Ch. 55.
[67] [1955] 1 W.L.R. 192.
[68] [1962] Ch. 531.
[69] *Pocock* v. *Reddington* (1801), 5 Ves. 794; *Styles* v. *Guy* (1849), 1 Mac. & G. 422; *Bethell* v. *Abraham* (1873), L.R. 17 Eq. 24.
[70] *Cock* v. *Goodfellow* (1722), 10 Mod. 489.

investment, the trustees must ensure that the consents are all obtained, and in the proper form. Furthermore, the persons whose consent is required must have knowledge of the nature of the intended investment.[71] This is simply an illustration of the general rule that all investment clauses, varying the statutory range of investment, are construed strictly. As a further illustration of this rule it may be mentioned that where a will gave power to trustees to invest " upon security of the funds of any company incorporated by Act of Parliament," and the trustees invested in the shares of a railway company incorporated by Act of Parliament, this was held to be a deviation from the investment clause, since the trustees had not secured their money upon the assets of the company, but had participated in the commercial adventure itself.[72] Where there is a clause permitting investment in the securities of any " railway or other public company," this permits the trustees to invest in the securities of any public company incorporated under the Companies Acts,[73] but only in securities of public companies in the United Kingdom.[74] Where the expression " companies in the United Kingdom " is used, this includes companies registered in the United Kingdom, but prosecuting their business abroad.[75] Even where the power given to invest in companies is very wide, the trustees must still exercise their discretion in investing, and they should consider the constitution of the company, more particularly in respect of rights of recourse against the shareholders.[76] If this discretion has in fact been exercised honestly, the fact that the shares are not fully paid up will not make them an improper investment.[77] An investment clause which gave the trustees power to invest in " stocks funds and securities " was held to give the trustees power to invest in the fully paid-up shares in a limited company.[78]

In recent years, there has been a tendency to draft increasingly wide investment clauses. One of such clauses purports to give the trustees power to invest at their absolute discretion as if they were the beneficial owners of the fund. In *Re Wragg*[79] P. O. Lawrence, J., held that such a clause was sufficiently wide to permit the trustees to go outside the range of trustee investments, and to purchase real estate. In *Re McEacharn*[80] trustees were given power to invest in " such stocks funds and securities " as they thought fit, and this was held to cover investment in fully paid shares of a limited company. In *Re Harari's Settlement Trusts*,[81] and in *Re Boys' Will Trusts*[82] the court thought that such a clause justified investments in all income-bearing property which the trustees honestly thought desirable. In *Re Power*,[83] the investment clause provided that " All moneys requiring to be invested under this my will may be invested by the trustee in any manner in which he may in his absolute

---

[71] *Re Massingberd's Settlement* (1890), 63 L.T. 296.
[72] *Harris* v. *Harris (No. 1)* (1861), 29 Beav. 107.
[73] *Re Sharp* (1890), 45 Ch.D. 286.
[74] *Re Castlehow*, [1903] 1 Ch. 352.
[75] *Re Hilton*, [1909] 2 Ch. 548.
[76] *New London and Brazilian Bank* v. *Brocklebank* (1882), 21 Ch.D. 302.
[77] *Re Johnson*, [1886] W.N. 72.
[78] *Re McEacharn's Settlement Trusts*, [1939] Ch. 858. See also *Re Boys' Will Trusts*, [1950] 1 All E.R. 624.
[79] [1919] 2 Ch. 58.
[80] [1939] Ch. 858.
[81] [1949] 1 All E.R. 430.
[82] [1950] 1 All E.R. 624.
[83] [1947] Ch. 572. *Cf. Re Harari's Settlement Trusts*, [1949] 1 All E.R. 430.

discretion think fit in all respects as if he were the sole beneficial owner of such moneys including the purchase of freehold property in England or Wales." The court held that the final words were inserted to enable the trustee to purchase land as an income-bearing investment, not for the purposes of occupation.

The more liberal construction now placed upon clauses of this kind is illustrated by Buckley, J.'s decision in *Re Peczenik's Settlement Trusts.*[84] The investment clause in the settlement provided that " the trustees shall stand possessed of the funds for the purpose of investing such funds in any shares stocks property or property holding company as the trustees in their discretion shall consider to be in the best interest " of the beneficiary. Buckley, J., decided that the clause authorised the trustees to invest in any shares, stock or property, adding [85]—

> It must, of course, be property of a kind capable of being treated as an investment, not property which is acquired merely for use and enjoyment. But, apart from that, it seems to me that clause (1) places no restriction upon the discretion of the trustees beyond saying that the investments must be investments in stocks or shares or something which can properly be described as property. The clause would not, I think, authorise investments upon personal security.

If the trustees are directly authorised to invest in, or to retain, certain specific types of security, the trustees are not liable if they do so,[86] and the same rule applies where they are directed to allow purchase-money to remain outstanding on an unsatisfactory security for the purpose of accommodating a purchaser.[87] Statute usually gives such authorisation in respect of replacement stock arising as a result of nationalisation of the enterprise in which the authorised stock was issued.[88] If a testator leaves unauthorised and wasting securities with an express trust for conversion, and confers a power on the trustees to retain them, then until conversion the tenant for life only receives 4 per cent. on the value of the securities at the death of the testator, whether the securities are of a wasting nature or not. Any surplus is treated as capital.[89] This rule, which applies only where there is an *express* trust for conversion and a power to retain, must be distinguished from the rule in *Howe* v. *Lord Dartmouth*,[90] which will be considered later, and which has similar consequences.

Finally, it should be noticed that under the Variation of Trusts Act 1958, trustees may apply to the court for a wider investment clause. This Act will be discussed later.

3. Custody of the Trust Property

There remains now for consideration the custody of the trust property by the trustee. In his care of the trust property, the trustee must exercise the

---

[84] [1964] 1 W.L.R. 720.
[85] [1964] 1 W.L.R. 723.
[86] *Cadogan* v. *Earl of Essex* (1854), 2 Drew. 277. But see *Re Rooke*, [1953] Ch. 716.
[87] *Re Hurst* (1890), 63 L.T. 665.
[88] *Municipal and General Securities Co. Ltd.* v. *Lloyds Bank Ltd.*, [1950] Ch. 212.
[89] *Re Chaytor*, [1905] 1 Ch. 233.
[90] (1802), 7 Ves 137 (Cases, p. 319).

same care and control as he would do if the property were his own.[91] Thus, a trustee is not liable if trust property is stolen, either from himself or his solicitor, always providing that his own conduct has not been negligent.[92] Again, although trustees are allowed to deposit money with a bank,[93] and they are not prima facie liable for the defaults of the bank, nevertheless, a trustee may be liable to a beneficiary for any loss, if he allows the money to remain in the private account of a co-trustee, or if the trustee placed the money in the bank when it was his plain duty to do something else with it, *e.g.* to invest it, or pay it into court.[94]

In one case,[95] a clause in a will, after appointing a bank as sole executor and trustee, authorised the trustee to be paid for its services, and then permitted it, " without accounting for any resultant profit," to " perform any service on behalf of my estate on the same terms as would be made with a customer." The bank left substantial trust funds with itself for a period on deposit, with interest at one-half per cent. This was held to be within the terms of the clause.

Title-deeds of trust property of all kinds should be retained by trustees under their joint control, and if they are not frequently in use, the best place for their custody is a bank or safe deposit. In the ordinary course of trust administration, however, it is sometimes necessary for the trustees to leave the title-deeds of real property with their solicitor, and if the occasion is a proper one, the trustees will not be liable for their loss whilst in the solicitor's possession. The Trustee Act 1925, s. 21, therefore gives the trustees power to deposit documents relating to the trust with a banker or other company whose business includes the safe custody of documents.

Section 30 provides that a trustee is not liable for the defaults of a person with whom documents are deposited under section 21, unless the loss was occasioned by the trustee's own wilful default.

The Trustee Act 1925, s. 19, gives the trustees power to insure against fire any building which forms part of the trust property, and to pay the premiums out of the trust income. The effect of this section is not to impose upon the trustees a duty to insure. It enables the trustees to insure if they think fit. If, after deliberation, they reach the conclusion that they should not insure, they are not liable if the property is destroyed by fire.[96] Section 20 of the Trustee Act 1925 governs the application of insurance moneys received in respect of trust property. Such moneys are to be treated as capital money, and are to be held upon trust corresponding as nearly as may be with the trust affecting the property in respect of which they were payable.

Subs. (4) of section 20 provides also that the money so received may be applied by the trustees in rebuilding, reinstating, replacing, or repairing the

---

[91] *Learoyd* v. *Whiteley* (1887), 12 App.Cas. 727. See also Paling, " The Trustee's Duty of Skill and Care " (1973) 37 *Conveyancer* 48. On the question of the trustee's duty of care where the property is in the hands of an agent, see pp. 238–241, *ante*. In *T. M. Fairclough & Sons Ltd.* v. *Berliner*, [1931] 1 Ch. 60, the fact that joint lessees were trustees holding under a statutory trust for the benefit of themselves as joint tenants in equity does not seem to have been regarded as possibly affecting their duties under a covenant to repair.

[92] *Morley* v. *Morley* (1678), 2 Ch.Cas. 2; *Jones* v. *Lewis* (1750), 2 Ves.Sen. 240.

[93] Trustee Act 1925, s. 11 (1).

[94] *Moyle* v. *Moyle* (1831), 2 Russ. & M. 710; *Wilkinson* v. *Bewick* (1858), 4 Jur.(N.S.) 1010.

[95] *Re Waterman's Will Trusts*, [1952] 2 All E.R. 1054.

[96] *Re McEacharn* (1911), 103 L.T. 900.

lost or damaged property, subject to any consents which may be required by the instrument, and in the case of capital money arising under the Settled Land Act, subject to the provisions of that Act in respect of the application of capital money.

C. THE POWER OF TRUSTEES TO SELL

Where there is a trust for sale, or the trustees have a power to sell trust property, they may sell either by private contract or by public auction, either the whole or any part of the trust property, under conditions which they consider appropriate [97] and a beneficiary may not impeach such a sale, unless the consideration was inadequate, and after the execution of the conveyance, the sale may not be impeached as against the purchaser, unless it appears that the purchaser was acting in collusion with the trustees at the time when the contract of sale was made.[98]

---

[97] Trustee Act 1925, s. 12.
[98] *Ibid.*, s. 13.

Chapter XVIII

THE TRUSTEE'S POWERS AND DUTIES IN THE ADMINISTRATION OF A TRUST—(continued)

A. THE RULE IN HOWE v. LORD DARTMOUTH

A TRUSTEE must never favour one beneficiary at the expense of another. It is his duty to act impartially and to hold the scales evenly between all beneficiaries. This has led to the elaboration of the principle which is generally known as the rule in *Howe* v. *Lord Dartmouth*,[1] and which may also be regarded as an illustration of the principle that it is the trustee's duty, unless otherwise directed, to convert all hazardous property into property of a secure and non-wasting character. This rule may be expressed as follows—

> Where residuary personalty is settled *by will* for the benefit of persons in succession, then it is the duty of the trustees to convert all property of a wasting, hazardous or reversionary character, into authorised securities which will produce income immediately, unless the will expressly or by necessary implication directs otherwise, or unless the will confers on the trustee a power to postpone the conversion for a definite period, and the trustee, after due deliberation, exercises it.[2]

The rule has no application to cases of intestacy, since section 33 (1) of the Administration of Estates Act imposes a statutory trust for sale.

Wasting securities, such as terminable annuities,[3] are converted in the interests of the remainderman; reversionary property is converted in the interests of the tenant for life.

The sale of the property, and the investment of the proceeds, ought to be effected at the earliest moment at which a reasonable price may be obtained. In the normal case, this means within a year of the testator's death and it is at this date that the estate is valued, in order that the tenant for life may receive a fair and (as far as possible) constant income from it. Thus, where a copyright is subject to the rule, it is valued at this date, and the tenant for life receives 4 per cent. of its value, any surplus being invested.[4] Thereafter, the burden of showing that the retention of the unauthorised property was justifiable rests on the executors or trustees, but, of course, a bad market or other such circumstance may be a sufficient justification. It may be, however, that the will or other instrument gives the trustees a power to postpone the sale for an *indefinite* period. Where this is so, the duty to deal equally between tenant for life and remainderman still exists, although it has been doubted whether there is conversion in such a case. " If there is no duty upon the executor to sell at once, or within a year, or at any

---

[1] (1802), 7 Ves. 137 (Cases, p. 319).
[2] *Cf. Macdonald* v. *Irvine* (1878), 8 Ch.D. 101, 112.
[3] *i.e.* annuities which come to an end after a specified period. See National Debt and Local Loans Act 1887, Sched. 1.
[4] *Re Evans' Will Trusts*, [1921] 2 Ch. 309. The same rule applies to terminable annuities: *Re Payne*, [1943] 2 All E.R. 675 ; *Re Hey's Settlement Trusts*, [1945] Ch. 294.

other time, I can see no reason for assuming a notional conversion at once, or within a year, or at any other time. The essential equity, however—the balance between the successive interests—remains equally compelling even where there is no immediate obligation to convert and property is retained for the benefit of the estate as a whole." In such a case, however, the estate is valued for the purpose of establishing the amount attributable to capital and income, not a year after the testator's death, but on the day of the testator's death.[5]

This rule, which incorporates the principle of equity that " Equality is Equity " as between beneficiaries, was explained by Lord Eldon in *Howe* v. *Lord Dartmouth* [6] as follows—

Where residuary personalty is left by will—

> . . . it is to be construed as to the perishable part, so that one shall take for life, and the others afterwards; and unless the testator directs the mode so that it is to continue, as it was, the Court understands, that it shall be put in such a state, that the others may enjoy it after the decease of the first; and the thing is quite equal; for it might consist of a vast number of particulars: for instance, a personal annuity, not to commence in enjoyment till the expiration of twenty years from the death of the testator, payable upon a contingency perhaps. If in this case it is equitable, that Long or Short Annuities should be sold, to give every one an equal chance, the Court acts equally in the other case; for those future interests are for the sake of the tenant for life to be converted into a present interest; being sold immediately, in order to yield an immediate interest to the tenant for life. As in the one case that, in which the tenant for life has too great an interest, is melted for the benefit of the rest, in the other that, of which, if it remained in specie, he might never receive any thing, is brought in; and he has immediately the interest of its present worth.

Before discussing the scope of the rule, however, it is necessary to observe that the cases have gradually established two rules which are logical corollaries of the one first stated, and which apply to the position pending conversion by the trustees. In some instances, a considerable interval will elapse between the date when the trust comes into operation and the time when conversion actually happens. These rules are—

(A) Where property ought to be converted by the trustees, then unless the testator has expressly or impliedly given the whole of the income to the tenant for life until conversion, the tenant for life is entitled: (1) to the whole of the income of the real property, including leaseholds,[7] and upon all authorised investments [8]; (2) if there is an express trust for conversion in the will, or the property ought to be converted under the rule in *Howe* v. *Lord Dartmouth*, the tenant for life is entitled from the date of the testator's

---

[5] *Per* Romer, J., *Re Parry*, [1947] Ch. 23, 45 (Cases, p. 321).

[6] (1802), 7 Ves. 137, 148 (Cases, p. 319). See also Sheridan, " *Howe* v. *Lord Dartmouth* Re-examined " (1952) 16 *Conveyancer* 349; Keeton, *Modern Developments in the Law of Trusts*, pp. 100–104.

[7] *Re Brooker*, [1926] W.N. 93, but see *post*, p. 264.

[8] Since the Trustee Investments Act 1961 these may now include stocks and shares.

death to 4 per cent.[9] interest on the value of unauthorised, wasting and reversionary property.

(B) As regards unauthorised securities and wasting property, which will generally yield more, the balance of income accrues to the capital. As regards reversionary and non-income-producing interests of all kinds, the amount which the property realises when it falls into possession must be apportioned between capital and income, and the income belongs to the tenant for life. The apportionment is made by determining what sum, at 4 per cent. interest, accumulating at compound interest with yearly rests, and put out on the day of the testator's death would, after deduction of income-tax, have amounted to the sum so received. The amount so ascertained is treated as capital, and the rest as income.[10]

As an illustration of this last rule, in *Re Hollebone*,[11] A sold his business for a price which was to be paid by ten half-yearly instalments. By his will A bequeathed his residuary estate upon trust for conversion with power to postpone. A's widow was tenant for life of the residue, and the court held that each instalment ought as from the testator's death to be apportioned between capital and income by ascertaining what sums, laid out at 4 per cent. interest at the day of the testator's death, and accumulating at compound interest with yearly rests and deducting income tax would, with the accumu-lated interest, amount, on the day when the instalment should be paid or be due, to the instalment. The sum so ascertained was to be treated as capital, the rest as income.[12] Exactly the same principle would have applied had there been no trust for sale, and no other direction relating to the instalments had appeared in the will.

In *Re Chance's Will Trusts*,[13] the rule in *Re Earl of Chesterfield's Trusts*[10] was applied to the payments of compensation made by the Central Land Board under Part I of the Town and Country Planning Act 1954 which were included in a residuary bequest for persons in succession.

In *Re Fawcett*,[14] Farwell, J., said—

> The rule in *Howe* v. *Lord Dartmouth*, in my judgment, was based upon the equitable idea of treating that which ought to be done as having been done, and accordingly in the early cases the general rule was that the tenant for life was entitled to whatever the investments, if they were sold and re-invested in Consols, would produce. To that extent, and to that extent only, he was entitled to payment on account of income. In more recent years the practice has generally been to give to the tenant for life interest at 4 per cent. upon the capital value of the unauthorized investments. The reason for the alteration in the rule was, I think, due to the fact that the range of authorized investments has been very greatly extended in comparatively recent years, and accordingly the Court took the view that a rate of interest which might be higher than

---

[9] *Re Baker*, [1924] 2 Ch. 271. Notwithstanding the present yields of trustee securities, the rate is still 4 per cent. to which it was raised from 3 per cent. in 1920: *Re Lucas*, [1947] Ch. 558, 563–564; *Re Parry*, [1947] Ch. 23 (Cases, p. 321).
[10] *Re Earl of Chesterfield's Trusts* (1883), 24 Ch.D. 643 (Cases, p. 320).
[11] [1919] 2 Ch. 93.
[12] Applying *Beavan* v. *Beavan* (1869), 24 Ch.D. 649n.
[13] [1962] Ch. 593.
[14] [1940] Ch. 402, 407–408.

that which was produced by Consols would be a reasonable rate to allow to tenants for life, since there was, at any rate, some possibility that trust funds could be invested in securities returning such income. The general, although not the universal, rule is now to allow 4 per cent. . . . In order to give effect to the rule it appears to me that in a case of this kind it is the duty of the trustees to have the unauthorized investments valued as at the end of the first year after the testatrix's death. During that year the executors are given time to deal with the estate as a whole. At the end of it comes the time when, in my judgment, any unauthorized investments which they still retain should be valued and the tenant for life becomes entitled to be paid 4 per cent. on the valuation of the whole of the unauthorized investments . . . the trustees will receive the whole of the dividends which the unauthorized investments pay and there will be no apportionment. Those dividends will be applied in the first instance in paying, so far as they go, 4 per cent. on the capital value of the unauthorized investments. If the income received on the unauthorized investments is more than sufficient to pay the 4 per cent., then the balance will be added to the capital and it will form part of the whole fund in the hands of the trustees. If, on the other hand, the income actually received from the unauthorized investments is not sufficient to pay 4 per cent. in each year to the tenants for life, they will not be entitled to immediate recoupment out of the capital, but when the unauthorized investments are sold the trustees will then have in their hands a fund representing the proceeds of sale of the unauthorized investments, together with any surplus income which may have accrued in the earlier years; out of those proceeds of sale the tenants for life will be entitled to be recouped so as to provide them with the full 4 per cent. during the whole period and they will be entitled to be refunded the deficit calculated at 4 per cent. simple interest but less tax. In that way . . . the rule can be worked out satisfactorily as between capital and income and the balance will be held as evenly as possible between those two opposing interests. No doubt the duty of the trustees is to realize the unauthorised securities as soon as conveniently may be, but until that has been done that, in my view, is the right way of dealing with the matter. The fact that there may be some investments which are of little or no value and which produce no income does not affect the position if the whole of the unauthorized investments are treated as one whole, and the value of the whole of those investments is ascertained and the income received from the whole of those investments is received by the trustees and applied in the way which I have stated.

The rule, it has been observed, applies only to residuary personalty left by will, where the testator has not otherwise expressly or impliedly directed.[15]

Where the reversionary estate comprises a share of a partnership business, it is not necessary that there should be an express direction to carry on the business, in order that the rule in *Howe* v. *Lord Dartmouth* should be

---

[15] *Re Van Straubenzee*, [1901] 2 Ch. 779. Thus, the tenant for life can claim no benefit for reversionary realty under the rule in *Re Earl of Chesterfield's Trusts: Re Woodhouse*, [1941] Ch. 332.

excluded.[16] The court discovers the testator's intention from construing the will.

Before 1926, it was settled that the rule in *Howe* v. *Lord Dartmouth* was applicable to leaseholds. These, therefore, should be sold, and until sale, the tenant for life should receive 4 per cent. of their capital value. Since 1925, the position has changed. If they are subject to an express trust for sale, whether by the will[17] or by statute,[18] they must be sold. Where leaseholds are held for persons by way of succession, not on an express trust for sale, they are settled land, subject to the provisions of the Settled Land Act 1925,[19] and accordingly, they need not be sold. If they are, then the proceeds are capital. In any event, long leaseholds are now authorised investments under section 73 (1) (xi) of the Settled Land Act[20] (and are not regarded as wasting or hazardous under the Trustee Investments Act 1961). Today, therefore, only short leaseholds, *i.e.* with less than sixty years to run, which are not settled land, need to be sold, where the rule in *Howe* v. *Lord Dartmouth* is applicable (*i.e.* where they are comprised in a residuary gift left for persons in succession). Even where they are to be sold under this rule, since 1925, the tenant for life is entitled to the whole of the income until sale under section 28 (2) of the Law of Property Act 1925, since, by virtue of section 205 (1) (ix), the term " land " includes leaseholds.[21]

The rule only applies to residuary bequests. If property is specifically given, the court understands that the intention of the testator was that the successive beneficiaries should enjoy the actual income of the property and will not direct a conversion, or an apportionment, even though, in consequence, an ultimate remainderman may receive nothing at all by reason of the wasting security having terminated.[22] Even if, in such a case, the trustee is given power to vary the securities, this is not held to give him power to invest in authorised securities, so reducing the income, for the power (in the absence of intention) was not given by the intention of varying the rights of the legatees.[23] So carefully does the court construe this rule, that in *Askew* v. *Woodhead*,[24] where there were leaseholds in respect of which the tenant for life was entitled to the whole of the income, and the leaseholds were compulsorily acquired under the Public Health Act 1875, in exercising their discretion under section 74 of the Lands Clauses Consolidation Act 1845 the Court of Appeal directed that the purchase money should be invested in an annuity to last as long as the lease would have done, to be paid to the person who would have received the rents and profits of the leaseholds.[25]

Furthermore, if an intention can be gathered from the will that the property shall be enjoyed *in specie*, even though it is not in strictness given

---

[16] *Stanier* v. *Hodgkinson* (1903), 73 L.J.Ch. 179.
[17] *Re Brooker*, [1926] W.N. 93 ; *Re Trollope's Will Trusts*, [1927] 1 Ch. 596.
[18] *Re Berton*, [1939] Ch. 200.
[19] Settled Land Act 1925, s. 1.
[20] *Re Gough*, [1957] Ch. 323.
[21] *Re Brooker, supra.* See further, Bailey, " Leaseholds and the Rule in *Howe* v. *The Earl of Dartmouth* " (1932) 4 *Cambridge Law Journal* 357.
[22] *Re Beaufoy's Estate* (1852), 1 Sm. & Giff. 20.
[23] *Lord* v. *Godfrey* (1819), 4 Madd. 455.
[24] (1880), 14 Ch.D. 27.
[25] See also *Re Lingard*, [1908] W.N. 107.

specifically, then it should not be converted[26]; and if various kinds of property are given, including some being given specifically, this raises the implication that the other property given was also intended to be enjoyed *in specie*.[27] The terms of each will must be considered carefully to discover what the true intention was.[28] Thus, in *Re Game*,[29] the residuary estate included freeholds and leaseholds, and the testator directed his trustees to pay the rents and profits to his wife for life. It was argued that this direction implied that the wife was entitled to the whole of the rents of the leaseholds, but Stirling, J., held that the word " rents " might be satisfied if applied to the freeholds only, and conversion was therefore directed. The position is, of course, different where the term " rents " is used, and there are leaseholds only. If trustees are directed to retain or sell part of the trust estate, this is construed as an expression of intention that in the meantime the tenant for life shall enjoy the whole of the income of that part,[30] and this rule extends to the postponement of the sale of the testator's business.[31] In *Macdonald* v. *Irvine*,[32] the testator bequeathed the income of his " entire estate " to the tenant for life. The court was of the opinion that if this meant " the whole estate " this was not a direction that the tenant for life should enjoy the whole of the income.

This rule has no application to settlements *inter vivos*, for, as Cozens-Hardy, J., pointed out in *Re Van Straubenzee*,[33] such instruments must be observed strictly in accordance with their terms. Hence, the inference is that the property must be enjoyed as settled. Furthermore, even in settlements by will, the rule directing conversion does not apply where the testator indicates that conversion should occur at some later date.[34] Moreover, comparatively slight indications of a contrary intention have been held sufficient to take the case out of the general rule, as where the will gave the trustees a direction that they should give the tenant for life a power of attorney to receive the income,[35] or where the testator directed his estate to be divided into certain portions on the death of the tenant for life.[36] The rule, however, must be applied unless there is a sufficiently clear intention to exclude it, and the burden of proof is upon that person who seeks to exclude it.[37]

The question of excluding the rule in *Howe* v. *Lord Dartmouth*[38] is one of considerable importance, since the effect of failing to exclude the rule is that all unauthorised securities, whether wasting or hazardous, must be sold, and the proceeds reinvested in authorised securities. This may affect the income of the tenant for life substantially and, in view of the fall in value

---

[26] *Bothamley* v. *Sherson* (1875), L.R. 20 Eq. 304; *Re Ovey* (1882), 20 Ch.D. 676, affirmed *sub nom. Robertson* v. *Broadbent* (1883), 8 App.Cas. 812; *Re Gough*, [1957] Ch. 323.
[27] *Bethune* v. *Kennedy* (1835), 1 My. & Cr. 114.
[28] *Re Gough*, [1957] Ch. 323.
[29] [1897] 1 Ch. 881.
[30] *Re Bates*, [1907] 1 Ch. 22; *Re Wilson*, [1907] 1 Ch. 394.
[31] *Re Crowther*, [1895] 2 Ch. 56; *Re Elford*, [1910] 1 Ch. 814.
[32] (1878), 8 Ch.D. 101.
[33] [1901] 2 Ch. 779.
[34] *Re Pitcairn*, [1896] 2 Ch. 199. As to the position where there is a statutory trust for sale on intestacy under s. 33 of the Administration of Estates Act 1925, see *Re Fisher*, [1943] Ch. 377.
[35] *Nevill* v. *Fortescue* (1848), 16 Sim. 333.
[36] *Re Barratt*, [1925] Ch. 550.
[37] *Macdonald* v. *Irvine* (1878), 8 Ch.D. 101.
[38] (1802), 7 Ves. 137 (Cases, p. 319).

of trustee stocks, it may also adversely affect the remainderman. Accordingly, the draftsman of a will should secure specific instructions on this point; and it may be added that the common form of bequest of residue excludes the rule.

There remains the further question of the application of the rule in *Howe* v. *Lord Dartmouth* [39] to wills in which there is an express trust for conversion. In *Re Berry* [40] Pennycuick, J., said—

> Broadly, the rule commonly known as the rule in *Howe* v. *Lord Dartmouth* [39] is applied not only to cases where there is no trust for conversion but to cases where there is a trust for conversion, so that if the residuary estate includes any item of property which is not an authorised investment, then, unless the will manifests a contrary intention, the life-tenant is only entitled to an income of some notional fund and not to the actual income arising from that item of property.

A mere power to postpone sale, which is now an incident of all trusts for sale, does not entitle the life tenant to the whole of the income from unsold unauthorised investments. In *Re Berry*,[41] where a trust for sale had been inserted into the will, it was held that, in spite of the language of two clauses relating to the enjoyment of income under the trust, the rule in *Howe* v. *Lord Dartmouth* [39] was not excluded, and therefore the tenant for life, the testator's widow, was only entitled to 4 per cent. upon the proceeds of the sale of the testator's business from the date of his death, to the date of the sale of the business (when the proceeds were invested in authorised investments), irrespective of the actual income earned.

That aspect of the rule which restricts the right of the tenant for life to the receipt of 4 per cent. on the present value of the property is based upon the maxim that equity regards as done that which ought to be done. In other words, from the standpoint of equity, conversion has already occurred. From this it follows that if the trustees have a discretion to postpone for a definite period, *e.g.* until the death of the tenant for life, there is no conversion in equity, and, therefore, in such a case the tenant for life is entitled to the whole of the income. Where, however, the power to postpone is inserted simply with the object of permitting the trustees to sell to the best advantage, as where no power to postpone sale for an indefinite period is given, then, as Romer, J., pointed out in *Re Parry*,[42] the trustees must still deal fairly as between tenant for life and remainderman, and the property must be valued, and capital and income at 4 per cent. apportioned, at the date of the testator's death.

Romer, J., in his lucid review of the authorities in *Re Parry*,[42] points out that for a number of years after the decision in *Howe* v. *Lord Dartmouth* [39] the courts were still troubled by the problem of the mode in which justice should be done between tenant for life and remainderman. No difficulty arose where the testator intended the beneficiaries to enjoy the property *in specie*. In other cases, however, the problem was what should be given to the tenant for life in the first year after the testator's death—

---

[39] (1802), 7 Ves. 137 (Cases, p. 319).   [40] [1962] Ch. 97, 106.
[41] [1962] Ch. 97, following *Re Chaytor*, [1905] 1 Ch. 233.
[42] [1947] Ch. 23 (Cases, p. 321).

In 1841 (as appears from *Taylor* v. *Clark*) [43] it was still possible for a tenant for life in cases where there was a trust for conversion of residue, followed by a settlement of the proceeds, to present a threefold argument and to cite high authority in support of each contention. One was that he was entitled to the income of the residue during the first year after the testator's death, without reference to the investment in which he found it. An alternative argument was that he was entitled to the income accruing during the first year after the testator's death on such parts of the testator's estate as were invested at his death upon authorized investments and on such parts as were afterwards so invested during the same year, but not to the income of property not so invested. A third alternative was that he was entitled during that year to a notional income consisting of the dividends on so much 3 per cent. stock as would have been produced during the year by the conversion of the property at the end of the year. [44]

This third possibility had already been chosen by Lord Lyndhurst in *Dimes* v. *Scott*, [45] and Wigram, V.-C., applied the same rule in *Taylor* v. *Clark*. [46] The same course was followed in *Morgan* v. *Morgan* [47] ten years later, a case in which there was no express trust for sale.

However, in *Brown* v. *Gellatly* [48] Lord Cairns pointed out that there was an important qualification to this rule. In that case the testator settled the residue of his estate, and part of it comprised ships, in respect of which he provided that, until sale, the executors should have power to operate them for profit. This, said Lord Cairns, showed that the testator contemplated that sale of them would be postponed for an indefinite period. In such a case, therefore, valuation would be from the date of the testator's death. This was not a new principle, for it had been applied by Lord Eldon to leaseholds in *Gibson* v. *Bott*, [49] although there were some intervening decisions inconsistent with it. *Brown* v. *Gellatly*, [48] however, has been followed in a succession of later cases, the last being *Re Parry* [50] itself, and must now be regarded as firmly established.

The apportionment does not apply to the income of freehold land, for here the tenant for life is entitled to the whole of the income irrespective of any *implied* intention on the part of the testator, [51] although it is always open to the testator expressly to direct otherwise.

The mode in which the apportionment operates may be considered from *Re Godden*. [52] There the residuary estate included a mortgage of a colliery, of which the testator was in possession. His trustees foreclosed, and the court decided that the profits from death to foreclosure must be regarded as

43 (1841), 1 Hare 161.
44 [1947] Ch. 33.
45 (1828), 4 Russ. 195.
46 (1841), 1 Hare 161.
47 (1851), 14 Beav. 72.
48 (1867), L.R. 2 Ch.App. 751.
49 (1802), 7 Ves. 89.
50 [1947] Ch. 23 (Cases, p. 321). See also *Re Woods*, [1904] 2 Ch. 4; *Re Chaytor*, [1905] 1 Ch. 233; *Re Owen*, [1912] 1 Ch. 519; *Re Beech*, [1920] 1 Ch. 40; *Re Baker*, [1924] 2 Ch. 271.
51 *Hope* v. *d'Hédouville*, [1893] 2 Ch. 361; *Re Searle*, [1900] 2 Ch. 829; *Re Oliver*, [1908] 2 Ch. 74.
52 [1893] 1 Ch. 292. See also *Brown* v. *Gellatly* (1867), L.R. 2 Ch.App. 751.

capital and income, which had arisen from a sum which, if put out at 4 per cent. at the testator's death, would have amounted to the sum then in the hands of the trustees. On that sum so ascertained, the tenant for life received 4 per cent. The balance of annual revenue from the colliery must be regarded as capital, on which again the tenant was entitled to 4 per cent. An illustration of the rule operating on reversionary interests or other property which produced no immediate interest is furnished by *Re Duke of Cleveland's Estate*,[53] where a debt which bore no interest was recovered by the trustees and was directed to be apportioned between capital and income.[54]

The rule of apportionment between tenant for life and remainderman has also a limited application where the trustees invest in unauthorised securities. Here, if the capital has not been diminished in consequence of the investment, the tenant for life is entitled to retain the whole of the income, for the capital value of the investment has already been determined, and since it has not been prejudicially affected by the unauthorised investment, the remainderman is not then entitled to have it increased,[55] although this was doubted in *Re Hill*.[56] On the other hand, if the capital has been diminished by the unauthorised investment, the position is that although the tenant for life cannot be compelled to refund any income which he has actually received, nevertheless he will not obtain any arrears which may be due to him, unless he brings into account all income he has received from the unauthorised investment.[57]

B. EXPRESS TRUSTS FOR SALE AND THE POWER TO POSTPONE

It has already been mentioned that the testator may exclude the rule in *Howe* v. *Lord Dartmouth*,[58] if he wishes, thereby providing that property shall be enjoyed in the form in which it is found at his death. The effect of such exclusion will be to give the tenant for life the whole of the income arising from the residuary estate, as it exists at the time of the testator's death. A distinct problem arises, however, where the testator imposes a trust for sale and conversion upon his residuary estate, but gives the trustees a discretion to postpone, and then excludes the rule in *Howe* v. *Lord Dartmouth* [58] thereby giving to the tenant for life the whole income of the residuary estate. In such a case, the rule in *Re Earl of Chesterfield's Trusts* [59] is also excluded. Nevertheless, it was held in *Rowlls* v. *Bebb* [60] that, notwithstanding such a clause, the equitable rule of apportionment will apply if the trustees have not exercised their discretion to postpone, until the discretion is exercised. This is of particular importance when the residuary estate includes income received from some other fund. If the executors of the will decide to postpone the sale of the right to receive the income then, until its sale, the income must

---

[53] [1895] 2 Ch. 542.
[54] See also *Re Earl of Chesterfield's Trusts* (1883), 24 Ch.D. 643 (Cases, p. 320); *Re Morley*, [1895] 2 Ch. 738.
[55] *Stroud* v. *Gwyer* (1860), 28 Beav. 130; *Re Appleby*, [1903] 1 Ch. 565.
[56] (1881), 50 L.J.Ch. 551.
[57] *Re Bird*, [1901] 1 Ch. 916.
[58] (1802), 7 Ves. 137 (Cases, p. 319).
[59] (1883), 24 Ch.D. 643 (Cases, p. 320).
[60] [1900] 2 Ch. 107.

be apportioned between capital and income; but on sale, the sum received is capital.[61] In *Re Guinness's Settlement* [62] there was a resulting trust of income from a settlement to a testator, passing into his residuary estate, which included a trust for sale and conversion, with a power to postpone. Goff, J., decided that until the executors decided to convert, all income received under the resulting trust was capital which must be apportioned under the rule in *Re Earl of Chesterfield's Trusts.*[59]

C. THE RULE IN *HOWE* v. *LORD DARTMOUTH* AND THE TRUSTEE INVESTMENTS ACT 1961

The Trustee Investments Act 1961 has brought about an important modification of that part of the rule in *Howe* v. *Lord Dartmouth* which applied to shares and debentures. Under the Act of 1961, shares and debentures, provided these fulfil certain conditions, may become wider range investments, where the trustees, after taking advice, decide to divide the trust fund into wider and narrower range investments. Where the fund is divided, it may therefore be the case that part of the residuary personalty qualifies as wider range investments. If this is so, then these investments, when appropriated to the wider range investments, are outside the rule in *Howe* v. *Lord Dartmouth*, and the tenant for life is entitled to the whole of the income.

D. THE APPORTIONMENT OF COMPANY PROFITS AND LIABILITIES

Section 5 of the Apportionment Act 1870 provides that " The word ' dividends ' includes (besides dividends strictly so called) all payments made by the name of dividend, bonus, or otherwise out of the revenue of trading or other public companies, divisible between all or any of the members of such respective companies, whether such payments shall be usually made or declared at any fixed times or otherwise; and all such divisible revenue shall, for the purposes of this Act, be deemed to have accrued by equal daily increment during and within the period for or in respect of which the payment of the same revenue shall be declared or expressed to be made, but the said word ' dividend ' does not include payments in the nature of a return or reimbursement of capital."

This definition may serve as a clue in the determination of what is income and what is capital where there is a settlement with successive interests. Such problems are frequently by no means easy to solve, since the company in which the shares are held will not itself take notice of any trust, and its distribution of profits may be prompted by quite different considerations, for example, the financial position of the company, the outlook for future years and the liability of distributions to income tax.

1. PAYMENT OF ARREARS OF DIVIDENDS

Where trustees hold ordinary shares, they will pay to the tenant for life all dividends declared in the years in which the life tenant's interest exists.

---

[61] *Re Hey's Settlement Trusts,* [1945] Ch. 294.
[62] [1966] 1 W.L.R. 1355.

A different kind of situation arises, however, in respect of fixed interest cumulative preference shares. Is the tenant for life for the time being, or his predecessor, entitled where arrears are paid after an interval in which there has been a change of tenant for life? This problem was considered by the Court of Appeal in *Re Wakley*,[63] in the light of the earlier decisions, and it was decided that all the dividends, when declared, belonged to the tenant for life at the time of declaration. In that case, the cumulative dividends were payable in respect of preferred and deferred ordinary shares, but the principle has been extended to cumulative preference shares. It was very clearly expressed in Warrington, L.J.'s judgment, as follows [64]—

> The first question to be considered is what is the nature of a shareholder's right to a cumulative dividend. It is, in my opinion, nothing more than a right to participate in profits available for dividend which in accordance with its regulations the company has from time to time determined to distribute. In fact the shareholder has no right to a dividend, whether cumulative or otherwise, until there are profits available, and the company by the proper authority has determined to distribute them. It follows that when profits are available and the company determines to distribute them it is the shareholder who is then entitled to the shares who takes the dividend, and not the person entitled to them in past years, though the dividend may in the case of cumulative dividend be large enough to cover the amount which would have been paid in past years if there had been profits available, but which was not paid because there were no such profits.

This decision confirmed the view of the problem which had been taken by Buckley, J., in *Re Taylor's Trusts*,[65] and which had already been followed by Astbury, J., in *Re Sale*,[66] and by Eve, J., in *Re Grundy*.[67] It has been consistently applied subsequently, and in *Re MacIver's Settlement*,[68] Farwell, J., applied it in a case where trustees were holders of cumulative preference shares, and by a scheme of arrangement sanctioned by the court the arrears of interest on these shares were cancelled in exchange for a surrender, by the ordinary shareholders, of part of their holdings to the preference shareholders. The ordinary shares so surrendered, said Farwell, J., must be treated as income, and must be paid over to the tenant for life.

2. DISTRIBUTION OF A RESERVE FUND

The situation which arises when the company distributes as dividend a reserve fund was considered by the Court of Appeal in *Re Thomas*.[69] Here again trustees held shares on behalf of a tenant for life and remainderman. So long as the reserve fund remained undistributed, the market value of the shares was a high one. It would necessarily be lower after distribution. Nevertheless, the Court of Appeal decided that the whole of the distribution

---

[63] [1920] 2 Ch. 205. See also Keeton, *Modern Developments in the Law of Trusts*, p. 105.
[64] [1920] 2 Ch. 221–222.
[65] [1905] 1 Ch. 734.
[66] [1913] 2 Ch. 697.
[67] (1917) 117 L.T. 470.
[68] [1936] Ch. 198. See also Keeton, *Modern Developments in the Law of Trusts*, p. 105.
[69] [1916] 2 Ch. 331.

belonged to the tenant for life. Lord Cozens-Hardy, M.R., pointed out that the company would have been completely within its rights in declaring a dividend and had applied the reserve fund in payment of that dividend. He said [70]—

> . . . in other words, they might have put into the pockets of the tenant for life under the present marriage settlement the whole or such part as they thought fit of this accumulated reserve fund, invested as it was. It was an inherent danger in the investment. The trustees in the present case were perfectly entitled to take the shares and to keep them—the instrument sanctioned it; but in every case of this kind there is a risk between tenant for life and remainderman of their rights being affected by resolutions of the company, so that their rights are not really such as they would be in a settlement where the trust estate is invested in ordinary trustee securities of that nature.

3. BONUSES IN CASH OR SPECIE

Two types of cases, which at first sight appear very similar, have been treated differently by the courts. They are (i) cases where the company distributes accumulated profits as a cash bonus, or as a bonus in some similar valuable form; and (ii) cases where the distribution takes the form of the issue of new shares in the company. Although these cases appear similar, they arise from different circumstances and they contemplate different results. The first case contemplates a special distribution, once and for all, out of profits. In the second case, there is an increase in the issued capital of the company, which will have the effect of increasing the number of shares entitling holders to participate in future dividends. In the first case, the payment is out of profits, and is an income payment, to which the tenant for life is entitled, and which is taxable as income. This is so, even if the company expressly describes the bonus as a capital distribution, as was the case in *Re Doughty*,[71] where the Court of Appeal followed *Re Bates*,[72] and *Hill* v. *Permanent Trustee Co. of New South Wales*.[73] Two years later Roxburgh, J., applied the same rule to money arising from the realisation of the capital assets of a company which had no power to increase its capital,[74] and in *Re Sechiari*,[75] Romer, J., applied the same rule to a " special capital profits dividend " payable out of the profit realised by an omnibus company on the sale of its undertaking to the British Transport Commission. In all these cases, the court acted on the principle expressed by Lord Russell of Killowen in *Hill* v. *Permanent Trustee Co. of New South Wales*[76]—

> A limited company not in liquidation can make no payment by way of return of capital to its shareholders except as a step in an authorized reduction of capital. Any other payment made by it by means of which

---

70 [1916] 2 Ch. 341.
71 [1947] Ch. 263. See also Keeton, *Modern Developments in the Law of Trusts*, pp. 105–108.
72 [1928] Ch. 682.
73 [1930] A.C. 720.
74 *Re Harrison's Will Trusts*, [1949] Ch. 678.
75 [1950] 1 All E.R. 417.
76 [1930] A.C. 720, 731. See also *Re Whitehead's Will Trusts*, [1959] Ch. 579. For the apportionment to be made in respect of repayments under a scheme of arrangement between a company and its debenture holders, see *Re Morris's Will Trusts*, [1960] 1 W.L.R. 1210.

it parts with moneys to its shareholders must and can only be made by
way of dividing profits. Whether the payment is called " dividend " or
" bonus," or any other name, it still must remain a payment on division
of profits.

Moneys so paid to a shareholder will (if he be a trustee) prima facie
belong to the person beneficially entitled to the income of the trust estate.

Four cases in 1951 threw some further light upon the application of this
principle. *Re Winder's Will Trusts*,[77] arose out of the same declaration of a
" special capital profits dividend " as was considered by Romer, J., in *Re
Sechiari*. In this case, the distribution was to be made on April 1, to follow
a meeting of shareholders summoned for March 17. The shareholder
died on February 27, six days after the notice concerning the meeting had
been sent out, and by his will, the stock formed part of a settled fund.
Romer, J. (who had decided *Re Sechiari*), held that in this case, income
accrued before the testator's death, and therefore it accrued to the capital
of the estate, following *Re Muirhead*.[78]

In *Re Duff's Settlements*,[79] the company from time to time allotted shares
at a premium, and where it did so, it transferred the premiums to a share
premium account, in accordance with section 56 of the Companies Act 1948.
The Court of Appeal held that where a trustee received a distribution from
this account, it must be treated as capital, not as income. This represents an
important change as compared with the position before 1948. As Jenkins, L.J.,
put it, in delivering the judgment of the court [80]—

> A fund representing share premiums received by a company, if
> distributed in cash before s. 56 came into operation, would . . . have
> been income in the hands of the recipient shareholders, notwithstanding
> its capital character when considered as a receipt of the company. But
> that was because, as the law then stood, such a fund constituted a profit
> available for distribution as dividend, and, except in liquidation, only
> capable of distribution on the ground that it was a profit so available. The
> rights of tenant for life and remainderman would thus have been deter-
> mined in favour of the former by reference to the character of the
> distribution, the origin of the fund distributed being irrelevant. The effect
> of s. 56, however, is to make such a distribution equivalent in law to an
> actual return of paid up share capital and capable of being validly
> effected only through the medium of precisely similar reduction pro-
> ceedings. It may therefore be said that s. 56 recognizes the essentially
> capital character of premiums received on the issue of shares, and gives
> effect to it by investing any distribution of the share premium account
> with the character of a capital distribution carried out by means of a
> notional reduction of paid up share capital. Thus, whether the origin
> of the share premium account or the mode and character of its distribu-
> tion be looked at, it seems to us that as between successive interests in
> settled shares the claims of capital are unanswerable.

[77] [1951] Ch. 916.
[78] [1916] 2 Ch. 181.
[79] [1951] Ch. 923.
[80] [1951] Ch. 932.

Yet another variation of the " special capital profits dividend " problem on nationalisation came before Vaisey, J., in *Re Kleinwort's Settlements*.[81] Vaisey, J., held, as others had done, that the payment of such a capital profits dividend out of sums received in exchange for shares on nationalisation was income, payable to the tenant for life, but the trustee had asked whether the court would exercise its jurisdiction to apportion the sum between tenant for life and remainderman. This Vaisey, J., refused to do, adding [82]—

> While it may well be that the suggested jurisdiction exists, and while I do not doubt the power of the court to exercise it in suitable special circumstances—although the court's interference may only be justified where the trustees could be said to have committed a breach of trust consisting either of some action or inaction on their part—here, in my judgment, there are no special circumstances; and I cannot think that there is anything in the nature of a general rule that profits distributed, in whatever shape, as dividends, and belonging under well-settled principles to the tenant for life, must be subject to an apportionment for the benefit of capital.

In *Re Rudd's Will Trusts*,[83] it was decided that the mere fact that the trustees ought to have foreseen the windfall does not mean that they have committed a breach of trust in failing to sell the stock *cum dividendo*.

4. THE ISSUE OF BONUS SHARES

The principles applicable to this type of distribution were long ago settled in the leading case of *Bouch* v. *Sproule*,[84] where all the earlier authorities were reviewed. In this case, a distinction was drawn by the House of Lords between cases in which a company has no power to increase its capital and cases in which the company possesses such a power. In the latter case, the House of Lords adopted the principle expressed by Fry, L.J., in the Court of Appeal [85]—

> When a testator or settlor directs or permits the subject of his disposition to remain as shares or stock in a company which has the power either of distributing its profits as dividend, or of converting them into capital, and the company validly exercises this power, such exercise of its power is binding on all persons interested under him, the testator or settlor, in the shares, and consequently what is paid by the company as dividend goes to the tenant for life, and what is paid by the company to the shareholder as capital, or appropriated as an increase of the capital stock in the concern, enures to the benefit of all who are interested in the capital.

To this Lord Herschell added [86]—

> And it appears to me that where a company has power to increase its

[81] [1951] Ch. 860.
[82] [1951] Ch. 863.
[83] [1952] 1 All E.R. 254.
[84] (1887), 12 App.Cas. 385. See also Keeton, *Modern Developments in the Law of Trusts*, pp. 108–10.
[85] (1885), 29 Ch.D. 635, 653.
[86] 12 App.Cas. 398.

capital and to appropriate its profits to such increase, it cannot be considered as having intended to convert, or having converted, any part of its profits into capital when it has made no such increase, even if a company having no power to increase its capital may be regarded as having thus converted profits into capital by the accumulation and use of them as such.

In such distributions the Inland Revenue is naturally interested, and the position from the tax point of view (which is also the position from the standpoint of tenant for life and remainderman) was more fully expressed in *I.R.C.* v. *Blott*,[87] which decided that profits of a company allotted in the form of bonus shares to a shareholder with no option to take the value of such shares in cash, were capital and not income. The House of Lords expressly decided also that the decision of *Bouch* v. *Sproule* applied, not only between tenant for life and remainderman, but also between Crown and taxpayer.

In *Blott's* case, however, it should be noticed, there was no provision for the payment of the bonus in cash if the shareholder did not want the shares. The introduction of such an option has been productive of much uncertainty, and in some cases has been sufficient to turn the distribution back again into income, under the principles considered in the preceding section.[88] The question turns ultimately upon the true intention of the company, as decided, not by the form of the transaction, but by its substance. Subject to this, however, the same rule has been applied to distributions of bonus debentures, in *I.R.C.* v. *Fisher's Executors*.[89]

In all these cases, the personal motive of individual shareholders, even if they hold a controlling interest in the company, is irrelevant.[90] The operative condition is the power and the intention to increase capital coupled with the exclusion of any real choice on the part of the shareholder to take cash in the alternative.

5. PROFITS ON RECONSTRUCTION

If, however, a company is reconstructed and a profit is realised, which is returned to the shareholders of the original company as surplus capital, this accrues to the capital fund of the trust, and not to the tenant for life.[91] Exactly the same principle applies where the trustees change the trust investments, and realise a profit. Conversely, where trustees held cumulative preference shares in a company, upon which there were several years' arrears of dividend, and the ordinary shareholders surrendered a block of ordinary shares in exchange for the renunciation by the preference shareholders of their arrears of dividends, the ordinary shares were held to accrue to the trustees holding preference shares as income accruing to the tenant for life.[92]

---

87 [1921] 2 A.C. 171.
88 *Re Malam*, [1894] 3 Ch. 578.
89 [1926] A.C. 395.
90 *Commissioner of Income Tax, Bengal* v. *Mercantile Bank of India Ltd.*, [1936] A.C. 478.
91 *Re Armitage*, [1893] 3 Ch. 337.
92 *Re MacIver's Settlement*, [1936] Ch. 198. On the general question of apportionments between capital and income, see Strachan, " Capital and Income (Lifeowner and Remainderman) " (1912) 28 *Law Quarterly Review* 175; Bailey, " Settled Shares in a Company—Income and Capital " (1951) 67 *Law Quarterly Review* 195; Strachan, " A Company's Capital or Income " (1930) 46 *Law Quarterly Review* 334; Keeton, *Modern Developments in the Law of Trusts*, pp. 110–111.

Where income on cumulative preference shares has fallen in arrears, and the tenant for life dies, his personal representatives have no claim against the shares for arrears if the dividends are subsequently paid up.[93] In *Re Walker's Settlement Trusts* [94] a light railway was promoted to serve an estate forming part of a settled estate. The railway was incorporated, and debenture stock was issued to the trustees of the settlement. The interest upon the stock fell into arrears, and when the railway company was wound up, the assets were insufficient to pay off the debenture stock and the arrears of interest. The court held, following *Re Atkinson* [95] (a case in which the interest on a mortgage had fallen into arrears, and the security had been sold, yielding less than the amount of the principal and the arrears of interest), that the sum recovered from the company must be apportioned between capital and income.

Again, in *Re Morris's Will Trusts* [96] Cross, J., held (following *Re Atkinson* [97]) that there must be an apportionment between capital and income of the proceeds of a complicated scheme of arrangement between a company and its debenture-holders, where trustees (with power to retain) held a substantial number of debentures for the benefit of a tenant for life and remainderman.

6. CALLS ON SHARES

On the other hand, where there are calls on shares forming part of the trust estate, these are payable out of the capital of the trust fund.[98] This is simply an illustration of the general rule that all capital charges are payable out of the corpus, whilst any interest on such charges is payable out of income, and if the current income is insufficient to discharge it, it may be paid out of subsequent income.[99] An annuity, or a sum payable by instalments, constitutes for this purpose a capital charge.

E. OTHER APPORTIONMENTS BETWEEN CAPITAL AND INCOME

The rule that the trustee must act impartially between beneficiaries is a general one, and has many applications other than that which is known as the rule in *Howe* v. *Lord Dartmouth*. Thus, it was held in *Raby* v. *Ridehalgh* [1] that trustees must not, in response to the solicitations of the tenant for life, invest trust funds exclusively in his interests, as for example by investing in a permitted, but not entirely secure, property, producing a high return, as by so doing they would be jeopardising the interests of the remainderman to whom, in consequence, they would become liable. In this case, the court did

---

93 *Re Sale*, [1913] 2 Ch. 697.
94 [1936] Ch. 280. For the apportionment between capital and income of compensation payable under the Coal Act 1938, see *Re Duke of Leeds*, [1947] Ch. 525 and *Williams* v. *Sharpe*, [1949] Ch. 595; as to value payments under the War Damage Act 1943, see *Re Scholfield's Will Trusts*, [1949] Ch. 341.
95 [1904] 2 Ch. 160.
96 [1960] 1 W.L.R. 1210.
97 [1904] 2 Ch. 160.
98 *Todd* v. *Moorhouse* (1874), L.R. 19 Eq. 69.
99 *Marshall* v. *Crowther* (1874), 2 Ch.D. 199; *Honywood* v. *Honywood*, [1902] 1 Ch. 347.
1 (1855), 7 De G. M. & G. 104.

not decide whether the investment was permitted: their lordships held the tenants for life liable to indemnify the trustees.

Another illustration of the general scope of the rule is afforded by *Cox* v. *Cox*.[2] C gave to the trustees of his marriage settlement a bond to secure the payment, three months after his death, of a sum to be held in trust for his widow for life, remainder to his children, with interest at 5 per cent. per annum from his death until payment. C died, and his estate was insufficient to pay the sum due. The court held that there must be a calculation of what sum, invested when the testator died, would, together with interest thereon at 4 per cent., have equalled the amount recovered from C's estate at the time that sum was paid, and that an apportionment must be made between tenant for life and remainderman on that basis.

All annual charges, however, are defrayed out of income. In this class of charges are included rates and taxes, and if the property is leasehold, anything incidental to the performance of the covenants; but the tenant for life is not liable for repairs necessary when his interest begins, nor for breaches of covenant arising before that time.[3] Where the trustees of a settlement were directed to continue a business for the benefit of persons in succession, and there was a loss during the lifetime of the first tenant for life, it was held that this should be made good out of profits made when a subsequent tenant for life was beneficially entitled.[4] The exact mode of apportionment depends upon the construction of the particular will, so that if it were the custom of a partnership to write off losses sustained from each partner's share of the capital, that custom would govern the respective rights of tenant for life and remainderman where one of the partners bequeathed his share in trust for persons in succession, and the tenant for life would not have to replenish the depleted capital, for the benefit of the remainderman, out of later profits.[5] Furthermore, the rule does not apply where losses are sustained whilst the business is being carried on simply as a prelude to sale, for in such a case any losses sustained are apportioned between capital and income,[6] according to the rule laid down in *Re Earl of Chesterfield's Trusts*.[7]

There is one important class of cases in which no apportionment is made, although it might naturally have been thought that this should be done. If a trustee, in changing trustee investments, sells stocks or shares just before dividend day, then a price will be paid which necessarily includes some allowance for accrued income. Nevertheless the sum received is placed exclusively to capital. Exactly the same rule applies where the trustee buys stocks or shares just before dividend day; here again the purchase-money is drawn exclusively from capital, although the trustees have in fact bought a right to a dividend which will very shortly be payable. The rule, which seems an unsatisfactory one, is now of general application,[8] and it applies even

---

[2] (1869), L.R. 8 Eq. 343.
[3] *Re Betty*, [1899] 1 Ch. 821; *Re Gjers*, [1899] 2 Ch. 54.
[4] *Upton* v. *Brown* (1884), 26 Ch.D. 588.
[5] *Gow* v. *Forster* (1884), 26 Ch.D. 672.
[6] *Re Hengler*, [1893] 1 Ch. 586.
[7] (1883), 24 Ch.D. 643 (Cases, p. 320).
[8] *Bostock* v. *Blakeney* (1789), 2 Bro.C.C. 653; *Scholefield* v. *Redfern* (1863), 2 Dr. & Sm. 173; *Freman* v. *Whitbread* (1865), L.R. 1 Eq. 266; *Re Clarke* (1881), 18 Ch.D. 160; *Bulkeley* v. *Stephens*, [1896] 2 Ch. 241; *Re Sir Robert Peel's Settled Estates*, [1910] 1 Ch. 389. In Scotland, an apportionment is always made in these circumstances.

though the contract note separately specifies how much is paid or received on account of accrued interest.[9] Of course, if the trustees embarked upon a policy of manipulating investments in favour of tenant for life or remainder-man, they would become liable for breach of trust to the injured party.

An early decision upon the point is *Bostock* v. *Blakeney*,[10] but this is not very helpful, for the rule is categorically stated without any reasons at all, and is quite clearly a well-established one, even at that early date. Possibly it was regularly applied in chambers, and the courts accepted it without question in ordinary cases, though there was an idea that special circumstances might call for special treatment. Thus, in *Lord Londesborough* v. *Somerville*,[11] a large sum of Consols was, for convenience, sold just before the transfer books closed, and the Master of the Rolls directed an apportionment. This was clearly regarded as exceptional, for in *Scholefield* v. *Redfern* [12] an apportionment was refused, Kindersley, V.-C., basing his action on the ground of convenience and saying—

> It is obvious that the reason why such equity on either side has never been administered habitually by this Court is that by attempting it a grievous burthen would be imposed upon the estates of testators, by reason of the complex investigation which it would lead to. The gain to either party would be far more than compensated by the expense which might be incurred in a complicated case, and for that reason, no doubt, the thing has never been done. I will not be the first to introduce the practice.

It is impossible to resist the conclusion that the learned Vice-Chancellor was exaggerating the difficulties in this case. Complicated investigations are not unknown in trust accounts and, in any case, the amount that the purchaser pays for accrued dividend is not difficult to ascertain, even where it is not expressly stated in the contract note. Two years later, however, in *Freman* v. *Whitbread*,[13] the same Vice-Chancellor reiterated his view, for the same reasons, notwithstanding that in the first case of *Bulkeley* v. *Stephens*,[14] decided just after *Scholefield* v. *Redfern*, Stuart, V.-C., had given relief to the tenant for life, on the ground that the sale of stock had been made under the authority of the court for the benefit of the estate.

In *Re Clarke*,[15] the trustees purchased stock with accrued dividend and the court held that the tenant for life was entitled to the whole of the dividend. The court also pointed out that in these cases the Apportionment Act 1870 had nothing to do with the case.

The whole of the earlier authorities were considered by Stirling, J., in the second decision in *Bulkeley* v. *Stephens*,[16] and the learned judge came to the conclusion that whilst in general no apportionment could be directed, yet the special circumstances of the case might give rise to a good claim for

---

9 *Re Walker*, [1934] W.N. 104.
10 (1789), 2 Bro.C.C. 653.
11 (1854), 19 Beav. 295.
12 (1863), 2 Dr. & Sm. 173, 183.
13 (1865), L.R. 1 Eq. 266.
14 (1863), 3 New Rep. 105.
15 (1881), 18 Ch.D. 160.
16 [1896] 2 Ch. 241.

relief. As to the general rule, Stirling, J., like his predecessors, based it upon the ground of difficulty in making the apportionment. The special circumstances in which the judge allowed an apportionment, however, were that the sale that had occurred was not strictly necessary for the execution of the trust, and had taken place under an order made in the absence of the legal representative of the tenant for life. For these reasons, therefore, Stirling, J., held that it would not be equitable to deprive him of his dividend.

It will be seen, therefore, that as the rule stood at the end of the nineteenth century, it was based simply upon the difficulty of apportionment, and the court would grant relief where special circumstances warranted it. These principles were directly applied in *Re Peel's Estates*.[17] Stock was purchased when a dividend had been earned and declared, but was not yet paid. Warrington, J., held that the dividend accrued to capital. There was no difficulty, and the circumstances warranted a deviation from the general rule.

In *Re Walker*,[18] India 5½ per cent. stock was sold by trustees, and the contract note stated that £34,397 8s. 10d. was paid for the stock, and £616 5s. was paid in respect of accrued interest. Clauson, J., held, however, that no apportionment could be made in favour of the tenant for life, basing his decision upon the absence of any special circumstances. This would seem to ignore the reason for the existence of the rule stated in *Scholefield* v. *Redfern*, and leaves open the question, what special circumstances are sufficient to justify a departure from the usual practice?

The learned judge himself attempted to answer this question in a later case.

In *Re Winterstoke's Will Trusts*,[19] the trustees sold securities *cum dividendo* after the death of the tenant for life. The amount involved was a very large one, and Clauson, J., directed the trustees to account, if so requested, for that sum which represented the value of the accrued dividend in the purchase price to the personal representatives of the deceased tenant for life. The learned judge said [20]—

> In small cases, I dare say even in large cases, it has no doubt been the practice, a practice possibly justified by certain dicta of Stirling J. in *Bulkeley* v. *Stephens*,[21] not to make this special reservation for the tenant for life or to account to his executors for the apportioned dividend; but it appears to me that when the question has been raised and there is no difficulty in ascertaining the figure which would be payable to the executors of the tenant for life, the trustees may properly deal and ought to deal with the matter in the way I have indicated, that is to say, by accounting to the executors of the tenant for life for the apportioned dividend.

This attempt to relax the rigidity of the rule was immediately challenged in *Re Firth*,[22] where Farwell, J., distinguished *Re Winterstoke's Will Trusts*, and, after observing that he did not think Clauson, J., meant to do more than say

---

17 *Re Sir Robert Peel's Settled Estates*, [1910] 1 Ch. 389.
18 [1934] W.N. 104.
19 [1938] Ch. 158.
20 [1938] Ch. 162.
21 [1896] 2 Ch. 241.
22 [1938] Ch. 517.

that there may be cases in which the court will depart from the general practice, he added [23]—

> I would point out that there is to my mind a serious difficulty in appreciating exactly what the learned judge meant in the case before him, because he says this: " but it appears to me that when the question has been raised and there is no difficulty in ascertaining the figure which would be payable to the executors of the tenant for life, the trustees may properly deal and ought to deal with the matter " in a particular way. For myself, I am unable to see what difference it can make, whether the calculation is an easy one or a difficult one. If the tenant for life has an equity which he has a right to assert in this court, his right cannot depend on whether the sum which has to be done is one which can be done easily, or which requires care and consideration. But however that may be, in my judgment nothing has altered the practice which has obtained for many years.

In this case, therefore, apportionment was refused. The matter cannot as yet be regarded as finally settled, however, for in *Re Maclaren's Settlement Trusts*,[24] it was pointed out that whilst in ordinary cases the rule was based on practical convenience, if its application caused glaring injustice, the court would direct an apportionment.

The question whether the cost of repairs or improvements to land and buildings held on trust are regarded as charges upon capital or upon income is now governed principally by the Settled Land Act 1925, Part IV, together with Schedule III and the decisions relevant thereto.[25] This is a technical question, of which only brief consideration can be given here.

The Settled Land Act, sections 83 and 84, authorises the expenditure of capital money for the execution of improvements authorised by the Act, and for any operation necessary for the carrying out of such purposes; and section 84 (1) provides that it is no longer necessary (as it was before 1926) to obtain the approval of the court or of the trustees of the settlement to a scheme before the tenant for life undertakes such improvements. Where the capital money is in the hands of the trustees, then unless they are otherwise authorised by the court, they must not apply it in payment for improvements, unless they have obtained a certificate from a competent surveyor, employed independently of the tenant for life, certifying that the work done has been properly executed, and what sum may be properly paid in respect of it. A certificate so given is conclusive in favour of the trustees as a discharge for any payment they may have made in pursuance of it.[26] The subsection contains two provisos—

> (*a*) In the case of improvements not authorised by Part I of the Third Schedule to this Act or by the settlement, the trustees may, if they think fit, and shall if so directed by the court, before they make any such application of capital money require that that money, or any part thereof, shall be repaid to them out of the income of the settled land by not more than

23 [1938] Ch. 529.
24 [1951] 2 All E.R. 414.
25 For an illustration, under s. 73 (1) of the Settled Land Act 1925, see *Re Duke of Wellington's Parliamentary Estates*, [1972] Ch. 374.
26 Settled Land Act 1925, s. 84 (2) (i).

fifty half-yearly instalments, the first of such instalments to be paid or to be deemed to have become payable at the expiration of six months from the date when the work or operation, in payment for which the money is to be applied, was completed;

(b) No capital money shall be applied by the trustees in payment for improvements not authorised by Parts I and II of the Third Schedule to this Act, or by the settlement, except subject to provision for the repayment thereof being made in manner mentioned in the preceding paragraph of this proviso.

The Third Schedule, mentioned in these provisos, sets out in detail a list of improvements, and is divided into three parts. Part I includes only those improvements which permanently increase the capital value of the land, and for which accordingly payment may be made out of capital money with no provision for replacement out of income. Part II comprises improvements, the cost of which either the trustees or the court *may*, but need not, require to be defrayed out of income by instalments, unless these are permitted to be paid for out of capital by the settlement itself. Part III includes those improvements which may not be paid for out of capital, unless the settlement expressly provides for it.

When the capital money is in court, the court may, if it thinks fit, on the report or certificate of the Minister of Agriculture, Fisheries and Food, or of a competent engineer or an able practical surveyor, approved by the court, or on such other evidence as the court may think sufficient, make such order as it thinks fit, for the application of the money towards payment for the improvement.[27]

Moreover, subsection (4) provides—

Where the court authorises capital money to be applied in payment for any improvement or intended improvement not authorised by Part I of the Third Schedule to this Act or by the settlement, the court, as a condition of making the order, may in any case require that the capital money or any part thereof, and shall as respects an improvement mentioned in Part III of that Schedule (unless the improvement is authorised by the settlement), require that the whole of the capital money shall be repaid to the trustees of the settlement out of the income of the settled land by a fixed number of periodical instalments to be paid at the times appointed by the court, and may require that any incumbrancer of the estate or interest of the tenant for life shall be served with notice of the proceedings.

There have been, since 1925, a number of decisions upon the question of improvements under sections 83–4, and permanent or structural repairs, and the allocation of the costs of them. In the first of these, *Re Gray*,[28] repairs of a substantial nature were effected in respect of a block of freehold flats comprised in a settlement. The court held that such repairs were authorised by section 102 (2) of the Settled Land Act 1925 and were properly payable out of income. It should be noticed that, in this case, the repairs were undertaken at the instance of trustees for sale, acting under the Law of

[27] Settled Land Act 1925, s. 84 (3).
[28] [1927] 1 Ch. 242.

Property Act 1925, section 28 (1). In *Re Conquest*,[29] permanent structural repairs were effected, and the court held: (1) that the effect of the Law of Property Act 1925, section 28 (1), was not only to confer on trustees for sale during a minority the powers of management specified in the Settled Land Act 1925, section 102, but also the powers exercisable by the tenant for life under section 84 of that Act of making improvements and paying for them out of capital.[30] In this case the court took the view that the work done fell within Part I of Schedule III, and that it should therefore be paid for out of capital. It appears from this decision that the powers conferred on trustees for sale under the Law of Property Act 1925, section 28 (1), may overlap. Where they do so, and the trustees have a choice of powers, they are guided by the equitable principles enunciated in *Re Hotchkys*.[31] These principles were stated by Lindley, L.J., in that case to be—

> . . . if it is shewn that it is judicious to make repairs, and the trustees come to the court for authority to make them, that authority will be given, but it will be given on equitable terms as to the mode of paying the expenses.[32]

There exists also another important rule relating to equitable apportionments of which brief mention must be made, although it is a rule applicable to the duties of personal representatives. The rule, which is known as the rule in *Allhusen* v. *Whittell*,[33] applies to the payment of the debts of a testator out of his estate, and has regard to the fact that where the debts are not paid immediately, the residue will be producing income, which is also applicable for the payment of debts. Now, in taking capital and income of residue for the payment of debts, the personal representatives must act impartially between tenant for life and remainderman, and therefore—

> . . . the true principle is, that, in bookkeeping which the court enters upon for the purpose of adjusting the rights between the parties, it is necessary to ascertain what part, together with the income of such part for a year, will be wanted for the payment of debts, legacies, and other charges, during the year; and the proper and necessary fund must be ascertained by including the income for one year which may arise upon the fund which may be so wanted.

To take a simple example, suppose the testator leaves £50,000 and debts of £4,000, and suppose that the sum of £50,000 produces £1,500 income. The apportionment is made by adding £1,500 to £50,000, and subtracting the debts of £4,000, leaving £47,500, which represents capital plus one year's interest at 3 per cent. Accordingly £46,116·50 is placed to capital, and the tenant for life receives £1,383·50 interest. The rule will not be applied where the

---

[29] [1929] 2 Ch. 353.

[30] See also *Re Duke of Northumberland*, [1951] Ch. 202; *Re Boston's Will Trusts*, [1956] Ch. 395.

[31] (1886), 32 Ch.D. 408, 420.

[32] *i.e.* as between income and capital. See also *Re Robins*, [1928] Ch. 721; *Re Lord Sherborne's Settled Estate*, [1929] 1 Ch. 345; *Re Whitaker*, [1929] 1 Ch. 662; *Re Smith*, [1930] 1 Ch. 88; *Re Jacques Settled Estates*, [1930] 2 Ch. 418; *Re Borough Court Estate*, [1932] 2 Ch. 39.

[33] (1867), L.R. 4 Eq. 295, 303 (Cases, p. 324). See also *Lambert* v. *Lambert* (1873), L.R. 16 Eq. 320.

testator shows a contrary intention, or where circumstances would make it inequitable to apply it.[34] An intention to exclude the rule must, however, be clearly expressed.[35]

Quite apart from these equitable rules of apportionment, there exist the provisions of the Apportionment Act, 1870, that "all rents, annuities, dividends, and other periodical payments in the nature of income (whether reserved or made payable under an instrument in writing or otherwise) shall, like interest on money lent, be considered as accruing from day to day, and shall be apportionable in respect of time accordingly." [36] This Act more particularly concerns executors and administrators, but it also affects the duties of trustees, especially on the death of a tenant for life, and it is not excluded by a power to postpone a trust for sale coupled with a direction that, pending sale, " the whole of the income of property actually producing income " shall be applied as from the testator's death as income.[37]

Where costs are incurred in the administration of a trust, these will normally be defrayed out of capital, unless the settlor has directed otherwise. Examples of such costs are costs incurred in the appointment of new trustees, conveyancing expenses and the cost of bringing and defending actions on behalf of the trust. If, however, expense is incurred in the determination of a matter which relates solely to the income of a trust, such expense will be a charge upon the income.[38] Income fees charged by a trust corporation in respect of settled legacies are payable out of the income of each legacy.[39]

It must also be noticed that if a trustee delays for an unreasonably lengthy period before investing trust money or handing it over to the persons entitled, he is chargeable with interest on the money, and this may be granted even where it has not been specially asked for.[40] The same rule is also applicable to personal representatives who are guilty of undue delay in distributing the estate after all outstanding claims have been satisfied, and it is no excuse for either an executor or a trustee to declare that he made no use of the money, which remained at the bank.[41] As far as the executor is concerned, this is a deviation from the earlier and laxer practice which permitted him to employ surplus assets for his own purposes without being called to account, but this was finally overruled by Lord North in *Ratcliffe* v. *Graves*.[42] It may be, however, that if the trustee employs the money in business, he makes a substantial profit. If this is so, the beneficiary may choose whether he will take the profits or charge interest for the use of his money.[43] Where the money has been used for purposes of trade, the rate of interest has frequently been 5 per cent.

---

[34] *Re McEuen*, [1913] 2 Ch. 704; *Re Wills*, [1915] 1 Ch. 769. For a criticism of the rule, see Strachan, " Rule in *Allhusen* v. *Whittell* " (1914) 30 *Law Quarterly Review* 481.

[35] *Re Ullswater*, [1952] Ch. 105.

[36] s. 2. For the definition of dividends, see s. 5 and p. 269, *ante*. See also Keeton, *Modern Developments in the Law of Trusts*, pp. 96-8.

[37] *Re Edwards*, [1918] 1 Ch. 142. See also *Re Wakley*, [1920] 2 Ch. 205; *Re Marjoribanks*, [1923] 2 Ch. 307; *Re Sandbach*, [1933] Ch. 505.

[38] *Re Marner's Trusts* (1866), L.R. 3 Eq. 432; *Re Evans' Trusts* (1872), L.R. 7 Ch.App. 609.

[39] *Re Roberts' Will Trusts*, [1937] Ch. 274, distinguishing *Re Hulton*, [1936] Ch. 536, and *Re Riddell*, [1936] Ch. 747. See also *Re Godwin*, [1938] Ch. 341.

[40] *Turner* v. *Turner* (1819), 1 Jac. & W. 39.

[41] *Younge* v. *Combe* (1798), 4 Ves. 101.

[42] (1683), 1 Vern. 196.

[43] *Docker* v. *Somes* (1834), 2 My. & K. 655.

compound interest.[44] In other cases, it has usually been 4 per cent., unless the trustee ought to have received more (*e.g.* where he improperly called in mortgages yielding more) or where he actually received more.[45] Whether simple or compound interest is levied seems to depend entirely upon the facts of the particular case, but if there is an express direction to accumulate, Lord Eldon observed that compound interest ought to be decreed.[46] It should be noticed, however, that an executor is not usually chargeable with interest during the first year which follows the testator's death, for the fund is not regarded as being distributable until the expiration of the executor's year.

F. THE RIGHTS AND DUTIES OF TRUSTEES IN RELATION TO THE DISTRIBUTION OF THE TRUST PROPERTY

The obvious duty of the trustee in relation to the distribution of the trust property is to pay the proper persons, and therefore the trustee must ensure he identifies the persons he must pay, either as creditors or as beneficiaries. The Trustee Act 1925, s. 27 [47] (replacing the Law of Property Amendment Act 1859, which applied to personal representatives only), sets out the procedure to be followed by trustees and personal representatives in ascertaining the existence and extent of claims against the estate. They must advertise in the *Gazette*, and also in a newspaper circulating in the district where the land is situated, and they must insert such other advertisements as would have been directed by the court, asking persons interested to send to the trustees within the time fixed by the trustees (which must not be less than two months from the last of the advertisements) giving particulars of claims. When this period has expired, the trustees may pay claims of which they then have notice, and distribute the estate, and they are not liable in respect of claims of which they then had no notice. Nothing in the section, however,

> (*a*) prejudices the right of any person to follow the property, or any property representing the same, into the hands of any person, other than a purchaser, who may have received it; or
>
> (*b*) frees the trustees or personal representatives from any obligation to make searches or obtain official certificates of search similar to those which an intending purchaser would be advised to make or obtain.

By section 28, it is provided that a trustee or personal representative who is acting for more than one trust or estate shall not, in the absence of fraud, be affected by notice of any instrument, matter, fact or thing in relation to any particular trust or estate if he has obtained notice thereof merely by reason of his acting or having acted for the purposes of another trust or estate.

The advertisement should be made as soon as possible after the death,[48] and a trustee or executor who has done what is required by the section

---

[44] *Burdick* v. *Garrick* (1870), L.R. 5 Ch.App. 233.

[45] *Jones* v. *Foxall* (1852), 15 Beav. 388, 392 ; *Burdick* v. *Garrick, supra.*

[46] *Raphael* v. *Boehm* (1804), 11 Ves. 92. Lord Erskine agreed : (1807), 13 Ves. 407. Lord Eldon reiterated his opinion : (1807), 13 Ves. 590.

[47] As amended by the Law of Property (Amendment) Act 1926, s. 7 and Sched.

[48] *Re Kay*, [1897] 2 Ch. 518.

enjoys the same protection as if he had administered the estate under an order of the court.[49]

If, however, the trustee has notice of a claim by a creditor, this is not barred simply because the creditor neglects to claim immediately in response to the advertisement.[50] On the other hand, a mere reply to the advertisement by a creditor does not preserve that claim from the operation of the Statutes of Limitation.[51]

If the trustees distribute among the persons entitled to the property, and then a debt of which they had no previous notice is claimed, they are entitled to call upon the beneficiaries to refund the property to the extent necessary to satisfy the debt, but if the trustees had notice of the claim, but nevertheless distributed, although they must pay the claim (unless statute-barred), they may not call upon the beneficiaries to refund, unless the liability was a remote possibility, such as a call in respect of prospering shares, not contemplated at the time of distribution.[52]

Furthermore, the right of any person to follow the property into the hands of a person other than a purchaser is preserved. This is also referred to in section 26 (2), which operates notwithstanding anything in the will or settlement to the contrary.

It is to be observed that section 27 only protects the trustee in respect of claims of which he has no notice. Obviously, he has notice of all interests directly arising out of the will or other trust instrument. It may be, however, that a beneficiary assigns his interest in a trust fund, and here section 137 of the Law of Property Act, extending the rule in *Dearle* v. *Hall*,[53] provides that the assignee of an equitable interest must give notice in writing to the trustees or estate owners, and the priorities of the encumbrancers are determined according to the dates when they gave notice. There may still be occasions, however, when a trustee is affected with constructive notice of an assignment,[54] and in such a case he would not be protected if he paid to the assignor.

Now that illegitimate children and their issue are ranked equally with legitimate children and their issue or parents on intestacy, for the purpose of saving gifts by will from lapsing when the donee predeceases the testator, and for the interpretation of a gift to a person's " child " or " children," additional problems may arise for trustees or personal representatives in ascertaining who are a relevant person's illegitimate offspring. Section 17 of the Family Law Reform Act 1969 deals with these problems by providing that trustees or personal representatives may convey or distribute any property to or among the persons entitled to it without having ascertained that there is no person who is or may be entitled to any interest in the property by virtue of the statutory extension of benefits to illegitimate children and their issue or fathers. They are not liable to any such person of whose claim they had no notice at the time of the conveyance or distribution, " but nothing in this

---

[49] *Re Frewen* (1889), 60 L.T. 953; *Hunter* v. *Young* (1879), 4 Ex.D. 256.
[50] *Scottish Equitable Life Assurance Soc.* v. *Beatty* (1889), 29 L.R. Ir. 290.
[51] *Re Stephens* (1889), 43 Ch.D. 39.
[52] *Jervis* v. *Wolferstan* (1874), L.R. 18 Eq. 18; *Whittaker* v. *Kershaw* (1890), 45 Ch.D. 320, 325.
[53] (1823), 3 Russ. 1 (Cases, p. 60).
[54] *e.g.* of an equitable assignment of a legal chose in action; see Marshall: *Assignment of Choses in Action*, pp. 105–106.

section shall prejudice the right of any such person to follow the property, or any property representing it, into the hands of any person, other than a purchaser, who may have received it."

If a beneficiary has gone abroad, and has not been heard of for seven years, there is a presumption that he is dead.[55] This, however, does not free the trustee from liability, for if the beneficiary reappears, the trustee will have to pay him,[56] and, therefore, the usual practice of the court in paying out is to require security, in case repayment should become necessary. Accordingly, the proper course for the trustee to adopt is to obtain a proper indemnity or to accumulate the fund, or to seek the direction of the court; and now, by section 63 of the Trustee Act 1925, it is provided that where the trustees[57] are in doubt, whether to pay a beneficiary in full, or whether the claimant is really entitled, they may pay the money or property into court, and the certificate of the officer of the court will discharge them from liability.

The desirability of taking advantage of this provision becomes evident from what has been said above concerning the presumption of death with regard to a missing beneficiary, particularly when it is remembered that there is no presumption of death without issue; therefore, when A and his issue are entitled, under a settlement *inter vivos*, or under a will or on intestacy, with a gift over to B, the fact that A has died without issue must be proved by proper evidence before distribution of B's share can safely be made.[58] A trustee should not, however, pay money into court without reasonable cause, or he may be made liable for costs.[59]

Where there is a reasonable doubt concerning the identity of a beneficiary under a trust, the trustee will usually be allowed the costs of payment into and out of court,[60] but in other cases he will have to pay the costs of the applicant.[61] In *Re Schnapper*,[62] a beneficiary under a trust, who was of German nationality and Prussian domicile, was ordered to be paid her legacy out of funds in court, on attaining the age of eighteen, which, by the law of the place of her domicile, was the age at which she became competent to receive it and to give receipts therefor.[63]

The position of a trustee who overpays some of his beneficiaries and underpays others has occasioned some discussion. He is, of course, liable to pay the true beneficiary but in general, in the absence of fraud or other fault, he is entitled to have the mistake rectified with the assistance of the court, but this general principle is modified by the decision in *Re Horne*.

The facts of *Re Horne*,[64] though simple, differed in one important essential from those in respect of which the rule just enunciated has been developed. In that case the trustee was himself one of the beneficiaries, and he inadvertently overpaid the other beneficiaries and underpaid himself. Before any

---

55 *Re Benjamin*, [1902] 1 Ch. 723 ; *Re Aldersey*, [1905] 2 Ch. 181.
56 *Lord Woodhouselee* v. *Dalrymple* (1861), 9 W.R. 475, 564.
57 Including personal representatives : Trustee Act 1925, s. 68 (17).
58 *Re Jackson*, [1907] 2 Ch. 354.
59 *Re Giles* (1886), 55 L.J.Ch. 695.
60 *Re Jones* (1857), 3 Drew. 679 ; *Re Headington's Trust* (1857), 27 L.J.Ch. 175.
61 *Re Woodburn's Will Trusts* (1857), 1 De G. & J. 333 ; *Re Elliot's Trusts* (1873), L.R. 15 Eq. 194.
62 [1928] Ch. 420, following *Re Hellmann's Will* (1866), L.R. 2 Eq. 363, and *Donohoe* v. *Donohoe* (1887), 19 L.R. Ir. 349.
63 Twenty-one was then the age of majority in England.
64 [1905] 1 Ch. 76.

rectification could be made, the trustee-beneficiary died, and it was held that his executors could neither recover the overpayments from the beneficiaries nor have them deducted from future income to be paid to the other beneficiaries. The reason for Warrington, J.'s judgment seems to be that to alter the position " would be very inconvenient, and a great hardship on the other legatees." This may be true, but it is scarcely a conclusive reason for refusing to ensure that a trust is carried out according to the intention of the settlor, and the learned judge himself had already admitted [65] that—

> If Richard Horne had not been himself a trustee, but only one of the beneficiaries, the case would be plainly covered by authority, and it would now have been the duty of the plaintiff, as the surviving trustee of this will, in administering the trusts of it for the future, to equalize the payments which have been made out of income.

That is the general rule, and *Re Horne* [66] must, therefore, be regarded as an exception to it, the trustee-beneficiary's position being altered for the worse because—

> Any equity that he might have had in his character of beneficiary is displaced by the fact that he is himself responsible for the mistake which has been made.[67]

Re Horne [66] has received consideration, and some criticism, in later cases, however. In *Re Ainsworth*,[68] the executors of a will wrongly and by mistake paid the legacy duty on a life interest in a settled legacy out of the capital of the legacy, instead of out of the income during the first four years of the life tenancy, as provided by the Legacy Duty Act 1796. The legacy had been bequeathed (on the termination of the life interest) to two special trustees, one of whom was one of the executors authorising the wrong payment, and the executor-trustee was held to be entitled, after a lapse of seven years, to set the mistake right by reducing the payments of future income to the tenant for life in order to make up the capital of the settled legacy, which had been diminished by the payment of legacy duty. There would have been little difficulty in reaching this decision but for *Re Horne*.[66] Joyce, J., commenting on that case, observed [69] that it—

> . . . is said to have established for the first time some general rule that prevents the error being set right in such circumstances as those of the present case. I am unable to accept this argument. Moreover, in these days innocent trustees acting bona fide are not treated with the severity of former days; and the case of *In re Horne* [66] was a totally different one from the present.

The essential point, of course, was that *Re Horne* [66] dealt with a trustee-beneficiary, who impoverished himself by his own mistake. *Re Ainsworth* [68] dealt with a trustee who was not a beneficiary, who had impoverished others by his mistake, and those persons naturally had a right to have the mistake rectified in their favour.

[65] [1905] 1 Ch. 79.
[66] [1905] 1 Ch. 76.
[67] [1905] 1 Ch. 81.
[68] [1915] 2 Ch. 96.
[69] [1915] 2 Ch. 104–5.

Re Musgrave[70] was decided on similar facts to *Re Ainsworth*.[68] A testator had directed that certain annuities should be paid "without deduction." The trustees paid the annuities for some years without deducting income tax, which is not covered by "without deduction." The trustees were not beneficiaries, and it was held that the trustees were entitled to deduct the tax, which should have been deducted, from future payments of the annuities. Neville, J., laid down the general principle concerning over-payment by a trustee, and then observed that a mistake as to the payment of income tax was a mistake of law, and not of fact, adding [71] that—

> ... in my opinion the mere fact that a mistake is an honest mistake of law, as long as it is not a mistake of public law, which everyone is bound to know, has not prevented the Courts from giving relief to one party as against the other ...

Re Horne[72] was again commented on, and the learned judge observed [73] that—

> ... it was said that that lays down the general principle that where a mistake has been made by the trustee he cannot get this adjustment against the cestui que trust. I do not think the learned judge put it so high as that. It has nothing to do with the decision of the case before me; clearly it can be supported on other grounds.

The learned judge was correct. *Re Horne*[72] was never intended to lay down a general principle on the relation of trustee and beneficiary. Warrington, J., expressly disclaimed any such intention.

Finally, in *Re Reading*,[74] Mrs. S., executrix of the last surviving executor of the testator, secured sole control of the distribution of the income arising out of the trusts of the will, purporting to appoint herself as trustee. The appointment was bad, but she nevertheless became a constructive trustee, and made distributions of income whereby she overpaid both herself and another. This was the converse case to *Re Horne*,[72] and an attempt to make that case apply failed, so that a redistribution was ordered. It is clear that there could be no ground for applying *Re Horne*,[72] since (1) the beneficiary who lost by the transaction was in no way responsible for the error; and (2) the duties which a trustee must observe towards his beneficiary have no counterpart in the relation of beneficiary to trustee. Furthermore, Mrs. S.'s overpayment of herself was a violation of the elementary rule that a trustee must not profit from his trust.

The rule to be derived from these decisions may, therefore, be stated as follows—Where a trustee is also a beneficiary, he is still bound by his mistake, where it results in an underpayment to himself. Where the trustee is not a beneficiary or where the trustee-beneficiary overpays himself, the mistake will be rectified.

As regards executors, the court will not generally order a legatee to refund

[70] [1916] 2 Ch. 417.
[71] [1916] 2 Ch. 424.
[72] [1905] 1 Ch. 76.
[73] [1916] 2 Ch. 425.
[74] [1916] W.N. 262.

personally to an executor [75]; nor will it order the legatee to refund where the executor has voluntarily overpaid the legatee, in spite of the latter's doubts whether so much was, in fact, payable.[76] However, an executor who distributes with notice of liabilities which may become due, but are not certain to materialise (*e.g.* future calls on shares) may, if he is compelled to pay them, recover them from the legatees,[77] but an executor will not generally be able to recover if the legatee has sold to a purchaser for value.[78] On the other hand, if an executor still retains property that he has appropriated to satisfy a legacy, he may, if compelled to pay a creditor for whom he has made no other provision, recover the debt from the appropriated property.[78]

In *Re Musgrave*,[79] it was noticed that the court would relieve against an overpayment due to a mistake of law, not being a mistake of public law, and in *Ex parte James*,[80] where money was paid to a trustee in bankruptcy under a mistake of law, the court ordered it to be refunded, on the principle that the Court of Bankruptcy ought to act in the way in which any high-minded man would act.

If the trustees are holding property on behalf of a beneficiary who is of full age and absolutely entitled, they must at his request transfer to him the entire trust fund. This point is illustrated by *Re Selot's Trust*,[81] where a French subject, who by French law had been declared a " prodigal," and was therefore subject to some restraint, claimed the fund, and it was held that since this status was unknown in English law, the trustees were not justified in withholding the property.

By the Trustee Act 1925, s. 26, trustees and personal representatives who transfer real property are given protection with respect to rents, covenants and other obligations which may exist in respect of the property if they have satisfied all liabilities and covenants up to the date when they transfer the property.

Under section 26, the term " lease " includes both an underlease and an agreement for a lease or underlease, " grant " includes a grant whether the rent is created by limitation, grant, reservation or otherwise, and also an agreement for a grant, whilst " lessee " and " grantee " include persons claiming under them.

It is important to remember in considering distributions by trustees that they must not only ascertain what are the proper distributions under the instrument, but also what is the effect of English law upon them, for a trustee is not excused for a mistake of English law, even if he has taken counsel's opinion upon the matter.[82] On the other hand, he is not deemed to know foreign law. Thus, in *Leslie* v. *Baillie*,[83] a testator died and his will was proved in England. By his will, the testator left a legacy to a married woman,

---

[75] *Downes* v. *Bullock* (1858), 25 Beav. 54; (1860), 9 H.L.C. 1.
[76] *Bate* v. *Hooper* (1855), 5 De G.M. & G. 338.
[77] *Whittaker* v. *Kershaw* (1890), 45 Ch.D. 320.
[78] *Noble* v. *Brett* (1858), 24 Beav. 499. As to the right of the underpaid or unpaid beneficiary to recover directly from the person wrongly paid, see Chap. XXV, s. C, 3, *post.*
[79] [1916] 2 Ch. 417, followed in *Re Dunville*, [1947] N.I. 50.
[80] (1874), L.R. 9 Ch.App. 609. See also *Re Wyvern Developments Ltd.*, [1974] 1 W.L.R. 1097, 1105, *per* Templeman, J.
[81] [1902] 1 Ch. 488.
[82] *Doyle* v. *Blake* (1804), 2 Sch. & Lef. 229, 243; *Re Knight's Trusts* (1859), 27 Beav. 45 Such a mistake might be a ground for relief under Trustee Act 1925, s. 61.
[83] (1843), 2 Y. & C.C.C. 91.

who was domiciled in Scotland. Before payment, the woman's husband died, and the testator's executors paid the legacy to the wife, being unaware of the fact that, by Scottish law, the legacy should have been paid to the husband's personal representatives, who therefore proceeded to sue the testator's executors. It was held that they were not to be deemed to know the law of Scotland, and that as they had not had express notice of this rule of Scottish law before they paid, and had discharged what had appeared to be their duty, they were not liable.

If a dispute exists between two persons with regard to a right to the trust fund, the trustee is entitled to retain the fund until the issue has been determined,[84] and a person who has made an improper claim to the fund may be made liable for costs.[85]

In *Re Edward's Will Trusts*[86] trustees were given property "upon trust to pay or transfer the same or any part thereof to such persons and for such purposes as the managing trustee shall in his absolute and uncontrolled discretion think fit." The question raised was whether this gave the managing trustee power to direct the transfer of the property to himself. Jenkins, J., held that the question to be decided was whether the power had been given to the trustee as an individual or *virtute officii*. If the power had been given to him as an individual, the trustee could take beneficially. Otherwise he must direct the transfer to other persons.

A clause which purports to give trustees a power to determine all questions arising under a will is void, as an attempt to oust the court's jurisdiction,[87] but a more limited power may be valid if exercised reasonably.[88]

A trustee will usually pay a share of the trust fund to the person directly entitled thereto. The Trustee Act 1925, however, now provides for several occasions where payment may be made to other persons than the one who is primarily entitled.

1. WHERE A PROTECTIVE TRUST EXISTS

Under section 33, where a protective trust exists, and the act or thing contemplated occurs, so that the interest of the principal beneficiary determines, the trustees may at their absolute discretion, and without being liable to account, apply the income for all or any one or more of the following persons—

(a) The principal beneficiary and his or her wife or husband, if any, and his or her children or more remote issue, if any; or

(b) If there is no wife or husband or issue of the principal beneficiary in existence, the principal beneficiary and the persons who would, if he were actually dead, be entitled to the trust property or the income thereof.

By virtue of the Family Law Reform Act 1969, s. 15 (3), children will now include illegitimate children and remoter issue will include persons who

---

84 *Hockey* v. *Western*, [1898] 1 Ch. 350.
85 *Re Primrose* (1857), 23 Beav. 590.
86 [1947] 2 All E.R. 521.
87 *Re Wynn*, [1952] Ch. 271.
88 *Dundee General Hospitals Board of Management* v. *Walker*, [1952] 1 All E.R. 896.

would have been regarded as issue had they or some other person through whom they are descended from the principal beneficiary been born legitimate.

It would appear that where the principal beneficiary under a discretionary protective trust becomes bankrupt, the trustees should not pay him or apply for his benefit more than is necessary for his bare support, or the trustee in bankruptcy will be able to claim it,[89] and if the trustees pay the income to a third person on a secret trust for the principal beneficiary, that arrangement may be set aside.[90]

2. MAINTENANCE UNDER THE TRUSTEE ACT 1925

Under section 31, the trustees have a wide power to apply income for the maintenance of a beneficiary during his minority. The power may be exercised by the trustees in respect of any interest, whether vested or contingent, provided that the interest carries the intermediate income. It also applies to intestacies [91] and is additional to any power conferred by the trust deed, but only so far as no contrary intention is expressed.[92] An express direction to accumulate is an expression of an intention to exclude the statutory powers of maintenance and advancement, and this is the situation even when the direction to accumulate is invalid under section 164 of the Law of Property Act 1925.[93]

The whole of section 31 may be varied by the settlor, even though some parts of it may appear to be couched in imperative language. For example, section 31 (1) (ii), after providing for maintenance out of income during infancy, directs—

> if such person [*i.e.* the beneficiary] on attaining the age of eighteen years has not a vested interest in such income, the trustees shall thenceforth pay the income of that property and of any accretion thereto under subsection (2) of this section to him, until he either attains a vested interest therein or dies, or until failure of his interest . . .

In *Re Turner's Will Trusts* [94] the settlor postponed the vesting of the beneficiary's interest until he attained the age of twenty-eight and further directed that sums not needed during this period should acrue to capital. The Court of Appeal held that this provision superseded the direction in section 31 (1) (ii), so that when the beneficiary died before attaining the age of 28, his executors had no claim upon the annual balances of income between the time when the beneficiary attained the age of majority and his death. Payments may be made to the parent or guardian for the infant's "maintenance, education, or benefit," up to the whole of the income, and they may be made even though there are other funds applicable for that purpose (*e.g.* under other trusts), and even though there is some person bound by law to maintain the infant (*e.g.* the father). In making payments, however, the trustees are directed to have regard to the general requirements

---

[89] *Holmes* v. *Penney* (1856), 3 K. & J. 90; *Re Coleman* (1888), 39 Ch.D. 443.
[90] *Holmes* v. *Penney, supra.*
[91] Administration of Estates Act 1925, s. 47 (1).
[92] Trustee Act 1925, s. 69 (2).
[93] *Re Erskine's Settlement Trusts*, [1971] 1 W.L.R. 162.
[94] [1937] Ch. 15 (Cases, p. 331), followed in *Re Watt's Will Trusts*, [1936] 2 All E.R. 1555; *Re Ransome*, [1957] Ch. 348.

of the infant, and, if possible, they should reach agreement with trustees of other funds applicable to the infant's maintenance, concerning the proportion to be borne by each fund. Where there is a surplus of income over expenditure for maintenance, this surplus is invested, and placed to capital, although at any time during infancy the trustees, if they wish, may use such accumulations as income. Section 31 (2) provides that if the infant beneficiary attains the age of twenty-one (now, under section 1 (3) of the Family Law Reform Act 1969, eighteen) years, or marries under that age, and his interest in such income during his infancy or until his marriage is a vested interest; or on attaining the age of eighteen years or on marriage under that age becomes entitled to the property from which such income arose in fee simple, absolute or determinable, or absolutely, or for an entailed interest, the trustees shall hold the accumulations in trust for such person absolutely. In any other case the trustees shall, notwithstanding that such person had a vested interest in such income, hold the accumulations as an accretion to the capital of the property from which such accumulations arose, and as one fund with such capital for all purposes.

The section applies only where the infant's interest carries the intermediate income of the property, but, unlike sections 42–43 of the Conveyancing Act of 1881, which it has replaced, it extends also to annuities. It should also be noticed that the trustees have power under section 31 to apply the income of contingent gifts for the maintenance of the infant, a provision which is repeated from the earlier Act, and which was described by Kay, L.J., in *Re Holford*[95] as " very arbitrary legislation," inasmuch as it allows the application for maintenance of income to which, if the infant never satisfies the contingency, he may never become entitled at all. Again, if a person for whose benefit the trustees have the power to apply income for maintenance does not acquire a vested interest at eighteen, it is provided by section 31 (1) (ii), a subsection which did not appear in the Conveyancing Act of 1881, that the beneficiary shall be entitled to the whole of the income, and of accretions thereto until the interest either fails, or becomes vested, or until the beneficiary dies. A further addition in section 31 is the proviso which directs trustees to have regard to the age of the infant, his general circumstances, and especially to what other income may be available for maintenance; and more particularly, if there are other trust funds available, the trustees should pay only a proportionate amount of the cost of maintenance. Whilst it should be remembered that payments are at the sole discretion of the trustees, that discretion must nevertheless be exercised, and in *Wilson* v. *Turner*,[96] the trustees, without exercising any discretion, paid the whole of the income to the infant's father, and the Court of Appeal held the father's estate liable to account for the income so received. So long as the trustee exercises his discretion in good faith, the court will not interfere with him in the exercise of this power.[97]

Subsection 31 (3) attempts to clarify the rules which decide whether gifts carry intermediate income or not, where nothing is expressed in the gift on

---

[95] [1894] 3 Ch. 30, 52.
[96] (1883), 22 Ch.D. 521.
[97] *Re Lofthouse* (1885), 29 Ch.D. 921 ; *Re Bryant*, [1894] 1 Ch. 324.

this point.[98] The language of the subsection is somewhat indirect, for it states—

> This section applies in the case of a contingent interest only if the limitation or trust carries the intermediate income of the property, but it applies to a future or contingent legacy by the parent of, or a person standing in loco parentis to, the legatee, if and for such period as, under the general law, the legacy carries interest for the maintenance of the legatee, and in any such case as last aforesaid the rate of interest shall (if the income available is sufficient, and subject to any rules of court to the contrary) be five pounds per centum per annum.

The Law of Property Act 1925, s. 175, provides that in respect of wills coming into operation after 1925, a contingent or future specific devise or bequest of property, real or personal, and a contingent residuary devise of freehold land to trustees on trust for persons whose interests are contingent or executory, carries the intermediate income, except so far as such income is otherwise expressly disposed of. It must be noticed that this section does not affect the rule that a contingent or future pecuniary legacy does not (in the absence of indication to the contrary) carry intermediate income. There exists, however, one exception to this rule: where in a will a father gives a pecuniary legacy to his son, or other person to whom he stands in loco parentis, upon a contingency which is either attaining an age not greater than full age, or marrying under that age, and no other sum is set aside in the will for the maintenance of the legatee, then in the absence of a contrary intention, that pecuniary legacy will be deemed to carry intermediate income.[99] This is the principle referred to in section 31 (3). The testator, however, may, by his will as a whole, demonstrate the intention that a child should be maintained out of the intermediate income of a pecuniary legacy, even when payment is postponed to some date after the child has attained his majority.[1]

Before 1926, a future or contingent devise, whether specific or residuary, did not carry the intermediate income, nor did future or contingent bequests of personalty unless either the gift was residuary, or the fund was directed in the will to be set aside for the beneficiary. Section 175 has therefore not altered the law governing interest on a future or contingent pecuniary legacy.

Section 175 does not make a vested future or deferred gift, whether or not it is defeasible, carry intermediate income, and that type of gift will not carry the intermediate income,[2] unless such an intention can be discovered from the words of the gift.[3] Where, therefore, such a gift is of residue, the income is undisposed of, and it will be dealt with as on intestacy, after it has been accumulated during the period in which the prior interests are in existence, or for 21 years, whichever is the shorter.

In Re McGeorge,[4] there was a pecuniary legacy with the proviso that it should not take effect until after the death of the testator's widow. There was

---

[98] For examples of language sufficient to carry intermediate income, see Re Churchill, [1909] 2 Ch. 431; Re Selby-Walker, [1949] 2 All E.R. 178.

[99] See Re Abrahams, [1911] 1 Ch. 108.

[1] Re Jones, [1932] 1 Ch. 642.

[2] Berry v. Geen, [1938] A.C. 575; Re Oliver, [1947] 2 All E.R. 162; Re Gillett's Will Trusts, [1950] Ch. 102.

[3] Re Geering, [1964] Ch. 136; Re Nash's Will Trusts, [1965] 1 W.L.R. 221.

[4] [1963] Ch. 544 (Cases, p. 325).

also a specific devise of agricultural land, with a proviso that if the devisee died in the lifetime either of the testator or of his widow, leaving issue, her issue could take in place of the devisee. The testator did not dispose of the income of either gift. Cross, J., held that both gifts were vested, but did not vest in possession until after the widow's death. The pecuniary legacy therefore did not carry interest until the date fixed for payment. The specific devise to the daughter was subject to a clause of defeasance, which could take effect in the widow's lifetime, and therefore although it carried the intermediate income under section 175 of the Law of Property Act 1925, that income must be accumulated, so that section 31 of the Trustee Act 1925 did not apply. Cross, J., also commented [5] upon one of the difficulties which had arisen in construing section 175—

> If a testator gives property to A after the death of B, then whether or not he disposes of the income accruing during B's life he is at all events showing clearly that A is not to have it. Yet if the future gift to A is absolute and the intermediate income is carried with it by force of this section, A can claim to have the property transferred to him at once, since no one else can be interested in it. The section, that is to say, will have converted a gift in remainder into a gift in possession in defiance of the testator's wishes. The explanation for the section taking the form it does is, I think, probably as follows. It has long been established that a gift of residuary personalty to a legatee in being on a contingency or to an unborn person at birth, carries the intermediate income so far as the law will allow it to be accumulated, but that rule has been held for reasons depending on the old land law not to apply to gifts of real property, and it was apparently never applied to specific dispositions of personalty. Section 175 of the Law of Property Act was plainly intended to extend the rule to residuary devises and to specific gifts whether of realty or of personalty. It is now, however, established at all events in courts of first instance that the old rule does not apply to residuary bequests whether vested or contingent which are expressly deferred to a future date which must come sooner or later.[6] There is a good reason for this distinction. If a testator gives property to X contingently on his attaining the age of 30 it is reasonable to assume, in the absence of a direction to the contrary, that he would wish X if he attains 30 to have the income produced by the property between his death and the happening of the contingency. If, on the other hand, he gives property to X for any sort of interest after the death of A, it is reasonable to assume that he does not wish X to have the income accruing during A's lifetime unless he directs that he is to have it. But this distinction between an immediate gift on a contingency and a gift which is expressly deferred was not drawn until after the Law of Property Act, 1925, was passed. There were statements in textbooks and even in judgments to the effect that the rule applied to deferred as well as to contingent gifts of residuary personalty.

---

5 [1963] Ch. 550–2.
6 *Re Oliver*, [1947] 2 All E.R. 162; *Re Gillett's Will Trusts*, [1950] Ch. 102; *Re Geering*, [1964] Ch. 136.

The legislature, when it extended this rule to residuary devises and specific gifts, must, I think, have adopted this erroneous view of the law. I would have liked, if I could, to construe the reference to " future specific devises " and " executory interest " in the section in such a way as to make it consistent with the recent cases on the scope of the old rule applicable to residuary bequests. But to do that would be to rectify the Act, not to construe it, and I see no escape from the conclusion that whereas before 1926 a specific or a residuary devise which was not vested in possession did not prima facie carry intermediate income at all, now such a gift may carry intermediate income in circumstances in which a residuary bequest would not carry it.

A contingent entailed interest, whether in realty or personalty, does not carry the intermediate income.[7]

The trustee's power to grant income for maintenance is made " subject to any prior interests or charges," so that a remainderman cannot be maintained out of the income of the tenant for life, without the latter's consent. If there is contained in the trust instrument an express trust for the accumulation of the income of a beneficiary's share, this will exclude the statutory power of maintenance,[8] but a direction to accumulate will not be implied merely from the absence of an express direction that the gift is to carry intermediate income.[9]

The receipt of the parent or guardian is a sufficient discharge of the trustee, and the Law of Property Act 1925, s. 21, now provides that a *married* infant can give the receipts for income.

In *Lowther* v. *Bentinck*,[10] where, however, the beneficiary was a man of thirty who had been married three years, it was held that payment of the beneficiary's debts was for his " benefit," within the meaning of an express advancement clause. Normally, however, this would not be a proper exercise of a power confined to " advancement," [11] nor is paying a person's debts necessarily for his " benefit." [12]

A complicated question of maintenance may arise where property is settled upon a class of such children as shall attain the age of majority, in equal shares, so that each child shall receive a proportionate share of the income on attaining full age, as if the class were then closed. In *Re King*,[13] where such a settlement was executed, Romer, J., ordered an apportionment of income for such members of the class as had attained twenty-one, on the basis of the number of children then existing. If the class subsequently increased, the income payable to those members who had attained 21 would be proportionately diminished. Further, in the case of those members of the class who had not attained 21, there would be a provisional division of the income, with the possibility that the proportion would diminish as from the birth of another member of the class; but the effect of such

---

[7] *Re Crossley's Settlement Trusts*, [1955] Ch. 627.
[8] *Re Alford* (1886), 32 Ch.D. 383 ; *Re Reade-Revell*, [1930] 1 Ch. 52 ; *Re Stapleton*, [1946] 1 All E.R. 323.
[9] *Re Leng*, [1938] Ch. 821.
[10] (1874), L.R. 19 Eq. 166.
[11] *Luard* v. *Pease* (1853), 22 L.J.Ch. 1069.
[12] *Re Price* (1887), 34 Ch.D. 603.
[13] [1928] Ch. 330.

provisional assignment of income to infant beneficiaries is to permit maintenance under section 31 of the Trustee Act 1925.

Re King was a decision upon a settlement governed by section 43 of the Conveyancing Act 1881, and in *Re Joel's Will Trusts*,[14] Goff, J., explored in detail the effect of the differences in wording between that section and section 31 of the Trustee Act 1925 in so far as they dealt with gifts to a class which varied in number. In *Re Joel's Will Trusts*, there were five young grandchildren at the time when exercise of a power of appointment constituted them beneficiaries with contingent interests, and three other grandchildren were subsequently born and added to the class. Goff, J., held that the shares of the infants (and hence the amount of income available for maintenance) were initially established when the appointment was made, and were subject to modification whenever the class was extended. If a grandchild died before obtaining a vested interest, the accumulations of income attributable to that grandchild's contingent share in the capital of the fund had to be dealt with in accordance with section 31 (2) (ii) of the Trustee Act 1925, the investments representing the accumulation of income being added to the general capital of the fund, notwithstanding that a grandchild born subsequently would acquire an interest in capital due to interest which arose before he was born. It was not, as Romer, J., in *Re King*[15] had suggested on section 43 of the Conveyancing Act 1881, reallocated on failure of the infant's contingent interest in the capital. Section 31 (2) permitted maintenance out of the income of a contingent interest, and accumulation of the balance of unapplied income. If the contingent interest failed, section 31 (2) (ii) nevertheless still governed the destination of the allocated income.

So long as the infant beneficiary's interest is liable to be modified by a future appointment to another beneficiary or by failure of the beneficiary to satisfy a condition, his interest cannot be said to be enjoyed by him " absolutely," as required by section 31 (2) (i) (*b*). In *Re Sharp's Settlement Trusts*,[16] a power of appointment had been given to trustees, exercisable amongst a class of beneficiaries, and in default of appointment, the fund was to be held in trust for such of the settlor's children as attained 21 in equal shares. All contingent interests carried the intermediate income. There was one exercise of the power of appointment, and the settlor had three children, P, R and J, and was unlikely to have more. The income of the fund had been allocated to the three children in equal shares. P was 21, and the income was paid directly to her. R attained the age of 21 in 1967, but before that date, his share had been accumulated. J was still under 21, and her share (subject to maintenance) was also being accumulated. Pennycuick, V.-C., held, following *Re King*[15] and *Re Joel's Will Trusts*,[17] that the accumulations did not form an accretion to the general corpus of the fund, but were held for R and J, subject to any future exercise of the power of appointment, and in J's case, subject to her attaining 21, as then provided in section 31 (2) (i) (*b*).

14 [1967] Ch. 14.
15 [1928] Ch. 330.
16 [1973] Ch. 331.
17 [1967] Ch. 14.

There is also another section of the Trustee Act 1925 of which advantage may be taken to provide money for the maintenance of an infant. Section 53 states that where an infant is beneficially entitled to any property, the court may, with a view to the application of the capital or income thereof for the maintenance, education or benefit of the infant, make an order appointing a person to convey such property. In *Re Gower's Settlement*,[18] Clauson, J., decided that advantage may be taken of the section to authorise the mortgage of an infant's entailed interest in remainder for the purpose of providing money for the maintenance of the infant, so as to bar the infant tenant in tail's issue and subsequent remaindermen as effectively as if the infant had been of full age, and had executed the required disentailing assurance.

Two general points on this section should be noticed—

(*a*) Section 31 of the Trustee Act relates only to the employment of income for maintenance, whilst section 53 permits capital to be used for that purpose in circumstances where there is no intermediate income.

(*b*) Section 31 can be utilised by the trustees entirely of their own discretion. Under section 53, an application to the court is necessary.

The existence of section 53 prompts the inquiry whether, apart from this section, capital can be applied for maintenance. Where the infant's interest is small, the court has frequently made such an order,[19] provided that the interest is in personalty. A similar order was made in respect of an infant's freehold estate in *Re Howarth*,[20] but in *Re Hambrough's Estate*[21] it was held that the court could not direct the execution of a disentailing assurance to effect a mortgage of the equitable interest of an infant tenant in tail. In this respect, therefore, the position is now altered by section 53 of the Trustee Act 1925, under which the court acted in *Re Gower's Settlement*.[22]

Whether the trustee or executor can himself make provision for maintenance out of capital without recourse to the court would appear to be very doubtful.

In *Lee* v. *Brown*,[23] Arden, M.R., said—

> . . . that principle has been established . . . that if an executor does without application what the Court would have approved, he shall not be called to account, and forced to undo that, merely because it was done without application.

This was a decision on a power of advancement, but it is an observation which must clearly be confined within limits, otherwise it might be construed as authorising an executor or trustee to purchase the trust property. In *Barlow* v. *Grant*[24] Lord Guildford, L.K., allowed an advancement of £16 a year for maintenance out of a legacy of £100, but in *Walker* v. *Wetherell*[25] Sir W. Grant said that executors and trustees could not do this without the sanction of the court, and the court would be reluctant to give

---

[18] [1934] Ch. 365. See also *Re Heyworth's Contingent Reversionary Interest*, [1956] Ch. 364.
[19] *Ex parte Green* (1820), 1 Jac. & W. 253; *Ex parte Swift* (1828), 1 Russ. & M. 575; *Ex parte Chambers* (1829), 1 Russ. & M. 577.
[20] (1873), L.R. 8 Ch.App. 415.
[21] [1909] 2 Ch. 620.
[22] [1934] Ch. 365.
[23] (1798), 4 Ves. 362, 369.
[24] (1684), 1 Vern. 255.
[25] (1801), 6 Ves. 473, 474.

its permission. The question is now of little importance in view of the statutory power enjoyed by the court under section 53 of the Trustee Act 1925.

3. THE POWER OF ADVANCEMENT [26]

(a) *The Statutory Power.* A new statutory power of advancement was conferred on trustees by section 32. Before 1926, it was customary to include an express power in the settlement, and even in the absence of such a power, the court would sanction an advance in a proper case. Now, however, a wide power has been conferred *in respect of personalty settlements* created after 1925,[27] including settlements contained in wills coming into effect after 1925, although made before 1926.[28] By virtue of the power given by section 32, trustees may pay up to half the beneficiary's share by way of advancement, whether the share is vested or contingent, and whether or not the interest is liable to be defeated by the exercise of a power of appointment or revocation. All sums advanced must be brought into account as part of the share, and no advancement may be made to prejudice any person entitled to a prior interest, unless that person is in existence and is of full age, and consents in writing to the advancement.

Section 32 speaks of " advancement or benefit," and in *Re Moxon's Will Trusts*,[29] Danckwerts, J., pointed out that the word " benefit " is the widest possible word, and it includes payments direct to the beneficiary. Nevertheless, the word does not absolve the trustees from making up their minds whether the payment as contemplated was for the benefit of the person advanced. Accordingly, where trustees knew that an advancement to a beneficiary was to be used for other purposes, they were held liable to repay the sum advanced.[30]

In *Pilkington* v. *I.R.C.*[31] Lord Radcliffe explained that the word " advancement " meant " the establishment in life of the beneficiary who was the object of the power or at any rate some step that would contribute to the furtherance of his establishment." He added that in nineteenth century conveyancing practice it had frequently been used in conjunction with other words of wide meaning, *e.g.* preferment or benefit. He also described an advancement as " any use of the money which will improve the material situation of the beneficiary." This, in the case of a wealthy person, could cover a gift to charity by the trustees on his behalf, where the beneficiary accepted a moral obligation to contribute.[32] The power is commonly—and validly—exercised to diminish the incidence of estate duty, by taking half the remainderman's share of the capital out of the trust at least seven years before the death of the tenant for life.[33]

---

[26] For a full discussion, see Waters, " The ' New ' Power of Advancement " (1958) 22 *Conveyancer* 413 ; Waters, " The Creation of Sub-trusts under a Power of Advancement " (1959) 23 *Conv.* 27 ; Waters, " *Re* Pilkington's Will Trusts : A Comment " (1959) 23 *Conv.* 423.
[27] *Re Batty*, [1952] Ch. 280 ; *Re Bransbury*, [1954] 1 W.L.R. 496.
[28] *Re Taylor's Will Trusts* (1950), 66 T.L.R. (Pt. 2) 507.
[29] [1958] 1 W.L.R. 165.
[30] *Re Pauling's Settlement Trusts*, [1964] Ch. 303.
[31] [1964] A.C. 612, 633 (Cases, p. 336).
[32] *Re Clore's Settlement Trusts*, [1966] 1 W.L.R. 955.
[33] For an example, see *Re Hastings-Bass*, [1974] 2 W.L.R. 904 (C.A.).

The statutory power applies only in so far as a contrary intention is not expressed in the instrument, and it takes effect subject to any terms there expressed.[34]

The effect of this section has therefore been to make the insertion of a power of advancement unnecessary in trusts of personalty, except where it is desired to vary the powers conferred by the section, but the power should be retained in settlements of land. What constitutes an advancement necessarily depends upon the circumstances of the transaction. In *Taylor* v. *Taylor*,[35] it was said that an advancement by way of portion was something given by a parent to establish the child in life, as distinct from a casual payment,[36] and sums given on marriage, or on entry into a profession, or to purchase a business, or to supply further capital for a business have at various times been considered to be advancements. Small sums or temporary assistance are, however, outside the scope of the provision. In *Taylor* v. *Taylor*,[35] it was held that a father's discharge of his son's debts did not constitute an advancement, but in *Re Blockley*[37] Pearson, J., was of opinion that a sum given by a father to his son to pay his debts could be so considered. It is submitted that there is no real conflict here, as the circumstances of one transaction might easily preclude it from being so considered, although in the other case, the nature of the debts and their amount might point to the fact that a discharge of them amounted to an advancement of the son.

In *Re Stimpson's Trusts*,[38] it was held that this section applied to land held on trust for sale, or the proceeds of sale, and in the same case it was pointed out that where the settlement provides that the interest of the tenant for life is given over on assignment, the giving of his consent to the advancement may occasion a forfeiture of his interest.[39]

In *Re Garrett*[40] Clauson, J., decided that the statutory power of advancement can be exercised in favour of an infant, although his interest is contingent upon the double event of attaining the age of twenty-one, and of surviving a previous life tenant.

Problems not infrequently arise where the prior interest is a protected life interest. Where the protected life interest is created under section 33 of the Trustee Act 1925, and the advancement is under section 32, consent by the tenant for life does not forfeit the interest of the tenant for life[41]; nor will it where the power of advancement is an express power. If the trust deed contains both a protected life interest and an express power of advancement, then " the consent to the exercise of one does not lead to the forfeiture by the consenting party of his life interest under the other." [42]

In *Re Craven's Estate* (*No. 2*),[43] there was an express power of advancement contained in a will, but limited by a proviso permitting advancement

[34] Trustee Act 1925, s. 69 (2). See p. 299, *post*.
[35] (1875), L.R. 20 Eq. 155.
[36] See also *Boyd* v. *Boyd* (1867), L.R. 4 Eq. 305; *Roper-Curzon* v. *Roper-Curzon* (1871). L.R. 11 Eq. 452; *Re Mead* (1918), 88 L.J. Ch. 86; *Pilkington* v. *I.R.C.*, [1964] A.C. 612.
[37] (1885), 29 Ch.D. 250.
[38] [1931] 2 Ch. 77.
[39] See, however, *Re Hodgson*, [1913] 1 Ch. 34.
[40] [1934] Ch. 477.
[41] Trustee Act 1925, s. 33 (1); *Re Rees*, [1954] Ch. 202.
[42] *Per* Harman, J., in *Re Shaw's Settlement*, [1951] Ch. 833, 840.
[43] [1937] Ch. 431.

only for one or more of the following purposes: (a) the purchase of a dwelling-house; (b) the purchase of a business or share in a business; (c) the purchase of an annuity; (d) the payment of the expenses of an illness or serious operation. The court held that this power would not cover the application of a sum of money by way of a deposit to permit the beneficiary to become a Lloyd's underwriter; and it was also held that the court could not sanction the transaction under section 57. For transactions to be approved under this section, they must be for the benefit of the trust as a whole, and not for a particular beneficiary alone.[44]

In *Re Collard's Will Trusts* [45] the statutory power of advancement was incorporated into the settlement by will of real and personal property, but with a proviso that no advancement should be made to a beneficiary for any purpose connected with business. Buckley, J., decided that, in order to avoid circuity of action, the trustees could advance land directly to a beneficiary, since they would have had power to advance money, and then sell him the land. He also held that an advancement made to avoid death duty was not an advancement connected with business (which would have been excluded from the ambit of the power).

An unusual problem relating to the effect of the statutory power of advancement upon a provision to accumulate income during the settlor's life was decided by the Court of Appeal in *I.R.C.* v. *Bernstein.*[46] The settlor, William Bernstein, in 1947, settled a fund on trust to accumulate the income during his life, and after his death on trust as to one-third for the children then living of the settlor by a specified beneficiary (who subsequently became his wife), and as to two-thirds, for that beneficiary absolutely. If the beneficiary died during the settlor's lifetime, the fund was to be held on trust for her children, living at the settlor's death, but if at his death there were living no children of himself and the beneficiary, then the fund was to be held on trust for the beneficiary absolutely. If she should die during the testator's lifetime and there were no children, then the fund was to be held on trust for the beneficiary's sister absolutely. The Inland Revenue Commissioners assessed the settlor to surtax in respect of income arising under the settlement, contending that by virtue of the statutory power of advancement under section 32 of the Trustee Act 1925 one-half of the property comprised in the settlement might become applicable for the benefit of the beneficiary, who had become the settlor's wife, and accordingly, one-half of the income of the settlement was under section 405 of the Income Tax Act 1952 to be regarded as the settlor's income. The Court of Appeal held that the trust for the accumulation of income during the settlor's lifetime showed an intention which conflicted with the power of advancement conferred by section 32 (1), which was accordingly excluded. The claim for tax therefore failed.

(b) *Special Powers of Advancement.* Notwithstanding the existence of

44 In *Re Forster's Settlement*, [1942] Ch. 199, the settlement contained a special power of advancement with the consent of the tenant for life, who was an enemy alien. It was held that the court could not direct the exercise of the power, without the consent of the tenant for life, which could not be given.

45 [1961] Ch. 293.

46 [1961] Ch. 399. As to when an express power of advancement will impliedly exclude the statutory power, see *Re Evans's Settlement*, [1967] 1 W.L.R. 1294.

the statutory power of advancement, special powers in trust instruments are common. A special power may be given where it is desired to give power to advance more than one-half of the interest, or where it is desired to give the power to the trustees independently of the tenant for life, or where there is a strict settlement of realty, or finally in instruments executed before 1926. If the special clause speaks of " advancement and benefit," the courts have held that " benefit " extends the possible purposes for which it may be used.[47] In *Re Bainbridge* [48] two powers of advancement were inserted in a will dated August 6, 1910. One power authorised the trustees to raise up to one-half of the expectant share of " any minor " for his advancement. The other was in the following terms: " From and after the death of my daughter . . . as to as well the capital as the income thereof upon trust for all or such one or more exclusively of the others or other of the children or remoter issue of my daughter . . . (such remoter issue to be born and take vested interests within 21 years after her death) at such age or time or respective ages or times if more than one in such shares and with such future or other trusts for their benefit and such provision for their respective advancement maintenance and education at the discretion of either my trustees or of any other persons or person and in such manner in all respects as my daughter . . . whether covert or discovert shall by any deed or deeds revocable or irrevocable or by will or codicil appoint." It was held that this power of advancement was not exercisable during the lifetime of the daughter, the tenant for life.

Whether the power of advancement is one conferred by section 32 or is a special power, it is also a fiduciary power, which can be exercised only for the benefit of the person advanced. It may be exercised by making either an out and out payment, or one for a specified purpose. Where the payment is made for a specified purpose, then it is the duty of the trustee to make reasonably sure that the specified purpose will be carried out.[49]

Several points affecting special powers of advancement were discussed in *Re Wills' Will Trusts*,[50] but possibly the one of most general interest was whether the trustees, in making an advancement, might create sub-trusts. The decisions have not always appeared to be entirely consistent, but Upjohn, J., pointed out that there are now a number of reported cases in which the courts have held that trustees may properly settle funds advanced under special powers of advancement. Of these *Roper-Curzon* v. *Roper-Curzon* [51] is the earliest and most interesting. In that case power was given to advance a son " for his advancement or preferment in the world." The son, after his marriage, and whilst studying for the law, asked for an advancement, and Lord Romilly, M.R., only approved the application when the son agreed to settle the funds advanced. Again in *Re Halsted's Will Trusts*,[52] there was a special power of advancement, and Farwell, J., decided that the trustees, in making an advancement, might settle a sum on the person advanced in order to benefit him, his wife and children, with an ultimate trust

47 *Re Halsted's Will Trusts*, [1937] 2 All E.R. 570.
48 [1948] Ch. 717.
49 *Re Pauling's Settlement Trusts*, [1964] Ch. 303.
50 [1959] Ch. 1.
51 (1871), L.R. 11 Eq. 452.
52 [1937] 2 All E.R. 570.

for the residue of the testator's estate. This case, it will be seen, raises the highly interesting question whether, in an advancement, there could be a settlement upon protective trusts, which, it is submitted, finds an answer in *Re Wills' Will Trusts.*

In *Re Ropner's Settlement Trusts,*[53] Harman, J., decided that under a special advancement clause trustees might settle the property upon the beneficiary to be advanced, for the purpose of avoiding heavy death duties. Harman, J., pointed out that it made no difference whether the person advanced was an infant or an adult. The test is whether the advancement will benefit the beneficiary. *Re Ropner* has also another point of interest. The tenant for life, whose consent was necessary for the advancement, had a protected life interest, and as counsel pointed out, a consent by him did not bring about a forfeiture of his life interest.

In *Re Meux*[54] there was a settlement of a sum raised under section 53, and Wynn-Parry, J., pointed out that it was the fact of settlement for the infant's benefit which distinguished this case from *Re Heyworth's Contingent Reversionary Interest,*[55] where Upjohn, J., refused to consent under section 53, since all that it was proposed to do was to hand over a cash sum to the infant absolutely. In *Re Meux*[54] there was extended discussion of what was meant by the phrase in section 53: " with a view to the application of the capital or income thereof for the maintenance, education, or benefit of the infant," and Wynn-Parry, J., quoted[56] Upjohn, J.'s words[57] in the former case—

> It covers not merely expenditure but capital investment such as the purchase of a house to live in or a share in a partnership, or even in some cases placing of money on deposit for an infant.[58] However, to bring the jurisdiction into play, there must be " a view to the application " of the capital or income for the maintenance, education or benefit of the infant. Mr. Jennings concedes that that phrase is equivalent to " for the purpose of applying." Shorn of the niceties of legal argument, this deed is intended to put an end to the trusts created by the settlement, by enlarging the interest of the life tenant to include some or all of the reversioners' interests by means of a sale of those reversionary interests for cash. The infant (inter alios) receives an immediate absolute interest in a sum of cash in exchange for a future contingent interest. The deed is not in the least degree entered into with a view to the application of, or for the purpose of applying, any capital or income of the infant for her benefit. If I sanctioned this scheme on behalf of the infant I should be reading the section as though it empowered the court to convey the property of an infant whenever it was for her benefit. Unfortunately the section only confers a more limited jurisdiction.

Of the decision in *Re Meux,*[54] Upjohn, J., said in *Re Wills' Will Trusts*[59]—

> . . . I think it is clear that Wynn-Parry J. would have come to a similar conclusion upon section 32 of the same Act. I have seen the settlement

[53] [1956] 1 W.L.R. 902.
[54] [1958] Ch. 154.
[55] [1956] Ch. 364.
[56] [1958] Ch. 165–6.
[57] [1956] Ch. 370.
[58] *Re Baron Vestey's Settlement,* [1951] Ch. 209.   [59] [1959] Ch. 1, 12.

approved by the judge. It was of the simplest kind and as stated in the judgment, it merely excluded the plaintiff's life interest and substituted an estate tail contingent on attaining 21 for a vested estate tail in the first defendant.

In *Re Lansdowne's Will Trusts* [60] Buckley, J., held that an application to disentail an infant's entailed interest as part of a variation of the trust under the Variation of Trusts Act 1958 was an application for the benefit of the infant under section 53.

In *Re Wills' Will Trusts* [61] it was argued by counsel that, on a true view of section 32, and in spite of decisions such as *Roper-Curzon* v. *Roper-Curzon* [62] and *Re Ropner*,[63] there was no power on the part of trustees to advance money by way of settlement. The problem, of course, is a different one under section 32, from that under section 53, for under section 32, the trustees may exercise their discretion without obtaining the court's sanction, which is required in section 53. On this point, Upjohn, J., said [64]—

> . . . these authorities do establish the proposition that trustees exercising a power of advancement may make settlements upon objects of the power if the particular circumstances of the case warrant that course as being for the benefit of the object of the power. What the authorities typified by *In re May*,[65] and *In re Mewburn* [66] establish to my mind is that any settlement made by way of advancement upon an object of the power by trustees must not conflict with the principle delegatus non potest delegare. Thus, unless upon its proper construction the power of advancement permits delegation of powers and discretions, a settlement created in exercise of the power of advancement cannot in general delegate any powers or discretions, at any rate in relation to beneficial interests, to any trustees or other persons, and in so far as the settlement purports to do so it is pro tanto invalid.

This would seem to give the answer to the question mentioned above, arising out of *Re Halsted's Will Trusts*,[67] *i.e.* whether trustees in making an advancement could make a settlement upon protective trusts. Subject to the qualifications which Upjohn, J., mentions, it would seem that they could not, since they would, in the event of the discretionary trust arising, be conferring on other trustees discretions which they should retain for themselves.

The question of sub-trusts was again considered, this time by the House of Lords, in *Pilkington* v. *I.R.C.*[68] This, however, was a decision upon the statutory power. The trustees of the settlement, for the purpose of avoiding death duties, wished to exercise the statutory power by placing the sum advanced within a new settlement, the income of which would be applied for the maintenance of the beneficiary until she was twenty-one, and thereafter, the income

60 [1967] Ch. 603.
61 [1959] Ch. 1.
62 (1871), L.R. 11 Eq. 452.
63 [1956] 1 W.L.R. 902.
64 [1959] Ch. 12–13.
65 [1926] Ch. 136.
66 [1934] Ch. 112.
67 [1937] 2 All E.R. 570.
68 [1964] A.C. 612 (Cases, p. 336). See also *Re Abrahams' Will Trusts*, [1969] 1 Ch. 463.

would be paid to her until she was thirty, when the capital would be paid over to her. If she should die under that age, the fund would be held for those of her children who should attain the age of twenty-one. The House of Lords held that there was nothing in section 32 which restricted the width or purpose of advancement. In particular, where an advancement was made to benefit a person, there was no ground for objection in the circumstance that others might also benefit, or where the money advanced was resettled. However, the exercise of the statutory power by paying money to be resettled is exercise of a special power, and must therefore conform to the rule against remoteness in the form in which it is applicable to special powers. Another such case on the statutory power is *Re Hastings-Bass*,[69] where the Court of Appeal held that the fact that the sub-settlement declared no effective beneficial trusts of capital, but created only a limited beneficial interest in income, did not deprive the transaction of the character of a valid exercise of the power of advancement.[70] They also decided that where some of the beneficial interests under the sub-settlement were void for perpetuity, other such interests not themselves infringing the rule could stand where, as here, those parts of the sub-settlement left standing were for the benefit of the remainderman within the meaning of section 32.

4. OTHER MATTERS AFFECTING PAYMENTS BY A TRUSTEE

Instead of receiving trust money in person, a beneficiary may appoint an agent or attorney to receive it on his behalf, and the authority of the agent need not necessarily arise from a deed or writing. Nevertheless, the trustee must ensure in such cases that the purported authority is genuine, for if the trustee pays on the strength of it, and the beneficiary in fact gave no such authority, the trustee is liable to the beneficiary.[71]

When the whole estate has been distributed, it is customary for the trustees to be released from all future claims. The release is usually by deed (at the expense of the trust fund) following an examination and settlement of the trust accounts, but it would seem that in strictness, in the absence of special circumstances, the trustee is not entitled to a release under seal even though such release is customarily given.[72] Thus, Kindersley, V.-C., said in *King* v. *Mullins*[73]—

> . . . in the case of a declared trust; where the trust is apparent on the face of a deed; the fund clear; the trust clearly defined: and the trustee is paying either the income or the capital or the fund; if he is paying it in strict accordance with the trusts, he has no right to require a release under seal. It is true that in the common case of executors, when the executorship is being wound up, it is the practice to give executors a release. An executor has a right to be clearly discharged, and not to be left in a posi-

---

[69] [1974] 2 W.L.R. 904.
[70] [1974] 2 W.L.R. 915, *per* Buckley, L.J., giving the judgment of the court.
[71] *Ashby* v. *Blackwell* (1765), 2 Eden 299. See also *Sloman* v. *Bank of England* (1845), 14 Sim. 475; *Welch* v. *Bank of England*, [1955] Ch. 508. As to the revocation, or attempted revocation of a power of attorney, the trustee not knowing of the revocation or attempt, see the Powers of Attorney Act 1971, ss. 4–6.
[72] *Re Cater's Trusts (No. 2)* (1858), 25 Beav. 366.
[73] (1852), 1 Drew. 308, 311. See also *Chadwick* v. *Heatley* (1845), 2 Coll. 137.

tion in which he may be exposed to further litigation; therefore he fairly says, unless you give me a discharge on the face of it protecting me, I cannot safely hand over the fund; and therefore it is usual to give a release; but such a claim on the part of a trustee would in strictness be improper, if he is paying in accordance with the letter of the trust. In such a case he would have no right to a release.

Before the trustees receive their discharge, they must allow the beneficiaries time to investigate the accounts [74] and any breaches of trust must be fully disclosed.[75]

If a release is given by a beneficiary who has just attained the age of majority, it may be advisable for him to be separately advised. Otherwise a question of undue influence may arise later.[76]

Where there is any doubt as to the proper persons to whom to pay trust money, the trustee, as an alternative to payment of the sum into court under section 63, or in cases where this would not be appropriate, may proceed to the determination of the question by way of originating summons. This enables trustees, executors, administrators, or their beneficiaries to procure the determination, without administration by the court of the estate or trust, of a number of questions arising out of or affecting trusts or persons interested in trusts, or to obtain an order for the administration of the estate without the formalities of an action. This mode of procedure is not applicable to questions of breach of trust, however, except by consent,[77] nor does the procedure apply where a person is claiming against the settlement. The procedure was formerly regarded as applicable only for the determination of simple questions,[78] but the present test is whether there is a conflict of evidence. In this connection it should be noticed that a clause has sometimes been inserted into a trust deed, giving a power to trustees to decide any doubt as to the identity of a beneficiary. Warrington, J., in *Re Raven*,[79] decided that such a clause was void in so far as it attempted to oust the jurisdiction of the court.

It remains to mention the " hotchpot clause," which is very frequently inserted in settlements for the purpose of producing an equality of distribution among beneficiaries, usually children or other issue. The chief question which arises for consideration in applying this clause is whether those beneficiaries who have been advanced must be charged with interest in bringing the sums they have already received into account. In *Re Rees* [80] and *Re Dallmeyer*,[81] the rule laid down was that where the testator makes an ordinary direction as to hotchpot, the interest is only chargeable on advances from the date of distribution (which, if there is a prior life interest, may obviously be postponed for a considerable period after the testator's death), and not from the date of advancement, whether the advancement was made by trustees in pursuance of the testator's directions, or by the testator himself in his lifetime. The rule

---

[74] *Wedderburn* v. *Wedderburn* (1838), 4 My. & Cr. 41, 50–1.
[75] *Cole* v. *Gibson* (1750), 1 Ves.Sen. 503, 507; *Walker* v. *Symonds* (1818), 3 Swanst. 1, 58.
[76] *Re Garnett* (1885), 31 Ch.D. 1.
[77] *Per* Lord Macnaghten in *Dowse* v. *Gorton*, [1891] A.C. 190, 202.
[78] *Re Giles* (1890), 43 Ch.D. 391; *Re Hargreaves* (1890), 43 Ch.D. 401.
[79] [1915] 1 Ch. 673.
[80] (1881), 17 Ch.D. 701.
[81] [1896] 1 Ch. 372.

was applied by Sargant, J., in *Re Forster-Brown*,[82] where a will contained a power of advancement and also a provision that advances should be brought into hotchpot on distribution of the fund. Furthermore, if the testator directs accumulation for a period after his death, the end of the period of accumulation is the date of distribution, and the estate for division is the amount of the estate at the expiration of the period of accumulation, not at the testator's death. For valuing the advance which has been made, the amount of the advance is calculated at the time when it was made, and not at the time of the testator's death or the date of distribution, so that if an encumbrance has been paid off by the child advanced, this must obviously be deducted.[83]

Sometimes life interests and reversionary interests have to be brought into hotchpot. The computation of these is frequently difficult, and there seems to be no uniform rule. If the actual value of the life interest is for any reason (*e.g.* death of the life tenant) precisely ascertainable, this is taken, otherwise the actuarial value must be accepted.[84]

[82] [1914] 2 Ch. 584.
[83] *Re Beddington*, [1900] 1 Ch. 771 ; *Re Crocker*, [1916] 1 Ch. 25.
[84] *Eales* v. *Drake* (1875), 1 Ch.D. 217 ; *Wheeler* v. *Humphreys*, [1898] A.C. 506 ; *Re Metcalf*, [1903] 2 Ch. 424 ; *Re West*, [1921] 1 Ch. 533 ; *Re North Settled Estates*, [1946] Ch. 13 ; *Re Thomson Settlement Trusts*, [1953] Ch. 414. In the valuation of advances for the purposes of the Administration of Estates Act 1925 different rules are applied.

CHAPTER XIX

THE TRUSTEE'S POWERS AND DUTIES IN THE
ADMINISTRATION OF A TRUST—*(continued)*

" A TRUSTEE MAY NOT PROFIT FROM HIS TRUST "

THE general rule that a trustee may not profit from his trust, and the corollary that if he does, he holds any profit so derived as a constructive trustee for his beneficiaries, has already been considered in discussing constructive trusts. Accordingly, it remains only to consider here the scope of the rule, which is very wide.[1] Three main aspects of the rule require separate treatment—

1. Derivation of a direct profit by the trustee from handling the trust property.

2. Sale of trust property by a trustee to himself or to a co-trustee; with a consideration of the circumstances in which a trustee may purchase a beneficiary's interest.

3. Payment of trustees for services rendered.

A. DERIVATION OF A DIRECT PROFIT

This would obviously be a violation of the fiduciary relation which exists for the benefit of the *cestui que trust,* and not for the benefit of the trustee. A good illustration is furnished by *Williams* v. *Barton,*[2] wherein a stockbroker's clerk, whose salary consisted of half the commission earned on business introduced by him, was held liable to account to a trust estate, of which he was a trustee, for the amount paid to him in respect of the business of the trust estate which he had introduced to the firm. This case should be distinguished from an earlier one, *Re Dover Coalfield Extension Ltd.,*[3] in which a trustee, whose qualification as director of a company was certain trust shares, was held to be under no obligation to account to the trust estate for his salary as director, since the salary was paid to him for personal services and qualities, and was not a profit from the handling of the shares. In reaching their decision, the Court of Appeal do not seem to have taken into account the decision of Kekewich, J., in *Re Francis,*[4] which was not cited. In that case, trustees held shares in a company, by virtue of which holding they became directors of the company. The learned judge held that they must account for their directors' fees to the trust estate, and that the sums so received must be treated as capital. The ground of the distinction between the two cases seems to be that in *Re Francis* the holding of the shares gave the trustees enough votes to elect themselves to directorships, whilst in the later case, it gave them the qualification, but they had been elected to office before they held any

---

[1] The question is discussed by Marshall, " Conflict of Interest and Duty " (1955) 8 *Current Legal Problems* 91.
[2] [1927] 2 Ch. 9.
[3] [1908] 1 Ch. 65.
[4] (1905), 74 L.J. Ch. 198.

trust shares, and these were registered in their names to enable them to continue as directors, so it was not by virtue of these shares that they then became entitled or continued to earn their fees.[5]

The matter cannot be regarded as finally settled yet, however, for in *Re Macadam*,[6] trustees who elected themselves directors were held liable to account to the trust estate for their fees; whilst, in *Re Gee*,[7] Harman, J., distinguishing *Re Dover Coalfield Extension Ltd.*,[8] and *Williams* v. *Barton*,[9] held that a trustee who is elected a director may retain his director's fees, even if he cast trust votes in favour of his own appointment, at least in cases where he would have been elected even if he had cast the trust votes for another candidate.

Furthermore, a trustee may not enter into competition with his trust, for he is placing himself in a position where his interest and his duty conflict. In *Re Thomson*,[10] the defendant was one of the executors and trustees of a will, in which a yachtbroker's business was bequeathed with instructions to the trustees to continue it. The defendant claimed the right to carry on a similar business in competition with the testator's, but the court restrained him. It should be noticed: (1) that the nature of the business was such as to render competition within the same town inevitable; and (2) the trustee opened the business after accepting the trust. Had the testator appointed the defendant his trustee knowing that the trustee conducted a business in competition with his own, the attitude of the court might have been different.

Again, in *Webb* v. *Earl of Shaftesbury*,[11] where valuable sporting rights were attached to a trust estate, Lord Eldon directed an inquiry whether these could be let for the profit of the beneficiaries. If they could not, the rights could not be enjoyed by the trustees. They should be held for the benefit of the heir. There was no discussion in the decision whether the trustees could have hired the sporting rights in default of other tenants, but on general principles it would seem that they could not. In *Pooley* v. *Quilter*,[12] it was held that if trustees or executors bought up debts or encumbrances to which the trust estate was subject for less than was actually due, they held the profit for the appropriate beneficiaries. The same rule also applies to dealings by a solicitor in respect of the property of his client.[13]

If an advowson forms part of an estate held on trust for sale, then, pending sale, the right of presentation is in the beneficiaries under the trust, not in the heir or other person entitled under a resulting trust.[14] In *Johnstone* v. *Baber*,[15] the beneficiaries were tenants in common, and it was held they must cast lots for the right to present.

In *Sugden* v. *Crossland*,[16] an incoming trustee paid his predecessor a sum

[5] Per Harman, J., *Re Gee*, [1948] Ch. 284, 293-6, where the earlier decisions are discussed.
[6] [1946] Ch. 73.
[7] [1948] Ch. 284; followed, *Re Llewellin's Will Trusts*, [1949] Ch. 225. See also *Re Northcote's Will Trusts*, [1949] 1 All E.R. 442.
[8] [1908] 1 Ch. 65.
[9] [1927] 2 Ch. 9.
[10] [1930] 1 Ch. 203.
[11] (1802), 7 Ves. 480.
[12] (1858), 2 De G. & J. 327.
[13] *Macleod* v. *Jones* (1883), 24 Ch.D. 289.
[14] *Hawkins* v. *Chappel* (1739), 1 Atk. 621.
[15] (1856), 6 De G.M. & G. 439.
[16] (1856), 3 Sm. & Giff. 192.

of money in consideration of his retirement, and it was held that this sum must also be treated as trust property. It is abundantly clear that a trustee cannot employ trust funds for commercial ventures of his own. If he does, he must account for the profits, or pay 5 per cent. interest.[17]

The rule preventing a trustee obtaining a profit from the trust estate, like the rule preventing his purchase of trust property, is not confined to express trustees. It applies to all who occupy a fiduciary position, including agents. and persons who act as agents although they in fact are not,[18] company directors, secretaries, promoters, solicitors,[19] and a number of others. Even if the beneficiaries under a trust die intestate without leaving any person who can take their interests by succession, or where the beneficiary is a corporation which is dissolved and no disposition of the beneficial interest is made, the trustee still cannot take the benefit of it. It belongs to the Crown as *bona vacantia*.[20]

Where a trustee or a person in a fiduciary position does make a profit from his trust the right of the beneficiary to compel him to account may be lost by laches or acquiescence. If the person who is entitled to the benefit of the rule understands his rights and is content with the position, it may be commercially to his advantage to accept the position, and forego his right. It is for him alone to decide how far he wishes to be protected, but the trustee, director or other person in a fiduciary position cannot claim the application of the rule as a protection.[21]

B. SALES OF TRUST PROPERTY BY A TRUSTEE TO HIMSELF OR TO A CO-TRUSTEE

A trustee (other than a tenant for life under the Settled Land Act [22]) and also many other persons [23] who occupy fiduciary positions are unable to purchase the trust property or, if the observations of Danckwerts, L.J., in *Holder* v. *Holder* [24] are to be regarded as general in their application, if the trustee does purchase, the sale may be set aside within a reasonable time at the instance of any beneficiary. This is a rule of most general application,[25] and it is not founded upon any question of fraud on the part of the trustee. It is the logical consequence of the position which he occupies.

The foundations of this rule were laid in *Fox* v. *Mackreth*,[26] but it was exhaustively examined and developed by Lord Eldon during his lengthy tenure of office as Lord Chancellor, and he may be regarded as having placed

---

[17] See, further, Chap. XXIV, s. A, *post.*

[18] *Lyell* v. *Kennedy* (1889), 14 App.Cas. 437; *Boardman* v. *Phipps*, [1967] 2 A.C. 45.

[19] *Brown* v. *I.R.C.*, [1965] A.C. 244.

[20] *Cave* v. *Roberts* (1836), 8 Sim. 214; *Re Higginson and Dean*, [1899] 1 Q.B. 325 (explained in *Re Sir Thomas Spencer Wells*, [1933] Ch. 29); Companies Act 1948, Sects. 354–5.

[21] *Bray* v. *Ford*, [1896] A.C. 44, 51; *Boulting* v. *Association of Cinematograph, Television and Allied Technicians*, [1963] 2 Q.B. 606.

[22] Settled Land Act 1925, s. 68. See *Re Pennant's Will Trusts*, [1970] Ch. 75.

[23] *Post*, pp. 312–315.

[24] [1968] Ch. 353.

[25] Where, however, a statutory trust for sale under the Law of Property Act 1925, s. 36 (1), arises out of a joint commercial enterprise, the prohibition may not be so extensive (*Re Foot and Hall Beddall & Co. Ltd.'s Agreement* (1945), 174 L.T. 83).

[26] (1788), 2 Bro.C.C. 400. See *Whelpdale* v. *Cookson* (1747), 1 Ves.Sen. 9; Ves.Sen. Supp. 8; and also the notes to *Fox* v. *Mackreth* in White and Tudor's *Leading Cases in Equity*.

it beyond the possibility of serious limitation. Thus, in *Ex parte Lacey*,[27] he observes—

> I disavow that interpretation of Lord *Rosslyn's* doctrine, that the trustee must make advantage. I say, whether he makes advantage, or not, if the connection does not satisfactorily appear to have been dissolved, it is in the choice of the *Cestuy que trusts,* whether they will take back the property, or not; if the trustee has made no advantage. It is founded upon this; that though you may see in a particular case, that he has not made advantage, it is utterly impossible to examine upon satisfactory evidence in the power of the Court, by which I mean, in the power of the parties, in ninety-nine cases out of a hundred, whether he has made advantage, or not. Suppose, a trustee buys any estate; and by the knowledge acquired in that character discovers a valuable coal-mine under it; and locking that up in his own breast enters into a contract with the *Cestuy que trust*: if he chooses to deny it, how can the Court try that against that denial?

In the very next case in the reports, *Lister* v. *Lister*,[28] Sir W. Grant, M.R., had to consider the case of trustees who had purchased trust property at an auction, and he held that it must be offered by auction again, the Master of the Rolls saying [29]—

> The rule is a rule of general policy, to prevent the possibility of fraud and abuse; for it may not always be possible to know, whether the property was undersold. I was not aware, that the *Lord Chancellor* had laid down a general rule as to the terms; that the property should be set up again at the risk of the trustee. It is a very important consideration, whether that is to be taken as a general rule. If it is, I must adhere to it: but if it turns upon special circumstances, I see no special circumstances in this case. These lots must be resold at all events. The only question is, whether they shall be put up at the price, at which the trustees purchased.

The report then continues—

> *Feb. 24th.* The cause having stood over, the *Master of the Rolls* said, he had mentioned it to the *Lord Chancellor*; and his Lordship said, he meant to lay down a general rule; and understood, it had been so established, in Lord *Thurlow's* time.

In *Ex parte James*,[30] Lord Eldon again returned to a consideration of the rule, and extended it to a purchase of a bankrupt's estate by the solicitor to the bankruptcy commission, observing [31]—

> This doctrine as to purchases by trustees, assignees, and persons having a confidential character, stands much more upon general principle than upon the circumstances of any individual case. It rests upon this; that the purchase is not permitted in any case, however honest the circumstances; the general interests of justice requiring it to be destroyed in every

---

27 (1802), 6 Ves. 625, 627 (Cases, p. 339). See also Sheridan, *Fraud in Equity*, pp. 107–13.
28 (1802), 6 Ves. 631.
29 6 Ves. 632–3.
30 (1803), 8 Ves. 337.
31 8 Ves. 345.

instance; as no Court is equal to the examination and ascertainment of the truth in much the greater number of cases.

In *Aberdeen Railway Co.* v. *Blaikie Brothers*,[32] the House of Lords fully affirmed the breadth of the principle enunciated by Lord Eldon, and applied it to dealings between a director and his company. Lord Cranworth, L.C., there stated [33]—

> A corporate body can only act by agents, and it is of course the duty of those agents so to act as best to promote the interests of the corporation whose affairs they are conducting. Such agents have duties to discharge of a fiduciary nature towards their principal. And it is a rule of universal application, that no one, having such duties to discharge, shall be allowed to enter into engagements in which he has, or can have, a personal interest conflicting, or which possibly may conflict, with the interests of those whom he is bound to protect.
>
> So strictly is this principle adhered to, that no question is allowed to be raised as to the fairness or unfairness of a contract so entered into.
>
> It obviously is, or may be, impossible to demonstrate how far in any particular case the terms of such a contract have been the best for the interest of the *cestui que* trust, which it was possible to obtain.
>
> It may sometimes happen that the terms on which a trustee has dealt or attempted to deal with the estate or interests of those for whom he is a trustee, have been as good as could have been obtained from any other person,—they may even at the time have been better.
>
> But still so inflexible is the rule that no inquiry on the subject is permitted. The English authorities on this head are numerous and uniform....
>
> It cannot be contended that the rule to which I have referred is one confined to the English law, and that it does not apply to Scotland.
>
> It so happens that one of the leading authorities on the subject is a decision of this House on an appeal from Scotland—I refer to the case of *The York Buildings Company* v. *Mackenzie*,[34] decided by your Lordships in 1795.
>
> There the respondent, Mackenzie, while he filled the office of " Common Agent " in the sale of the estates of the appellants, who had become insolvent, purchased a portion of them at a judicial auction; and though he had remained in possession for above eleven years after the purchase, and had entirely freed himself from all imputation of fraud, yet this House held that filling as he did an office which made it his duty both to the insolvents and their creditors to obtain the highest price, he could not put himself in the position of purchaser, and so make it his interest that the price paid should be as low as possible.
>
> This was a very strong case, because there had been acquiescence for above eleven years; the charges of fraud were not supported, and the purchase was made at a sale by auction. Lord Eldon and Sir William Grant were counsel for the respondent, and no doubt everything was

---

[32] (1854), 1 Macq. 461. See also *York Buildings Co.* v. *Mackenzie* (1795), 8 Bro.P.C. 42.
[33] 1 Macq. 471.
[34] 8 Bro.P.C. 42.

urged which their learning and experience could suggest in favour of the respondent.

But this House considered the general principle one of such importance and of such universal application, that they reversed the decree of the Court of Session, and set aside the sale.[35]

In *Holder* v. *Holder*[36] all three Lords Justices of Appeal considered the observations of Lord Eldon in *Ex parte Lacey and Ex parte James,* and in spite of those observations, Danckwerts, L.J., adopted the view[37] that the true rule is not that a trustee may not purchase trust property, but that the sale is voidable within a reasonable time at the instance of any beneficiary. This was also the foundation of the unanimous decision of the Court of Appeal in *Holder* v. *Holder,* that a sale of trust property to a trustee who had ineffectively attempted to renounce his trusteeship, and who had performed only minor acts of administration, could purchase the trust property, and that the purchase could not be impeached by a beneficiary. All three Lords Justices thought the rule was not so rigid as it had formerly been thought to be, and Danckwerts, L.J., pointed out that such transactions were not void, but voidable. Further, it is the case that the court may allow a trustee to bid for trust property, or in appropriate circumstances, purchase it.[38]

The rule applies to property of all kinds, whether real or personal, whether in possession or in reversion. Moreover, the trustee may not sell to a person who is, in fact, a trustee for himself[39]; and all other circuitous arrangements to achieve the same result are equally invalid.[40] In particular, where the trustee has contracted to sell to a third person, he cannot re-purchase from that third person, so long as the contract remains executory.[41] On the other hand, a *bona fide* sale to a third person in the hope of subsequently acquiring the property from him is valid, provided that no agreement existed between trustee and purchaser at the time of the sale.

The strictness with which the rule has been applied is well illustrated by the decision of the Judicial Committee of the Privy Council in *Wright* v. *Morgan.*[42] A testator left the residue of his estate, comprising land and the stock on it, on trust to sell and divide the proceeds amongst his widow, his sons and daughters. He appointed his widow and his sons H and D to be his executors and trustees. There was a clause in the will postponing public sale

[35] The fact that Lord Eldon and Sir William Grant appeared in this case may in fact be responsible for the frequent references to it during the period in which they were, respectively, Lord Chancellor and Master of the Rolls, *e.g. Ex parte Lacey* (1802), 6 Ves. 625, 630, note (2). As far as the position of company directors *vis-à-vis* their company is concerned, this now depends upon the Companies Acts and the decisions thereon which have seemed to deviate somewhat from the principle enunciated above. See, further, *Transvaal Lands Co. Ltd.* v. *New Belgium (Transvaal) Land and Development Co. Ltd.,* [1914] 2 Ch. 488, where the authorities are discussed. A right to purchase granted *before* the trust arises may be exercised: *Re Mulholland's Will Trusts,* [1949] 1 All E.R. 460.

[36] [1968] Ch. 353 (Cases, p. 340).

[37] Expressed, *e.g.,* in Snell's *Equity* (26th ed., p. 259) and Sheridan, *Fraud in Equity,* pp. 107–8.

[38] *Tennant* v. *Trenchard* (1869), L.R. 4 Ch.App. 537. See, further, Hinde, " Purchase of Trust Property by a Trustee with the Approval of the Court " (1961) 3 *Melbourne University Law Review* 15.

[39] *Campbell* v. *Walker* (1800), 5 Ves. 678; (1807), 13 Ves. 601.

[40] *Whitcomb* v. *Minchin* (1820), 5 Madd. 91; *Re Bloye's Trust* (1849), 1 Mac. & G. 488, 495.

[41] *Williams* v. *Scott,* [1900] A.C. 499.

[42] [1926] A.C. 788.

until the property had been offered at a valuation to H and refused by him. After the testator's death, D purchased H's share in the estate, together with the option to purchase the trust estate. Moreover, D resigned his trusteeship after agreeing to purchase, but before completion. The Privy Council refused to allow the transaction to stand, as it violated the rule invalidating purchases of trust property by a trustee. Although H had been given an option to purchase, this option was not assignable to another trustee. On the other hand, where an option is first given to a person who is *subsequently* appointed a trustee by the settlor, the option remains exercisable.[43]

Since one of the reasons for the rule is the presumption of the trustee's superior knowledge of the value of the trust property, two further consequences follow. Whilst a trustee cannot purchase the trust property through an agent, neither can he purchase it as agent for a third party, for, as Lord Eldon observed in *Ex parte Bennett*,[44] " the Court can with as little effect examine, whether that was done by making an undue use of the information, received in the course of their duty, in the one case as in the other." Secondly, a trustee, for the same reason, may not retire from the trust in order to purchase trust property. In *Re Boles and British Land Company's Contract*,[45] Buckley, J., held that a trustee who had retired from the trust twelve years before was entitled to purchase trust property, there being no evidence that he was taking advantage of knowledge gained whilst a trustee. Similarly, a trustee who has disclaimed a trust without ever having acted may purchase.[46]

Again, a trustee for sale cannot lease to himself since this is, in effect, a partial sale, and when the lease is set aside, he may be made to account for all profits.[47]

It has been stated that the beneficiary can set aside the sale without proof of loss, and this he may do, not only as against the trustee himself, but also against all subsequent purchasers who have notice of the flaw in the title.[48] In fact, the only safe course for a trustee who wishes to purchase trust property from his co-trustees is to apply to the court for leave to purchase. This will only be given where the sale is clearly to the advantage of the beneficiaries.[49] If this appears, the fact that the beneficiary is an infant will not prevent the court from giving permission, if it is necessary for the property to be sold.[50]

The rule even goes so far as to provide that a trustee cannot purchase in the name of his children,[51] although the mere fact that the purchaser is related to the trustee is not of itself a ground for setting the transaction aside[52]; and it should be observed that a trustee may sell to a company of which he is a shareholder,[53] although even here the beneficiary may attack it. Thus, in

---

[43] *Re Mulholland's Will Trusts*, [1949] 1 All E.R. 460.
[44] (1805), 10 Ves. 381, 400.
[45] [1902] 1 Ch. 244.
[46] *Stacey* v. *Elph* (1833), 1 My. & K. 195. See also *Clark* v. *Clark* (1884), 9 App.Cas. 733.
[47] *Ex parte Hughes* (1802), 6 Ves. 617.
[48] *Aberdeen Town Council* v. *Aberdeen University* (1877), 2 App.Cas. 544.
[49] *Farmer* v. *Dean* (1863), 32 Beav. 327.
[50] *Campbell* v. *Walker* (1800), 5 Ves. 678; (1807), 13 Ves. 601.
[51] *Gregory* v. *Gregory* (1815), G. Coop. 201; (1821), Jac. 631. See also Fleming, " Can a Trustee Sell to his Wife? " (1949) 13 *The Conveyancer* 248.
[52] *Coles* v. *Trecothick* (1804), 9 Ves. 234.
[53] *Silkstone and Haigh Moor Coal Co.* v. *Edey*, [1900] 1 Ch. 167.

Farrar v. *Farrars Ltd.*,[54] three mortgagees sold the mortgaged property to a company of which one of them was a shareholder, and also the promoter and solicitor. Although the sale was upheld, since the mortgagees had obtained the best price possible in the circumstances, the court held that the mortgagees must undertake the task of showing that the transaction was a proper one. It is noteworthy that a mortgagee is not a trustee of his power of sale, and it would, therefore, seem an irresistible conclusion that where the vendor is a trustee, the duty is at least as high as that of an encumbrancer who is exercising his power of sale.

The general rule here enunciated applies also to all persons who occupy a fiduciary position, although perhaps not with the same rigidity as to trustees. Thus, an executor or administrator should not normally purchase the assets of the deceased,[55] although it would appear that if he acts entirely openly, and with the assent of all interested parties, and the best price was obtained, the sale may be allowed to stand, if the beneficiaries at the time of the sale knew the whole of the relevant facts.[56] In *John* v. *Jones*,[57] a sale by an administratix to her son was held invalid on the grounds of relationship.

It has already been noticed that under the old bankruptcy laws an assignee in bankruptcy was entirely prohibited from purchasing the bankrupt's property,[58] and this is now expressly provided for in the Bankruptcy Rules,[59] and the incapacity has been extended to the partner of the trustee in bankruptcy.[60]

Agents whose employment is such that they acquire special knowledge of the circumstances affecting the property of their principal are also debarred from purchasing it, unless they can show that they have acted in perfect fairness, have given full value, and have put their principals in possession of all the knowledge relating to the property which they possess.[61] Similarly, if an agent has an interest in a sale to a third party, he must disclose it in full.[62] It is, of course, a cardinal rule of agency that the agent should account to his principal for any unauthorised commission or profit made by the agent on the transaction.[63] This last rule extends to partners, since each partner is an agent for the others in respect of partnership business.[64] There is, however, nothing to prevent a surviving partner from purchasing the share of a deceased partner, provided that the transaction is an entirely fair one [65]; and where a partner himself sells his share to a co-partner, he must put the co-partner into possession of all the material facts.[66]

The relationship of solicitor and client has been the subject of particular

---

[54] (1888), 40 Ch.D. 395. *Cf. Belton* v. *Bass, Ratcliffe and Gretton Ltd.*, [1922] 2 Ch. 449.

[55] *Hall* v. *Hallet* (1784), 1 Cox 134; *Watson* v. *Toone* (1820), 6 Madd. 153; *Re Harvey* (1888), 58 L.T. 449; *Beningfield* v. *Baxter* (1886), 12 App.Cas. 167.

[56] *Watson* v. *Toone, supra; Champion* v. *Rigby* (1830), 1 Russ. & M. 539; *Baker* v. *Read* (1854), 18 Beav. 398; *Smedley* v. *Varley* (1857), 23 Beav. 358.

[57] (1876), 34 L.T. 570.

[58] *Ex parte Bennett* (1805), 10 Ves. 381.

[59] Rule 349.

[60] *Ex parte Forder*, [1881] W.N. 117; *Re Moore* (1881), 51 L.J.Ch. 72.

[61] *Lowther* v. *Lord Lowther* (1806), 13 Ves. 95, 103; *Charter* v. *Trevelyan* (1844), 11 Cl. & Fin. 714. See also Sheridan, *Fraud in Equity*, pp. 113-115.

[62] *Liquidators of Imperial Mercantile Credit Association* v. *Coleman* (1873), L.R. 6 H.L. 189.

[63] *De Bussche* v. *Alt* (1878), 8 Ch.D. 286.

[64] *Featherstonhaugh* v. *Fenwick* (1810), 17 Ves. 298; *Beningfield* v. *Baxter* (1886), 12 App. Cas. 167.

[65] *Chambers* v. *Howell* (1847), 11 Beav. 6.

[66] *Law* v. *Law*, [1905] 1 Ch. 140.

scrutiny in regard to the question: In what circumstances, if at all, may the solicitor purchase the property of his client, or sell his own property to a client? The general rule was stated by Wigram, V.-C., in *Edwards* v. *Meyrick*,[67] as follows—

The rule of equity which subjects transactions between solicitor and client to other and stricter tests than those which apply to ordinary transactions is not an isolated rule, but is a branch of a rule applicable to all transactions between man and man, in which the relation between the contracting parties is such as to destroy the equal footing on which such parties should stand.... In the case of *Gibson* v. *Jeyes*[68] there was evidence that the client was of advanced age, and of much infirmity, both in mind and body, that the consideration was inadequate—and of various other circumstances. Lord Eldon there shews that each of these circumstances gave rise to its appropriate duty on the part of the attorney. In other cases where an attorney has been employed to manage an estate he has been considered as bound to prove that he gave his employer the benefit of all the knowledge which he had acquired in his character of manager or professional agent, in order to sustain a bargain made for his advantage.[69] But, as the communication of such knowledge by the attorney will place the parties upon an equality, when it is proved that the communication was made, the difficulty of supporting the transaction is *quoad hoc* removed. If, on the other hand, the attorney has not had any concern with the estate respecting which the question arises the particular duties to which any given situation of confidence might give rise cannot of course attach upon him, whatever may be the other duties which the mere office of attorney may impose. If the attorney, being employed to sell, becomes himself the purchaser, his duties and his interests are directly opposed to each other, and it would be difficult—and without the clearest evidence that no advantage was taken by the attorney of his position, and that the vendor had all the knowledge which could be given him in order to form a judgment, it would be impossible—to support the transaction. In other cases the relation between the parties may simply produce a degree of influence and ascendancy, placing the client in circumstances of disadvantage; as where he is indebted to the attorney, and is unable to discharge the debt. The relative position of the parties in such a case must at least impose upon the attorney the duty of giving the full value for the estate, and the *onus* of proving that he did so. If he proves the full value to have been given the ground for any unfavourable inference is removed. The case may be traced through every possible variation until we reach the simple case where, though the relation of solicitor and client exists in one transaction, and, therefore, personal influence or ascendancy may operate in another, yet the relation not existing *in hâc re*, the rule of equity to which I am now adverting may no longer apply.

The nature of the proof, therefore, which the Court requires must

---

[67] (1842), 2 Hare 60, 69–70. See also *Spencer* v. *Topham* (1856), 22 Beav. 573.
[68] (1801), 6 Ves. 266.
[69] *Cane* v. *Lord Allen* (1814), 2 Dow 289.

depend upon the circumstances of each case, according as they may have placed the attorney in a position in which his duties and his pecuniary interests were conflicting, or may have given him a knowledge which his client did not possess, or some influence or ascendancy or other advantage over his client; or, notwithstanding the existence of the relation of attorney and client, may have left the parties substantially at arm's length and on an equal footing. . .[70]

It will be seen that the equitable rule really rests upon the supposition that the solicitor may obtain some unwarranted advantage as a result of undue influence, and under the head of " Undue Influence " it has, therefore, been considered already. The law on this topic was reviewed in *Wright* v. *Carter*,[71] where it was held that a solicitor may purchase, under the conditions stated by Wigram, V.-C., if the price is fair, the client was fully informed, and the client had competent independent advice from another solicitor, who does all that is necessary to protect his client's interests.

There exists one important exception to the general rule that a trustee is absolutely prohibited from purchasing the trust estate. Under the Settled Land Act 1925 a tenant for life has the legal estate vested in him on trust for all the beneficiaries under the settlement. Nevertheless, by section 68 of that Act, he may sell, lease or mortgage the settled land to himself.

SETTING ASIDE THE PURCHASE

Wherever a trustee has wrongfully acquired trust property, a beneficiary may set aside the sale, not only as against the trustee himself, but also as against anyone who has acquired it from the trustee, with notice that the trustee purchased it in breach of trust. The beneficiary will repay the price at which the trustee bought it, with interest at 4 per cent., against which there must be set off the rents and profits, or an occupation rent for the property, for the period during which the trustee was in possession of it.[72] The trustee is entitled to have an allowance for improvements and repairs upon which he has expended his own money, and which are substantial and which improve the value of the property.[73]

If the trustee had sold to a third party, who took without notice of the trustee's breach of trust, and the trustee has made a profit, he must account to the trust for the profit.

The beneficiary's right to set aside the sale may be lost by his acquiescence. The effectiveness of this will depend upon his knowledge of the facts—whether it also depends upon his knowledge of the legal consequences of these facts depends upon the circumstances. In *Holder* v. *Holder*[74] Harman, L.J., said that there was no hard and fast rule that ignorance of a legal right is a bar.

---

70 *Welles* v. *Middleton* (1784), 1 Cox 112; *Gibson* v. *Jeyes* (1801), 6 Ves. 266; *Hatch* v. *Hatch* (1804), 9 Ves, 292; *Bellew* v. *Russel* (1809), 1 B. & B. 96; *Wood* v. *Downes* (1811), 18 Ves. 120; *Montesquieu* v. *Sandys* (1811), 18 Ves. 302; *Hunter* v. *Atkins* (1834), 3 My. & K. 113; *Holman* v. *Loynes* (1854), 4 De G.M. & G. 270; *O'Brien* v. *Lewis* (1863), 32 L.J. Ch. 569; *Re Haslam and Hier-Evans*, [1902] 1 Ch. 765; *Wright* v. *Carter*, [1903] 1 Ch. 27.
71 [1903] 1 Ch. 27 (Cases, p. 238).
72 *Re Sherman*, [1954] Ch. 653.
73 *Ex parte Bennett* (1805), 10 Ves. 381.
74 [1968] Ch. 353 (Cases, p. 340). Harman, L.J., accepted the view of Wilberforce, J., in *Re Pauling's Settlement Trusts*, [1962] 1 W.L.R. 86.

The whole of the circumstances must be looked at to see whether it is just that the complaining beneficiary should succeed against the trustee.

Where one of several beneficiaries seeks to set aside the trustee's purchase, he cannot insist that the property be reconveyed to the vendor trustees without the consent of the other beneficiaries, and where this is not forthcoming, the court will order a resale. If the resale showed a profit to the trust, the purchasing trustee will be held to account, with allowances for improvement.

Purchase of a Beneficiary's Interest by a Trustee

The purchase of a beneficiary's interest by a trustee stands on rather a different footing from a purchase of trust property by a trustee from himself or a co-trustee. Here there is no absolute prohibition, but the trustee must take no advantage whatever of his position. He must give the beneficiary the fullest information relating to his interest, and furthermore, it would seem that the sale will always be voidable if the consideration is in the opinion of the court inadequate.[75] Before the transaction takes place, either the relation of trustee and beneficiary should have been terminated,[76] or alternatively the parties should be at arm's length, and the *cestui que trust* should clearly understand the nature of the transaction, and agree to waive all objections.[77] Each case will obviously depend upon its own merits, but probably the best illustration of the circumstances in which such a sale was held to be valid is furnished by *Coles* v. *Trecothick*,[78] wherein the beneficiary took complete charge of the sale (which was by auction), approving the auctioneer, the plan of sale and the price, and the sale was held good.

On the other hand, in *Dougan* v. *Macpherson*,[79] two brothers, A and B, were beneficiaries under a trust. A was also a trustee, but B was not, and A purchased B's interest without showing him a valuation of the trust estate made for the purpose of obtaining a loan on A's share. If the valuation was correct, B's share was worth considerably more than A paid for it. When B subsequently went bankrupt, B's trustee in bankruptcy succeeded in setting aside the sale.

Remedies of the Beneficiary

The relief granted to a beneficiary, where the trustee purchases from the beneficiary, is, of course, equitable, and therefore the beneficiary should seek it with reasonable promptitude after becoming acquainted with the real nature of the transaction. If, however, the beneficiary is subject to a disability, he cannot be considered as in a position effectively to prosecute his rights until that disability has ended.[80] Moreover, whilst the beneficiary remains in ignorance of the fact that the trustee was the purchaser, it is clear that *laches* will not bar the beneficiary's remedy.[81]

[75] *Ex parte Lacey* (1802), 6 Ves. 625, 626 (Cases, p. 339); *Coles* v. *Trecothick* (1804), 9 Ves. 234; *Luff* v. *Lord* (1864), 34 Beav. 220; *Williams* v. *Scott*, [1900] A.C. 499; *Dougan* v. *Macpherson*, [1902] A.C. 197.
[76] *Downes* v. *Grazebrook* (1817), 3 Mer. 200, 208.
[77] *Randall* v. *Errington* (1805), 10 Ves. 423, 427.
[78] (1804), 9 Ves. 234. See also *Clarke* v. *Swaile* (1762), 2 Eden 134; *Morse* v. *Royal* (1806), 12 Ves. 355.
[79] [1902] A.C. 197.
[80] *Campbell* v. *Walker* (1800), 5 Ves. 678; (1807), 13 Ves. 601.
[81] *Chalmer* v. *Bradley* (1819), 1 Jac. & W. 51.

If the beneficiary does not prosecute his rights within a reasonable time after becoming aware of the true facts, and not being subject to any disability, he is treated as acquiescing in the transaction and that it was in all respects fair.[82] No exact period has been prescribed by the court, since there is no statute of limitations applicable, but in general the court will not reopen a transaction which has stood for twenty years,[83] although in some cases relief has not been granted when a lesser period has supervened.[84]

In general, the beneficiary is entitled to have the property reconveyed to him, either by the trustee,[85] or by a person who has purchased from the trustee with notice of the voidability of the original sale.[86] The trustee is entitled to an allowance for repairs and improvements which are permanent,[87] but the interests of lessees and others who have dealt with the trustee before the sale (except purchasers with notice) are not prejudiced by the beneficiary's action.[88]

In some cases, more especially where an assignee in bankruptcy has purchased, it has been held that the property should be put up for auction again, at the price at which the trustee purchased; if there is no bidding, the trustee should be held to his bargain.[89]

If the trustee has resold to a bona fide purchaser for value without notice of the invalidity, the sale cannot then be impeached, but the trustee will be compelled to account for the difference between the price he gave and the price he received,[90] or alternatively for the difference between the price paid and the true value, with interest at 4 per cent.[91]

C. PAYMENT TO A TRUSTEE FOR HIS SERVICES

It is a general rule of Equity that a trustee must administer his trust gratuitously, and this is the case notwithstanding the fact that the completion of his undertaking may involve considerable time and much personal inconvenience.[92] The reason for this rule, according to Lord Talbot, is that otherwise the estate would be rendered of little value in consequence of administration costs; and furthermore, it is exceedingly difficult to estimate the value of one man's time and trouble, as compared with another's.[93] Another reason for the rule was expressed by Chitty, J., in *Re Barber*[94] (wherein it was declared to extend also to executors) as follows—

> Now, undoubtedly, a solicitor who is a trustee is not allowed to make a profit out of his trusteeship, and the same rule applies to him in regard to executorship. He stands, in respect of this general principle, in the same

---

[82] *Morse* v. *Royal* (1806), 12 Ves. 355.
[83] *Barwell* v. *Barwell* (1865), 34 Beav. 371.
[84] *Gregory* v. *Gregory* (1815), G. Coop. 201; (1821), Jac. 631; *Baker* v. *Read* (1854), 18 Beav. 398.
[85] *Aberdeen Town Council* v. *Aberdeen University* (1877), 2 App.Cas. 544.
[86] *Dunbar* v. *Tredennick* (1813), 2 B. & B. 304.
[87] *York Buildings Co.* v. *Mackenzie* (1795), 8 Bro.P.C. 42.
[88] See *Lister* v. *Lister* (1802), 6 Ves. 631.
[89] *Lister* v. *Lister* (1802), 6 Ves. 631, 633.
[90] *Fox* v. *Mackreth* (1788), 2 Bro.C.C. 400.
[91] *Lord Hardwicke* v. *Vernon* (1799), 4 Ves. 411; *Hall* v. *Hallet* (1784), 1 Cox 134.
[92] *Barrett* v. *Hartley* (1866), L.R. 2 Eq. 789; *Re Thorpe*, [1891] 2 Ch. 360.
[93] *Robinson* v. *Pett* (1734), 3 P.Wms. 249.
[94] (1886), 34 Ch.D. 77, 80–1 (Cases, p. 342). See also *New* v. *Jones* (1833), 1 Mac. & G. 668n.; *Barrett* v. *Hartley* (1866), L.R. 2 Eq. 789.

position as a broker, commission agent, or the like, who may be appointed
trustee or executor, and who may transact some of the business relating to
the estate which requires the assistance of either broker, commission
agent, or the like; and if the executor or trustee transacts business of that
kind for the estate, he is allowed, of course, his costs out of pocket, that
is to say, the expenditure, but not anything for his time or trouble. That
principle is based upon this consideration, that the Court of Equity will
not allow a man to place himself in a position in which his interest and
duty are in conflict. If it were not the rule, a trust estate might be heavily
burdened by reason of business being done by a trustee or executor
employing himself as commission agent for the estate. The difficulty
would be in saying in each particular case that the business was not
required to be done.

Furthermore, it may be noticed that a trustee will not, in general, be
appointed receiver of the trust estate at a salary,[95] whilst if a trustee is a
banker, and is not authorised to charge, he cannot, as trustee, borrow money
from himself as banker, at compound interest, even although this is the normal
usage of banker and customer.[96]

It may be that the solicitor-trustee, instead of undertaking the work himself, employs a partner to perform it. This was considered in *Re Doody*,[97]
where Stirling, J., observed [98]—

> . . . as a general rule, neither a solicitor trustee nor a firm of which the
> trustee is a member can receive out of the trust estate profit costs by way
> of remuneration for transacting legal business in connection with the
> trust.

> To this general rule there are some exceptions, to one of which I
> may refer at once. It was decided by Lord *Hatherley*, when Vice-
> Chancellor, in *Clack* v. *Carlon*,[99] that a solicitor trustee may employ his
> partner to act as solicitor for himself and his co-trustees with reference
> to the trust affairs, and may pay him the usual charges, provided that it
> has been expressly agreed between himself and his partner that he him-
> self shall not participate in the profits or derive any benefit from the
> charges. Nothing short of this will be sufficient. In particular it was
> decided in *Christophers* v. *White*,[1] that the general rule applies, although
> all the business has been transacted by the partners of the solicitor trustee,
> and not by the trustee himself.

In *Re Gates*,[2] a solicitor-trustee employed his firm (including himself) to
act as solicitors to the trust, and Clauson, J., held that as the trust instrument
contained no power to charge, the firm could not charge profit costs, even
though there was an agreement that the solicitor-trustee should have no share
of them. In *Re Hill*,[3] the Court of Appeal were of the same opinion.

[95] *Re Bignell*, [1892] 1 Ch. 59.
[96] *Crosskill* v. *Bower* (1863), 32 Beav. 86.
[97] [1893] 1 Ch. 129.
[98] At pp. 134–135.
[99] (1861), 30 L.J. Ch. 639.
[1] (1847), 10 Beav. 523. See also *Re Corsellis* (1887), 34 Ch.D. 675.
[2] [1933] Ch. 913.
[3] [1934] Ch. 623. See also *Re French Protestant Hospital*, [1951] Ch. 567.

To the general rule stated above, the following exceptions have in course of time been established.

1. By Agreement with the Beneficiaries

A trustee is entitled to contract with his beneficiaries, provided they are all *sui juris* and absolutely entitled to the entire trust estate, that he shall be paid. This is a contract which must be concluded without any pressure whatever by the trustee upon the beneficiary, and it is regarded with suspicion by the court. Furthermore, it must be concluded before the trustee has entered into the administration of the trust.[4] There would seem to be nothing to prevent a single adult beneficiary agreeing to pay, but that would affect his interest only.

2. By Authority of the Court

The court may, in very special circumstances, and where the trustee is put to exceptional trouble, direct that the trustee shall be paid, but it will only do this where the trustee's services are exceptionally beneficial to the estate. Thus, in *Re Freeman's Settlement Trusts*,[5] two of the three trustees were in Canada, and the third was the agent of the estate. He declined to be appointed unless he was paid, and the court allowed him 5 per cent. on the rents he collected. It may be assumed, however, that since a general power of appointing agents is conferred by the Trustee Act 1925, the occasions when the court will authorise payment of a private trustee will now be even more infrequent.

3. The Public Trustee, Judicial Trustees, and Trust Corporations

The Public Trustee and judicial trustees are entitled to charge for their services, whether or not there is any power contained in the trust instrument to charge. In the case of the Public Trustee, the remuneration is regulated by statute, while in the case of a judicial trustee it is fixed by the court.[6] When a trust corporation (other than the Public Trustee) is appointed, a power to charge is invariably given, but apart from it there is no statutory power to charge, and therefore they are not often appointed subsequently, unless all the beneficiaries are of full age, and consent. If the court appoints a trust corporation, however, it may authorise it to charge what remuneration the court thinks fit.[7] Thus, in *Re Young Estates*,[8] the court appointed a trust corporation to be administrator *de bonis non*, and authorised it to make the usual scale charges.

The difficulties arising from the absence of a power to charge if the trustee

---

4 *Ayliffe* v. *Murray* (1740), 2 Atk. 58; *Re Sherwood* (1840), 3 Beav. 338; *Douglas* v. *Archbutt* (1858), 2 De G. & J. 148.

5 (1887), 37 Ch.D. 148. See also *Marshall* v. *Holloway* (1820), 2 Swanst. 432.

6 Public Trustee Act 1906, s. 9, as amended by Public Trustee (Fees) Act 1957; Public Trustee (Fees) Order 1969, as amended by Orders listed on p. 57, *ante*. Judicial Trustees Act 1896, s. 1; Judicial Trustee Rules 1972, rule 16.

7 Trustee Act 1925, s. 42; *Re Masters*, [1953] 1 W.L.R. 81. (In this case, at p. 83, Danckwerts, J., said: " Apart from the statutory jurisdiction conferred by section 42 of the Trustee Act, 1925, it is also quite plain there is inherent jurisdiction in the court to authorize remuneration of a trustee, whether appointed by the court or not.") See also *Re Barbour's Settlement*, [1974] 1 All E.R. 1188.

8 (1934), 103 L.J.P. 75.

is a trust corporation are emphasised by the decision of the Court of Appeal in *Forster* v. *Williams Deacon's Bank Ltd.*[9] In that case, under a trust in which the trustees had no power to charge for their services, a sole trustee wished to retire in favour of the defendant bank. He executed a deed by which he purported to appoint the bank as (a) managing trustee, and (b) custodian trustee. Under the Public Trustee Act 1906 a custodian trustee may always charge for services. The Court of Appeal held, however, that the bank could not split its functions in this way. If the deed operated at all, it operated to create the bank sole trustee, in which case the inability to charge remained. This case was followed in *Arning* v. *James*[10] in which it was decided that the purported appointment was a complete nullity.

A practical consequence of these decisions appears in *Re Squire's Settlement,*[11] where the Public Trustee had been appointed custodian trustee, and it was desired to appoint him as an ordinary trustee. Evershed, J., held that it was necessary to discharge the Public Trustee from his custodian trusteeship before his appointment as full trustee.

4. The Rule in *Cradock* v. *Piper* [12]

It has been observed that a solicitor is in the same position as any other person as regards his inability to charge for his services. There exists, however, a curious limitation upon this exception, known as the rule in *Cradock* v. *Piper*,[12] which may be stated as follows—

> . . . where there is work done in a suit not on behalf of the trustee, who is a solicitor, alone, but on behalf of himself and a co-trustee, the rule will not prevent the solicitor or his firm from receiving the usual costs, if the costs of appearing for and acting for the two have not increased the expense; that is to say, if the trustee himself has not added to the expense which would have been incurred if he or his firm had appeared only for his co-trustee.[13]

The reason for this rule is stated [14] by Cotton, L.J., to be—

> . . . that it is not the business of a trustee, although he is a solicitor, to act as solicitor for his co-trustee. But the exception in *Cradock* v. *Piper* is limited expressly to the costs incurred in respect of business done in an action or a suit, and it may be an anomaly that that exception should apply to such a case, and should not apply to business done out of Court by the solicitor for himself as trustee and his co-trustee. But there may be this reason for it, that in an action, although costs are not always hostilely taxed, yet there may be a taxation where parties other than the trustee-solicitor may appear and test the propriety of the costs, and the Court can disallow altogether the costs of any proceedings which may appear to be vexatious or improperly taken.

Although the rule (which extends to litigation only) has been subjected to

[9] [1935] Ch. 359.
[10] [1936] Ch. 158.
[11] (1946), 115 L.J. Ch. 90.
[12] (1850), 1 Mac. & G. 664.
[13] *Per* Cotton, L.J., *Re Corsellis* (1887), 34 Ch.D. 675, 681.
[14] *Re Corsellis* (1887), 34 Ch.D. 675, 682.

some criticism, it is now firmly established,[15] but it is regarded as anomalous, and though its consequences will not be unduly circumscribed, the principle will not be extended.[16] It does not apply to a liquidator who is a solicitor, and who conducts legal proceedings on behalf of himself and his co-liquidator.[17]

5. Possibly where the Trust Property is Abroad and the Law of the Foreign Country Allows Payment

By an Act of the Jamaica Assembly of 1740, trustees and agents, amongst others, were permitted to charge a commission for their services. In *Chambers* v. *Goldwin*,[18] a Jamaican trustee delegated the management of the trust property in Jamaica to an agent and returned to England. Lord Eldon held that he could not have his commission whilst he remained in England, leaving open the question whether he would have been entitled to recover the commission for the time when he was resident in Jamaica and in entire management of the estates.

Some further light was thrown on this question in *Re Northcote's Will Trusts*.[19] A testator, domiciled in England, left assets both in England and in the United States. The executors took out an English grant, and were required by the revenue authorities to take out a grant in the State of New York to collect the American assets. Under the law of the State of New York, they were allowed an agency commission, which they deducted before transferring the American assets to themselves as English executors. The court held they were entitled to keep the commission, which was money which never formed part of the English assets. They had taken out an American grant in order to obtain the American assets, and their rights under that grant were governed by the law of the State of New York.

6. Where the Trustee is permitted by the Trust Instrument to Charge for his Services

If the settlement permits the trustee to charge for his services, he may of course be paid; and if the settlement is by will, payment is regarded as a legacy to the trustee.[20] From this, it follows that if the solicitor attests the will, he loses his right to charge [21] (since a person who attests a will may not take a benefit under it), and he cannot charge profit costs if the estate is insolvent.[22]

In *Re Royce's Will Trusts* [23] a solicitor attested a will, which allowed a solicitor-trustee to charge for his services, and which also contained a clause permitting the trustees to pay themselves 5 per cent. of the income for their trouble. After the will was proved, the surviving trustee appointed the solicitor who had attested the will, to be a new trustee in place of a trustee who had

---

[15] *Broughton* v. *Broughton* (1855), 5 De G.M. & G. 160; *Lincoln* v. *Windsor* (1851), 9 Hare 158; *Re Barber* (1886), 34 Ch.D. 77 (Cases, p. 342).
[16] Per Lindley, L.J., *Re Corsellis* (1887), 34 Ch.D. 675, 687–8.
[17] *Re R. Gertzenstein Ltd.*, [1937] Ch. 115.
[18] (1804), 9 Ves. 254, 271.
[19] [1949] 1 All E.R. 442.
[20] *Ellison* v. *Airey* (1748), 1 Ves.Sen. 111, 115; *Re Thorley*, [1891] 2 Ch. 613. As to estate duty on a bequest for life to trustees of a will, see *Public Trustee* v. *I.R.C.*, [1960] A.C. 398.
[21] *Re Barber* (1886), 34 Ch.D. 77; *Re Pooley* (1888), 40 Ch.D. 1.
[22] *Re White*, [1898] 2 Ch. 217.
[23] [1959] Ch. 626.

died. The Court of Appeal held: (1) that, *at the time when the will was attested,* the solicitor received no benefit under the will, and his attestation did not affect the validity of a later benefit; (2) that the solicitor-trustee could not only charge for his services, but was also entitled to a share of the 5 per cent. of the income.

Charging clauses are construed strictly, so that if a solicitor or other agent is entitled to charge for " professional services " only those services which are strictly within the term may be charged for.[24] Wider clauses are scrutinised carefully, although if drawn sufficiently widely, the taxing master has power to allow costs for services not strictly professional.[25] In *Re Chalinder and Herrington,*[26] the clause stated that the solicitor should be allowed " all professional and other charges for his time and trouble notwithstanding his being such executor and trustee." The court held that this did not entitle the solicitor to charge for work not professional, which could have been done personally by a trustee who was not a solicitor. In *Re Chapple,*[27] Kay, J., commenting on the form which includes the words " including all business of whatever kind not strictly professional, but which might have been performed or would necessarily have been performed in person by a trustee not being a solicitor," he said that a clause of this description should not be inserted by a solicitor in a will unless the testator has expressly instructed him to insert those very words.

An action by a beneficiary against a professional trustee for excessive charges under a charging clause is an action for an account, and not for breach of trust, and in such an action, a beneficiary is entitled to an account as of right, without furnishing particulars of the amounts which it is claimed are excessive.[28]

Although most charging clauses are inserted for the benefit of trustees who are also solicitors, they may be made applicable to many other professional or business men. For example, in *Re Wertheimer* [29] a trustee who was a keeper of antiquities at the British Museum was held to be entitled under a charging clause to charge a commission on the sales of the testator's works of art.

Where a testator authorised the trustees of a charity which he had established to receive a salary of £1,000 for their services, the House of Lords decided that this was " earned income " for the purposes of the Income Tax Acts.[30]

D. THE TRUSTEE'S RIGHT TO INDEMNITY

Although not entitled to payment for his services, a trustee is entitled to reimburse himself for his expenses, incurred in the administration of the trust, and the Trustee Act 1925, s. 30 (2), now expressly provides that " A trustee may reimburse himself or pay or discharge out of the trust premises all expenses incurred in or about the execution of the trusts or powers." This

---

[24] *Clarkson* v. *Robinson*, [1900] 2 Ch. 722; *Re Chalinder and Herrington*, [1907] 1 Ch. 58.
[25] *Re Ames* (1883), 25 Ch.D. 72; *Re Fish*, [1893] 2 Ch. 413.
[26] *Supra.*
[27] (1884), 27 Ch.D. 584, 587.
[28] *Re Wells*, [1962] 1 W.L.R. 874.
[29] (1912), 106 L.T. 590.
[30] *Dale* v. *I.R.C.*, [1954] A.C. 11.

has rendered unnecessary any indemnity clause, which used to provide that a trustee should not be liable for the acts and defaults of a co-trustee,[31] and should have a right to recover his necessary expenses from the estate.[32] Thus, if the trustee is under an obligation to pay calls on trust shares, the trustee can recover the amount from the estate.[33] So also, where a testator has directed his executors or trustees to continue his business (but not otherwise), they have a right of indemnity against the estate. If the creditors of the deceased have assented to the continuance of the business, the trustees' right of indemnity takes precedence of their claims also.[34]

The right of indemnity is a first charge on the trust estate, both of corpus and income, taking precedence of the beneficiaries' interests; and the trustee has a lien to enforce it.[35] The fact that the beneficiary is subject to a disability makes no difference to the right.[36]

The lien which the trustee possesses does not extend to agents employed by him. They must look to him for payment.[37]

The right of the trustee to indemnity is normally proprietary and not personal; that is to say, it is limited to the amount of the trust property, but where the beneficiary is *sui juris* and absolutely entitled, " the right of the trustee to indemnity by him against liabilities incurred by the trustee by his retention of the trust property has never been limited to the trust property; it extends further, and imposes upon the cestui que trust a personal obligation enforceable in equity to indemnify his trustee." [38] This is obviously because the trustee in such a case is no more than an agent, to fulfil the orders of his beneficiary. It should be observed, however, that trustees of members' clubs are not within this principle, inasmuch as it is a condition of membership that members shall not be liable beyond the amount of their subscriptions.[39]

The trustee's right to indemnity in respect of litigation prosecuted by him as trustee requires special consideration. Wherever he has obtained leave of the court to sue or defend as a trustee, he will be entitled to an indemnity in respect of costs; and leave will always be given where the litigation is in the interests of the trust estate.[40] Even where leave of the court has not been obtained before the action is brought, the trustee will still be entitled to his costs where the action was properly brought for or on behalf of the trust estate, although in such a case the onus of proving this will be upon the trustee.[41] Thus, in *Walters* v. *Woodbridge*,[42] beneficiaries sought to set aside a decree for a compromise, alleging fraud on the part of one of the trustees in obtaining the decree, but when the charge failed to receive the support of the court, the bill was dismissed, and costs were awarded against the beneficiary.

[31] Now included in Trustee Act 1925, s. 30 (1), *post*, Chap. XXIV, s. E.
[32] See *Westley* v. *Clarke* (1759), 1 Eden 357.
[33] *James* v. *May* (1873), L.R. 6 H.L. 328 ; *Hobbs* v. *Wayet* (1887), 36 Ch.D. 256.
[34] *Dowse* v. *Gorton*, [1891] A.C. 190.
[35] *Stott* v. *Milne* (1884), 25 Ch.D. 710.
[36] *Re Andrews* (1885), 30 Ch.D. 159.
[37] *Staniar* v. *Evans* (1886), 34 Ch.D. 470.
[38] *Per* Lord Lindley, *Hardoon* v. *Belilios*, [1901] A.C. 118, 124. There is also a right of indemnity against the beneficiary personally where the beneficiary was the creator of the trust: *Matthews* v. *Ruggles-Brise*, [1911] 1 Ch. 194.
[39] *Wise* v. *Perpetual Trustee Co. Ltd.*, [1903] A.C. 139.
[40] *Stott* v. *Milne* (1884), 25 Ch.D. 710.
[41] *Re Beddoe*, [1893] 1 Ch. 547.
[42] (1878), 7 Ch.D. 504.

As he could not pay, the court ordered them to be paid out of the trust estate, since the trustee had been defending the estate as well as his character. In *Turner* v. *Hancock*,[43] Jessel, M.R., pointed out that it is not the function of the court to discourage persons from becoming trustees by inflicting costs upon them if they have performed their duties properly, or even if they have committed an innocent breach of trust. On the other hand, if the trustee has brought an action as a trustee, which is of a distinctly speculative nature, and which is unsuccessful, he will not usually be allowed his costs, even though he has acted in good faith, and under legal advice.[44]

What may properly be regarded as expenses of the trustee lies ultimately within the discretion of the taxing master,[45] but it should be remembered that trustees now possess under sections 23 and 25 of the Trustee Act 1925 wide powers to appoint agents, where a prudent man would do so on his own behalf, and the expenses incurred in employing these persons are out-of-pocket expenses of the trustee.[46] In *Re Raybould*,[47] a trustee continued the colliery business of his testator, and in doing so let down the surface, so that heavy damages were awarded against him. These were held to be expenses which could be recovered out of the trust estate. This case also illustrates the application of the doctrine of subrogation to third persons to whom trustees are indebted. This doctrine allows a creditor of a trustee to stand in the trustee's place, and recover directly from the trust estate, and this is what happened in *Re Raybould*.[48] Equity, however, will not allow a trustee to be indemnified out of the trust estate if he is himself in default to the estate, from which it follows that in such a case the creditor himself would be unable to recover from the estate by virtue of the doctrine, although he would still have his remedy against the trustee. But if there are several trustees, some of whom are in default, and some are not, the creditor is entitled to be subrogated to those trustees who are not in default.[49]

In *Re Ormrod's Settled Estate*,[50] a trustee was allowed his costs incurred in opposing in Parliament a bill affecting the trust estate, whilst in *How* v. *Earl Winterton*,[51] a subscription to a voluntary school, made to avoid the increased expense of a school-board, was allowed; and in *Hamilton* v. *Tighe*,[52] the court allowed costs incurred in establishing a right to a several fishery which formed part of the trust estate.

It would appear that in general a trustee will not be ordered to pay costs, unless he has acted dishonestly, vexatiously or unreasonably, or where he refuses or neglects to perform his duty, and this is the direct cause of the proceedings which are instituted.[53] On the other hand, the trustee may be

---

[43] (1882), 20 Ch.D. 303, 305.
[44] *Re England's Settlement Trusts*, [1918] 1 Ch. 24.
[45] This discretion is absolute on the question of *quantum*, but it is subject to review by the court where a question of principle is involved: *Re Robertson*, [1949] 1 All E.R. 1042. See also *Re Grimthorpe*, [1958] Ch. 615.
[46] *Re Bennett*, [1896] 1 Ch. 778.
[47] [1900] 1 Ch. 199.
[48] As to the trustee's agents as creditors, see p. 323, *ante.*
[49] *Re Frith*, [1902] 1 Ch. 342.
[50] [1892] 2 Ch. 318.
[51] (1902), 51 W.R. 262.
[52] [1898] 1 I.R. 123.
[53] *Loyd* v. *Spillet* (1734), 3 P.Wms. 344; *Earl of Hardwicke* v. *Vernon* (1808), 14 Ves. 504; *Taylor* v. *Glanville* (1818), 3 Madd. 176; *Marshall* v. *Sladden* (1851), 4 De G. & Sm. 468; *Moore* v. *Prance* (1851), 9 Hare 299; *Re Chapman* (1897), 72 L.T. 66.

deprived of his costs, or of part of them, for much less serious reasons, as where he defends an action without obtaining leave, and the court considers that it should not have been defended.[54]

It has been stated that, except where there is a sole beneficiary, *sui juris,* the trustee's right to indemnity is against the trust estate only. It should be added, however, that if a trustee incurs expense at the request of a beneficiary, and the trust estate proves insufficient to indemnify him, the trustee may then recover against the beneficiary personally, provided that the latter is not subject to a disability.[55]

The trustee should keep a strict account of his expenses, although failure to do so will not necessarily be fatal. In the old case of *Hethersell* v. *Hales,*[56] the trustee failed to do so, but put in a general claim for £2,500. The court, after full consideration, allowed the trustee £2,000.

Finally, it may be stated as a general principle that a trustee has no claim for indemnity for expenses incurred not in fulfilment of his duties as a trustee,[57] and if he has committed a breach of trust he may not exercise his right before he has made reparation to the trust estate in respect of it.

E. THE TRUSTEE'S DUTY TO ACCOUNT AND FURNISH INFORMATION

Every accounting party, including trustees, personal representatives and agents, must be ready with his accounts when properly called upon. It is also the duty of a trustee to furnish the beneficiary with all reasonable information concerning the manner in which the trust property is being handled. This will include a diary relating to the administration of the estate.[58] If the trustee declines information when called upon, the beneficiary may apply to the court, and the trustee will then be ordered to pay the costs of the application personally.[59] The beneficiary's right to inspect the accounts may be exercised by himself or by his solicitor,[60] but if he requires a copy, that will be supplied at his expense,[61] and the employment of a solicitor by the beneficiary will also be at the beneficiary's expense. If the beneficiary is not in possession he is only entitled to a capital account, and in this connection the question of apportionment should be watched. Similarly, if the beneficiary requires information of such a nature that it does not require to have been incorporated in the account, and the procuring of which involves expense, the beneficiary must again defray it.

Where a trust corporation is both trustee and banker, its successors in the trust should be placed in no worse position with regard to information concerning the bank account than they would have been if a third party had been the banker.[58]

Sometimes the principle that a trustee is bound to furnish the beneficiary

---

54 *Re Beddoe,* [1893] 1 Ch. 547.
55 *Balsh* v. *Hyham* (1728), 2 P.Wms. 453; *Jervis* v. *Wolferstan* (1874), L.R. 18 Eq. 18; *Fraser* v. *Murdoch* (1881), 6 App.Cas. 855; *Whittaker* v. *Kershaw* (1890), 45 Ch.D. 320.
56 (1679), 2 Ch.Rep. 158.
57 *Leedham* v. *Chawner* (1858), 4 K. & J. 458.
58 *Tiger* v. *Barclays Bank Ltd.,* [1952] 1 All E.R. 85.
59 *Re Skinner,* [1904] 1 Ch. 289; *Re Linsley,* [1904] 2 Ch. 785.
60 *Kemp* v. *Burn* (1863), 4 Giff. 348.
61 *Ottley* v. *Gilby* (1845), 8 Beav. 602.

with all relevant information may conflict with the principle that trustees exercising a discretionary power are not compelled to disclose their reasons for doing so to the beneficiaries. This was the problem in *Re Londonderry's Settlement* [62] where the beneficiaries requested the trustees to produce the minutes of meetings in which decisions upon the exercise of discretionary powers were reached; and also correspondence between trustees and individual beneficiaries. The Court of Appeal held that the trustees were not bound to produce confidential documents which related to the exercise of their discretion. Salmon, L.J., in discussing what are " trust documents," of which the beneficiary can require production, after remarking that they had never been comprehensively defined, stated [63] that they had three characteristics—

(1) they are documents in the possession of the trustees as trustees;

(2) they contain information about the trust which the beneficiaries are entitled to know;

(3) the beneficiaries have a proprietary interest in the documents, so that they are entitled to see them.

But he added that he doubted whether the beneficiaries were entitled to see parts of a document which contained information which the beneficiaries were not entitled to know, and such parts would therefore be excluded from a document which was otherwise liable to be produced.

Special problems relating to the production of documents may arise where trustees are also directors of a company in which there are trust shares. In *Butt* v. *Kelson* [64] the Court of Appeal held that one of several beneficiaries was not entitled to call upon trustees who were the sole directors of a company to use their powers as if the powers were held on trust for that beneficiary, and also that where a beneficiary asked for the production of documents relating to the affairs of the company, he must first specify the documents he wished to see; secondly, make out a proper case for their production; and, thirdly, it must be ascertained that there was no valid objection by other beneficiaries, or by the directors from the point of view of the company. If these conditions were satisfied, then the directors should allow the documents to be inspected. If all the beneficiaries are agreed, and the trustees hold enough shares to prevail at a company general meeting, the beneficiaries, by controlling the trustees' votes as registered shareholders, could effectively control the trustees as directors.

Any person who has an interest in the trust property may demand information, whether his interest is vested or contingent. [65] However, in *Low* v. *Bouverie*, [65] it was pointed out that it is no part of the trustee's duty to inform an intending assignee of the beneficiary's interest of the manner in which the beneficiary has dealt with his interest, in order to facilitate the squandering of the beneficiary's interest, but now the Law of Property Act 1925,

---

[62] [1965] Ch. 918 (Cases, p. 345).

[63] [1965] Ch. 938.

[64] [1952] Ch. 197.

[65] *Low* v. *Bouverie*, [1891] 3 Ch. 82 (Cases, p. 343); *Re Tillott*, [1892] 1 Ch. 86. As to the information which the Public Trustee must give when acting as an ordinary, judicial, or custodian trustee, see Public Trustee Rules 1912, rule 29; and on trust accounts generally see Chandler's *Trust Accounts*, and Hanbury, " Forms of Account against Executors and Trustees " (1936), 52 *Law Quarterly Review* 365.

s. 137 (8), provides that a trustee may be required to produce notices of dealings with equitable interests to any person interested in such property.

If the beneficiary is about to assign his interest, it has been suggested that the intending assignee is not a person interested in the trust property,[66] but even if this is so, it could be argued that, as a result of the decision of the House of Lords in *Hedley Byrne & Co. Ltd.* v. *Heller & Partners Ltd.,*[67] a trustee who makes an honest misrepresentation negligently may be liable to the person to whom it is addressed. A person to whom an inquiry is addressed may keep silent; or alternatively he could reply with the clear qualification that he accepted no responsibility for the statement; but if he does answer, without such a qualification, then, in the view of the House of Lords, he must exercise such care in replying as the circumstances require. However, the duty to answer carefully does not apply to all questions and, since the *Hedley Byrne* case, *Low* v. *Bouverie* has been approved by the Privy Council [68] and by the House of Lords,[69] though not in cases of trustees.

In *Horton* v. *Brocklehurst (No. 2),*[70] a trustee who was aware of the manner in which his co-trustee was keeping the accounts, and who permitted a beneficiary to act on the assumption that he sanctioned his co-trustee's keeping of the accounts, was held liable to make good the defalcations of his co-trustee, who had incorrectly kept the accounts.

Again, where a beneficiary required information from a trustee, and the trustee gave only partial information, concealing other information, so that the beneficiary in consequence acquiesced in an act of the trustee, it was held that the beneficiary was not bound, because he had acquiesced as a result of imperfect knowledge.[71] Moreover, when a beneficiary attains his majority, it is the trustee's duty to inform him of his rights, and acquiescence by him does not bind him until he is fully informed after attaining full age.[72]

The Trustee Act 1925, s. 22 (4), provides that trustees may, at their absolute discretion, but not more than once in three years, unless the nature of the trust makes another practice desirable, have their accounts audited at the cost of the trust estate, out of either capital or income. The trustee is, of course, entitled to employ an agent to keep the trust accounts. Furthermore, the Public Trustee Act 1906, s. 13 (1), provides—

> Subject to rules under this Act and unless the court otherwise orders, the condition and accounts of any trust shall, on an application being made and notice thereof given in the prescribed manner by any trustee or beneficiary, be investigated and audited by such solicitor or public accountant as may be agreed on by the applicant and the trustees or, in default of agreement, by the public trustee or some person appointed by him:
>
> Provided that (except with the leave of the court) such an investigation

---

[66] See further on this section, Gower, " The Present Position of the Rule in *Dearle* v. *Hall* " (1935), 20 *The Conveyancer* 137.

[67] [1964] A.C. 465.

[68] *Mutual Life and Citizens' Assurance Co. Ltd.* v. *Evatt*, [1971] A.C. 793. *Cf. Esso Petroleum Co. Ltd.* v. *Mardon* (1974), *The Times* newspaper, August 2.

[69] *Woodhouse A.C. Israel Cocoa Ltd. S.A.* v. *Nigerian Produce Marketing Co. Ltd.*, [1972] A.C. 741.

[70] (1858), 29 Beav. 504.

[71] *Ryder* v. *Bickerton* (1743), 3 Swanst. 80n.; *Walker* v. *Symonds* (1818), 3 Swanst. 1.

[72] *Hawkesley* v. *May*, [1956] 1 Q.B. 304.

or audit shall not be required within twelve months after any such previous investigation or audit, and that a trustee or beneficiary shall not be appointed under this section to make an investigation or audit.[73]

Some light is thrown on the procedure to be followed in auditing the accounts of judicial trustees by the decision in *Re Ridsdel*.[74] A trustee had paid a sum of £223 10s. in compromise of a claim in contract made against him. The auditor disallowed the item, but the court held that the disallowance was wrong. Where the auditor finds a payment on the face of it improper (said the court), *e.g.* an unauthorised investment, it is his duty to disallow the payment. Where, however, the payment is authorised, either by the instrument or by law, and the trustee considers it should have been made, the auditor would exceed his function if he disallowed it. If the auditor considers the propriety of such a payment open to doubt, his proper course is to leave it in the account, with a note calling attention to any circumstances which might give rise to a claim on the part of the beneficiaries.

---

[73] The procedure to be followed by an applicant under this section is set out in the Public Trustee Rules 1912, rules 31–34. If an applicant improperly insists upon an investigation under the section, the court may order him to pay the costs (*Re Oddy*, [1911] 1 Ch. 532, 536).
[74] [1947] Ch. 597.

Chapter XX

THE BENEFICIARY IN RELATION TO THE TRUST

A. THE POSITION OF A BENEFICIARY IN RELATION TO THE TRUST

The general rule that a trustee must not take heed of one beneficiary to the detriment of others has already been discussed. Put in another way, the rule implies that although a trustee may be the servant of all the beneficiaries, he is not the servant of any one of them, but an arbitrator, who must hold the scales evenly. The trustee also has another duty. He must consider the interest of the estate as a whole.[1] Equity, however, has always recognised the principle that if there is only a single beneficiary, who is *sui juris* and absolutely entitled, he may terminate and resettle the trust at his pleasure, and furthermore, if the trustee incurs liabilities in carrying out his beneficiary's instructions, he can recover, not only out of the trust property, but against the beneficiary personally. The same position follows where all the beneficiaries, being *sui juris* and absolutely entitled, unite to instruct the trustee to deviate from the terms of his trust. Moreover, it makes no difference in the latter case whether the beneficiaries are entitled as joint tenants, as tenants in common, or in succession.[2]

Again, the rule applies, not only to simple trusts, where the trustee has become, in the circumstances, a mere repository of the legal title, but also to special trusts, where the settlor may have intended that the trustee should fulfil certain duties, provided always that there is no person other than the sole beneficiary interested in the maintenance of the trust.[3] This is illustrated by the well-known case of *Saunders* v. *Vautier*,[4] where a trustee was directed to accumulate the income upon a legacy until a specified date. The court held that as soon as the beneficiary became of age, since he was ultimately entitled to the income, he could call at any time for the transfer to him of the capital sum. Similarly, in *Re Browne's Will*,[5] personal representatives were directed to employ Consols in the purchase of a life annuity for a woman, to be held to her separate use without power of anticipation. The court held that, as the woman was unmarried at the time when the will took effect, the restraint being at that time of no effect, she was entitled to the transfer to her of the Consols, with no fetter on their disposal. It is necessary to distinguish these cases, however, from cases in which some other person will benefit by an intermediate gift of income, or in which the interests remain contingent until the occurrence of a future event, *e.g.* a gift to such members of a class of persons as shall be living when the youngest attains the age of 21, in equal

---

[1] *Re Hayes' Will Trusts*, [1971] 1 W.L.R. 758.
[2] *Palairet* v. *Carew* (1863), 32 Beav. 564; *Re White*, [1901] 1 Ch. 570.
[3] *Re George Whichelow Ltd.*, [1954] 1 W.L.R. 5; *Re Powles*, [1954] 1 W.L.R. 336.
[4] (1841), Cr. & Ph. 240. A gift of income in perpetuity to a charity does not necessarily give a right to the corpus: *Re Levy*, [1960] Ch. 346. See, further, Keeton and Sheridan, *The Modern Law of Charities*, 2nd Ed., p. 240.
[5] (1859), 27 Beav. 324.

shares. Here, obviously, no member of the class can claim absolute control of his share until the last member has attained the age of 21.

A further illustration is afforded in some discretionary trusts. In *Re Smith*,[6] trustees of a will were directed to apply at their absolute discretion the whole or any part of a fund for the benefit of A, and the rest of the fund, so far as it was not so applied, for the benefit of B. Romer, J., held that A and B were together to be regarded as the sole objects of the discretionary trust, and were together entitled to have the whole fund applied for their benefit, and therefore, A and B both being *sui juris*, they together could transfer the property as if they owned it. In the course of his judgment,[7] Romer, J., emphasised the following points—

> (1) 'Where there is a trust to apply the whole or such part of a fund as trustees think fit to or for the benefit of A, and A has assigned his interest under the trust, or becomes bankrupt, although his assignee or his trustee in bankruptcy stand in no better position than he does and cannot demand that the fund shall be handed to them, yet they are in a position to say to A: "Any money which the trustees do in the exercise of their discretion pay to you, passes by the assignment or under the bankruptcy." But they cannot say that in respect of any money which the trustees have not paid to A or invested in purchasing goods or other things for A, but which they apply for the benefit of A in such a way that no money or goods ever gets into the hands of A.'

> (2) 'Where there is a trust under which trustees have a discretion as to applying the whole or part of a fund to or for the benefit of a particular person, that particular person cannot come to the trustees, and demand the fund; for the whole fund has not been given to him but only so much as the trustees think fit to let him have. But when the trustees have no discretion as to the amount of the fund to be applied, the fact that the trustees have a discretion as to the method in which the whole of the fund shall be applied for the benefit of the particular person does not prevent that particular person from coming and saying: "Hand over the fund to me." '

> (3) 'What is to happen where the trustees have a discretion whether they will apply the whole or only a portion of the fund for the benefit of one person, but are obliged to apply the rest of the fund, so far as not applied for the benefit of the first named person, to or for the benefit of a second named person? There, two people together are the sole objects of the discretionary trust and, between them, are entitled to have the whole fund applied to them or for their benefit. It has been laid down by the Court of Appeal in the case to which I have referred [8] that, in such a case as that you treat all the people put together just as though they formed one person for whose benefit the trustees were directed to apply the whole of a particular fund.'

Where a beneficiary who is *sui juris* and absolutely entitled mortgages his

6 [1928] Ch. 915. See also *Green* v. *Spicer* (1830), 1 Russ. & M. 395; *Younghusband* v. *Gisborne* (1844), 1 Coll. 400; *Re Nelson* (1918), [1928] Ch. 920n.
7 [1928] Ch. 918–20.
8 *Re Nelson*, [1928] Ch. 920n.

interest or several beneficiaries collectively absolutely entitled mortgage their share to one mortgagee, the question arises whether the mortgagee can terminate the trust, and call for the transfer of the legal estate to himself. The view taken by the court is that, so long as the equity of redemption subsists (that is to say until the mortgagee forecloses, or exercises his power of sale), the mortgagor may also be regarded as retaining an interest in the trust, and therefore the mortgagee cannot require the transfer; but if he sold the entire interest of the beneficiaries under his power of sale, the purchaser obviously could.[9]

When a statutory trust for sale exists, or where the instrument so provides, the trustees are under an obligation to consult the wishes of the beneficiaries of full age in the exercise of their powers,[10] and if they fail to do so, they may be restrained by injunction from taking action without consultation.[11]

It should be mentioned that where beneficiaries are entitled in succession so that the trustees may become liable for estate duty on the death of one or more of them, the beneficiaries' right to call for a distribution of the trust property under the rule in *Saunders* v. *Vautier*[12] is subject to the trustees' lien on the property in respect of liability for estate duty.[13]

B. THE BENEFICIARY'S RIGHT TO POSSESSION

It has been stated in an earlier chapter that the nature of the trustee's estate is such that he is entitled to the custody of the title deeds. It was assumed in such a case that the legal estate was vested in the trustees; that is to say, since 1925, that the land is not settled land, for in such a case, the legal estate is now generally vested in the tenant for life, and an incident of that estate will be possession of the title deeds. Where the title deeds are in the hands of the trustees, however, the beneficiary is entitled to their production for inspection, even although he has an interest only in the proceeds of sale.[14]

As far as possession of land subject to a trust is concerned, the position has changed somewhat since 1925 owing to the fact that nearly all trusts of land are now either trusts for sale or settlements under the Settled Land Act. Before 1926, if there was a passive trust, the beneficiary could compel the trustee to give him possession,[15] and if the trustee ejected him, the court could compel the trustee to account for the whole of the rents which he could have recovered from the tenants.[16] Where, however, the trust was not for one beneficiary only, but there were other interests besides those of the tenant for life, the court had absolute discretion before 1926 to order whether the trustee or the tenant for life should have actual possession, and if the latter, then upon what terms.[17] This position was not altered by the Settled Land Act

---

[9] See *Re Cooper and Allen's Contract for Sale to Harlech* (1876), 4 Ch.D. 802; *Re Bell*, [1896] 1 Ch. 1; *Hockey* v. *Western*, [1898] 1 Ch. 350.

[10] *Re House*, [1929] 2 Ch. 166; *Bull* v. *Bull*, [1955] 1 Q.B. 234. Law of Property Act 1925, s. 26 (3). *Cf. Barclay* v. *Barclay*, [1970] 2 Q.B. 677.

[11] *Waller* v. *Waller*, [1967] 1 W.L.R. 451.

[12] (1841), Cr. & Ph. 240.

[13] *Re Joynson's Will Trusts*, [1954] Ch. 567.

[14] *Davis* v. *Earl of Dysart* (1855), 20 Beav. 405, 414; *Re Cowin* (1886), 33 Ch.D. 179; *Gough* v. *Offley* (1852), 5 De G. & Sm. 653. See also *Tiger* v. *Barclays Bank Ltd.*, [1952] 1 All E.R. 85; *Butt* v. *Kelson*, [1952] Ch. 197.

[15] *Brown* v. *How* (1740), Barn.C. 354.   [16] *Kaye* v. *Powel* (1791), 1 Ves.Jun. 408.

[17] *Jenkins* v. *Milford* (1820), 1 Jac. & W. 629; *Taylor* v. *Taylor* (1875), L.R. 20 Eq. 297.

of 1882, although after that date the court exercised its discretion with increased freedom in favour of the tenant for life.[18]

Now, by virtue of section 29 of the Law of Property Act 1925, trustees for sale may delegate their powers of leasing and management to a *cestui que trust* for the time being beneficially entitled in possession to the net rents and profits of the land *during his life or for any less period*, and in section 30 it is provided that if the trustees do not so delegate their powers, the beneficiary may apply to the court. It would appear that in delegating these powers, the trustees also give possession. The power of leasing is exercised by the beneficiary only in the names and on behalf of the trustees. The trustees are not liable for the acts or defaults of the *cestui que trust*, but in respect of the exercise of the power of leasing by the beneficiary the latter is deemed to be in the position of a trustee, though not, apparently, a trustee for sale.

As far as the tenant for life under the Settled Land Act 1925 is concerned, he will be automatically entitled to possession when his interest vests in possession.[19]

If a beneficiary under a trust is occupying a leasehold house which is part of the trust property, his period of occupation may count, under section 6 of the Leasehold Reform Act 1967, towards the qualifying five-year period under the Act, by virtue of which the tenant may acquire enfranchisement or an extension of the lease.

Where the trust estate includes chattels, settled for the benefit of persons in succession, the tenant for life is also entitled to the use and control of them for the period of his interest; and such chattels do not vest in the trustee in bankruptcy of the tenant for life [20] because they are regarded as being in the possession of the trustees, who are able to maintain an action for conversion against a wrongdoer. Use and possession, without qualification by the terms of the settlement, would include enjoyment by the tenant for life in his own or any other person's house, and also letting them out on hire,[21] but if heirlooms are annexed to a mansion house, the heirlooms can only be hired out with the house.[22] The right of beneficiaries under a statutory trust for sale to possession of the land was considered in *Bull* v. *Bull*.[23] In that case there had been a joint purchase in unequal shares of a dwelling-house by a mother and son. The court held that they were tenants common in equity, and as the son had attempted to eject the mother, the court held that, until sale, each of them was entitled, concurrently with the other, to the possession of the premises, so that neither could eject the other.

C. THE BENEFICIARY'S RIGHT TO COMPEL
TRANSFER BY THE TRUSTEES

A sole beneficiary who is *sui juris* and absolutely entitled may compel the trustee to convey the legal estate as he directs. He may, for example, compel

---

18 *Re Wythes*, [1893] 2 Ch. 369; *Re Bagot's Settlement*, [1894] 1 Ch. 177; *Re Newen*, [1894] 2 Ch. 297.
19 See Settled Land Act 1925, s. 19, and notes thereto in Wolstenholme and Cherry's *Conveyancing Statutes*.
20 *Barker* v. *Furlong*, [1891] 2 Ch. 172.
21 *Marshall* v. *Blew* (1741), 2 Atk. 217.
22 *Cadogan* v. *Kennett* (1776), Cowp. 432, 436.
23 [1955] 1 Q.B. 234.

the transfer of shares held by the trustees to him.[24] If the trustee refuses, the beneficiary may apply to the court, and the trustee will have to pay the costs of the application unless there are reasonable grounds for his refusal.[25] Furthermore, if the beneficiary in such a case has sold his equitable interest the purchaser may also call for a conveyance from the trustee, on the same terms.[26] In such cases, however, the trustee must always satisfy himself that the beneficiary or the purchaser is the only person interested, and he cannot be compelled to give conveyance of parts of the trust estate at various times. Furthermore, the trustee cannot be compelled to transfer the estate by any other description than that by which the conveyance was made to him.[27] Again, in *Hannah* v. *Hodgson*,[28] under a trust, a mother, the tenant for life, had a power of appointment among her children, and in default of appointment the children took. She appointed to some, but not to others, and then, with her husband, the remainderman for life, and the appointees, she called upon the trustees to convey. The trustees had reason to suppose that there had been fraud on the power, resulting from an unfair bargain between the appointor and the appointees, and they refused to convey. The court supported their attitude, and held, further, that they were entitled to their costs. There must, however, be reason for the suspicion. The mere possibility of fraud does not entitle the trustees to refuse to convey.

D. THE ACCELERATION OF BENEFICIAL INTERESTS UNDER TRUSTS

It has long been an established doctrine in the law of wills that where there is a gift in remainder, following upon a life interest, and the life interest fails to take effect, *e.g.* by disclaimer, then the remainder is accelerated, and the beneficiary is entitled to it forthwith.[29] A similar situation would arise where the person entitled to the life interest had witnessed the will, and so was unable to take,[30] or where the life tenant was unable to take because he refused to comply with a condition.[31]

In *Re Scott*,[32] however, Warrington, J., held that the principle did not apply to real estate, where the limitations were legal (and where there were prior contingent remainders capable of being preserved if the right people were born), although it certainly applied to equitable limitations of real estate.[33] In *Re Hatfeild's Will Trusts*,[34] Harman, J., pointed out that the correctness of Warrington, J.'s distinction, in respect of legal interests in real estate, had been doubted, and he refused to follow it, since the 1925 legislation had abolished the distinction between equitable and legal limitations. In the case before him, the testator in 1938 devised freehold property to his cousin, H, for life, with

24 *Re Marshall*, [1914] 1 Ch. 192; *Re Sandeman's Will Trusts*, [1937] 1 All E.R. 368; *Re Weiner*, [1956] 1 W.L.R. 579.
25 *Re Ruddock* (1910), 102 L.T. 89.
26 *Angier* v. *Stannard* (1834), 3 My. & K. 566.
27 *Goodson* v. *Ellisson* (1827), 3 Russ. 583, 594; *Holford* v. *Phipps* (1841), 3 Beav. 434.
28 (1861), 30 Beav. 19. See also *King* v. *King* (1857), 1 De G. & J. 663.
29 *Re Scott*, [1911] 2 Ch. 374.
30 *Jull* v. *Jacobs* (1876), 3 Ch.D. 703.
31 *D'Eyncourt* v. *Gregory* (1864), 34 Beav. 36.
32 [1911] 2 Ch. 374.
33 *Re Conyngham*, [1921] 1 Ch. 491.
34 [1958] Ch. 469.

remainder to H's sons successively in tail, with remainder to another cousin, A, for life, with remainder to A's sons successively in tail, with remainder to a third cousin, C, in fee simple; and he gave his residuary estate to trustees upon certain trusts. The testator died in 1941, and H died without issue in April 1950. By deed dated August 11, 1950, A, who at that time had no son, disclaimed his interest under the will. C, who would have received the ultimate fee simple, died in 1951. The question to be decided was (i) whether until the birth of a son to A, or until his death, the income of the settled property should be paid to C's personal representatives; or (ii) whether it should be regarded as income of the contingent interest of A's unborn son, by virtue of section 175 (1) of the Law of Property Act 1925, to be held on trust for any future son of A; or, finally (iii) whether it should form part of the residue. Harman, J., decided that, until the birth of the son to A, the income of the settled property from H's death should be paid to the personal representatives of C, whose interest in the remainder had been accelerated by A's disclaimer.

Acceleration by the release of prior life interests in favour of children is a common feature of the modern law of trusts. In *Re Kebty-Fletcher's Will Trusts*,[35] and again in *Re Harker's Will Trusts*,[36] it was held that this has no effect on the class of children who are entitled to take. It does not have the effect, as it did in *Andrews* v. *Partington*,[37] of excluding children unborn at the time when the release of the life interest occurred, when the children then born acquired a vested interest.

Until recently, the doctrine of acceleration had not been regarded as having any application to trusts created by deed. However, in *Re Flower's Settlement Trusts*,[38] it was suggested that it might be applicable to a settlement *inter vivos*. The facts are complicated, but the question at issue was whether there was a passing of a fund at the date of the settlor's death, so as to attract estate duty. Upjohn, J., and the Court of Appeal both decided that in this case there was no acceleration, but Jenkins, L.J., said [39]—

> . . . although all the authorities to which we have been referred have been concerned with wills, Mr. Cross submits—and I do not think that Mr. Pennycuick disputes—that there is no reason for applying any different rule to a settlement inter vivos. As to that I would say that I am disposed to agree that the principle must be broadly the same; but I cannot help feeling that it may well be more difficult, in the case of a settlement, to collect the intention necessary to bring the doctrine of acceleration into play.

Accordingly the precise circumstances in which the doctrine applies to trusts remains to be explored. In *Re Dawson's Settlement* [40] Goff, J., applied the doctrine to an *inter vivos* settlement in which, the life interest of a former wife of the settlor having failed, the contingent interests of the children were accelerated.

---

[35] [1969] 1 Ch. 339.
[36] [1969] 1 W.L.R. 1124.
[37] (1791), 3 Bro.C.C. 401.
[38] [1957] 1 W.L.R. 401.
[39] [1957] 1 W.L.R. 405.
[40] [1966] 1 W.L.R. 1456.

CHAPTER XXI

TRUSTS AND TAXATION

ONE of the most striking legal changes of recent times has been the progressive modification of the trust concept to serve changed social conditions. Today, land is no longer the most important item of property which can be made the subject of a trust. It is commercial property of all kinds, but more especially stocks, shares, insurance policies and similar property. Moreover, whilst formerly, in a family settlement, the main purpose of the settlor was to preserve the corpus of the fund settled, so that it might be enjoyed successively by various members of his family, today, although that purpose is still an important one, his major object will be, by means of a settlement, to reduce the incidence of taxation upon his property.

Generally, in preparing a settlement, the draftsman has had in mind that it is affected by four distinct kinds of taxation. These are: (1) stamp duties; (2) estate duty; (3) income tax; and (4) capital gains tax. In the future, there may be two further taxes to be considered. In his budget statement in the spring of 1974, the Chancellor of the Exchequer foreshadowed the introduction of a capital transfer tax in the autumn of 1974, to apply to chargeable gifts made after the date of his spring statement. What gifts will be chargeable, and what the rates of tax will be, are the subject of a White Paper published in August 1974 and summarised in the Preface. The tax will reduce the usefulness of the creation or variation of trusts for the purpose of avoiding or reducing estate duty. A Green Paper on a wealth tax, *i.e.* a tax *on capital* (as opposed to the existing tax *on capital gains*) was also published in August 1974, and is also summarised in the Preface.[1]

1. STAMP DUTIES

These are taxes on documents, and the Stamp Act 1891, together with later Acts, defines the various classes of documents, and the stamp duty payable on each class. For practical purposes, there are two classes of duty: (a) fixed duties, usually small, and (b) ad valorem duties, which affect settlements and many kinds of gift, and which are now substantial. If, therefore, the object of the settlement is to save taxation, the possible saving must be considered in relation to the stamp duty payable upon the transaction.

2. ESTATE DUTY

There have, in the past, been a number of death duties, *e.g.* estate duty, legacy duty, succession duty and settled estate duty. The Finance Act 1949, s. 27, abolished all such duties except estate duty, which is chargeable[2] upon all property which " passes " on death. " Passing " is a wide term,

---

[1] See also Lovell, " Reflections on a Unified Estate and Gift Tax Regime " (1974) *British Tax Review* 141 ; Ray, " Capital Transfer Tax " (1974) 124 *New Law Journal* 785 (to be cont.). The literature upon taxation and settlements is extensive. The reader is referred particularly to Wheatcroft, *The Taxation of Gifts and Settlements*, and Potter and Monroe, *Tax Planning With Precedents*. See also Keeton, *Modern Developments in the Law of Trusts*, pp. 112–128. Bale, " Whither Death Duties " (1974) Public Law 121.

[2] Under the Finance Act 1894, Part I, as amended.

with a technical meaning. It not only covers property which the deceased himself leaves on death, but any other property which changes hands, or in which rights are modified, in consequence of his death. Moreover, in recent times estate duty has been imposed upon a number of transfers of property undertaken by the deceased in his lifetime, with the object of avoiding duty. In general, transactions of substance which have occurred within seven years of death may be reopened in this way. Estate duty rises steadily with the size of the estate. It will be abolished if the capital transfer tax is introduced.

3. INCOME TAX

The present law relating to income tax is to be found primarily in the Income and Corporation Taxes Act 1970 (a lengthy and complicated statute), and in later Finance Acts, together with their interpretation by the courts and decisions by the courts on earlier Acts. There is no general definition of " income " in the Act of 1970, or any other Act. " Income," in its legal sense, differs in important respects from any layman's conception of it. In general, it is taken to be the opposite of " capital." Where income tax is levied on the income of individuals from some gilt-edged stocks it is deducted at source at the standard rate. If, therefore, the recipient is entitled to some of the reliefs or allowances that can be set against the tax, there may be a case for claiming repayment of a portion of it from the Revenue. The same applies to tax credits on dividends.

Surtax was a tax, additional to income tax, payable by persons (but not corporations) whose income exceeded a specified amount. For those in very high income groups, the arrangement of income in order to minimise the effect of the higher rates of income tax (replacing surtax) has become a problem of major importance, and a variety of methods, some of them of very considerable complexity, have been used from time to time.

In considering the validity of any arrangement to minimise the effect of our modern machinery of taxation, the attitude of the courts is of major importance. This has often been discussed by the courts, and although from time to time individual judges have appeared to lean slightly towards the Revenue, the general attitude of the judiciary has not varied. A taxing statute is one which deprives the subject of money or property to which otherwise he would be fully entitled. It is therefore the duty of the Revenue to show that the transaction is within the very letter of the statute imposing the tax; otherwise, the transaction is immune. The judiciary has set its face firmly against any claim of the Revenue that a transaction, though not covered by the words of the statute, is nevertheless within its spirit.[3] Two modern expressions of the judicial attitude may be mentioned. In *Levene* v. *I.R.C.*,[4] Lord Sumner said—

> It is trite law that His Majesty's subjects are free, if they can, to make their own arrangements, so that their cases may fall outside the scope of the taxing Acts. They incur no legal penalties and, strictly speaking, no moral censure if, having considered the lines drawn by the Legislature

[3] See, *e.g.*, Lord Cairns in *Partington* v. *Attorney-General* (1869), L.R. 4 H.L. 100, 122.
[4] [1928] A.C. 217, 227.

for the imposition of taxes, they make it their business to walk outside them.

One consequence of this has been that taxing statutes are usually lengthy, and their language is frequently involved, since the draftsman is attempting to include a number of devices which might otherwise escape taxation. The courts are, therefore, required to undertake some exceedingly complicated exercises in construction. Nevertheless, the attitude of the judge remains unaltered. In the words of Lord Simonds, in *Lord Vestey's Executors* v. *I.R.C.*[5]—

> The determination of these appeals involves a consideration of certain sections of two Acts of Parliament [Finance Acts 1936, s. 18, and 1938, s. 38] which were designed to bring within the ambit of taxation to income tax and sur-tax income which otherwise would escape that burden. For that reason and because the ways of those who would avoid liability to tax are often devious and obscure, the sections are framed in language of the widest and most general scope and in the case of one of the Acts (I refer to the Finance Act, 1936, s. 18 (4)) the operative sub-sections are reinforced by a provision which appears to exhort the assessing authority, and presumably the court, to let the balance, wherever possible, be weighted against the taxpayer. But, this notwithstanding, I think that it remains the taxpayer's privilege to claim exemption from tax unless his case is fairly brought within the words of the taxing section . . .

Corporations do not now pay income tax, their profits being assessed to a flat rate of corporation tax, now governed principally by the Income and Corporation Taxes Act 1970.

4. INCOME TAX AND THE BENEFICIARY'S INTEREST

So far as trusts are concerned, special principles, distinct from those evolved in courts of equity, have always been applicable to the levy of income tax. In his speech in the House of Lords in *Williams* v. *Singer*,[6] Viscount Cave, L.C., said—

> The fact is that if the Income Tax Acts are examined, it will be found that the person charged with the tax is neither the trustee nor the beneficiary as such, but the person in actual receipt and control of the income which it is sought to reach. The object of the Acts is to secure for the State a proportion of the profits chargeable, and this end is attained (speaking generally) by the simple and effective expedient of taxing the profits where they are found. If the beneficiary receives them he is liable to be assessed upon them. If the trustee receives and controls them, he is primarily so liable. If they are under the control of a guardian or committee for a person not sui juris or of an agent or receiver for persons resident abroad, they are taxed in his hands. But in cases where a trustee or agent is made chargeable with the tax the statutes recognize the fact that he is a trustee or agent for others and

[5] [1949] 1 All E.R. 1108, 1112–3.
[6] [1921] 1 A.C. 65, 72–73.

he is taxed on behalf of and as representing his beneficiaries or principals. This is made clear by the language of many sections of the Act of 1842. For instance, section 41 provides that a person not resident in Great Britain shall be chargeable " in the name of " his trustee or agent. Section 44 refers to the trustee or agent of any person as being assessed " in respect of " such person, and gives him a right to retain the tax out of any money of such person coming to his hands. Section 51, under which trustees and others are bound to make returns, refers to the event of the beneficiary being charged either " in the name of " the trustee or other person making the return, or in his own name. Section 53 refers to the trustee or agent as being charged " on account " of the beneficiary; and similar expressions are found in other sections. In short, the intention of the Acts appears to be that where a beneficiary is in possession and control of the trust income and is sui juris, he is the person to be taxed; and that while a trustee may in certain cases be charged with the tax, he is in all such cases to be treated as charged on behalf or in respect of his beneficiaries, who will accordingly be entitled to any exemption or abatement which the Acts allow.

Lord Watson's remarks related to the situation where a beneficiary abroad is entitled to income under an English trust. In the converse case, of a beneficiary entitled to income under a foreign trust, the question may also be affected by the application of foreign law. In *Drummond* v. *Collins*[7] the House of Lords decided that income from a foreign trust is assessable in the hands of the beneficiary as income arising from dominion or foreign assets under case 5 of Schedule D. In *Baker* v. *Archer-Shee*[8] Lady Archer-Shee was entitled to a life interest under a settlement made by her father (an American), the settlement being administered by a trust company in the State of New York, and the investments being (from the standpoint of English law) foreign investments. Her husband was assessed under cases 4 and 5 of Schedule D in respect of the gross income received by the New York trusts. He contended that he was assessable only in respect of the net sum remitted by the trustees to his wife, in the United Kingdom (which was nil). Since the trust was administered in New York, the law applicable to its administration was the law of the State of New York, which in this appeal was assumed (for lack of expert evidence) to be identical with English law. The House of Lords therefore decided that, under the English Income Tax Acts, Lady Archer-Shee being the beneficiary, her husband was assessable in respect of the interest and dividends of all the securities forming the trust fund, the House of Lords thus directly applying the reasoning of Viscount Cave in *Williams* v. *Singer*.[9] The assumption of the identity of English law on this point with that of the State of New York was erroneous, however, and in *Archer-Shee* v. *Garland*,[10] Lady Archer-Shee's husband raised the same question a second time in respect of three further years of assessment. This time expert evidence was given on the law of the State of

---

[7] [1915] A.C. 1011.
[8] [1927] A.C. 844. See also *Ransom* v. *Higgs*, [1973] 1 W.L.R. 1180.
[9] [1921] 1 A.C. 65.
[10] [1931] A.C. 212. See also the Income and Corporation Taxes Act 1970, s. 122.

New York, which was applicable to the administration of the trust, and to the nature of the beneficiary's interest. This evidence established that Lady Archer-Shee's interest was limited to the receipt of a net sum after administration, and accordingly, on this ground only, her husband was successful in his claim that he was chargeable only on the net sum remitted to her in the United Kingdom (as the legislation stood then).

5. CAPITAL GAINS TAX

A decade ago Finance Acts introduced into English law the principle of taxing capital gains, and this has had important consequences in the management of trust funds. Until the year 1971–2, short-term gains were liable to income tax and surtax, but all capital gains are now subject to capital gains tax.

Capital gains tax was introduced by the Finance Act 1965, and it has produced some problems of very great difficulty for trustees. Charities are exempt from tax.[11]

By section 19, tax is chargeable on the disposal of all assets (with a number of exceptions) after April 5, 1965. It is applicable to (a) residents and persons ordinarily resident in the United Kingdom; and (b) persons non-resident in the United Kingdom if they carry on a trade through a branch or agency here, in respect of gains accruing through the sale of assets by the branch or agent. The flat rate of tax is thirty per cent. of the gain. Losses are deductible, and by section 21, as an alternative to the flat rate, where it is to the benefit of the person charged, he may elect that one half of the net chargeable gains, or his net chargeable gains less £2,500 (whichever is the greater), shall be treated as ordinary unearned income, and the other half or £2,500, as the case may be, shall be exempt. Chargeable assets are all forms of property, including debts, options, foreign currency, incorporeal property, and any form of property created by the person disposing of it, or otherwise coming to be owned without being acquired.[12] Disposal includes part disposal, which in turn includes the creation of a lesser interest in it. Assets transferred by or to a trust constitute a disposal and are therefore subject to tax, but not transfers by way of security.

Section 22 (5) provides that where a trustee holds property for another person absolutely entitled as against the trustee, or for any person who would be so entitled but for being an infant or other person under disability, the property is treated, so far as assessment of tax is concerned, as the property of the beneficiary, and as if the disposal of it were carried out by him; but this subsection does not extend to an infant whose interest is contingent upon attaining a specified age, even though that age is the age of majority.[13] In all other cases, trustees must pay the flat rate of tax.

Death of the asset holder was originally treated as a disposal, but that is not a chargeable disposal in the case of deaths after March 30, 1971.[14]

[11] Finance Act 1965, s. 35.
[12] s. 22 (1).
[13] *Tomlinson* v. *Glyns Executor and Trustee Co.*, [1970] Ch. 112.
[14] s. 24 of the 1965 Act, as amended by the Finance Act 1971, s. 59 and Sched. 12, paras. 1–3. See, further, Lovell, " The Abolition of the Charge to Capital Gains Tax on Death " (1973) *British Tax Review* 27.

Section 25 makes detailed provision for the application of capital gains tax under this Act to trusts and settlements. Once again, trustees are regarded as a continuing body, resident in the United Kingdom unless the general administration of the trust is conducted outside the United Kingdom, and a majority of the trustees are not ordinarily resident in the United Kingdom. Section 25 (2) provides that the creation of a trust is a disposal of the assets settled, notwithstanding that the settlor retains an interest in the property, or that the settlement is a declaration of trust whereby the assets remain legally vested in the settlor. The property is regarded as transferred for a consideration equal to the market value whenever a beneficiary becomes absolutely entitled to it. When a life interest terminates, there is no charge to capital gains tax. Estate duty is payable, if the estate is large enough, and the general scheme of the Finance Act 1971 is to make estate duty and capital gains tax mutually exclusive.

Section 25 (9) enables capital gains tax to be recovered from a beneficiary. Should the trustees fail to pay the tax within six months, and transfer the asset to a beneficiary, the tax can be recovered from the beneficiary at any time within two years of the tax becoming payable.

Before making any distribution of capital to beneficiaries, trustees therefore must now ascertain what capital gains have been made, and what tax is payable. Advancement of part of the trust capital, so as to take that capital out of the trust, is a disposal of that amount. If a capital transfer tax is introduced, advancements are expected to be chargeable.

It is now necessary to examine briefly how these various taxes may affect the main types of settlement. These are: (1) deeds of covenant; (2) family settlements; (3) marriage settlements; (4) discretionary trusts.

A. DEEDS OF COVENANT

Covenants are exceedingly common, and they certainly exceed half a million in number, the bulk of them being executed in favour of charities. They are of two kinds, being either for payments of capital or for payments of income. Covenants for payment of capital do not give rise to many problems of taxation. Stamp duty is payable on the covenant, at the rate of 25p per £100 of capital settled. No income tax problems arise. Any liability on such a covenant outstanding at the death of the settlor is not allowed as a debt for computation of estate duty, unless the covenant was executed for money, or money's worth, a limitation which therefore excludes marriage as a consideration for the covenant.[15] Moreover, a payment made during the settlor's lifetime under a voluntary deed of covenant is regarded as a gift at the date of payment, so that it ranks for estate duty unless made more than seven years before the death (or to a charity).

Covenants for the transfer of income are by far the most common type of deed of covenant. Frequently, it is provided that they cease on the settlor's death, and in such a case, estate duty is not usually payable. Where, however, the covenant is to continue after the settlor's death, the question whether it can be regarded as a debt payable by the estate is answered in the same way

---

[15] *Lord Vestey's Executors* v. *I.R.C.*, [1949] 1 All E.R. 1108, 1112–3.

as it is in respect of capital covenants. Moreover, payments made within seven years of the settlor's death also attract estate duty (unless in favour of a charity or unless the gift is within one of the following four exceptions)—

(1) Gifts made in consideration of marriage.[16]

(2) Gifts which are proved to the satisfaction of the Commissioners to be part of the normal expenditure of the settlor, and to have been reasonable, having regard to the amount of his income.[17]

(3) Gifts not exceeding £100 in the aggregate.

(4) Gifts not exceeding £500 in the aggregate, which do not include any interest in settled property, and in which *bona fide* possession of the property is assumed by the donee immediately, and is retained to the entire exclusion of the settlor.

The first three exceptions are contained in section 59 (2) of the Finance (1909–10) Act 1910, the fourth was introduced by the Finance Act 1949, s. 33.

Under an income covenant, income is transferred from one person to another. In consequence, the covenantor pays the sum due under the covenant, after first deducting the tax at the basic rate, whilst the donee reclaims from the Revenue any repayment which may be due to him in respect of exemptions and reliefs to which he may be entitled or pays any additional tax to which he may be liable at a higher rate. When the payer deducts tax, he does not actually hand over extra cash to the Revenue if he has an income on which he has paid income tax at the basic rate or at a higher rate, as he is treated as having already paid the tax on the payments under the covenant. If the covenantor is liable to tax at a high rate, the covenantee, if able to reclaim tax, can only reclaim at the basic rate. Hence, the higher the basic rate is in any given year, the higher the covenantee's net income in cases of reclaim. This is particularly important for charities, which are not liable to income tax at all, and hence can reclaim the whole of the basic rate.

These benefits, however, are only available if the deed of covenant satisfies certain conditions. These are—

(1) The covenant must be stated to last for a period which can exceed six years.[18] However, a covenant expressed to be payable to a person for seven years " if he and the covenantor so long live " satisfies this condition.

(2) The deed of covenant should not include a power of revocation.[19]

(3) The payments should not be made to, or applied for, the benefit of an unmarried child of the settlor during infancy.[20] Covenants in favour of the children of another person do, however, enable tax to be reclaimed.

(4) The payments must be distributed within the financial year in which they are made, so that the income disposed of by the covenant appears as someone else's in the same financial year.[21] (This condition applies only in very limited circumstances.)

---

[16] See, now, the Finance Acts 1963, s. 53, and 1968, s. 36.

[17] See, now, the Finance Act 1968, s. 37.

[18] Income and Corporation Taxes Act 1970, s. 434 (1).

[19] *Ibid.*, s. 445 (1).

[20] *Ibid.*, Sect. 437, as amended by the Finance Act 1971, Sect. 16. " Child " includes a step-child, an adopted child, and an illegitimate child: 1970 Act, s. 444 (1). See also *I.R.C.* v. *Russell* (1955), 36 T.C. 83.

[21] Income and Corporation Taxes Act 1970, s. 450. But see s. 457.

(5) The payment must not be a " pension " within section 182 of the Act of 1970. " Pension " here has a specialised meaning, and a covenant for a pension for a retired employee or his dependants probably gives a deduction for tax purposes to the settlor.[22]

(6) A deed of covenant by a husband in favour of a wife living with him does not reduce the husband's taxable income by the covenanted (or any) amount.[23] Moreover, by section 448 of the Act of 1970, a deed of covenant establishing a trust in favour of a discretionary class of persons, of whom the spouse of the covenantor is one, is also ineffective for tax purposes.

B. FAMILY SETTLEMENTS

The family settlement of former times, based upon the tenure of freehold land, has, in the past half century, given place to a different kind of family settlement, in which the principal assets are stocks, shares, units in unit trusts, property bonds and other varieties of personalty investment, and in which one of the main objects of the settlor is to diminish the incidence of taxation, both upon the income of the beneficiaries, and also upon the estate as a whole, on its transmission on the death of the settlor.

Generally, therefore, a family settlement will be executed by a person who has a wife, children, and possibly grandchildren. Its primary effect will be to distribute the property in varying interests among the members of his family, thus diminishing his income and also the capital of his estate, which will pass on his death. The methods by which such a plan can be achieved are varied, and often very complex. Only one or two of the more common features of family settlements, and the effect of taxation upon them, can therefore be mentioned. It must be stressed, however, that any settlement is valueless from the standpoint of reducing the incidence of taxation, if the settlor himself retains any interest in, or control over, the property which he is purporting to transfer for the benefit of his family. Furthermore, it is essential that the settlement, once executed, should be irrevocable. Even if the settlement fulfils these conditions, it is then necessary that the settlor should survive the making of the settlement for seven years in order to make it completely immune from estate duty unless the settlement is in favour of a charity, in which case, if it does not exceed £50,000, it is immediately free of such duty (Finance Act 1972, s. 121).

The reservation of even a small interest by the settlor will render the settlement ineffective to save estate duty; and moreover, section 11 (1) of the Customs and Inland Revenue Act 1889 requires *bona fide* possession by the beneficiaries of the interests conferred (a direction which is by no means clear, if the beneficiary is an infant who is entitled to a reversionary interest), and also requires that no benefit shall be reserved to the settlor " by contract or otherwise." [24]

If, under the settlement, property is given to an infant beneficiary, so that he becomes entitled to it on attaining the age of eighteen, but prior to that he had only a contingent interest, then if the beneficiary dies before he attains

---

[22] See Potter and Monroe, *op. cit.*

[23] Income and Corporation Taxes Act 1970, ss. 37 and 42.

[24] See also the Finance Act 1969, s. 36 (2); *St. Aubyn* v. *Attorney-General*, [1952] A.C. 15. As to who is a settlor, see *Mills* v. *I.R.C.*, [1974] 2 W.L.R. 325.

the age of eighteen, no estate duty is payable on his death.[25] If the interest given to the beneficiary is contingent upon attaining an age greater than eighteen, and he dies after attaining eighteen but before the interest becomes vested, estate duty is payable, because under section 31 (1) of the Trustee Act 1925 the beneficiary is entitled to the income from the age of eighteen onwards.[26] If, therefore, as in *Re Turner's Will Trusts*,[27] a beneficiary's interest is made contingent upon attaining an age greater than the age of majority, and between reaching majority and the attainment of the specified age, the settlement provides that the beneficiary is not entitled to the income, then estate duty would not be payable if the beneficiary died after attaining the age of majority, but before the age specified for the interest to vest in him.

Where a settlement is made, and the settlor fails to survive the required seven years, the property settled must be included for purposes of estate duty, as at the date of the settlor's death.[28] That property, however, will probably have changed its form, and also its value, in the interval between the execution of the settlement and the settlor's death, and section 38 (8) of the Finance Act 1957 now provides that the property which is deemed to pass for estate duty purposes is the property which is in fact governed by the settlement at the time of the settlor's death.

One of the objects of a family settlement will also be to achieve a saving, not only of estate duty, but also of the settlor's income tax. This, however, is by no means a simple problem to solve, if the beneficiaries are (as they frequently will be) the settlor's children. For a saving of tax to be achieved, the settlement must satisfy all the provisions of sections 437–444 of the Income and Corporation Taxes Act 1970. These deal with (a) settlements on children generally; (b) revocable settlements and settlements where the settlor retains an interest; and (c) a number of other cases.

Broadly, the general position in such a settlement is that the income of the child under the settlement during his minority is treated as the income of the settlor. If this provision is to be avoided, it is necessary that the income should be accumulated. Even accumulated income may, however, still be regarded as the settlor's income unless it satisfies the conditions laid down in ss. 438–439 of the Act of 1970.

In addition to satisfying these provisions, dispositions of income must also be irrevocable, and the settlor must not have reserved any interest for himself out of the property settled.[29]

Assuming that the settlement, when executed, had successfully met all the requirements specified above for the exclusion of income from the settlor's own income, the question will then arise of the payment of income tax in respect of the income of the settled property.

Trustees of all trusts are required to make a return of income in respect of funds administered by them, together with a statement of charges, administration expenses, and the mode in which the income is divided among

---

[25] Finance Act 1894, s. 2 (1) (*b*) (i), as enacted by the Finance Act 1969, s. 36 (2).
[26] *Re Jones' Will Trusts*, [1947] Ch. 48, decided when the age of majority was twenty-one.
[27] [1937] Ch. 15.
[28] Customs and Inland Revenue Acts 1881, s. 38, and 1889, s. 11 (1); Finance Acts 1894, s. 2 (1) (*c*), and 1968, s. 35 (1) and Sched. 14, para. 1.
[29] See *Vandervell* v. *I.R.C.*, [1967] 2 A.C. 291.

the beneficiaries. When the trustees pay income to the beneficiaries they deduct income tax at the basic rate, and if the beneficiary is entitled to reliefs, he may reclaim them himself, and if he is liable to pay tax at a higher rate, he will be assessed himself. An infant beneficiary is entitled to the same reliefs and allowances as an adult, but if the infant is entitled to income from a settlement, his parent may in consequence lose part or all of his claim to child allowance, if the infant's income exceeds £115.[30] The infant beneficiary will also be liable to pay income tax at a higher rate than the basic rate, if his income *from all sources* brings him into that tax class.[31]

It is a common practice in modern settlements to direct that income of an infant beneficiary should be accumulated until the infant attains the age of twenty-one or some later age. Such an accumulation is necessary if tax is to be saved to the settlor, when the settlor is also the parent of the beneficiary. It is customary in such cases to make the interest contingent upon the attainment of the specified age, for if the interest is vested, it is regarded as the infant's, and tax is payable on it, though allowances and reliefs can be claimed, but if the interest is contingent, the income from it cannot be regarded as the infant's, and accordingly no reliefs or allowances can be claimed, but tax will have to be paid by the trustees, so this only makes a saving if the infant's rate would have been higher.

Many modern settlements, moreover, contain provisions for the benefit of children as a class, including not only existing children, but children not yet born. In such a case, it appears to be necessary to provide that the class shall close, and become ascertained, at a specified date, which is usually the attainment by the eldest child of the age of majority.

C. MARRIAGE SETTLEMENTS

A marriage settlement may be regarded, from the settlor's point of view, as one type of family provision, its operation being restricted, however, simply to the child who is entering into the marriage, and the family of that child. One benefit which is secured by such a settlement is exemption from the seven-year rule governing gifts, which otherwise would now be liable to estate duty. Section 59 (2) of the Finance (1909–10) Act 1910 provides that this rule does not apply to some gifts in consideration of marriage; although this exemption is not applicable where the settlor reserves a life interest in the property settled.[32] The exemption is enjoyed in respect of the property of the parties to the marriage, which they themselves settle, and also by gifts made by a parent, grandparent, or possibly other close relatives of one of the parties.

In *I.R.C.* v. *Rennell*,[33] a father, on the marriage of his daughter, settled a large fund on discretionary trusts for the benefit of *all* his children and their issue. The House of Lords decided that the entire beneficial interests under this settlement were exempt from estate duty, under section 59 (2) of

---

[30] Income and Corporation Taxes Act 1970, s. 10.
[31] See *I.R.C.* v. *Countess of Longford*, [1928] A.C. 252. As to higher rates of tax on accumulations under section 31 of the Trustee Act 1925, see *Stanley* v. *I.R.C.*, [1944] K.B. 255.
[32] For a full discussion of this exemption, see Potter and Monroe, *op. cit.* For financial limits of the exemption, see the Finance Act 1968, s. 36.
[33] [1964] A.C. 173.

the Finance (1909–10) Act 1910, but the wide effect of this decision was restricted by section 53 of the Finance Act 1963.

One other point of considerable importance in connection with marriage settlements relates to the surrender of life interests. In the common form of marriage settlement, it was customary to settle property on the parties for their joint lives, then upon the survivor for life, with remainders to the children. If, however, a grandparent settled property upon his child, X (a party to the marriage), for life, with remainder to X's children, and X released either the whole or part of his life interest in favour of the grand-child, it was held in *I.R.C.* v. *Buchanan* [34] that X, by so releasing his life interest, either wholly or in part, became himself a settlor, within the meaning of section 21 (9) of the Finance Act 1936 (now section 444 (1) of the Income and Corporation Taxes Act 1970), and the income of the fund so released was therefore treated as X's income for tax purposes. Accordingly, any possible tax benefit was lost.

D. DISCRETIONARY TRUSTS

In recent years there has been a large increase in the use of discretionary trusts in settlements, either for descendants or for employees or former employees. Savings in income tax may be achieved, provided that the settlor is prepared to transfer property outright to trustees, and to exclude from benefit, not only himself, but also his wife. As the object of a dis-cretionary trust has no right to any income, endowing the trustees with a wide discretion [35] enables them to minimise the family tax by making payments to those paying the lowest rates: each recipient will pay tax only on what he receives. [36]

By the Finance Act 1973, s. 16, where there is a discretionary trust or a trust for accumulation (not being a trust for charity or for pensions or other retirement benefits), and there is income in excess of what is properly used for the trustees' administrative expenses, the trustees must pay income tax at the additional rate as well as at the basic rate. By section 59 (2), the additional rate is that referred to in the Finance Act 1971, s. 32 (1), the current rate being set out in the Finance Act 1972, s. 66.

If the discretionary trust is established at least seven years before the settlor's death (and, where there are successive transfers of property to the trustees, each transfer must satisfy this requirement), there will be no estate duty when the settlor dies. Before recent legislation, there was also no estate duty on the fund on the death of an object of a discretionary trust, because, as the object had no right to receive anything, no property passed on his death, [37] provided the trustees did indeed have a complete discretion. [38] By virtue of the Finance Act 1969, s. 36, and the Finance Act 1970, s. 31, subject to minor exceptions, every time an object of a discretionary trust dies estate

---

[34] [1958] Ch. 289.

[35] For an example, see *Re Weir's Settlement Trusts*, [1971] Ch. 145.

[36] But see the Finance Act 1973, ss. 15–17.

[37] See *Gartside* v. *I.R.C.*, [1968] A.C. 553; *I.R.C.* v. *Holmden*, [1968] A.C 685; *Sainsbury* v. *I.R.C.*, [1970] Ch. 712; *Re Weir's Settlement Trusts*, [1971] Ch. 145.

[38] As to the application of the rule against perpetuities to discretionary trusts, see p. 154, *ante*.

duty is paid on that fraction of the fund which is equal to the fraction of the income of the fund, during the whole period the deceased was an object, actually paid to the deceased.[39] The period cannot exceed seven years prior to the death of the object or to the date on which he ceased to be eligible to benefit under the trust.

Discretionary trusts of considerable complexity have been created in recent years, sometimes in favour of very wide classes. Care must be taken in drafting such discretions to ensure that they do not fail for uncertainty.[40]

[39] See, further, Lovell, " Discretionary Trusts and Estate Duty—The Dutiable Slice " (1970), *British Tax Review* 220; Goldberg, " The Curious Case of the Finance Act 1969 and Sub-Trusts " (1971) *British Tax Review* 117; Cohen, " Discretionary Trusts and Estate Duty " (1971) 35 *Conveyancer* 82.

[40] As to the rules governing certainty, see pp. 102–103, *ante*.

CHAPTER XXII

THE VARIATION OF BENEFICIAL INTERESTS IN TRUSTS

A. METHODS OF VARIATION

THE increasing pressure of taxation upon interests created by trusts has not only been responsible for the developments in the law of trusts which have been outlined in the previous chapter; it has also been responsible for attempts to reframe interests in trusts already in existence. In a number of cases, where the remaindermen are an ascertained class, and are of full age, such rearrangements of trust interests can be carried out by agreement between the beneficiaries, but when the interests of children or unborn persons are involved, an application to the court is necessary.

The methods adopted to minimise either income tax or estate duty, or both, have been varied, but most of them have involved one or more of the following—

(1) The surrender by a life-tenant in possession of his interest to the remainderman. When this occurs, the estate surrendered merges with the remainder, and provided the life-tenant survives for seven years, the estate duty which would have been payable on the life-tenant's death is not payable.[1]

(2) The surrender of a reversionary life interest to the life-tenant. Estate duty will also be governed by the seven-year rule.[1]

(3) The disclaimer of a life interest, bequeathed by will. Such a disclaimer is, however, a disposition of the property, so will not avoid estate duty on the death of the person disclaiming unless he survives the disclaimer by at least seven years.[2]

(4) The release of an annuity, arising by will.

(5) The exercise by the trustees of their power of advancement, either under section 32 of the Trustee Act 1925 or conferred by the settlement. The limits upon the exercise of this power have been discussed earlier.

(6) The division of the trust fund between the life-tenant and the remainderman. This will follow the valuation of the respective interests of tenant for life and remainderman. Sometimes the tenant for life has also been given a power of appointment amongst the remaindermen, with a gift over to them in default of appointment. In such a case, the tenant for life may release his power, in order to facilitate the partition.[3]

(7) A further possibility is that there may be a sale of a reversion to the tenant for life. These transactions, however, are now affected by section 38 of the Finance Act 1969, so that if the tenant for life dies within seven years, estate duty is payable upon the sum equal to the money paid in respect of the purchase.

To these seven methods of varying the provisions of a settlement,[4] there

---

[1] Finance Act 1894, s. 2 (1) (*b*), as substituted by the Finance Act 1969, s. 36 (2).
[2] Finance Act 1940, s. 45 (2); *Re Stratton's Disclaimer*, [1958] Ch. 42.
[3] *Re Radcliffe*, [1892] 1 Ch. 227; *Re Greaves*, [1954] Ch. 434.
[4] They are discussed more fully in Potter and Monroe, *op. cit.*, pp. 226–37.

should be added that wherever such a variation involved an application to the court, the opportunity might have been taken, prior to the Trustee Investments Act 1961, to ask for the insertion of a wider investments clause, if the settlement did not originally contain one.

Such an application, it has been pointed out, is necessary, wherever the interest of an infant or unborn person is affected by the proposed rearrangement of the beneficial interests. Prior to the Variation of Trusts Act 1958 the powers of the court to consent to such rearrangements might have been derived from one of the following sources:

(a) The inherent jurisdiction of the court to sanction compromises on behalf of an infant where there is a genuine dispute affecting the infant's interest. This jurisdiction may be invoked, even though the effect of sanctioning the compromise is to reduce the liability upon some of the interests in the settlement to estate duty. There must, however, be a genuine dispute.[5]

Quite distinct from this inherent jurisdiction to sanction compromises, however, the court also has inherent jurisdiction to sanction some special act, which might perhaps include the variation of an interest, in respect of a trust in accordance with what are termed " salvage principles." This is discussed more fully in connection with the decision of the House of Lords in *Chapman* v. *Chapman,*[5] where the observations of Romer, L.J., on this point in *Re New* [6] were approved.

(b) Section 57 of the Trustee Act 1925. Although the terms of this section appear to be very wide, it is nevertheless now clear that this section is appliable only to matters of management or administration, and it is therefore not open to the court to sanction the variation of trust interests, at any rate in any ordinary case.[7]

(c) Section 64 of the Settled Land Act 1925. This section is drawn more widely than section 57 of the Trustee Act 1925, although it is only applicable to land, whether held in strict settlement or upon trust for sale.

(d) Finally, under section 24 of the Matrimonial Causes Act 1973, the Family Division has a wide jurisdiction to order the variation of trust interests contained in any ante-nuptial or post-nuptial settlement made by the parties.[8] On an application to vary a post-nuptial settlement, the court must consider the position of both spouses and of any infant children of the marriage.[9] The Act only authorises the court to act for the benefit of living persons, so that there can be no variation where one of the parties has died between the time when the summons was issued and the hearing.[10]

The whole question of the extent of the court's jurisdiction was examined by the House of Lords in *Chapman* v. *Chapman.*[11]

---

[5] *Chapman* v. *Chapman*, [1954] A.C. 429 (Cases, p. 309); *Re Lord Hylton's Settlement*, [1954] 1 W.L.R. 1055; *Re Powell-Cotton's Resettlement*, [1956] 1 W.L.R. 23.

[6] [1901] 2 Ch. 534.

[7] *Chapman* v. *Chapman*, [1954] A.C. 429; *Re Forster's Settlement*, [1954] 1 W.L.R. 1450; *Re Cockerell's Settlement Trusts*, [1956] Ch. 372. See also Marshall, " Deviations from the Terms of a Trust " (1954), 17 *Modern Law Review* 420.

[8] For an example, see *Radziej* v. *Radziej*, [1968] 1 W.L.R. 1928. See also p. 366, *post*.

[9] *Meldrum* v. *Meldrum*, [1971] 1 W.L.R. 5.

[10] *Thomson* v. *Thomson*, [1896] P. 263; *D'Este* v. *D'Este*, [1973] Fam. 55.

[11] [1954] A.C. 429. (Cases, p. 309). See also *Allen* v. *Distillers Co (Biochemicals) Ltd.*, [1974] Q.B. 384.

B. *CHAPMAN* v. *CHAPMAN*

The decision of the House of Lords in *Chapman* v. *Chapman* temporarily checked a movement to bring the law of trusts in practice a little more into harmony with the changed conditions of the mid-twentieth century. Indeed, its restrictive effect produced so much criticism that a committee to inquire into its effects was promptly constituted.

When *Chapman* v. *Chapman* was considered by the Court of Appeal,[12] it was one of three appeals which were considered together. All three had certain common features, but there were also differences between them. The principal common feature was that, if the court was able to assent to the scheme put before it in each case, a substantial sum in death duties could be avoided. The *Chapman* appeal related to three settlements. By the first, of March 15, 1944, Colonel Sir Robert Chapman and his wife, Lady Chapman, settled land or the proceeds of the sale thereof and other property. Clauses 2, 3 and 4 of the settlement read as follows—

> 2. The trustees shall stand possessed of the trust premises (subject to clauses 3 and 4 following) for all or any the child or children of the settlors' son Robert Macgowan Chapman who shall attain the age of twenty-one years or die under that age leaving issue and if more than one in equal shares as tenants in common.
>
> 3. Provided always that until the youngest child of the said Robert Macgowan Chapman shall have attained the age of twenty-five years if that event shall happen within twenty-one years from the date hereof or until the expiration of twenty-one years from the death of the survivor of the settlors if the youngest surviving child of the said Robert Macgowan Chapman shall not then have attained the age of twenty-five years the trustees shall retain the trust premises and shall apply such part as they in their discretion shall think fit of the income thereof for or towards the common maintenance education or other benefits of the children of the said Robert Macgowan Chapman for the time being living whether minors or adults or for or towards the maintenance education or other benefit of any one or more of them to the exclusion of the other or others and shall (subject as hereinafter mentioned) accumulate the surplus of such income until the time for distribution by investing the same and the resulting income thereof in any investments hereby authorised in augmentation of the capital of the trust premises to be held upon the same trusts as the original trust premises but so that the trustees may apply the accumulations of any preceding year or years in or towards the maintenance education or benefit of all or any of the said children in the same manner as such accumulations might have been applied had they been income arising from the original trust funds in the then current year. Provided always that after each child of the said Robert Macgowan Chapman has attained his or her majority the surplus income of his share in the trust premises not expended by virtue of the foregoing powers of this clause shall not be accumulated but shall be paid to such child.

12 [1953] Ch. 218.

4. Provided also that the trustees may at any time with the consent in writing of the settlors raise any part or parts not exceeding in the whole one half of the then expectant or presumptive or vested share of any child whether minor or adult of the said Robert Macgowan Chapman in the trust premises under the trust hereinbefore contained and pay or apply the same to him or her for his or her advancement or otherwise for his or her exclusive benefit in such manner as the trustees shall think fit and as to the part or parts so raised the maintenance and other trusts of the last preceding clause shall cease to be applicable and no interest on any such advance shall be charged to any child so advanced in the accounts of the trust.

In the second settlement, dated February 8, 1950, Lady Chapman settled further property on substantially the same trusts as those declared by the 1944 settlement for the benefit of Mr. Robert Macgowan Chapman's children. The third settlement, dated February 10, 1950, was made on the occasion of the marriage of Henry James Nicholas Chapman (a son of Sir Robert and Lady Chapman) with Anne Barbara Croft. By it Lady Chapman settled property upon trusts for the children of that marriage, and upon similar trusts for the children of any subsequent marriage of Nicholas, and it was provided that in the event of the failure of these trusts the trustees should pay over the trust funds to the trustees of the settlement of February 8, 1950, to be held on the trusts of that settlement.

Robert Macgowan Chapman was, at the date of the action, married to Barbara May Chapman, and there were three children of the marriage, born in 1941, 1944 and 1946. There were at the time no children of Nicholas' marriage.

In March 1952, the value of the funds comprised in the three settlements was approximately £77,000, and because of the discretionary trusts for the common maintenance of Mr. Robert Chapman's children, contained in clause 3 of the 1944 settlement and clause 4 of the settlement of 1950, the trustees of the settlements were advised that a claim for estate duty would arise in respect of the funds comprised in the 1944 settlement (amounting to £43,300) on the death of the survivor of Sir Robert Chapman (then aged 72) and Lady Chapman (then aged 65) and in respect of the funds comprised in the 1950 settlement upon the death of Lady Chapman. The trustees of the third settlement were advised that if the substituted limitation contained in that settlement was valid and became effective, a claim for estate duty would arise in respect of their fund also. The total amount of estate duty involved would amount to nearly £30,000.

In these circumstances a scheme of arrangement was prepared with the object of avoiding these anticipated claims. This could only be effective if the first two settlements were freed from the provisions for common maintenance contained in clause 3 of the first, and clause 4 of the second, and it was therefore proposed that the trustees should, with the sanction of the court, advance their funds to the trustees of a new settlement containing similar trusts, but with those clauses omitted. It was also proposed that the trustees of the third settlement should, on the failure of the trusts therein contained, similarly transfer their funds to the trustees of the new settlement.

This scheme, therefore, which required the consent of the court to release the interests of the infant children of Mr. Robert Macgowan Chapman and also possible unborn children of Robert and Nicholas, who might at some future time have been beneficiaries under the settlements, was brought before Harman, J., in chambers, by way of originating summons on July 28, 1952, and Harman, J., refused to sanction it, on the ground that he had no jurisdiction to do so, either under the inherent jurisdiction of the court, or under section 57 of the Trustee Act 1925. The trustees appealed.

A majority of the Court of Appeal, Evershed, M.R., and Romer, L.J., upheld the decision of Harman, J. They took the view that there was no authority to sanction the scheme under section 57 which, in their view, only empowers the court to make orders with reference to the management or administration by trustees of the trust property. The scheme proposed in this case did not arise out of any administrative or managerial difficulty affecting the trust assets. It was really a scheme for rewriting the trust interests to avoid death duties.

It was, however, strongly pressed on behalf of the trustees that the court had an unlimited jurisdiction in relation to the property of infants and unborn beneficiaries, which it would exercise whenever a suitable case for intervention is placed before it. This contention is summarised by Evershed, M.R., as follows [13]—

> It was the argument of counsel for all the appellants (founded on Jeffrey L.C.'s case, *Earl of Winchelsea* v. *Norcliffe* [14] and other early cases, including *Pierson* v. *Shore* [15] before Hardwicke L.C. and *Inwood* v. *Twyne* [16] before Northington L.C.) that the jurisdiction of the court to modify or vary trusts and to direct the trustees accordingly was unlimited provided: (1) that all persons interested who were sui juris assented, and (2) that it was clearly shown to be for the advantage or convenience of all persons interested who were not sui juris, including persons unborn or not presently ascertainable; in other words, that the court has unlimited jurisdiction in relation to the property of infants, including the beneficial interests of infants and unborn cestuis que trustent under a settlement, and will exercise that jurisdiction so as to secure any benefit or advantage for the infants or unborn persons, which they could have themselves secured had they been in esse and sui juris, even to the extent of sanctioning a departure from the beneficial trusts of the trust instrument from which the interests in question are derived.

The majority of the Court of Appeal were unable to agree that the inherent jurisdiction went so far. In particular, Lord Evershed thought that the decisions in *Re New* [17] and *Re Tollemache* [18] were against it. To the principle that the court's jurisdiction does not extend to the remoulding of beneficial interests he thought that there were only two exceptions: (1) trusts intended for the benefit of a family, but where the settlor has provided for income to be

---

[13] [1953] Ch. 233.
[14] (1686), 1 Vern. 435.
[15] (1739), 1 Atk. 480.
[16] (1762), Amb. 417.
[17] [1901] 2 Ch. 534.
[18] [1903] 1 Ch. 457.

accumulated for a while: in such cases the court will allow maintenance out of income directed to be accumulated [19]; and (2) cases where there is a genuine compromise between beneficiaries in respect of their rights under a settlement: here the court will approve the compromise on behalf of infants and unborn persons. The best-known illustration of the exercise of this jurisdiction is *Re Trenchard*.[20] A rearrangement of interests to avoid a liability to estate duty which would otherwise exist is not, however, a compromise but a substitution of new beneficial interests for those which existed before.

From this view Denning, L.J., dissented. He thought that the early cases, from the time of Lord Chancellor Jeffreys onwards, showed that the court did possess such an inherent jurisdiction, which it exercised in the interests of infants. In his view, therefore, cases in which maintenance had been authorised, where there was no provision for maintenance in the will or settlement, and cases in which the court had sanctioned compromises on behalf of infants and unborn persons were simply specific illustrations of the exercise of a general jurisdiction. He also added that whenever the court has, of its own motion, placed limitations on its own jurisdiction, *e.g.* in respect of lifting restraints on anticipation,[21] or in respect of the sale of heirlooms,[22] or in respect of the power of trustees to concur in the reconstruction or amalgamation of companies in which they held shares,[23] the legislature has been ready to intervene to remove these self-imposed limitations.[24] Finally he added [25]—

> I would therefore myself allow the appeal in all three cases; and I am the more ready to do so because I am told that the Chancery judges in chambers have in the past exercised their jurisdiction in similar cases in a very beneficent manner, and this is confirmed by the approval given to the schemes in *In re Salting*,[26] by Eve J., and in *In re Mair*,[27] by Farwell J., and in an unreported decision of Simonds J. in 1938 under the inherent jurisdiction which was drawn to our attention. The jurisdiction has been so freely exercised that the rejection of the schemes in the present cases has taken Lincoln's Inn by surprise, so much so that many proposed schemes have been held up pending our decision. The practice of the profession in these cases is the best evidence of what the law is; indeed, it makes law. It would be most disturbing if we were to say that the Chancery judges for many years have been acting without jurisdiction. What would be the result? I suppose that the schemes could be ignored by the Revenue and by all persons not sui juris, which would be a very unsatisfactory state of affairs. It is not right to unsettle the jurisdiction of the court on these matters unless some high principle demands it, and I see none.

---

[19] *Havelock* v. *Havelock* (1881), 17 Ch.D. 807; *Re Collins* (1886), 32 Ch.D. 229; *Re Walker*, [1901] 1 Ch. 879.

[20] [1902] 1 Ch. 378.

[21] *Robinson* v. *Wheelwright* (1856), 6 De G. M. & G. 535.

[22] *D'Eyncourt* v. *Gregory* (1876), 3 Ch.D. 635.

[23] *Re New*, [1901] 2 Ch. 534; *Re Tollemache*, [1903] 1 Ch. 457.

[24] Conveyancing Act 1881, s. 39; Law of Property Act 1925, s. 169 (married women); Settled Land Act 1925, s. 67 (heirlooms); Trustee Act 1925. ss. 10 (3) and 57 (shares).

[25] [1953] Ch. 279.

[26] [1932] 2 Ch. 57.

[27] [1935] Ch. 562.

By a majority, therefore, the appeal in the *Chapman* case failed. The *Downshire* [28] appeal, however, raised different questions. Once again there was a proposal that interests under a settlement (one of them being the protected life interest of the Marquess of Downshire) should be exchanged for various other interests which would arise under the rewritten settlement. In this case, however, the property was settled under the Settled Land Act 1925, and although Roxburgh, J., held in chambers that he had no jurisdiction, either under the inherent jurisdiction of the court or under section 64 of the Settled Land Act 1925, the Court of Appeal took a different view. The court agreed that this transaction could not be effected by the inherent jurisdiction of the court, but they were prepared to regard the scheme in this case as a genuine compromise, and also as within the terms of section 64, and said [29]—

> The jurisdiction under section 64 of the Settled Land Act, 1925, is, in our judgment, in some respects more ample in regard to the subject-matter to which it relates than is section 57 of the Trustee Act, 1925. If this result is regarded as unexpected, we point out that the language of the two sections is to a material degree dissimilar, and the conclusions which we have formed are based on what we regard, in each case, as the natural meaning of the words used.

In the *Downshire* appeal, therefore, the court accepted jurisdiction under section 64, and sanctioned the reframed settlement as a compromise of interests.

The *Blackwell* [30] appeal arose out of a voluntary settlement, made in 1933, by which the plaintiff settled a trust fund on protective trusts on himself for life, with remainder to his children or remoter issue, as he should appoint, and in default of appointment, for his children in unequal shares, with an ultimate trust for his testamentary appointees. The plaintiff had one son, born in 1951. The value of the settled fund was £83,000 on which, on the plaintiff's death, estate duty would be payable at 65 per cent. The plaintiff asked the court to sanction a scheme whereby he surrendered his life interest in half the settled fund, so as to accelerate the interests in remainder, upon terms that his life interest in the other half of the fund was not thereby forfeited. Once again Roxburgh, J., had held that there was no jurisdiction to sanction such a scheme, but once again the Court of Appeal took the view that, although section 57 of the Trustee Act 1925 was not wide enough to cover it, the scheme was essentially a compromise, similar in essentials to that in *Re Downshire Settled Estates*,[31] although, in this case, it was referred to the judge with liberty to the parties to amend the scheme and to make it more appropriate for the court to sanction it under its inherent jurisdiction.

It will be apparent that, in these three appeals, the majority of the court felt that it had gone as far as it could towards sanctioning these schemes. One was approved under section 64 of the Settled Land Act 1925; one would be ultimately approved as a compromise under the court's inherent jurisdiction, although it was too wide to qualify for approval under section 57 of the

---

[28] *Re Downshire Settled Estates*, [1953] Ch. 218.
[29] [1953] Ch. 253–254.
[30] *Re Blackwell's Settlement Trusts*, [1953] Ch. 218.
[31] [1953] Ch. 218.

Trustee Act 1925. The House of Lords, however, was less responsive to the desires of the trustees and other interested parties. Since only the Chapman scheme had been rejected by the Court of Appeal, there was a further appeal to the House of Lords in this case only, and the House of Lords unanimously upheld the decision of the majority of the Court of Appeal. The principal ground upon which the majority of the members of the House of Lords based their view was that, although the court undoubtedly had power to sanction compromises on behalf of infant beneficiaries, the scheme in *Chapman* v. *Chapman* [32] could not properly be regarded as a compromise, since there was no real dispute between any of the beneficiaries as to the extent of their rights. What was sought to be done was, by way of bargain, to rearrange the beneficial interests. This, however, failed to solve the conundrum propounded by Lord Cohen who, although he did not dissent, expressed certain reservations concerning the conclusions reached by other members of the House in the following terms [33]—

> My Lords, I am not satisfied that the court, in sanctioning a compromise in the strict sense, is not exercising a jurisdiction to alter beneficial rights. It is true that in such a case the right has not been defined, but the right of the beneficiary is a right to that to which, upon its true construction, the will or settlement entitles him. The very essence of a compromise is that it may give each party something other than that which the will or settlement would, on its true construction, confer on him.

Lord Cohen also disposed of the problem concerning the validity of earlier exercises of the jurisdiction raised by Denning, L.J., in the passage from his judgment which has already been quoted. Lord Cohen said [34]—

> I cannot sit down without expressing my doubt whether there is any foundation for the suggestion made by Denning L.J. that the effect of your Lordships' decision may be that schemes sanctioned in the past could be ignored by the Revenue and all persons not sui juris. The High Court is a superior court and the control of trustees is a matter within its jurisdiction. It would take a great deal of argument to satisfy me that its orders were a nullity and that trustees were not fully protected by orders made by that court in the exercise of that trust jurisdiction even though your Lordships may, in a later case, have said that the jurisdiction had been wrongly exercised.

Happily, no court has been subsequently called upon to consider an argument upon the effect of an order made by a superior court, either in excess of, or without jurisdiction to make it.

Behind the technical arguments upon the question whether the earlier decisions were simply illustrations of the exercise of a general inherent jurisdiction or whether they were to be regarded simply as specific cases in which a court would act was the broader question of the use of this jurisdiction to

[32] [1954] A.C. 429 (Cases, p. 309).
[33] [1954] A.C. 472.
[34] [1954] A.C. 474.

mitigate the rigours of modern taxation. This point was dealt with by Lord Morton of Henryton at the conclusion of his speech, where he observed [35]—

> . . . if the court had power to approve, and did approve, schemes such as the present scheme, the way would be open for a most undignified game of chess between the Chancery Division and the legislature. The alteration of one settlement for the purposes of avoiding taxation already imposed might well be followed by scores of successful applications for a similar purpose by beneficiaries under other settlements. The legislature might then counter this move by imposing fresh taxation upon the settlements as thus altered. The beneficiaries would then troop back to the Chancery Division and say, " Please alter the trusts again. You have the power, the adults desire it, and it is for the benefit of the infants to avoid this fresh taxation. The legislature may not move again." So the game might go on, if the judges of the Chancery Division had the power which the appellants claim for them, and if they thought it right to make the first move.

Other judges have been less apprehensive. In *Re Simmons* [36] Danckwerts, J., held that section 64 of the Settled Land Act 1925 permitted him to authorise the trustees of a trust for sale of land to assent to a scheme whereby the tenant for life obtained a larger capital sum in lieu of certain other interests, on the ground that the powers conferred by section 64 were exercisable (subject to the approval of the court) by trustees for sale by virtue of section 28 (1) of the Law of Property Act 1925.

The decision of the House of Lords in *Chapman* v. *Chapman*, taken in conjunction with the decisions of the Court of Appeal in the *Blackwell* [37] and *Downshire* [37] appeals, left the law in an uncertain and unsatisfactory state, and accordingly the question of the extent of the court's jurisdiction in these cases was, in March 1957, referred to the Law Revision Committee, who were unanimously of opinion that the law should be restored to the position which had existed before the decision of the House of Lords was given.

C. THE VARIATION OF TRUSTS ACT 1958

The recommendations of the Law Revision Committee were embodied in the Variation of Trusts Act 1958. Section 1 (1) of this Act reads—

> Where property, whether real or personal, is held on trusts arising, whether before or after the passing of this Act, under any will, settlement or other disposition, the court may if it thinks fit by order approve on behalf of—
>
> (*a*) any person having, directly or indirectly, an interest, whether vested or contingent, under the trusts who by reason of infancy or other incapacity is incapable of assenting, or
>
> (*b*) any person (whether ascertained or not) who may become entitled, directly or indirectly, to an interest under the trusts as being at

[35] [1954] A.C. 468.
[36] [1956] Ch. 125.
[37] [1953] Ch. 218.

a future date or on the happening of a future event a person of any
specified description or a member of any specified class of persons, so
however that this paragraph shall not include any person who would
be of that description or a member of that class, as the case may be,
if the said date had fallen or the said event had happened at the date
of the application to the court, or

(c) any person unborn, or

(d) any person in respect of any discretionary interest of his under
protective trusts where the interest of the principal beneficiary has not
failed or determined,

any arrangement (by whomsoever proposed, and whether or not there is
any other person beneficially interested who is capable of assenting thereto) varying or revoking all or any of the trusts, or enlarging the powers
of the trustees of managing or administering any of the property subject to
the trusts:

Provided that except by virtue of paragraph (d) of this subsection the
court shall not approve an arrangement on behalf of any person unless
the carrying out thereof would be for the benefit of that person.

It will be seen that the general principle underlying this section is that the
court shall have power to assent to variations of provisions in settlements on
behalf of persons who lack the power themselves to do so. This includes
mentally defective beneficiaries.[38] Persons of full age must, as before, decide
for themselves whether they will assent. The Act does not in any way affect
the powers which the Court already enjoys under section 57 of the Trustee
Act 1925, or the Settled Land Act 1925, section 64. In *Re Poole's Settlements
Trusts*,[39] Roxburgh, J., pointed out that under section 1 of the Act of 1958 the
court has jurisdiction to have regard to the interests of future unborn persons.

Jurisdiction

Whilst the courts in Northern Ireland do not possess jurisdiction under the
Act,[40] it has been held that where the trust property is land and the trustees
live in England at the time of the application, the English courts may vary a
settlement made in Northern Ireland.[41] Ungoed-Thomas, J., in his decision,
pointed out that a similar power to vary had been conferred by section 5 of
the Matrimonial Causes Act 1859, and it had been decided [42] that the court
could vary settlements whatever the law applicable to them. It would seem
that a similar construction will be applied to the construction of the Variation
of Trusts Act 1958, and that any foreign settlement may be varied if the
trustees, and possibly the property, are within the jurisdiction.

How the Application to Vary May Arise

Very extensive use has already been made of the powers conferred by the

[38] Variation of Trusts Act 1958, s. 1 (3). *Re Sanderson's Settlement Trusts*, [1961] 1
W.L.R. 36.
[39] [1959] 1 W.L.R. 651, 656–657.
[40] Variation of Trusts Act 1958, s. 2 (2). (They have a similar jurisdiction under the
Trustee Act (Northern Ireland) 1958, s. 57.)
[41] *Re Ker's Settlement Trusts*, [1963] Ch. 553. See also *Re Paget's Settlement*, [1965] 1
W.L.R. 1046.
[42] *Forsyth* v. *Forsyth*, [1891] P. 363.

Act, and it was appropriate that the first decision under it was *Chapman* v. *Chapman (No. 2)*.[43] This was heard by Vaisey, J., who stated that it was important that all interests which it was sought to bind should be represented by counsel. The court then made an order approving on behalf of infant beneficiaries and unborn children the scheme which had produced so much difficulty in the Court of Appeal and the House of Lords in 1954, and in respect of which the House of Lords had held that it had no inherent jurisdiction to consent to a variation. In this application there could be no agreement between the beneficiaries, since none of them were *sui juris,* and accordingly it was the trustees who made the application.

Section 1 (1) of the Act provides that anyone (including the settlor)[44] can be an applicant. Often the beneficiaries will make the application. In *Re Druce's Settlement Trusts*[45] it was initiated by the trustees, and despite the fact that the application was successful, Russell, J., pointed out that—

> . . . in general, the trustees should not be the applicants in applications to vary beneficial trusts, unless they are satisfied that the proposals are beneficial to the persons interested and have a good prospect of being approved by the court, and further, that if they do not make the application no one will. In particular, it would not be right if it became the general practice for such applications to be made by the trustees upon the supposition that should the application fail it will be more probable (though not, of course, certain) that the costs of all parties will be directed to be met out of the trust funds.
>
> Arising out of the discussion about trustees as applicants, a question was to some extent canvassed—to what extent should trustees be the initiators or movers of schemes to be put before the court for the variation of beneficial interests. I would deprecate any suggestion that trustees must content themselves in every case with leaving it to the beneficiaries (or, if infants, their parents or guardians) to initiate or put forward such schemes, although, on the other hand, failure to do so themselves would scarcely be a breach of trust. But the initiation of and other steps leading to a final scheme may be very costly and may prove abortive. In general, such steps should be left to the beneficiaries (except in so far as inevitably joined in by the trustees) unless the trustees are satisfied that such steps are liable to produce beneficial results, and that no beneficiary is able or willing to take them.

If part of the trust funds may ultimately be held on charitable trusts, the Attorney General should be a respondent.[46] But it is unnecessary to join persons who, in certain circumstances, would be the settlor's next of kin, although they were not so at the date of the application. Such persons may never be beneficiaries, and their interests are looked after by the trustees.[47] Subject to this, however, all interests should be separately represented.[48]

[43] [1959] 1 W.L.R. 372.
[44] *Re Tinker's Settlement,* [1960] 1 W.L.R. 1011.
[45] [1962] 1 W.L.R. 363, 371.
[46] *Re Longman's Settlement Trusts,* [1962] 1 W.L.R. 455; *Re Lister's Will Trusts,* [1962] 1 W.L.R. 1441.
[47] *Re Moncrieff's Settlement Trusts,* [1962] 1 W.L.R. 1344.
[48] *Re Rouse's Will Trusts,* [1959] 1 W.L.R. 372.

Where there are beneficiaries who are *sui juris,* there may be a formal contract between them, but this is not necessary. " I think that the word ' arrangement '," said Lord Evershed, M.R., in *Re Steed's Will Trusts,*[49] " is deliberately used in the widest possible sense so as to cover any proposal which any person may put forward for varying or revoking the trusts " and the other members of the Court of Appeal agreed. In that case, the proposal was put forward by a beneficiary in face of the opposition of the trustees, and it is of considerable importance in determining the extent to which the court will support a beneficiary who wishes to override the exercise of a discretion by the trustees, conferred by the will creating the settlement. The trustees had been about to sell a farm under their discretionary powers, when the beneficiary interposed an application to vary under the Variation of Trusts Act 1958. The Court of Appeal declined to approve this variation, and held that if the trustees contemplated a proper exercise of their discretion the court would not override it through the exercise of their own powers under the Act.

One point which did not arise in this case, but which may be relevant in similar cases, is that section 1 (1) of the Act provides that whilst the beneficial interests may be varied or revoked, the powers of the trustees cannot be curtailed; they can only be enlarged.

Beneficiaries on whose behalf the Court may Consent

Section 1 (1) (a) of the Act provides that the court may consent on behalf of various classes of person. The first of these is one having, directly or indirectly, an interest, whether vested or contingent, under trusts who by reason of infancy or other incapacity is incapable of assenting. In *Re Whittall*[50] Brightman, J., said—

> . . . where an infant beneficiary is a defendant to an application under the Variation of Trusts Act 1958, the guardian ad litem of the infant has the duty, under proper legal advice, to apprise himself fully of the nature of the application, of the existing beneficial interest of the infant, and of the manner in which that interest is proposed to be affected, and to inform the solicitor whom he has retained in the matter, of the course which he, the guardian, considers, in the light of the legal advice given to him, should be taken on behalf of the infant.

Apart from infancy, the usual ground of incapacity is mental unsoundness under the Mental Health Act 1959. In such a case, application may be made to the Court of Protection for an assent on behalf of the patient.[51] Whilst the court, acting under the Variation of Trusts Act 1958, has power to approve an arrangement on behalf of all incapable adults, whether or not a receiver has been appointed, where in fact a receiver *has* been appointed, the Court of Protection is the proper court to decide whether the arrangement is for the benefit of the patient, and in deciding the Court of Protection will endeavour to do what the patient would have done, had the patient been of sound mind.[52]

---

[49] [1960] Ch. 407, 419.
[50] [1973] 1 W.L.R. 1027, 1031.
[51] Variation of Trusts Act 1958, s. 1 (3); *Re Sanderson's Settlement Trusts,* [1961] 1 W.L.R. 36.
[52] *Re C. L.,* [1969] 1 Ch. 587.

Where there is an application for a variation put forward by beneficiaries who are *sui juris,* it is desirable that parties who are not *sui juris* (on whose behalf the court is being asked to consent) should be separately represented.[53]

A person having an indirect interest will usually be a person interested in a sub-settlement, but other problems may also arise. For example, in *Re Suffert's Settlement* [54] it was suggested that an infant who had a possibility of taking under a gift to the next of kin of a living person might have an interest within the paragraph, although this point was not decided.

The second class of persons in respect of whom the court may consent is specified in section 1 (1) (*b*) where there is an important proviso, which was discussed in *Re Suffert.* By the terms of a settlement a daughter had a protected life interest, with a power to appoint the capital and income on trust for her children. The settlement also provided that if the daughter had no child who attained a vested interest, the trust fund should be subjected to a general testamentary power of appointment vested in the daughter, and in default of such appointment, the fund should be held for the persons who would have been entitled under the Administration of Estates Act 1925, at the daughter's death, if she had died intestate and unmarried. The daughter, who was sixty-one years of age and unmarried, and who had three first cousins, all over twenty-one, sought to vary the trusts, and Buckley, J., decided that the arrangement was one which might be approved on behalf of any persons who might be entitled under the settlement, who were not in existence. On the other hand, he was not prepared to approve on behalf of two absent cousins, who would take in default of appointment, as next of kin, as they were within the proviso, being members of the class (*i.e.* next of kin), if the event (*i.e.* the daughter's death) had happened at the date of the application; it was necessary for them to consent on their own behalf.

Section 1 (1) (*c*) contains the power of the court to consent on behalf of unborn persons, and section 1 (1) (*d*) provides that the court may consent on behalf of any person who has a discretionary interest under a protective trust, where the interest of the principal beneficiary has not determined. " Any person " here will include any unascertained or unborn person,[55] and " any discretionary interest " means any interest arising on the determination of the protected life interest. Reference to the proviso in section 1 (1) will show that in giving a consent under (*d*) the court is not obliged to consider the interests of such beneficiaries, whose interests are usually within the care of the trustees.[56] In *Re Burney's Settlement Trusts* [57] Wilberforce, J., approved the variation of a marriage settlement under which the husband had received a protected life interest. One of the elements of the variation was that the protected life interest was enlarged into a life interest, free of the protective trusts. Wilberforce, J., pointed out that in approving the variation, the interests of those who might have benefited under the protective trusts could not be disregarded altogether. All such cases, therefore, must be considered individually.[58]

53 *Re Whigham's Settlement Trusts,* [1971] 1 W.L.R. 831.
54 [1961] Ch. 1.
55 *Re Turner's Will Trusts,* [1960] Ch. 122.
56 *Re Munro's Settlement Trusts,* [1963] 1 W.L.R. 145. See also *Re Whittall,* [1973] 1 W.L.R. 1027.   57 [1961] 1 W.L.R. 545.
58 For another example, see *Re Berry's Settlement,* [1966] 1 W.L.R. 1515.

In *Re Munro's Settlement Trusts* [59] the same judge gave further consideration to this question, which has also been discussed by other judges,[60] and he
pointed out that whilst, in general, it would be reasonable to assume that the
trustees had taken note of the interests of persons who might be interested
under the discretionary trusts, nevertheless in cases where it could be seen
that some distinction might arise between the beneficiaries in existence and
those not in existence, it would be proper to insist upon separate representation of existing interests, and the trustees would be the best persons to point
out to the court that they could not properly represent the interests both of
persons in existence and unborn persons.

It is only under section 1 (1) (*d*) that the court may consent in respect of
persons who are ascertained and *sui juris*. In other cases, such persons (as
appeared in *Re Suffert*) [61] must consent for themselves.

The Court's Consent

The court has a wide discretionary power to give or withhold consent to
proposed variations, but there are limits to it.[62] For example, the court will
not order a resettlement of an infant's interest, though it may postpone its
vesting and, in a suitable case, impose a protected life interest upon it.[63] Nor
may the court insert a provision contrary to public policy, *e.g.* in restraint of
marriage. At the same time, in considering the application of this principle to
the variation of a settlement, it will consider it from the same standpoint as it
does in respect of settlements generally, that is to say, it will look at the intentions of the parties, and in particular, to the question whether restraint of
marriage is the primary object of the settlement, or an incidental or possible
consequence of it.[64]

Subject to overriding considerations such as these, the court has a general
discretion, which it will exercise in favour of variation in any proper case,
ensuring at the same time that each beneficiary gets advantage from the rearrangement.[65] This is not solely a matter of actuarial calculation. " The court
is also concerned whether the arrangement as a whole, in all the circumstances, is such that it is proper to approve it. The court's concern involves,
inter alia, a practical and businesslike consideration of the arrangement, including the total amounts of the advantages which the various parties obtain,
and their bargaining strength." [66] In *Re Tinker's Settlement* [67] Russell, J.,
thought that there must always be some financial advantage to the beneficiaries on whose behalf the court was asked to consent, but in *Re C. L.*[68]
Cross, J., doubted this. In his view, " benefit " in the Variation of Trusts Act
1958 meant what it did when used in connexion with advancements.

59 [1963] 1 W.L.R. 145.
60 *Re Druce's Settlement Trusts*, [1962] 1 W.L.R. 363 ; *Re Moncrieff's Settlement Trusts*,
[1962] 1 W.L.R. 1344.
61 [1961] Ch. 1. See p. 359, *ante*.
62 For a review of the cases, see Harris, " Ten Years of Variation of Trusts " (1969) 33
Conveyancer 113 and 183. See also Keeton, *Modern Developments in the Law of Trusts*,
pp. 172–179.
63 *Re T.'s Settlement Trusts*, [1964] Ch. 158.
64 *Re Michelham's Will Trusts*, [1964] Ch. 550.
65 See *Re Brook's Settlement*, [1968] 1 W.L.R. 1661.
66 *Per* Ungoed-Thomas, J., *Re Van Gruisen's Will Trusts*, [1964] 1 W.L.R. 449, 450.
67 [1960] 1 W.L.R. 1011.
68 [1969] 1 Ch. 587.

In *Re Cohen's Will Trusts* [69] the arrangement to which the court was asked to consent was an arrangement to vary the trusts of a will in which, in the unlikely event of one of the testator's children dying before the testator's widow, then aged nearly eighty, the arrangement would not be advantageous to the next generation. The question to be decided was whether some provision ought to be inserted to guard against this contingency. Danckwerts, J., said that some degree of risk was inherent in all such variations, and he approved this one without ordering a provision to be inserted.

In a later application, also entitled *Re Cohen's Settlement Trusts* [70] Stamp, J., explained the position of the court in deciding whether to assent to a variation in the following way—

> Apart from the Act of 1958, the trusts of a settlement can only be effectively varied as against those who consent to the variation, and what I think the Act of 1958 envisages is the court supplying the consent of those whose consents will in the event be necessary but whose actual consent by reason of their disability, or because they have not appeared on the scene, cannot be obtained. The consents which are contemplated to be given by the court are, in my judgment, precisely those consents which under a deed of family arrangement or variation would have to be obtained before the trustees could safely act upon it, but at present cannot be obtained. In order to ascertain what those consents are one must, in my judgment, consider all possible events and all persons who would or might become entitled on the happening of those events. Only if all the latter have consented could the trust fund safely be distributed in accordance with the deed of family arrangement. . . .
>
> Before concluding this judgment it is right that I should refer particularly to an argument which was addressed to me to the effect that, in considering the interests of a class of infants and similarly, so it was urged, a class of unborn persons, counsel appearing for the infants and the court are concerned with the interests of the class as a whole and not with the individual members of it. I must protest against any such conception of the duties of counsel appearing for infants or the duty of the court in considering whether a variation is for their benefit. In my judgment, the court has to be satisfied in the case of each individual infant that on balance the proposed variation is for his benefit. Similarly, in my judgment, the court must be satisfied that the proposed variation is for the benefit of any individual person who may hereafter come into existence and become interested under the trusts of the settlement. . . . The court does not have to be satisfied that by the effect of a proposed variation each individual infant is bound to be better off than he would otherwise have been, but that that infant is making a bargain which is a reasonable one and one which an adult would be prepared to make. Nevertheless the bargain which the court approves must, in my judgment, be a bargain which appears to be advantageous to each individual infant. If the infants whose interests to be considered are all in the same position, the benefit of one will no doubt be the benefit of all; but if this is not so,

[69] [1959] 1 W.L.R. 865.
[70] [1965] 1 W.L.R. 1229, 1234, 1236. See also *Re Brook's Settlement*, [1968] 1 W.L.R. 1661.

there is, in my judgment, no justification for assuming that because the variation is for the benefit of one it must be for the benefit of all.

Accordingly, in this case, Stamp, J., refused to consent to the proposed variation because there was a possibility that there might be a beneficiary who would get no benefit whatsoever in the proposed rearrangement. In *Re Holt's Settlement*,[71] however, Megarry, J., preferred the view of Danckwerts, J., to that of Stamp, J., and consented to the variation even though there was a risk that some unborn person might not benefit from it.

Clauses which may be varied

It should first be pointed out that section 1 (1) of the Act has been construed widely, to permit the revocation of the existing trusts, and to substitute new trusts, provided that the new trusts can be regarded as a variation of the old ones, but not where wholly new trusts are contemplated.[72]

Investment Clauses. The Act has been freely used to give trustees wider powers of investment by the insertion of new clauses, or by the modification of existing ones. In *Re Byng's Will Trusts*,[73] Vaisey, J., made an order approving the substitution for the original investment clause in a will of a new investment clause, permitting the trustees to invest up to the whole of the trust funds in ordinary or deferred shares or stock of any company quoted on the Stock Exchange of London, New York, Montreal, Melbourne, or Johannesburg, provided that such company had an issued and paid up capital of not less than £500,000, the clause including new issues of such shares or stock. Vaisey, J., pointed out that in applications to vary investments, one of two courses might be followed: either to add a few words to the existing clause, or to redraft the whole investment clause, excluding any out of date matter and adding new powers. He thought that in the great majority of cases the most convenient course would be to produce a new clause.[74] In *Re Coates' Trusts*,[75] Harman, J., made an order enlarging the powers of investment of the trustees in the following terms—

> The court in pursuance of the power conferred by the [Variation of Trusts Act, 1958] doth hereby approve the arrangement set forth in the schedule . . .

There were, in fact, four trusts. In three of them, the clause was amended. In the fourth, the old clause was revoked, and a new one substituted. In this application, Harman, J., pointed out that before the passing of the Variation of Trusts Act 1958, the court had exercised a similar jurisdiction to confer wider investment powers, for charities under the Charitable Trusts Acts,[76] and for other trusts, possibly under section 57 of the Trustee Act 1925.[77] This had been doubted, although it was not open to question that the court could, under

---

[71] [1969] 1 Ch. 100.
[72] *Per* Wilberforce, J., *Re T.'s Settlement Trusts,* [1964] Ch. 158, 162, adopted but distinguished by Megarry, J., *Re Ball's Settlement Trusts,* [1968] 1 W.L.R. 899, 903.
[73] [1959] 1 W.L.R. 375. See also *Re Thompson's Will Trusts,* [1960] 1 W.L.R. 1165.
[74] [1959] 1 W.L.R. 382.
[75] [1959] 1 W.L.R. 375.
[76] *Re Royal Society's Charitable Trusts,* [1956] Ch. 87.
[77] *Re Shipwrecked Fishermen and Mariners' Royal Benevolent Society,* [1959] Ch. 220.

section 57 of the Act of 1925, direct the sale of existing securities, and the investment of the proceeds in specified new ones.[78]

Since the passing of the Trustee Investments Act 1961, a new problem has arisen for consideration, *i.e.* in view of the wider powers conferred by the Act of 1961, may trustees now be granted even wider powers of investment as a result of an application under the Variation of Trusts Act 1958? In *Re Cooper's Settlement,*[79] Buckley, J., thought that such applications should now be acceded to only where there were special circumstances—a view which was shared by Cross, J., in *Re Kolb's Will Trusts.*[80] There is scope for considerable difference of opinion upon what constitute special circumstances. Where, however, the effect of the application was to bring the clause substantially into accord with the provisions of the Trustee Investments Act 1961, the application was granted.[81]

Powers of Appointment. A power of appointment can be extinguished in a number of ways. It can be extinguished (a) expressly by a deed of release, or by a contract not to exercise the power; or (b) impliedly, by any dealing with the property by the donee of the power which is inconsistent with its further exercise.[82] Advantage has been taken of the Variation of Trusts Act 1958 to secure the release of powers. In *Re Christie-Miller's Marriage Settlement*[83] one of the elements in the variation of a marriage settlement was the release of a power of appointment, held by a husband in favour of the children of his brothers and sisters. The trustees had made the husband a party to the application, but not the objects of the power. Wilberforce, J., held that there was no need to join the objects, since the husband was always free to release the power, thereby extinguishing the possible interests of the objects of it. Again in *Re Ball's Settlement Trusts*[84] there was an express release of a power by deed, which therefore effectively bound non-parties.

The effect of approval by the court of a release by the appointor, where the possible objects of the power were not parties to the proceedings, was considered by Plowman, J., in *Re Courtauld's Settlement.*[85] There had been no release by deed on the part of the appointor, and the question was raised whether, without express release, the power could be regarded as extinguished. Plowman, J., held that, although he could not decide that the arrangement bound persons who were not parties to the proceedings, a possible future appointee would have so slender a chance of establishing that the power continued to exist, notwithstanding the order, that the power could be regarded as extinguished.

In variations involving powers of appointment, any arrangement whereby the appointor obtains a benefit from the exercise of the power may constitute a fraud on the power, although this may be negatived in cases where it can be shown that there is no intention to benefit him. In *Re Robertson's Will*

---

[78] [1959] 1 W.L.R. 378.
[79] [1962] Ch. 826.
[80] [1962] Ch. 531.
[81] *Re Clarke's Will Trusts,* [1961] 1 W.L.R. 1471.
[82] *Foakes* v. *Jackson,* [1900] 1 Ch. 807.
[83] [1961] 1 W.L.R. 462.
[84] [1968] 1 W.L.R. 899.
[85] [1965] 1 W.L.R. 1385.

Trusts [86] the testator devised and bequeathed part of his estate to his son for life on protective trusts, and after the son's death, to such of the son's issue as he should by deed or will appoint; and in default of appointment to the son's children equally. The son (the applicant) wished to make some immediate capital provision for his children, and he was advised that since he had a protected life interest he could not do this without applying to the court under the Variation of Trusts Act. It was proposed that he should exercise his power of appointment in favour of his three children equally, and that the court should be asked to approve an arrangement dividing the fund between the applicant and his children in accordance with the actuarial value of their interests. The arrangement benefited not only the children, but also the applicant, but Russell, J., held that the appointment by the applicant was not a fraud on a power, since his predominant intention was to benefit his three children. In all such cases, however, if it appears that there may be a fraud on a power, the approval of the arrangement will be withheld until an investigation has been made, and the absence of fraud established. [87]

In *Re Drewe's Settlement*, [88] as part of a general variation of trusts, a power of appointment, exercisable by deed or will, was limited to exercise by deed, with the consent of the trustees, after advice by counsel.

Deletion of a Forfeiture Clause. The court has power under the Act to delete a forfeiture clause (*e.g.* on becoming a Roman Catholic), although not all forfeiture clauses are intrinsically undesirable. [89]

Protected Life Interests. In *Re Burney's Settlement Trusts* [90] Wilberforce, J., approved the variation of a marriage settlement embodying the enlargement of a protected life interest into an ordinary life interest, and the same judge also approved a similar change in *Re Munro's Settlement Trusts*. [91] The problem of the interests of persons who might be affected by this change has already been discussed.

Although the court will not, under the Act, resettle an infant's interest, it may nevertheless postpone its vesting, and insert a protected life interest, if there is strong evidence that this is for the infant's benefit.

Protective trusts may also raise other problems. In *Re Westminster Bank Ltd.'s Declaration of Trusts* [92] a settlor had directed that the income of one third of the fund should be held on protective trusts for his daughter, D, during her life, and on the determination of her life interest, on a discretionary trust for herself, her husband, children and any other beneficiaries under the trust deed. D, who was born in 1911, asked that the trustees should be allowed to deal with her share in the settlement on the assumption that she would have no more children. After receiving medical and other evidence, Wilberforce, J., agreed, observing that the court would now be rather cautious in accepting that the cases had established any rule about the age at which a woman ceased to be capable of child-bearing. Nevertheless, in *Re Pettifor's Will Trusts* [93]

[86] [1960] 1 W.L.R. 1050.
[87] *Re Wallace's Settlements*, [1968] 1 W.L.R. 711.
[88] [1966] 1 W.L.R. 1518.
[89] *Re Remnant's Settlement Trusts*, [1970] Ch. 560.
[90] [1961] 1 W.L.R. 545. See also *Re Baker's Settlement*, [1964] 1 W.L.R. 336.
[91] [1963] 1 W.L.R. 145.
[92] [1963] 1 W.L.R. 820.
[93] [1966] Ch. 257.

Pennycuick, J., decided that trustees could safely distribute a fund on the basis that a woman over seventy years of age was incapable of child-bearing, and that it was inappropriate for the trustees to seek to invoke the Variation of Trusts Act 1958 to provide against the contingency that she might have a child.

Powers of Maintenance and Advancement. On an application under section 1 the court may sanction the insertion of a power of advancement, similar to the statutory power, into a protected life interest, in a case where the settlor died before the passing of the Trustee Act 1925.[94] It is possible to think of applications to vary both the statutory power of advancement, and the statutory power of maintenance.

Entailed Interests. The court will authorise the barring of an infant's entailed interest under section 53 of the Trustee Act 1925 as part of a variation of a trust under the Variation of Trusts Act 1958.[95]

Where, as part of an arrangement for variation, it was agreed that a tenant in tail in remainder should bar the entail, and there was no protector of the settlement, it was held that the consent of the court was unnecessary to the disentailment.[96]

Discretionary Trusts. An arrangement under the Act may simply extend the terminal date for the exercise of a discretionary power.[97] In *Re Steed's Will Trusts*,[98] Harman, J., settled a point of considerable importance. He had been asked to approve under the Variation of Trusts Act 1958, at the instance of beneficiaries, an arrangement which would have the effect of overriding discretionary powers committed to the trustees, and which they continued to exercise. Harman, J., held that the court had no power under the Act either to overrule the trustees or to take their discretion from them. He accordingly refused to make an order, and the Court of Appeal approved this view.

Transfer of Trust Abroad. A new and valuable application of the Act occurred in *Re Seale's Marriage Settlement*.[99] The husband and wife, for whom a marriage settlement had been executed, had emigrated with their family to Canada. Buckley, J., decided that he had power under the Act to approve a variation, appointing a Canadian trust corporation in place of the English trustees, and transferring the property to trustees of a Canadian settlement, which was substantially similar to the English settlement. In this case, there was no question of tax avoidance, for the whole family had emigrated to Canada, and the children had been brought up as Canadians. In *Re Weston's Settlements*,[1] in which there was an application to transfer the trust funds to Jersey, and to appoint as trustees Jersey residents, the motive of the transfer was to save tax, although once again the settlor and the beneficiaries had moved to Jersey with the intention of living there. The Court of Appeal

---

[94] *Re Lister's Will Trusts*, [1962] 1 W.L.R. 1441.
[95] *Re Bristol's Settled Estates*, [1965] 1 W.L.R. 469. See also *Re Lansdowne's Will Trusts*, [1967] Ch. 603.
[96] *Re Darnley's Will Trusts*, [1970] 1 W.L.R. 405, following *Re Blandy Jenkins' Estate*, [1917] 1 Ch. 46.
[97] *I.R.C.* v *Holmden*, [1968] A.C. 685.
[98] [1960] Ch. 407.
[99] [1961] Ch. 574. See also *Re Windeatt's Will Trusts*, [1969] 1 W.L.R. 692.
[1] [1969] 1 Ch. 223. (There is no law of trusts in Jersey.)

held that there was power to approve the variation although it would not necessarily do so if there were an application to transfer the trust to a jurisdiction unversed in English trust law; and in this case, the arrangement was not sanctioned.

Rectification to Add a Beneficiary. In *Re Tinker's Settlement* [2] the original settlement had omitted to provide for the children of one of the beneficiaries. Russell, J., held that the Variation of Trusts Act could not be used to achieve a rectification of the original settlement, since it would have the effect of taking away some part of the interests of other children and unborn persons, instead of benefiting them.

Variation of Provisions in order to minimise Taxation. Reduction of the burden of taxation, especially where there have been important changes in taxation since the trust was established, is one of the primary objects of the majority of applications. It is no ground for objection to the proposed variation that this will be the result of the application. [3]

Variation of Settlements in Matrimonial Proceedings. Under sections 24–26 of the Matrimonial Causes Act 1973, the court has power to vary the provisions of a settlement made in favour of a party to the marriage, on or after divorce, annulment or judicial separation. Such a variation is made for the benefit of the parties and, if there are children, of the children of the marriage. The power may be exercised even if the effect of exercising it will be to reduce the amount of tax otherwise payable. [4] These powers only arise where the court itself has pronounced the decree, and not where it has been pronounced by a foreign court. They exist in respect of both ante-nuptial and post-nuptial marriage settlements, and other kinds of property adjustment order, *e.g.* to transfer or settle it, may be made in respect of anything owned by either spouse.

---

[2] [1960] 1 W.L.R. 1011.
[3] *Re Roberts' Settlement Trust,* [1961] T.R. 401; *re Clitheroe's Settlement Trusts,* [1959] 1 W.L.R. 1159; *Re Lloyd's Settlement,* [1967] 2 W.L.R. 1078. For variation to minimise capital gains tax, see *Re Sainsbury's Settlement,* [1967] 1 W.L.R. 476.
[4] *Thomson* v. *Thomson and Whitmee,* [1954] P. 384.

CHAPTER XXIII

THE EMERGENCY JURISDICTION OF THE COURT

A. THE COURT'S INTEREST

IT has always been the doctrine of equity that the court has a general supervisory jurisdiction in respect of trusts. This inherent jurisdiction allows the court, in an emergency, to authorise acts of administration by the trustees, for which they would otherwise not have authority, either under the rules of equity or by statute. Such an application by the trustees to the court may arise because the settlor did not foresee it, and failed to provide for it, or because the beneficiaries lack the capacity to consent. Before the passing of the Trustee Act 1925 which, by section 10 (3) (as amended by section 9 of the Trustee Investments Act 1961), permits trustees to concur in the amalgamation and reconstruction of companies, difficulties frequently arose when trustees who were authorised by the settlor to retain, or purchase, shares in specified companies, were asked to concur in the reconstruction or amalgamation of the company. Since a clause directing the acquisition or retention of shares in Company A would not be construed to extend to shares in Company AB, or even to shares of a different character in Company A, trustees were unable to concur, and upon a number of occasions, they invoked the assistance of the court. This was only available where the circumstances were such that no speculative element was present; in *Re Morrison,*[1] for example, the court refused to sanction an agreement whereby the trustees concurred in reorganising a business in which the testator had been a partner into a limited liability company. The effect of doing so would have been to exchange the testator's interest in the business for shares and debentures in the new company, which would have constituted an important departure from the terms of the will. On the other hand, in *West of England and South Wales District Bank* v. *Murch*[2] an arrangement whereby an executrix and trustee exchanged a share in a partnership for cash, shares in a limited liability company, and the extinguishment of a number of debts, was supported by the court as a compromise.

The whole question was examined by the Court of Appeal in *Re New*[3] where the court permitted the trustees of three trusts to concur in a scheme for the reconstruction of a company in which the trustees held shares which the testator had authorised them to retain. By the terms of the agreement these shares were to be exchanged for shares in the new company, and these were not authorised either by the will, or by statute. The Court of Appeal directed that the trustees must apply for leave, if they wished to retain the shares beyond a year. Romer, L.J., in the course of the judgment, pointed out that the court's permission was given only because the case was one which

[1] [1901] 1 Ch. 701.
[2] (1883), 23 Ch.D. 138.
[3] [1901] 2 Ch. 534.

the settlor could not reasonably have been supposed to foresee and further, that the acts of the trustees were in the circumstances extremely proper. This case which, as Cozens-Hardy, L.J., remarked in *Re Tollemache*,[4] " constitutes the high-water mark of the exercise by the Court of its extraordinary jurisdiction in relation to trusts," furnishes a good example of a sound business arrangement of which the court will approve, but Romer, L.J., in *Re New*,[5] was careful to emphasise the limits which bounded the court's jurisdiction—

> It is a matter of common knowledge that the jurisdiction we have been referring to, which is only part of the general administrative jurisdiction of the Court, has been constantly exercised, chiefly at chambers. Of course, the jurisdiction is one to be exercised with great caution, and the Court will take care not to strain its powers. It is impossible, and no attempt ought to be made, to state or define all the circumstances under which, or the extent to which, the Court will exercise the jurisdiction; but it need scarcely be said that the Court will not be justified in sanctioning every act desired by trustees and beneficiaries merely because it may appear beneficial to the estate; and certainly the Court will not be disposed to sanction transactions of a speculative or risky character. But each case brought before the Court must be considered and dealt with according to its special circumstances. As a rule, these circumstances are better investigated and dealt with in chambers. Very often they involve matters of a delicate and private nature, the publication of which is not requisite on any good ground and might cause great injury to the trust estate.

Although the trustees now possess a statutory power to concur in company reconstructions and amalgamations, without application to the court, there are other administrative matters in which it may be desirable to invoke the court's inherent jurisdiction. For example, in a case where a testator directed the trustees to sell property at a specified time, the court authorised the trustees to postpone the sale where it appeared that the sale would operate to the detriment of the trust estate.[6]

More recently, in *Re Royal Society's Charitable Trusts*,[7] the Royal Society sought authority to consolidate a number of trust funds of which it was the trustee into one combined fund, and to enlarge the scope of permissible investments in respect of such fund beyond that permitted by the general law. It was held that, although the matter did not come within section 57 of the Trustee Act 1925 nor within the court's general jurisdiction, yet at the instance of *charitable* trustees, where the Attorney-General consented or did not object, the court had jurisdiction to make an order by way of a scheme. In *Lloyds Bank Ltd.* v. *Attorney-General*[8] Roxburgh, J., approved a similar scheme.

B. SALVAGE PRINCIPLES

One particular application of the court's inherent jurisdiction occurs where what are known as " salvage principles " are applied. For example, if it is

---

4 [1903] 1 Ch. 955, 956.
5 [1901] 2 Ch. 534, 545–6.
6 *Re New*, [1901] 2 Ch. 534, 544.
7 [1956] Ch. 87.

8 [1959] 1 W.L.R. 755.

necessary to use capital money for the repair of trust property by raising a mortgage, this will be authorised, where the alternative would be to permit the property to go to ruin.[9] The court has also authorised the payment of premiums on a settled insurance policy from capital,[10] and has permitted a settled policy to be surrendered [10] or sold,[11] where it was no longer possible to pay the premiums.

C. INFANTS

The court has authorised the payment of maintenance for an infant out of income directed to be accumulated, and even out of capital, where the infant was absolutely entitled, or where other interested parties consented.

Of more general importance, however, is the power of the court to approve, on behalf of infants and unborn persons, compromises of disputes relating to trust property. This power was extensively discussed by the Court of Appeal and by the House of Lords in *Chapman* v. *Chapman*,[12] and it was there emphasised that the compromise must be of a genuine dispute.[13] In *Re Powell-Cotton's Resettlement*,[14] there was a complicated investment clause, the effect of which was doubtful. The trustees took out a summons to determine its effect, and immediately afterwards, applied for leave to compromise the proceedings by the substitution of a new, and wider, investment clause. Danckwerts, J., refused to sanction the change, on the grounds that no real compromise of a genuine dispute had been disclosed and that, if it were a genuine compromise, it was not one which the court ought to approve. The Court of Appeal affirmed his decision, but only on the second ground.

D. THE TRUSTEE ACT 1925, SECTION 57

Section 57 of the Trustee Act 1925 is drafted in very wide terms, and it confers jurisdiction on the court to approve, either generally or in particular instances, acts of the trustees for which they would otherwise lack authority. In *Re Downshire Settled Estates*,[15] Lord Evershed, M.R., observed—

> ... the object of section 57 was to secure that trust property should be managed as advantageously as possible in the interests of the beneficiaries and, with that object in view, to authorize specific dealings with the property which the court might have felt itself unable to sanction under the inherent jurisdiction, either because no actual 'emergency' had arisen or because of inability to show that the position which called for intervention was one which the creator of the trust could not reasonably have foreseen; but it was no part of the legislative aim to disturb the rule that the court will not rewrite a trust, or to add to such exceptions to that rule as had already found their way into the inherent jurisdiction.

There are some important limits to the exercise of this jurisdiction. First, the transaction contemplated must be for the benefit of the trust as a whole.

9 *Re Jackson* (1882), 21 Ch.D. 786; *Neill* v. *Neill*, [1904] 1 I.R. 513.
10 *Beresford* v. *Beresford* (1857), 23 Beav. 292.
11 *Hill* v. *Trenery* (1856), 23 Beav. 16.
12 [1954] A.C. 429 (Cases, p. 309). See pp. 348–355, *ante*.
13 *Cf. Re Lord Hylton's Settlement*, [1954] 1 W.L.R. 1055.
14 [1956] 1 W.L.R. 23.
15 [1953] Ch. 218, 248.

In *Re Craven's Estate* (*No. 2*) [16] a will authorised trustees to apply the whole or part of a beneficiary's share by way of advancement for the purpose of buying a business or a share in a business. The beneficiary wished to become a Lloyd's underwriter, and he asked the trustees to advance him the amount of his deposit. Farwell, J., held: (1) that the transaction was not within the terms of the power of advancement, not being the purchase of a business, or of a share in a business; and (2) that he had no power under section 57 to authorise it, since it could not be regarded as for the benefit of the trust as a whole. He explained [17]—

> Section 57 is undoubtedly framed in very wide terms. It is intended to apply to cases where the powers expressly given by the instrument creating the trust are insufficient to enable that to be done which it is expedient to do in the interests of the beneficiaries under the trust which the trustees have to administer, but which without this power could not be done at all. The language, as I have said, is very wide. It is: ' Where in the management or administration of any property vested in trustees, any sale, lease, mortgage, surrender, release, or other disposition, or any purchase, investment, acquisition, expenditure, or other transaction.' Pausing there for a moment, to come within the section the matter must be one which arises in the management or administration of property vested in trustees; but so long as the matter does so arise, there is nothing in those words which limits the power of the Court under the section. Then the section goes on: ' is in the opinion of the court expedient, but the same cannot be effected by reason of the absence of any power for that purpose ' etc., the Court may authorize it to be done. The word ' expedient ' there quite clearly must mean expedient for the trust as a whole. It cannot mean that however expedient it may be for one beneficiary if it is inexpedient from the point of view of the other beneficiaries concerned the Court ought to sanction the transaction. In order that the matter may be one which is in the opinion of the Court expedient, it must be expedient for the trust as a whole.

A further limit to the power of the court under section 57 is that the court cannot sanction the modification of beneficial interests under the trust.[18] Where, however, no modification of beneficial interests is involved, the court will approve a scheme which has the effect of saving estate duty by authorising the sale of a reversion.[19]

Since the passing of the Trustee Investments Act 1961, the court will not now approve an investment clause giving wider powers than those conferred by the Act, unless there are special circumstances. In any case, such applications are now better made under the Variation of Trusts Act 1958.[20]

The court has, under this section, authorised the partition of property, where the trustees lacked power to do so [21]; or the blending of trust funds arising

---

16 [1937] Ch. 431.
17 [1937] Ch. 436.
18 *Chapman* v. *Chapman*, [1954] A.C. 429 (Cases, p. 309).
19 *Re Cockerell's Settlement Trusts*, [1956] Ch. 372.
20 *Re Coates' Trusts*, [1959] 1 W.L.R. 375. See pp. 362-363, *ante*.
21 *Re Thomas*, [1930] 1 Ch. 194.

under different wills, but held for the same trusts.[22] In *Re Salting* [23] the plaintiff was entitled to the income of a legacy that was liable to forfeiture if he attempted to alienate. He applied to court, under section 57, for authority to permit the trustees to raise a sum out of the legacy, to discharge his debts, on his effecting a policy of assurance on his life to secure repayment. Eve, J., held that such an order should be made, and that this would not bring about a forfeiture of the legatee's interest, so long as he paid the premiums, and the trustees were not called upon to apply any part of the settled income for the purpose.

In *Re Mair* [24] the arrangement was similar to that in *Re Salting*, and the only two beneficiaries who were adversely affected were the possible future husbands of two married women, aged 69 and 70. Since it was unlikely that any claim by such persons would ever arise, their possible interests were disregarded, when the court gave its sanction under section 57.

In *Re Forster's Settlement* [25] advantage was taken of section 57 to enable the trustees to buy up the interest of the tenant for life in unusual circumstances. Under a settlement made in 1919, F had received a protected life interest, with remainder to his then wife for life, and thereafter as to capital and income, to the issue of F by any marriage, as F should appoint, with remainders over in favour of F's children who attained 21 or (being female) married. There were no children by the first marriage, which was dissolved in 1924. F remarried in 1927, and there were several children of this marriage. F died in 1941 without exercising the power of appointment, and when money was required for the maintenance of the children, £2,100 was obtained between 1942 and 1945 by mortgages sanctioned by the court, from D, on terms that the loans should not be called in until one year after the death of F's first wife. D died in 1952, and his executors pressed for repayment of the loan, and in 1953, there was a claim for £500 death duties, which the trustees had overlooked on F's death. It was agreed by all the beneficiaries that the trusts of the settlement should be determined, and a summons was taken out to sanction the execution of a draft deed of family arrangement, whereby the first wife was to sell her life interest to the trustees at a price favourable to the trust, the children of full age were to be paid out, and the share of an infant beneficiary was to be accumulated until he attained 21. Harman, J., held that, although he could not authorise this under the inherent jurisdiction of the court, he could nevertheless do so under section 57, as an expedient act in the management of the trust. This comes very near to altering the beneficial interests under the trust, but Harman, J., stressed that the court had already sanctioned four transactions relating to the trust, and which had affected the beneficial interest of the remainderman. Presumably, if such a scheme now came before the court, without prior applications, it would be under the Variation of Trusts Act 1958.

E. THE SETTLED LAND ACT 1925, SECTION 64

Section 57 of the Trustee Act 1925 applies to land held on trust for sale, and in respect of such land, it has been extended by the Settled Land and Trustee

[22] *Re Harvey*, [1941] 3 All E.R. 284. [23] [1932] 2 Ch. 57.
[24] [1935] Ch. 562. [25] [1954] 1 W.L.R. 1450.

Acts (Court's General Powers) Act 1943, as amended by the Emergency Laws (Miscellaneous Provisions) Act 1953, s. 9. It has no application to settled land, in respect of which section 64 of the Settled Land Act 1925 (as amended by the Settled Land and Trustee Acts (Court's General Powers) Act 1943, and by the Statute Law (Repeals) Act 1969, s. 1 and Sched., Part III) provides—

> (1) Any transaction affecting or concerning the settled land, or any part thereof, or any other land (not being a transaction otherwise authorised by this Act, or by the settlement) which in the opinion of the court would be for the benefit of the settled land, or any part thereof, or the persons interested under the settlement, may, under an order of the court, be effected by a tenant for life, if it is one which could have been validly effected by an absolute owner.
>
> (2) In this section ' transaction ' includes any sale, exchange, assurance, grant, lease, surrender, reconveyance, release, reservation, or other disposition, and any purchase or other acquisition, and any covenant, contract, or option, and any application of capital money, and any compromise or other dealing, or arrangement . . .

Although at first sight the effect of section 64 seems to be similar to that of section 57 of the Trustee Act 1925, it is, in fact, wider, and the word " transaction " as used in the section is one of the widest import.[26] For a transaction to be approved, it must be for the benefit of the settled land, or for some part of it, or for the benefit of persons interested under the settlement. Further, the transaction must affect or concern the settled land, or any other land, and the test is satisfied by a transaction which operates indirectly upon the settled land, provided the effect is real. It was because of the more ample operation of section 64 that the Court of Appeal could sanction the variation of beneficial interests in *Re Downshire Settled Estates*,[27] and that this decision was not adversely affected by the decision of the House of Lords in *Chapman* v. *Chapman*.[28] The wider effect of the section was again demonstrated by the decision of Danckwerts, J., in *Re Simmons*.[29] In that case the court authorised the distribution of capital to the tenant for life on the remaindermen being compensated by the extinguishment of a power of appointment, given to the tenant for life, in respect of property remaining in the settlement, where the object of the transaction was to diminish estate duty which was otherwise payable.

Under section 64 (2) the court has power to authorise the application of capital money in any way it thinks fit, provided the transaction is beneficial to the land, or to those interested under the settlement. In *Re Scarisbrick Resettlement Estates*,[30] Cohen, J., held that he had power under the section, as amended by section 1 of the Settled Land and Trustee Acts (Court's General Powers) Act 1943, to authorise the tenant for life to raise a sum of £10,000 out of capital to allow him and his family to live in the principal mansion house, and to undertake the necessary repairs, the transaction being for the benefit of persons interested in the settled land.

26 *Re Chapman's Settled Estates*, [1953] Ch. 218, 252.
27 [1953] Ch. 218.   28 [1954] A.C. 429 (Cases, p. 309).
29 [1956] Ch. 125.   30 [1944] Ch. 229.

PART III

BREACH OF TRUST

CHAPTER XXIV

THE EXTENT OF THE TRUSTEE'S LIABILITY FOR BREACH OF TRUST

A. BREACH OF TRUST AND THE MEASURE OF LIABILITY

A BREACH of trust consists in some improper act, neglect, default, or omission of a trustee in respect of the trust property or of a beneficiary's interest in it. There are, therefore, very many kinds of breaches of trust, resulting either from direct intermeddling with the trust property for improper purposes, or from a failure to exercise proper prudence in discharging a duty, or from the *mala fide* exercise of a discretion. In all these cases the trustee must make good the loss to the trust fund. Thus, if the trustee makes an improper investment, or pays the wrong person in mistake for a beneficiary, he must replace the amount lost, with interest, which is fixed at the discretion of the court, but which has long been 4 per cent.[1] Again, a credit in the bank account of a company, which is under the control of the directors, is held by them on trust for the company's purposes, and if they apply it otherwise, they commit a breach of trust.[2]

A number of illustrations of this rule have already been given, in considering the duties of trustees, which, whether imposed by law or by the settlement, must be exactly discharged. Thus, in *Re Massingberd's Settlement*,[3] trust money was invested in Consols, and the trustees were empowered to vary the investments, *with the consent of the tenant for life*. The trustees sold the Consols and then, with the consent of the life tenant, invested in an unauthorised security. Later, they realised the unauthorised security, and reinvested in an authorised security, but without the consent of the tenant for life. Meanwhile, the Consols had risen in price, and the court held that since in both transactions the trustees had deviated from the terms of the settlement, they must place the beneficiaries in the same position as if no such deviation had occurred, and replace the Consols, paying the increase in price out of their own pockets. In *Re Pauling's Settlement Trusts* [4] the trustees were liable for the purchase of a house in the Isle of Man for the occupation of a beneficiary, and for an improper advance to a beneficiary. Again, it has been noticed that it is the duty of the trustee to invest trust money in authorised securities as soon as possible, and if he allows it to remain uninvested in his hands, he

[1] *Re Beech*, [1920] 1 Ch. 40; *Re Baker*, [1924] 2 Ch. 271.
[2] *Re City Equitable Fire Insurance Co. Ltd.*, [1925] Ch. 407; *Selangor United Rubber Estates Ltd.* v. *Cradock (No. 3)*, [1968] 1 W.L.R. 1555.
[3] (1890), 63 L.T. 296.
[4] [1964] Ch. 303.

will nevertheless be liable for the loss in interest,[5] at the rate of 4 per cent. simple interest. If, on the other hand, the trustees, either at law or under the settlement, had a duty to accumulate, they will be liable for compound interest.[6] Again, if a trustee has improperly called in trust money on a mortgage yielding 5 per cent., he is liable for loss in interest,[7] and the same rate is charged where he unnecessarily sells stock.[8]

In all the cases so far considered, it will be observed that the measure of damages is based on the loss to the trust fund. In some instances of breach of trust, however, there may have been no loss at all. Here, the trustee is under a duty to account to the beneficiaries for all the profit he has made. Thus, if the trustee invests in unauthorised securities at a higher rate than 4 per cent., and sells out without loss, he cannot retain the difference between 4 per cent. and the higher yield for himself. It is an accretion to the trust fund, notwithstanding the fact that if there had been a deficiency in the income, or a loss on realisation of the securities, the trustee would have had to make it good.[6] Further, the trustee is not able to set off the profit of one transaction in breach of trust against the loss on another.[9]

The liability of a trustee who invests trust money in his trade or business has been noticed in an earlier chapter, and it was there indicated that the trustee was chargeable with 5 per cent. interest upon the money so employed, or alternatively, the beneficiaries can, at their choice, call upon the trustee to account for all the profits he has actually received, if they have reason to suppose that he has made more.[10] If the money has been employed by the trustee in trade, compound interest may be obtained,[11] but in *Burdick* v. *Garrick*,[12] where a solicitor-trustee employed trust moneys in his business, putting them to the firm's credit at the bank, the Court of Appeal only allowed simple interest. Lord Hatherley pointed out [13] that in trade it may be presumed that compound interest has been earned, whilst capital used in a solicitor's business not infrequently yields no interest at all. It should be added that where a trustee improperly lends trust money to a tradesman who knows that it is trust money, although the capital can of course be recovered, the beneficiary cannot claim the profits from the trader.[14]

Finally, if the trustee has been guilty of actual fraud or other grave misconduct in relation to the trust property, thereby depriving the beneficiary of the income, the court may order him to pay 5 per cent. compound interest with yearly rests. Half-yearly rests have exceptionally been directed, but the court is reluctant to do this.[15] The principle, as expressed by Lord Cranworth in *Attorney-General* v. *Alford*,[16] is that—

[5] *Stafford* v. *Fiddon* (1857), 23 Beav. 386; *Re Goodenough*, [1895] 2 Ch. 537; *Re Barclay*, [1899] 1 Ch. 674.
[6] *Re Emmet's Estate* (1881), 17 Ch.D. 142.
[7] *Jones* v. *Foxall* (1852), 15 Beav. 388.
[8] *Pocock* v. *Reddington* (1801), 5 Ves. 794.
[9] See pp. 375–376, *post.*
[10] *Jones* v. *Foxall*, *supra*; *Burdick* v. *Garrick* (1870), L.R. 5 Ch.App. 233.
[11] *Vyse* v. *Foster* (1872), L.R. 8 Ch.App.309, 329; *Re Davis*, [1902] 2 Ch. 314.
[12] (1870), L.R. 5 Ch.App. 233.
[13] L.R. 5 Ch.App. 242.
[14] *Stroud* v. *Gwyer* (1860), 28 Beav. 130.
[15] Per Lord Hatherley in *Burdick* v. *Garrick* (1870), L.R. 5 Ch.App. 233, 241.
[16] (1855), 4 De G.M. & G. 843, 852.

... the Court would be justified in dealing in point of interest very hardly with an executor because it might fairly infer that he used the money in speculation, by which he either did make five per cent., or ought to be estopped from saying that he did not ...

It is sometimes extremely difficult to discover whether the acts of the trustees resulting in a breach of trust were merely negligent, or were actually corrupt and dishonest. Nevertheless, the court will examine the whole of the facts, and if extenuating circumstances, such as the fact that the breach was caused simply by want of judgment, or the absence of personal advantage, can be discovered, the lower rate of interest will usually be charged.[17]

Interest, whether simple or compound, may be awarded against the trustees even though it is not asked for in the pleadings.[18]

B. THE PERIOD IN RESPECT OF WHICH A TRUSTEE'S LIABILITY MAY EXIST

When a new trustee is appointed, he is entitled to assume, unless there are suspicious circumstances putting him upon an inquiry, that the existing trustees have performed their functions properly.[19] Should he discover, however, that a breach of trust has been committed, he must secure satisfaction from the former trustees, and also get in any part of the trust estate that is still outstanding.[20] Apparently the only circumstance that will justify a failure to do this is the fact that it will be futile to institute proceedings against the former trustees.[21]

When a trustee retires, he does not in this way escape liability for breaches of trust committed whilst he was a trustee, unless his colleagues, by releasing him from such liability, choose to shift his responsibility to themselves[22]; and further, if a co-trustee contemplates a breach of trust, and the trustee retires in order to avoid liability, he will still be regarded as liable, for it was his duty to do all he could to prevent the breach.[23] In such a case, however, it is necessary to prove that the trustee contemplated the breach of trust which his co-trustee subsequently committed, and that he retired on account of it. It is not sufficient that the breach was the outcome of his retirement.[24] Apart from these special circumstances, a trustee is not liable for breaches of trust committed after he retired from the trust.

It must also be noticed in considering the extent of the trustee's liability, that if the trustee commits two distinct breaches of trust, one of which results in a loss to the trust estate, whilst there is a gain on the other, he cannot set off the gain on the one against the loss on the other.[25] On the other hand,

---

[17] *Tebbs* v. *Carpenter* (1816), 1 Madd. 290; *Crackelt* v. *Bethune* (1820), 1 Jac. & W. 586, 588.

[18] *Johnson* v. *Prendergast* (1860), 28 Beav. 480; *Re Barclay*, [1899] 1 Ch. 674.

[19] *Ex parte Geaves* (1856), 8 De G.M. & G. 291.

[20] *Hobday* v. *Peters* (*No. 3*) (1860), 28 Beav. 603.

[21] *Re Forest of Dean Coal Mining Co.* (1878), 10 Ch.D. 450.

[22] The retiring trustee cannot compel them to give him such a release: *Tiger* v. *Barclays Bank Ltd.*, [1951] 2 K.B. 556.

[23] *Webster* v. *Le Hunt* (1861), 9 W.R. 918; *Palairet* v. *Carew* (1863), 32 Beav. 564; *Clark* v. *Hoskins* (1868), 37 L.J.Ch. 561.

[24] *Head* v. *Gould*, [1898] 2 Ch. 250.

[25] *Wiles* v. *Gresham* (1854), 2 Drew. 258; *Dimes* v. *Scott* (1824), 4 Russ. 195; *Re Barker* (1898), 77 L.T. 712.

if in a single transaction which is a breach of trust, the trustee first sustains a loss, and then realises a profit, he is only liable in respect of the final result of the transaction, and not for the loss in respect of a particular part of it. Thus, in *Fletcher* v. *Green*,[26] trustees, in breach of trust, lent money on a mortgage. The property was sold and the money paid into court and invested in Consols, which then rose in value. The trustees were allowed to set off the rise in the value of the Consols against the loss resulting from the sale of the mortgaged property. Here, gain and loss obviously resulted from different stages of the same transaction.

Repairing a breach of trust on the eve of bankruptcy is not necessarily a fraudulent preference within section 44 (1) of the Bankruptcy Act 1914. In *Re Lake*,[27] a solicitor-trustee of a settlement misappropriated trust money, and then, immediately before his bankruptcy, he deposited in the trust box, voluntarily, and without the knowledge of his beneficiaries, certain debentures of his own, together with a memorandum which admitted the breach of trust, and then expressed the trustee's gratitude to the beneficiaries for their forbearance during his financial difficulties, stating that the deposit was made with the intention of repairing the breach of trust. It was held that the bankrupt had not made a fraudulent preference, his dominating motive being the intention to repair the wrong he had committed.

The same rule applies to the agent of a trustee. Thus, in *Ex parte Taylor*,[28] a broker employed by trustees of a marriage settlement to sell securities and reinvest the proceeds, forged certain transfers for his own purposes, and instead of reinvesting, appropriated the proceeds. The trustees pressed him to complete, whereupon he informed them of the forgery. The trustees told him that unless he immediately handed over the proceeds of sale, they would prosecute him for embezzlement. He acquiesced, and the court held that this reparation for a wrong did not amount to a fraudulent preference.

C. THE EFFECT OF THE TRUSTEE'S BANKRUPTCY ON LIABILITY FOR BREACH OF TRUST

Where a trustee who has been guilty of a breach of trust becomes bankrupt, the loss may be proved against his estate,[29] and if interest would have been awarded against him, this also may be proved.[30] If the bankrupt was one of several trustees, who were jointly implicated in the breach of trust, the beneficiaries may prove against the bankrupt's estate for the entire loss, even though the bankrupt did not benefit by the breach of trust.[31] In such a case, however, the trustee in bankruptcy may compel contribution from the other trustees, even where the bankrupt could not himself have done so, being prevented by his own fraud.[32] If two trustees are bankrupt, the beneficiaries may prove in the bankruptcy of each for the whole of the loss, but not so as

[26] (1864), 33 Beav. 426.
[27] [1901] 1 Q.B. 710.
[28] (1886), 18 Q.B.D. 295.
[29] *Keble* v. *Thompson* (1790), 3 Bro.C.C. 112; *Dornford* v. *Dornford* (1806), 12 Ves. 127; Bankruptcy Act 1914, s. 30.
[30] *Dornford* v. *Dornford, supra.*
[31] *Ex parte Shakeshaft* (1791), 3 Bro.C.C. 197.
[32] See *Muckleston* v. *Brown* (1801), 6 Ves. 52, 68.

to receive more than the amount of the loss itself.[33] Again, if a trustee improperly lends money on the mortgage of certain securities, and then becomes bankrupt, the beneficiary may prove for the whole of the debt, and retain the securities also, not being put to his election between abandoning either the mortgage or the debt.[34]

The Partnership Act 1890, s. 13, provides—

> If a partner, being a trustee, improperly employs trust property in the business or on the account of the partnership, no other partner is liable for the trust-property to the persons beneficially interested therein:
>
> Provided as follows: —
>
> (1) This section shall not affect any liability incurred by any partner by reason of his having notice of a breach of trust; and
>
> (2) Nothing in this section shall prevent trust money from being followed and recovered from the firm if still in its possession or under its control.

It will be seen that this section only protects the other partners where they have no notice. Accordingly, where a trustee is a partner, and lends trust money to his firm, if he becomes insolvent, the beneficiaries can prove either against the joint property of the firm, or against the estate of the bankrupt trustee, *and* against the estate of any other partner who has participated in the breach of trust; but the beneficiaries may not usually prove against the firm estate as well as against the separate estates of trustee and partners participating in the breach.[35]

If a trustee lends trust money to a firm of which he is not a member, and then becomes bankrupt, the beneficiaries may prove against the partnership estate for this; but if the trustee lent it to one of the partners, and the others had no notice that it was trust money, proof is against the separate estate of that partner only.[36]

By virtue of section 28 of the Bankruptcy Act 1914 the liability of a trustee in respect of breaches of trust is terminated by his discharge, except in respect of those breaches of trust which are fraudulent. Where a trustee is compelled to pay costs in a suit wherein he is found guilty of a fraudulent breach of trust, these costs are outside the scope of section 28, and the trustee's discharge frees him from liability in respect of these.[37] The negligence of a trustee, as a result of which a co-trustee appropriates trust money, is not a fraudulent breach of trust.[38]

Where money is recovered for a breach of trust in the bankruptcy of a trustee, the question of apportionment between capital and interest has occasioned some variation in practice, but in *Cox* v. *Cox*,[39] it was pointed out that the true principle was that neither the tenant for life nor the remainderman should gain an advantage at the expense of the other, and, therefore, their respective interests must be calculated as follows—

[33] *Keble* v. *Thompson* (1790), 3 Bro.C.C. 112.
[34] *Ex parte Geaves* (1856), 8 De G.M. & G. 291.
[35] *Ex parte Watson* (1814), 2 V. & B. 414; *Ex parte Barnewall* (1855), 6 De G.M. & G. 801.
[36] *Ex parte Apsey* (1791), 3 Bro.C.C. 265.
[37] *Re Greer*, [1895] 2 Ch. 217.   [38] *Re Smith*, [1893] 2 Ch. 1.
[39] (1869), L.R. 8 Eq. 343. (Not following Lord Romilly's rule in *Stroud* v. *Gwyer* (1860), 28 Beav. 130.)

What principal, if invested on the day of the obligor's death (the date from which the interest was to run) at 4 per cent. would amount with interest to the sum so recovered? Interest at 4 per cent. on this principal, or in other words, the difference between the principal and the amount, will then go to the tenant for life, and the rest must be treated as principal.

D. LIABILITY OF THE ESTATE OF A DECEASED TRUSTEE

Where a trustee commits a breach of trust, and dies before he has repaired it, his personal representatives are liable to the extent of the assets they have received.[40] Furthermore, the beneficiaries under the trust may follow the assets into the hands of the legatees of the deceased trustee to the extent necessary to make good the breach of trust.

E. A TRUSTEE'S LIABILITY FOR THE ACTS OF HIS CO-TRUSTEE

In the performance of joint acts on behalf of the trust, all trustees are jointly and severally liable. Sometimes, however, a trustee may be able to act on his own account, or he may have been entrusted with particular duties for the trust by the trustees as a whole. In such cases, it becomes necessary to consider whether the other trustees are liable for his acts or defaults.

In general, such a trustee is liable only for his own acts or defaults, and in actual fact there are no real exceptions to this rule.[41] If a trustee is made liable for the wrongful acts of a co-trustee, the reason is because he himself has in some way been at fault. This is reflected in the following observations of Lord Westbury in *Wilkins* v. *Hogg*.[42]

> There were three modes in which a trustee would become liable according to the ordinary principles: 1. Where, being recipient, he hands over money without securing its due application. 2. Where he permits a co-trustee to receive money without making due inquiry as to his dealing with it. 3. Where he becomes aware of a breach of trust, either committed or meditated, and abstains from taking the needful steps to obtain restitution or redress.

This was always the rule of equity,[43] and it has now been embodied in statute, for the Trustee Act 1925, s. 30 (1), provides—

> A trustee shall be chargeable only for money and securities actually received by him notwithstanding his signing any receipt for the sake of conformity, and shall be answerable and accountable only for his own acts, receipts, neglects, or defaults, and not for those of any other trustee, nor for any banker, broker, or other person with whom any trust money or securities may be deposited, nor for the insufficiency or deficiency of

[40] *Devaynes* v. *Robinson* (1857), 24 Beav. 86.
[41] Except possibly where a trustee delegates his trusts under section 25 of the Trustee Act 1925, as replaced by the Powers of Attorney Act 1971, s. 9.
[42] (1861), 5 L.T. 467, 470.
[43] *Westley* v. *Clarke* (1759), 1 Eden 357.

any securities, nor for any other loss, unless the same happens through his own wilful default.

A liquidator of a company, however, is not a trustee within section 30.[44]

In *Re City Equitable Fire Insurance Co. Ltd.*,[45] Warrington, L.J., approved the observations of Romer, J., to the effect that—

> ... a person is not guilty of " wilful neglect or default " unless he is conscious that in doing the act which is companied of, or in omitting to do the act which it is said he ought to have done, he is committing a breach of his duty, and also, as he said, recklessly careless whether it is a breach of duty or not.

The point becomes clearer by contrasting *Hanbury* v. *Kirkland*[46] with *Re Munton*.[47] In the former case, one of three trustees informed his co-trustees that he had an opportunity of investing the trust property in a 5 per cent. mortgage, and he requested his co-trustees to execute a power of attorney to himself to enable him to transfer the trust stock on the mortgage security being completed. The co-trustees complied, without making any inquiry. The trustee sold the stock and absconded, and it was held that the trustees who signed the power of attorney were responsible, Shadwell, V.-C., observing—

> ... the trustees, without further inquiry, without exercising a single act of discretion, execute the power of attorney.

On the other hand, in *Re Munton*,[47] a retiring trustee, acting on the advice of his own independent solicitors, joined with two co-trustees, one of whom was a solicitor acting for the trust, in executing a joint power of attorney authorising certain brokers to sell and transfer all or any part of some stock, and to receive the purchase money. They then handed the power to the solicitor-trustee, who gave it to the brokers. These sold the fund and handed to him alone the whole of the proceeds, which he misappropriated. The Court of Appeal, upholding the decision of Astbury, J., held that, as the power contained no authority to pay the solicitor-trustee alone, the retiring trustee was not liable for the solicitor-trustee's default.

The effect of signing for conformity is now specifically considered in the section. All trustees must normally join in the performance of a trust, and in general are deemed to have done so.[48] In particular, all trustees must join in giving receipts, and in receiving capital money. It has been recognised, however, that trustees may appoint one of themselves to receive rents, for joint collection would in many cases be impossible. Accordingly, in *Townley* v. *Sherborne*,[49] where one of the trustees had received the rents and had then become impoverished, it was pointed out that his co-trustee was not liable simply because he had joined in giving receipts; but if the co-trustee had subsequently allowed the trust money to remain for a long period in the hands of his colleague, he would have been held liable on this account. This is

---

44 *Re Windsor Steam Coal Co. (1901) Ltd.*, [1928] Ch. 609.
45 [1925] Ch. 407, 434, 525. See p. 239, *ante*.
46 (1829), 3 Sim. 265, 271.
47 [1927] 1 Ch. 262 (Cases, p. 308).
48 See *Re Flower and the Metropolitan Board of Works* (1884), 27 Ch.D. 592.
49 (1634), Bridg. J. 35.

exactly the position under the Trustee Act 1925, s. 30, of a trustee who signs for conformity.[50] The trustee who seeks to evade liability must show, however, that he never received the money.[51]

The position of executors is in this respect a little different from that of trustees. Each executor has full authority to handle the pure personalty of the testator alone, and to give a good discharge.[52] Accordingly, if a co-executor signs a receipt, this is stronger evidence that he actually handled the money than it would be in the case of a trustee, and he will be held liable if he allowed the money to remain for an undue length of time in the hands of his colleague even though he never actually received it.[53] Again, he will be liable for any act which unnecessarily puts assets under the sole control of a co-executor if loss occurs.[54]

It is by no means unusual for a trust instrument to include an indemnity clause, varying the statutory indemnity contained in section 30 of the Trustee Act 1925. Such a clause will usually confer on the trustee a greater protection than the statutory provision. For example, in *Wilkins* v. *Hogg*[55] the indemnity clause, after providing that the trustee should be liable only for his own acts and defaults, went on to exempt him from any obligation to see to the due application of money by a co-trustee. When a co-trustee failed to deposit trust money in the joint names of trustees and then, after an interval, converted it to his own use, Lord Westbury, L.C., on appeal, held that the other trustees could not be made liable for the misappropriation.

F. THE TRUSTEE'S RIGHT OF INDEMNITY OR CONTRIBUTION FROM A CO-TRUSTEE

The duty of trustees to act jointly has already been mentioned, and in order that the trust estate shall be bound, the agreement of the trustees must be unanimous, for there is no power in the majority to bind a minority, unless the trust instrument so declares or unless the trust is charitable. All investments and mortgages should therefore be in their joint names,[56] unless this is impossible, as where shares formed part of the trust property, and these by the regulations of the company could only be registered in the name of a single person.[57] It follows from this, therefore, that the liability of trustees for joint acts or defaults is joint and several; that is to say, the beneficiaries may proceed against one or more of the trustees for the whole amount, or against all, whilst if judgment is obtained against all, it may be enforced against one or more. Accordingly, if a judgment against two trustees has been partially satisfied by one, and the other then becomes bankrupt, the beneficiaries may prove in his bankruptcy for the whole amount, and not for the balance, although obviously not more than the balance can be recovered.[58] This rule

---

[50] See also *Brice* v. *Stokes* (1805), 11 Ves. 319; *Walker* v. *Symonds* (1818), 3 Swanst. 1; *Consterdine* v. *Consterdine* (1862), 31 Beav. 330; *Lewis* v. *Nobbs* (1878), 8 Ch.D. 591; *Carruthers* v. *Carruthers*, [1896] A.C. 659.

[51] *Brice* v. *Stokes*, supra.

[52] Law of Property Act 1925, s. 27 (2).

[53] *Joy* v. *Campbell* (1804), 1 Sch. & Lef. 328, 341; *Re Gasquoine*, [1894] 1 Ch. 470.

[54] *Doyle* v. *Blake* (1804), 2 Sch. & Lef. 229.   [55] (1861), 5 L.T. 467.

[56] *Lewis* v. *Nobbs* (1878), 8 Ch.D. 591.

[57] *Consterdine* v. *Consterdine* (1862), 31 Beav. 330.

[58] *Edwards* v. *Hood-Barrs*, [1905] 1 Ch. 20.

of joint and several liability extends not only to express trustees, but also to all who meddle with the trust property. Thus, in *Cowper* v. *Stoneham*,[59] it was held that, if trustees committed the execution of their trust to solicitors, who received trust money and invested it in their business, both the trustees and the solicitors would be equally liable, and that the beneficiaries could recover against the solicitors alone.

As between the trustees themselves, however, the general rule is that there is a right of contribution,[60] unless they have been guilty of fraud.[61] It seems doubtful, however, whether there is a right of contribution in respect of the costs of the action, although obviously where a breach of trust has been made out, the court may make an order in respect of costs.[62] Where one of the trustees has died, the right of contribution may be exercised against his personal representatives.[63]

In three cases, a trustee who has committed a breach of trust will have to go further, and indemnify his co-trustees against the whole of the consequences of the breach. The first of these is where the trustee through whose activity the loss is sustained is a solicitor, who is acting as solicitor to the trust for himself and his co-trustees, so that the breach of trust is committed on his advice.[64] It is essential in such cases that the breach of trust should have been committed solely in consequence of the advice of the solicitor-trustee; thus, in *Head* v. *Gould*,[65] the co-trustee, a woman, urged the solicitor-trustee to enable her to commit a breach of trust for the benefit of her brother, and here the court declined to give her an indemnity.

The second case of an indemnity arises in respect of a trustee who, in the words of Cotton, L.J., in *Bahin* v. *Hughes*,[66] " has himself got the benefit of the breach of trust, or between whom and his co-trustees there has existed a relation, which will justify the Court in treating him as solely liable for the breach of trust." Such cases obviously cannot be defined with complete precision.

Thirdly, if one of the trustees is also a beneficiary under the trust, the breach will, as far as possible, be satisfied out of his interest. This is illustrated by *Chillingworth* v. *Chambers*,[67] where two trustees invested on insufficient security, and thus became jointly and severally liable to the beneficiaries for the loss. One trustee having made good the loss, he sought to recover contribution from his co-trustee, but this was refused, as he had become entitled to a share in the trust estate as his wife's successor. The principle is that a trustee beneficiary who has assented to and profited by the breach of trust [68] must bear the loss to the extent of his share. However, after his interest has been exhausted, it seems that the right of contribution arises again *pro tanto*.

In *Robinson* v. *Harkin* [69] it was pointed out that a trustee's right to indem-

59 (1893), 68 L.T. 18.
60 *Lingard* v. *Bromley* (1812), 1 V. & B. 114; *Birks* v. *Micklethwait* (1864), 33 Beav. 409.
61 See *Bahin* v. *Hughes* (1886), 31 Ch.D. 390; *Jackson* v. *Dickinson*, [1903] 1 Ch. 947.
62 *Re Linsley*, [1904] 2 Ch. 785.
63 *Jackson* v. *Dickinson*, [1903] 1 Ch. 947.
64 *Lockhart* v. *Reilly* (1856), 25 L.J.Ch. 697; *Re Turner*, [1897] 1 Ch. 536; *Re Linsley*, *supra*.
65 [1898] 2 Ch. 250.
66 (1886), 31 Ch.D. 390, 396.
67 [1896] 1 Ch. 685 (Cases, p. 347). See also *Moxham* v. *Grant*, [1900] 1 Q.B. 88.
68 Kay, L.J., pp. 701–702, speaks of " exclusive benefit."
69 [1896] 2 Ch. 415.

nity or contribution is like a surety's right to sue a co-surety for contribution, so that the Limitation Act 1939 only begins to run when a judgment for the breach has been obtained.

G. CRIMINAL AND OTHER PROCEEDINGS AGAINST A TRUSTEE FOR BREACH OF TRUST

The Theft Act 1968, which has remodelled and simplified the law of theft, contains two subsections imposing criminal liability upon a trustee and upon any person who dishonestly appropriates trust property. Such a wrongful appropriation includes any dealing with property as would previously have amounted to a taking, embezzlement, conversion or fraudulent misappropriation by a trustee. " Property " has an extremely comprehensive meaning, and although a person may not usually steal land, he may do so " when he is a trustee or personal representative, or is authorised by power of attorney, or as liquidator of a company, or otherwise, to sell or dispose of land belonging to another, and he appropriates the land or anything forming part of it by dealing with it in breach of the confidence reposed in him." (Section 4 (2) (a).) By section 5 (2), " Where property is subject to a trust, the persons to whom it belongs shall be regarded as including any person having a right to enforce the trust, and an intention to defeat the trust shall be regarded accordingly as an intention to deprive of the property any person having that right." This, therefore, includes a beneficiary who has no present interest in the trust property.

Where a solicitor-trustee misappropriates trust money, the court has jurisdiction to order him to be struck off the rolls.[70]

It must also be observed that whilst the Debtors Act 1869 largely abolished arrest and imprisonment for debt, certain classes of persons are excepted from the benefit of this provision. Among them are trustees or persons acting in a fiduciary capacity in default in respect of a court order to such a person to pay any sum in his possession or under his control. By section 4 it is provided that no person so excepted can be imprisoned for more than one year. This period runs from the date of imprisonment, notwithstanding release during the period and subsequent rearrest. An order for attachment on a default is in the nature of a punishment for that offence, and therefore a second order cannot be made in respect of the same default, inasmuch as the offence has been purged.[71]

The term " person acting in a fiduciary capacity " is wide. It does not mean " acting in a fiduciary capacity to the plaintiff," but so acting towards anyone.[72] It includes an auctioneer in respect of the proceeds of sale of property,[73] and also the London agent of a country solicitor, where the agent fails to pay money into court as ordered; but a partner does not occupy a fiduciary position in respect of money received by him on behalf of the partnership.[74]

[70] *Thompson* v. *Finch* (1856), 8 De G.M. & G. 560.
[71] *Church's Trustee* v. *Hibbard*, [1902] 2 Ch. 784.
[72] *Marris* v. *Ingram* (1879), 13 Ch.D. 338.
[73] *Crowther* v. *Elgood* (1887), 34 Ch.D. 691.
[74] *Piddocke* v. *Burt*, [1894] 1 Ch. 343.

A trustee who has once been in possession of the money, but has spent it, is liable to attachment. He may not avoid liability by alleging that it is no longer in his possession or under his control.[75] Accordingly, in *Re Bourne*,[76] an executor who was also a debtor to the estate was regarded as having paid money to himself as executor, and as holding the debt in a fiduciary capacity, so rendering him liable to attachment, but the court held that it would not make an order therefor if his conduct was free from all moral blame. Similarly, an order will not be made where the trustee has merely made default in getting in the trust money.[77]

Attachment is not merely a civil proceeding. It is of a punitive nature,[78] and therefore it may be ordered notwithstanding the fact that the trustee has become bankrupt, and that the Bankruptcy Act 1914, s. 7, provides that after the making of a receiving order, no creditor shall have any remedy against the person or property of the defendant.[79]

The Debtors Act 1878 provides that a court may inquire into the case of a defaulting trustee, and grant or refuse, either absolutely or upon terms, any application for a writ of attachment, or other process. In several cases after that Act, attachment was refused for various reasons, for example that the trustee had no means to pay, but Kay, J., in *Re Knowles*,[80] made an order where the trustee had been fraudulent, notwithstanding the fact that he appeared to be without means, thus adopting the view of Jessel, M.R., in *Marris* v. *Ingram*.[81] Where, however, there has been no fraud, but merely erroneous application of trust funds, the order will not usually be granted.[82]

[75] *Re Smith*, [1893] 2 Ch. 1.
[76] [1906] 1 Ch. 697.
[77] *Ferguson* v. *Ferguson* (1875), L.R. 10 Ch.App. 661.
[78] *Per* Jessel, M.R., *Marris* v. *Ingram* (1879), 13 Ch.D. 338, 341–343.
[79] See *Re Wray* (1887), 36 Ch.D. 138; *Re Edye* (1891), 63 L.T. 762; *Re Smith, supra.*
[80] (1883), 52 L.J.Ch. 685.
[81] (1879), 13 Ch.D. 338.
[82] *Holroyde* v. *Garnet* (1882), 20 Ch.D. 532; *Earl of Aylesford* v. *Earl Poulett*, [1892] 2 Ch. 60.

CHAPTER XXV

SPECIAL RIGHTS OF A BENEFICIARY IN DEFENCE
OF HIS INTEREST

A. THE RIGHT TO COMPEL PERFORMANCE OF THE
TRUST, OR TO PREVENT A THREATENED
BREACH

IF the trustee fails to take all due steps in defence of the trust estate, a beneficiary may intervene, and compel the trustee to lend his name for the purpose of bringing any actions that will be necessary.[1] Again, if a trustee fails to renew leaseholds, the court will compel him to do so on the suit of a beneficiary.[2] Further, if the trustees are about to sell at an undervalue, the court will restrain the sale by injunction[3]; and the court will also grant an injunction and appoint a receiver where the character of the trustee is such as to imperil the trust fund,[4] or where, as in *Earl Talbot* v. *Scott*,[5] the acceptance by the trustees of a second trust, inconsistent with the first, threatened the proper fulfilment by them of the first trust.

If the number of trustees has been reduced by the death or retirement of trustees, and the failure to appoint new ones, a beneficiary, whether tenant for life or remainderman, may require new trustees to be appointed.[6]

In *Keeling* v. *Child*,[7] where the beneficiary offered substantial reasons for his allegation that the trustee would not properly perform his trust, the court compelled the trustee to give security therefor.

Any beneficiary may intervene to have his interest properly protected, whether he has a vested or a contingent interest,[8] although it would seem that a person who has merely a possibility of a future interest cannot exercise this right.[9] The value of this wide right inherent in the beneficiary is emphasised by the fact that a beneficiary can only sue a debtor to the trust estate in exceptional circumstances. Failing such special circumstances, the beneficiary's course is to sue the trustee for the execution of the trusts, and then to apply for leave to sue in his own name.[10]

A beneficiary may ask for the removal of a trustee, and for the appointment of another in his place, for good reason. Such proceedings may be by originating summons or, where the proceedings are likely to be contentious, by writ.[11]

---

[1] *Foley* v. *Burnell* (1783), 1 Bro.C.C. 274, but in *T.M. Fairclough & Sons Ltd.* v. *Berliner*, [1931] 1 Ch. 60, this was not done. See (1931) 47 *Law Quarterly Review* 173.
[2] *Bennett* v. *Colley* (1832), 5 Sim. 181, 192.
[3] *Anon.* (1821), 6 Madd. 10. See also *Milligan* v. *Mitchell* (1833), 1 My. & K. 446.
[4] *Everett* v. *Prythergch* (1841), 12 Sim. 363.
[5] (1858), 4 K. & J. 139; but see *Berry* v. *Keen* (1883), 51 L.J.Ch. 912.
[6] *Hibbard* v. *Lamb* (1756), Amb. 309; *Buchanan* v. *Hamilton* (1801), 5 Ves. 722; *Finlay* v. *Howard* (1842), 2 Dr. & War. 490.
[7] (1678), Rep.t. Finch 360.
[8] *Re Sheppard's Will Trusts* (1862), 4 De G.F. & J. 423.
[9] *Davis* v. *Angel* (1862), 4 De G.F. & J. 524. (Discussed in *Clowes* v. *Hilliard* (1876), 4 Ch. D. 413.)
[10] *Sharpe* v. *San Paulo Railway Co.* (1873), L.R. 8 Ch.App. 597.
[11] *Re Sir Lindsay Parkinson & Co. Ltd. Settlement Trusts*, [1965] 1 W.L.R. 372.

Certain characteristic equitable remedies may also be asked for by a beneficiary against his trustee. In the first place, the court may grant an injunction wherever the trustee contemplates a breach of trust, even though the act may be remedial in its consequences.[12] For example, section 26 (3) of the Law of Property Act 1925 provides that trustees for sale shall, so far as practicable, give effect to the wishes of the beneficiaries if of full age. Failure to consult them, or some of them, therefore amounts to a breach of trust, which can be restrained by injunction, even if a husband as sole trustee, and his wife is the only other beneficiary.[13] Again, an injunction will be granted against a bankrupt trustee who seeks to obtain possession of trust property.[14]

Secondly, it is within the discretion of the court to appoint a receiver, on the application of a beneficiary, whenever it is " just or convenient " to do so.[15] An order for a receiver will be made wherever there is evident actual or prospective violation of the duties of the trustee, resulting in serious danger to the trust property.[16] Thus, loss of part of the trust estate, through failure to get it in, affords good grounds [17]; so does the failure of the trustees to agree, so that the trust cannot be properly administered,[18] or refusal of the trustee to act,[19] or denial of the trust.[20] Mere poverty of the trustee is not a ground for appointing a receiver,[21] but if it is associated with bad character, misconduct, or acts of waste, it will be a relevant factor.[22]

Finally, whenever trust property is endangered, as for example where it is invested in unauthorised and hazardous securities, the court may, upon the admission of the trustee that the fund is in his co-trustee's hands, order the amount to be paid into court by the trustee who is not holding the fund, if that trustee admits that the fund has not been properly applied.[23] Application may be made by any person interested in the fund, even though only contingently [24]; but the plaintiff's title must be beyond any real dispute.[25]

It will be observed that the trustee must admit that the fund is in his hands. If he admits receipt of the money, but states that he has made payments out, this may be verified, and payment in of the balance ordered,[26] although the admission may justify an order for payment in of the whole sum.[27] In *Freeman* v. *Cox* [28] an unchallenged affidavit made by the plaintiff was held to constitute a sufficient admission, but in *Neville* v. *Matthewman,*[29] Lord Herschell said that this principle would not be extended. Letters written by the

---

[12] *Milligan* v. *Mitchell* (1833), 1 My. & K. 446; *Balls* v. *Strutt* (1841), 1 Hare 146.
[13] *Waller* v. *Waller*, [1967] 1 W.L.R. 451.
[14] *Bowen* v. *Phillips*, [1897] 1 Ch. 174.
[15] Supreme Court of Judicature (Consolidation) Act 1925, s. 45 (1). As to receivers generally see Keeton and Sheridan, *Equity*, pp. 509–517.
[16] *Middleton* v. *Dodswell* (1806), 13 Ves. 266; *Barkley* v. *Lord Reay* (1842), 2 Hare 306, 308.
[17] *Richards* v. *Perkins* (1838), 3 Y. & C. Ex. 299.
[18] *Bagot* v. *Bagot* (1841), 10 L.J.Ch. 116; *Swale* v. *Swale* (1856), 22 Beav. 584.
[19] *Tait* v. *Jenkins* (1842), 1 Y. & C.C.C. 492.
[20] *Sheppard* v. *Oxenford* (1855), 1 K. & J. 491.
[21] *Howard* v. *Papera* (1815), 1 Madd. 142.
[22] *Everett* v. *Prythergch* (1841), 12 Sim. 363.
[23] *Wiglesworth* v. *Wiglesworth* (1852), 16 Beav. 269.
[24] *Freeman* v. *Fairlie* (1812), 3 Mer. 29.
[25] *Bartlett* v. *Bartlett* (1845), 4 Hare 631; *Marryat* v. *Marryat* (1854), 23 L.J. Ch. 876.
[26] *Hollis* v. *Burton*, [1892] 3 Ch. 226.
[27] *Re Benson*, [1899] 1 Ch. 39.
[28] (1878), 8 Ch.D. 148.
[29] [1894] 3 Ch. 345, 352–353.

trustee before the action and containing the admission are, however, quite sufficient,[30] and a verbal admission has been accepted.[31]

A solicitor of a trustee, if he receives money with notice of the trust, may also be ordered to pay it into court, since his title is no better than the trustee's.[32]

B. IF THE TRUSTEE IS ALSO A BENEFICIARY, HIS INTEREST MAY BE IMPOUNDED

The liability of the beneficial interest of a trustee to indemnify a co-trustee where there has been a breach of trust has already been considered.[33] It remains to notice that the liability of the trustee's interest to forfeiture is rather wider than was there stated. If there has been a breach of trust, the trustee will not be able to receive any part of his interest under the trust until the breach has been made good, and this applies not only to interests to which the trustee was directly entitled, but to interests he may have acquired by purchase or succession,[34] and furthermore, an assignee of a beneficial interest from a trustee is subject to the same disability, even though the breach has occurred after assignment of the interest.[35]

If a trustee of two separate trusts commits a breach of trust in respect of the first, and is a beneficiary under the second, but not under the first, his interest in the second fund will not be impounded to make good the breach of trust in respect of the first.[36]

C. FOLLOWING THE TRUST PROPERTY

That the beneficiary has always a personal remedy against the trustee for breaches of trust has already been noticed. The beneficiary, however, possesses a more powerful remedy. He may follow the trust property. This equitable principle has three aspects. In the first place, it implies that even though the trustee has parted with the actual trust property, yet so long as the proceeds of the disposition of that property are identifiable, the beneficiary can recover them from the hands of the trustee. In the second aspect, the doctrine implies that the beneficiary may, subject to conditions, follow the trust property into the hands of third persons. Thirdly, he may follow trust property into the hands of another beneficiary. Finally, independently of these remedies, he may have a personal remedy against another beneficiary or a stranger, to whom trust money has been wrongly paid.[37]

1. Following the Trust Property in a Changed Form in the Hands of the Trustee

Where the trustee has wrongfully sold trust property, it makes no difference what form the proceeds of sale assume, the beneficiary can always recover

---

30 *Hampden* v. *Wallis* (1884), 27 Ch.D. 251.
31 *Re Beeny*, [1894] 1 Ch. 499.
32 *Staniar* v. *Evans* (1886), 34 Ch.D. 470; *Re Carroll*, [1902] 2 Ch. 175.
33 p. 381, *ante*.
34 *Jacubs* v. *Rylance* (1874), L.R. 17 Eq. 341; *Doering* v. *Doering* (1889), 42 Ch.D. 203; *Re Dacre*, [1916] 1 Ch. 344.
35 *Doering* v. *Doering*, *supra*.
36 *Re Towndrow*, [1911] 1 Ch. 662.
37 See also Keeton and Sheridan, *Equity*, pp. 518–529.

them so long as they are identifiable, and furthermore, any gain which accrues in the process belongs to the beneficiary, whilst any loss is debited to the trustee. It was at one time thought that if the trustee sold the trust property, and paid the proceeds into his account at the bank, the beneficiary could not recover them, since " money has no earmark," but this doctrine is now entirely discredited.[38]

The position is simple where the proceeds of sale remain distinct from any other property.[39] More difficult questions arise, however, when (as is often the case) the trustee mixes trust moneys with his own, and then employs them in some enterprise in breach of trust. In *Re Hallett's Estate*[40] Jessel, M.R., observed—

> The modern doctrine of Equity as regards property disposed of by persons in a fiduciary position is a very clear and well-established doctrine. You can, if the sale was rightful, take the proceeds of the sale, if you can identify them. If the sale was wrongful, you can still take the proceeds of the sale, in a sense adopting the sale for the purpose of taking the proceeds, if you can identify them. There is no distinction, therefore, between a rightful and a wrongful disposition of the property, so far as regards the right of the beneficial owner to follow the proceeds. But it very often happens that you cannot identify the proceeds. The proceeds may have been invested together with money belonging to the person in a fiduciary position, in a purchase. He may have bought land with it, for instance, or he may have bought chattels with it. Now, what is the position of the beneficial owner as regards such purchases? I will, first of all, take his position when the purchase is clearly made with what I will call, for shortness, the trust money, although it is not confined, as I will shew presently, to express trusts. In that case, according to the now well-established doctrine of Equity, the beneficial owner has a right to elect either to take the property purchased, or to hold it as a security for the amount of the trust money laid out in the purchase; or, as we generally express it, he is entitled at his election either to take the property, or to have a charge on the property for the amount of the trust money. But in the second case, where a trustee has mixed the money with his own, there is this distinction, that the *cestui que trust,* or beneficial owner, can no longer elect to take the property, because it is no longer bought with the trust-money simply and purely, but with a mixed fund. He is, however, still entitled to a charge on the property purchased, for the amount of the trust-money laid out in the purchase; and that charge is quite independent of the fact of the amount laid out by the trustee. The moment you get a substantial portion of it furnished by the trustee, using the word "trustee" in the sense I have mentioned, as including all persons in a fiduciary relation, the right to the charge follows. That is the modern doctrine of Equity.

---

[38] *Re Hallett's Estate* (1880), 13 Ch.D. 696.
[39] *Taylor* v. *Plumer* (1815), 3 M. & S. 562; *Ex parte Dumas* (1754), 2 Ves.Sen. 582; *Re Patten and the Guardians of the Poor of Edmonton Union* (1883), 52 L.J.Ch. 787.
[40] (1880), 13 Ch.D. 696, 708-9 (Cases, p. 351).

In *Re Hallett's Estate,* it was decided that where a trustee, or other person with a fiduciary character, pays trust moneys into his own account, thereby mixing the moneys with his own, and subsequently withdraws money for his own purposes, he must be deemed to be drawing out his own money, so that the beneficiaries can claim the balance as trust money, as against the trustee's other creditors. In other words, there is a presumption against an intention on the part of the trustee that he is about to commit a breach of trust. Thus, in *Re Oatway,*[41] a trustee paid trust moneys into his current account, and then drew out to purchase an investment. He subsequently spent the balance for his own purposes. The court held that the trustee's personal representatives could not argue that the investment had been made out of the trustee's own money, and that the money subsequently spent was trust money. This presumption applied, and the investment represented trust money. As regards beneficiary and trustee of the same trust, therefore, the rule in *Clayton's Case*[42] has no application. This rule was evolved, as Maitland observes,[43] " for the purpose of settling the liabilities of partners in banking firms " though it has since been extended to several other types of commercial transaction. In *Clayton's Case,* C, a customer of a bank, had a balance of £1,713 in his favour, on the death of D, a partner in the bank. After D's death, C drew out more than £1,713, and then paid in sums to a larger amount still. The surviving partners of the bank then became insolvent, and C sought to recover from D's estate. The court held, however, that the sums paid out to C after D's death must be appropriated to the £1,713 due to C, and therefore D's estate was free from liability, for the £1,713 due at his death had been discharged, while the sums which C subsequently paid in constituted a new debt, for which the surviving partners alone were liable.

It must be noticed however—

1. That the rule in *Clayton's Case* probably applies to the account of a trustee, as between beneficiaries under two separate trusts,[44] and as between two *cestuis que trust,*[45] though it is open to argument that such beneficiaries rank on the account *pari passu.*

2. Although there is a presumption against a breach of trust by a trustee, there is no similar presumption that a trustee intends to repair a breach of trust.

Thus, in *James Roscoe (Bolton) Ltd.* v. *Winder,*[46] a trustee mixed trust moneys with his own, and then withdrew money, so that at length the trust account was diminished. Later still, he paid in further sums of his own money, and the court held that the beneficiaries could not claim these unless they could prove that the sums had been paid in with the intention of replacing the trust money.

The trust property can be followed, not only into the hands of the trustee himself, but also into the hands of his trustee in bankruptcy, even although

41 [1903] 2 Ch. 356.
42 (1816), 1 Mer. 572.
43 *Equity* (rev. Brunyate), p. 219.
44 *Re Hallett's Estate* (1880), 13 Ch.D. 696, 729, *per* Jessel, M.R., 738, *per* Baggallay, L.J. (Cases, p. 351); *Hancock* v. *Smith* (1889), 41 Ch.D. 456.
45 *Re Stenning,* [1895] 2 Ch. 433.
46 [1915] 1 Ch. 62.

the trustee only acquired it on the eve of bankruptcy, for the purpose of absconding with it.[47] Where a succession of transactions have occurred, whereby the trust property has changed its form several times, the general onus is on the beneficiary of proving the transactions whereby the successive conversions took place.[48] An interesting example of the application of this doctrine is furnished by *Robertson* v. *Morrice*,[49] where a trustee held stock in trust, and also similar stock of his own, and confused them. He sold stock from the mixed fund from time to time, and at his death the amount of stock left was less than the amount which should have been subject to the trust. The court held that the whole of the remaining stock must be appropriated to the trust.

There are some other problems to be considered where a trustee mixes his own money with trust funds, and buys property with some or all of it. Since the equities between himself and the beneficiaries are unequal, the beneficiaries are entitled to a first charge on the whole of the fund. Accordingly, although under the rule in *Hallett's* case [50] the trustee is presumed to have bought the property primarily with his own money, so that what is left in the account (or so much as is necessary) is considered to be trust money, if the trustee subsequently spends what is left on his own behalf, the charge against the purchased property still protects the beneficiary's interest. Moreover, if the property purchased has increased in value, the charge is not for the actual amount of the trust money used, but for the part of the increased value which is proportionate to the original amount of trust money used. Further, with regard to the actual amounts employed, where the trustee has mixed trust money with his own, then the onus is on the trustee to show what money of his has been employed and until he does so the fund, or what has been purchased with it, is presumed to be the trust fund.[51]

But in a case in which the trustee mixed trust moneys in her bank account but used substantial overdraft facilities in order to purchase property which gained in value, it was held that although the beneficiaries had a charge on the account for the trust money, mixed in the account, they had no claim for any share of the enhanced value of the property.[52]

It was at one time doubted whether beneficiaries could follow trust funds into the form of real estate, since the purchase could usually only be proved by parol evidence, but it is now settled that the relief afforded by equity is on the ground of fraud, a constructive trust arising, and these are not within the Statute of Frauds [53] (now section 53 (1) (*b*) of the Law of Property Act 1925). It is always open to the beneficiary to claim the land (or other investment) and then to claim the loss, if any, from the trustee. Whether trust money has actually been invested in the purchase of land or not is often a little difficult to determine. Where, however, the amount of the trust fund is nearly identical with the purchase price, there is a presumption that the fund has been so

---

[47] *Frith* v. *Cartland* (1865), 2 H. & M. 417.
[48] *Harford* v. *Lloyd* (1855), 20 Beav. 310.
[49] (1845), 9 Jur. 122.
[50] (1880), 13 Ch.D. 696 (Cases, p. 351). See pp. 387–388, *ante*.
[51] *Lupton* v. *White* (1808), 15 Ves. 432; *Gray* v. *Haig* (1855), 20 Beav. 219; *Cook* v. *Addison* (1869), L.R. 7 Eq. 466.
[52] *Re Tilley's Will Trusts*, [1967] Ch. 1179.
[53] *Lane* v. *Dighton* (1762), Amb. 409; *Lench* v. *Lench* (1805), 10 Ves. 511, 517.

used,[54] and also where the trustee's means are clearly insufficient for the purchase, unaided by trust money [55] (although the possibility of a purchase with a mixed fund should not be excluded). The mere fact that a trustee has trust money under his control, however, is not sufficient to stamp any purchase made by him with the trust.[56]

It is clear from the opening words of Jessel, M.R.'s observations in *Re Hallett's Estate,* cited above, that the rule of following trust property, in this aspect, extends not only to express trustees, but also to all persons in a fiduciary capacity, including factors, and many types of agents. In the absence of special circumstances,[57] however, a fiduciary relationship does not exist between banker and customer.[58]

The limiting factor in this doctrine is illustrated by *Re Hallett & Co.,*[59] where a transaction was completed by a set-off in the accounts, the money not being actually received in any form. Here, the doctrine of identification could not be applied; it depends upon a defined subject-matter which can be followed.

It will be noticed that this rule governing the following of trust property in the hands of a trustee is important mainly where the trustee is insolvent, since in other cases the beneficiary's remedy against the trustee himself is normally sufficient.

The two extremely important decisions of *Sinclair* v. *Brougham* [60] and *Re Diplock* [61] have done much to explain the principles upon which *Re Hallett's Estate* [62] rests. In *Re Diplock,*[61] the Court of Appeal contrasted the remedy of " tracing " in equity with the machinery of the common law. They pointed out that the common law approached the problem in " a strictly materialistic way. It could only appreciate what might almost be called the ' physical ' identity of one thing with another. It could treat a person's money as identifiable so long as it had not become mixed with other money. It could treat as identifiable with the money other kinds of property acquired by means of it, provided that there was no admixture of other money. It is noticeable that in this latter case the common law did not base itself on any known theory of tracing such as that adopted in equity. It proceeded on the basis that the unauthorized act of purchasing was one capable of ratification by the owner of the money . . ." [63] Another limitation suggested was that money was not identifiable once it had been paid into a banking account, although on this the Court of Appeal commented that " If it is possible to identify a principal's money with an asset purchased exclusively by means of it we see no reason for drawing a distinction between a chose in action such as a banker's debt to his customer and any other asset." [64] If the acquisition of one can be ratified, so can the acquisition of the other.

---

[54] *Perry* v. *Phelips* (1798), 4 Ves. 108; (1810), 17 Ves. 173. See also *Harford* v. *Lloyd* (1855), 20 Beav. 310.
[55] *Ryall* v. *Ryall* (1739), 1 Atk. 59; Amb. 413.
[56] *Sealy* v. *Stawell* (1868), I.R. 2 Eq. 326, 347.
[57] *Re Brown* (1889), 60 L.T. 397.
[58] *Foley* v. *Hill* (1848), 2 H.L.C. 28.   [59] [1894] 2 Q.B. 237.
[60] [1914] A.C. 398.
[61] [1948] Ch. 465 (C.A.); [1951] A.C. 251 (H.L.) *sub nom. Ministry of Health* v. *Simpson.* See also Keeton, *Modern Developments in the Law of Trusts,* pp. 314–320.
[62] (1880), 13 Ch.D. 696 (Cases, p. 351).
[63] [1948] Ch. 518. *Cf.* Lord Parker in *Sinclair* v. *Brougham,* [1914] A.C. 398, 441.
[64] [1948] Ch. 519.

The Court of Appeal also made three other points distinguishing the common law from the equity attitude—

1. The common law did not recognise equitable claims to property, whether money or any other form of property.

2. The narrowness of the limits within which the common law operated was linked with the limited nature of common law remedies. In particular, the device of the declaration of charge was unknown to the common law.

3. It was the materialistic approach of the common law, together with the limited range of remedies, which prevented the common law from identifying money in a mixed fund. Once A's money had been mixed with B's, identification physically became impossible, and the only remedy was then a claim for damages.[65]

Equity approached the problem more abstractly, and had no difficulty in recognising the continued notional existence of distinct funds which were physically mixed. This amalgam, in proper circumstances, could be resolved into its constituent elements. Whilst, however, the equitable relief is personal in the sense that equity acts *in personam,* it presupposes the continued existence of the fund itself. If, for example, the fund has been spent on a dinner, equity can do nothing.

A further problem, of some importance, was raised in *Sinclair* v. *Brougham*[66] and *Re Diplock,*[67] indicating a wider application of the principle underlying *Re Hallett's Estate.*[68] Can money be recovered in equity, if the mixing has been undertaken by an innocent volunteer, or is it confined to cases where a fiduciary relationship exists between the claimant and the person mixing the fund? In *Re Diplock*[67] the Court of Appeal took the view that the decision in *Sinclair* v. *Brougham*[66] sanctioned the wider principle that where an innocent volunteer mixes money of his own with money which in equity belongs to another person, or is found in possession of such a mixture, although that other person cannot claim a charge on the mass superior to the claim of the volunteer he is entitled, nevertheless, to a charge ranking *pari passu* with the claims of the volunteer. This is, in fact, a deduction from Lord Parker's observations in *Sinclair* v. *Brougham,* and it is explained by the Court of Appeal in the following terms[69]—

> Equity regards the rights of the equitable owner as being " in effect rights of property " though not recognized as such by the common law. Just as a volunteer is not allowed by equity in the case, e.g., of a conveyance of the legal estate in land, to set up his legal title adversely to the claim of a person having an equitable interest in the land, so in the case of a mixed fund of money the volunteer must give such recognition as equity considers him in conscience (as a volunteer) bound to give to the interest of the equitable owner of the money which has been mixed with the volunteer's own. But this burden on the conscience of the volunteer is not such as to compel him to treat the claim of the equitable

---

[65] For an argument that equity and law should be fused on this question, see Babafemi, " Tracing Assets: A Case for the Fusion of Common Law and Equity in English Law " (1971) 34 *Modern Law Review* 12.

[66] [1914] A.C. 398.

[67] [1948] Ch. 465 (C.A.); [1951] A.C. 251 (H.L.).

[68] (1880), 13 Ch.D. 696 (Cases, p. 351).

[69] [1948] Ch. 524.

owner as paramount. That would be to treat the volunteer as strictly as if he himself stood in a fiduciary relationship to the equitable owner which ex hypothesi he does not. The volunteer is under no greater duty of conscience to recognize the interest of the equitable owner than that which lies upon a person having an equitable interest in one of two trust funds of " money " which have become mixed towards the equitable owner of the other. Such a person is not in conscience bound to give precedence to the equitable owner of the other of the two funds.

This principle, in the view of the Court of Appeal, is illustrated by the decision in *Sinclair* v. *Brougham*.[66] The dispute in that case was between share-holders and depositors in respect of a miscellaneous mass of assets distribut-able by the liquidator in the winding up of a building society. The deposits had been made, and the assets were used, in connection with a banking busi-ness carried on in the name of the society, but *ultra vires*. Each of the two classes claimed priority over the other, but the House of Lords held that the principle upon which *Hallett's* case [68] was founded directed that the two classes should share rateably. Again, in *Re Diplock* itself, trustees of a will had wrongly paid money to charities, who were thought to be beneficiaries, but in fact were not. Some of the charities had innocently mixed such moneys with their own funds. The Court of Appeal held that the charities were not pre-cluded from setting up their own claims in respect of the moneys contributed by them to the mixed fund, so that they and the true beneficiaries could claim *pari passu* in the fund. Where, however, the moneys received by the charity had not been mixed with the moneys of the charity, but had been expended on the alteration or improvement of their own assets (*e.g.* by creating build-ings on their own land, or by discharging debts of the charity) the trust money could not be separated from the money of the charities, so that in these cases, the right of the true beneficiaries under the will to follow the assets *in rem* was lost. A practical difficulty which arises is how to establish into what forms the trust property has been converted. This problem is simplified by the fact that, where appropriate, discovery will be granted *before* delivery of the statement of claim.[70]

2. Following the Trust Property Itself into the Hands of Third Parties

The right of the beneficiary to follow trust property with which the trustee has parted depends upon the nature of an equitable interest in property, as recognised and protected by a court of equity, and the position is that where a trustee parts with trust property *in breach of trust,* the recipient of that property will be bound by the trust unless he can show (1) that he has obtained the legal title; (2) that he was a *bona fide* purchaser for valuable considera-tion; and (3) that he received no notice that the transaction was a breach of trust before the transfer was complete.[71] Thus, James, L.J., observed in *Pilcher* v. *Rawlins* [72]—

---

[70] *Speyside Estate and Trust Co. Ltd.* v. *Wraymond Freeman (Blenders) Ltd.*, [1950] Ch. 96.
[71] For a highly-interesting historical review of this doctrine, see Bailey, " Trusts and Titles " (1942) 8 *Cambridge Law Journal* 36.
[72] (1872), L.R. 7 Ch.App. 259, 268–269. See also *Cave* v. *Cave* (1880), 15 Ch.D. 639.

I propose simply to apply myself to the case of a purchaser for valuable consideration, without notice, obtaining, upon the occasion of his purchase, and by means of his purchase deed, some legal estate, some legal right, some legal advantage; and according to my view of the established law of this Court, such a purchaser's plea of a purchase for valuable consideration without notice is an absolute, unqualified, unanswerable defence, and an unanswerable plea to the jurisdiction of this Court. Such a purchaser . . . may be interrogated and tested to any extent as to the valuable consideration which he has given in order to shew the *bona fides* or *mala fides* of his purchase, and also the presence or the absence of notice; but when once he has gone through that ordeal, and has satisfied the terms of the plea of purchase for valuable consideration without notice, then . . . this Court has no jurisdiction whatever to do anything more than to let him depart in possession of that legal estate, that legal right, that legal advantage which he has obtained . . . In such a case a purchaser is entitled to hold that which, without breach of duty, he has had conveyed to him.

This proposition is a direct consequence of the application of the maxim " Where the equities are equal, the law prevails," for the purchaser has obobtained the legal estate without any privity to the breach of trust, and equity will not, therefore, curtail his enjoyment of it in favour of the beneficiary. This is the limiting factor in relation to the enjoyment of equitable interests in property, but the onus of proving *bona fide* purchase for value rests upon the purchaser.[73]

The doctrine of notice has little application to chattels, since investigation of title has never been necessary on transfer. Maitland observed of this aspect of the rule [74]—

Finally, as regards equitable rights in moveable goods, corporeal chattels, we hear very much less. Doubtless if I bought a piece of plate from a trustee knowing that he held it on trust for E, E might enforce his right against me, and this would be so even though I purchased in market overt. But a purchaser of moveable goods is not expected to investigate his vendor's title. Of course if he buys from one who is not owner, and the sale does not take place in market overt or fall within the rules introduced by the Factors' Acts he gets a bad title. But though this be so, equity has not been able to say of corporeal chattels as it has said of land and of trust funds that the prudent purchaser makes an investigation of title. Corporeal chattels are outside the realm of constructive notice. In *Joseph* v. *Lyons*,[75] an attempt was made to apply that doctrine to goods, but the Court of Appeal would not hear of it. Cotton L.J. said " I think that the doctrine as to constructive notice has gone too far and I shall not extend it "—and Lindley L.J. " It seems to me that the modern doctrine as to constructive notice has been pushed too far, and I do not feel inclined to extend it."

[73] *G. L. Baker Ltd.* v. *Medway Building & Supplies Ltd.*, [1958] 1 W.L.R. 1216.
[74] *Equity* (rev. Brunyate), p. 146.
[75] (1884), 15 Q.B.D. 280.

A good illustration of the operation of the doctrine of notice in regard to trust estates is furnished by *Cave* v. *Cave*.[76] There a sole trustee of a marriage settlement, who was a solicitor, appropriated trust moneys, and used them, in breach of trust, to buy land, the conveyance being taken in the name of his brother. The brother then mortgaged the property by way of legal mortgage to A, and later to B by way of equitable mortgage. Neither A nor B had notice of the trust; and the court held that A's legal mortgage had priority to the interests of the beneficiaries, but that these had priority over B's equitable mortgage, in accordance with the rule that as between holders of conflicting equitable interests, the equities being equal, the equitable interest which is first in time prevails. This case, therefore, affords a striking illustration of the importance of the legal estate.[77] A further example of the rule is afforded by the case where a trustee wrongfully applies trust money in the purchase of land which he then sells to another person who buys without notice of the trust. If, before the estate has been conveyed, the beneficiaries claim the property, the beneficiaries' prior equity must be preferred to the purchaser's.[78]

The same point was also considered by Farwell, L.J., in *Burgis* v. *Constantine*,[79] where he observed—

> As has been pointed out by Lord Cairns in *Shropshire Union Railways and Canal Co.* v. *The Queen*,[80] the mere fact that a person has transferred the legal ownership of stock or shares or other property, real or personal, to a trustee, and given him the title deeds, or the securities, or other indicia of title, does not justify any one in assuming that the person to whom such transfer is made is the beneficial owner. If the trustee does, in fact, deal with the property, and convey the legal ownership to a bona fide purchaser or mortgagee for value without notice, the cestui que trust has to bear the loss.[81] If such a subsequent purchaser or mortgagee does not get the legal estate it is because he has not taken those precautions which the law allows him in order to protect himself from all risks; and he cannot set up the apparent ownership of the trustee as evidence of any misconduct or negligence on the part of the beneficial owner, because it is in accordance with the usages of mankind that the legal estate in property should be conveyed to, and the indicia of title deposited with, trustees, and no other member of the community, therefore, is entitled to allege that such a course of action constitutes any invitation to him from which a duty towards him can be inferred.

The doctrine of notice as regards trusts of land has been modified by the machinery of the property legislation of 1925.

Maitland [82] suggested that if the trustee recovered the property in his capacity of trustee for another trust, he might hold free from notice, as a stranger

---

[76] (1880), 15 Ch.D. 639.
[77] If this problem had arisen since 1925, B's mortgage would have been a legal term not protected by deposit of the deeds. In such circumstances he would not have been postponed to the beneficiaries.
[78] See *Joyce* v. *De Moleyns* (1845), 2 Jo. & Lat. 374; *Newton* v. *Newton* (1868), L.R. 4 Ch.App. 143; *Re Morgan* (1881), 18 Ch.D. 93.
[79] [1908] 2 K.B. 484, 501–502.
[80] (1875), L.R. 7 H.L. 496, 505.
[81] *i.e.* of the property. He still has his personal remedy against the trustee.
[82] *Equity* (rev. Brunyate), p. 118.

who purchased would, and this would seem to be provided for by the Trustee Act 1925, s. 28, which states—

A trustee or personal representative acting for the purposes of more than one trust or estate shall not, in the absence of fraud, be affected by notice of any instrument, matter, fact or thing in relation to any particular trust or estate if he has obtained notice thereof merely by reason of his acting or having acted for the purposes of another trust or estate.

The importance of this section in respect of a trust corporation handling the affairs of many trusts is obvious.

Moreover, a purchaser without notice from a purchaser with notice takes the legal estate free from the beneficiary's interests, for his own good faith shelters him.[83] It would appear, however, that an exception exists in favour of a charitable trust, for in respect of those trusts a purchaser without notice from a purchaser with notice is bound by the trust.[84]

If the purchaser has no notice of the trust at the time of the purchase, but receives notice before conveyance, he is nevertheless bound by the trust.[85] It should be noticed that this rule is confined strictly to land. Thus, when a trustee mortgaged shares to a mortgagee who had no notice of the trust when he received the transfer and the share certificate, but who received notice of the trust before becoming the registered owner of the shares, it was held that the mortgagee took free from the trust, for the transfer was like the conveyance of a legal estate to become vested on the performance of a condition.[86]

What constitutes notice is now considered in the Law of Property Act 1925, ss. 198 and 199, and the Land Charges Act 1972, which state that a purchaser shall not be prejudicially affected by notice of any instrument, matter, fact, or thing unless (1) if it is an instrument registrable under the Land Charges Act, it is so registered—if it is not registered, it is void as against the purchaser; or (2) it is within his own knowledge, or would have come to his knowledge if such inquiries and inspections had been made as ought reasonably to have been made by him; or (3) in the same transaction, with respect to which a question of notice to the purchaser arises, it has come to the knowledge of his counsel, solicitor, or other agent acting as such, or would have come to the knowledge of his solicitor or agent, if such inquiries and inspections had been made as ought reasonably to have been made. There are, therefore, several kinds of notice—

1. Where the purchaser actually has knowledge of the equitable interest or the interest is registered under the Land Charges Act. This is actual notice.

2. Where the agent of the purchaser acquires knowledge in the course of the transaction. This is usually termed imputed notice.

3. Where the purchaser or his agent did not have knowledge, but would have had if they had made proper inquiries. This is constructive notice.

---

[83] *Mertins* v. *Jolliffe* (1756), Amb. 311, 313; *Salsbury* v. *Bagott* (1677), 2 Swanst. 603, 608.

[84] *East Greensteds Case* (1633), Duke 64, 65; *Sutton Colefield Case* (1635), Duke 68. See also *Commissioners of Charitable Donations and Bequests* v. *Wybrants* (1845), 2 Jo. & Lat. 182, 194; *Re Alms Corn Charity*, [1901] 2 Ch. 750.

[85] See *Taylor* v. *Russell*, [1892] A.C. 244.

[86] *Dodds* v. *Hills* (1865), 2 H. & M. 424.

Concerning actual notice some diversity of opinion has existed. It has been said that the notice (if not consisting of registration) must proceed from a party interested in the transaction or his agent,[87] but whilst a purchaser would probably be safe in disregarding mere gossip, the position seems to be that if he had such information as should have affected the judgment of a prudent man he will be deemed to have had actual notice,[88] no matter from what source the information proceeds.

As regards constructive notice, Wigram, V.-C., in *Jones* v. *Smith*,[89] divided the cases which might arise into the two following classes—

> (1) Cases in which the party charged has had actual notice that the property in dispute was in fact charged, incumbered, or in some way affected, and the court has thereupon bound him with constructive notice of facts and instruments, to a knowledge of which he would have been led by an inquiry after the incumbrance, or other circumstances affecting the property, of which he had actual notice.

> (2) Cases in which the court has been satisfied from the evidence before it that the party charged had designedly abstained from inquiry for the purpose of avoiding notice—a purpose which, if proved, would clearly show that he had a suspicion of the truth, and a wilful determination not to learn it.

To this second class must now be added cases wherein the purchaser is culpably negligent in failing to make the usual inquiries.[90]

In illustration of the first class of case, in *Davis* v. *Hutchings*,[91] trustees distributed a beneficiary's share to their solicitor, who had informed them that the beneficiary had assigned his share to him. The trustees did not require the solicitor to produce the assignment, in which it was stated that the assignment was subject to a prior charge, of which the trustees received no other notice. It was held that the trustees had constructive notice of the prior charge.

It is necessary to observe that notice of the existence of an instrument is not always notice of its contents. Thus, as Jessel, M.R., observes in *Patman* v. *Harland* [92]—

> There is a class of cases, of which I think *Jones* v. *Smith* [93] is the most notorious, where the purchaser was told of a deed which might or might not affect the title, and was told at the same time that it did not affect the title. Supposing you are buying land of a married man, as in *Jones* v. *Smith*,[93] and you are told at the same time that there is a marriage settlement, but the deed does not affect the land in question, you have no constructive notice of its contents, because although you know there is a settlement you are told it does not affect the land. If every marriage settlement necessarily affected all a man's land then you would have constructive notice, but as a settlement may not relate to his land at all, or

---

[87] See *Barnhart* v. *Greenshields* (1853), 9 Moo.P.C. 18; *Reeves* v. *Pope*, [1914] 2 K.B. 284.
[88] *Lloyd* v. *Banks* (1868), L.R. 3 Ch.App. 488.
[89] (1841), 1 Hare 43, 55.
[90] *West* v. *Reid* (1843), 2 Hare 249, 257; *Hudston* v. *Viney*, [1921] 1 Ch. 98.
[91] [1907] 1 Ch. 356.
[92] (1881), 17 Ch.D. 353, 356–357. The particular point decided in this case has been overruled by the Law of Property Act 1925, s. 44 (5). See further on this subsection: *Shears* v. *Wells*, [1936] 1 All E.R. 832.
[93] (1841), 1 Hare 43, 55.

only to some other portions of it, the mere fact of your having heard of a settlement does not give you constructive notice of its contents, if you are told at the same time it does not affect the land.

The second class of cases arises out of the duty of the purchaser to investigate the vendor's title for the statutory period, and to require production not only of the abstract, but of the title deeds. If he fails to do this, he is nevertheless affected with notice of the contents thereof, unless, having required production, the purchaser receives from the vendor an adequate reason for non-production.[94]

As regards imputed notice, the important rule of section 199 of the Law of Property Act 1925 is that the agent must have received notice whilst employed in that transaction.

It should be observed that absence of notice only protects the purchaser for value. A volunteer is bound by the trust whether he has notice of it or not.[95]

It has been stated that absence of notice will not protect a *bona fide* purchaser for value who fails to obtain the legal estate; that is to say, that in relation to an equitable incumbrancer, the *cestui que trust* will normally be preferred. It need scarcely be added, however, that this rule will not be applied so as to enable the *cestui que trust* to commit what amounts to a fraud upon the incumbrancer. Thus, in *Re King's Settlement*,[96] X, in order to keep the trusts of a settlement off the title, conveyed property to A and B by deed of gift in consideration of his love and affection for them. A and B simultaneously executed a deed poll, declaring trusts in favour of X and others. The conveyance and title deeds were then handed to A and B, whilst the deed poll was retained by X's solicitor. Later, A and B, purporting to act as absolute owners, created equitable incumbrances in favour of M and N, who gave value and had no notice of the trust. Farwell, J., held that inasmuch as X's conveyance to A and B contained a direct representation which necessarily implied that the grantees were absolute owners, both X and the other beneficiaries claiming under him were estopped from denying that statement, and their interests under the trust were accordingly postponed to those of M and N.[97]

A further question which has occasioned some difficulty is the extent to which a purchaser is bound by notice of a doubtful equity. Where the equity is clear, the purchaser is bound by notice of it, but there may be, in the words of Lord Northington, in *Cordwell* v. *Mackrill*,[98] an equity which depends upon " the mere construction of words, which are uncertain in themselves, and the meaning of which often depends on their locality." How far this doctrine goes is not altogether clear, for in *Thompson* v. *Simpson*,[99] Sugden, L.C., regarded the decision in *Cordwell* v. *Mackrill*[1] as of no great authority, and said, in effect, that where the construction which a court of equity would put upon the

---

[94] *Plumb* v. *Fluitt* (1791), 2 Anst. 432 ; *Agra Bank Ltd.* v. *Barry* (1874), L.R. 7 H.L. 135.
[95] See *Mansell* v. *Mansell* (1732), 2 P.Wms. 678 ; *Spurgeon* v. *Collier* (1758), 1 Eden 55.
[96] [1931] 2 Ch. 294.
[97] The decision in this case seems to have been reached on the assumption that the legal estate was in the trustees, but it vested in the tenants for life under the Property Acts. See (1932) 48 *Law Quarterly Review* 11.
[98] (1766), 2 Eden 344, 347–348.
[99] (1841), 1 Dr. & War. 459, 491.
[1] (1766), 2 Eden 344.

words was not really in doubt, the equity resulting would be enforced, no matter how difficult the construction might be, but not after lapse of time if there was anything equivocal or ambiguous. Lord Northington's observations are clearly not intended as a loophole for any maxim that although a man is deemed to know the law, he may not necessarily be taken as understanding the operation of equity, for in *Parker* v. *Brooke* [2] a testator gave leasehold property to his daughter to her separate use, but without the interposition of a trustee. The husband entered into possession and mortgaged it, and the purchaser was bound by the wife's equitable interest, being deemed to know the effect of the will in equity. On the other hand, in *Hardy* v. *Reeves*,[3] a residuary legatee remained undisturbed in possession of a copyhold estate for nineteen years. Actually, the estate had been mortgaged to the testator in fee, and at the end of this period, the heir recovered the land and mortgaged it. The residuary legatee omitted to assert his title for nine years, and then, when he instituted a suit, and proved his claim, it was held that the mortgagee from the heir took without notice of the right of the residuary legatee, for it was not a clear equity. It is only to cases of this sort that Lord Northington's observations can refer, and they are to-day of very infrequent occurrence.

3. Following the Trust Property into the Hands of Another Beneficiary

If a trustee makes a mistake in paying a beneficiary, either by paying the wrong person, or by paying one beneficiary too much, at the expense of another beneficiary, the beneficiary who has suffered injury in consequence has two distinct remedies—

1. He can sue the trustee personally, and in such a case the trustee may have recourse against the beneficiary who has been wrongly paid or overpaid. This has already been considered.[4]

2. The injured beneficiary may proceed directly against the person who has been paid wrongly or the beneficiary who has been overpaid.

The whole of the law relating to this second remedy was exhaustively considered by the Court of Appeal in *Re Diplock*,[5] a case which was the direct consequence of the decision of the House of Lords in *Chichester Diocesan Fund and Board of Finance (Inc.)* v. *Simpson*.[6] In that case, a testator had left his residuary estate to " such charitable institution or institutions or other charitable or benevolent object or objects in England " as the executors should select. The House of Lords decided that the words included non-charitable as well as charitable objects, and the gift therefore failed for uncertainty. Before the decision of the House of Lords was given, however, the executors had distributed most of the residuary estate to a number of charities. The next of kin therefore claimed the property from the executors, and after these claims had been compromised with the approval of the court, the next of kin sought to recover the balance of the residue from the charities who had wrongly received it. The charities had treated the sums received from

---

[2] (1804), 9 Ves. 583.

[3] (1799), 4 Ves. 466; (1800), 5 Ves. 426.

[4] *Ante*, pp. 285–287.

[5] [1948] Ch. 465 (Cases, p. 356); [1951] A.C. 251, *sub nom. Ministry of Health* v. *Simpson* (Cases, p. 355).

[6] [1944] A.C. 341.

the *Diplock* estate in different ways. In the majority of cases, they had been paid into the general account of the charities. Some of these were in credit, others were overdrawn (either secured or unsecured). In a few cases, payment was made into a special account. In one or two cases, it was earmarked for a particular purpose. The next of kin prosecuted two types of claim. He claimed, first, *in rem*, by way of tracing the fund, by virtue of the principle underlying *Hallett's* case.[7] This has already been discussed, and it was established in *Diplock's* case that the remedy of tracing, or the remedy *in rem*, as it was termed in that case, was available to recover property wrongfully (even if innocently) transferred by trustee to volunteers, whether or not the volunteer himself has changed the form of the property, or has mixed it with property of his own. Amongst such volunteers are overpaid beneficiaries, or (as in the *Diplock* case) persons or institutions who have received the property upon the erroneous assumption that they are beneficiaries, when in law they are not. This remedy is available both to beneficiaries under trusts,[8] and legatees under wills.

Where the volunteer retains the property in an unmixed form, it is still impressed by a trust, and it must be restored when the beneficiary claims it. If, however, the volunteer has mixed the property of the trust with his own, the beneficiary has a charge upon the mixed fund for the value of the trust property. The principle applicable to such cases, however, differs from that applicable to trustees, against whom a beneficiary traces, for the volunteer, so long as he has taken innocently, may also set up a claim in respect of his own property and where he does, he and the beneficiary will share the proceeds *pari passu.*

The next of kin claimed, secondly, *in personam*, against the charities, as an underpaid beneficiary under the will. Three short points raised in the case may be noticed. In the first place, where claims co-exist, as here, against the executor or trustee and the overpaid beneficiary, the injured beneficiary's primary remedy is against the trustee. It is only when the remedy against the trustee has been exhausted that the remedy against an innocent, but wrongly-paid, beneficiary arises. Secondly, the mistake of payment made by the executor was strictly a mistake of law, and not of fact; nevertheless relief was available in equity. A third point was that the Court of Appeal decided that the claim of the next of kin was not liable to be defeated because recipients turned out to have no title, and were strangers to the estate. Their consciences were just as much affected as if they had been beneficiaries under the will.

The importance of the remedy of tracing by a beneficiary against a volunteer, quasi-beneficiary, or overpaid beneficiary was diminished in respect of claims *against personal representatives* by the acceptance, by the House of Lords in the *Diplock* case, of a direct personal remedy.

Once again, this remedy is only available when the beneficiary has exhausted his remedies against the personal representatives. It was described by the Court of Appeal in the *Diplock* case [9] in the following terms—

---

[7] (1880), 13 Ch.D. 696 (Cases, p. 351). See pp. 387–388, *ante*.

[8] For an unsuccessful attempt to construct a trust of an unproved claim in a company liquidation in order to make the claim good by means of this remedy, see *Butler* v. *Broadhead*, [1974] 3 W.L.R. 27.

[9] *Re Diplock*, [1948] Ch. 465, 502–503.

> . . . it seems to us . . . that the equity may be available equally to an unpaid or underpaid creditor, legatee, or next-of-kin. Second, it seems to us that a claim by a next-of-kin will not be liable to be defeated merely (*a*) in the absence of administration by the court: or (*b*) because the mistake under which the original payment was made was one of law rather than fact; or (*c*) because the original recipient, as things turned out, had no title at all and was a stranger to the estate; though the effect of the refund in the last case will be to dispossess the original recipient altogether rather than to produce equality between him and the claimant and other persons having a like title to that of the recipient. In our judgment there is no authority either in logic or in decided cases for such limitations to the equitable right of action. In our judgment also there is no justification for such limitations to be found in the circumstances which give rise to the equity. And as regards the conscience of the defendant upon which in this as in other jurisdictions equity is said to act, it is prima facie at least a sufficient circumstance that the defendant, as events have turned out, has received some share of the estate to which he was not entitled. . . .
>
> On the other hand, to such a claim by an unpaid beneficiary, there is, in our judgment, at least in circumstances such as the present, one important qualification. Since the original wrong payment was attributable to the blunder of the personal representatives, the right of the unpaid beneficiary is in the first instance against the wrongdoing executor or administrator: and the beneficiary's direct claim in equity against those overpaid or wrongly paid should be limited to the amount which he cannot recover from the party responsible. In some cases the amount will be the whole amount of the payment wrongly made, e.g., where the executor or administrator is shown to be wholly without assets or is protected from attack by having acted under an order of the court.

The earliest cases dealing with the right of an unpaid creditor or legatee to go direct against a legatee are *Nelthrop* v. *Hill*,[10] *Grove* v. *Banson*,[11] and *Chamberlain* v. *Chamberlain*.[12] These were considered by Lord Nottingham in *Noel* v. *Robinson*.[13] In this case and in *Newman* v. *Barton* [14] the principle was established that an unpaid or underpaid legatee may sue, but where the original payment by the executor was made voluntarily, there is no right to recover, unless there was originally a deficiency of assets. (That is to say, that where the assets were sufficient, and the executor paid voluntarily, the underpaid legatee must look to him alone.) This view was adopted by Jekyll, M.R., in a case in 1718 [15] and it was accepted and explained by the court in *Fenwicke* v. *Clarke*.[16] The right of the underpaid legatee, as established by these early cases, exists independently of any knowledge, real or assumed, on the part of the overpaid legatee that his title may be defeasible in favour of other

[10] (1669), 1 Ch.Cas. 135.
[11] (1669), 1 Ch.Cas. 148.
[12] (1675), 1 Ch.Cas. 256.
[13] (1682), 1 Vern. 90.
[14] (1690), 2 Vern. 205.
[15] *Anon.* 1 P.Wms. 495. See also *Orr* v. *Kaines* (1750), 2 Ves.Sen. 194.
[16] (1862), 4 De G.F. & J. 240.

persons. It exists simply in virtue of the overpayment. Moreover, it is not limited by the fact that there must be, or must have been, administration of the estate by the court.[17]

In *David* v. *Frowd* [18] there was a claim by the plaintiff that she was the sole next of kin of the deceased, and as such was entitled to recover back the estate from the defendants, to whom it had been wrongly distributed. Leach, M.R., held that she was not precluded by an administration decree from making her claim, and the defendants were thus under an obligation to refund.

Again, in *Re Rivers* [19] the plaintiff claimed to be entitled to a share in a reversionary legacy of £200 payable on the death of the plaintiff's mother in 1917, under the will of a testator who died in 1863. The defendants were the personal representatives of one of the residuary legatees, William Rivers. A grant of letters of administration with the will annexed was made to the tenant for life of the residue (who died in 1885). An administration action was instituted in 1868, and an order was made for the carrying over of £266 13s. 4d. three per cent. annuities to a separate account, entitled " the annuity account," of the plaintiff's mother. It had no doubt been the intention of the testator that the fund retained to answer the annuity (which was £8 per annum) would on her death provide the legacy of £200 bequeathed to the plaintiff, but no provision was made in the administration action, the order providing that, on the death of the plaintiff's mother, the fund of annuities should become part of the testator's general residue. In 1917, the proceeds of sale of the £266 13s. 4d. annuities fell far short of £200, after payment of costs. Accordingly, the plaintiff claimed direct against the defendants as overpaid residuary legatees for the balance; and Eve, J., held that this claim succeeded, as the plaintiff could not be bound or prejudiced by proceedings to which she was not a party.

It followed, therefore, in *Re Diplock* [20] that so far as the claims *in personam* were concerned, the next of kin was entitled to recover from the charities, as persons wrongly paid, the rateable excess over the sums already recovered from the trustees, the amount recoverable being recovered without interest. The Court of Appeal also held that the twelve-years period of limitation for executors under section 20 of the Limitation Act 1939 was applicable to these claims. Even at this point, however, the stubbornly-fought litigation was not at an end. There was no appeal from the Court of Appeal's decision on the question of tracing, but the Minister of Health who, in consequence of the nationalisation of the hospitals, stood in place of the original defendants, decided to contest the decision of the Court of Appeal on the availability of the personal remedy. The House of Lords, however, found itself in agreement with the Court of Appeal,[21] but was careful to confine the remedy *in personam* to cases where the executor has paid wrongly, without discussing the position of a trustee who may have made a similar mistake.

---

[17] *Re Diplock*, [1948] Ch. 465, 488–489. Wynn-Parry, J., at first instance had thought otherwise.
[18] (1833), 1 My. & K. 200. See also *Mohan* v. *Broughton*, [1900] P. 56.
[19] [1920] 1 Ch. 320.
[20] [1948] Ch. 465.
[21] *Ministry of Health* v. *Simpson*, [1951] Ch. 251 (Cases, p. 355).

CHAPTER XXVI

LIMITATIONS ON THE LIABILITY OF A TRUSTEE

A. PROTECTION WHERE THE TRUSTEE HAS ACTED REASONABLY AND HONESTLY

THE court has power to relieve a trustee or executor who has committed a breach of trust, in certain circumstances. The Trustee Act 1925, s. 61, replacing earlier legislation, provides—

> If it appears to the court that a trustee, whether appointed by the court or otherwise, is or may be personally liable for any breach of trust, whether the transaction alleged to be a breach of trust occurred before or after the commencement of this Act, but has acted honestly and reasonably, and ought fairly to be excused for the breach of trust and for omitting to obtain the directions of the court in the matter in which he committed such breach, then the court may relieve him either wholly or partly from personal liability for the same.

The court will not lay down any general rules governing the exercise of its discretion [1] but the onus of proof that he has acted reasonably and honestly is on the trustee. It should also be noticed that section 448 of the Companies Act 1948 gives the court power to grant relief to a company director, officer or auditor in similar circumstances.

Some illustrations of the circumstances in which the court has given or refused relief under section 3 of the Judicial Trustees Act 1896 (which section 61 of the Trustee Act 1925 has replaced), will serve to explain the manner in which the court utilises its powers of relief. In *Re Kay*,[2] an executor whose testator had left an estate of £22,000, with apparent liabilities amounting only to about £100, paid immediately to the testator's widow a legacy of £300, and permitted her to receive a portion of the income of the estate in accordance with the terms of the will. This was done before the executor advertised for claims, and it appeared that the testator was liable in respect of a claim for fraudulent misappropriation which, when satisfied, rendered the estate insolvent. The court held that the appropriation of the legacy and the payment of the income until service of the writ were reasonable and excusable, but that payment of income after that date was not.

The trustee must act reasonably as well as honestly, and the burden of showing this is on the trustee.[3] In dealings with the trust property reference will be made to the conduct of a prudent man of business, so that where a debt was owing to the estate which was small, and the debtor was of good standing,

---

[1] *Re Allsop*, [1914] 1 Ch. 1, 7. See also *Re Kay*, [1897] 2 Ch. 518; *Re Stuart*, [1897] 2 Ch. 583; *Perrins* v. *Bellamy*, [1899] 1 Ch. 797; *Re Turner*, [1897] 1 Ch. 536; *Re Mackay*, [1911] 1 Ch. 300; *Re Windsor Steam Coal Co. (1901) Ltd.*, [1929] 1 Ch. 151.

[2] *Supra*. See also *Re Brookes*, [1914] 1 Ch. 558. For a full discussion of this section, and the decisions upon it, see Sheridan, " Excusable Breaches of Trust " (1955) 19 *Conveyancer (N.S.)* 420.

[3] *Re Stuart*, [1897] 2 Ch. 583.

the trustee was held to be excused for not taking prompt steps to sue him,[4] and the same view was taken where the trustee failed to sue because he thought the proceedings would have been unsuccessful.[5] On the other hand, a trustee who makes an investment without obtaining certain necessary consents does not act reasonably,[6] nor does he if he allows a co-trustee who is a solicitor to persuade him to make an unauthorised investment (though he will usually have a right of indemnity),[7] and a trustee will not be excused if he fails to obtain the valuation prescribed by the Trustee Act 1925, s. 8, when investing in real securities.[8]

In *Perrins* v. *Bellamy*,[9] trustees, under a mistake of law, believed they possessed a power of sale, and sold settled leaseholds, thereby diminishing the income of the tenant for life, but it was held that in the circumstances (they had been advised by a solicitor that they had power to sell, and by a surveyor that it was undesirable to retain the properties) they were entitled to relief. Again, in *Re Allsop*,[10] a trustee, acting upon a mistaken construction of the will, but on legal advice, distributed to the wrong persons and was relieved. On the other hand, in *National Trustees Co. of Australasia Ltd.* v. *General Finance Co. of Australasia Ltd.*,[11] trustees who were remunerated as such were wrongly advised by their solicitors to make a distribution which, in fact, they had no power to make. The court pointed out that a trustee does not automatically become entitled to relief on showing that he has acted reasonably and honestly. Each case depends on its own facts, and relief is always within the discretion of the court.[12] The court has no power under this section to condone a breach of trust *in advance*, no matter how reasonable and honest the proposed course of conduct may be.[13] Further, a higher standard of diligence and knowledge of affairs is required from a paid trustee than from one who is unpaid.[14]

A good illustration of what is meant by the words " reasonably and honestly " is afforded by *Khoo Tek Keong* v. *Ch'ng Joo Tuan Neoh*.[15] By the terms of the will under which the trust arose, the trustees were given power to invest trust moneys in such investments as they in their absolute discretion thought fit. The sole surviving trustee lent money at interest on the security of deposited jewellery without independent valuations, and made other loans without security. The Privy Council held that the loans upon the security of the jewellery were not breaches of trust in the absence of proof that the security was insufficient when the loans were made, but that the unsecured loans were made in breach of trust; and they further held that the trustee was not entitled to relief, because, although he had acted honestly, he had not acted reasonably,

---

4 *Re Grindey*, [1898] 2 Ch. 593.
5 *Re Roberts* (1897), 76 L.T. 479.
6 *Chapman* v. *Browne*, [1902] 1 Ch. 785.
7 *Re Turner*, [1897] 1 Ch. 536.
8 *Re Stuart*, [1897] 2 Ch. 583.
9 [1899] 1 Ch. 797.
10 [1914] 1 Ch. 1.
11 [1905] A.C. 373 (Cases, p. 361). Similarly, in *Re Diplock*, [1948] 1 Ch. 465, the trustees paid the wrong beneficiaries, but they were not entitled to relief under s. 61.
12 *Marsden* v. *Regan*, [1954] 1 W.L.R. 423.
13 *Re Tollemache*, [1903] 1 Ch. 955.
14 *Re Waterman's Will Trusts*, [1952] 2 All E.R. 1054; *Re Pauling's Settlement Trusts*, [1964] Ch. 303; *Re Rosenthal*, [1972] 1 W.L.R. 1273.
15 [1934] A.C. 529 (Cases, p. 363).

for he had not considered whether the unsecured loans were dispositions which it was prudent for him to make as a trustee, but had satisfied himself with the knowledge that the testator himself had made such loans in his lifetime.

It is not necessary specially to plead the section in defence to an action for breach of trust; the benefit of it may be claimed at the trial.[16]

B. CONCURRENCE OF THE BENEFICIARY IN THE BREACH OF TRUST

If the beneficiary was *sui juris*, and had full knowledge of the circumstances, and yet concurred in the breach of trust, he cannot proceed against the trustee in respect of the breach.[17] Again, if, having no contemporary knowledge of the breach, yet on subsequently learning of it, he adopts it, with full knowledge of the facts, and takes the profits, here again the beneficiary may not proceed against the trustee.[18] In both cases it is assumed that the beneficiary is an entirely free agent, no pressure having been put upon him by the trustee.[19] It is essential that the beneficiary should be *sui juris* for the concurrence to be effective. An infant can proceed against a trustee for breach of trust even though he has concurred in it,[20] unless he has been guilty of fraud. This last exception is well illustrated by *Overton* v. *Banister*.[21] An infant beneficiary obtained a sum of stock, to which she was entitled on attaining her majority, from the trustees by fraudulently representing she was of full age. Later, having come of age, she sued the trustees to compel them to pay over the stock again. The court held that she could not enforce the second payment for, although the receipt of an infant is not a good discharge, yet the infant, having misrepresented her age, could not set up the invalidity of the receipt.

In *Re Pauling's Settlement Trusts*,[22] Wilberforce, J., discussed in detail the law governing the position of a beneficiary who has concurred, and who subsequently sues for the breach of trust. In the first place, the court must examine all the circumstances in which that concurrence was given, in order to discover whether it is fair and equitable that he should subsequently sue. Secondly, it is not necessary that the beneficiary should know that he is concurring in a breach of trust, provided that he fully understands what he is concurring in; nor is it necessary that he himself should have profited from the breach of trust.

It need hardly be stated that where one beneficiary has acquiesced in the breach of trust, another may proceed against the trustee in respect of it, and the court may in such a case order that the trustee be indemnified out of the interest of the concurring beneficiary, unless the latter is subject to a disability.[23] The matter is now governed by section 62 of the Trustee Act 1925, which provides that where a trustee commits a breach of trust at the instigation

---

[16] *Singlehurst* v. *Tapscott Steamship Co. Ltd.*, [1899] W.N. 133.
[17] *Life Association of Scotland* v. *Siddal* (1861), 3 De G.F. & J. 58; *Re Deane* (1889), 42 Ch.D. 9; *Fletcher* v. *Collis*, [1905] 2 Ch. 24.
[18] See *Crichton* v. *Crichton*, [1896] 1 Ch. 870.
[19] *Bowles* v. *Stewart* (1803), 1 Sch. & Lef. 209.
[20] *Wilkinson* v. *Parry* (1828), 4 Russ. 272, 276.
[21] (1844), 3 Hare 503.
[22] [1962] 1 W.L.R. 86, 107–108. (This point was not discussed by the Court of Appeal.)
[23] *Raby* v. *Ridehalgh* (1855), 7 De G.M. & G. 104; *Sawyer* v. *Sawyer* (1885), 28 Ch.D. 595.

or request or with the consent in writing of a beneficiary, the court may, if it thinks fit, make such order as to the court seems just for impounding all or any part of the interest of the beneficiary in the trust estate by way of indemnity to the trustee or persons claiming through him.

In *Griffith* v. *Hughes*,[24] it was decided that neither the instigation nor the request need be in writing, but only the consent, to be within the section. The court will not impound the beneficiary's interest unless the beneficiary clearly realised that the action contemplated amounted to a breach of trust,[25] and the order, when made, takes priority over the interest of a mortgagee whose charge was created after the breach of trust.[26] The object of the section is to enlarge the power of the court as to indemnifying trustees.[27]

Moreover, it is not necessary that a beneficiary should reap benefit from the breach of trust which he instigates, or to which he consents. Thus, if a remainderman induces the trustee to commit a breach of trust for the benefit of the tenant for life, the remainderman's interest may be impounded.[28]

Where a trustee is exercising his right to impound a beneficiary's interest to make good a breach of trust which he has instigated, he is not entitled to insist on remaining a trustee in order to exercise the right. A former trustee, who has been removed, may exercise it.[29]

C. THE TRUSTEES AND THE STATUTES
OF LIMITATION

1. *The Position of Trustees before* 1940

The old rule of equity was that mere lapse of time would never free an express trustee from liability for breach of trust,[30] and this rule was reproduced in the Judicature Act 1873, s. 25 (2). Moreover, it would appear that this rule applied also to some constructive trustees, and particularly to persons who received trust property knowingly.[31] On the other hand, some constructive trustees could take advantage of statutory limitation of actions. Thus, it was held in *Knox* v. *Gye* [32] that a surviving partner, as a trustee for the share of a deceased partner, could plead the benefit of the Statute of Limitations. Nevertheless, the rule of concealed fraud applied to them.

Furthermore, a beneficiary might find that his remedy was lost in consequence of his laches or acquiescence,[33] and it would also seem that the Court of Chancery would decline to reopen transactions after a considerable period of time, more particularly where most of the parties were dead and the receipts lost.[34]

The Real Property Limitation Act of 1833, s. 25, provided, however, that—

> . . . when any Land or Rent shall be vested in a Trustee upon any express Trust, the Right of the Cestuique Trust, or any Person claiming

---

24 [1892] 3 Ch. 105 (Cases, p. 366).
25 *Re Somerset*, [1894] 1 Ch. 231.
26 *Bolton* v. *Curre*, [1895] 1 Ch. 544.   27 *Ibid.*, p. 549.
28 *Per* Lindley, L.J., in *Chillingworth* v. *Chambers*, [1896] 1 Ch. 685, 700 (Cases, p. 347).
29 *Re Pauling's Settlement Trusts (No. 2)*, [1963] Ch. 576 (Cases, p. 349).
30 *Hovenden* v. *Lord Annesley* (1806), 2 Sch. & Lef. 607, 633.
31 See *Soar* v. *Ashwell*, [1893] 2 Q.B. 390.
32 (1872), L.R. 5 H.L. 656, 675.
33 *Rolfe* v. *Gregory* (1864), 4 De G.J. & S. 576.
34 *St. John* v. *Turner* (1700), 2 Vern. 418; *Bright* v. *Legerton* (1861), 2 De G.F. & J. 606.

through him, to bring a Suit against the Trustee, or any Person claiming through him, to recover such Land or Rent, shall be deemed to have first accrued, according to the Meaning of this Act, at and not before the Time at which such Land or Rent shall have been conveyed to a Purchaser for a valuable Consideration, and shall then be deemed to have accrued only as against such Purchaser and any Person claiming through him.

The effect of this section is to preserve the right of the *cestui que trust* under an express trust to follow trust property into the hands of his trustee and persons claiming through him after any interval of time, except that when a trustee conveyed property to a purchaser for valuable consideration, the title of that purchaser, and subsequent purchasers from him, could only be invalidated within twenty years (reduced by the Real Property Limitation Act of 1874 [35] to twelve years) from the date of the first purchase (if indeed it could be invalidated at all, for a *bona fide* purchaser for value *without notice* would have a good title). Moreover, even where the purchaser's title thus became good after twelve years, the personal right of the beneficiary against the trustee in respect of the breach of trust survived. [36] It should be added that this section only applied to express trusts of lands and rents. A lease for value was a conveyance within the Act. [37] Those constructive trusts which are within the terms of the decision in *Soar* v. *Ashwell* [38] were within section 25, but not other constructive trusts, as for example that which arises where a trustee renews a lease in his own name. [39] Such a trustee could plead lapse of time as a general bar, since in most cases the constructive trustee is claiming adversely to the *cestui que trust*. [40] On the other hand, a person who is not an express trustee, but enters into possession and assumes the character of a trustee under an express trust was within the section, [41] and in *Barnes* v. *Addy*, [42] a stranger to the trust who actively and knowingly participated in the trustee's breach of trust was said to be suitable to be dealt with as an express trustee.

There are several *dicta* which suggest that the twelve-year period after which the purchaser from the trustee obtained a good title was prolonged where the beneficiary was under a disability, or his interest was reversionary. [43]

In 1888, however, a new departure was taken in the Trustee Act of that year, and section 8 of that Act (now repealed) read—

(1) In any action or other proceeding against a trustee or any person claiming through him, except where the claim is founded upon any fraud or fraudulent breach of trust to which the trustee was party or privy, or is to recover trust property, or the proceeds thereof still retained by the

---

[35] Now the Limitation Act 1939.
[36] *Attorney-General* v. *Flint* (1844), 4 Hare 147; *East Stonehouse U.D.C.* v. *Willoughby Bros. Ltd.*, [1902] 2 K.B. 318, 335.
[37] *Attorney-General* v. *Davey* (1854), 4 De G. & J. 136.
[38] [1893] 2 Q.B. 390.
[39] *Re Dane's Estate* (1871), I.R. 5 Eq. 498.
[40] *Beckford* v. *Wade* (1805), 17 Ves. 87, 97; *Re Lacy*, [1899] 2 Ch. 149.
[41] *Life Association of Scotland* v. *Siddal* (1861), 3 De G.F. & J. 58, cited in *Soar* v. *Ashwell*, [1893] 2 Q.B. 396.
[42] (1874), L.R. 9 Ch.App. 244.
[43] *Thompson* v. *Simpson* (1841), 1 Dr. & War. 459. See also *Re Earl of Devon's Settled Estates*, [1896] 2 Ch. 562. The residuary legatee does not claim through the trustee of a will: *Leahy* v. *De Moleyns*, [1896] 1 I.R. 206; *Re Richardson*, [1920] 1 Ch. 423.

trustee, or previously received by the trustee and converted to his use, the following provisions shall apply:

(a) All rights and privileges conferred by any statute of limitations shall be enjoyed in the like manner and to the like extent as they would have been enjoyed in such action or other proceeding if the trustee or person claiming through him had not been a trustee or person claiming through him:

(b) If the action or other proceeding is brought to recover money or other property, and is one to which no existing statute of limitations applies, the trustee or person claiming through him shall be entitled to the benefit of and be at liberty to plead the lapse of time as a bar to such action or other proceeding in the like manner and to the like extent as if the claim had been against him in an action of debt for money had and received, but so nevertheless that the statute shall run against a married woman entitled in possession for her separate use, whether with or without a restraint upon anticipation, but shall not begin to run against any beneficiary unless and until the interest of such beneficiary shall be an interest in possession.

(2) No beneficiary, as against whom there would be a good defence by virtue of this section, shall derive any greater or other benefit from a judgment or order obtained by another beneficiary than he could have obtained if he had brought such action or other proceeding and this section had been pleaded.

The construction of this section provoked a good deal of difficulty and uncertainty. The first question to be answered was: To what kinds of trustees did the benefit of the statute extend? In section 1 of the Act of 1888 it was stated that the term included an executor or administrator, and a trustee whose trust arose by construction or implication of law, as well as an express trustee, but not the official trustee of charitable funds. Later decisions extended the statute's provisions to the director of a company,[44] and a mortgagee as far as any balance of the proceeds of sale of the mortgaged property was concerned,[45] but it did not apply to the trustee in bankruptcy[46] nor to the liquidator of a company in voluntary liquidation.[47] The relation of this section to the old equitable rule that an express trustee may not plead the benefit of the Statutes of Limitation must not be lost sight of. A constructive trustee might plead the benefit of the period of limitation, even though he had enriched himself at the expense of the trust estate; an express trustee and certain others classed with him could not, but might plead the benefit of section 8 of the Trustee Act 1888 in certain classes of case where they had not enriched themselves through the breach of trust. Some constructive trustees, however, fell within the Trustee Act 1888 and not within the old equitable rule. This is illustrated by *Soar* v. *Ashwell*.[48] Trustees handed trust money to a solicitor for investment, and he misappropriated it. The Court of

---

[44] *Re Lands Allotment Co. Ltd.*, [1894] 1 Ch. 616.
[45] *Thorne* v. *Heard*, [1895] A.C. 495 (Cases, p. 368).
[46] *Re Cornish*, [1896] 1 Q.B. 99.
[47] *Re Windsor Steam Coal Co. (1901) Ltd.*, [1928] Ch. 609; affirmed on other grounds, [1929] 1 Ch. 151.
[48] [1893] 2 Q.B. 390. See also *Re Timmis*, [1902] 1 Ch. 176.

Appeal held that he was not entitled to the protection accorded by the equitable rule, and obviously this was not a case to which the Trustee Act 1888 applied. Bowen, L.J., said [49]—

> It has been established beyond doubt . . . that a person occupying a fiduciary relation, who has property deposited with him on the strength of such relation, is to be dealt with as an express, and not merely a constructive, trustee of such property.

The old equitable rule relating to constructive trustees who have enriched themselves at the expense of the trust estate was preserved by section 25 (2) of the Judicature Act 1873, but this has been repealed by the Limitation Act 1939 with the result that section 19 in its reference to a " trustee " simply now puts express and constructive trustees of all kinds on the same basis, so that all trustees who have enriched themselves at the expense of the trust estate are now unable to plead any period of limitation. Thus, in *Tintin Exploration Syndicate Ltd.* v. *Sandys*,[50] *de facto* directors of a company paid money to one of themselves without authority. The court held that the *de facto* directors so enriched must account on the footing of express trustees, and so were not protected by any period of limitation.

It will be observed that section 8 (1) of the Act of 1888 deprived the trustee of the benefit of lapse of time wherever he had committed fraud, or wherever he retained the trust property or its proceeds in his hands. In *Re Landi* [51] the personal representatives of a tenant in common who died in 1923 claimed against the other tenant in common who had received the entire profits of the land from 1923 to 1935, and the court held that, as the Law of Property Act 1925 made tenants in common trustees, no Statute of Limitations ran in favour of one of them who retained the rents and profits of the land.

The object of subsection (1) (*a*) of section 8 has also been the subject of some conjecture. It could hardly be applicable to negligent breaches of trust, since these were not within the Statute of Limitations of 1623 at all, that statute applying only to actions arising out of contract and tort, and in any case negligent breaches of trust were within subsection 1 (*b*). In *Re Bowden*,[52] a newly appointed trustee brought an action against former trustees in respect of losses arising out of investments on insufficient security made more than six years before. Fry, L.J., observed [53] that this was not a case within subsection (1) (*a*) since, ". . . if a person had not been a trustee, he could not be sued for a breach of trust," and further, there was no right conferred by any Statute of Limitations (other than section 8 itself) in respect of breaches of trust. In *How* v. *Earl of Winterton*,[54] however, Lindley, L.J., in order to attach some meaning to the subsection, said that there might possibly be claims (such as those for an account) where some Statute of Limitations might be applicable, had not the claim been against a trustee.

---

[49] [1893] 2 Q.B. 397. See also *North American Land and Timber Co. Ltd.* v. *Watkins*, [1904] 1 Ch. 242; [1904] 2 Ch. 233.

[50] (1947), 177 L.T. 412 (decided on s. 19 of the Limitation Act 1939).

[51] [1939] Ch. 828.

[52] (1890), 45 Ch.D. 444.

[53] 45 Ch.D. 450.

[54] [1896] 2 Ch. 626, 639. See also *Robinson* v. *Harkin*, [1896] 2 Ch. 415.

A further explanation of the curious phraseology of subsection 8 (1) (*a*) was offered by Warrington, L.J., in *Re Richardson*.[55] He pointed out that in *Burdick* v. *Garrick* [56] an agent was prevented from pleading the Statute of Limitations because he was also a trustee. The subsection, said Warrington, L.J., was drafted to remove that disability.

It will be observed that the right of the trustee under subsection 1 (*b*) did not in any way alter the position where an existing Statute of Limitations was applicable. Now an executor was within the scope of section 8, but there were other statutes which protected him, and section 8 (1) (*b*) would therefore only operate where he acted as trustee. This is illustrated by *Re Swain*.[57] Executors and trustees of a will were under an obligation to sell the estate, including the testator's business. They delayed for some years, until the youngest child attained twenty-one. Eight years after this date an action was brought in respect of the delay in selling the business, and the resulting loss. Actions in respect of legacies could, under section 8 of the Real Property Limitation Act 1874 (now section 20 of the Limitation Act 1939), be brought within twelve years, but the court held that this was not an action in respect of a legacy, but an action in respect of a breach of trust within the Trustee Act 1888, section 8 (1) (*b*), and therefore the beneficiaries had delayed too long.

In *Re Richardson* [58] a testator died in 1909, leaving as his executors his widow and X. Under the will, the widow was entitled absolutely to the residuary estate, and the functions of the executors ceased in 1910. No formal accounts were delivered by X to the widow, but he told her of what had been done, and at the end of 1910 gave her a book containing all the particulars of her property. She died in 1917, and in 1918 the beneficiaries under her will (of which X was also an executor) brought an action against him for the administration of the husband's estate, and for an account. They did not allege, however, that any part of it had been misapplied. The defendant relied on the Trustee Act 1888, s. 8, but the Court of Appeal decided that the action was one to recover a legacy under section 8 of the Real Property Limitation Act 1874, and so as there was an existing Statute of Limitations applicable, section 8 (1) (*b*) of the Trustee Act 1888 did not apply (nor did any other section of that Act), and further that the twelve years under the Act of 1874 not having expired, the plaintiffs were entitled to an account. Lord Sterndale, M.R., commenting on section 8 (1) (*a*) of the Trustee Act 1888, said [59]—

> I take that to mean this: If a person has committed what Rigby L.J. in *How* v. *Lord Winterton* [60] calls a breach of duty which, whether he were a trustee or not, would give rise to an action against him, and there is in existence a statute which would be in those circumstances an answer to that action, then the person against whom the action is brought shall not be debarred from that defence because he is a trustee or executor, executor being included in the word " trustee," but he shall be able, so to speak, to put off the character of trustee altogether and avail himself of the defence

55 [1920] 1 Ch. 423, 441.
56 (1870), L.R. 5 Ch.App. 233.
57 [1891] 3 Ch. 233. See also *Re Timmis*, [1902] 1 Ch. 176.
58 [1920] 1 Ch. 423.
59 [1920] 1 Ch. 434.
60 [1896] 2 Ch. 626.

just as though he were not a trustee and were only an ordinary person who had committed that breach of duty.

On section 8 (1) (b) the Master of the Rolls observed [61]—

> That is the other branch, if I may call it so, of the protecting legislation. The first (a) is the case where there is a breach of duty which would give rise to an action whether the man were a trustee or not and for which there is an existing statute of limitations. The second (b) is where there is no statute of limitations applying at all to the action when it is brought. If this be an action to recover a legacy it does not come within (a) and for this reason, that this action for a legacy would not lie against the defendant except as executor. It therefore is not a case which comes within (a). No doubt where executors have received a legacy and have admitted that they held that legacy for legatees, an action might lie against them at common law for money had and received, but that is not an action to recover a legacy generally, and such an action could only lie against the defendant because he was an executor, and, therefore, a trustee within the meaning of sub-s. (a).
>
> Now, if this be an action to recover a legacy and does not come within (a) can it come within (b)? It seems to me it cannot, because it is then an action to recover money or other property, but it is not an action to which no existing statute of limitations applies, because the Real Property Limitation Act of 1874 does apply, and, therefore, if this be an action to recover a legacy in my opinion the Trustee Act, 1888, does not apply at all.

The trustee could claim the benefit of the statute, notwithstanding the fact that the trustee's agent has committed fraud, provided that the trustee himself is innocent of it. In *Thorne* v. *Heard*,[62] the solicitor of a trustee embezzled trust funds, through the negligence of the trustee. This was held by the House of Lords to be insufficient to make the trustee " party or privy " to the fraud.

The type of transaction contemplated by subsection (1) (b) is illustrated by *Re Somerset*.[63] In 1878 trustees committed a non-fraudulent breach of trust, by investing in real securities in excess of the permitted margin. In 1892 the tenant for life and the remainderman brought an action to make good the amount invested, and it was held that, although the remainderman had a good cause of action, that of the tenant for life was barred, as his right had accrued at the date when the breach of trust was committed, unless he was then subject to a disability. Where the trustee thus replaces money for the benefit of the remainderman, the trustee is entitled to keep any interest as to which statute bars a claim by the estate of the tenant for life.[64] Thus, it appears that, with regard to innocent breaches of trust, time runs in favour of the trustee unless the trustee has concealed the true facts from the knowledge of the beneficiary. Furthermore, time begins to run against the remainderman only when his interest falls into possession.[65]

---

[61] [1920] 1 Ch. 434–435.
[62] [1895] A.C. 495 (Cases, p. 368).
[63] [1894] 1 Ch. 231.
[64] *Re Fountaine*, [1909] 2 Ch. 382.
[65] *Re Pauling's Settlement Trusts*, [1964] Ch. 303.

In an action by a trustee for contribution from a co-trustee, time only begins to run when the claim of the *cestui que trust* in respect of the breach has been finally established.[66]

In *Mara* v. *Browne*,[67] a married woman was tenant for life under a settlement during the joint lives of herself and her husband, and was also entitled to a reversionary life interest on the death of her husband, by a resulting trust. When she sued the trustee the court held that, although she had been in possession more than six years without suing, under her first title, she could nevertheless sue in respect of her second title, the statutory six years not having elapsed since she acquired it.

2. *The Limitation Act* 1939

The Limitation Act 1939 (which came into force on July 1, 1940), represents a courageous attempt to simplify the complexities of the law relating to limitation of actions. Section 19 of the Act of 1939 replaces, with verbal alterations, section 8 of the Trustee Act 1888, and section 20 replaces section 8 of the Real Property Limitation Act 1874. The two sections read as follows—

19.—(1) No period of limitation prescribed by this Act shall apply to an action by a beneficiary under a trust, being an action—

(*a*) in respect of any fraud or fraudulent breach of trust to which the trustee was a party or privy; or

(*b*) to recover from the trustee trust property or the proceeds thereof in the possession of the trustee, or previously received by the trustee and converted to his use.[68]

(2) Subject as aforesaid, an action by a beneficiary to recover trust property or in respect of any breach of trust, not being an action for which a period of limitation is prescribed by any other provision of this Act, shall not be brought after the expiration of six years from the date on which the right of action accrued:

Provided that the right of action shall not be deemed to have accrued to any beneficiary entitled to a future interest in the trust property, until the interest fell into possession.

(3) No beneficiary as against whom there would be a good defence under this Act shall derive any greater or other benefit from a judgment or order obtained by any other beneficiary than he could have obtained if he had brought the action and this Act had been pleaded in defence.

20.—Subject to the provisions of subsection (1) of the last foregoing section, no action in respect of any claim to the personal estate of a deceased person or to any share or interest in such estate, whether under a will or on intestacy, shall be brought after the expiration of twelve years from the date when the right to receive the share or interest accrued, and no action to recover arrears of interest in respect of any legacy, or damages in respect of such arrears, shall be brought after the expiration of six years from the date on which the interest became due.

The language of section 19 of the Act of 1939 is simpler than that of section 8 of the Act of 1888, and the section was presumably drafted with many of the

---

66 *Robinson* v. *Harkin*, [1896] 2 Ch. 415.
67 [1895] 2 Ch. 69; [1896] 1 Ch. 199.
68 This is illustrated by *Re Howlett*, [1949] Ch. 767.

problems arising under the Act of 1888 in mind. The two sections, it will be noticed, preserve the two periods of limitation for executors and trustees. The twelve-year period for executors covers only acts done by executors as executors. Where, however, an executor becomes a trustee, in the normal sense, he will then be able to take advantage of the six-year period of limitation. Thus, the statutory definition of " trustee," which includes the personal representative, does not apply to sections 19 and 20 of the Limitation Act, because the context otherwise requires.[69]

The term " trustee " covers both express and constructive trustees, but not trustees in bankruptcy or liquidators of companies, but it has been held to include a *de facto* director of a company,[70] and it will include any person who takes trust property with notice of the trust. Where there is a fraudulent breach of trust, and a person receives trust property innocently, he may claim the benefit of the period of limitation.[71]

Although under this Act, time never runs in favour of a trustee who has been fraudulent, or who has converted the property to his own use, the claim of the beneficiary may still be barred by laches and acquiescence.

The following observations on the section may be offered—

(1) Section 19 (3) of the Act of 1939 is identical in effect with section 8 (2) of the Act of 1888.

(2) Problems such as those which arose in *Re Swain*,[72] *Re Timmis*[73] and *Re Richardson*[74] will be solved in the same way under sections 19 and 20 of the Act of 1939 as they were under section 8 of the Act of 1888 and section 8 of the Real Property Limitation Act of 1874. In the *Diplock* case,[75] for example, since the action was to recover the residuary estate, the twelve-year period under section 20 was applicable.

(3) The intention of the phrase " not being an action for which a period of limitation is prescribed by any other provision of this Act " in section 19 (2) of the Act of 1939 is to remove the disability upon a trustee which was established in *Burdick* v. *Garrick*.[76]

Innocent breaches of trust may take a great variety of forms. In *Re Diplock*,[77] the personal representatives had paid the residuary estate to charities, who were subsequently discovered to have no title to it. They include a failure to invest in accordance either with the statutory requirements or the investments clause; investment on insufficient security,[78] failure to accumulate income, as the settler had directed,[79] failure to use care in the exercise of a power of advancement,[80] and many other matters.

---

[69] As to persons intermeddling with an estate, see Hinks, " Executors *De Son Tort* and the Limitation of Actions " (1974) *The Conveyancer* 176, 181–186.
[70] *Tintin Exploration Syndicate Ltd.* v. *Sandys* (1947), 177 L.T. 412.
[71] *G.L. Baker Ltd.* v. *Medway Building and Supplies Ltd.*, [1958] 1 W.L.R. 1216.
[72] [1891] 3 Ch. 233.
[73] [1902] 1 Ch. 176.
[74] [1920] 1 Ch. 423.
[75] [1951] A.C. 251. See pp. 398–401, *ante*.
[76] (1870), L.R. 5 Ch.App. 233.
[77] [1948] Ch. 465.
[78] *Re Bowden* (1890), 45 Ch.D. 444 ; *Re Somerset*, [1894] 1 Ch. 231.
[79] *How* v. *Earl of Winterton*, [1896] 2 Ch. 626.
[80] *Re Pauling's Settlement Trusts*, [1964] Ch. 303.

CHAPTER XXVII

TRUSTS IN THE CONFLICT OF LAWS

A. *PENN* v. *LORD BALTIMORE*

IT is an obvious and necessary general principle of the conflict of laws that no court will entertain an action for the determination of the title to, or the right to possession of, land situated out of England, or for the recovery of damages for trespass to such foreign land. In the last edition of Dicey and Morris's *Conflict of Laws*,[1] there is a full discussion of the possible origin of this rule in English law, but it is self-evident that if any other rule were to prevail, it might have the consequence that English courts would be concerned to secure the execution of decrees which operate directly within the territorial orbit of another state—a situation which would produce many inconvenient consequences. Nevertheless, there exist two important exceptions to this general rule, both derived from the practice of the old Court of Chancery in respect of its equitable jurisdiction, especially in relation to trusts. The first of these exceptions was established by the decision of Lord Hardwicke in *Penn* v. *Lord Baltimore*,[2] and it arises out of a logical application of the maxim, " Equity acts *in personam*." It is that an English court of equity has jurisdiction to hear an action against a person in respect of land situated out of England, if that action arises out of a contract or out of an equity between the parties. Thus, in *Penn* v. *Lord Baltimore*, the suit in Chancery arose out of the grant of a charter in respect of land situated in British North America, which, from the standpoint of the English court, was foreign land. The entire scope of this jurisdiction was defined by Parker, J., in a well-known passage in his judgment in *Deschamps* v. *Miller*,[3] where he said—

> In my opinion the general rule is that the Court will not adjudicate on questions relating to the title to or the right to the possession of immovable property out of the jurisdiction. There are, no doubt, exceptions to the rule, but, without attempting to give an exhaustive statement of those exceptions, I think it will be found that they all depend on the existence between the parties to the suit of some personal obligation arising out of contract or implied contract, fiduciary relationship or fraud, or other conduct which, in the view of a Court of Equity in this country, would be unconscionable, and do not depend for their existence on the law of the locus of the immovable property. Thus, in cases of trusts, specific performance of contracts, foreclosure, or redemption of mortgages, or in the case of land obtained by the defendant by fraud, or other such unconscionable conduct as I have referred to, the Court may very well

---

[1] 9th ed., pp. 516–518.

[2] (1750), 1 Ves.Sen. 444. See, generally, Keeton and Sheridan, *Equity*, pp. 13–17.

[3] [1908] 1 Ch. 856, 863–864. See also *Gorash* v. *Gorash*, [1949] 4 D.L.R. 296 (Canada); *Inglis* v. *Commonwealth Trading Bank of Australia* (1972), 20 F.L.R. 30, commented on by Pryles, " Jurisdiction over Foreign Immovables " (1973) 22 *International and Comparative Law Quarterly* 756.

assume jurisdiction. But where there is no contract, no fiduciary relationship, and no fraud or other unconscionable conduct giving rise to a personal obligation between the parties, and the whole question is whether or not according to the law of the locus the claim of title set up by one party, whether a legal or equitable claim in the sense of those words as used in English law, would be preferred to the claim of another party, I do not think the Court ought to entertain jurisdiction to decide the matter.

It will be seen, therefore, that the whole foundation of this jurisdiction rests upon the breach of an equitable obligation *in personam* by a person whom the court can reach, namely, one who is, whether permanently or temporarily, within the jurisdiction of a court of equity.[4] Even so framed, the rule governing this jurisdiction has been criticised as going very far, when the rules upon which the conflict of laws is founded are considered. As Lord Esher put it, it " seems to me to be open to the strong objection, that the Court is doing indirectly what it dare not do directly "[5] and Dicey,[6] Falconbridge and others have pointed out that if the jurisdiction were pressed it could very well lead to embarrassing conflicts with the courts of the *situs*.

It is undeniable that in the present century courts of equity have shown a caution that was not always apparent in the eighteenth and early nineteenth centuries, although Hanbury's suggestion [7] that the jurisdiction is now limited to cases where the land, which is the object of the proceedings, is actually British territory is unduly restrictive. Indeed, in principle, this could scarcely be the position, for Cheshire, who discusses the limits of the principle of *Penn* v. *Lord Baltimore* very fully, points out that this jurisdiction *in personam* is not limited to cases affecting foreign land.[8] Such cases are simply specific instances of the invocation of a general jurisdiction *in personam*, which has been used to issue injunctions to restrain foreign proceedings,[9] and even to restrain a person from taking advantage of a foreign judgment, obtained in violation of equitable principles,[10] as well as, recently, to grant specific performance of a contract for the sale of foreign land.[11] In all such cases the test is neither the nationality of the defendant nor the place where the property, whether moveable or immoveable, is situated, but merely whether the defendant is within the jurisdiction of the court, so that he can be reached by the court's decree. It is in the exercise of this far-reaching jurisdiction that it is possible to trace the last survival of the high status of the Court of Chancery, and of those administrative powers which were such a striking feature of its jurisdiction in former times. Even so late as 1838, Shadwell, V.-C., said in *Bent* v. *Young*,[12] " I consider that in the contemplation of the Court of Chancery, every foreign Court is an Inferior Court " and although a modern equity judge might not express himself so forcibly, many of the consequences of that former pre-eminence remain.

---

4 *Ewing* v. *Orr-Ewing* (1883), 9 App.Cas. 34, 40.
5 *Companhia de Moçambique* v. *British South Africa Co.*, [1892] 2 Q.B. 358, 404–405.
6 9th ed., p. 522.   7 *Modern Equity*, 9th ed., p. 35.
8 *Private International Law*, 8th ed., p. 499.
9 e.g. *Lord Portarlington* v. *Soulby* (1834), 3 My. & K. 104. See also *Cohen* v. *Rothfield*, [1919] 1 K.B. 410; *Orr-Lewis* v. *Orr-Lewis*, [1949] P. 347.
10 e.g. *Ellerman Lines Ltd.* v. *Read*, [1928] 2 K.B. 144.
11 *Richard West and Partners (Inverness) Ltd.* v. *Dick*, [1969] 2 Ch. 424.
12 (1838), 9 Sim. 180, 191.

Even today, however, the jurisdiction of courts of equity is founded upon the same principles as in earlier days. For example, under the Variation of Trusts Act 1958, the English courts have exercised jurisdiction to vary the trusts of a Northern Ireland settlement, where the trustees and the trust property were in England,[13] and Ungoed-Thomas, J., in that case pointed out that in the execution of trusts, an English court executes the trusts of a foreign settlement in accordance with the foreign law. Variation, however, does not carry out the trusts of a settlement but varies or alters them in accordance with the powers conferred by English law, and the court has varied foreign marriage settlements under section 25 of the Matrimonial Causes Act 1950. Where, however, a trust contains substantial foreign elements, the court will consider carefully whether it is proper for it to exercise jurisdiction.[14]

Both Dicey and Cheshire emphasise the fact that although the jurisdiction is very wide, there are, nevertheless, important limitations. In the first place, there is the overriding consideration that there must exist some personal equity between the parties. This limitation, therefore, excludes any possibility of adjudicating upon direct questions of title to land situated abroad. Further, either the defendant must be present in England or, if he is not so present, the court must be able to reach him by service of a writ or notice (as, for example, where a person domiciled or ordinarily resident in England is for the time being out of England). Thirdly, the equitable jurisdiction will not assist if the decree granted would be directly contrary to the *lex situs*. This, however, is by no means as easy to determine as might appear at first sight. It is clear, for example, that if the equity recognised by the English court of equity is entirely unrecognised by the *lex situs*, the court will grant a decree. This is established by a long line of cases, of which the most important of the earlier ones is *Re Courtney*,[15] and one of the latest is *Re Anchor Line (Henderson Bros.) Ltd. (No. 2)*.[16]

Finally, it must be pointed out that the jurisdiction cannot, in general, affect third parties. Equity will only proceed against the actual person whose own conduct has brought him within the orbit of the court's jurisdiction. This is described by Cheshire as " privity of obligation," between plaintiff and defendant, arising out of some transaction between them. The plainest illustration of this is *Norris* v. *Chambres*.[17] In that case, Sadleir, an Englishman, contracted to buy land in Prussia from Simons (also an Englishman) and paid a deposit. Simons refused to complete, and sold to Chambres, who bought with notice of the earlier contract in favour of Sadleir. Sadleir's representative then brought an action in England, claiming he was entitled to an equitable lien on the land, arising out of his contract. In Prussia, no such equitable lien existed. Sir John Romilly, M.R., held that as the decree would necessarily affect the rights of Chambres, who was not a party to the original contract out of which the equity arose, no decree would be granted; Sadleir must obtain redress in the Prussian courts, or fail. This was upheld on appeal

---

13 *Re Ker's Settlement Trusts*, [1963] Ch. 553.

14 *Re Paget's Settlement*, [1965] 1 W.L.R. 1046. As to the current legislation governing variation of property in matrimonial proceedings, see p. 366, *ante*.

15 (1840), Mont. & Ch. 239, 250.

16 [1937] Ch. 483.

17 (1861), 29 Beav. 246.

to the Lord Chancellor.[18] However, if third parties themselves become affected by the personal equity, they may be made the objects of a decree. This occurred in *Mercantile Investment and General Trust Co.* v. *River Plate Trust, Loan, and Agency Co.,*[19] where a company had created an equitable charge in favour of debenture holders, and had then sold land " subject ... to the mortgage, lien, or charge now existing." The charge was void under the *lex situs* for want of registration, but the English court held that it could grant a decree against the purchasers at the suit of the debenture holders. Once this distinction is made, however, a difficulty arises. Granted that in the later case the purchase was expressly subject to the charge, nevertheless in *Norris* v. *Chambres* the sale was admitted to be made to a purchaser who had notice of a prior contract, and who might therefore have been reasonably regarded as affected by the equitable obligation. Although in *Mercantile, etc., Trust* v. *River Plate Trust,* Davey, Q.C., *arguendo,* said that the case was exactly covered by *Norris* v. *Chambres,* if North, J.'s judgment is read, it is hard to resist the inference that *Norris* v. *Chambres* was wrongly decided, since the effect of Chambres purchasing with notice of the prior contract does not seem to have been appreciated.

B. THE CONVERSE OF *PENN* v. *LORD BALTIMORE*

What is the attitude of an English court when presented with a situation which is the converse of *Penn* v. *Lord Baltimore, i.e.* when a foreign court grants a decree, based on a personal equity between the parties, but affecting land situated in England? One might think that such a situation might arise frequently. Nevertheless, no decision on this point exists in the reports of English courts. There is, however, a decision of the Supreme Court of Canada, *Duke* v. *Andler,*[20] which was fully discussed by Gordon [21] in 1933. Briefly, the decision in that case was that a decree of a Californian court, affecting land situated in British Columbia, and arising out of fraud by the defendant, would not be recognised by the courts of British Columbia. On principle, the decision is hard to challenge. The Californian court, in pronouncing its decree, was adjudicating on personal equities between parties to the suit, and it must make its decree effective without the aid of any foreign court. This point was clearly put by Lord Cottenham, L.C., in *Re Courtney,*[22] where he said—

> If indeed the law of the country where the land is situate should not permit or not enable the defendant to do what the court might otherwise think it right to decree, it would be useless and unjust to direct him to do the act; but where there is no such impediment the courts of this country, in the exercise of their jurisdiction over contracts made here, or in administering equities between parties residing here, act upon their own rules, and are not influenced by any consideration of what the effect of such contracts might be in the country where the lands are situate, or of the

---

[18] (1861), 3 De G.F. & J. 583. See also *Norton* v. *Florence Land and Public Works Co.* (1877), 7 Ch.D. 332.
[19] [1892] 2 Ch. 303.
[20] [1932] 4 D.L.R. 529.
[21] " The Converse of *Penn* v. *Lord Baltimore* " 49 *Law Quarterly Review* 547.
[22] (1840), Mont. & Ch. 239, 250–251.

manner in which the courts of such countries might deal with such equities.

Gordon also pointed out that, although American authority on this problem is not extensive, in two cases, *Carpenter* v. *Strange*,[23] and *Fall* v. *Eastin*,[24] the Supreme Court has decided that a decree *in personam* of a state court affecting title to real estate in another state is destitute of extraterritorial effect.

C. THE PROPER LAW OF A SETTLEMENT [25]

The proper law of a settlement may be defined as the law which governs its formal validity and its construction. On this question, the English decisions are few, and they do not establish a clear rule. In *Re Ker's Settlement Trusts*,[26] for example, the settlement was assumed to be an Irish settlement, and the point was not argued. In *Re Paget's Settlement*,[27] a settlor, domiciled in England when the settlement was made, executed in England a settlement drawn up in the United States, in which all the trusts were administered in the state of New York, in which almost all the trust funds were situated, and in which all the trustees were American. A court of the state of New York decided that the validity and effect of the settlement were governed by English law, but Cross, J., while agreeing that the decision of the New York court would have great weight with an English court, added that the contrary view, that the settlement was governed by the law of the state of New York, was not argued, although on the face of the settlement, there were indications which supported it. Accordingly, he did not decide this point.

In *Re Paget's Settlement*,[27] the trust was of moveables. Where, however, the trust is of immoveables, it is a rule of most general application that all matters relating to its creation and validity, whether the trust arises *inter vivos* or by will, are governed by the *lex situs*, i.e. the law of the country where the property is situated. This includes land held under a trust for sale. In *Re Fitzgerald* [28] part of the trust property of the settlement was heritable bonds, which have always been classed as immoveables, and all three members of the Court of Appeal agreed that the validity of the settlement, to this extent, must be governed by Scots law. Since the settlement had come into existence, some of the heritable bonds had been sold, and the proceeds had been invested in English securities, but this did not affect the law applicable to this part of the settlement.

Since land held under a trust for sale is treated in the conflict of laws as an immoveable, it would at first sight seem logical to treat capital money arising from the sale of land as a moveable, notwithstanding the provisions of section 75 (5) of the Settled Land Act 1925. However, in *Re Cutcliffe's Will Trusts*,[29] the English court decided that stock representing the proceeds of sale of English settled land must be treated as an immoveable, where the

---

[23] (1891), 141 U.S. 87.
[24] (1909), 215 U.S. 1.
[25] For a fuller treatment, see Graveson, *Conflict of Laws*, Chapter 17.
[26] [1963] Ch. 553.
[27] [1965] 1 W.L.R. 1046.
[28] [1904] 1 Ch. 573.
[29] [1940] Ch. 565.

intestate died domiciled in Ontario. This decision has been criticised on the ground that the doctrine of conversion is a domestic rule of English law, but Dicey points out that, whilst the decision in *Re Berchtold* [30] applied only to judge-made domestic law, the rule applicable in *Re Cutcliffe's Will Trusts* was statutory, and was expressed in terms applicable also to the conflict of laws.

Where the trust is either wholly or partly of moveables, different considerations are applicable, and in the United States, where this question has been frequently before the courts, a great variety of views have been expressed. In the first place, a distinction must be drawn between trusts *inter vivos* and testamentary trusts. In *Re Fitzgerald* [31] a marriage contract in Scottish form was entered into on the marriage of a domiciled Englishman with a domiciled Scotswoman, with limitations valid under Scots law, but not under English law. The trustees resided in England, which remained the domicile of the husband. Part of the property was money which was invested in Consols. The Court of Appeal held that, as the settlement was in Scots form, and as the bulk of the property (the heritable bonds) was governed by Scots law, the intention of the parties was that the whole of the settlement should be governed by Scots law. Cozens-Hardy, L.J., observed [32]—

> As a general rule the law of the matrimonial domicil is applicable to a contract in consideration of marriage. But this is not an absolute rule. It yields to an express stipulation that some other law shall apply.

And in this case, it yielded to the intention of the partner, as discovered from the settlement itself.

In *Iveagh* v. *I.R.C.* [33] one of the problems to be decided was the proper law of a voluntary settlement, made in England (when the whole of Ireland was part of the United Kingdom) of shares and other securities, which was managed in Ireland. At the date of the settlement, all parties were domiciled in Ireland. After commenting on the difficulties of reaching any decision, Upjohn, J., concluded that the decisive factor was that the settlement was made to benefit a family in Ireland, and accordingly the proper law of the settlement was the law of the Republic of Ireland.

Where trusts are created by will, the testamentary capacity of the testator is governed by the law of the testator's domicile at the time of his death. The question of the formal validity of a will of moveables (or immoveables) is a complicated one, which is governed by the Wills Act 1963. [34] In *Philipson-Stow* v. *I.R.C.*, [35] Lord Denning said—

> ... whilst I would agree that the *construction* of a will depends on the intention of the testator, I would say that in no other respect does his intention determine the law applicable to it.
>
> Let me take first the case where there is a disposition of *movable* property by will. There is no doubt that the proper law regulating the disposition of *movables* is the law of the domicile of the testator at the

---

[30] [1923] 1 Ch. 192.
[31] [1904] 1 Ch. 573.
[32] [1904] 1 Ch. 587.
[33] [1954] Ch. 364.
[34] See Dicey and Morris, *Conflict of Laws*, 9th ed., pp. 594–600; Graveson, *Conflict of Laws*, 6th ed., p. 568 *et seq.*
[35] [1961] A.C. 727, 760–761.

time of his death. In the leading case on this subject [36] Lord Cranworth used the word " regulate " in this very connection. When a person dies domiciled abroad, he said, " in every case the succession to personal property will be *regulated* not according to the law of this country, but to that of his domicile " . . . There is perhaps an exception in regard to the *construction* of his will: for if a question arises as to the interpretation of the will and it should appear that the testator has changed his domicile between making his will and his death, his will may fall to be *construed* according to the law of his domicile at the time that he made it; though in all other respects it would be governed by the law of his domicile at the date of his death.

In *Re Levick's Will Trusts,* [37] the testator, who was domiciled in South Africa, made a will in England in the English form, and established trusts for the benefit of his wife for life, and after her death upon protective trusts as to one half for his son, and then upon other trusts. The testator died abroad in 1937, and the son died in 1961, domiciled in England. Part of the trust fund comprised American dollar securities, the remainder being property in England. Plowman, J., held that the proper law regulating a disposition of moveables was the law from which the validity of the disposition was derived. This was the law of the country of the testator's domicile at the time of his death. Since this was South Africa, the law of South Africa was therefore applicable to the disposition, and not English law.

D. THE ADMINISTRATION OF A TRUST OF MOVEABLES

The law governing the administration of a trust of moveables is the law of the country where the administration is to be carried out. This is primarily the country where the trustees carry on the work of the trust.[38] Thus in both *Baker* v. *Archer-Shee* [39] and in *Archer-Shee* v. *Garland* [40] the House of Lords accepted the principle that the law applicable to administration was the law of the state of New York, where the trustees carried on the work of the trust, but in the first case they assumed (wrongly) that the law of New York state was identical with English law, whilst in the second, they received expert evidence to establish what the law of New York state was.

E. ADMINISTRATION OF AN ESTATE WHICH INCLUDES IMMOVEABLES SITUATED ABROAD [41]

It has never been doubted that where executors or trustees are administering the estate of a person who died leaving property within the jurisdiction, the court has jurisdiction also to decide matters relating to property, whether moveable or immoveable, situated abroad. In this case, the English court of

[36] *Enohin* v. *Wylie* (1862), 10 H.L.C. 1, 19.
[37] [1963] 1 W.L.R. 311.
[38] *Re Cigala's Settlement Trusts* (1878), 7 Ch.D. 351 ; *Re Smyth,* [1898] 1 Ch. 89.
[39] [1927] A.C. 844.
[40] [1931] A.C. 212.
[41] See also Croucher, " Trusts of Moveables in Private International Law " (1940) 4 *Modern Law Review* 111.

equity will even decide questions of title. Although, as Dicey points out, this rule, or rather exception to a general rule, has never been precisely defined, there is, nevertheless, abundant authority to support it. Moreover, it is a principle quite distinct from that in *Penn* v. *Lord Baltimore*, for in the case of the administration of estates with assets abroad, no question of fiduciary relationship or personal equity need arise at all. One or two illustrations will make the scope of the rule clear.

In *Earl Nelson* v. *Lord Bridport*,[42] the King of the Two Sicilies had granted land in Sicily to Lord Nelson and the heirs of his body, with power to appoint successors by will. By his will, which also extended to Lord Nelson's property in England, Nelson devised land to trustees for his brother for life, with various remainders. After Lord Nelson's death, the Government of the Two Sicilies passed a law, the effect of which was to invalidate these provisions of the will, and to make the persons in possession of the land the absolute owners thereof. In accordance with this law, the admiral's brother devised the land to his daughter, but the remainderman under Lord Nelson's settlement claimed the land under the settlement. The English court held that it possessed jurisdiction to settle this question, arising as it did under the original will, but it also held that the law applicable was the *lex situs*. Accordingly, the daughter of the admiral's brother was entitled to the estate, as against the claim of the remainderman under the admiral's will.

Re Piercy[43] is a further illustration of the application of the same principle. Piercy, a domiciled Englishman, was the owner of land in Sardinia. He made an English will, by virtue of which he left all his property to his executors and trustees, on trust to sell and convert it, and to hold the bulk of the proceeds for his children for their lives, with remainders to their issue. By Italian law, disposition of the land by will was invalid. North, J., held that he had jurisdiction to determine who was entitled to the land in Sardinia. So far, there was no difficulty, but the actual decision of North, J., in this case on the application of Italian law has been subjected to considerable criticism. Thus, Cheshire,[44] accepting Beale's criticism, and applying in its entirety the principle that rights over land are governed by the *lex situs,* comments: " The unsophisticated might conclude that the land must be allowed to remain subject to Italian law, and that any move to subject it, directly or indirectly, to the English trusts would be contrary to principle as being a contravention of the *lex situs*. North, J., however, was of a different opinion. He admitted, indeed, that the land was subject to Italian law as long as it remained unsold, but, apart from that concession, he directed the trustees to sell the land and to hold the proceeds upon the trusts declared by the will. His reasoning, ingenious if not sound, was that by Italian law it was not illegal for the testator to direct the sale of his land, that Italian law *qua* the *lex situs* would continue to govern the land in the hands of the purchaser, but that it had nothing whatever to do with the proceeds of sale, for by that time the land would have been placed outside the scope of the will.

---

[42] (1846), 8 Beav. 547. See also *Abdul Hameed Sitti Kadija* v. *De Saram*, [1946] A.C. 208 (Cases, p. 192).
[43] [1895] 1 Ch. 83.
[44] *Private International Law* (8th ed.), p. 487–488.

" What probably weighed with the learned judge was that the land had become money under the equitable doctrine of conversion, but, as Beale points out, whether such a conversion had been effected depends upon the *lex situs,* and by Italian law the answer was most definitely in the negative."

The second paragraph of this criticism is extremely difficult to follow. Careful perusal of North, J.'s judgment fails to reveal the slightest indication that he was influenced by the equitable doctrine of conversion, which is never mentioned. Conversely, there is evident throughout the judgment a most careful regard for the effect of Italian law, in so far as it is applicable to the will. There is no suggestion in Italian law, so far as it was stated in argument or judgment, that the trustees have power to sell for one purpose, and not for another; and further, Cheshire, in arguing that the will should stand or fall as a whole, apparently overlooks the fact that the will applied to both real and personal estate, and that, since the law governing the moveables was English law, no question was, or could be, raised upon its efficacy in respect of moveables. North, J.'s problem was therefore to discover what could be ranked as moveables for the purposes of the trusts.

The solution of this problem, it may be hazarded, was not as easy as Beale and Cheshire suggest. One of the difficulties in cases of this type is to discover exactly what the foreign law is. The relevant sections of the Italian Code were set out in the case. They established the following rules:

1. Successions by law or will, whether as regards the order of succession, or as to the measure of the rights of succession, or as to the intrinsic validity of the disposition, are regulated by the national law of the person whose estate is in question, whatever the property or wherever it may be situated.

2. The substance and effect of testamentary dispositions are regulated by the national law of the persons making them.

3. But, notwithstanding the preceding rules, in no case may the laws, Acts or judgments of a foreign country, nor any private dispositions, derogate from the prohibitive laws of Italy concerning either the persons, property or the Acts, nor from the laws in any way concerning public order and morality.

4. Any condition imposed on an heir or legatee, no matter how expressed, that he is to retain property and hand it to a third person, is a trust substitution, and, as such, is forbidden.

5. The invalidity of a trust substitution does not affect the validity of the institution of the heir or legatee, to which it is attached. But all trust substitutions are void.

After considering the provisions of the code, and the opinions of Italian jurists, North, J., decided that the devise to the trustees and the trust for sale were valid, but since by Italian law there could be no trust substitution, the attempt to settle the children's shares was not, in so far as it related to Italian land, valid, and the interests of the children were therefore absolute. The point in issue in the case was, therefore, to what trusts the purchase money resulting from sale of the land, and the rents and profits until sale, were subject.

North, J., attacks the problem in the following way. He says it is not necessary to decide whether the trustees or the children are heirs, since either way the will is good. If the trustees are heirs, then under rules 4 and 5, they take, but everything else is trust substitution and, therefore, invalid. On the other hand, if the children, not the trustees, are heirs, then they take, but subject to the power given to the trustees by Italian law to sell without interference on the part of persons interested in the estate.

Either way, therefore, the trustees are empowered to sell the land. When they sell it, the proceeds are to be invested in English securities, and held by the English trustees in favour of certain beneficiaries named by the will. The proceeds then enjoy the same status under the will as any other moveables. It is interesting to notice that North, J., dealt with the specific objection that patrimonial land sold is still, by Italian law, patrimony. So it is, says North, J., if in fact the person in whom the proceeds of sale vest is subject to Italian law. But the English trustees are not.

It is respectfully suggested, therefore, that the argument of Beale and Cheshire does not accurately reflect the successive steps in North, J.'s judgment, which turns upon a direct application of Italian law to the land. Once the land has been sold, the English will necessarily governs the actions of the English trustees with regard to the proceeds of sale, as much as it does with regard to other moveables.

In a later case, *Re Duke of Wellington,*[45] the English court of equity again accepted jurisdiction to decide questions of title to foreign land. Once again the question, as in *Nelson* v. *Bridport,* arose out of a grant of foreign estates to one of our two great commanders during the Napoleonic wars. The first Duke of Wellington was also created, by the Spanish monarchy, Duke of Ciudad Rodrigo in 1812, and there was a grant of Spanish estates to the Duke of Ciudad Rodrigo, his heirs and successors. No problems upon the devolution of this estate arose until 1943, when the sixth Duke of Wellington and Ciudad Rodrigo was killed in action, being then a bachelor. Thereupon the Dukedom of Wellington passed to the uncle of the sixth Duke, and the Dukedom of Ciudad Rodrigo to the sister of the sixth Duke. By a Spanish will, dated May 6, 1942, the sixth Duke had left his Spanish estates and personalty to the person who, being issue of the first Duke of Wellington and Ciudad Rodrigo, " will on my decease become Duke of Wellington and Ciudad Rodrigo for his absolute benefit." He also made an English will, dated December 6, 1942, disposing of the remainder of his property, and excepting therefrom the property disposed of by Spanish will. The English court of equity held that it had jurisdiction to decide this question, and on the question of the law applicable, the Court of Appeal accepted the reasoning of Wynn-Parry, J., at first instance.[46]

As far as the Spanish will was concerned, Wynn-Parry, J., held that the gift failed, since there was no one who could satisfy the description contained in it. Accordingly, it was necessary to determine in whom the moveables and immoveables disposed of by that will vested. As far as moveables were concerned, the law applicable was English law, since the testator was domiciled in England. The immoveables, however, were governed by Spanish law, and the determination of who, under Spanish law, was entitled was a matter of complexity, involving the question whether Spanish law recognises and applies

45 [1948] Ch. 118.
46 [1947] Ch. 506.

the doctrine of *renvoi*. After receiving expert evidence, which conflicted in important particulars, Wynn-Parry, J., decided that it would be contrary to the spirit of the Spanish Civil Code to hold that in such a case Spanish law would accept the *renvoi* which the English law makes to it as the *lex situs*. Accordingly, the question was decided by reference to English law. The gift in the Spanish will having failed, the present Duke of Wellington was entitled under the English will to the Spanish property, both immoveable and moveable, ineffectually disposed of under the Spanish will.

F. TRANSFER OF TRUST ABROAD

In *Re Seale's Marriage Settlement*,[47] Buckley, J., decided that the court had jurisdiction under the Variation of Trusts Act 1958 to order that the assets of an English trust should be transferred to the trustees of a Canadian trust for the same beneficiaries, all of whom lived in Canada. In reaching this decision, Buckley, J., pointed out that in *Re Liddiard* [48] the will of an English testator had provided that the residue of the estate should be divided amongst his children and their issue. All of them were resident in Australia. Malins, V.-C., ordered that the estate should be transferred to Australian trustees, whose intention was to sell the English investments, and to invest the money in Australia. In that case, however, the trust remained an English trust and, in general, an English court is reluctant to appoint trustees all of whom are out of the jurisdiction. On the other hand, in *Re Seale's Marriage Settlement* the effect of the transfer was that the trust became situate in Canada, and therefore became subject to the jurisdiction of the Canadian courts, and to Canadian law.

In *Re Weston's Settlements* [49] the court refused to assent to the transfer of an English trust to Jersey, for the purpose of avoiding United Kingdom tax, there being no law of trusts in Jersey.

G. CHARITABLE TRUSTS SITUATED ABROAD [50]

A quite separate group of problems arises with respect to the administration of charitable trusts situated abroad. Here, problems of administration, involving the proper control of trustees, sometimes present insoluble difficulties. A good illustration of this is afforded by *New* v. *Bonaker*.[51] A testator, domiciled in England, bequeathed North American stock to the President and Vice-President of the United States, and the Governor of Pennsylvania, upon trust to build a college in Pennsylvania where moral philosophy should be taught, and where a professor should be engaged to inculcate and advocate the natural rights of the black people of every clime and country until they should be restored to an equality in civil rights with their white brethren throughout the Union. The will was made in 1825, and the testator died in 1828, but there was a provision for accumulation of income, so that it was

47 [1961] Ch. 574.
48 (1880), 14 Ch.D. 310.
49 [1969] 1 Ch. 223.
50 See generally, Delany, " Charitable Trusts and the Conflict of Laws " (1961) 10 *International and Comparative Law Quarterly* 385.
51 (1867), L.R. 4 Eq. 655.

not until 1861 that proceedings were instituted. Prior to their institution, however, there had been correspondence with the President and Vice-President of the United States, and with the Governor of Pennsylvania, all of whom had declined the trust, on the ground that it was of doubtful utility, and that the fund was in any case inadequate. Unless the inadequacy is so great, however, as to amount to impossibility of performance, this is no ground for the court to refuse to give effect to a trust, nor will the fact that the named trustees disclaim bar its execution, since others should then be selected. Malins, V.-C., accepted both these propositions, but, somewhat optimistically, suggested [52] that the object of the promotion of civil equality between the blacks and whites in the United States " cannot be carried into effect, because the equality of the black people has already been substantially established throughout the Union." This, however, was not the sole ground of the decision. He took the refusal of the three officials named in the trust to be an indication that the trust was unacceptable in the United States, and, therefore, incapable of achievement. This seems to be a sound conclusion on the facts.

On the other hand, in *Re Robinson*,[53] the testator devised and bequeathed the residue of his property to the German Government for the benefit of German soldiers disabled in the First World War, with an alternative gift, if the first should be void, to General Smuts for the benefit of Boer soldiers disabled in the South African War. Here, the object being charitable, and the trustees named being willing to accept, the court held that there was no power to direct a scheme. In such cases, where the trustee is abroad, the practice was to hand over the fund, to be applied to the trusts of the will. Where, however, the trustee is in England, but the trust is to be administered abroad, the court will direct a scheme; and in *Re Colonial Bishoprics Fund, 1841* [54] the court directed the *cy-près* modification of a charitable scheme, where a general charitable intent had been shown, but the original object could no longer be achieved.

H. CAPACITY

Questions have sometimes arisen in the administration of trusts concerning the status and capacity of a party. Dicey and Morris, in *The Conflict of Laws*,[55] express one tenable view as follows—

> The existence, at any rate, of a status imposed by the law of a person's domicile ought in general to be recognised in other countries, though the courts of such countries may exercise their discretion in giving operation to the results of such status.

In particular, English courts have not normally given effect to a status, existing under foreign law, but not under English law, which is penal.

In so far as the law of trusts is concerned, such incapacity may be that of a settlor, a trustee or a beneficiary. In *Re Selot's Trust*,[56] the English court refused to give effect to Article 513 of the French Code, establishing the status

[52] L.R. 4 Eq. 660.
[53] [1931] 2 Ch. 122.
[54] [1935] Ch. 148.
[55] 9th ed., p. 229.
[56] [1902] 1 Ch. 488.

of prodigal in respect of a beneficiary, and in *Re Langley's Settlement Trusts*,[57] the English court refused to give effect to the declaration of incompetency of the Supreme Court of the State of California, made in respect of a settlor, who retained powers of withdrawal in respect of a fund settled by a settlement, the proper law of which was English law. In such cases, therefore, the English court applies English law.[58]

I. TAXATION

A difficult and complicated problem upon the effect of the rules of the conflict of laws upon tax legislation in respect of beneficial interests under trusts was decided in *Re Latham*.[59] By a Canadian settlement of 1931, the proper law of which was Canadian law, Canadian securities (situate in Canada) were settled, as to one-quarter, on trusts, after the death of the settlor and his wife, to revert to remainder of the fund. The remaining three-quarters, after the settlor's death, was to be divided into three equal parts for the settlor's three children. One of such parts was settled on the settlor's son, P on protective trusts, and after his death, equally for his children.

The settlor died in 1931, and his wife in 1950, both being domiciled in England. On the wife's death, estate duty became payable under the Finance Act 1894 on the one-fourth share in the fund in which the wife had an interest. In so far as the one-third share of this one-fourth part of the fund was concerned, which passed to P, duty was never paid. P died in 1955, domiciled in England, bequeathing his entire estate to R, his only child.

A deduction was claimed from the assets of the estate of P for duty on that estate for the amount of the estate duty which should have been paid by P on the death of the settlor's wife, and for interest on that sum for the period between her death and the death of P.

One of the several questions to be decided was whether the estate of P had a right to reimbursement against P's share in the trust fund established by the settlement of 1931. P himself, as a limited owner, would clearly have had such a right, as a limited owner under section 9 (6) of the Finance Act 1894, and Wilberforce, J., held that the right could also be exercised by the limited owner's executors. However, since the settlement was a Canadian settlement, it was not possible for English legislation, such as section 9 (6), to interfere with the rights created by such a settlement, and to confer on one of the beneficiaries a charge over trust property inconsistent with the rights of the beneficiaries under the proper law of the settlement. Accordingly, P's executors had no right to reimbursement against the capital of P's share in the trust fund under section 9 (6). However, assuming Canadian law to be the same as English law on this point, there was an equitable obligation under the general law applying to the settlement of property in succession, which entitled P and his executors to claim that such portion of the estate duty as represented the charge in respect of the capital of P's share in the trust fund should be paid out of capital, so that on this ground P's estate had a right to reimbursement.

[57] [1962] Ch. 541.
[58] See also *Re Waite's Settlement Trusts*, [1958] Ch. 100.
[59] [1962] Ch. 616.

J. TAXATION AND FOREIGN CHARITABLE TRUSTS

In *Camille and Henry Dreyfus Foundation Inc.* v. *Inland Revenue Commissioners* [60] the House of Lords decided that exemption from income tax, enjoyed by charities, is limited to a body of persons or a trust established in the United Kingdom for charitable purposes only and it excludes a body or trust established elsewhere.

[60] [1956] A.C. 39.

PART IV

TRUSTEE ACT 1925

[15 GEO. 5 CH. 19]

ARRANGEMENT OF SECTIONS

PART I

INVESTMENTS

PART II

GENERAL POWERS OF TRUSTEES AND PERSONAL REPRESENTATIVES

General Powers

427

Indemnities

Maintenance, Advancement and Protective Trusts

PART III

APPOINTMENT AND DISCHARGE OF TRUSTEES

PART IV

POWERS OF THE COURT

Appointment of new Trustees

Vesting Orders

TRUSTEE ACT 1925

[15 GEO. 5 CH. 19]

AN Act to consolidate certain enactments relating to trustees in England and
Wales   [9th April 1925]

BE it enacted by the King's most Excellent Majesty, by and with the advice
and consent of the Lords Spiritual and Temporal, and Commons, in this
present Parliament assembled, and by the authority of the same as follows—

PART I

INVESTMENTS

1. [*The whole of section 1 of the Trustee Act 1925 has been repealed and
replaced by the Trustee Investments Act 1961, which is reproduced in full at
pp. 469–486, post.*]

2. **Purchase at a premium of redeemable stocks; change of character of
investment.**—(1) A trustee may under the powers of this Act invest in any
of the securities mentioned or referred to in section one of this Act, notwithstanding that the same may be redeemable, and that the price exceeds the
redemption value.

[*The proviso is repealed by the Trustee Investments Act 1961.*]

(2) A trustee may retain until redemption any redeemable stock, fund, or security which may have been purchased in accordance with the powers of this Act, or any statute replaced by this Act.

References to statutes of the Republic of Ireland and Northern Ireland are preceded by the abbreviations R.I. and N.I. respectively.

R.I.: Trustee Act 1893, s. 2. N.I.: Trustee Act (Northern Ireland) 1958, s. 1.

3. **Discretion of trustees.** Every power conferred by the preceding sections shall be exercised according to the discretion of the trustee, but subject to any consent or direction required by the instrument, if any, creating the trust or by statute with respect to the investment of the trust funds.

R.I.: Trustee Act 1893, s. 3. N.I.: Trustee Act (Northern Ireland) 1958, s. 2.

4. **Power to retain investment which has ceased to be authorised.** A trustee shall not be liable for breach of trust by reason only of his continuing to hold an investment which has ceased to be an investment authorised by the trust instrument or by the general law.

R.I.: Trustee Act 1893 Amendment Act 1894, s. 4. N.I.: Trustee Act (Northern Ireland) 1958, s. 3.

5. **Enlargement of powers of investment.**—(1) A trustee having power to invest in real securities may invest and shall be deemed always to have had power to invest—

[*Section 5 (1) (a) is repealed by the Trustee Investments Act 1961.*]

(*b*) on any charge, or upon mortgage of any charge, made under the Improvement of Land Act, 1864.

(2) A trustee having power to invest in real securities may accept the security in the form of a charge by way of legal mortgage, and may, in exercise of the statutory power, convert an existing mortgage into a charge by way of legal mortgage.

(3) A trustee having power to invest in the mortgages or bonds of any railway company or of any other description of company may invest in the debenture stock of a railway company or such other company as aforesaid.

[*Subsections (4)–(6) of section 5 are repealed by the Trustee Investments Act 1961.*]

R.I.: Trustee Act 1893, s. 5. N.I.: Trustee Act (Northern Ireland) 1958, ss. 1, 4 and 5.

6. **Power to invest in land subject to drainage charges.** A trustee having power to invest in the purchase of land or on mortgage of land may invest in the purchase or on mortgage of any land notwithstanding the same is charged with a rent under the powers of the Landed Property Improvement (Ireland) Act, 1847, or by an absolute order made under the Improvement of Land Act, 1864, unless the terms of the trust expressly provide that the land to be purchased or taken in mortgage shall not be subject to any such prior charge.

[*Section 6 is given as amended by the Statute Law Revision Act 1963.*]

R.I.: Trustee Act 1893, s. 6. N.I.: Trustee Act (Northern Ireland) 1958, s. 6.

7. **Investment in bearer securities.**—(1) A trustee may, unless expressly prohibited by the instrument creating the trust, retain or invest in securities

payable to bearer which, if not so payable, would have been authorised investments:

Provided that securities to bearer retained or taken as an investment by a trustee (not being a trust corporation [1]) shall, until sold, be deposited by him for safe custody and collection of income with a banker or banking company.

A direction that investments shall be retained or made in the name of a trustee shall not, for the purposes of this subsection, be deemed to be such an express prohibition as aforesaid.

(2) A trustee shall not be responsible for any loss incurred by reason of such deposit, and any sum payable in respect of such deposit and collection shall be paid out of the income of the trust property.

R.I.: Trustee Act 1893, s. 7. N.I.: Trustee Act (Northern Ireland) 1958, s. 7.

8. **Loans and investments by trustees not chargeable as breaches of trust.** —(1) A trustee lending money on the security of any property on which he can properly lend shall not be chargeable with breach of trust by reason only of the proportion borne by the amount of the loan to the value of the property at the time when the loan was made, if it appears to the court—

(a) that in making the loan the trustee was acting upon a report as to the value of the property made by a person whom he reasonably believed to be an able practical surveyor or valuer instructed and employed independently of any owner of the property, whether such surveyor or valuer carried on business in the locality where the property is situate or elsewhere [2]; and

(b) that the amount of the loan does not exceed two third parts of the value of the property as stated in the report; and

(c) that the loan was made under the advice of the surveyor or valuer expressed in the report.[3]

(2) A trustee lending money on the security of any leasehold property shall not be chargeable with breach of trust only upon the ground that in making such a loan he dispensed either wholly or partly with the production or investigation of the lessor's title.[4]

(3) A trustee shall not be chargeable with breach of trust only upon the ground that in effecting the purchase, or in lending money upon the security, of any property he has accepted a shorter title than the title which a purchaser is, in the absence of a special contract, entitled to require, if in the opinion of the court the title accepted be such as a person acting with prudence and caution would have accepted.

---

[1] See s. 68 (18).

[2] The trustee must believe the surveyor or valuer to be able, whilst he must in fact be employed independently of the owner of the property (*Re Somerset*, [1894] 1 Ch. 231; *Re Dive*, [1909] 1 Ch. 328).

The trustee must use his judgment in selecting the surveyor or valuer. He may not leave the selection to his solicitor (*Re Walker* (1890), 59 L.J.Ch. 386, 391; *Fry* v. *Tapson* (1884), 28 Ch.D. 268). Whilst it is no longer necessary to select the surveyor from the locality, local knowledge may be material in determining ability (*Fry* v. *Tapson, supra*).

[3] The power to invest in real securities is a power to lend money on mortgage, and not a power to invest in the purchase of land (*Re Wakeman*, [1945] Ch. 177); but a trustee for sale of land, where some of the land is retained, may purchase land with the proceeds of sale (*Re Wellsted's Will Trusts*, [1949] Ch. 296).

[4] On the precautions to be taken in investing on the security of leaseholds, see *Re Salmon* (1889), 42 Ch.D. 351.

(4) This section applies to transfers of existing securities as well as to new securities and to investments made before as well as after the commencement of this Act.[5]

R.I.: Trustee Act 1893, s. 8. N.I.: Trustee Act (Northern Ireland) 1958, s. 8.

9. Liability for loss by reason of improper investment.—(1) Where a trustee improperly advances trust money on a mortgage security which would at the time of the investment be a proper investment in all respects for a smaller sum than is actually advanced thereon, the security shall be deemed an authorised investment for the smaller sum, and the trustee shall only be liable to make good the sum advanced in excess thereof with interest.[6]

(2) This section applies to investments made before as well as after the commencement of this Act.

R.I.: Trustee Act 1893, s. 9. N.I.: Trustee Act (Northern Ireland) 1958, s. 9.

10. Powers supplementary to powers of investment.—(1) Trustees lending money on the security of any property on which they can lawfully lend may contract that such money shall not be called in during any period not exceeding seven years from the time when the loan was made, provided interest be paid within a specified time not exceeding thirty days after every half-yearly or other day on which it becomes due, and provided there be no breach of any covenant by the mortgagor contained in the instrument of mortgage or charge for the maintenance and protection of the property.

(2) On a sale of land for an estate in fee simple or for a term having at least five hundred years to run by trustees or by a tenant for life or statutory owner, the trustees, or the tenant for life or statutory owner [7] on behalf of the trustees of the settlement, may, where the proceeds are liable to be invested, contract that the payment of any part, not exceeding two-thirds, of the purchase money shall be secured by a charge by way of legal mortgage or a mortgage by demise or sub-demise for a term of at least five hundred years (less a nominal reversion when by sub-demise), of the land sold, with or without the security of any other property, such charge or mortgage, if any buildings are comprised in the mortgage, to contain a covenant by the mortgagor to keep them insured against loss or damage by fire to the full value thereof.

The trustees shall not be bound to obtain any report as to the value of the land or other property to be comprised in such charge or mortgage, or any advice as to the making of the loan, and shall not be liable for any loss which may be incurred by reason only of the security being insufficient at the date of the charge or mortgage; and the trustees of the settlement shall be bound to give effect to such contract made by the tenant for life or statutory owner.

---

[5] S. 8 is a relieving section and should be liberally construed (*Re Solomon*, [1912] 1 Ch. 261, 271). See also *Re Stuart*, [1897] 2 Ch. 583, and *Palmer* v. *Emerson*, [1911] 1 Ch. 758, where it is pointed out that failure to fulfil the requirements of the section will not necessarily exclude the trustees from the operation of s. 61.

[6] On this section, see *Re Somerset*, [1894] 1 Ch. 231; *Re Turner*, [1897] 1 Ch. 536; *Shaw* v. *Cates*, [1909] 1 Ch. 389.

[7] *i.e.* a person having the powers of a tenant for life (Settled Land Act 1925, s. 117 (1) (xxvi)).

(3) Where any securities [8] of a company are subject to a trust, the trustees may concur in any scheme or arrangement—

(*a*) for the reconstruction of the company;

(*b*) for the sale of all or any part of the property and undertaking of the company to another company;

(*bb*) for the acquisition of the securities of the company, or of control thereof, by another company;

(*c*) for the amalgamation of the company with another company;

(*d*) for the release, modification, or variation of any rights, privileges or liabilities attached to the securities or any of them;

in like manner as if they were entitled to such securities beneficially, with power to accept any securities of any denomination or description of the reconstructed or purchasing or new company in lieu of or in exchange for all or any of the first-mentioned securities; and the trustees shall not be responsible for any loss occasioned by any act or thing so done in good faith, and may retain any securities so accepted as aforesaid for any period for which they could have properly retained the original securities.[9]

[*Section* 10 (3) (*bb*) *was added by the Trustee Investments Act* 1961, *s.* 9(1).]

(4) If any conditional or preferential right to subscribe for any securities in any company is offered to trustees in respect of any holding in such company, they may as to all or any of such securities, either exercise such right and apply capital money subject to the trust in payment of the consideration, or renounce such right, or assign for the best consideration that can be reasonably obtained the benefit of such right or the title thereto to any person including any beneficiary under the trust, without being responsible for any loss occasioned by any act or thing so done by them in good faith:

Provided that the consideration for any such assignment shall be held as capital money of the trust.

(5) The powers conferred by this section shall be exercisable subject to the consent of any person whose consent to a change of investment is required by law or by the instrument, if any, creating the trust.

(6) Where the loan referred to in subsection (1), or the sale referred to in subsection (2), of this section is made under the order of the court, the powers conferred by those subsections respectively shall apply only if and as far as the court may by order direct.

N.I.: Trustee Act (Northern Ireland) 1958, s. 10.

11. **Power to deposit money at bank and to pay calls.**—(1) Trustees may, pending the negotiation and preparation of any mortgage or charge, or during any other time while an investment is being sought for, pay any trust money into a bank to a deposit or other account, and all interest, if any, payable in respect thereof shall be applied as income.

(2) Trustees may apply capital money subject to a trust in payment of the calls on any shares subject to the same trust.

R.I.: Trustee Act 1893, s. 1, as substituted by the Trustee (Authorised Investments) Act 1958, s. 1. N.I.: Trustee Act (Northern Ireland) 1958, s. 11.

---

[8] Defined in s. 68 (13).

[9] The restrictive interpretation of this subsection contained in *Re Walker's Settlement*, [1935] Ch. 567 has been removed by s. 9 (1) of the Trustee Investments Act 1961.

PART II

GENERAL POWERS OF TRUSTEES AND PERSONAL REPRESENTATIVES

General Powers

12. **Power of trustees for sale to sell by auction, &c.**—(1) Where a trust for sale or a power of sale of property is vested in a trustee, he may sell or concur with any other person in selling all or any part of the property, either subject to prior charges or not, and either together or in lots, by public auction or by private contract, subject to any such conditions respecting title or evidence of title or other matter as the trustee thinks fit, with power to vary any contract for sale, and to buy in at any auction, or to rescind any contract for sale and to re-sell, without being answerable for any loss.[10]

(2) A trust or power to sell or dispose of land [11] includes a trust or power to sell or dispose of part thereof, whether the division is horizontal, vertical, or made in any other way.

(3) This section does not enable an express power to sell settled land to be exercised where the power is not vested in the tenant for life or statutory owner.

R.I.: Trustee Act 1893, s. 13. N.I.: Trustee Act (Northern Ireland) 1958, s. 12.

13. **Power to sell subject to depreciatory conditions.**—(1) No sale made by a trustee shall be impeached by any beneficiary upon the ground that any of the conditions subject to which the sale was made may have been unnecessarily depreciatory, unless it also appears that the consideration for the sale was thereby rendered inadequate.

(2) No sale made by a trustee shall, after the execution of the conveyance, be impeached as against the purchaser upon the ground that any of the conditions subject to which the sale was made may have been unnecessarily depreciatory, unless it appears that the purchaser was acting in collusion with the trustee at the time when the contract for sale was made.

(3) No purchaser, upon any sale made by a trustee, shall be at liberty to make any objection against the title upon any of the grounds aforesaid.

(4) This section applies to sales made before or after the commencement of this Act.

R.I.: Trustee Act 1893, s. 14. N.I.: Trustee Act (Northern Ireland) 1958, s. 13.

14. **Power of trustees to give receipts.**—(1) The receipt in writing of a trustee for any money, securities, or other personal property or effects payable, transferable, or deliverable to him under any trust or power shall be a sufficient discharge to the person paying, transferring, or delivering the same and shall effectually exonerate him from seeing to the application or being answerable for any loss or misapplication thereof.

---

[10] Thus, trustees may sell leaseholds in lots by a grant of an underlease with a nominal reversion (*Re Judd and Poland and Skelcher's Contract*, [1906] 1 Ch. 684). The trustees must sell to the maximum advantage of the beneficiaries, but they may adopt any usual mode of sale.

[11] As to what is land, see s. 68 (6).

(2) This section does not, except where the trustee is a trust corporation, enable a sole trustee to give a valid receipt for—

(*a*) the proceeds of sale or other capital money arising under a trust for sale of land;

(*b*) capital money arising under the Settled Land Act, 1925.[12]

[*Section* 14 (2) (*a*) *is given as amended by the Law of Property (Amendment) Act* 1926, *s*. 7 *and Sched.*]

(3) This section applies notwithstanding anything to the contrary in the instrument, if any, creating the trust.

R.I.: Trustee Act 1893, s. 20. N.I.: Trustee Act (Northern Ireland) 1958, s. 14.

15. **Power to compound liabilities.** A personal representative, or two or more trustees acting together, or, subject to the restrictions imposed in regard to receipts by a sole trustee not being a trust corporation, a sole acting trustee where by the instrument, if any, creating the trust, or by statute, a sole trustee is authorised to execute the trusts and powers reposed in him, may, if and as he or they think fit—

(*a*) accept any property, real or personal, before the time at which it is made transferable or payable; or

(*b*) sever and apportion any blended trust funds or property; or

(*c*) pay or allow any debt or claim on any evidence that he or they think sufficient; or

(*d*) accept any composition or any security, real or personal, for any debt or for any property, real or personal, claimed; or

(*e*) allow any time of payment of any debt; or

(*f*) compromise, compound, abandon, submit to arbitration, or otherwise settle any debt, account, claim, or thing whatever relating to the testator's or intestate's estate or to the trust [13];

and for any of those purposes may enter into, give, execute, and do such agreements, instruments of composition or arrangement, releases, and other things as to him or them seem expedient, without being responsible for any loss occasioned by any act or thing so done by him or them in good faith.

R.I.: Trustee Act 1893, s. 21. N.I.: Trustee Act (Northern Ireland) 1958, s. 15.

16. **Power to raise money by sale, mortgage, &c.**—(1) Where trustees are authorised by the instrument, if any, creating the trust or by law to pay or apply capital money subject to the trust for any purpose or in any manner, they shall have and shall be deemed always to have had power to raise the money required by sale, conversion, calling in, or mortgage of all or any part of the trust property for the time being in possession.

---

[12] A sole personal representative can, however, give a valid receipt (Administration of Estates Act 1925, s. 2 (1)).

[13] For an example of such a compromise, see *Re Ezekiel's Settlement Trusts*, [1942] Ch. 230. A judicial trustee has the power to compromise with a debtor (*Re Ridsdel*, [1947] Ch. 597). The Public Trustee has no more power than an ordinary trustee to compromise with himself (*Re New Haw Estate Trusts* (1912), 107 L.T. 191). Furthermore, a trustee must act in good faith, and without negligence (*Re Greenwood* (1911), 105 L.T. 509).

(2) This section applies notwithstanding anything to the contrary contained in the instrument, if any, creating the trust, but does not apply to trustees of property held for charitable purposes, or to trustees of a settlement for the purposes of the Settled Land Act, 1925, not being also the statutory owners.

N.I.: Trustee Act (Northern Ireland) 1958, s. 16.

17. **Protection to purchasers and mortgagees dealing with trustees.** No purchaser or mortgagee, paying or advancing money on a sale or mortgage purporting to be made under any trust or power vested in trustees, shall be concerned to see that such money is wanted, or that no more than is wanted is raised, or otherwise as to the application thereof.

N.I.: Trustee Act (Northern Ireland) 1958, s. 17.

18. **Devolution of powers or trusts.**—(1) Where a power or trust is given to or imposed on two or more trustees jointly, the same may be exercised or performed by the survivors or survivor of them for the time being.

(2) Until the appointment of new trustees, the personal representatives or representative for the time being of a sole trustee, or, where there were two or more trustees of the last surviving or continuing trustee, shall be capable of exercising or performing any power or trust which was given to, or capable of being exercised by, the sole or last surviving or continuing trustee, or other the trustees or trustee for the time being of the trust.

(3) This section takes effect subject to the restrictions imposed in regard to receipts by a sole trustee, not being a trust corporation.

(4) In this section " personal representative " does not include an executor who has renounced or has not proved.

R.I.: Trustee Act 1893, s. 22, and Conveyancing Act 1911, s. 8. N.I.: Trustee Act (Northern Ireland) 1958, s. 18.

19. **Power to insure.**—(1) A trustee may insure against loss or damage by fire any building or other insurable property to any amount, including the amount of any insurance already on foot, not exceeding three fourth parts of the full value of the building or property, and pay the premiums for such insurance out of the income thereof or out of the income of any other property subject to the same trusts without obtaining the consent of any person who may be entitled wholly or partly to such income.[14]

(2) This section does not apply to any building or property which a trustee is bound forthwith to convey absolutely to any beneficiary upon being requested to do so.

R.I.: Trustee Act 1893, s. 18. N.I.: Trustee Act (Northern Ireland) 1958, s. 19.

20. **Application of insurance money where policy kept up under any trust, power or obligation.**—(1) Money receivable by trustees or any beneficiary under a policy of insurance against the loss or damage of any property subject to a trust or to a settlement within the meaning of the Settled Land Act, 1925, whether by fire or otherwise, shall, where the policy has been kept up under

---

[14] If the trustees, after consideration, decide not to insure, they are not liable if the property is destroyed by fire (*Re McEacharn* (1911), 103 L.T. 900).
On the scope of the section, see *Re Earl of Egmont's Trusts*, [1908] 1 Ch. 821.

any trust in that behalf or under any power statutory or otherwise, or in performance of any covenant or of any obligation statutory or otherwise, or by a tenant for life impeachable for waste, be capital money for the purposes of the trust or settlement, as the case may be.

(2) If any such money is receivable by any person, other than the trustees of the trust or settlement, that person shall use his best endeavours to recover and receive the money, and shall pay the net residue thereof, after discharging any costs of recovering and receiving it, to the trustees of the trust or settlement, or, if there are no trustees capable of giving a discharge therefor, into court.

(3) Any such money—

(a) if it was receivable in respect of settled land within the meaning of the Settled Land Act, 1925, or any building or works thereon, shall be deemed to be capital money arising under that Act from the settled land, and shall be invested or applied by the trustees, or, if in court, under the direction of the court, accordingly;

(b) if it was receivable in respect of personal chattels settled as heirlooms within the meaning of the Settled Land Act, 1925, shall be deemed to be capital money arising under that Act, and shall be applicable by the trustees, or, if in court, under the direction of the court, in like manner as provided by that Act with respect to money arising by a sale of chattels settled as heirlooms as aforesaid;

(c) if it was receivable in respect of property held upon trust for sale, shall be held upon the trusts and subject to the powers and provisions applicable to money arising by a sale under such trust;

(d) in any other case, shall be held upon trusts corresponding as nearly as may be with the trusts affecting the property in respect of which it was payable.

(4) Such money, or any part thereof, may also be applied by the trustees, or, if in court, under the direction of the court, in rebuilding, reinstating, replacing, or repairing the property lost or damaged, but any such application by the trustees shall be subject to the consent of any person whose consent is required by the instrument, if any, creating the trust to the investment of money subject to the trust, and, in the case of money which is deemed to be capital money arising under the Settled Land Act, 1925, be subject to the provisions of that Act with respect to the application of capital money by the trustees of the settlement.

(5) Nothing contained in this section prejudices or affects the right of any person to require any such money or any part thereof to be applied in rebuilding, reinstating, or repairing the property lost or damaged, or the rights of any mortgagee, lessor, or lessee, whether under any statute or otherwise.

(6) This section applies to policies effected either before or after the commencement of this Act, but only to money received after such commencement.

N.I.: Trustee Act (Northern Ireland) 1958, s. 20.

21. Deposit of documents for safe custody. Trustees may deposit any documents held by them relating to the trust, or to the trust property, with any banker or banking company or any other company whose business includes the undertaking of the safe custody of documents, and any sum payable in respect of such deposit shall be paid out of the income of the trust property.

N.I.: Trustee Act (Northern Ireland) 1958, s. 22.

22. Reversionary interests, valuations, and audit.—(1) Where trust property includes any share or interest in property not vested in the trustees, or the proceeds of the sale of any such property, or any other thing in action, the trustees on the same falling into possession, or becoming payable or transferable may—

> (*a*) agree or ascertain the amount or value thereof or any part thereof in such manner as they may think fit;
>
> (*b*) accept in or towards satisfaction thereof, at the market or current value, or upon any valuation or estimate of value which they may think fit, any authorised investments;
>
> (*c*) allow any deductions for duties, costs, charges and expenses which they may think proper or reasonable;
>
> (*d*) execute any release in respect of the premises so as effectually to discharge all accountable parties from all liability in respect of any matters coming within the scope of such release;

without being responsible in any such case for any loss occasioned by any act or thing so done by them in good faith.

(2) The trustees shall not be under any obligation and shall not be chargeable with any breach of trust by reason of any omission—

> (*a*) to place any distringas notice or apply for any stop or other like order upon any securities or other property out of or on which such share or interest or other thing in action as aforesaid is derived, payable or charged; or
>
> (*b*) to take any proceedings on account of any act, default, or neglect on the part of the persons in whom such securities or other property or any of them or any part thereof are for the time being, or had at any time been, vested [15];

unless and until required in writing so to do by some person, or the guardian of some person, beneficially interested under the trust, and unless also due provision is made to their satisfaction for payment of the costs of any proceedings required to be taken:

Provided that nothing in this subsection shall relieve the trustees of the obligation to get in and obtain payment or transfer of such share or interest or other thing in action on the same falling into possession.

(3) Trustees may, for the purpose of giving effect to the trust, or any of the provisions of the instrument, if any, creating the trust or of any statute, from time to time (by duly qualified agents) ascertain and fix the value of any trust property in such manner as they think proper, and any valuation so made in good faith shall be binding upon all persons interested under the trust.

---

[15] If the trustees genuinely believe that the proceedings will be fruitless, they are excused the necessity of taking proceedings to enforce payment (*Clack* v. *Holland* (1854), 19 Beav. 262, 271; *Re Brogden* (1888), 38 Ch.D. 546).

(4) Trustees may, in their absolute discretion, from time to time, but not more than once in every three years unless the nature of the trust or any special dealings with the trust property make a more frequent exercise of the right reasonable, cause the accounts of the trust property to be examined or audited by an independent accountant, and shall, for that purpose, produce such vouchers and give such information to him as he may require; and the cost of such examination or audit, including the fee of the auditor, shall be paid out of the capital or income of the trust property, or partly in one way and partly in the other, as the trustees, in their absolute discretion, think fit, but, in default of any direction by the trustees to the contrary in any special case, costs attributable to capital shall be borne by capital and those attributable to income by income.

N.I.: Trustee Act (Northern Ireland) 1958, s. 23.

23. **Power to employ agents.**—(1) Trustees or personal representatives may, instead of acting personally, employ and pay an agent, whether a solicitor, banker, stockbroker, or other person, to transact any business or do any act required to be transacted or done in the execution of the trust, or the administration of the testator's or intestate's estate, including the receipt and payment of money, and shall be entitled to be allowed and paid all charges and expenses so incurred, and shall not be responsible for the default of any such agent if employed in good faith.

(2) Trustees or personal representatives may appoint any person to act as their agent or attorney for the purpose of selling, converting, collecting, getting in, and executing and perfecting insurances of, or managing or cultivating, or otherwise administering any property, real or personal, moveable or immoveable, subject to the trust or forming part of the testator's or intestate's estate, in any place outside the United Kingdom or executing or exercising any discretion or trust or power vested in them in relation to any such property, with such ancillary powers, and with and subject to such provisions and restrictions as they may think fit, including a power to appoint substitutes, and shall not, by reason only of their having made such appointment, be responsible for any loss arising thereby.

(3) Without prejudice to such general power of appointing agents as aforesaid—

(a) A trustee may appoint a solicitor to be his agent to receive and give a discharge for any money or valuable consideration or property receivable by the trustee under the trust, by permitting the solicitor to have the custody of, and to produce, a deed having in the body thereof or endorsed thereon a receipt for such money or valuable consideration or property, the deed being executed, or the endorsed receipt being signed, by the person entitled to give a receipt for that consideration;

(b) A trustee shall not be chargeable with breach of trust by reason only of his having made or concurred in making any such appointment; and the production of any such deed by the solicitor shall have the same statutory validity and effect as if the person appointing the solicitor had not been a trustee;

(c) A trustee may appoint a banker or solicitor to be his agent to receive and to give a discharge for any money payable to the trustee under or by virtue of a policy of insurance, by permitting the banker or solicitor to have the custody of and to produce the policy of insurance with a receipt signed by the trustee, and a trustee shall not be chargeable with a breach of trust by reason only of his having made or concurred in making any such appointment:

Provided that nothing in this subsection shall exempt a trustee from any liability which he would have incurred if this Act and any enactment replaced by this Act had not been passed, in case he permits any such money, valuable consideration, or property to remain in the hands or under the control of the banker or solicitor for a period longer than is reasonably necessary to enable the banker or solicitor, as the case may be, to pay or transfer the same to the trustee.

This subsection applies whether the money or valuable consideration or property was or is received before or after the commencement of this Act.[16]

R.I.: Trustee Act 1893, s. 17. N.I.: Trustee Act (Northern Ireland) 1958, s. 24.

24. Power to concur with others. Where an undivided share in the proceeds of sale of land directed to be sold, or in any other property, is subject to a trust, or forms part of the estate of a testator or intestate, the trustees or personal representatives may (without prejudice to the trust for sale affecting the entirety of the land and the powers of the trustees for sale in reference thereto) execute or exercise any trust or power vested in them in relation to such share in conjunction with the persons entitled to or having power in that behalf over the other share or shares, and notwithstanding that any one or more of the trustees or personal representatives may be entitled to or interested in any such other share, either in his or their own right or in a fiduciary capacity.

N.I.: Trustee Act (Northern Ireland) 1958, s. 25.

25. Power to delegate trusts.—(1) Notwithstanding any rule of law or equity to the contrary, a trustee may, by power of attorney,[17] delegate for a period not exceeding twelve months the execution or exercise of all or any of the trusts, powers and discretions vested in him as trustee, either alone or jointly with any other person or persons.

(2) The persons who may be donees of a power of attorney under this section include a trust corporation but not (unless a trust corporation) the only other co-trustee of the donor of the power.

(3) An instrument creating a power of attorney under this section shall be attested by at least one witness.

(4) Before or within seven days after giving a power of attorney under this section the donor shall give written notice thereof (specifying the date on which the power comes into operation and its duration, the donee of the

---

[16] On the relation of s. 23 to the earlier law, see Re Vickery, [1931] 1 Ch. 572 (Cases, p. 304); Green v. Whitehead, [1930] 1 Ch. 38; Re Lucking's Will Trusts, [1968] 1 W.L.R. 866.
[17] A statutory declaration by the donor must be filed with each power of attorney: Practice Direction, [1960] 1 W.L.R. 355.

power, the reason why the power is given and, where some only are delegated, the trusts, powers and discretions delegated) to—

(*a*) each person (other than himself), if any, who under any instrument creating the trust has power (whether alone or jointly) to appoint a new trustee; and

(*b*) each of the other trustees, if any;

but failure to comply with this subsection shall not, in favour of a person dealing with the donee of the power, invalidate any act done or instrument executed by the donee.

(5) The donor of a power of attorney given under this section shall be liable for the acts or defaults of the donee in the same manner as if they were the acts or defaults of the donor.

(6) For the purpose of executing or exercising the trusts or powers delegated to him, the donee may exercise any of the powers conferred on the donor as trustee by statute or by the instrument creating the trust, including power, for the purpose of the transfer of any inscribed stock, himself to delegate to an attorney power to transfer but not including the power of delegation conferred by this section.

(7) The fact that it appears from any power of attorney given under this section, or from any evidence required for the purposes of any such power of attorney or otherwise, that in dealing with any stock the donee of the power is acting in the execution of a trust shall not be deemed for any purpose to affect any person in whose books the stock is inscribed or registered with any notice of the trust.

(8) This section applies to a personal representative, tenant for life and statutory owner as it applies to a trustee except that subsection (4) shall apply as if it required the notice there mentioned to be given—

(*a*) in the case of a personal representative, to each of the other personal representatives, if any, except an executor who has renounced probate;

(*b*) in the case of a tenant for life, to the trustees of the settlement and to each person, if any, who together with the person giving the notice constitutes the tenant for life;

(*c*) in the case of a statutory owner, to each of the persons, if any, who together with the person giving the notice constitute the statutory owner and, in the case of a statutory owner by virtue of section 23 (1) (*a*) of the Settled Land Act 1925, to the trustees of the settlement.

[*Section 25 is given as amended by the Powers of Attorney Act 1971, s. 9 (1).*]
N.I.: Trustee Act (Northern Ireland) 1958, s. 26.

Indemnities

26. **Protection against liability in respect of rents and covenants.**—(1) Where a personal representative or trustee liable as such [18] for—

(*a*) any rent, covenant, or agreement reserved by or contained in any lease; or

(*b*) any rent, covenant or agreement payable under or contained in any grant made in consideration of a rentcharge; or

---

[18] For an illustration of this, see *Whitehead* v. *Palmer*, [1908] 1 K.B. 151.

(c) any indemnity given in respect of any rent, covenant or agreement referred to in either of the foregoing paragraphs;

satisfies all liabilities under the lease or grant which may have accrued and been claimed, up to the date of the conveyance hereinafter mentioned, and, where necessary, sets apart a sufficient fund to answer any future claim that may be made in respect of any fixed and ascertained sum which the lessee or grantee agreed to lay out on the property demised or granted, although the period for laying out the same may not have arrived, then and in any such case the personal representative or trustee may convey the property demised or granted to a purchaser, legatee, devisee, or other person entitled to call for a conveyance and thereafter—

(i) he may distribute the residuary real and personal estate of the deceased testator or intestate, or, as the case may be, the trust estate (other than the fund, if any, set apart as aforesaid) to or amongst the persons entitled thereto, without appropriating any part, or any further part, as the case may be, of the estate of the deceased or of the trust estate to meet any future liability under the said lease or grant;

(ii) notwithstanding such distribution, he shall not be personally liable in respect of any subsequent claim under the said lease or grant.

[*Section* 26 (1) *is given as amended by the Law of Property (Amendment) Act* 1926, *s.* 7 *and Sched.*]

(2) This section operates without prejudice to the right of the lessor or grantor, or the persons deriving title under the lessor or grantor, to follow the assets of the deceased or the trust property into the hands of the persons amongst whom the same may have been respectively distributed, and applies notwithstanding anything to the contrary in the will or other instrument, if any, creating the trust.

(3) In this section " lease " includes an underlease and an agreement for a lease or underlease and any instrument giving any such indemnity as aforesaid or varying the liabilities under the lease; " grant " applies to a grant whether the rent is created by limitation, grant, reservation, or otherwise, and includes an agreement for a grant and any instrument giving any such indemnity as aforesaid or varying the liabilities under the grant; " lessee " and " grantee " include persons respectively deriving title under them.

R.I.: Law of Property Amendment Act 1859, ss. 27, 28. N.I.: Trustee Act (Northern Ireland) 1958, s. 27.

27. Protection by means of advertisements.—(1) With a view to the conveyance to or distribution among the persons entitled to any real or personal property, the trustees of a settlement or of a disposition on trust for sale or personal representatives, may give notice by advertisement in the Gazette, and in a newspaper circulating in the district in which the land is situated, and such other like notices, including notices elsewhere than in England and Wales, as would, in any special case, have been directed by a court of competent jurisdiction in an action for administration, of their intention to make such conveyance or distribution as aforesaid, and requiring any person interested to send to the trustees or personal representatives within the time, not being less than two months, fixed in the notice or, where more than one notice is given, in the last of the notices, particulars of his claim in respect of the property or any part thereof to which the notice relates.[19]

[*Section* 27 (1) *is given as amended by the Law of Property* (*Amendment*) *Act* 1926, *s.* 7 *and Sched.*]

(2) At the expiration of the time fixed by the notice the trustees or personal representatives may convey or distribute the property or any part thereof to which the notice relates, to or among the persons entitled thereto, having regard only to the claims, whether formal or not, of which the trustees or personal representatives then had notice and shall not, as respects the property so conveyed or distributed, be liable to any person of whose claim the trustees or personal representatives have not had notice at the time of conveyance or distribution; but nothing in this section—

(*a*) prejudices the right of any person to follow the property, or any property representing the same, into the hands of any person, other than a purchaser, who may have received it; or

(*b*) frees the trustees or personal representatives from any obligation to make searches or obtain official certificates of search similar to those which an intending purchaser would be advised to make or obtain.

(3) This section applies notwithstanding anything to the contrary in the will or other instrument, if any, creating the trust.

R.I.: Law of Property Amendment Act 1859, s. 29. N.I.: Trustee Act (Northern Ireland) 1958, s. 28.

28. **Protection in regard to notice.** A trustee or personal representative acting for the purposes of more than one trust or estate shall not, in the absence of fraud, be affected by notice of any instrument, matter, fact or thing in relation to any particular trust or estate if he has obtained notice thereof merely by reason of his acting or having acted for the purposes of another trust or estate.

N.I.: Trustee Act (Northern Ireland) 1958, s. 29.

29. [*Section* 29 *was repealed by the Powers of Attorney Act* 1971, *s.* 11 (2) *and Sched.* 2.]

R.I.: Trustee Act 1893, s. 23.

30. **Implied indemnity of trustees.**—(1) A trustee [20] shall be chargeable only for money and securities actually received by him notwithstanding his signing any receipt for the sake of conformity, and shall be answerable and accountable only for his own acts, receipts, neglects, or defaults, and not for those of

---

[19] Advertisement should be made as soon as possible (*Re Kay*, [1897] 2 Ch. 518). A trustee who has complied with the section enjoys the same protection as if he had administered the estate under an order of the Court (*Re Frewen* (1889), 60 L.T. 953). Where a trustee already has notice of a claim by a creditor, the claim is not barred simply because the creditor neglects to reply promptly to the advertisement (*Re Beatty's Estate* (1889), 29 L.R. Ir. 290, 296). Nevertheless, a mere reply to an advertisement does not preserve the claim from the operation of the Statutes of Limitation (*Re Stephens* (1889), 43 Ch.D. 39). See also *Re Holden*, [1935] W.N. 52, and *Re Letherbrow*, [1935] W.N. 34 and 48.

There is no need to advertise for claims by illegitimate children or persons claiming through them: Family Reform Act 1969, s. 17.

[20] A liquidator of a company is not a trustee for the purposes of this section (*Re Flower and the Metropolitan Board of Works* (1884), 27 Ch.D. 592).

any other trustee, nor for any banker, broker, or other person with whom any trust money or securities may be deposited, nor for the insufficiency or deficiency of any securities, nor for any loss, unless the same happens through his own wilful default.[21]

(2) A trustee may reimburse himself or pay or discharge out of the trust premises all expenses incurred in or about the execution of the trusts or powers.

R.I.: Trustee Act 1893, s. 24. N.I.: Trustee Act (Northern Ireland) 1958, s. 31.

Maintenance, Advancement and Protective Trusts

31. **Power to apply income for maintenance and to accumulate surplus income during a minority.**—(1) Where any property is held by trustees in trust for any person for any interest whatsoever, whether vested or contingent,[22] then, subject to any prior interests or charges affecting that property [23]—

(i) during the infancy of any such person, if his interest so long continues, the trustees may, at their sole discretion,[24] pay to his parent or guardian, if any, or otherwise apply for or towards his maintenance, education, or benefit,[25] the whole or such part, if any, of the income of that property as may, in all the circumstances, be reasonable, whether or not there is—

(a) any other fund applicable to the same purpose; or

(b) any person bound by law to provide for his maintenance or education; and

(ii) if such person on attaining the age of eighteen years has not a vested interest in such income,[26] the trustees shall thenceforth pay the income of that property and of any accretion thereto under subsection (2) of this section to him, until he either attains a vested interest therein or dies, or until failure of his interest:

Provided that, in deciding whether the whole or any part of the income of the property is during a minority to be paid or applied for the purposes aforesaid, the trustees shall have regard to the age of the infant and his requirements and generally to the circumstances of the case, and in particular to what other income, if any, is applicable for the same purposes; and where trustees have notice that the income of more than one fund is applicable for those purposes, then, so far as practicable, unless the entire income of the

---

[21] As to what constitutes " wilful default," see *Re City Equitable Fire Insurance Co. Ltd.*, [1925] Ch. 407, 434, 525, and *Re Lucking's Will Trusts*, [1968] 1 W.L.R. 866.

[22] A gift may still be contingent, even though it is coupled with an express provision for the " advancement and education " of the beneficiary (*Re Rogers*, [1944] Ch. 297).

[23] Thus a remainderman cannot be maintained without the tenant for life's consent (*Re Alford* (1886), 32 Ch.D. 383 ; *Re Reade-Revell*, [1930] 1 Ch. 52, considered and distinguished in *Re Leng*, [1938] Ch. 821).

[24] Whilst payments are at the discretion of the trustee the discretion must nevertheless be exercised (*Wilson* v. *Turner* (1883), 22 Ch.D. 521). If the trustee exercises his discretion in good faith, the court will not interfere (*Re Lofthouse* (1885), 29 Ch.D. 921 ; *Re Bryant*, [1894] 1 Ch. 324).

[25] Payment of the beneficiary's debts *may* be a " benefit " (*Lowther* v. *Bentinck* (1874), L.R. 19 Eq. 166, but this was an exceptional case, *Luard* v. *Pease* (1853), 22 L.J.Ch. 1069; *Re Price* (1887), 34 Ch.D. 603).

[26] In *Re Turner's Will Trusts*, [1937] Ch. 15 (followed in *Re Watt's Will Trusts*, [1936] 2 All E.R. 1555) the Court of Appeal held that this discretion may be varied by a clause in the trust instrument (overruling *Re Spencer*, [1935] Ch. 533 and *Re Ricarde-Seaver's Will Trusts*, [1936] 1 All E.R. 580). See also *Re Ransome*, [1957] Ch. 348.

funds is paid or applied as aforesaid or the court otherwise directs, a proportionate part only of the income of each fund shall be so paid or applied.

(2) During the infancy of any such person, if his interest so long continues, the trustees shall accumulate all the residue of that income in the way of compound interest by investing the same and the resulting income thereof from time to time in authorised investments, and shall hold those accumulations as follows: —

(i) If any such person—

(a) attains the age of eighteen years, or marries under that age, and his interest in such income during his infancy or until his marriage is a vested interest [27]; or

(b) on attaining the age of eighteen years or on marriage under that age becomes entitled to the property from which such income arose in fee simple, absolute or determinable, or absolutely, or for an entailed interest; the trustees shall hold the accumulations in trust for such person absolutely, but without prejudice to any provision with respect thereto contained in any settlement by him made under any statutory powers during his infancy, and so that the receipt of such person after marriage, and though still an infant, shall be a good discharge; and

(ii) In any other case the trustees shall, notwithstanding that such person had a vested interest in such income, hold the accumulations as an accretion to the capital of the property from which such accumulations arose, and as one fund with such capital for all purposes, and so that, if such property is settled land, such accumulations shall be held upon the same trusts as if the same were capital money arising therefrom;

but the trustees may, at any time during the infancy of such person if his interest so long continues, apply those accumulations, or any part thereof, as if they were income arising in the then current year.[28]

(3) This section applies in the case of a contingent interest only if the limitation or trust carries the intermediate income of the property, but it applies to a future or contingent legacy by the parent of, or a person standing in loco parentis to, the legatee, if and for such period as, under the general law, the legacy carries interest for the maintenance of the legatee, and in any such case as last aforesaid the rate of interest shall (if the income available is sufficient, and subject to any rules of court to the contrary) be five pounds per centum per annum.[29]

(4) This section applies to a vested annuity in like manner as if the annuity were the income of property held by trustees in trust to pay the income thereof

---

[27] As to the distinction between a vested interest subject to divesting and a contingent interest, see *Re Mallinson Consolidated Trusts*, [1974] 2 All E.R. 530.

[28] For the application of this subsection where these are contingent gifts to a fluctuating class of infants, see *Re King*, [1928] Ch. 330; *Re Joel's Will Trusts*, [1967] Ch. 14; *Re Sharp's Settlement Trusts*, [1973] Ch. 331.

[29] As to what gifts carry intermediate income, see Law of Property Act 1925, s. 175; *Re Abrahams*, [1911] 1 Ch. 108; *Re Raine*, [1929] 1 Ch. 716; and *Re Jones*, [1932] 1 Ch. 642. *Re Selby-Walker*, [1949] 2 All E.R. 178; *Re Gillett's Will Trusts*, [1950] Ch. 102; *Re Crossley's Settlement Trusts*, [1955] Ch. 627; *Re McGeorge*, [1963] Ch. 544 (Cases, p. 325); *Re Geering*, [1964] Ch. 136; *Re Nash's Will Trusts*, [1965] 1 W.L.R. 221.

An express trust for accumulation excludes this section (*Re Reade-Revell*, [1930] 1 Ch. 52; *Re Stapleton*, [1946] 1 All E.R. 323), even though the direction is invalid under s. 164 of the Law of Property Act 1925 (*Re Erskine's Settlement Trusts*, [1971] 1 W.L.R. 162; but not an implied trust for accumulation (*Re Leng*, [1938] Ch. 821)).

to the annuitant for the same period for which the annuity is payable, save that in any case accumulations made during the infancy of the annuitant shall be held in trust for the annuitant or his personal representatives absolutely.

(5) This section does not apply where the instrument, if any, under which the interest arises came into operation before the commencement of this Act.

[*The age of eighteen was substituted for the age of twenty-one in subss. (1) and (2) by the Family Law Reform Act 1969, s. 1 (3) and Sched. 1.*]

R.I.: Conveyancing Act 1881, ss. 42, 43. N.I.: Trustee Act (Northern Ireland) 1958, s. 32.

32. **Power of advancement.**—(1) Trustees may at any time or times pay or apply any capital money subject to a trust, for the advancement [30] or benefit, in such manner as they may, in their absolute discretion, think fit, of any person entitled to the capital of the trust property or of any share thereof, whether absolutely or contingently on his attaining any specified age or on the occurrence of any other event, or subject to a gift over on his death under any specified age or on the occurrence of any other event, and whether in possession or in remainder or reversion, and such payment or application may be made notwithstanding that the interest of such person is liable to be defeated by the exercise of a power of appointment or revocation, or to be diminished by the increase of the class to which he belongs:
Provided that—

(*a*) the money so paid or applied for the advancement or benefit of any person shall not exceed altogether in amount one-half of the presumptive or vested share or interest of that person in the trust property; and

(*b*) if that person is or becomes absolutely and indefeasibly entitled to a share in the trust property the money so paid or applied shall be brought into account as part of such share; and

(*c*) no such payment or application shall be made so as to prejudice any person entitled to any prior life or other interest, whether vested or contingent, in the money paid or applied unless such person is in existence and of full age and consents in writing to such payment or application. [31]

(2) This section applies only where the trust property consists of money or securities or of property held upon trust for sale [32] calling in and conversion, and such money or securities, or the proceeds of such sale calling in and conversion are not by statute or in equity considered as land, or applicable as capital money for the purposes of the Settled Land Act, 1925.

(3) This section does not apply to trusts constituted or created before the commencement of this Act. [33]

N.I.: Trustee Act (Northern Ireland) 1958 s. 33.

---

[30] As to what constitutes an advancement, see *Taylor* v. *Taylor* (1875), L.R. 20 Eq. 155; *Boyd* v. *Boyd* (1867), L.R. 4 Eq. 305; *Roper-Curzon* v. *Roper-Curzon* (1871), L.R. 11 Eq. 452; *Re Blockley* (1885), 29 Ch.D. 250; *Re Mead* (1918), 88 L.J.Ch. 86. On this, see *Re Stimpson's Trusts*, [1931] 2 Ch. 77; *Re Garrett*, [1934] Ch. 477; *Re Craven's Estate (No. 2)*, [1937] Ch. 431; and *Re Gourju's Will Trusts*, [1943] Ch. 24. On the meaning of " benefit," see *Re Moxon's Will Trusts*, [1958] 1 W.L.R. 165. An advancement may include a gift to charity: *Re Clore's Settlement Trusts*, [1966] 1 W.L.R. 955.

[31] A consent by a protected life tenant does not involve a forfeiture of his interest: *Re Shaw's Settlement*, [1951] Ch. 833.

[32] On which, see *Re Stimpson's Trusts*, [1931] 2 Ch. 77.

[33] *Re Batty*, [1952] Ch. 280. But it applies to wills made before 1926, but coming into operation after 1925: *Re Taylor's Will Trusts* (1950), 66 T.L.R. (Pt. 2) 507; *Re Bransbury*,

33. **Protective trusts.**—(1) Where any income, including an annuity or other periodical income payment, is directed to be held on protective trusts [34] for the benefit of any person (in this section called " the principal beneficiary ") for the period of his life or for any less period, then, during that period (in this section called the " trust period ") the said income shall, without prejudice to any prior interest, be held on the following trusts, namely—

(i) Upon trust for the principal beneficiary during the trust period or until he, whether before or after the termination of any prior interest, does or attempts to do or suffers any act or thing, or until any event happens, other than an advance [35] under any statutory or express power, whereby, if the said income were payable during the trust period to the principal beneficiary absolutely during that period, he would be deprived of the right to receive the same or any part thereof, in any of which cases, as well as on the termination of the trust period, whichever first happens, this trust of the said income shall fail or determine;

(ii) If the trust aforesaid fails or determines during the subsistence of the trust period, then, during the residue of that period, the said income shall be held upon trust for the application thereof for the maintenance or support, or otherwise for the benefit, of all or any one or more exclusively of the other or others of the following persons (that is to say)—

(a) the principal beneficiary and his or her wife or husband, if any, and his or her children [36] or more remote issue, if any [37]; or
(b) if there is no wife or husband or issue of the principal beneficiary in existence, the principal beneficiary and the persons who would, if he

---

[1954] 1 W.L.R. 496. As to the duty of a trustee in making an advancement, see *Re Pauling's Settlement Trusts*, [1964] Ch. 303. For advancements by way of resettlement, see *Pilkington* v. *Inland Revenue Commissioners*, [1964] A.C. 612 (Cases, p. 336). For the effect of an express incorporation of the statutory powers of maintenance and advancement in a trust for accumulation, followed by a class gift to grandchildren who should attain the age of 21 or marry, see *Re Henderson's Trusts*, [1969] 1 W.L.R. 651, in which the Court of Appeal considered its earlier decision in *Re Deloitte*, [1919] 1 Ch. 209.

[34] Where this phrase is used, s. 33 is regarded as being incorporated (*Re Isaacs* (1948), 92 S.J. 336).

[35] In *Re Wittke*, [1944] Ch. 166, the beneficiary under the protective trust and her husband lived in France during the war, so becoming " enemies " within the Trading with the Enemy Act 1939. This resulted in a forfeiture of the life interest, and future payments must be made to the Custodian of Enemy Property. In *Re Furness*, [1944] 1 All E.R. 575, the forfeiture clause was in a different form, and forfeiture was thereby avoided. See also *Re Pozot's Settlement Trusts*, [1952] Ch. 427.

For a forfeiture on the appointment of a receiver in lunacy, see *Re Custance's Settlements*, [1946] Ch. 42, but this decision was overruled by *Re Westby's Settlement*, [1950] Ch. 296, and see now Law Reform (Miscellaneous Provisions) Act 1949, s. 8. For a forfeiture on sequestration of the tenant for life's property, see *Re Baring's Settlement Trusts*, [1940] Ch. 737 ; and for a forfeiture on settlement of part of the income, see *Re Dennis's Settlement Trusts*, [1942] Ch. 283 ; and *Re O'Connor*, [1948] Ch. 628. For a forfeiture of a husband's protected life interest, following an order of the High Court charging it, see *Re Richardson's Will Trusts*, [1958] Ch. 504.

[36] The meaning of " children " and " issue " in s. 33 (1) (ii) has been amended by the Family Law Reform Act 1969, s. 15 (3), which provides that, in s. 33, the reference to children and other issue shall have effect as if :—" (a) the reference to the children or more remote issue of the principal beneficiary included a reference to any illegitimate child of the principal beneficiary and to anyone who would rank as such issue if he, or some other person through whom he is descended from the principal beneficiary, had been born legitimate ; and (b) the reference to the issue of the principal beneficiary included a reference to anyone who would rank as such issue if he, or some other person through whom he is descended from the principal beneficiary, had been born legitimate."

[37] If the principal beneficiary has become bankrupt, and the trustees pay or apply for his benefit more than is necessary for his bare support, the trustee in bankruptcy will be able to claim it (*Holmes* v. *Penney* (1856), 3 K. & J. 90; *Re Coleman* (1888), 39 Ch.D. 443).

were actually dead, be entitled to the trust property or the income thereof or to the annuity fund, if any, or arrears of the annuity, as the case may be;

as the trustees in their absolute discretion, without being liable to account for the exercise of such discretion, think fit.

(2) This section does not apply to trusts coming into operation before the commencement of this Act, and has effect subject to any variation of the implied trusts aforesaid contained in the instrument creating the trust.

(3) Nothing in this section operates to validate any trusts which would, if contained in the instrument creating the trust, be liable to be set aside.[38]

N.I.: Trustee Act (Northern Ireland) 1958, s. 34.

Part III

Appointment and Discharge of Trustees

34. Limitation of the number of trustees.—(1) Where, at the commencement of this Act, there are more than four trustees of a settlement of land, or more than four trustees holding land on trust for sale, no new trustees shall (except where as a result of the appointment the number is reduced to four or less) be capable of being appointed until the number is reduced to less than four, and thereafter the number shall not be increased beyond four.

(2) In the case of settlements and dispositions on trust for sale of land made or coming into operation after the commencement of this Act—

(*a*) the number of trustees thereof shall not in any case exceed four, and where more than four persons are named as such trustees, the four first named (who are able and willing to act) shall alone be the trustees, and the other persons named shall not be trustees unless appointed on the occurrence of a vacancy;

(*b*) the number of the trustees shall not be increased beyond four.

(3) This section only applies to settlements and dispositions of land, and the restrictions imposed on the number of trustees do not apply—

(*a*) in the case of land vested in trustees for charitable, ecclesiastical, or public purposes [39]; or

(*b*) where the net proceeds of the sale of the land are held for like purposes; or

(*c*) to the trustees of a term of years absolute limited by a settlement on trusts for raising money, or of a like term created under the statutory remedies relating to annual sums charged on land.

35. Appointments of trustees of settlements and dispositions on trust for sale of land.—(1) Appointments of new trustees of conveyances on trust for sale on the one hand and of the settlement of the proceeds of sale on the

---

[38] Thus, a settlement by a person upon *himself* until bankruptcy, and then on discretionary trusts is still invalid. See *Higinbotham* v. *Holme* (1812), 19 Ves. 88; *Re Burroughs-Fowler*, [1916] 2 Ch. 251.

[39] As to these see *Re Cleveland Literary and Philosophical Society's Land*, [1931] 2 Ch. 247.

other hand, shall, subject to any order of the court, be effected by separate instruments, but in such manner as to secure that the same persons shall become the trustees of the conveyance on trust for sale as become the trustees of the settlement of the proceeds of sale.

(2) Where new trustees of a settlement are appointed, a memorandum of the names and addresses of the persons who are for the time being the trustees thereof for the purposes of the Settled Land Act, 1925, shall be endorsed on or annexed to the last or only principal vesting instrument by or on behalf of the trustees of the settlement, and such vesting instrument shall, for that purpose, be produced by the person having the possession thereof to the trustees of the settlement when so required.

(3) Where new trustees of a conveyance on trust for sale relating to a legal estate are appointed, a memorandum of the persons who are for the time being the trustees for sale shall be endorsed on or annexed thereto by or on behalf of the trustees of the settlement of the proceeds of sale, and the conveyance shall, for that purpose, be produced by the person having the possession thereof to the last-mentioned trustees when so required.

(4) This section applies only to settlements and dispositions of land.

36. **Power of appointing new or additional trustees.**—(1) Where a trustee, either original or substituted, and whether appointed by a court or otherwise, is dead, or remains out of the United Kingdom for more than twelve months, or desires to be discharged from all or any of the trusts or powers reposed in or conferred on him, or refuses or is unfit to act therein, or is incapable of acting therein, or is an infant, then, subject to the restrictions imposed by this Act on the number of trustees,—

(*a*) the person or persons nominated for the purpose of appointing new trustees by the instrument, if any, creating the trust; or

(*b*) if there is no such person, or no such person able and willing to act, then the surviving or continuing trustees or trustee for the time being, or the personal representatives of the last surviving or continuing trustee;

may, by writing, appoint one or more other persons (whether or not being the persons exercising the power) to be a trustee or trustees in the place of the trustee so deceased remaining out of the United Kingdom, desiring to be discharged, refusing, or being unfit or being incapable, or being an infant, as aforesaid.[40]

[40] Remaining out of the United Kingdom for more than twelve months is construed strictly (*Re Walker*, [1901] 1 Ch. 259), and the absent trustee may be removed against his will (*Re Stoneham Settlement Trusts*, [1953] Ch. 59). A trustee who is resident abroad may be appointed under s. 36 (1) where this is in the interests of the beneficiaries: *Re Whitehead's Will Trusts*, [1971] 1 W.L.R. 833.

Bankruptcy will usually make a trustee "unfit to act"; at any rate where the trustee is called upon to handle money (*Re Roche* (1842), 2 Dr. & War. 287; *Re Wheeler and De Rochow*, [1896] 1 Ch. 315, 322).

On what is meant by "incapable of acting," see *Withington* v. *Withington* (1848), 16 Sim. 104; *Re Harrison's Trusts* (1852), 22 L.J.Ch. 69; *Re Watts* (1851), 20 L.J.Ch. 337.

A lunatic, even if not so found, is "incapable of acting" (*Re East* (1873), L.R. 8 Ch.App. 735; *Re Elizabeth Blake*, [1887] W.N. 173). A trustee who suffers from a prolonged, incapacitating illness may also be incapable of acting (*Re Weston's Trusts*, [1898] W.N. 151).

Personal representatives who have completed the administration may appoint under this section: *Re Cockburn's Will Trusts*, [1957] Ch. 438; but an executor who has not proved the will may not: *Re Crowhurst Park*, [1974] 1 W.L.R. 583.

(2) Where a trustee has been removed under a power contained in the instrument creating the trust, a new trustee or new trustees may be appointed in the place of the trustee who is removed, as if he were dead, or, in the case of a corporation, as if the corporation desired to be discharged from the trust, and the provisions of this section shall apply accordingly, but subject to the restrictions imposed by this Act on the number of trustees.

(3) Where a corporation being a trustee is or has been dissolved, either before or after the commencement of this Act, then, for the purposes of this section and of an enactment replaced thereby, the corporation shall be deemed to be and to have been from the date of the dissolution incapable of acting in the trusts or powers reposed in or conferred on the corporation.

(4) The power of appointment given by subsection (1) of this section or any similar previous enactment to the personal representatives of a last surviving or continuing trustee shall be and shall be deemed always to have been exercisable by the executors for the time being (whether original or by representation) of such surviving or continuing trustee who have proved the will of their testator or by the administrators for the time being of such trustee without the concurrence of any executor who has renounced or has not proved.

(5) But a sole or last surviving executor intending to renounce, or all the executors where they all intend to renounce, shall have and shall be deemed always to have had power, at any time before renouncing probate, to exercise the power of appointment given by this section, or by any similar previous enactment, if willing to act for that purpose and without thereby accepting the office of executor.

(6) Where a sole trustee, other than a trust corporation, is or has been originally appointed to act in a trust, or where, in the case of any trust, there are not more than three trustees (none of them being a trust corporation) either original or substituted and whether appointed by the court or otherwise, then and in any such case—

    (a) the person or persons nominated for the purpose of appointing new trustees by the instrument, if any, creating the trust; or

    (b) if there is no such person, or no such person able and willing to act, then the trustee or trustees for the time being;

may, by writing, appoint another person or other persons to be an additional trustee or additional trustees, but it shall not be obligatory to appoint any additional trustee, unless the instrument, if any, creating the trust, or any statutory enactment provides to the contrary, nor shall the number of trustees be increased beyond four by virtue of any such appointment.

(7) Every new trustee appointed under this section as well before as after all the trust property becomes by law, or by assurance, or otherwise, vested in him, shall have the same powers, authorities, and discretions, and may in all respects act as if he had been originally appointed a trustee by the instrument, if any, creating the trust.

(8) The provisions of this section relating to a trustee who is dead include the case of a person nominated trustee in a will but dying before the testator, and those relative to a continuing trustee include a refusing or retiring trustee, if willing to act in the execution of the provisions of this section.

(9) When a trustee is incapable, by reason of mental disorder within the meaning of the Mental Health Act, 1959, of exercising his functions as trustee and is also entitled in possession to some beneficial interest in the trust property, no appointment of a new trustee in his place shall be made by virtue of paragraph (*b*) of subsection (1) of this section unless leave to make the appointment has been given by the authority having jurisdiction under Part VIII of the Mental Health Act, 1959.

[*Subsection* (9) *was substituted by the Mental Health Act* 1959, *s.* 149 (1) *and Sched.* 7, *Pt.* I.]

R.I.: Trustee Act 1893, s. 10. N.I.: Trustee Act (Northern Ireland) 1958, s. 35.

37. Supplemental provisions as to appointment of trustees.—(1) On the appointment of a trustee for the whole or any part of trust property—

(*a*) the number of trustees may, subject to the restrictions imposed by this Act on the number of trustees, be increased; and

(*b*) a separate set of trustees, not exceeding four, may be appointed for any part of the trust property held on trusts distinct from those relating to any other part or parts of the trust property, notwithstanding that no new trustees or trustee are or is to be appointed for other parts of the trust property, and any existing trustee may be appointed or remain one of such separate set of trustees, or, if only one trustee was originally appointed, then, save as hereinafter provided, one separate trustee may be so appointed; and

(*c*) it shall not be obligatory, save as hereinafter provided, to appoint more than one new trustee where only one trustee was originally appointed, or to fill up the original number of trustees where more than two trustees were originally appointed, but, except where only one trustee was originally appointed, and a sole trustee when appointed will be able to give valid receipts for all capital money, a trustee shall not be discharged from his trust unless there will be either a trust corporation or at least two individuals to act as trustees to perform the trust [41]; and

(*d*) any assurance or thing requisite for vesting the trust property, or any part thereof, in a sole trustee, or jointly in the persons who are the trustees, shall be executed or done.

(2) Nothing in this Act shall authorise the appointment of a sole trustee, not being a trust corporation, where the trustee, when appointed, would not be able to give valid receipts for all capital money arising under the trust.

R.I.: Trustee Act 1893, s. 10. N.I.: Trustee Act (Northern Ireland) 1958, s. 36.

38. Evidence as to a vacancy in a trust.—(1) A statement, contained in any instrument coming into operation after the commencement of this Act by which a new trustee is appointed for any purpose connected with land, to the effect that a trustee has remained out of the United Kingdom for more than

---

[41] This subsection does not apply where there is no appointment of a new trustee, but merely a discharge of an existing trustee (*Chamberlain* v. *Inland Revenue Commissioners*, [1945] 2 All E.R. 351).

twelve months or refuses or is unfit to act, or is incapable of acting, or that he is not entitled to a beneficial interest in the trust property in possession, shall, in favour of a purchaser of a legal estate, be conclusive evidence of the matter stated.

(2) In favour of such purchaser any appointment of a new trustee depending on that statement, and any vesting declaration, express or implied, consequent on the appointment, shall be valid.

N.I.: Trustee Act (Northern Ireland) 1958, s. 37.

39. **Retirement of trustee without a new appointment.**—(1) Where a trustee is desirous of being discharged from the trust, and after his discharge there will be either a trust corporation or at least two individuals to act as trustees to perform the trust, then, if such trustee as aforesaid by deed declares that he is desirous of being discharged from the trust, and if his co-trustees and such other person, if any, as is empowered to appoint trustees, by deed consent to the discharge of the trustee, and to the vesting in the co-trustees alone of the trust property, the trustee desirous of being discharged shall be deemed to have retired from the trust, and shall, by the deed, be discharged therefrom under this Act, without any new trustee being appointed in his place.

(2) Any assurance or thing requisite for vesting the trust property in the continuing trustees alone shall be executed or done.

R.I.: Trustee Act 1893, s. 11. N.I.: Trustee Act (Northern Ireland) 1958, s. 38.

40. **Vesting of trust property in new or continuing trustees.**[42]—(1) Where by a deed a new trustee is appointed to perform any trust, then—

(a) if the deed contains a declaration by the appointor to the effect that any estate or interest in any land subject to the trust, or in any chattel so subject, or the right to recover or receive any debt or other thing in action so subject, shall vest in the persons who by virtue of the deed become or are the trustees for performing the trust, the deed shall operate, without any conveyance or assignment, to vest in those persons as joint tenants and for the purposes of the trust the estate interest or right to which the declaration relates; and

(b) if the deed is made after the commencement of this Act and does not contain such a declaration, the deed shall, subject to any express provision to the contrary therein contained, operate as if it had contained such a declaration by the appointor extending to all the estates interests and rights with respect to which a declaration could have been made.

(2) Where by a deed a retiring trustee is discharged under the statutory power without a new trustee being appointed, then—

(a) if the deed contains such a declaration as aforesaid by the retiring and continuing trustees, and by the other person, if any, empowered to appoint trustees, the deed shall, without any conveyance or assignment,

---

[42] S. 40 does not apply where a personal representative, who is also a sole trustee, but who has not executed a written assent in his own favour, appoints a new trustee (*Re King's Will Trusts,* [1964] Ch. 542).

operate to vest in the continuing trustees alone, as joint tenants, and for the purposes of the trust, the estate, interest, or right to which the declaration relates; and

(*b*) if the deed is made after the commencement of this Act and does not contain such a declaration, the deed shall, subject to any express provision to the contrary therein contained, operate as if it had contained such a declaration by such persons as aforesaid extending to all the estates, interests and rights with respect to which a declaration could have been made.

(3) An express vesting declaration, whether made before or after the commencement of this Act, shall, notwithstanding that the estate, interest or right to be vested is not expressly referred to, and provided that the other statutory requirements were or are complied with, operate and be deemed always to have operated (but without prejudice to any express provision to the contrary contained in the deed of appointment or discharge) to vest in the persons respectively referred to in subsections (1) and (2) of this section, as the case may require, such estates, interests and rights as are capable of being and ought to be vested in those persons.

(4) This section does not extend—

(*a*) to land conveyed by way of mortgage for securing money subject to the trust, except land conveyed on trust for securing debentures or debenture stock [43];

(*b*) to land held under a lease which contains any covenant, condition or agreement against assignment or disposing of the land without licence or consent, unless, prior to the execution of the deed containing expressly or impliedly the vesting declaration, the requisite licence or consent has been obtained, or unless, by virtue of any statute or rule of law, the vesting declaration, express or implied, would not operate as a breach of covenant or give rise to a forfeiture;

(*c*) to any share, stock, annuity or property which is only transferable in books kept by a company or other body, or in manner directed by or under an Act of Parliament.

In this subsection " lease " includes an underlease and an agreement for a lease or underlease.

(5) For purposes of registration of the deed in any registry, the person or persons making the declaration expressly or impliedly, shall be deemed the conveying party or parties, and the conveyance shall be deemed to be made by him or them under a power conferred by this Act.

(6) This section applies to deeds of appointment or discharge executed on or after the first day of January, eighteen hundred and eighty-two.

R.I.: Trustee Act 1893, s. 12. N.I.: Trustee Act (Northern Ireland) 1958, s. 39.

[43] On this, see *London and County Banking Co.* v. *Goddard*, [1897] 1 Ch. 642, 649. A separate deed is required to convey a mortgage term.

PART IV

POWERS OF THE COURT

Appointment of new Trustees

41. Power of court to appoint new trustees.—(1) The court may, whenever it is expedient to appoint a new trustee or new trustees, and it is found inexpedient difficult or impracticable so to do without the assistance of the court, make an order appointing a new trustee or new trustees either in substitution for or in addition to any existing trustee or trustees, or although there is no existing trustee.[44]

In particular and without prejudice to the generality of the foregoing provision, the court may make an order appointing a new trustee in substitution for a trustee who is incapable, by reason of mental disorder within the meaning of the Mental Health Act, 1959, of exercising his functions as trustee. or is a bankrupt, or is a corporation which is in liquidation or has been dissolved.

[*Subsection* (1) *is given as amended by the Mental Health Act* 1959, *s.* 149 (1) *and Sched.* 7, *Pt.* I, *and by the Criminal Law Act* 1967, *s.* 10 (2) *and Sched.* 3, *Pt.* III.]

(2) The power conferred by this section may, in the case of a deed of arrangement within the meaning of the Deeds of Arrangement Act, 1914, be exercised either by the High Court or by the court having jurisdiction in bankruptcy in the district in which the debtor resided or carried on business at the date of the execution of the deed.

(3) An order under this section, and any consequential vesting order or conveyance, shall not operate further or otherwise as a discharge to any former or continuing trustee than an appointment of new trustees under any power for that purpose contained in any instrument would have operated.

(4) Nothing in this section gives power to appoint an executor or administrator.[45]

R.I.: Trustee Act 1893, s. 25. N.I.: Trustee Act (Northern Ireland) 1958, s. 40.

42. Power to authorise remuneration. Where the court appoints a corporation, other than the Public Trustee, to be a trustee either solely or jointly with another person, the court may authorise the corporation to charge such remuneration for its services as trustee as the court may think fit.[46]

N.I.: Trustee Act (Northern Ireland) 1958, s. 41.

43. Powers of new trustee appointed by the court. Every trustee appointed by a court of competent jurisdiction shall, as well before as after the trust property becomes by law, or by assurance, or otherwise, vested in him, have

---

[44] The court will appoint a new trustee under this section in place of an existing trustee where there is friction between the trustees (*Re Henderson*, [1940] Ch. 764), or where the trustee is a bankrupt (*Re a Solicitor*, [1952] Ch. 328). But the court will not appoint a new trustee where there is some person able and willing to do so (*Re Higginbottom*, [1892] 3 Ch. 132).

[45] But when a sole administrator has cleared the estate, the court will then appoint a trustee to act with him (*Re Ponder*, [1921] 2 Ch. 59).

[46] Thus, where the court made a grant of administration *de bonis non*, it gave the trust corporation a power to charge the authorised scale (*Re Young Estates* (1934), 103 L.J.P. 75; and see *Re Masters*, [1953] 1 W.L.R. 81).

the same powers, authorities, and discretions, and may in all respects act as if he had been originally appointed a trustee by the instrument, if any, creating the trust.

R.I.: Trustee Act 1893, s. 37. N.I.: Trustee Act (Northern Ireland) 1958, s. 42.

Vesting Orders

44. Vesting orders of land. In any of the following cases, namely:—

(i) Where the court appoints or has appointed a trustee, or where a trustee has been appointed out of court under any statutory or express power;

(ii) Where a trustee entitled to or possessed of any land or interest therein, whether by way of mortgage or otherwise, or entitled to a contingent right therein, either solely or jointly with any other person—

(a) is under disability [47]; or

(b) is out of the jurisdiction of the High Court; or

(c) cannot be found, or, being a corporation, has been dissolved;

(iii) Where it is uncertain who was the survivor of two or more trustees jointly entitled to or possessed of any interest in land;

(iv) Where it is uncertain whether the last trustee known to have been entitled to or possessed of any interest in land is living or dead;

(v) Where there is no personal representative of a deceased trustee who was entitled to or possessed of any interest in land, or where it is uncertain who is the personal representative of a deceased trustee who was entitled to or possessed of any interest in land;

(vi) Where a trustee jointly or solely entitled to or possessed of any interest in land, or entitled to a contingent right therein, has been required, by or on behalf of a person entitled to require a conveyance of the land or interest or a release of the right, to convey the land or interest or to release the right, and has wilfully refused or neglected to convey the land or interest or release the right for twenty-eight days after the date of the requirement;

(vii) Where land or any interest therein is vested in a trustee whether by way of mortgage or otherwise, and it appears to the court to be expedient;

the court may make an order (in this Act called a vesting order) vesting the land or interest therein in any such person in any such manner and for any such estate or interest as the court may direct, or releasing or disposing of the contingent right to such person as the court may direct:

Provided that—

(a) Where the order is consequential on the appointment of a trustee the land or interest therein shall be vested for such estate as the court may direct in the persons who on the appointment are the trustees; and

(b) Where the order relates to a trustee entitled or formerly entitled jointly with another person, and such trustee is under disability or out of the jurisdiction of the High Court or cannot be found, or being a corporation has been dissolved, the land interest or right shall be vested in such

---

[47] Where only one of several trustees is under disability, the court will only make an order vesting the property in the remaining trustees in exceptional circumstances. (*Re Harrison's Settlement Trusts*, [1965] 1 W.L.R. 1492.)

other person who remains entitled, either alone or with any other person the court may appoint.

R.I.: Trustee Act 1893, s. 26. N.I.: Trustee Act (Northern Ireland) 1958, s. 43.

45. Orders as to contingent rights of unborn persons. Where any interest in land is subject to a contingent right in an unborn person or class of unborn persons who, on coming into existence would, in respect thereof, become entitled to or possessed of that interest on any trust, the court may make an order releasing the land or interest therein from the contingent right, or may make an order vesting in any person the estate or interest to or of which the unborn person or class of unborn persons would, on coming into existence, be entitled or possessed in the land.

R.I.: Trustee Act 1893, s. 27. N.I.: Trustee Act (Northern Ireland) 1958, s. 44.

46. Vesting order in place of conveyance by infant mortgagee. Where any person entitled to or possessed of any interest in land, or entitled to a contingent right in land, by way of security for money, is an infant, the court may make an order vesting or releasing or disposing of the interest in the land or the right in like manner as in the case of a trustee under disability.

R.I.: Trustee Act 1893, s. 28. N.I.: Trustee Act (Northern Ireland) 1958, s. 45.

47. Vesting order consequential on order for sale or mortgage of land. Where any court gives a judgment or makes an order directing the sale or mortgage of any land, every person who is entitled to or possessed of any interest in the land, or entitled to a contingent right therein, and is a party to the action or proceeding in which the judgment or order is given or made or is otherwise bound by the judgment or order, shall be deemed to be so entitled or possessed, as the case may be, as a trustee for the purposes of this Act, and the court may, if it thinks expedient, make an order vesting the land or any part thereof for such estate or interest as that court thinks fit in the purchaser or mortgagee or in any other person:

Provided that, in the case of a legal mortgage, the estate to be vested in the mortgagee shall be a term of years absolute.

R.I.: Trustee Act 1893, s. 30, and Trustee Act 1893 Amendment Act 1894, s. 1. N.I.: Trustee Act (Northern Ireland) 1958, s. 47.

48. Vesting order consequential on judgment for specific performance, &c. Where a judgment is given for the specific performance of a contract concerning any interest in land, or for sale or exchange of any interest in land, or generally where any judgment is given for the conveyance of any interest in land either in cases arising out of the doctrine of election or otherwise, the court may declare—

(a) that any of the parties to the action are trustees of any interest in the land or any part thereof within the meaning of this Act; or

(b) that the interests of unborn persons who might claim under any party to the action, or under the will or voluntary settlement of any deceased person who was during his lifetime a party to the contract or transaction concerning which the judgment is given, are the interests of persons who, on coming into existence, would be trustees within the meaning of this Act;

and thereupon the court may make a vesting order relating to the rights of those persons, born and unborn, as if they had been trustees.

R.I.: Trustee Act 1893, s. 31. N.I.: Trustee Act (Northern Ireland) 1958, s. 48.

49. **Effect of vesting order.** A vesting order under any of the foregoing provisions shall in the case of a vesting order consequential on the appointment of a trustee, have the same effect—

(*a*) as if the persons who before the appointment were the trustees, if any, had duly executed all proper conveyances of the land for such estate or interest as the court directs; or

(*b*) if there is no such person, or no such person of full capacity, as if such person had existed and been of full capacity and had duly executed all proper conveyances of the land for such estate or interest as the court directs [48];

and shall in every other case have the same effect as if the trustee or other person or description or class of persons to whose rights or supposed rights the said provisions respectively relate had been an ascertained and existing person of full capacity, and had executed a conveyance or release to the effect intended by the order.

R.I.: Trustee Act 1893, s. 32. N.I.: Trustee Act (Northern Ireland) 1958, s. 49.

50. **Power to appoint person to convey.** In all cases where a vesting order can be made under any of the foregoing provisions, the court may, if it is more convenient, appoint a person to convey the land or any interest therein or release the contingent right, and a conveyance or release by that person in conformity with the order shall have the same effect as an order under the appropriate provision.

R.I.: Trustee Act 1893, s. 33. N.I.: Trustee Act (Northern Ireland) 1958, s. 50.

51. **Vesting orders as to stock and things in action.**—(1) In any of the following cases, namely : —

(i) Where the court appoints or has appointed a trustee, or where a trustee has been appointed out of court under any statutory or express power;

(ii) Where a trustee entitled, whether by way of mortgage or otherwise, alone or jointly with another person to stock or to a thing in action—

(*a*) is under disability; or

(*b*) is out of the jurisdiction of the High Court; or

(*c*) cannot be found, or, being a corporation, has been dissolved; or

---

[48] So, if an order is made appointing a person to convey the entailed interest in possession of an infant, the effect is to bar the entail and remainders over (*Re Gower's Settlement,* [1934] Ch. 365).

(*d*) neglects or refuses to transfer stock or receive the dividends or income thereof, or to sue for or recover a thing in action, according to the direction of the person absolutely entitled thereto for twenty-eight days next after a request in writing has been made to him by the person so entitled; or

(*e*) neglects or refuses to transfer stock or receive the dividends or income thereof, or to sue for or recover a thing in action for twenty-eight days next after an order of the court for that purpose has been served on him;

(iii) Where it is uncertain whether a trustee entitled alone or jointly with another person to stock or to a thing in action is alive or dead;

(iv) Where the stock is standing in the name of a deceased person whose personal representative is under disability;

(v) Where stock or a thing in action is vested in a trustee whether by way of mortgage or otherwise and it appears to the court to be expedient;

the court [49] may make an order [50] vesting the right to transfer or call for a transfer of stock, or to receive the dividends or income thereof, or to sue for or recover the thing in action, in any such person as the court may appoint:

Provided that—

(*a*) Where the order is consequential on the appointment of a trustee, the right shall be vested in the persons who, on the appointment, are the trustees; and

(*b*) Where the person whose right is dealt with by the order was entitled jointly with another person, the right shall be vested in that last-mentioned person either alone or jointly with any other person whom the court may appoint.

(2) In all cases where a vesting order can be made under this section, the court may, if it is more convenient, appoint some proper person to make or join in making the transfer:

Provided that the person appointed to make or join in making a transfer of stock shall be some proper officer of the bank, or the company or society whose stock is to be transferred.

(3) The person in whom the right to transfer or call for the transfer of any stock is vested by an order of the court under this Act, may transfer the stock to himself or any other person, according to the order, and the Bank of England and all other companies shall obey every order under this section according to its tenor.

(4) After notice in writing of an order under this section it shall not be lawful for the Bank of England or any other company to transfer any stock to which the order relates or to pay any dividends thereon except in accordance with the order.

(5) The court may make declarations and give directions concerning the manner in which the right to transfer any stock or thing in action vested under the provisions of this Act is to be exercised.

---

[49] The county court has jurisdiction if the fund to be dealt with does not exceed £5,000 in amount or value: County Courts Act 1959, s. 52 (3) and Sched. 1, as amended by the Administration of Justice Act 1969, s. 5.

[50] Similar orders may be made under the Local Government Act 1972, s. 146 (1) (*c*).

(6) The provisions of this Act as to vesting orders shall apply to shares in ships registered under the Acts relating to merchant shipping as if they were stock.[51]

R.I.: Trustee Act 1893, s. 35. N.I.: Trustee Act (Northern Ireland) 1958, s. 51.

52. Vesting orders of charity property. The powers conferred by this Act as to vesting orders may be exercised for vesting any interest in land, stock, or thing in action in any trustee of a charity or society over which the court would have jurisdiction upon action duly instituted, whether the appointment of the trustee was made by instrument under a power or by the court under its general or statutory jurisdiction.

R.I.: Trustee Act 1893, s. 39. N.I.: Trustee Act (Northern Ireland) 1958, s. 52.

53. Vesting orders in relation to infant's beneficial interests. Where an infant is beneficially entitled to any property the court may, with a view to the application of the capital or income thereof for the maintenance, education, or benefit of the infant, make an order—

(a) appointing a person to convey such property [52]; or

(b) in the case of stock, or a thing in action, vesting in any person the right to transfer or call for a transfer of such stock, or to receive the dividends or income thereof, or to sue for and recover such thing in action, upon such terms as the court may think fit.

N.I.: Trustee Act (Northern Ireland) 1958, s. 53.

54. Jurisdiction in regard to mental patients.—(1) Subject to the provisions of this section, the authority having jurisdiction under Part VIII of the Mental Health Act, 1959, shall not have power to make any order, or give any direction or authority, in relation to a patient who is a trustee if the High Court has power under this Act to make an order to the like effect.

(2) Where a patient is a trustee and a receiver appointed by the said authority is acting for him or an application for the appointment of a receiver has been made but not determined, then, except as respects a trust which is subject to an order for administration made by the High Court, the said authority shall have concurrent jurisdiction with the High Court in relation to—

(a) mortgaged property of which the patient has become a trustee merely by reason of the mortgage having been paid off;

(b) matters consequent on the making of provision by the said authority for the exercise of a power of appointing trustees or retiring from a trust;

---

[51] When shares are liable to calls, the direction to the trustees to transfer into their own names will be omitted. (*Re New Zealand Trust and Loan Co.*, [1893] 1 Ch. 403.)

[52] Thus, in *Re Gower's Settlement*, [1934] 1 Ch. 365, the court authorised the mortgage of an infant's entailed interest in remainder for maintenance.

The court may not, however, authorise a sale, either under s. 53 or under its inherent jurisdiction, *merely* because it is for the infant's benefit: *Re Heyworth's Contingent Reversionary Interest*, [1956] Ch. 364. In *Re Bristol's Settled Estates*, [1965] 1 W.L.R. 469, and in *Re Lansdowne's Will Trusts*, [1967] Ch. 603, the court authorised under this section the barring of an infant's entailed interest as part of a variation of a settlement under the Variation of Trusts Act 1958. See also *Re Meux*, [1958] Ch. 154.

(*c*) matters consequent on the making of provision by the said authority for the carrying out of any contract entered into by the patient;

(*d*) property to some interest in which the patient is beneficially entitled but which, or some interest in which, is held by the patient under an express, implied or constructive trust.

The Lord Chancellor may make rules with respect to the exercise of the jurisdiction referred to in this subsection.

(3) In this section " patient " means a patient as defined by section one hundred and one of the Mental Health Act, 1959, or a person as to whom powers are exercisable and have been exercised under section one hundred and four of that Act.

[*Section* 54 *was substituted by the Mental Health Act* 1959, *s.* 149 (1) *and Sched.* 7, *Pt.* I.]

55. Orders made upon certain allegations to be conclusive evidence. Where a vesting order is made as to any land under this Act or under Part VIII of the Mental Health Act, 1959, as amended by any subsequent enactment, or under any Act relating to lunacy in Northern Ireland, founded on an allegation of any of the following matters namely—

(*a*) the personal incapacity of a trustee or mortgagee; or

(*b*) that a trustee or mortgagee or the personal representative of or other person deriving title under a trustee or mortgagee is out of the jurisdiction of the High Court or cannot be found, or being a corporation has been dissolved; or

(*c*) that it is uncertain which of two or more trustees, or which of two or more persons interested in a mortgage, was the survivor; or

(*d*) that it is uncertain whether the last trustee or the personal representative of or other person deriving title under a trustee or mortgagee, or the last surviving person interested in a mortgage is living or dead; or

(*e*) that any trustee or mortgagee has died intestate without leaving a person beneficially interested under the intestacy or has died and it is not known who is his personal representative or the person interested;

the fact that the order had been so made shall be conclusive evidence of the matter so alleged in any court upon any question as to the validity of the order; but this section does not prevent the court from directing a reconveyance or surrender or the payment of costs occasioned by any such order if improperly obtained.

[*Section* 55 *is given as amended by the Mental Health Act* 1959, *s.* 149 (1) *and Sched.* 7, *Pt.* I.]

R.I.: Trustee Act 1893, s. 40. N.I.: Trustee Act (Northern Ireland) 1958, s. 54.

56. Application of vesting order to property out of England. The powers of the court to make vesting orders under this Act shall extend to all property in any part of His Majesty's dominions except Scotland.

R.I.: Trustee Act 1893, s. 41. N.I.: Trustee Act (Northern Ireland) 1958, s. 55.

Jurisdiction to make other Orders

57. **Power of court to authorise dealings with trust property.**—(1) Where in the management or administration of any property vested in trustees, any sale, lease, mortgage, surrender, release, or other disposition, or any purchase, investment, acquisition, expenditure, or other transaction, is in the opinion of the court expedient, but the same cannot be effected by reason of the absence of any power for that purpose vested in the trustees by the trust instrument, if any, or by law, the court may by order confer upon the trustees, either generally or in any particular instance, the necessary power for the purpose, on such terms, and subject to such provisions and conditions, if any, as the court may think fit and may direct in what manner any money authorised to be expended, and the costs of any transactions, are to be paid or borne as between capital and income.[53]

(2) The court may, from time to time, rescind or vary any order made under this section, or may make any new or further order.

(3) An application to the court under this section may be made by the trustees, or by any of them, or by any person beneficially interested under the trust.

(4) This section does not apply to trustees of a settlement for the purposes of the Settled Land Act, 1925.

N.I.: Trustee Act (Northern Ireland) 1958, s. 56.

58. **Persons entitled to apply for orders.**—(1) An order under this Act for the appointment of a new trustee or concerning any interest in land, stock, or thing in action subject to a trust, may be made on the application of any person beneficially interested in the land, stock, or thing in action, whether under disability or not, or on the application of any person duly appointed trustee thereof.

(2) An order under this Act concerning any interest in land, stock, or thing in action subject to a mortgage may be made on the application of any person beneficially interested in the equity of redemption, whether under disability or not, or of any person interested in the money secured by the mortgage.

R.I.: Trustee Act 1893, s. 36. N.I.: Trustee Act (Northern Ireland) 1958, s. 58.

59. **Power to give judgment in absence of a trustee.** Where in any action the court is satisfied that diligent search has been made for any person who, in the character of a trustee, is made a defendant in any action, to serve him

---

[53] For the effect of an authorisation by the court under this section, see *Re Mair*, [1935] Ch. 562. The transaction must benefit the whole trust. (*Re Craven's Estate (No. 2)*, [1937] Ch. 431.)

For the sale of trust assets under this section, see *Re Cockerell's Settlement Trusts*, [1956] Ch. 372.

The court will not exercise the power to permit trustees to vary the trusts to reduce the incidence of taxation. (*Chapman* v. *Chapman*, [1954] A.C. 429 (Cases, p. 309); *Re Downshire Settled Estates*, [1953] Ch. 218.) The section allows the court to authorise trustees to purchase a beneficiary's interest. (*Re Forster's Settlement*, [1954] 1 W.L.R. 1450.) See also *Re Lord Hylton's Settlement*, [1954] 1 W.L.R. 1055. The court will not authorise a sale of stocks under this section where the trust instrument includes a power of sale. (*Re Pratt's Will Trusts*, [1943] Ch. 326; *Municipal and General Securities Co. Ltd.* v. *Lloyds Bank Ltd.*, [1950] Ch. 212.) For the court's power to authorise a wider range of investments see *Re Shipwrecked Fishermen and Mariners' Royal Benevolent Society*, [1959] Ch. 220.

with a process of the court, and that he cannot be found, the court may hear and determine the action and give judgment therein against that person in his character of a trustee as if he had been duly served, or had entered an appearance in the action, and had also appeared by his counsel and solicitor at the hearing, but without prejudice to any interest he may have in the matters in question in the action in any other character.

R.I.: Trustee Act 1893, s. 43. N.I.: Trustee Act (Northern Ireland) 1958, s. 59.

60. **Power to charge costs on trust estate.** The court may order the costs and expenses of and incident to any application for an order appointing a new trustee, or for a vesting order, or of and incident to any such order, or any conveyance or transfer in pursuance thereof, to be raised and paid out of the property in respect whereof the same is made, or out of the income thereof, or to be borne and paid in such manner and by such persons as to the court may seem just.

R.I.: Trustee Act 1893, s. 38. N.I.: Trustee Act (Northern Ireland) 1958, s. 60.

61. **Power to relieve trustee from personal liability.** If it appears to the court that a trustee, whether appointed by the court or otherwise, is or may be personally liable for any breach of trust, whether the transaction alleged to be a breach of trust occurred before or after the commencement of this Act, but has acted honestly and reasonably, and ought fairly to be excused for the breach of trust and for omitting to obtain the directions of the court in the matter in which he committed such breach, then the court may relieve him either wholly or partly from personal liability for the same.[54]

R.I.: Irish Land Act 1903, s. 51. N.I.: Trustee Act (Northern Ireland) 1958, s. 61.

62. **Power to make beneficiary indemnify for breach of trust.**—(1) Where a trustee commits a breach of trust at the instigation or request or with the consent in writing of a beneficiary, the court may, if it thinks fit, make such order as to the court seems just, for impounding all or any part of the interest of the beneficiary in the trust estate by way of indemnity to the trustee or persons claiming through him.[55]

[54] The court will not lay down any general rules for the exercise of its discretion under this section (see *Re Kay*, [1897] 2 Ch. 518; *Re Stuart*, [1897] 2 Ch. 583; *Perrins* v. *Bellamy*, [1899] 1 Ch. 797; *Re Turner*, [1897] 1 Ch. 536; *Re Grindey*, [1898] 2 Ch. 593; *Re Mackay*, [1911] 1 Ch. 300; *Re Allsop*, [1914] 1 Ch. 1; *Re Brookes*, [1914] 1 Ch. 558).
The burden of showing that he has acted reasonably, as well as honestly, is on the trustee (*Re Stuart, supra*).
Making unauthorised investments is not acting reasonably (*Re Turner, supra*; *Khoo Tek Keong* v. *Ch'ng Joo Tuan Neoh*, [1934] A.C. 529) (Cases, p. 363). The court cannot under this section authorise a breach of trust *in advance* (*Re Tollemache*, [1903] 1 Ch. 955).
The section does not give relief against improper distribution of the trust fund, to a person claiming as assignee, without asking to see his title (*Davis* v. *Hutchings*, [1907] 1 Ch. 356).
[55] Neither the instigation nor the request need be in writing (*Griffith* v. *Hughes*, [1892] 3 Ch. 105 (Cases, p. 366)). The court will not impound the interest, unless the beneficiary knew that the action amounted to a breach of trust (*Re Somerset*, [1894] 1 Ch. 231).
The interest of a remainderman who instigates a breach of trust for the tenant for life may be impounded (*Chillingworth* v. *Chambers*, [1896] 1 Ch. 685, 700 (Cases, p. 347)). The right to impound may be exercised by a former trustee: *Re Pauling's Settlement Trusts (No. 2)*, [1963] Ch. 576 (Cases, p. 349).

[*Subsection* (1) *is given as amended by the Married Women* (*Restraint upon Anticipation*) *Act* 1949, *s.* 1 (4) *and Sched.* 2.]

(2) This section applies to breaches of trust committed as well before as after the commencement of this Act.

R.I.: Trustee Act 1893, s. 45. N.I.: Trustee Act (Northern Ireland) 1958, s. 62.

Payment into Court

63. **Payment into court by trustees.**—(1) Trustees, or the majority of trustees, having in their hands or under their control money or securities belonging to a trust, may pay the same into court.

[*Subsection* (1) *is given as amended by the Administration of Justice Act* 1965, *s.* 36 (4) *and Sched.* 3.]

(2) The receipt or certificate of the proper officer shall be a sufficient discharge to trustees for the money or securities so paid into court.

(3) Where money or securities are vested in any persons as trustees, and the majority are desirous of paying the same into court, but the concurrence of the other or others cannot be obtained, the court may order the payment into court to be made by the majority without the concurrence of the other or others.

(4) Where any such money or securities are deposited with any banker, broker, or other depositary, the court may order payment or delivery of the money or securities to the majority of the trustees for the purpose of payment into court.

(5) Every transfer payment and delivery made in pursuance of any such order shall be valid and take effect as if the same had been made on the authority or by the act of all the persons entitled to the money and securities so transferred, paid, or delivered.

R.I.: Trustee Act 1893, s. 42. N.I.: Trustee Act (Northern Ireland) 1958, s. 63.

PART V

GENERAL PROVISIONS

64. **Application of Act to Settled Land Act Trustees.**—(1) All the powers and provisions contained in this Act with reference to the appointment of new trustees, and the discharge and retirement of trustees, apply to and include trustees for the purposes of the Settled Land Act, 1925, and trustees for the purpose of the management of land during a minority, whether such trustees are appointed by the court or by the settlement, or under provisions contained in any instrument.

(2) Where, either before or after the commencement of this Act, trustees of a settlement have been appointed by the court for the purposes of the Settled Land Acts, 1882 to 1890, or of the Settled Land Act, 1925, then, after, the commencement of this Act—

(*a*) the person or persons nominated for the purpose of appointing new trustees by the instrument, if any, creating the settlement, though no trustees for the purposes of the said Acts were thereby appointed; or (*b*) if there is no such person, or no such person able and willing to act, the surviving or continuing trustees or trustee for the time being for the purposes of the said Acts or the personal representatives of the last surviving or continuing trustee for those purposes,

shall have the powers conferred by this Act to appoint new or additional trustees of the settlement for the purposes of the said Acts.

(3) Appointments of new trustees for the purposes of the said Acts made or expressed to be made before the commencement of this Act by the trustees or trustee or personal representatives referred to in paragraph (*b*) of the last preceding subsection or by the persons referred to in paragraph (*a*) of that subsection are, without prejudice to any order of the court made before such commencement, hereby confirmed.

R.I.: Trustee Act 1893, s. 47. N.I.: Trustee Act (Northern Ireland) 1958, s. 64.

65. [*Section 65 was repealed by the Criminal Law Act 1967, s. 10 (2) and Sched. 3, Pt. I.*]

R.I.: Trustee Act 1893, s. 48.

66. **Indemnity to banks, &c.** This Act, and every order purporting to be made under this Act, shall be a complete indemnity to the Bank of England, and to all persons for any acts done pursuant thereto, and it shall not be necessary for the Bank or for any person to inquire concerning the propriety of the order, or whether the court by which the order was made had jurisdiction to make it.

R.I.: Trustee Act 1893, s. 49. N.I.: Trustee Act (Northern Ireland) 1958, s. 65.

67. **Jurisdiction of the " court."**—(1) In this Act " the court " means the High Court, or the county court, where those courts respectively have jurisdiction.

(2) The procedure under this Act in county courts shall be in accordance with the Acts and rules regulating the procedure of those courts.

[*Section 67 is given as amended by the Courts Act 1971, s. 56 (4) and Sched. 11, Pt. II.*]

R.I.: Trustee Act 1893, s. 46. N.I.: Trustee Act (Northern Ireland) 1958, s. 66.

68. **Definitions.**—(1) In this Act, unless the context otherwise requires, the following expressions have the meanings hereby assigned to them respectively, that is to say:—

(1) " Authorised investments " mean investments authorised by the instrument, if any, creating the trust for the investment of money subject to the trust, or by law;

(2) " Contingent right " as applied to land includes a contingent or executory interest, a possibility coupled with an interest, whether the object of the gift or limitation of the interest, or possibility is or is not ascertained,

also a right of entry, whether immediate or future, and whether vested or contingent;

(3) " Convey " and " conveyance " as applied to any person include the execution by that person of every necessary or suitable assurance (including an assent) for conveying, assigning, appointing, surrendering, or otherwise transferring or disposing of land whereof he is seised or possessed, or wherein he is entitled to a contingent right, either for his whole estate or for any less estate, together with the performance of all formalities required by law for the validity of the conveyance; " sale " includes an exchange;

(4) " Gazette " means the London Gazette;

(5) " Instrument " includes Act of Parliament;

(6) " Land " includes land of any tenure, and mines and minerals, whether or not severed from the surface, buildings or parts of buildings, whether the division is horizontal, vertical or made in any other way, and other corporeal hereditaments; also a manor, an advowson, and a rent and other incorporeal hereditaments, and an easement, right, privilege, or benefit in, over, or derived from land, but not an undivided share in land; and in this definition " mines and minerals " include any strata or seam of minerals or substances in or under any land, and powers of working and getting the same, but not an undivided share thereof; and " hereditaments " mean real property which under an intestacy occurring before the commencement of this Act might have devolved on an heir;

(7) " Mortgage " and " mortgagee " include a charge or chargee by way of legal mortgage, and relate to every estate and interest regarded in equity as merely a security for money, and every person deriving title under the original mortgage;

(8) [*Paragraph* (8) *was repealed by the Administration of Justice Act* 1965, *s.* 17 (1) *and Sched.* 1.]

(9) " Personal representative " means the executor, original or by representation, or administrator for the time being of a deceased person;

(10) " Possession " includes receipt of rents and profits or the right to receive the same, if any; " income " includes rents and profits; and " possessed " applies to receipt of income of and to any vested estate less than a life interest in possession or in expectancy in any land;

(11) " Property " includes real and personal property, and any estate share and interest in any property, real or personal, and any debt, and any thing in action, and any other right or interest, whether in possession or not;

(12) " Rights " include estates and interests;

(13) " Securities " include stocks, funds, and shares; and " securities payable to bearer " include securities transferable by delivery and endorsement;

[*Paragraph* (13) *is given as amended by the Administration of Justice Act* 1965, *s.* 17 (1) *and Sched.* 1.]

(14) " Stock " includes fully paid up shares, and so far as relates to vesting orders made by the court under this Act, includes any fund, annuity, or security transferable in books kept by any company or society, or by instrument of transfer either alone or accompanied by other formalities, and any share or interest therein;

(15) " Tenant for life," " statutory owner," " settled land," " settlement," " trust instrument," " trustees of the settlement," " term of years absolute " and " vesting instrument " have the same meanings as in the Settled Land Act, 1925, and " entailed interest " has the same meaning as in the Law of Property Act, 1925;

[*Paragraph* (15) *is given as amended by the Mental Health Act* 1959, *s.* 149 (2) *and Sched.* 8, *Pt.* I.]

(16) " Transfer " in relation to stock or securities, includes the performance and execution of every deed, power of attorney, act, and thing on the part of the transferor to effect and complete the title in the transferee;

(17) " Trust " does not include the duties incident to an estate conveyed by way of mortgage, but with this exception the expressions " trust " and " trustee " extend to implied and constructive trusts, and to cases where the trustee has a beneficial interest in the trust property, and to the duties incident to the office of a personal representative, and " trustee " where the context admits, includes a personal representative, and " new trustee " includes an additional trustee;

(18) " Trust corporation " means the Public Trustee or a corporation either appointed by the court in any particular case to be a trustee, or entitled by rules made under subsection (3) of section four of the Public Trustee Act, 1906, to act as custodian trustee;

(19) " Trust for sale " in relation to land means an immediate binding trust for sale, whether or not exercisable at the request or with the consent of any person, and with or without power at discretion to postpone the sale; " trustees for sale " mean the persons (including a personal representative) holding land on trust for sale;

(20) " United Kingdom " means Great Britain and Northern Ireland.

(2) Any reference in this Act to paying money or securities into court shall be construed as referring to paying the money or transferring or depositing the securities into or in the Supreme Court or into or in any other court that has jurisdiction, and any reference in this Act to payment of money or securities into court shall be construed—

(a) with reference to any order of the High Court, as referring to payment of the money or transfer or deposit of the securities into or in the Supreme Court; and

(b) with reference to an order of any other court, as referring to payment of the money or transfer or deposit of the securities into or in that court.

[*Subsection* (2) *was added by the Administration of Justice Act* 1965, *s* 17 (1) *and Sched.* 1.]

R.I.: Trustee Act 1893, s. 50. N.I.: Trustee Act (Northern Ireland) 1958, s. 67.

69. **Application of Act.**—(1) This Act, except where otherwise expressly provided, applies to trusts including, so far as this Act applies thereto, executorships and administratorships constituted or created either before or after the commencement of this Act.

(2) The powers conferred by this Act on trustees are in addition to the powers conferred by the instrument, if any, creating the trust, but those powers,

unless otherwise stated, apply if and so far only as a contrary intention is not expressed in the instrument, if any, creating the trust, and have effect subject to the terms of that instrument.

(3) This Act does not affect the legality or validity of anything done before the commencement of this Act, except as otherwise hereinbefore expressly provided, and except that the enactments mentioned in the First Schedule to this Act shall be deemed always to have had effect subject to the provisions set forth in that Schedule.

N.I.: Trustee Act (Northern Ireland) 1958, s. 68.

70. **Enactments repealed.** Without prejudice to the provisions of section thirty-eight of the Interpretation Act, 1889:

(*a*) Nothing in this repeal shall affect any vesting order or appointment made or other thing done under any enactment so repealed, and any order or appointment so made may be revoked or varied in like manner as if it had been made under this Act;

(*b*) References in any document to any enactment repealed by this Act shall be construed as references to this Act or to the corresponding enactments in this Act.

[*Section* 70 *is given as amended by the Statute Law Revision Act* 1950.]
N.I.: Trustee Act (Northern Ireland) 1958, s. 69.

71. **Short title, commencement, extent.**—(1) This Act may be cited as the Trustee Act, 1925.

(2) [*Subsection* (2) *was repealed by the Statute Law Revision Act* 1950.]

(3) This Act, except where otherwise expressly provided, extends to England and Wales only.

(4) The provisions of this Act bind the Crown.

R.I.: the Trustee Act 1893 does not bind the Crown. N.I.: Trustee Act (Northern Ireland) 1958, s. 70.

FIRST SCHEDULE [1]

RETROSPECTIVE AMENDMENTS

(1) The investments mentioned in paragraphs (*d*), (*i*) and (*k*) of section one of the Trustee Act, 1893, and in the corresponding provisions of any enactment replaced by that Act, shall be deemed always to have included investments mentioned in paragraphs (*d*), (*i*) and (*k*) of subsection (1) of section one of this Act.

(2) In subsection (3) of section twelve of the Trustee Act, 1893, and in the enactment which it replaced, the expression " customary land " shall be deemed never to have included land in regard to which a tenant had power to dispose of the legal estate by deed, and the expression " land conveyed by way of mortgage " shall be deemed never to have included land conveyed in trust for securing debentures or debenture stock.

[1] N.I.: First Schedule (1958 Act).

(3) Section forty-seven of the Trustee Act, 1893, shall be deemed always to have had effect as if after the words " Settled Lands Acts, 1882 to 1890," there had been inserted the words " and trustees for the purposes of section forty-two of the Conveyancing Act, 1881."

(4) Subsection (1) of section eight of the Conveyancing Act, 1911, shall be deemed always to have had effect as if at the end thereof there had been inserted the words " or other the trustees or trustee for the time being of the trust."

SECOND SCHEDULE

ENACTMENTS REPEALED

[*The Second Schedule was repealed by the Statute Law Revision Act* 1950.]
N.I. : Second Schedule (1958 Act).

TRUSTEE INVESTMENTS ACT 1961

[9 AND 10 ELIZ. 2 CH. 62]

ARRANGEMENT OF SECTIONS

[R.I.: Trustee Act 1893, s. 1, as substituted by the Trustee (Authorised Investments) Act 1958. N.I.: Trustee Act (Northern Ireland) 1958, s. 1, and Trustee (Amendment) Act (Northern Ireland) 1962.]

TRUSTEE INVESTMENTS ACT, 1961

[9 AND 10 ELIZ. 2 CH. 62]

An Act to make fresh provision with respect to investment by trustees and persons having the investment powers of trustees, and by local authorities, and for purposes connected therewith.   [3rd August, 1961]

BE it enacted by the Queen's most Excellent Majesty, by and with the advice and consent of the Lords Spiritual and Temporal, and Commons, in this present Parliament assembled, and by the authority of the same, as follows—

1. New powers of investment of trustees.—(1) A trustee may invest any property in his hands, whether at the time in a state of investment or not, in

469

any manner specified in Part I or II of the First Schedule to this Act or, subject to the next following section, in any manner specified in Part III of that Schedule, and may also from time to time vary any such investments.

(2) The supplemental provisions contained in Part IV of that Schedule shall have effect for the interpretation and for restricting the operation of the said Parts I to III.

(3) No provision relating to the powers of the trustee contained in any instrument (not being an enactment or an instrument made under an enactment) made before the passing of this Act shall limit the powers conferred by this section, but those powers are exercisable only in so far as a contrary intention is not expressed in any Act or instrument made under an enactment, whenever passed or made, and so relating or in any other instrument so relating which is made after the passing of this Act.

For the purposes of this subsection any rule of the law of Scotland whereby a testamentary writing may be deemed to be made on a date other than that on which it was actually executed shall be disregarded.

(4) In this Act " narrower-range investment " means an investment falling within Part I or II of the First Schedule to this Act and " wider-range investment " means an investment falling within Part III of that Schedule.

2. Restrictions on wider-range investment.—(1) A trustee shall not have power by virtue of the foregoing section to make or retain any wider-range investment unless the trust fund has been divided into two parts (hereinafter referred to as the narrower-range part and the wider-range part), the parts being, subject to the provisions of this Act, equal in value at the time of the division; and where such a division has been made no subsequent division of the same fund shall be made for the purposes of this section, and no property shall be transferred from one part of the fund to the other unless either—

(a) the transfer is authorised or required by the following provisions of this Act, or

(b) a compensating transfer is made at the same time.

In this section " compensating transfer," in relation to any transferred property, means a transfer in the opposite direction of property of equal value.

(2) Property belonging to the narrower-range part of a trust fund shall not by virtue of the foregoing section be invested except in narrower-range investments, and any property invested in any other manner which is or becomes comprised in that part of the trust fund shall either be transferred to the wider-range part of the fund, with a compensating transfer, or be reinvested in narrower-range investments as soon as may be.

(3) Where any property accrues to a trust fund after the fund has been divided in pursuance of subsection (1) of this section, then—

(a) if the property accrues to the trustee as owner or former owner of property comprised in either part of the fund, it shall be treated as belonging to that part of the fund;

(b) in any other case, the trustee shall secure, by apportionment of the accruing property or the transfer of property from one part of the fund to the other, or both, that the value of each part of the fund is increased by the same amount.

Where a trustee acquires property in consideration of a money payment the acquisition of the property shall be treated for the purposes of this section as investment and not as the accrual of property to the trust fund, notwithstanding that the amount of the consideration is less than the value of the property acquired; and paragraph (a) of this subsection shall not include the case of a dividend or interest becoming part of a trust fund.

(4) Where in the exercise of any power or duty of a trustee property falls to be taken out of the trust fund, nothing in this section shall restrict his discretion as to the choice of property to be taken out.

3. Relationship between Act and other powers of investment.—(1) The powers conferred by section one of this Act are in addition to and not in derogation from any power conferred otherwise than by this Act of investment or postponing conversion exercisable by a trustee (hereinafter referred to as a " special power ").

(2) Any special power (however expressed) to invest property in any investment for the time being authorised by law for the investment of trust property, being a power conferred on a trustee before the passing of this Act or conferred on him under any enactment passed before the passing of this Act, shall have effect as a power to invest property in like manner and subject to the like provisions as under the foregoing provisions of this Act.

(3) In relation to property, including wider-range but not including narrower-range investments—

(a) which a trustee is authorised to hold apart from—

(i) the provisions of section one of this Act or any of the provisions of Part I of the Trustee Act, 1925, or any of the provisions of the Trusts (Scotland) Act, 1921, or

(ii) any such power to invest in authorised investments as is mentioned in the foregoing subsection, or

(b) which became part of a trust fund in consequence of the exercise by the trustee, as owner of property falling within this subsection, of any power conferred by subsection (3) or (4) of section ten of the Trustee Act, 1925, or paragraph (o) or (p) of subsection (1) of section four of the Trusts (Scotland) Act, 1921,

the foregoing section shall have effect subject to the modifications set out in the Second Schedule to this Act.

(4) The foregoing subsection shall not apply where the powers of the trustee to invest or postpone conversion have been conferred or varied—

(a) by an order of any court made within the period of ten years ending with the passing of this Act, or

(b) by any enactment passed, or instrument having effect under an enactment made, within that period, being an enactment or instrument relating specifically to the trusts in question; or

(c) by an enactment contained in a local Act of the present Session;

but the provisions of the Third Schedule to this Act shall have effect in a case falling within this subsection.

4. Interpretation of references to trust property and trust funds.—(1) In this Act " property " includes real or personal property of any description, including money and things in action:

Provided that it does not include an interest in expectancy, but the falling into possession of such an interest, or the receipt of proceeds of the sale thereof, shall be treated for the purposes of this Act as an accrual of property to the trust fund.

(2) So much of the property in the hands of a trustee shall for the purposes of this Act constitute one trust fund as is held on trusts which (as respects the beneficiaries or their respective interests or the purposes of the trust or as respects the powers of the trustee) are not identical with those on which any other property in his hands is held.

(3) Where property is taken out of a trust fund by way of appropriation so as to form a separate fund, and at the time of the appropriation the trust fund had (as to the whole or a part thereof) been divided in pursuance of subsection (1) of section two of this Act, or that subsection as modified by the Second Schedule to this Act, then if the separate fund is so divided the narrower-range and wider-range parts of the separate fund may be constituted so as either to be equal, or to bear to each other the same proportion as the two corresponding parts of the fund out of which it was so appropriated (the values of those parts of those funds being ascertained as at the time of appropriation), or some intermediate proportion.

(4) In the application of this section to Scotland the following subsection shall be substituted for subsection (1) thereof—

" (1) In this Act ' property ' includes property of any description (whether heritable or moveable, corporeal or incorporeal) which is presently enjoyable, but does not include a future interest, whether vested or contingent."

5. Certain valuations to be conclusive for purposes of division of trust fund.— (1) If for the purposes of section two or four of this Act or the Second Schedule thereto a trustee obtains, from a person reasonably believed by the trustee to be qualified to make it, a valuation in writing of any property, the valuation shall be conclusive in determining whether the division of the trust fund in pursuance of subsection (1) of the said section two, or any transfer or apportionment of property under that section or the said Second Schedule, has been duly made.

(2) The foregoing subsection applies to any such valuation notwithstanding that it is made by a person in the course of his employment as an officer or servant.

6. Duty of trustees in choosing investments.—(1) In the exercise of his powers of investment a trustee shall have regard—

(a) to the need for diversification of investments of the trust, in so far as is appropriate to the circumstances of the trust;

(b) to the suitability to the trust of investments of the description of investment proposed and of the investment proposed as an investment of that description.

(2) Before exercising any power conferred by section one of this Act to invest in a manner specified in Part II or III of the First Schedule to this Act, or before investing in any such manner in the exercise of a power falling within subsection (2) of section three of this Act, a trustee shall obtain and consider proper advice on the question whether the investment is satisfactory having regard to the matters mentioned in paragraphs (a) and (b) of the foregoing subsection.

(3) A trustee retaining any investment made in the exercise of such a power and in such a manner as aforesaid shall determine at what intervals the circumstances, and in particular the nature of the investment, make it desirable to obtain such advice as aforesaid, and shall obtain and consider such advice accordingly.

(4) For the purposes of the two foregoing subsections, proper advice is the advice of a person who is reasonably believed by the trustee to be qualified by his ability in and practical experience of financial matters; and such advice may be given by a person notwithstanding that he gives it in the course of his employment as an officer or servant.

(5) A trustee shall not be treated as having complied with subsection (2) or (3) of this section unless the advice was given or has been subsequently confirmed in writing.

(6) Subsections (2) and (3) of this section shall not apply to one of two or more trustees where he is the person giving the advice required by this section to his co-trustee or co-trustees, and shall not apply where powers of a trustee are lawfully exercised by an officer or servant competent under subsection (4) of this section to give proper advice.

(7) Without prejudice to section eight of the Trustee Act, 1925, or section thirty of the Trusts (Scotland) Act, 1921 (which relate to valuation, and the proportion of the value to be lent, where a trustee lends on the security of property) the advice required by this section shall not include, in the case of a loan on the security of freehold or leasehold property in England and Wales or Northern Ireland or on heritable security in Scotland, advice on the suitability of the particular loan.

7. Application of sections 1–6 to persons, other than trustees, having trustee investment powers.—(1) Where any persons, not being trustees, have a statutory power of making investments which is or includes power—

(a) to make the like investments as are authorised by section one of the Trustee Act, 1925, or section ten of the Trusts (Scotland) Act, 1921, or

(b) to make the like investments as trustees are for the time being by law authorised to make,

however the power is expressed, the foregoing provisions of this Act shall with the necessary modifications apply in relation to them as if they were trustees:

Provided that property belonging to a Consolidated Loans Fund or any other fund applicable wholly or partly for the redemption of debt shall not by virtue of the foregoing provisions of this Act be invested or held invested in any manner specified in paragraph 6 of Part II of the First Schedule to this Act or in wider-range investments.

(2) Where, in the exercise of powers conferred by any enactment, an authority to which paragraph 9 of Part II of the First Schedule to this Act applies uses money belonging to any fund for a purpose for which the authority has power to borrow, the foregoing provisions of this Act, as applied by the foregoing subsection, shall apply as if there were comprised in the fund (in addition to the actual content thereof) property, being narrower-range investments, having a value equal to so much of the said money as for the time being has not been repaid to the fund, and accordingly any repayment of such money to the fund shall not be treated for the said purposes as the accrual of property to the fund:

Provided that nothing in this subsection shall be taken to require compliance with any of the provisions of section six of this Act in relation to the exercise of such powers as aforesaid.

(3) In this section " Consolidated Loans Fund " means a fund established under section fifty-five of the Local Government Act, 1958, and includes a loans fund established under section two hundred and seventy-five of the Local Government (Scotland) Act, 1947, and " statutory power " means a power conferred by an enactment passed before the passing of this Act or by any instrument made under any such enactment.

8. Application of sections 1–6 in special cases.—(1) In relation to persons to whom this section applies—

(*a*) notwithstanding anything in subsection (3) of section one of this Act, no provision of any enactment passed, or instrument having effect under an enactment and made, before the passing of this Act shall limit the powers conferred by the said section one;

(*b*) subsection (1) of the foregoing section shall apply where the power of making investments therein mentioned is or includes a power to make some only of the investments mentioned in paragraph (*a*) or (*b*) of that subsection.

(2) This section applies to—

(*a*) the persons for the time being authorised to invest funds of the Duchy of Lancaster;

(*b*) any persons specified in an order made by the Treasury by statutory instrument, being persons (whether trustees or not) whose power to make investments is conferred by or under any enactment contained in a local or private Act.

(3) An order of the Treasury made under the foregoing subsection may provide that the provisions of sections one to six of this Act (other than the provisions of subsection (3) of section one) shall, in their application to any persons specified therein, have effect subject to such exceptions and modifications as may be specified.

9. Supplementary provisions as to investments.—(1) In subsection (3) of section ten of the Trustee Act, 1925, before paragraph (*c*) (which enables trustees to concur in any scheme or arrangement for the amalgamation of a company in which they hold securities with another company, with power to accept securities in the second company) there shall be inserted the following paragraph—

"(*bb*) for the acquisition of the securities of the company, or of control thereof, by another company."

(2) It is hereby declared that the power to subscribe for securities conferred by subsection (4) of the said section ten includes power to retain them for any period for which the trustee has power to retain the holding in respect of which the right to subscribe for the securities was offered, but subject to any conditions subject to which the trustee has that power.

10. Powers of Scottish trustees supplementary to powers of investment.— Section four of the Trusts (Scotland) Act, 1921 (which empowers trustees in trusts the execution of which is governed by the law in force in Scotland to do certain acts, where such acts are not at variance with the terms or purposes of the trust) shall have effect as if, in subsection (1) thereof, after paragraph (*n*), there were added the following paragraphs—

"(*o*) to concur, in respect of any securities of a company (being securities comprised in the trust estate), in any scheme or arrangement—

(i) for the reconstruction of the company,

(ii) for the sale of all or any part of the property and undertaking of the company to another company,

(iii) for the acquisition of the securities of the company, or of control thereof, by another company,

(iv) for the amalgamation of the company with another company, or

(v) for the release, modification, or variation of any rights, privileges or liabilities attached to the securities or any of them,

in like manner as if the trustees were entitled to such securities beneficially; to accept any securities of any denomination or description of the reconstructed or purchasing or new company in lieu of, or in exchange for, all or any of the first mentioned securities; and to retain any securities so accepted as aforesaid for any period for which the trustees could have properly retained the original securities;

(*p*) to exercise, to such extent as the trustees think fit, any conditional or preferential right to subscribe for any securities in a company (being a right offered to them in respect of any holding in the company), to apply capital money of the trust estate in payment of the consideration, and to retain any such securities for which they have subscribed for any period for which they have power to retain the holding in respect of which the right to subscribe for the securities was offered (but subject to any conditions subject to which they have that power); to renounce, to such extent as they think fit, any such right; or to assign, to such extent as they think fit and for the best consideration that can reasonably be obtained, the benefit of such right or the title thereto to any person, including any beneficiary under the trust."

11. Local Authority investment schemes.—(1) Without prejudice to powers conferred by or under any other enactment, any authority to which this section applies may invest property held by the authority in accordance with a scheme submitted to the Treasury by any association of local authorities and approved by the Treasury as enabling investments to be made collectively without in substance extending the scope of powers of investment.

(2) A scheme under this section may apply to a specified authority or to a specified class of authorities, may make different provisions as respects different authorities or different classes of authorities or as respects different descriptions of property or property held for different purposes, and may impose restrictions on the extent to which the power conferred by the foregoing subsection shall be exercisable.

(3) In approving a scheme under this section, the Treasury may direct that the Prevention of Fraud (Investments) Act, 1958, or the Prevention of Fraud (Investments) Act (Northern Ireland), 1940, shall not apply to dealings undertaken or documents issued for the purposes of the scheme, or to such dealings or documents of such descriptions as may be specified in the direction.

(4) The authorities to which this section applies are—

(a) in England and Wales, the council of a county, a borough, a district or a parish, a river authority, the Common Council of the City of London, the Greater London Council and the Council of the Isles of Scilly;

(b) in Scotland, a local authority within the meaning of the Local Government (Scotland) Act, 1947;

(c) in any part of Great Britain, a joint board or joint committee constituted to discharge or advise on the discharge of the functions of any two or more of the authorities mentioned in the foregoing paragraphs (including a joint committee established by those authorities acting in combination in accordance with regulations made under section 7 of the Superannuation Act 1972);

(d) in Northern Ireland, a district council established under the Local Government Act (Northern Ireland) 1972 and the Northern Ireland Local Government Officers' Superannuation Committee established under the Local Government (Superannuation) Act (Northern Ireland), 1950.

[*Section* 11 *is given as amended by the London Government Act* 1963, *ss.* 83 (1) *and* 93 (1) *and Scheds.* 17 *and* 18, *the Water Resources Act* 1963, *s.* 136 (1) *and Sched.* 13, *the Superannuation Act* 1972, *s.* 29 (1) *and Sched.* 6, *the Local Government Act* 1972, *s.* 272 (1) *and Sched.* 30, *and the Transfer of Functions* (*Local Government, etc.*) (*Northern Ireland*) *Order* 1973, *Art.* 3 *and Sched.* 2.]

12. Power to confer additional powers of investment.—(1) Her Majesty may by Order in Council extend the powers of investment conferred by section one of this Act by adding to Part I, Part II or Part III of the First Schedule to this Act any manner of investment specified in the Order.

(2) Any Order under this section shall be subject to annulment in pursuance of a resolution of either House of Parliament.

13. Power to modify provisions as to division of trust fund.—(1) The Treasury may by order made by statutory instrument direct that, subject to subsection (3) of section four of this Act, any division of a trust fund made in pursuance of subsection (1) of section two of this Act during the continuance in force of the order shall be made so that the value of the wider-range part at the time of the division bears to the then value of the narrower-range part such proportion, greater than one but not greater than three to one, as may be prescribed by the order; and in this Act " the prescribed proportion " means the proportion for the time being prescribed under this subsection.

(2) A fund which has been divided in pursuance of subsection (1) of section two of this Act before the coming into operation of an order under the foregoing subsection may notwithstanding anything in that subsection be again divided (once only) in pursuance of the said subsection (1) during the continuance in force of the order.

(3) If an order is made under subsection (1) of this section, then as from the coming into operation of the order—

(*a*) paragraph (*b*) of subsection (3) of section two of this Act and subparagraph (*b*) of paragraph 3 of the Second Schedule thereto shall have effect with the substitution, for the words from " each " to the end, of the words, " wider-range part of the fund is increased by an amount which bears the prescribed proportion to the amount by which the value of the narrower-range part of the fund is increased ";

(*b*) subsection (3) of section four of this Act shall have effect as if for the words " so as either " to " each other " there were substituted the words " so as to bear to each other either the prescribed proportion or."

(4) An order under this section may be revoked by a subsequent order thereunder prescribing a greater proportion.

(5) An order under this section shall not have effect unless approved by a resolution of each House of Parliament.

14. Amendment of section 27 of Trusts (Scotland) Act, 1921.—So much of section twenty-seven of the Trusts (Scotland) Act, 1921, as empowers the Court of Session to approve as investments for trust funds any stocks, funds or securities in addition to those in which trustees are by that Act authorised to invest trust funds shall cease to have effect.

15. Saving for powers of Court.—The enlargement of the investment powers of trustees by this Act shall not lessen any power of a court to confer wider powers of investment on trustees, or affect the extent to which any such power is to be exercised.

16. Minor and consequential amendments and repeals.—(1) The provisions of the Fourth Schedule to this Act (which contain minor amendments and amendments consequential on the foregoing provisions of this Act) shall have effect.

(2) The enactments mentioned in the Fifth Schedule to this Act are hereby repealed to the extent specified in the third column of that Schedule.

17. Short title, extent and construction.—(1) This Act may be cited as the Trustee Investments Act, 1961.

(2) Sections eleven and sixteen of this Act shall extend to Northern Ireland, but except as aforesaid and except so far as any other provisions of the Act

apply by virtue of subsection (1) of section one of the Trustee Act (Northern Ireland) 1958, or any other enactment of the Parliament of Northern Ireland, to trusts the execution of which is governed by the law in force in Northern Ireland, this Act does not apply to such trusts.

(3) So much of section sixteen of this Act as relates to the National Savings Bank and to trustee savings banks shall extend to the Isle of Man and the Channel Islands.

[*Subsection* (3) *is given as amended by the Post Office Act* 1969, *s.* 94 (2) (*c*) *and Sched.* 6, *Pt.* III.]

(4) Except where the context otherwise requires, in this Act, in its application to trusts the execution of which is governed by the law in force in England and Wales, expressions have the same meaning as in the Trustee Act, 1925.

(5) Except where the context otherwise requires, in this Act, in its application to trusts the execution of which is governed by the law in force in Scotland, expressions have the same meaning as in the Trusts (Scotland) Act, 1921.

SCHEDULES

FIRST SCHEDULE

MANNER OF INVESTMENT

PART I

NARROWER-RANGE INVESTMENTS NOT REQUIRING ADVICE

1. In Defence Bonds, National Savings Certificates, Ulster Savings Certificates, Ulster Development Bonds, National Development Bonds and British Savings Bonds.

[*Paragraph 1 is given as amended by S.I. 1962 No. 2611, S.I. 1964 No. 703 and S.I. 1968 No. 470.*]

2. In deposits in the National Savings Bank, ordinary deposits in a trustee savings bank and deposits in a bank or department thereof certified under subsection (3) of section nine of the Finance Act, 1956.

[*Paragraph 2 is given as amended by the Post Office Act 1969, s. 94 (2) (c) and Sched. 6, Pt. III.*]

PART II

NARROWER-RANGE INVESTMENTS REQUIRING ADVICE

1. In securities issued by Her Majesty's Government in the United Kingdom, the Government of Northern Ireland or the Government of the Isle of Man, not being securities falling within Part I of this Schedule and being fixed-interest securities registered in the United Kingdom or the Isle of Man, Treasury Bills or Tax Reserve Certificates.

2. In any securities the payment of interest on which is guaranteed by Her Majesty's Government in the United Kingdom or the Government of Northern Ireland.

3. In fixed-interest securities issued in the United Kingdom by any public authority or nationalised industry or undertaking in the United Kingdom.

4. In fixed-interest securities issued in the United Kingdom by the government of any overseas territory within the Commonwealth or by any public or local authority within such a territory, being securities registered in the United Kingdom.

References in this paragraph to an overseas territory or to the government of such territory shall be construed as if they occurred in the Overseas Service Act, 1958.

5. In fixed-interest securities issued in the United Kingdom by the International Bank for Reconstruction and Development, being securities registered in the United Kingdom. In fixed-interest securities issued in the United Kingdom by the Inter-American Development Bank. In fixed-interest securities issued in the United Kingdom by the European Investment Bank or by the European Coal and Steel Community, being securities registered in the United Kingdom.

[*Paragraph 5 is given as amended by S.I. 1964 No. 1404 and S.I. 1972 No. 1818.*]

6. In debentures issued in the United Kingdom by a company incorporated in the United Kingdom, being debentures registered in the United Kingdom.

7. In stock of the Bank of Ireland. In Bank of Ireland 7 per cent. loan stock 1986–91.

[*Paragraph 7 is given as amended by S.I. 1966 No. 401.*]

8. In debentures issued by the Agricultural Mortgage Corporation Limited or the Scottish Agricultural Securities Corporation Limited.

9. In loans to any authority to which this paragraph applies charged on all or any of the revenues of the authority or on a fund into which all or any of those revenues are payable, in any fixed-interest securities issued in the United Kingdom by any such authority for the purpose of borrowing money so charged, and in deposits with any such authority by way of temporary loan made on the giving of a receipt for the loan by the treasurer or other similar officer of the authority and on the giving of an undertaking by the authority that, if requested to charge the loan as aforesaid, it will either comply with the request or repay the loan.

This paragraph applies to the following authorities, that is to say—

(*a*) any local authority in the United Kingdom;

(*b*) any authority all the members of which are appointed or elected by one or more local authorities in the United Kingdom;

(*c*) any authority the majority of the members of which are appointed or elected by one or more local authorities in the United Kingdom, being an authority which by virtue of any enactment has power to issue a precept to a local authority in England and Wales, or a requisition to a local authority in Scotland, or to the expenses of which, by virtue of any enactment, a local authority in the United Kingdom is or can be required to contribute;

(*d*) the Receiver for the Metropolitan Police District or a combined police authority (within the meaning of the Police Act, 1946);

(*e*) the Belfast City and District Water Commissioners;

(*f*) the Great Ouse Water Authority;

(*g*) any district council in Northern Ireland.

[*Paragraph 9 (f) was added by S.I. 1962 No. 658 and paragraph 9 (g) by S.I. 1973 No. 1332.*]

10. In debentures or in the guaranteed or preference stock of any incorporated company, being statutory water undertakers within the meaning of the Water Act, 1945, or any corresponding enactment in force in Northern Ireland, and having during each of the ten years immediately preceding the calendar year in which the investment was made paid a dividend of not less than $3\frac{1}{2}$ per cent. on its ordinary shares.

[*By the Finance Act 1973, s. 58, the Treasury may by order make such amendments in para. 10, and in any enactment or instrument modifying para. 10, as appear to them required in consequence of the repeal by the Finance Act 1972 of the provisions relating to the deduction of income tax from distributions made by companies. Such an order is subject to annulment on resolution of either House.*]

Paragraph 10 *is given as amended by S.I.* 1973 *No.* 1393, *made under s.* 58 *of the Finance Act* 1973.]

11. In deposits by way of special investment in a trustee savings bank or in a department (not being a department certified under subsection (3) of section nine of the Finance Act, 1956) of a bank any other department of which is so certified.

12. In deposits in a building society designated under section one of the House Purchase and Housing Act, 1959.

13. In mortgages of freehold property in England and Wales or Northern Ireland and of leasehold property in those countries of which the unexpired term at the time of investment is not less than sixty years, and in loans on heritable security in Scotland.

14. In perpetual rent-charges charged on land in England and Wales or Northern Ireland and fee-farm rents (not being rent-charges) issuing out of such land, and in feu-duties or ground annuals in Scotland.

PART III

WIDER-RANGE INVESTMENTS

1. In any securities issued in the United Kingdom by a company incorporated in the United Kingdom, being securities registered in the United Kingdom and not being securities falling within Part II of this Schedule.

2. In shares in any building society designated under section one of the House Purchase and Housing Act, 1959.

3. In any units, or other shares of the investments subject to the trusts, of a unit trust scheme in the case of which there is in force at the time of investment an order of the Board of Trade under section seventeen of the Prevention of Fraud (Investments) Act, 1958, or of the Ministry of Commerce for Northern Ireland under section sixteen of the Prevention of Fraud (Investments) Act (Northern Ireland), 1940.

PART IV

SUPPLEMENTAL

1. The securities mentioned in Parts I to III of this Schedule do not include any securities where the holder can be required to accept repayment of the principal, or the payment of any interest, otherwise than in sterling.

2. The securities mentioned in paragraphs 1 to 8 of Part II, other than Treasury Bills or Tax Reserve Certificates, securities issued before the passing of this Act by the Government of the Isle of Man, securities falling within paragraph 4 of the said Part II issued before the passing of this Act or securities falling within paragraph 9 of that Part, and the securities mentioned in paragraph 1 of Part III of this Schedule, do not include—

(*a*) securities the price of which is not quoted on a recognised stock exchange within the meaning of the Prevention of Fraud (Investments) Act, 1958, or the Belfast stock exchange;

(*b*) shares or debenture stock not fully paid up (except shares or debenture stock which by the terms of issue are required to be fully paid up within nine months of the date of issue).

3. The securities mentioned in paragraph 6 of Part II and paragraph 1 of Part III of this Schedule do not include—

(a) shares or debentures of an incorporated company of which the total issued and paid up share capital is less than one million pounds;

(b) shares or debentures of an incorporated company which has not in each of the five years immediately preceding the calendar year in which the investment is made paid a dividend on all the shares issued by the company, excluding any shares issued after the dividend was declared and any shares which by their terms of issue did not rank for the dividend for that year. For the purposes of sub-paragraph (b) of this paragraph a company formed—

(i) to take over the business of another company or other companies, or

(ii) to acquire the securities of, or control of, another company or other companies,

or for either of those purposes and for other purposes shall be deemed to have paid a dividend as mentioned in that sub-paragraph in any year in which such a dividend has been paid by the other company or all the other companies, as the case may be.

4. In this Schedule, unless the context otherwise requires, the following expressions have the meanings hereby respectively assigned to them, that is to say—

" debenture " includes debenture stock and bonds, whether constituting a charge on assets or not, and loan stock or notes;

" enactment " includes an enactment of the Parliament of Northern Ireland;

" fixed-interest securities " means securities which under their terms of issue bear a fixed rate of interest;

" local authority " in relation to the United Kingdom, means any of the following authorities—

(a) in England and Wales, the council of a county, a borough, an urban or rural district or a parish, the Common Council of the City of London, the Greater London Council and the Council of the Isles of Scilly;

(b) in Scotland, a local authority within the meaning of the Local Government (Scotland) Act, 1947;

(c) in Northern Ireland, the council of a county, a county or other borough, or an urban or rural district;

" ordinary deposits " and " special investment " have the same meanings respectively as in the Trustee Savings Banks Act, 1954;

" securities " includes shares, debentures, Treasury Bills and Tax Reserve Certificates;

" share " includes stock;

" Treasury Bills " includes bills issued by Her Majesty's Government in the United Kingdom and Northern Ireland Treasury Bills.

[*Paragraph* 4 *is given as amended by the London Government Act* 1963, *ss.* 83 (1) *and* 93 (1) *and Scheds.* 17 *and* 18, *the National Loans Act* 1968, *s.* 24 (2) *and Sched.* 6, *Pt.* I, *and the Local Government Act* 1972, *s.* 272 (1) *and Sched.* 30.]

5. It is hereby declared that in this Schedule " mortgage," in relation to freehold or leasehold property in Northern Ireland, includes a registered charge which, by virtue of subsection (4) of section forty of the Local Registration of Title (Ireland) Act, 1891, or any other enactment, operates as a mortgage by deed.

6. References in this Schedule to an incorporated company are references to a company incorporated by or under any enactment and include references to a body of persons established for the purpose of trading for profit and incorporated by Royal Charter.

7. The references in paragraph 12 of Part II and paragraph 2 of Part III of this Schedule to a building society designated under section one of the House Purchase and Housing Act, 1959, include references to a permanent society incorporated under the Building Societies Acts (Northern Ireland) 1874 to 1940 for the time being designated by the Registrar for Northern Ireland under subsection (2) of that section (which enables such a society to be so designated for the purpose of trustees' powers of investment specified in paragraph (*a*) of subsection (1) of that section).

SECOND SCHEDULE

MODIFICATION OF SECTION 2 IN RELATION TO PROPERTY FALLING WITHIN SECTION 3 (3)

1. In this Schedule " special-range property " means property falling within subsection (3) of section three of this Act.

2.—(1) Where a trust fund includes special-range property, subsection (1) of section two of this Act shall have effect as if references to the trust fund were references to so much thereof as does not consist of special-range property, and the special-range property shall be carried to a separate part of the fund.

(2) Any property which—

(*a*) being property belonging to the narrower-range or wider-range part of a trust fund, is converted into special-range property, or

(*b*) being special-range property, accrues to a trust fund after the division of the fund or part thereof in pursuance of subsection (1) of section two of this Act or of that subsection as modified by sub-paragraph (1) of this paragraph,

shall be carried to such a separate part of the fund as aforesaid; and sub-sections (2) and (3) of the said section two shall have effect subject to this sub-paragraph.

3. Where property carried to such a separate part as aforesaid is converted into property other than special-range property—

(*a*) it shall be transferred to the narrower-range part of the fund or the wider-range part of the fund or apportioned between them, and (*b*) any transfer of property from one of those parts to the other shall be made which is necessary to secure that the value of each of those parts of the fund is increased by the same amount.

THIRD SCHEDULE

PROVISIONS SUPPLEMENTARY TO SECTION 3 (4)

1. Where in a case falling within subsection (4) of section three of this Act, property belonging to the narrower-range part of a trust fund—

(*a*) is invested otherwise than in a narrower-range investment, or

(*b*) being so invested, is retained and not transferred or as soon as may be reinvested as mentioned in subsection (2) of section two of this Act,

then, so long as the property continues so invested and comprised in the narrower-range part of the fund, section one of this Act shall not authorise the making or retention of any wider-range investment.

2. Section four of the Trustee Act, 1925, or section thirty-three of the Trusts (Scotland) Act, 1921 (which relieve a trustee from liability for retaining an investment which has ceased to be authorised), shall not apply where an investment ceases to be authorised in consequence of the foregoing paragraph.

FOURTH SCHEDULE

MINOR AND CONSEQUENTIAL AMENDMENTS

1.—(1) References in the Trustee Act, 1925, except in subsection (2) of section sixty-nine of that Act, to section one of that Act or to provisions which include that section shall be construed respectively as references to section one of this Act and as including references to section one of this Act.

(2) References in the Trusts (Scotland) Act, 1921, to section ten or eleven of that Act, or to provisions which include either of those sections, shall be construed respectively as references to section one of this Act and as including references to that section.

[*Paragraph 2 was repealed by the Building Societies Act, 1962, s. 131 and Sched. 10.*]

3. The following enactments and instruments, that is to say—

(*a*) subsection (3) of section seventy-four of the Third Schedule to the Water Act, 1945, and any order made under that Act applying the provisions of that subsection;

(*b*) any local and personal Act which, or any order or other instrument in the nature of any such Act which, modifies paragraph (*l*) of subsection (1) of section one of the Trustee Act, 1925,

shall have effect as if for any reference to the said paragraph (*l*) there were substituted a reference to paragraph 10 of Part II of the First Schedule to this Act.

[*Paragraphs* 4 *and* 5 *were repealed by the National Savings Bank Act* 1971, *s.* 28 (1) *and Sched.* 2.]

6. For the reference in subsection (2) of section one of the House Purchase and Housing Act, 1959, to paragraph (*a*) of subsection (1) of that section there shall be substituted a reference to paragraph 12 of Part II and paragraph 2 of Part III of the First Schedule to this Act.

FIFTH SCHEDULE

REPEALS

Session and Chapter	Short Title	Extent of Repeal
63 & 64 Vict. c. 62.	The Colonial Stock Act, 1900.	Section two.
2 Edw. 7. c. 41.	The Metropolis Water Act, 1902.	In section seventeen, subsection (4).
11 & 12 Geo. 5. c. 58.	The Trusts (Scotland) Act, 1921.	Sections ten and eleven. In section twelve, subsections (3) and (4). In section twenty-seven, the words from " including such regulations " to the end of the section.
15 & 16 Geo. 5. c. 19.	The Trustee Act, 1925.	Section one. In section two, the proviso to subsection (1). In section five, paragraph (*a*) of subsection (1) and subsections (4) to (6).
18 & 19 Geo. 5. c. 43.	The Agricultural Credits Act, 1928.	Section three.
19 & 20 Geo. 5. c. 13.	The Agricultural Credits (Scotland) Act, 1929.	Section three.
20 & 21 Geo. 5. c. 5.	The Colonial Development Act, 1929.	In section three, subsection (3).
24 & 25 Geo. 5. c. 47.	The Colonial Stock Act, 1934.	The whole Act.
8 & 9 Geo. 6. c. 12.	The Northern Ireland (Miscellaneous Provisions) Act, 1945.	Sections four to six.
11 & 12 Geo. 6. c. 7.	The Ceylon Independence Act, 1947.	In the Second Schedule, paragraph 4.
12, 13 & 14 Geo. 6. c. 1.	The Colonial Stock Act, 1948.	In section two, subsection (3).
2 & 3 Eliz. 2. c. 62.	The Post Office Savings Bank Act, 1954.	In section four, subsection (4).
5 & 6 Eliz. 2. c. 6.	The Ghana Independence Act, 1957.	In the Second Schedule, paragraph 4.
5 & 6 Eliz. 2. c. 60.	The Federation of Malaya Independence Act, 1957.	In the First Schedule, paragraph 8.
6 & 7 Eliz. 2. c. 47.	The Agricultural Marketing Act, 1958.	In section sixteen, in paragraph (*a*), the words from " or for the time " to " Act."
6 & 7 Eliz. 2. c. 55.	The Local Government Act, 1958.	Section fifty-four.
6 & 7 Eliz. 2. c. 64.	The Local Government and Miscellaneous Financial Provisions (Scotland) Act, 1958.	Section sixteen.
7 & 8 Eliz. 2. c. 33.	The House Purchase and Housing Act, 1959.	In section one, paragraph (*a*) of subsection (1), and subsection (5).
8 & 9 Eliz. 2. c. 52.	The Cyprus Act, 1960.	In the Schedule, in paragraph 9, sub-paragraphs (1), (3) and (4).
8 & 9 Eliz. 2. c. 55.	The Nigeria Independence Act, 1960.	In the Second Schedule, paragraph 4.
9 & 10 Eliz. 2. c. 16.	The Sierra Leone Independence Act, 1961.	In the Third Schedule, paragraph 5.

Table of Statutes referred to in this Act

Short Title	Session and Chapter
Local Registration of Title (Ireland) Act, 1891 . . .	54 & 55 Vict. c. 66.
Trusts (Scotland) Act, 1921	11 & 12 Geo. 5. c. 58.
Trustee Act, 1925	15 & 16 Geo. 5. c. 19.
Local Government Superannuation Act, 1937 . .	1 Edw. 8 & 1 Geo. 6. c. 68.
Local Government Superannuation (Scotland) Act, 1937 .	1 Edw. 8 & 1 Geo. 6. c. 69.
Building Societies Act, 1939	2 & 3 Geo. 6. c. 55.
Water Act, 1945	8 & 9 Geo. 6. c. 42.
Police Act, 1946	9 & 10 Geo. 6. c. 46.
Local Government (Scotland) Act, 1947 . . .	10 & 11 Geo. 6. c. 43.
Post Office Savings Bank Act, 1954	2 & 3 Eliz. 2. c. 62.
Trustee Savings Bank Act, 1954	2 & 3 Eliz. 2. c. 63.
Finance Act, 1956	4 & 5 Eliz. 2. c. 54.
Overseas Service Act, 1958	6 & 7 Eliz. 2. c. 14.
Prevention of Fraud (Investments) Act, 1958 . .	6 & 7 Eliz. 2. c. 45.
Local Government Act, 1958	6 & 7 Eliz. 2. c. 55.
House Purchase and Housing Act, 1959 . . .	7 & 8 Eliz. 2. c. 33.
Building Societies Act, 1960	8 & 9 Eliz. 2. c. 64.

INDEX

A

ABSCONDING TRUSTEE—
unfit to act, 228

ACCOUNT—
trustee's duty to, 308, 325 *et seq.* (See also TRUST ACCOUNTS)

ACCUMULATIONS—
rule relating to, 128 *et seq.*
    appropriate period, determination a question of construction, 130, 131
    direction to accumulate longer than permitted period, effect of, 131
    implied as well as express directions, applies to, 130
    minority not to be reckoned in allowable period, 130, 132
    presumptions affecting child bearing, 131
trustees' power as to, 291
    direction to accumulate to an age exceeding 18, whether trustees bound to pay income
        after attainment of, 291

ADMINISTRATION OF FOREIGN ESTATE, 419 *et seq.*

ADMINISTRATOR (See also PERSONAL REPRESENTATIVES)—
constructive trustee as, 207 *et seq.*
executor, of, cannot administer estate of original testator, 221
Public Trustee as, 57

ADVANCEMENT—
death duties, for avoidance of, 297, 301
presumption of—
    earlier distinctions now abandoned, 176, 177
    father and daughter, 177
    father and son, 176, 177, 181, 189
    husband and wife, 177–79, 189
    illegitimate children, to, 180
    mother and child, 179
    near relationship, existence of, 176, 189
    person *in loco parentis* and nominal purchaser, 179, 180
    question of intent, a, 176, 177
    rebuttal by evidence of actual intention, 180
    subsequent acts and statements, effect of, 180, 181
protective trusts, by way of, whether trustees have power to make, 302
special powers of, 299 *et seq.*
statutory power, 297 *et seq.*
trustees' power to make sub-trusts on, 300 *et seq.*
valuation of advances, 305
what constitutes, 297, 298

ADVERTISEMENT—
claims on trust fund, for, protection of trustees, 283, 284

ADVOWSON—
trust estate, forming part of, 307
trust for purchase of, 136

AGENCY—
trust distinguished from, 16
use, relationship to, 18

AGENT—
constructive trustee, as, 211, 215 *et seq.*
employment of—
    personal representatives, by, 237 *et seq.*
    trustee, by, 237 *et seq.* (See also DELEGATION BY TRUSTEE)
        professional agent, 237, 238
        valuer, 238
illegality of transaction, cannot set up, as excuse for retention, 116
trust property, cannot purchase, 310 *et seq.*

ALIEN—
British ship, cannot hold interest in, 54
cestui que trust, as, 54
trustee, as, 52
    domiciled abroad, where, 52

487

G

GUARDIAN—
undue influence over ward, 122

H

HANBURY, 414

HEADSTONES—
bequest for repair of, 135, 138, 163

HEIRLOOMS—
mansion-house, annexed to, hire of, 332

HORSE—
trust for maintenance of, 135, 136, 138

" HOTCHPOT "—
interest on sums already received, 304–5
life interest brought into, valuation of, 305
reversion brought into, valuation of, 305

HOWE v. *LORD DARTMOUTH*, RULE IN—
apportionment of capital and income pending conversion—
reversionary interests, 262
unauthorised securities, 262
conversion directed at later date, no application where, 265
definition of, 260
exclusion of, 265–6
express trust to convert, application where, 266, 267, 268, 269
freeholds always outside, 267
inter vivos settlements outside, 265
leaseholds, whether applicable to, 264
property given specifically, no application to, 264
residuary personalty left by will—
application to, 260 *et seq.*
trustee's duty to convert, 260 *et seq.*
Trustee Investments Act 1961, effect on, 269
will shows intention that property is to be enjoyed in specie, no application where, 264–5

HUSBAND—
purchase by, in name of wife, presumption of advancement, 177–9
purchase by wife in name of, no presumption of advancement, 177–9
wife, and, mutual wills by, 181 *et seq.* (See also RESULTING TRUSTS)

I

IDIOT—
trust, how far capable of creating, 49

ILLEGAL—
purpose, trusts for, effect, 114 *et seq.*

ILLEGITIMATE CHILDREN (See TRUSTS)

IMMORALITY—
trusts contemplating—
not void, when, 113
void, when, 113

IMPLIED TRUST (See also RESULTING TRUSTS)
by law, 35
constructive trust, distinguished from, 173
development of, 28
express trust, and, distinction one of degree, 173
nature of, 28, 35, 36
precatory trust as an, 173
presumed intention, depends on, 173
resulting trusts, in relation to, 36, 37, 173
Statute of Frauds does not apply to, 175, 188

IMPLIED USE, 22

IMPROVEMENTS, 279–81
payment for—
capital money, out of—
deposited in court, 280
repayment by tenant for life, 279–80

M

MAINTENANCE—
    capital, application of, for, 296
        order of court, whether necessary, 296
    effect of direction to accumulate, 132
    mortgage of infant's entailed interest in remainder for, 296
    trustees' power to apply income of trust for, 290 *et seq.*, 369
        accumulations of residue, trusts on which held, 290
        considerations determining amount, 290-1
        contingent gifts, income of, 291
    vesting orders of property of infant for, 296

MARRIAGE—
    agreement in consideration of, 86
    articles, construction of, 78
        executory trust in, distinguished from executory trusts in wills, 78-81
        " heirs of the body," 80
    consideration, as, 85
    fraudulent misrepresentation, induced by, settlement not set aside, 120
    mutual wills, effect of, 181 *et seq.*
    property jointly acquired, trusts arising where, 174 *et seq.*
    settlement, volunteers, position of, 86
    trust in contemplation of—
        marriage subsequently declared void, 116
        marriage subsequently not celebrated, 116
    trust in restraint of, 113
    trust until, 113

MARRIAGE SETTLEMENTS, 344, 345
    bankruptcy, effect of subsequent, 146
    variation of, by court, 366
    volunteers, position of, 86

MARRIED WOMAN—
    after-acquired property, covenanted to be settled by, trustees' duty to ensure it is settled, 243
    mother and married daughter, undue influence, no presumption of, between, 122
    presumption of advancement in relation to, 177-9, 189
    restraint on anticipation, abolition of, 48
    separate estate—
        abolition of, 48
        doctrine of, 48
    settlor, as, 47, 48
    trustee—
        acquisition of property as, 51
        disclaimer of office by, 220
        disposal of property as, 51

MASSES FOR THE DEAD—
    bequest of personalty for, validity, 160, 161

MENTAL DEFECTIVE—
    power of court to assent to variation of trusts on behalf of, 358
    settlement by, under direction of court, 49

MENTAL PATIENT—
    settlement by, under discretion of court, 49
    trust, how far capable of creating, 49
    trustee, is capable of acting as, 228

MISREPRESENTATION (See also FRAUD)
    fraudulent, inducing marriage, settlement not set aside, 120
    innocent, trust set aside on ground of, 119
    trust established as result of, set aside, 120

MISTAKE—
    of law, trustee making, 287, 288, 392 *et seq.*
        remedies of beneficiary against, 287, 288, 398 *et seq.*
    trust established as result of—
        rectified, when, 118-9
            settlor's attention not called to unusual limitation, 118
        set aside, 117-9

MIXED FUNDS—
    trustee mixing trust monies with his own—
        no presumption of intention to repair a breach of trust, 388
        presumption against breach of trust, 388